MASS VIOLENCE IN AMERICA

MEMPHIS RIOTS AND MASSACRES

ARNO PRESS & THE NEW YORK TIMES

New York · 1969

Reprinted from a copy in the

*

*

Library of Congress Catalog Card No. 79–90202

*

Manufactured in the United States of America

Editorial Note

NATIONS, LIKE MEN, ARE SOMETIMES INTERESTED IN BURYING THE PAST.

In early 1968, after more than five years marked by political assassinations, racial uprisings, campus disorders, mass demonstrations and the violent suppression of protest, *The New York Times Magazine* asked a group of distinguished scholars to reply to the question, "Is America by nature a violent society?" In answer, University of Chicago anthropologist Clifford Geertz wrote:

> "We do not know very well what kind of society we live in, what kind of history we have had, what kind of people we are. We are just now beginning to find out, the hard way . . ."

The proposition was astonishing but correct: what was least understood about domestic political violence was its role in American history. It was common knowledge that the United States had had a Revolution, a Civil War, some trouble with the Indians and a period of labor-management conflict. But one could search the shelves of the nation's great libraries without discovering more than a handful of works on the subject of violence in American history, and these hopelessly out of date.

Historians had generally ignored or soft-pedaled the history of farmer uprisings, native vigilantism, labor-management struggles, ethnic conflicts and race riots; comparative work in the history of social conflict was particularly weak. Sociologists and political scientists in the grip of "consensus" theory tended to treat episodes of mass violence in America as insignificant or aberrational—temporary exceptions to the norm of peaceful progress. Psychologists and behavioral scientists discussed "mob violence" in terms which suggested that riots, revolts, insurrections and official violence were the products of individual or group pathology. All such interpretations had the effect not only of minimizing group violence in America, but of depriving it of political content—hence, of relevance to the present.

As a result, as late as 1968, the rich, multifarious and often terrifying history of domestic political violence was still largely *terra incognita*. So long as most Americans wished to keep certain skeletons locked away in their closets, few scholars would attempt to open doors. Conversely, once the American people, frightened yet emboldened by the sudden reappearance of intense social conflict, began to ask new questions about the past, so did the scholars.

Our purpose in helping Arno Press and *The New York Times* select and publish significant documents in the history of political violence has not been to compound past errors by overemphasizing the role of conflict in American history. On the contrary, our aim has been to provide materials which will aid in the search for an accurate perspective on the present. MASS VIOLENCE IN AMERICA includes eyewitness reports, government documents and other descriptive and analytic material relating to mass political violence in the United States. These documents not only provide information—they give the "feel" or "flavor" of past eras of civil disorder by evoking the emotional and political context in which revolts took place. Most of them have long been out of print and are obtainable, if at all, only in the nation's largest libraries.

The scope of this series is wide, ranging from accounts of Indian warfare to descriptions of labor-management violence, from narratives of colonial insurrections to reports on modern racial uprisings. It is not, however, limitless, nor were the constituent volumes carelessly selected. The principle of coherence which guided the selections is implicit in the phrase "mass political violence." "Mass" denotes activity engaged in by large groups rather than individuals acting alone; "political" suggests a relationship between such activity and competition among domestic groups for power, property and prestige; and "violence" is narrowly construed as resulting in physical damage to persons or property. In short, the materials reproduced herein are intended to illuminate the resort to violence by American groups seeking to change or to preserve the status quo. Although historical, they are of interest to any who wishes to understand the causes, nature and direction of domestic political violence, whether they be social scientists, historians or just interested Americans.

Of course, we are particularly hopeful that these volumes will prove useful to those now engaged in curriculum-revision and the teaching of high school and college courses in the area of American studies. What Christopher Jencks and David Reisman term "the Academic Revolution" has made difficult demands on all educators, not the least of which is the demand for courses which are both relevant to the condition of modern America and of the highest academic quality. These volumes are meant to provide raw material for such courses—primary source matter which will help both instructors and students to deepen and enrich their views of the American experience.

Most important, the editors and publisher recognize that these volumes appear during a national crisis which is also a crisis of the spirit, a time in which the public response to various manifestations of civil disorder is increasingly governed by anger, fear and hysteria. In such an atmosphere it is important to recognize that one is not alone in time—that such events have taken place before in America and, unless fundamental changes in our social and political life take place, will probably recur in the future. Our fondest hope is that this work, and others like it, will help to keep alive, in a time of growing unreason, the spirit of reasoned inquiry.

RICHARD E. RUBENSTEIN
The Adlai Stevenson Institute
Chicago, Illinois

ROBERT M. FOGELSON
Harvard-MIT Joint Center
for Urban Studies
Cambridge, Massachusetts

MEMPHIS RIOTS AND MASSACRES

THE

REPORTS OF THE COMMITTEES

OF THE

HOUSE OF REPRESENTATIVES,

MADE DURING THE

FIRST SESSION THIRTY-NINTH CONGRESS,

1865-'66.

WASHINGTON:
GOVERNMENT PRINTING OFFICE.
1866.

MEMPHIS RIOTS AND MASSACRES.

JULY 25, 1866.—Ordered to be printed.

Mr. E. B. WASHBURNE, from the Select Committee on the Memphis Riots, made the following

REPORT.

The special committee of the House, charged with an investigation into all matters connected with the riots at Memphis, which took place on the first days of May, 1866, and particularly to inquire into the origin, progress, and termination of the riotous proceedings ; the names of parties engaged in it ; the acts of atrocity perpetrated ; the number of killed and wounded, and the amount and character of the property destroyed, having completed their labors, now beg leave to submit their report :

The committee reached Memphis on the 22d day of May last, and immediately proceeded with their investigations. They examined a hundred and seventy witnesses, whose testimony, with the various exhibits, is herewith submitted, and which will make a volume of, it is estimated, twelve hundred printed pages.

On their arrival the committee found that Major General Stoneman, commanding the department of Tennessee, headquarters at Memphis, had instituted a commission for the purpose of making substantially the same investigations in regard to the riotous proceedings your committee were directed to make. That commission consisted of Brevet Brigadier General B. P. Runkle, superintendent of the Freedmen's Bureau for the district of Memphis; Captain A. W. Allyn, 16th United States infantry; Brevet Major W. J. Colburn, assistant quartermaster in the volunteer service ; and M. J. Wright, a citizen of Memphis. This commission had nearly completed its labors, and its investigations seem to have been of the most thorough and searching character.

In order to insure a fair hearing on the part of the citizens of Memphis, Major General Stoneman, with great propriety, placed upon the commission, in addition to the military men, Marcus J. Wright, one of the most prominent citizens of that city, and a man who had held the position of brigadier general in the rebel army.

The committee also found that Brevet Major General Clinton B. Fisk, of the volunteer service, and assistant commissioner of the Freedmen's Bureau for the States of Kentucky and Tennessee, had instituted a commission consisting of Colonel Charles F. Johnson, subsequently uniting with him Major Gilbraith, who had been sent out by Major General O. O. Howard, of the Freedmen's Bureau at Washington, for the purpose of instituting an investigation into matters connected with the riots. This commission also prosecuted its labors with great zeal, thoroughness, and fidelity. The committee desire to state that they received from Major General Stoneman, Brevet Major General Fisk, and Brevet Brigadier General Runkle every assistance possible for them to render in the discharge of their duties. They were greatly aided in their labors by the records of the investigations made by the respective commissions, embracing the testimony of very many witnesses whom it was impossible for the committee to examine, both for want of sufficient time, and from the fact that many of them had scattered off and were not to be found. The testimony of all witnesses bearing upon the subject, taken by those commissions, except where the same witnesses were examined by the committee, was verified as being such testimony, made a part of the record, and is submitted to the House with the testimony taken by the committee.

MAJOR GENERAL STONEMAN'S TESTIMONY.

The testimony first taken was that of Major General George Stoneman, from which it appears that the whole military force stationed at Memphis consisted of a detachment of the 16th United States infantry, not more than one hundred and fifty strong, and that this force was not more than sufficient to guard the large amount of government property at Memphis against the large numbers of thieves, robbers, incendiaries, and the Irish police of that city.

Previous to this time the people of Memphis had been clamoring for a withdrawal of all the United States troops, boasting that they were perfectly competent to take care of themselves. General Stoneman had, therefore, turned the city and that section of country over to the civil authorities, as far as it was practicable, holding them responsible for good order, peace, and quiet. At the first breaking out of the riotous proceedings, on the afternoon of Tuesday, the 1st day of May, General Stoneman was called upon by the sheriff of the county, and requested to use the United States troops under his command for quelling them. As there had theretofore been so urgent a demand upon the part of the people to have the troops withdrawn, General Stoneman desired to know what means the city authorities had taken to quell the disturbances; and he further desired that the question should be tested whether the civil authorities could take care of themselves, and preserve order as it had been claimed they could and would do. Subsequent to this, irresponsible parties, representing themselves as coming from the mayor and aldermen of the city, made application to the general for the use of the troops. His reply was, that if the mayor wanted the use of the troops, or wanted assistance, and would address him a communication to that effect, it should receive due attention. Shortly after, and on the same day, the mayor requested General Stoneman to order a force of troops to co-operate with the constabulary force of the city in case of any further continued lawlessness; to which General Stoneman replied immediately that he had but a small force at his command, which was in camp at Fort Pickering, and the mayor could communicate with the commanding officer at the fort in case he should find need of assistance. He would, however, prefer that the troops should be called upon only in case of extreme necessity, as he desired to see whether they could keep peace and order themselves without the intervention of the military authorities, as they had asserted they could in a communication previously made.

RIOTOUS PROCEEDINGS.

The riotous proceedings continuing, the regular forces were called out on Tuesday night, and they scattered and dispersed the rioters, as will more fully appear by reference to the testimony of Captain Allyn, in command of regular troops, Captain Dornin, and Lieutenant Clifford. The next morning, May 2, General Stoneman was called on by Judge Leonard, judge of the county court, who, after stating that they were skirmishing down in South Memphis, made application to have arms turned over to a posse of citizens, then being formed. The general told him he had no arms to be used for that purpose; that all arms used must be under his control, and that in no event would he turn over arms to citizens, without being assured that they would be used for proper purposes, and placed in the hands of proper parties—of men who would act under the direction of the military authorities. The reply of General Stoneman was a very proper one, for, as he states, this posse, when brought to him by Judge Leonard, proved to be a heterogeneous mass, some of them firemen, some ex-confederate soldiers, and some did not belong to anything but the rabble of the town. Judge Leonard said he thought he could vouch for these men, but after taking a look at them, General Stoneman became satisfied that if he, the judge, could vouch for them, he, the general, could not, and declined to put any arms into their hands.

The mob continuing its outrages through Wednesday and Wednesday night, on Thursday a meeting was held by a number of citizens, who resolved that the mayor of the city and sheriff of the county, together with the chairman of the meeting, be authorized to summon a force of sufficient number, to act in concert with the military, which should constitute a patrol for the protection of the city, &c. General Stoneman, on the same day, addressed a communication to the mayor and city council of Memphis, stating that circumstances compelled him to interfere with the civil affairs of the city, and forbidding any persons without his authority to assemble together any posse, armed or unarmed, white or colored. That, however, did not include the police force of the city, so long as it could be relied on to preserve the peace. This interference by the military authorities seems to have had an immediate and most salutary effect, for all parties who had been assembled together by the civil authorities for any purpose whatever immediately dispersed and went home. There were no more formidable riotous proceedings after this, although there were many isolated acts of murder, robbery, and maltreatment both of white and colored persons. There were apprehensions, however, as appears from the testimony of General Stoneman and others, on the part of a good many persons, that a general conflagration would take place, and that the town would be burned down. Several northern people came to him and expressed their fears that measures would be taken to drive all northern people out of the city, though the general does not seem to have shared in those fears. The teachers of colored schools and preachers for colored churches came to him and represented that their schools and churches had been burned down; that some of them had been threatened and others warned, asking him for protection and troops to guard their places. Not having troops enough for such purpose, he told them that if they would go to the troops they should have protection, or if they desired to leave the city they should have transportation to wherever they wanted to go. Many, and, in fact, nearly all of them, availed themselves of the opportunity and left the city.

The guards which were placed in the city on Thursday night, with strict orders to disperse any party assembling together for any purpose whatever, prevented the assembling of any such parties, if there was any intention of so doing, which the general thought, from information subsequently obtained, there was; that people had come over from Arkansas and different sections of the country, leading him to believe there would have been trouble on Thursday night if no precautions had been taken.

It was very natural, after the pertinacious demands of the people of Memphis to have the troops withdrawn, and their boastful pretences that they could take care of themselves, that General Stoneman should have been disinclined to interfere until it should be fully demonstrated to him that the public safety imperatively required it. It is to be regretted, however, that he had not at an earlier period of the lawless and murderous proceedings taken the same resolute steps that he subsequently adopted, as he, no doubt, would have done, had he comprehended the full proportions of the riots and the true character of the city government of Memphis, and of the controlling influences of that city.

MAJOR GENERAL STONEMAN AND THE CITY AUTHORITIES.

After the riotous proceedings were at an end, General Stoneman constituted a commission of investigation; as has been stated, and on the same day addressed the following communication to the mayor:

HEADQUARTERS DEPARTMENT OF TENNESSEE,
Memphis, Tennessee, May 5, 1866.

SIR: I have the honor to request information upon the following points, viz:

1. What efforts have been made or steps taken by the city authorities of the city of Memphis to apprehend and bring to trial and punishment the perpetrators of the outrages which have disgraced the city of Memphis during the past week, and what assurances can be given me that the murderers and incendiaries will be arrested and punished?

2. What steps or measures have been taken by the city authorities, or the citizens of Memphis, to remunerate individuals and the United States government for losses sustained and expenses incurred caused by the recent riotous proceedings of the people of this city, and are you able to assure me that all claims for such losses and expenses will be promptly paid by the city?

3. Can and will you furnish me with a statement, showing the sources from which the city derives its revenue, with the amount or amounts derivable from each source?

4. Are the city authorities able and competent to prohibit and prevent persons, under whatever pretext, from carrying and using arms? I am reliably informed that the city recorder has assured the people of Memphis that they will not hereafter be prohibited from carrying and using fire-arms.

5. What security can you give me that the rights and privileges of the colored population of this city and surroundings shall be respected and protected; and what disposition has been made of the large number of negroes who have been arrested by the police during the past week?

I have to request that you will do me the favor to give me all the information possible, and such assurances as circumstances warrant, as future action will be based upon your reply to this communication.

In conclusion, I have to assure you, and, through you, the people of Memphis, that if they cannot govern themselves as a law-abiding and Christian community, they will be governed, and that hereafter it will be my duty and privilege to see that there are no more riotous proceedings or conduct, either on the part of whites or blacks, or city authorities.

I am, sir, very respectfully, your obedient servant,

GEO. STONEMAN,
Major General, Commanding.

His Honor JOHN PARK,
    Mayor of the City of Memphis.

The committee desire to say that, in their judgment, General Stoneman is deserving of the highest commendation for his prompt and determined action in demanding this information, and in warning the mayor and people of Memphis that if they could not govern themselves as a "law abiding and Christian community," *they would be governed,* and that it would be his duty and privilege to put a stop to further riotous proceedings. The answer of the mayor is of a very unsatisfactory and discreditable character, and too long to be inserted in this report. It is, however, set out in the testimony of General Stoneman It will be seen that the mayor states that the city authorities have taken no steps or measures to remunerate individuals or the United States government for losses sustained by the riotous proceedings, and that he is advised of no law or ᵗatute authorizing any such appropriation of money; and takes it for granted that no action will be had. He is also advised that no claim for such losses had been or would be entertained or recognized by any tribunal of competent jurisdiction as constituting a meritorious claim against the civil authorities.

Order having been restored in the city, and the excitement of the community consequent upon the riot having abated, shortly afterwards the military control of the city was withdrawn, though without formal public notice, and the civil authorities exercised their functions as before the riot The further testimony of General Stoneman is particularly referred to, as entitled to great weight, coming from a military man, not complicated with the political or other questions of the day.

THE CHARACTER OF THE ATROCITIES.

The proportions of what is called the "riot," but in reality the massacre, proved to be far more extended, and the circumstances surrounding it of much greater significance, than the committee had any conception of before they entered upon their investigation.

Most of the newspapers in the city had grossly misrepresented nearly everything connected with it, while great efforts had been made by the citizens to belittle it into a simple row between some discharged negro soldiers and the Irish police. It was called in derision the "nigger riot," while, in fact, in the language of General Stoneman, the negroes had nothing to do with it after the first day, except to be killed and abused. "They assembled in no bodies, and were engaged in no riotous proceedings."

Nothing could be more false and malicious than the charge that the riotous proceedings grew out of the teachings of the Freedmen's Bureau officers and of the teachers of the colored schools and the preachers in the churches of the colored people. From the observation of your committee the affairs of the Freedmen's Bureau in Tennessee have been most admirably managed by Major General Fisk and his subordinates, and the best possible influence has been exercised on the colored people.

The outbreak of the disturbance resulting from collision between some policemen and discharged colored soldiers ·was seized upon as a pretext for an organized and bloody massacre of the colored people of Memphis, regardless of age, sex, or condition, inspired by the teachings of the press, and led on by sworn officers of the law composing the city government, and others. The mob, finding itself under the protection and guidance of official authority, and sustained by a powerful public sentiment behind, actuated by feelings of the most deadly hatred to the colored race, and particularly those who wore the uniform of the republic, proceeded with deliberation to the commission of crimes and the perpetration of horrors which can scarcely find a parallel in the history of civilized or barbarous nations, and must inspire the most profound emotions of horror among all civilized people. The. testimony taken in this regard is very full, and is believed by the committee, as a general thing, to be entitled to the fullest confidence. The story of the shocking events of those terrible days, the 1st and 2d of May, told by colored witnesses who escaped the fury of the mob, was simple, affecting, and, no doubt, truthful. The whole evidence discloses the killing of men, women, and children—the innocent, unarmed, and defenceless pleading for their lives and crying for mercy; the wounding, beating, and maltreating of a still greater number; burning, pillaging, and robbing; the consuming of dead bodies in the flames, the burning of dwellings, the attempts to burn up whole families in their houses, and the brutal and revolting ravishings of defenceless and terror-stricken women.

COMMENCEMENT.

The riotous proceedings are considered to have commenced on Tuesday afternoon, May 1 ; but the causes that proximately led to it will be more fully considered in a subsequent part of this report. The affair of Monday afternoon, April 30, between some policemen and discharged negro soldiers, cannot be considered as the commencement of the riot ; but as indicating a state of feeling which led to the violence of the afternoon of the next day, and which was only a repetition on a larger scale of what had happened before.

It seems from the testimony of Ellen and Rachel Dilts, two witnesses who were in a position to know the facts about which they testified, that four policemen were walking down the street and met three or four colored men ; some words followed ; the negroes turned out to allow the policemen to pass, when one of them fell down and a policeman fell over him. That appeared to exasperate the policemen, who drew pistols and knives. The colored man who had fallen started to go away, when one of the policemen ran after him and stuck him over the head with his pistol, breaking the breech of it. The other colored men seeing their companion thus beaten became excited, and one of them struck the policeman over the head with a stick. This colored man was in turn hit on his head by a policeman with a brick. The parties then separated, going in opposite directions.

The causes which led to the riot, independent of the state of feeling which had been fostered by the press, was the animosity existing between the Irish population of Memphis, which embraces nearly all the members of the city government, and the colored population, large numbers of whom had come into the city since its occupation by the Union authorities. A regiment of colored troops (the 3d heavy artillery) had been stationed at Memphis for a long time, and the families of many of the soldiers had gathered there. In the vicinity of Fort Pickering, where these troops were stationed, and immediately east of it, great numbers of these colored people had squatted and built their little cabins.*

Many of the families of the soldiers were living in these cabins. This was outside the corporate limits of the city of Memphis, and was called South Memphis. The natural hostility between the Irish and negroes seems to have been aggravated by the fact that it had been the duty of the colored troops to patrol the city, bringing them into contact more or less with the Irish police; and it came to pass that whenever a colored man was arrested for any cause, even the most frivolous, and sometimes without cause, by the police, the arrest was made in a harsh and brutal manner, it being usual to knock down and beat the arrested party. Such treatment tended, of course, greatly to exasperate the negroes. The police waited with an evident anxiety for the time to arrive when the colored troops should be mustered out of the service, and should have no adequate means of defence. Unfortunately, when that time arrived the men were detained for some time after they were discharged waiting to be paid off. Their arms had been taken from them, but by some means quite a number of them had obtained possession of pistols ; but having been mustered out, and the restraints of military discipline having in a measure been removed, the soldiers, with nothing to do, would leave the fort in large numbers, and wander about in those parts of the city usually inhabited by colored people, congregating in saloons, and indulging, more or less, in drinking.

THE FIRST OUTBREAK.

On the day the riot first broke out your committee sift from the large mass of testimony taken on that subject the following facts : About a week before the riot, according to the testimony of Dr. Sharp, there had been an arrest made

* Personal observation.

of a colored man, in the neighborhood of the fort, without cause. The colored man was knocked down, most cruelly beaten, and carried off on a dray. It was then that the colored soldiers made threats that if ever the police came up again and arrested a man in that way they would resent it.

It was about the middle of the afternoon of Tuesday, May 1, that a crowd of some hundred of these negroes had congregated on South street. They appeared to have been on a "regular spree," but, according to the testimony of one witness, were not doing any harm; yet the committee are bound to state that the weight of the evidence is that their behavior was riotous and disorderly, and fully justified the interposition of the civil authorities. When the police came on the ground these colored soldiers were cheering for "Abe Lincoln," to which a policeman replied, "Your old father, Abe Lincoln, is dead and damned." Then followed the arrest of two colored men by the police in an orderly manner. At this time the colored man who a week before had been arrested by the police, as heretofore stated, discovered among the policemen making the arrests the very man who had arrested him, and he became very much excited. The colored soldiers began previously to gather around the policemen, threatening them in an excited manner, and calling out "Club them," "Shoot them." Then, as police marched off with the men they had arrested, these colored soldiers began fire their revolvers in the air. Whereupon the police, possibly thinking the soldiers were firing at them, turned around and began firing at the crowd of colored soldiers. Then followed a general discharge of revolvers between the colored soldiers and police, and one of the soldiers was heard to say a policeman had been shot, and other soldiers shouted to the crowd, " They have killed one of our men." Thereupon the negroes became still more excited and advanced towards the police, but soon returned saying they had killed one of the officers.

RENEWAL OF DISTURBANCES.

Some time after this the police returned with re-enforcements, and the colored soldiers had also increased their numbers to an extent exceeding that of the police. Then followed a promiscuous running fight between the police and colored soldiers, the soldiers calling on the policemen to "halt," and firing at them. One colored man, with a Spencer rifle, came up to an officer, calling out, "Halt, you white son of a bitch," and fired at him. In this last affair there were no white men killed, and whether any colored men were or not does not clearly appear. When it closed, it was about dark; the colored soldiers went directly to the fort, and were not out again during the night. The police, however, went to town for re-enforcements, and returned again about 10 o'clock that night with about two hundred men, composed of the police and what was called a "posse comitatus." On reaching the ground of the previous disturbance they found nobody on the streets and nothing to oppose them. All the riotous and bad conduct on the part of the negroes had ceased some hours before. Then the police and posse commenced an indiscriminate robbing, burning and murdering, full details of which will be found in the testimony, and which will be referred to somewhat at length in this report.

When the negroes went back into the fort the riotous proceedings were at an end,a s far as they were concerned. In the row which previously took place several on both sides seem to have been injured. Among the white men, Dunn, the fireman, and Stephens, the policeman, were killed. Another policeman, by the name of Slatterly, received a flesh wound in the legs, and another had his fingers grazed by a ball. There is much conflicting testimony as to how these men were wounded or killed. The committee are satisfied, however, that Dunn was killed by one of his own friends. This is from the direct testimony of James Carrol Mitchell, an intelligent colored man, who testified as to the facts from his personal knowledge, and who saw him shot by one John Pendergrast

He saw Pendergrast fire at Dunn as he was going towards the colored soldiers and as he came up heard him exclaim, " I have made a mistake ; I have shot one of our men ; I thought it was a d—d yellow nigger." This testimony of Mitchell was far more clear and circumstantial than that of any other witness on the subject, and if believed, and the committee have no doubt of its truth, would settle the question as to who killed Dunn.

The testimony as to the killing of the policeman Stephens is conflicting. Dr. Creighton, who had been serving in Union hospitals during the entire war, and who was called in consultation with Dr. Irwin and Dr. Keller, states that the wound was in the upper third of the thigh, the course of the ball having been backwards and downwards; that his impression was and is that he was not shot by a negro, nor by anybody but himself. Stephens told them that he was thirty yards from the crowd firing upon him, and that he fell through the bridge and was shot at exactly that time. Dr. Creighton says that, from the direction of the wound, it could not have been fired except from a vertical position. He says they could not find the ball, but that in putting his finger into the wound he had to feel longitudinally, and that the ball could not have taken that course without having been fired from a vertical position. Another reason why he thought it must have been from his own pistol was, that the wound appeared to be powder-marked. Dr. Keller, who had his attention called to the powder-mark, said the man was an Irishman, and was so dirty he could not tell whether the portion blackened was a powder-mark or not. Dr. Creighton says it was the only black spot on his leg, and was just such a mark as would be made by a powder-burn. Dr. Keller, who had been a surgeon in the rebel service, states that the wound was evidently inflicted by a second party; that it could not, he imagined, have been done by Stephens himself; that the shot must have been almost horizontal. Dr. Irwin, who was in consultation, heard the wounded man say he fell through a bridge at the time he was shot, and he made the suggestion at the time that his own pistol might have caused the wound. (See testimony of Drs. Creighton, Irwin, and Keller.)

SHOOTING NEGROES.

During the affair in which these white men received their wounds many colored men were beaten, fired upon, and wounded. Dr. Sharp says that at this time he saw the policemen firing and shooting every negro they met. He saw one negro being chased and thirty shots fired at him; saw policemen shooting at him and beating him with their pistols and clubs. He saw another negro lying on the ground who had been shot through the shoulder, and heard that a number of citizens shot him, making the remark that every one of them (negroes) would be killed. At this very period of time also there was a negro killed on the Bayou bridge by a policeman, and two others also appeared to have been killed at this time; that on the return of the crowd to town they made an indiscriminate charge on men, women, and children.

It has been stated that the riot, as far as the colored people were concerned, was ended by dark on Tuesday evening, at the time the colored soldiers left the ground and went into the fort, and there was no shadow of excuse for any further acts of violence on the part of the police or posse. Everything was quiet on the ground when the large number of policemen and posse returned to it at 10 o'clock that evening. The colored soldiers were in the fort, where they could have been arrested had it been deemed desirable or necessary, and where the assistance of the military could have been had in securing the prompt arrest of every man concerned in the riotous proceedings. But this police force and posse from that time became the mob, and commenced an indiscriminate robbery, burning and slaughter.

BRUTAL MURDER OF JACKSON GOODELL.

Among the first victims to the bloodthirsty spirit of the mob on Tuesday night was Jackson Goodell, a drayman, in no way connected with the soldiers. Coming home from his work at the close of the day, at the request of his wife, who was sick, he went out of the house to a store to get some meal for supper. As he was going into the store, two policemen came out of a grocery next door, and followed him with revolvers. To get away from them he slipped through the house and came out at another door. These policemen saw him and caught him, called him "a d—d rascal," and knocked him down his head falling in the gutter. They struck him fifteen or twenty times, the testimony being that any one of the blows would have killed almost any white man. Then they shot him after he was down. His wife was soon after notified that her husband was killed. She went out and found him on the ground groaning. She pressed her hand to his breast and called him, but "he never spoke." The people in the neighborhood were so frightened at the demonstrations of the mob that none of them dared aid her in bringing him into the house, and she was finally advised that she had better go in or she would be killed, for the policemen were going to kill every negro they could catch. While she was sitting by her wounded husband holding his head in her hands, three policemen came along, and one of them said, "Here is a d—d nigger; if he is not dead we will finish him." She went out in the morning, but he was not there, and she was afterwards informed that four men had taken him off in the night, and was advised that she had better go to the station-house and see about it. She went, and after much difficulty she was enabled, by peeping through the bars of the window, to see her husband lying there dead. With a refinement of cruelty the station-house keeper refused to allow her to go inside, and also refused to give up the body to her for burial, although she begged for it in the most piteous terms. The testimony of Lavinia Goodell as to this murder is corroborated by that of John E. Moller, who states that he saw them knock down the negro man, and that in the crowd was a policeman on horseback, who was a sergeant or lieutenant, and who said, "*Kill them altogether; the God d—d niggers ought to be all killed, no matter whether the small or big ones.*"

WHAT THE RIOT WAS.

This witness Moller, states that the riot was a well-appointed thing; that they had been working on it for a long time. He thought so for the reason that they had been talking about the riots of the negroes at Christmas, the talk coming from just such men as he saw engaged in the riots, the strongest rebels that could be found, guerillas and such, who were in fact trying to incite the negroes to acts of vengeance by telling them that they were "the boys that saved the country," and that they ought to have just the same privileges as white men; that if the white men would not give such rights to them they ought to take them; that they had taken Port Hudson, and could take their rights, too. The negroes, however, were too sensible to be betrayed into following the advice of these rebels, whose hatred and treacheries they understood full well. The policemen, said Mr. Moller, were nothing more than a set of lawless thieves; the whole city government was Irish, and was of about the same character. And this testimony of Mr. M. was corroborated by the testimony of many other witnesses. Among other reasons for the opinion of the witness was that the policemen were trying to come in conflict with the negroes all the time; that there is a certain class of rebels who are seeking to place obstacles in the way of the government, *who would be very polite, would deprecate any violence, but would use these low-lived Irish rascals as their tools;* that these were the men who came from the country and offered their services for the purpose of keeping order, but did it for nothing else than to get a chance to arm themselves. (See testimony of Lavinia Goodell, C. M. Cooley, and John E. Moller.

ROBBERY OF ALBERT HARRIS.

Among the flagrant cases of robbery on Tuesday night was that of Albert Harris, a shoemaker. Early in the evening about eight men came to his house, two or three of them being policemen, under the pretext of searching for arms. They ransacked his house, broke open his trunks, and robbed him of $350 of his own money, the fruits of his hard earnings, of $50 placed in his care, and $10 belonging to another man. His wife seeing policemen in this gang of robbers, tried to get them to interfere, but they drew their pistols, and pointed them at the side of her head. When they were going off, Albert begged them not to carry away his money; it was all he had, and he had "worked hard for it." They derisively told him to go to the *Freedmen's Bureau* in the morning and he would get it. The witness particularly impressed the committee as a most honest, respectable, and industrious man, and other witnesses testified to his most excellent character. It is a somewhat remarkable fact connected with the robbery of Albert Harris, that during the whole day he had seen two men around the grocery store of one Finne, on the opposite corner. These two men, whose names were ascertained to be Wilson and Tyler, were put in possession of Finne's store by the sheriff, who had an execution against his goods, and they were fully identified by Albert Harris as belonging to the party who committed the robbery, and there is evidence going to show that one of Mr. Finne's boys was cognizant of, if not a party to, the transaction, he having given the robbers a candle and some matches to go over there to Harris's house. (See testimony of Albert Harris and William Cole.)

A COLORED HOSPITAL FIRED INTO.

To show the character and spirit of these police, and of the citizens who had joined them in their deeds of violence and blood, it may be stated that on their return, after their difficulties with the negroes on Tuesday afternoon, as they were passing the hospital of the Freedmen's Bureau, there were some colored patients sitting outside, and these policemen and citizens fired a volley right among them, wounding two, one of them a boy, whose limbs had been paralyzed for two years, who was shot in the shoulder, and the other was wounded in the leg. This act of barbarity, firing into a hospital, in violation of all laws of civilized warfare, shows the character of the men engaged in it.

THE MOB AND WHITE PEOPLE.

The robberies and maltreatment of Tuesday night were not confined entirely to the colored population. The policemen and mob went to the house of Patrick Grady, a white man, who kept a grocery in a negro neighborhood, undertaking at the same time to k ll a negro. They afterwards broke down the door and robbed him of $200 in money and $90 worth of groceries, abusing the woman of the house and offering violence to a little girl and her negro nurse, telling the woman of the house, when she remonstrated, that they would burn the house down in five minutes if she didn't shut up.

THE APPEARANCE OF THE MOB.

The character of the crowd that went to the scene of the disturbance on Thursday was an index of what it would be likely to do. They hurried forward very rapidly; some of them with unsheathed knives in their hands, others with revolvers in plain sight, and others with them attached to their belts, and holding them to keep them from flapping against their hips. One or two had shotguns, or something of the kind. Meeting a colored man, a policeman seized him, jerking him up against a wall, and commenced beating him, swearing most furiously that he would blow his brains out and shoot him through. The crowd were full of threats against the colored people; such as, "You d——d niggers ought to be shot. You ought to be driven out of the place."

WHAT REV. MR. TADE SAW.

No witness seems to have had a better opportunity for observation than the Rev. Mr. Tade, who testified before the committee. On Wednesday morning Mr. Tade took particular pains to be in a position where he could see all the movements in that part of the town where the difficulties had occurred the night before, and where they were threatened to be renewed on Wednesday. It should be stated that at the time the police and what was called the posse arrived on the ground of the previous disturbance, all was entirely quiet; there were no colored people in sight, and no demonstration whatever. The colored soldiers had all gone into the fort, and a few were watching out from the parapet. Nobody was left but women and children, and a very few old men.

When the posse came down, Sheriff Winters, who raised it and who virtually admitted its questionable character, by stating that he summoned good men, but that they did not go, armed it at the store of Henry Folsom, an ironmonger on Main street. According to the description given by the Bulletin newspaper it was quite apparent that a majority of the citizens were armed and ready for any emergency. "Rifles, shot-guns, revolvers, Derringers, bowie-knives, and almost every conceivable weapon, were brought into use, and citizens were seen moving about armed cap-a-pie and ready to proceed to the scene of action and determined to quell the riot at whatever hazard." A great effort was made by the newspapers in sympathy with the rioters, and by those connected with the mob, to show that on Wednesday morning the negroes, and particularly the negro soldiers, were in a hostile attitude, and attempts have been made to show that the military force under Captain Allyn acted in concert with the mob in putting down this alleged force of negroes.

Nothing is more false than this last assertion, as will be seen by the testimony of Captain Allyn and Lieutenant Clifford. The great object of the military force seemed to be to protect the negroes as far as possible from the violence of the mob, by keeping them inside the fort. When the mob came down and commenced shooting, burning, and robbing, a very small number of colored soldiers, two of them having muskets and the others pistols, wrought up to the highest pitch of excitement on account of the outrages committed upon their families and the burning of their property, ventured out in the direction of the mob and fired many scattering shots, none of which took effect. But the charge made, that any considerable number of negroes were in hostile array or as constituting any portion of the mob, was utterly without foundation. To be sure a man by the name of Upmann, who professed to have been once an officer in the regular army, but who had, no doubt, left the army for the good of the service, pretended to have seen "three, four, or five hundred" of these colored soldiers outside of the fort, and in "something like a line of battle," all which shocked the nerves of this ex-officer of the regular army, and, as it appeared, a receiver of a land office in Minnesota under Polk, and at present a member of the "democratic party." But his testimony was shown to be utterly false by Captain Dornin and Lieutenant Clifford, of the regular army, and many persons who were in a position to know what the facts were.

ATTORNEY GENERAL WALLACE.

The police and the posse, under Sheriff Winters and Attorney General Wallace, became a mob on Wednesday morning, and were guilty of violence, murders, burnings, and robberies. The voice of this mob was the voice of revenge and threats of vengeance against the colored people. It was in favor of killing all the colored people, or of driving them out, and also of killing or driving out all those who sympathized with them. That portion of the mob led by Attorney General Wallace came upon the ground at about 11 o'clock. Most of his crowd were citizens; several of them were on horseback, and some of them were drunk. Immediately a crowd filed off to a point where there were some shanties, near by, and then shots were heard in that direction, and shouts of "kill him," "shoot him;" and when the crowd returned they said there were "two damned niggers out of the way." In a few minutes afterwards two shanties were on fire. After this achievement, the crowd went into a grocery "to wet their whistles," and celebrate their successes. Mr. Tade said that during this time there was not a colored man in sight, but the disposition of the crowd seemed to be to shoot colored children and to maltreat or to kill any colored person who came along. They drove the colored men out of their shanties, and if they started to run would shoot them down indiscriminately. Captain Allyn also testified at seeing this same Attorney General Wallace harangue his men in a violent manner, and urge them to arm. No language of denunciation is too severe to characterize the conduct of a high officer of the law in thus lending himself to become a leader of a bloodthirsty mob in the work of massacre, incendiarism, and robbery.

THE COWARDICE OF THE MOB.

Your committee were not able to get at the witness who was represented to have witnessed a scene near the fort on Wednesday morning, when a negro went out of the fort with a flag of truce in the direction of the mob, and told them they wanted no disturbance, but if they would go away all would be quiet. Upon that the crowd made a movement as if to follow him up. A party of colored men on the earthworks, seeing the man who had gone out attacked, as they supposed, fired back, the balls striking a little way short of the crowd and throwing up some dust. Thereupon the cowardice of the mob, which could shoot down unarmed men and defenceless women and children and burn their houses, was shown by breaking and running with all their might, their revolvers sticking out behind, and crying out, "*The niggers have risen and are going to take Memphis.*"

BURNING OF THE LINCOLN CHAPEL.

The Rev. Mr. Tade, a man of earnest character and Christian spirit, deeply interested in educating and christianizing the colored race, had erected with his own hands a building for a chapel and school-house for the colored people. He had dedicated it in the immortal name of that man whose fiat had stricken the shackles from four millions of slaves. He called it the "Lincoln chapel." This sacred edifice, bearing that name, and erected for that noble purpose, was dedicated on the 1st day of January of this year under very interesting auspices, a crowd gathering on that occasion more than sufficient to fill three such churches. The school taught there was an orderly one. There had never been the least disturbance made or objection raised to it. The only crowds that had ever gathered about there were crowds of southern people who had stopped in front of the door to hear the children sing.

The Rev. Mr. Tade seemed to have thoroughly engaged in his work. He pursued it with the spirit of a Christian, and as he was a leading man so engaged, it is well to know something of his teachings. When called upon by an old preacher of Memphis, of twenty years' standing, for the purpose of teaching him "how to preach to niggers," he replied that he knew only one way, and that was to preach to them when they met together on the Sabbath as dying men, and that he did not even know them as "niggers," but as men. When asked by this person why he called this place the "Lincoln chapel," he replied that there were "Asbury chapels," and "Wesley chapels," and he did not know but Lincoln was as good a saint as any of them. When questioned by a minority of the committee whether he did not, in his intercourse with the colored population, talk with them about their civil and political rights, and instruct them as to what these were, he replied that he did not remember anything of the kind. He had sometimes, in speaking to their literary societies of young men, made allusions to what they might be and ought to be, and told them that their privileges would come eventually if they took the proper stand, and would work and improve themselves as they had an opportunity of doing; and further, that his instructions had been as to their present duties, and not in reference to their civil or political standing; and especially to deport themselves quietly, peaceably, industriously, saving all they could for the support of themselves and their children, and abiding the results that would be wrought out. In reply to a question calling for his views on the right of suffrage, he said he was in favor of a limited suffrage—that is, a suffrage which should be equal to all, without distinction of color, and that he would be heartily in favor of the proposition of President Johnson, which was understood to have been announced to Governor Sharkey, of Mississippi, that all who had borne arms in defence of the Union, or had property to the amount of two hundred and fifty dollars, and could read and write, should have the right of suffrage. He thought he and the President agreed on that subject. As showing his spirit, and the spirit of those who had been more nearly connected, the following is quoted from his testimony:

"What became of your little flock that worshipped in 'Lincoln chapel?'
"Some of them have gone away and have not come back.
"Have you had any place of worship since that?
"I went out on Thursday morning after the burning to the ruins of the chapel. Quite a number of the parents came out and a large number of the children. They seemed to be very much troubled on account of it, expressed strong feelings of attachment, and so on.
"What was the spirit in which they received this thing?
"The spirit was great sorrow and depression.
"Was it a feeling mingled with one of vengeance and retaliation, or was it a Christian feeling?
"There was not a word or look or expression of envy or hatred. I told them not to be discouraged; *that there were ashes enough there to build another Lincoln chapel.* I told them we would meet the next night on the opposite side of the street, in the shade of some cottonwood trees."

RAPE.

The crowning acts of atrocity and diabolism committed during these terrible nights were the ravishing of five different colored women by these fiends in human shape, independent of other attempts at rape. The details of these outrages are of too shocking and disgusting a character to be given at length in this report, and reference must be had to the testimony of the parties. It is a singular fact, that while this mob was breathing vengeance against the negroes and shooting them down like dogs, yet when they found unprotected colored women they at once "conquered their prejudices," and proceeded to violate them under circumstances of the most licentious brutality.

FRANCES THOMPSON.

The rape of Frances Thompson, who had been a slave and was a cripple, using crutches, having a cancer on her foot, is one to which reference is here made. On Tuesday night seven men, two of whom were policemen, came to her house. She knew the two to be policemen by their stars. They were all Irishmen. They first demanded that she should get supper for them, which she did. After supper the wretches threw all the provisions that were in the house which had not been consumed out into the bayou. They then laid hold of Frances, hitting her on the side of the face and kicking her. A girl by the name of

LUCY SMITH,

about sixteen years old, living with her, attempted to go out at the window. One of the brutes knocked her down and choked her. They then drew their pistols, and said they would shoot them and fire the house if they did not let them have their way. The woman, Frances Thompson, was then violated by four of the men, and so beaten and bruised that she lay in bed for three days. They then took all the clothes out of the trunk, one hundred dollars in greenbacks belonging to herself, and two hundred dollars belonging to another colored woman, which had been left to take care of her child, besides silk dresses, bed-clothing, &c. They were in the house nearly four hours, and when they left they said they intended "to burn up the last God damned nigger, and drive all the Yankees out of town, and then there would be only some rebel niggers and butternuts left." The colored girl, Lucy Smith, who was before the committee, said to be sixteen or seventeen years old, but who seemed, from her appearance, to be two or three years younger, was a girl of modest demeanor and highly respectable in appearance. She corroborated the testimony of Frances Thompson as to the number of men who broke into the house and as to the policemen who were with them. They seized her (Lucy) by the neck and choked her to such an extent that she could not talk for two weeks to any one. She was then violated by one of the men, and the reason given by another for not repeating the act of nameless atrocity was, that she was so *near dead he would not have anything to do with her.* He thereupon struck her a severe blow upon the side of the head. The violence of these wretches seemed to be aggravated by the fact that the women had in their room some bed-covering or quilting with red, white, and blue, and also some picture of Union officers. They said, "You niggers have a mighty liking for the damned Yankees, but we will kill you, and you will have no liking for any one then." This young girl was so badly injuired that she was unable to leave her bed for two weeks.

Another case is that of

REBECCA ANN BLOOM,

who was ravished on the night of the 2d of May. She was in bed with her husband, when five men broke open her door and came into her house. They professed to have authority to arrest Mr. Bloom, and threatened to take him to the station-house unless he should pay them a forfeit of twenty-five dollars. Not having the money, he went out to raise it, and while absent one of the men assaulted the wife and threatened to kill her if she did not let him do as he wished. Brandishing his knife, and swearing she must submit to his wishes, he accomplished his brutal purpose. This is from the testimony of Mrs. Bloom, taken before the Freedmen's Bureau commission, and is corroborated by the testimony of Elvira Walker, taken before the committee, and also by Mrs. Bloom's husband, Peter Bloom.

Another case is that of

LUCY TIBBS.

A party of seven men broke into her house on Tuesday night and demanded to know where her husband was. She had with her two little children of the ages of five and two years, respectively. She implored them not to do anything to her, as she was just there with her "two little children." While the others of the party were plundering the house, one man threatened to kill her if she did not submit to his wishes; and although another man, discovering her situation, interfered, and told him to let that woman alone—that she was not in a situation for doing that, the brute did not desist, but succeeded in violating her person in the presence of the other six men. She was obliged to submit, as the house was full of men, and she thought they would kill her, as they had stabbed a woman the previous night in her neighborhood.

WHAT LUCY TIBBS SAW.

This woman lived in the immediate neighborhood, and was in the situation to see, and did see, a great deal that transpired during the riotous proceedings. This witness was intelligent and well-appearing, and the committee was strongly impressed with the truth and fairness of her testimony. She saw two colored soldiers shot down on Tuesday night, not ten rods apart. One of the men, she states, was killed by John Pendergrast, who keeps a grocery in her neighborhood. She was looking right at him when he shot the man. After being shot the soldier made an effort to get up the bayou, and Pendergrast went to a policeman, got another pistol and shot him in his mouth. This man had no sooner been killed by Pendergrast—the witness being within a few feet at the time—than another colored man came in sight. *They beat him and kept him down until they loaded their pistols then they shot him three times, burst his head open and killed him.* She knew of four colored people being killed, their bodies lying within two hundred yards of her house for two days and nights, beside the body of Rachel Hatcher, to whom allusion is made in another part of this report. She testifies to other matters, and particularly to the conduct of Policeman Roach, one of the most murderous of them all, and who is understood still to be in Memphis. She testifies also to the shooting of a colored man by a white man of the name of Galloway, and of another colored man, by the name of Charley Wallace, being shot by a Mr. Cash. Her brother, Robert Taylor, a member of the 59th regiment, was killed on Tuesday afternoon. He had $300 in possession of his sister, the witness, of which she was robbed. She states further, in regard to a man that lived in the next house to her, that he was called outside of his house and shot down. They shot him three times, and then said, " Damn you, that will learn you how to leave your old master and mistress," and took $25 from his pocket. His name was Fayette Dickerson. The white men she knew in this crowd of murderers and robbers were the old man Pendergrast and his two sons, Mr. Cash, a boy called Charley Toller, and also a wretch by the name of Charley Smith, who professed to have belonged to the Union army, and who had been teaching a school of colored people, but who had now joined these other men in their robberies and murders. Another case of rape is that of

HARRIET ARMOR.

On Wednesday morning, in open day, two men came into her room. One of them, by the name of Dunn, living on South street, under the pretext of hunting for arms, entered and barred the door, and both of them violated her. This outrage was attended with circumstances of too disgusting and shocking a character to be mentioned except by the most distant allusion. The testimony of this witness is substantially corroborated by other witnesses.

SHOOTING AND BURNING OF RACHEL HATCHER.

The shooting and burning of a colored girl by the name of Rachel Hatcher was one of the most cruel and bloody acts of the mob. This girl Rachel was about sixteen years of age. She was represented by all to be a girl of remarkable intelligence, and of pure and excellent character. She attended school, and such had been her proficiency that she herself had become a teacher of the smaller scholars. Her mother, Jane Sneed, testified before the committee that on Tuesday night the mob came to her house, took a man out, took him down to the bridge and shot him. They then set fire to the house of an old colored man by the name of Adam Lock, right by the house of the witness. Her daughter, Rachel, seeing the house of a neighbor on fire, proposed to go and help get the things out. While in the house, engaged in an act of benevolent heroism, the savages surrounded the burning building, and with loaded revolvers threatened to shoot her. In piteous tones she implored them to let her come out; but one of the crowd—the wretch Pendergrast—said, "No; if you don't go back I will blow your damned brains out." As the flames gathered about her she emerged from the burning house, when the whole crowd "fired at her as fast as they could." She was deliberately shot, and fell dead between the two houses. Her clothes soon took fire, and her body was partially consumed, presenting a spectacle horrible to behold. The mother of Rachel was, in the mean time, inside her own house trying to get out a man who was wounded that night, and who she was afraid would be burnt up. When she came back she saw the dead body of her daughter, the blood running out of her mouth. There was an Irishman about her house at this time by the name of Callahan, with the largest pistol in his hand she had ever seen. He demanded that her husband should come out until he could shoot him. But his life was saved at that moment by the appearance of two regulars, who told them to go to the fort.

CALLAHAN AND M'GINN.

Among the parties who robbed the houses of Sneed and Adam Lock were Callahan, one George McGinn, and a young man whose name witness did not know. Callahan was seen to go off with a feather-bed on one arm and a pistol in the other hand, and the young man was seen to have on the hoop skirt and the Balmoral skirt of the girl Rachel who was killed the night before. These facts are testified to by a German woman of the name of Garey, whose husband was a confectioner. At the time these things were carried off a large crowd ran into Callahan's store, and he came out with bottles and things and treated them. The crowd was very noisy, and made a great many threats. They said the next night they wanted to kill these "d—d Yankee niggers"—calling such people as this German witness "Yankee niggers."

OTHER BURNINGS AND SHOOTINGS.

Witnesses testified as to the circumstances of other burnings and shootings. A house containing women and little children was set on fire, and was then surrounded by armed men. Scorched by the extending flames the terrified inmates rushed out, but only to be fired upon when fleeing from their burning dwelling. It was reported that the arm of a little child was shot off. A woman and her little son were in a house which was fired. She begged to be permitted to come out, but the murderer (Pendergrast) shot at her. She got down on her knees and prayed him to let her out. She had her little son in there with her. They told her that if she did not go back they would kill her. McGinn was in this crowd, and the scene moved even his adamantine heart to mercy. He said, "This is a very good woman; it is a pity to burn her up. Let her come out." She came out with her boy; but it happened he had on *blue clothes.* That seemed to madden them still more. They pushed him back and said, "Go back, you d—n son of a b—h." Then the poor heart-broken mother fell on her knees and prayed them to let the child out; *it was the only child she had;* and the boy was finally permitted to escape from the flames. Pendergrast went into a grocery and gave ammunition to a policeman to load his pistol. They then started up a negro man who ran up the bayou, and told him to come to them. He was coming up to them, when they put a pistol to his mouth, shot his tongue off, killing him instantly. This man's name was Lewis Robertson.

ATTEMPT TO BURN LUCY HUNT.

One Chris. Pigeon, an Irishman, went with others to the house of Lucy Hunt, a colored woman, and threatened if they could not get in they would burn them all up. They did set fire to the house in which Lucy lived, and when she attempted to come out they pushed her back into the fire three or four times. One of them caught her by the throat and said he was going to burn her up. One of the gang put his pistol to her head and said, "G—d d—n you, if you leave I will shoot you." She thinks she owes her life to the appearance of some soldiers. They broke open her trunk and robbed her of $25, the proceeds of sixteen months' work at the fort, where she had been cooking for a company of soldiers. And they not only robbed her of her money, but of all her clothes, and everything she had, leaving her nearly naked and penniless.

MARY BLACK AND MARIA SCOTT.

They also broke into the house of Mary Black on Wednesday night. This same Pigeon was in the crowd. They poured turpentine on the bed and set the house on fire. There was in the house opposite Mary Black, at the time, a little girl twelve years old, and an old colored woman by the name of Maria Scott. After they had set fire to the house they attempted to keep them in, and when asked to let them out they replied, they intended to burn them up. Witness had no doubt they would have done so had it not been for the appearance of the regulars.

SHOOTING OF JOSEPH WALKER.

Among the instances of shooting and killing was that of Joseph Walker, a colored man who was returning home from his work during the riotous proceedings, and going round by way of the Tennessee and Mississippi railroad depot. The depot agent, a man by the name of Palmer, ordered him to halt, while Palmer's brother, from the top of a car, called out, "Shoot the d—n son of a b—h." He thereupon pulled out his pistol and shot at him three times, but hit him only once. The ball was in the body of witness at the time he was before the committee, the doctor having been unable to extract it. He was so badly injured that he has been unable to work since. He has a wife, sister, mother, brother and child, all of whom are dependent on him for support. The ruffians who shot this man hold responsible positions under the Tennessee and Mississippi Railroad Company, and the attention of the officers of that company is called to that fact, so that if the laws cannot be vindicated in bringing them to punishment, it may be seen whether they will be employed by a railroad company that seeks support from the public. The testimony is, that after Joseph Walker had escaped from these men they went after another black man whom they saw dodging round the bayou.

THE KILLING OF BEN. DENNIS.

Perhaps there is nothing that can more fully illustrate the feeling in the city of Memphis than the impunity with which the most brutal and dastardly crimes were committed upon white persons also, and upon those not even remotely connected with the riotous proceedings than the murder of Dennis on Thursday, after the riots were substantially at an end. It seems that Dennis was a man of respectable connexions, and of a good disposition, who had served a year in the rebel army; that he went into a saloon to take a drink, and while there met a colored barber, who was an old acquaintance, and spoke to him in a kind and friendly manner. At this time an Irishman

2

was sitting behind a screen, eating his dinner, and when he heard the kind words of Dennis to the negro he rushed out and demanded to know how Dennis dared to talk that way to a negro. Dennis made some reply, when the Irishman deliberately shot him. He fell on the floor and died in ten minutes. The murderer was escorted to the station-house, and according to the testimony of the station-keeper was retained there for a term of *five or ten minutes*, and no one appearing against him, he was set at liberty. The statement is, though not in proof, that while at the station-house, some one made the remark that he had "only shot a nigger," and that was no cause for his detention. No further effort has been made to bring this murderer to justice.

ATTEMPT TO BURN MARY JORDAN AND HER CHILDREN.

There are but few acts of the mob which equal in barbarism that of the outrage committed upon Mary Jordan. She had just lost her husband, and was in her house with her three children, the youngest of which being seven months old, and very sick. They had been shooting down colored people in her neighborhood, and she was very much frightened, expecting that she would herself be shot down. While she and her three children, the oldest of which being only sixteen years, were in her house, the mob set fire to a house adjoining, and the flames communicated to her dwelling. They refused to allow her or her children to come out. She started out, and told her children to follow her. Her eldest daughter said : "Mother, you will be shot." She replied she had rather be shot than burned. While she was escaping from the flames into the streets it was raining, and she could get no shelter. Her child got wet, and afterwards died. She states there were policemen in that crowd, as she knew them by the stars they wore. She lost everything she had. When, however, the house was all in flames, she ran out with her little children, with her baby in her arms. They fired at her, the bullets coming all around her, and she would have been hit had she not ran around the corner of the house and got out of the way. While running away with her baby in her arms a man put a pistol to her breast and asked her what she was doing. She told him she was trying to save her baby.

THE MURDER OF LONG.

Scarcely a more brutal murder was committed than that of Shade Long. He with his wife and two children were in their house while a mob of twenty or thirty men came to it and demanded admittance. Long was very sick, and had been in bed for two weeks. They broke into the house, and told him to get up and come out, that they were going to shoot him. He told them he was very sick. They replied they did not "care a d—n." They took him out of doors, and told him that if he had anything to say, to "say it very quick;" that they were going to kill him. They asked him if he had been a soldier. He replied that he had not, but had been in the employ of the government. Then one of them stepped back and shot him, putting a pistol to his head, and firing three times. He scuffled about a little and looked as if he was trying to get back to the house, when they told him that if he did "not make haste and die" they would shoot him again. Then one of them kicked him, and another shot him after he was down. They shot him through the head every time. They then robbed the poor woman of fifty-five dollars in paper money and fifteen dollars in silver, and went away.

THE SHOOTING OF WOMEN AND CHILDREN.

The shooting of Rachel Hatcher and the subsequent burning of her body has already been alluded to in detail. Adeline Miller, a colored girl, about twenty years old, on the first evening of the mob was standing at the door of a family grocery kept by an Italian named Cicalla. She seems to have been discovered by some person in the mob at a distance, who deliberately fired at her, the ball taking effect and killing her instantly.

Rhoda Jacobs, a young girl twenty years old, lived with her mother, who had three other young children living with her. On one night during the riots a gang of five or six men came to the door and demanded admittance. They pretended to be looking for some man. One of the ruffians pulled out his pistol and told the mother that if she did not light the candle quick he would shoot her brains out. The light disclosed that there was somebody in a bed behind the door, and it turned out to be this girl Rhoda, with her little sister, who was eight years old. Seeing the man with the pistol she screamed out, "O! I am a woman! I am a woman! don't shoot!" But that did not stay the hand of the assassin, who deliberately fired into the bed. The witness was before the committee, and in answer to the question, "Where did he shoot you?" says, "The ball came into my arm between my elbow and shoulder, went through my arm, grazed two of my fingers, went through between the lips of my little sister lying in bed with me, entered my breast, *and the bullet is right there now.*"

This girl could not identify any of the parties. She looked at the pistol in the hands of a man and said she was so afraid they would shoot her mother that she did not think of herself at all; that he had his pistol at her mother's head, and had it cocked. The little girl was not much hurt, the ball only grazing her lips. After accomplishing this brilliant feat they left the house. The mother then describes the scene as follows:

"I looked at my daughter and thought that death was upon her. The ball had gone through her arm, had hit her fingers, and shot into her breast, and, what I did not see till afterwards, the ball had glanced the child's lips. I fixed up my daughter's wounds by the *light of the burning house* on the other side of the street, and put them all to bed. I put out my lamps for fear they would come back again. It was a fuss all the time, and I dared not put my head out." (See testimony of Celia Simmonds.)

A gang consisting, among others, of Mike Cotton, S. D. Young, and Billy Barber, together with a policeman, went to the house of Richard Lane, colored man, in which he kept a saloon. They demanded a light, and while Mrs. Lane was getting one they asked her husband for arms, and upon his denying that he had any they deliberately shot him through the shoulder, the ball being afterwards cut out below in his back. As they were going out one of the fiends deliberately shot their little girl through the right arm. In the language of the mother, the little child "screamed dreadfully and bled awfully, and looked just as though she had been dipped in a tub of blood." The mother seeing her husband and child thus wounded and bleeding, commenced screaming, whereupon the crowd left.

Jane Goodloe testified before General Stoneman's commission that the mob shot into her house on the evening of the first of May and wounded her in the breast.

ATTEMPTS TO BURN WHITE CHILDREN.

The vindictive and revengeful feelings of the mob were not limited to the colored people, but they extended to such white people as had manifested particular friendship to the colored race by interesting themselves in their schools and churches, and in their welfare generally. Mr. and Mrs. Cooper were English people; they had put up a building, a portion of which was to be let for a colored school, which was to be taught by a Mr. Glasgow, who had been a soldier in the Union army. Mr. Cooper was called an "abolitionist," because they said he was doing too much for the colored people, and spoke occasionally in their chapel. A gang of policemen and citizens came into the neighborhood in a threatening attitude. Being appealed to by Mrs. Cooper to know what they were going to do, they said they were going to kill her husband and Mr. Glasgow, for they would have no abolitionists in the south. While they were talking to her, at some distance from her house, and assuring her that they would not hurt her or her children, the house, with her four little children in it, was deliberately set on fire, and while her husband and Mr. Glasgow attempted to put it out the mob fired at them several times. A policeman headed this crowd of incendiaries, whose intention, Mrs. Cooper thinks, was to burn up her children. The building and all the furniture was burned, and Mr. Cooper fled from the city to save his life.

TEACHERS OF COLORED SCHOOLS.

The most intense and unjustifiable prejudice on the part of the people of Memphis seems to have been arrayed against teachers of colored schools and against preachers to colored people. They would not teach the colored people themselves, and seemed to think it a reflection upon them that benevolent persons and societies outside should undertake the work. The preachers seemed to be men of earnest piety and sincere convictions, and to be actuated by the highest and best motives. Many of the teachers of the schools were young ladies from the northern States, graduates of the best northern schools, of intelligence, of education, and of the most unblemished characters, and who, responding to the convictions of duty, had, at the call of benevolent individuals and societies, left their homes, gone to Memphis, and entered upon the task of educating and elevating a down-trodden and oppressed race. In the face of scorn and obloquy they proceeded, even at the peril of their own lives, to the work assigned them; and with consciences so void of offence and lives so pure and blameless, that while subject to persecution and insult, neither hatred nor calumny was ever able to stain their reputations or to blacken their characters; and yet these people, guilty of no crime, engaged in a work of benevolence and Christianity, were themselves obliged to flee from the city for personal safety; and as they left, they were guided in their pathway by the light reflected from their burning school-houses.

THE SCHOOLS.

At the breaking out of the riots the number of schools was twelve, and the number in attendance was about 1200, taught by twenty-two teachers. The superintendent of these schools was a Mr. Orin E. Waters, whose testimony was taken by the committee, and is hereby referred to. The teachers were employed by the American Baptist Missionary Association, the Western Freedmen's Aid Commission, the American Missionary Association, two or three independent associations, and two or three were established independent of any associations. Twelve school-houses, or places where schools were taught, were burned during the riot, and the value of each was estimated at $2,500, besides the apparatus, furniture, &c. Mr. Waters testifies as to the teachers leaving on account of the threats of the mob that they would burn them out and kill them. Their offence was that they were teaching colored children; and although these schools had been going on for three years, there had never been a single instance in which any difficulty had been created on the part of any person connected with them, and the character and conduct of the scholars had been uniformly good. The progress of the scholars in their studies was said to be remarkable. The colored children evinced very great eagerness and interest in their studies. As an instance of the low prejudice against the teachers, your committee quote the following anonymous communication which was sent around three or four days after the riots :

"MEMPHIS, TENNESSEE, *May* 6, 1866.

'To ―――― ―――― :

"You will please to notice that we have determined to rid our community of negro fanatics and philanthropic teachers of our former slaves. You are one of the number, and it will be well for you if you are absent from the city by the 1st of June. Consult your safety.

"ANONYMOUS."

It might also be stated that the mob were not satisfied with burning school-houses and churches, but they burned also a building belonging to the government, used by the Western Freedmen's Aid Commission as a storehouse for supplies for freedmen. The total amount of stores destroyed, and of property belonging to that commission, was $4,597 35. Your committee were glad to learn that, to supply the place of the school-houses burned by the mob, Major General Fisk had, on behalf of the Freedmen's Bureau, with commendable energy, built a large school-house for the use of the colored schools.

THE CHURCHES BURNED.

Four churches were burned during the riots. One was a large brick building ; another was a large frame structure, with a brick basement, and two others were used as churches and school-houses. And although all the churches and places of worship of the colored people were destroyed by the mob, no effort whatever seems to have been made by the people of Memphis to supply, even temporarily, the want created. So far as your committee were able to ascertain, no church within the control of the white people was open for their worship.

THREATS AGAINST THE MEMPHIS POST AND FREEDMEN'S BUREAU.

The mob seemed to be very much exasperated against the Memphis Post newspaper. It is a loyal paper, defends the government, and is edited and published exclusively by men who have served in the Union army and risked their lives in defence of the government. Testimony was taken to show the threats of the mob to burn down the office and "clean out" the establishment. Mr. Galloway, who had been an officer in the rebel army, testified before the General Stoneman commission that he was the chief editor of the Memphis Avalanche. The mob seems to have thoroughly understood the feelings and sentiments of Mr. Galloway, for he states in his testimony that on the night of the second of May a proposition was made to him by a party of one hundred or one hundred and fifty men to mob the Post printing office. The mob seeing him pass in the street, shouted for the Avalanche, and some parties in the crowd seized hold of him, Galloway, the editor, to raise him on their shoulders. He says he heard cries from individual men in the crowd to "mob the Post." But he appealed to them to desist, stating that he was opposed to anything of that kind, and that the proceeding would injure *them* and *him*. It would, therefore, seem that his objections to mobbing the Post were not grounded upon the objection that any injury might be done to the Post or to the cause of good order and public decency, but because it would injure the mob and Mr. Galloway. The character of this crowd who shouted for the Avalanche, and proposed to carry this editor upon their shoulders, may be judged from what Galloway himself says, that while this discussion was going on relative to mobbing the Post, a negro passed and he saw three shots fired at him from the crowd. He did not know whether he was wounded or not. When leaving the crowd he also saw three shots fired at a passing hack driven by a negro and heard the bullets strike the windows. (See testimony of Mr. C. Galloway.) Such were the threats made against the Freedmen's Bureau that a guard was required to be detailed for its protection.

Your committee have only gone into detail in their statement of a few of the many cases of outrages about which they took testimony, and they must refer generally to the very voluminous testimony which has been taken. To go over every case would be a substantial repetition of acts of terrible brutality and cruelty. Hardly any crime seems to have been omitted. There were burglary, robbery, arson, mayhem, rape, assassination, and murder, committed under circumstances of the most revolting atrocity, the details of which in every case are fully set out in the testimony. In many cases negroes were murdered and their bodies remained on the ground for forty-eight hours, and had reached a stage of decomposition before they were buried; the relatives and friends of the murdered parties being afraid to appear on the street to claim the dead bodies, and the authorities permitted them to remain longer than they would have permitted the body of a dead dog to remain on the street.

TREATMENT OF U. S. MARSHAL RYDER.

Your committee beg leave to call attention to the testimony of Colonel Martin T. Ryder, United States marshal for the State of Tennessee. Colonel Ryder has been a Union man from the beginning. He was appointed to the office of marshal by the present Executive. The fact that he was what is called a "radical" man seems to have excited against him the prejudice of the mob. It may be here stated that all men are stigmatized as "radicals" and "abolitionists" who assert their love for the government and the flag, and who do not pander to rebels and sympathize with the rebel cause. While about the city during the riots endeavoring to keep peace, a man came up to him and asked him what he was doing there. He told him he was an officer trying to keep the peace; to which the man replied, "I know who you are;" and, having a pistol in his hand, called him an "abolitionist," and said that it was men like him that commenced these disturbances, and that he would as soon take his life as that of a "nigger," for it was men like him (Ryder) that caused all the trouble. This man then turned to the crowd and told them that this man Ryder, United States marshal, holding his appointment from the President, was a "damned Yankee abolitionist," and that he was worse than a nigger. He thereupon struck Ryder on the head and tried to knock him down. In answer to a question from the committee why he was called an "abolitionist," Colonel Ryder says that he supposes it was because he was an officer of the government; that the reason why he was called a "damned Yankee" was because that name was given to every supporter of the government.

COUNTY AND CITY OFFICERS.

Your committee have alluded in general terms to the conduct of the officers of the law in connexion with the proceedings of the mob, but deem it their duty more fully to particularize the conduct of some of these parties. While the enormity of the outrages and crimes committed during the riots and massacres have been fully acknowledged, a great effort has been made to show that they had resulted from the character of the city government, and the bad conduct of the city officials. And as these officers were elected by and owed their existence to the vote of the people, and as great numbers of the citizens of Memphis have been disfranchised under the laws of the State of Tennessee, the argument was that the citizens generally being thus disfranchised, and being in a very large majority, having no voice in the elections, could not be held responsible for the action of the city government.

The committee might admit the force of that reasoning, and, without going into the question of the propriety of disfranchising rebels who had been doing all in their power to break down the government, submit as an answer to the objection in this regard that the same man who is now mayor of Memphis, John Park, as appears by an official statement of the register of the city, which will be found in the appendix to this report, was first elected mayor in June, 1861, just after the breaking out of the rebellion, and when the secessionists had full and absolute control of the city. John Park was then elected mayor, receiving 1,631 out of 3,143 votes. In 1862 John Park was elected without opposition, there being but a very small vote cast. In 1863 he was again elected, by 1,553 votes out of 2,348. In 1864 the United States held military possession of the city. In June, 1865, and a little more than a year since, this same John Park was again elected, receiving 1,356 out of 2,191 votes. It will be seen that Park got only 275 votes less for mayor in 1865 than he did in 1861, when there was no disfranchising law in operation. Much stress was laid upon the fact that since Park's first election as mayor, he had become very drunken and worthless; but your committee can give but little weight to that suggestion, for it appears that he might have easily been defeated, had the people of Memphis who were entitled to vote exercised that right and voted against him; but they appeared to be satisfied to have him elected, and did not go to the polls to vote against him.

Mr. Richards, the city recorder, states that "they staid away more in consequence of their indifference and disinclination, than on account of being prohibited by law."

The city government was utterly and completely Irish in nearly all its branches: the mayor was an Irishman; the recorder was an Irishman; nine out of sixteen of the city council were Irish; and out of one hundred and eighty members of the police force, one hundred and sixty-three were Irish, and all the members of the police committee were Irish. The fire department was nearly all Irish. The persons composing the police force were of the most unworthy and disreputable character; monsters in crime, iniquity, and cruelty, and who during the riots committed acts that place vandalic barbarity far in the shade.

JOHN PARK.

John Park, the mayor, seems to have been utterly unequal to the occasion, either from sympathy with the mob, or on account of drunkenness during the whole time. He appeared on the ground with the mob in company with one Charles S. Cameron, who was subsequently called before your committee to prove the good character of the people of Memphis, and they were both, according to the testimony of Mr. John Oldridge, "three-quarters drunk," and were walking arm in arm. Park certainly did nothing to suppress the riot; and so far as his influence was concerned, it tended to incite it still further, disgracing himself, if he could be disgraced, and stamping with undying infamy the city of which he was the dishonored chief magistrate.

JOHN C. CREIGHTON.

The ringleader of this work of murder, incendiarism, and butchery was undoubtedly John C. Creighton, the judge of the recorder's court of the city of Memphis. He was among the earliest engaged in the riotous proceedings, and continued a leading spirit throughout, and must justly be held guilty of all the shocking crimes perpetrated. It seems he was first elected recorder in 1863, and has held that office since that time. According to the testimony of McElvaine, he had murdered a man six months before, although he had been discharged on the ground of justifiable homicide. It is shown by the testimony, that on the evening of the first day of the riot he was roaming around on horseback inciting the mob.

Alexander Mitcheler testified before the Freedmen's Bureau commission that he was making a speech to the crowd, in which he said: "*Boys, I want you to go ahead and kill the last damned one of the nigger race, and burn up the cradle, God damn them. They are very free, indeed, but, God damn them, we will kill and drive the last one of them out of the city.*"

Frederick A. Meyers testified before the same commission that he heard Recorder Creighton make a speech to the crowd to the effect, "*that every one of the citizens should get arms, organize, and go over to the nigger district, and that he was in favor of killing every God-damn nigger.*"

Sheriff Winters testified that he heard Recorder Creighton say, "*that during this riot he would not fine any one for carrying concealed weapons;*" and George Todd, that he heard Creighton make a speech in which he said, "*By God I am a brave man; we are not prepared now, but let us prepare to clean every God-damn son of a bitch out of town;*" and a crowd thereupon gave three cheers, and said they would vote for John C. Creighton. This witness further states that after this harangue, a negro was noticed, and some one in the crowd halloed out "kill him; kill the damned son of a bitch;" and that some four or five shots were fired at him. Lieutenant Clifford, of the 16th regulars, saw Creighton with the mob and heard him make a speech about killing every "God d——d nigger he saw," and proclaiming he would not "fine a white man for carrying arms."

In extenuation of the fact of such a man being recorder, it was argued that he could not have been elected to that office were it not for the fact that so many of the citizens had been disfranchised; that he had only been elected by the votes of the Irish, who managed, through perjury or otherwise, to become registered voters. But this would appear to be contradicted by the fact that, according to the testimony of Colonel Martin T. Ryder, United States Marshal of the State of Tennessee, two prominent citizens of Memphis—S. D. Walker and Mr. Poston—had petitioned the President that he, Ryder, should be removed, and that Creighton should be appointed marshal in his place, on account of his political influence in the city. And Marland H. Perkins also testified that this same man Creighton occupies a position as one of the vice-presidents of the Johnson club of Memphis, and that John Park is another one of the vice-presidents of the same club.

SHERIFF T. M. WINTERS.

T. M. Winters, sheriff of the county of Shelby, interfered as a conservator of the peace; and while your committee would not call in question his intentions, so far as suppressing the mob and restoring the peace was concerned, they consider that he was, at least, peculiarly unfortunate; that he permitted bad and lawless men to impose themselves upon him as a posse, so that when he went upon the ground to restore peace and order, it turned out, according to the testimony, that the parties he had with him were "ragamuffins" and boys, armed with shotguns and the like, and all appeared to be drunk, with the exception of Winters himself, who, witness says he believes, was the only sober man in the crowd. There is no doubt their sympathies were with the mob, for, as before remarked in this report, Sheriff Winters testifies that the best men he called upon to join his posse would not go. The testimony of J. T. Stanford, who had been in the rebel army, and was a deputy of Mr. Winters, is here referred to as illustrating "how not to do it." He was at the head of a posse to put down the "negro riot," and as he proceeded with his force to the scene of this supposed negro riot, he states that he saw one old negro who came running from under a house, saw several shots fired at him, and then saw him fall. Thereupon this officer of the law said he *was not there to suffer that;* that he should go back and get more men, and would arrest every one who would do anything of that kind; and he thereupon went back to town and reported "*that they were not doing exactly what it was intended they should do.*" He says, further, that he got on the ground on Wednesday morning, and that he found no riot when he got down there, although there were a great many people scattered around on the hills, and that there were no riotous proceedings among the colored people; and he saw from them no demonstrations of any kind.

CHIEF OF POLICE GARRETT.

There is nothing particularly to impugn the good faith of Mr. Garrett, the chief of police, but he seems entirely to have lost control of his force, and to have made but feeble attempts to regain it. Wherever he was heard of, however, he seemed to be doing all he could to protect the colored people from the assaults and violence of his brutal policemen.

OTHER OFFICERS CONNECTED WITH THE MOB.

Many of the officers of the law connected with the mob were identified as being conspicuous as leaders in the riotous proceedings, and among them one O'Hearn, a constable, identified by the witness Oldridge as having been the head of a gang of incendiaries. Oldridge heard O'Hearn calling some of his party who went and set fire to a negro school-house. But the burning of the school-house would endanger the building adjoining, and the man who occupied it came out and begged the crowd not to put fire to the school-house, as it would burn his own building; whereupon O'Hearn called out "Shoot the g—d d——d son of a b——h. If he comes out, I will shoot him myself."

The school-house was finally consumed, and while it was burning an Irish policeman named John Mickey, who had on a federal overcoat, and had a revolver in his hand, was heard to say: "May the man that sit that on fire niver be sick, God bless him. It's the only place I've had to say me prayers for the last three months, and the divil a place have I now; I'll have to say me prayers on the sidewalk"

This gang of O'Hearn's seems to have been organized, for he gave the command like this: "Number ones fall in!" And they were heard to say they were "going to burn Caldwell Hall, and every nigger building, and every nigger church, and every G—d d—n s—n of a b—h that taught a nigger;" and that "if they had the editor of the Post there they would put him into the middle of the fire." Caldwell Hall was used as a negro church and school building.

DAVID ROACH

seems to have been one of the most blood-thirsty of the policemen and scoundrels engaged in the massacre. Cynthia Townsend testifies that she saw him shoot a negro man, who was driving a dray, in the side of his head. Billy Johnson testifies that he saw this Roach shoot a negro soldier by the name of Jim, and also saw him shoot another colored man just as he was coming out of his mother's yard. "He shot him three times, and killed him dead." Other witnesses testify as to further acts of violence, robbery, and incendiarism on the part of this man Roach. The witness, Hannah Robinson, saw him at the head of a mob of twenty men, and after he had robbed her of twenty-five dollars, she heard him say, "This is white man's day."

JOHN EGAN

headed a gang who broke into the house of Molly Davis, driving the inmates out and burning down the house and all its contents. Other policemen were identified with many acts of outrage, it appearing, from nearly all the witnesses, that the policemen were in the crowds that committed the outrages; that they were generally ringleaders, and that they were most brutal and violent in their conduct and behavior. They were also engaged in the burning of school-houses and churches. And it may be said in this connexion that many of the firemen of the city were identified as being engaged with the mob. There is certainly no doubt that they were in sympathy with it. They made no effort whatever to extinguish the fires of the burning churches and school-houses; and when on the ground at all, it was not to put out burning churches and school-houses, but to prevent the adjoining buildings from taking fire. Mr. Tade heard a policeman in the crowd say "You damned niggers ought to be shot, and ought to be driven out of the place."

M'CORMICK

seems to have been a hero among the policemen on these days. A witness testifies that he saw him, surrounded by other policemen, shoot a colored man, afterwards knock him down, and strike him with a carbine, breaking it into three pieces; and after the man was down, he was "shot into a half-dozen times." This act seems to have made a hero of McCormick among his brother policemen, who was thereupon congratulated by them and looked upon as a leader.

THE CITIZENS OF MEMPHIS.

In their investigations the committee allowed the utmost latitude of examination to show what were the sentiments of the people of Memphis in regard to the riots, and also touching their feelings toward northern people. It was readily admitted that "gentlemen of property and standing" are not usually in favor of mobs and mob violence, particularly when they have reason to believe that they may become the victims by the destruction of their property or violence to their own persons; that there were a large number of these citizens of Memphis who heartily reprobated the riot there can be no doubt, but they were so far overborne by the opposite and controlling sentiment that their voice was not effectual. At the request of a minority of the committee several of the citizens of Memphis were called before them to testify in regard to the feeling of the better class of citizens in relation to the riot, as well as their feelings toward northern people and colored people. The old citizens, Mr. Miller, Mr. Ayers, Judge Smith, Mr. Wright, Colonel Dupre, and Mr. Gridley, testified from their standpoint with great fairness. Mr. Miller admitted that there was a little jealousy toward northern people there, particularly when such northern people were disposed to be a little "fussy" in their political matters, though in business matters they seemed in many cases to get along very well together. He complained of the operation of the franchise law, which debarred the better class of citizens from voting, while the Irish swore every man a loyal citizen right through— "swore to anything and everything that was asked." He had tried to get up a meeting for the purpose of disapproving the riots and hunting out the rioters and punishing them, and making compensation for the burnings done, but his proposition was not responded to, and he thought some of his friends were a little cold on the subject, and disposed to throw off the responsibility. Mr. Miller said that no movement had been made to punish the outrages by citizens or through the courts, and it did not look as though there would be.

Martin Gridley, a native of New York, who had been a citizen of Memphis for the past twenty-six years, testified that there was no hostility to northern people in Memphis, unless it was to their politics; and his idea was that if such northern people undertook to interfere or advance doctrines which were *obnoxious to the majority* there would be great prejudice against them. The fact that they should advocate the disfranchisement of the southern people who participated in the rebellion had created great hostility to them. Upon questioning, Mr. Gridley further stated that the feeling toward Union men at the breaking out of the war was hostile; that such men were called abolitionists and politicians. He also admitted that the Union men in Memphis now were called "abolitionists," just as they were before the war broke out, and that the same class of people who were obnoxious to the southerners prior to the rebellion were obnoxious to them now.

TWO SWIFT WITNESSES.

In marked contrast with the testimony of the old citizens of Memphis was the testimony of two men recently from the north, called before the committee by the minority of the committee—Charles S. Cameron and Marland H. Perkins, both of whom had been in the Union service. The character of Mr. Cameron is illustrated by the testimony of John Oldridge, and also by the testimony of Perkins, who states that he (Cameron) was ordered before a military commission charged with "drunkenness." The testimony of these two witnesses is referred to that it may be judged whether or not that, while wearing the national uniform and receiving the pay of the government, they were not in heart, sympathy, and hope with the rebels. It is no wonder that southern gentlemen should feel a contempt for northern men, when they find one of them, like Perkins, becoming so swift a witness in their behalf—the apologist for crime and blood; who calls red-handed rebels by the tender name of "confederates;" who does not believe that a man who has been in arms against his government is a rebel, and should be "punished according to the law for the crime of treason," nor that Jeff. Davis should be punished for the crime of treason. This man, Perkins, "outheroded Herod" in his denunciations of the loyal and patriotic Union men of Tennessee. His assaults upon the true loyalty of the country, his avowed sympathy with rebels and traitors, and his flippant testimony in regard to the massacre, will enable all honorable men to place a true estimate upon his character.

STATE OF AFFAIRS AT MEMPHIS.

In inquiring into the origin of the riotous proceedings the committee took a good deal of testimony in regard to the state of public feeling in that city, and the necessity of retaining there

UNITED STATES TROOPS

to uphold the authority of the government, and protect the lives, liberty, and property of citizens of the United States.

The fact that up to the time your committee left Memphis, which was more than a month after these massacres had taken place, not a single step had been taken to vindicate the law by the civil authorities, is considered to be one of the most alarming signs of the times. That no effort should have been made by the civil authorities to bring to justice the perpetrators of these stupendous and multiplied outrages is a burning and lasting disgrace to the officers of the law, and a blot on the American name.

All the witnesses testify as to the improbability, if not impossibility, of convicting any of the parties guilty of the outrages. Judge Hunter, of the criminal court at Memphis, who knows the course of criminal justice in that city, says that the chances of convicting white men for outrages upon negroes would be very remote. General Stoneman had heard of no steps being taken by the civil authorities to bring the criminals to justice; that the outrages had not been denounced in the newspapers as he had hoped they would be, nor had any public meeting been assembled to express condemnation of the riotous proceedings. He had told the people, repeatedly, that they had better have taxed the city millions of dollars and thrown it into the Mississippi, than to have had such a thing happen, and that the best thing they could do was to have some expression of opinion as would satisfy the country and world that such outrages were not countenanced by the people of Memphis. General Stoneman further states that he had written to his superior officers that he did not believe the perpetrators of the outrages during the Memphis riots would ever be punished unless the strong arm of the federal government was made use of for that purpose.

Reference is particularly had to the testimony of General Stoneman, touching the necessity of troops in Memphis, and in the State of Tennessee, in order to protect all classes of people in their rights and persons, and he does not believe, with the present officers and executors of the civil law now in power, they could be protected if the military force should be entirely withdrawn. He was led to believe that there would have been indiscriminate slaughter of the colored people during the mob, had it not been for the presence of the United States troops in the city. He thinks that there was a disposition on the part of "numbers of the mob" to interfere with the white people engaged in educating and christianizing the colored people. Captain Allyn, of the 16th regular infantry, commanding the post at Memphis, testified before your committee that his impression was, that if there had been no United States troops at Memphis at the time of the riots, ten thousand troops would have been needed there a few days afterwards, for the reason that, there being no fear of any organized force for the preservation of order, the mob would have had things their own way. In answer to the question, "What would have followed," Captain Allyn answers:

"A universal massacre here, a universal burning, and the Union people of the city would have been compelled to leave; and had they not left, they would have been killed, their houses burned, and I am inclined to think that there would have been an organized attempt to get possession of the State government; this is my impression from all I saw and heard, and from the many circumstances which came to my knowledge. As soon as it was known abroad that these men had got the mastery, people would have flocked in from the country, and it might have spread through other sections."

THE REBELS DEMAND RIGHTS.

General Stoneman says he was in East Tennessee at the time of the surrender of Lee's and Johnston's armies; that a large proportion of the people of Tennessee, who had been connected with the rebellion, passed through East Tennesse on their way home. At that time they appeared to be satisfied with the results of their efforts, and were willing to go home and keep out of sight if they were let alone. But subsequent to the election which had been held, these people had been instructed by office-seekers to believe that they had *rights as well as privileges*. At first they were satisfied with the *privileges* without the *rights;* now they are not satisfied unless they have the *rights*. And in reply to a question whether these people had surrendered the doctrines they once held of the right of secession, as one of the issues settled by the war, he states that they were willing apparently to accept it, as they had appealed to the last high court of nations; but that the *principle* of secession, as he learned through the newspapers of Tennesse, is still advocated by newspaper editors. They say they do not admit that they were wrong, as that would be to stultify themselves; that they were willing to admit they were mistaken, but not that they were wrong. They have surrendered the doctrine of secession upon the principle that might makes right. The general states that he does not believe the feelings of the people of Tennessee, in regard to the principle of secession, have changed any more than his would have changed had he been the conquered party.

A large majority would recognize the facts as they exist, but they were not willing to say that they were wrong, or that they have committed treason and should be punished. General Stoneman says that he considers the change that has taken place on the part of the people of Tennessee to be owing to the teachings of demagogues and office-seekers and a portion of the press, and that he believes the returned rebels look upon the administration as friendly to them.

It is a significant fact that although General Stoneman occupied a distinguished position throughout the war, and is looked upon as, perhaps, one of the most "conservative" of the officers of the regular army, and although stationed and living in Memphis with his family, he knew nothing of the social status of that city, and that he knew of no regular officer of the United States army who occupied any social position among that people, or went into society; that he did not know any officer of the United States army who had been received into society there; and this applied to himself as well as to others. He stated, however, that, judging from his own feelings, there would be a diffidence on the part of the officers of the army in mixing with society there, for the reason that it would not be very agreeable, as they would not be as welcome as they would wish to be, or as they had been accustomed to be.

COLONEL RYDER'S OPINION.

Colonel Ryder, the United States marshal of Tennessee, who, it is supposed, must have thorough knowledge about the matters he testifies to, states that, in his opinion, it would not be safe there for colored people or for white people like himself if the troops were taken away. He says that while he might live there himself, there are a great many in town who could not live there; that personal violence might not be used against them, but that the people would act in such a way as to keep patrons from their business and compel them to leave the city; that they would be pointed out by the Avalanche, and other newspapers, as persons attending Union meetings; that the Avalanche had advised that "small-pox" should be written over their doors because they attended unconditional Union meetings. He further stated that if there were to be a repetition of the riots of the 1st of May, the white men would be attacked as well as the negroes. He had heard talk in the streets that the white men were more to blame than the negroes, and that if justice was to be done the violence should be visited upon the white men. He heard this remark made in regard to himself: "Damn him; he is as black as a nigger."

TESTIMONY OF JUDGE LEWIS.

Your committee beg leave to refer to the testimony taken by them of Judge Barbour Lewis, who was an officer in the Union service. and whose testimony gives an interesting and, as your committee believe, a truthful account of the existing state of things in Memphis. Judge Lewis, as a northern man, did not deem it necessary to suppress his sentiments, or yield up his manhood, although he lived in Memphis; nor to

"crook the pregnant hinges of the knee,
That thrift might follow fawning."

In regard to the withdrawal of the United States troops from the city, the judge states that, unless adequate protection could be had from the establishment of the Metropolitan police force, no northern man who sympathized with Congress could remain in that city in any comfort; that he should consider it hazardous for such a person to remain, especially of any prominent man known and marked as sympathizing with the republicans and the north. Judge Lewis is the chairman of the republican committee in Memphis, and further states that if the troops should be withdrawn he would leave the place; that he and many of his friends have talked over the matter, and that it has been generally agreed that northern men of national ideas could not remain there without the protection of the military—that it had been said a thousand times of the earnest, loyal men who had fought in the late war, that they would not and could not remain there if the military are withdrawn; that many of them were threatened during the late riots, and that the newspapers had spoken of them as "enemies, tyrants, and oppressors of the south;" that this had had the effect of intensifying the bitterness felt toward northern men, and he thought that if the troops should be withdrawn a thousand men, besides women and children, would have to leave Memphis.

Mr. Stanbrough, an old resident, who had been a Union man from the beginning, says, if the troops were withdrawn he could not speak the sentiments of his heart; that he and twenty more of his friends would have to go away; that he had heard people say they could push General Stoneman and his handful of troops into the Mississippi river before he knew it. He says that if the general was to remove the forces from Memphis, he would not stay there, that people were so unfriendly to the flag of their country.

Dr. Brooks, who had been a surgeon in the United States service, states that he believes if the troops were withdrawn all northern men holding what are considered objectionable sentiments would have to leave; that he had heard men talk in this way, when speaking of Union people: "By G—d, we will clean you all out. Just get the troops away, and we'll show you when we get things into our own hands." He states that the conduct of a portion of the press had been to excite a feeling of hostility toward people who entertained what are called radical sentiments; that they advised placing a sign of "small-pox" over their doors, and advised that the people should not patronize them, and that these papers had, by every kind of ingenuity, sought to bring contempt upon northern men.

COLORED WITNESSES.

Your committee was glad to find that the value of the testimony of colored persons was appreciated, and that the minority of the committee called many colored persons, male and female, who had been slaves, to testify in regard to the treatment they had received from their old masters, and from the better class of the citizens of Memphis. They bore testimony to the kind treatment that had generally been extended to them by the better class of citizens. One of these witnesses, Prince Moultrie, seems to have had but a poor opinion of the "low-down people" engaged in the riotous proceedings, and in answer to a question as to how he considered an Irishman in comparison with himself, answered that he thought the Irishman *very much below him.*

THE CAUSE OF THE RIOT.—THE NEWSPAPERS.

As has been stated in this report, the riotous proceedings had their immediate cause in a difficulty between Irish police and colored soldiers. The more remote cause may be found in the prejudice which has grown up between the two races. The feelings of hatred and revenge toward the colored race, which have been fostered by the Irish and by large numbers of people in the south, seem to have been intensified since the negro became free. The colored race have been subject to great abuse and ill-treatment. In fact, they have had no protection from the law whatever. All the testimony shows that it was impossible for a colored man in Memphis to get justice against a white man. Such is the prejudice against the negro that it is almost impossible to punish a white man by the civil courts for any injury inflicted upon a negro. It was in the testimony before the committee that several months prior to their arrival in Memphis a negro was most brutally and inhumanly murdered publicly in the streets by a policeman by the name of Maloney. The officer in command at Memphis, Major General John E. Smith, knowing full well that Maloney would not be punished through the civil tribunals, had him tried by a military commission, by which he was found guilty and sentenced to imprisonment in Nashville. It appears that afterwards the murderer Maloney was brought before United States Judge Trigg, at Nashville, on a writ of *habeas corpus*, and the judge, without giving any notice whatever to General Thomas, that there might be a fair hearing of the question, made haste to discharge him from imprisonment, and he is now at large, " unwhipt of justice." There can be no doubt that the feeling which led to the terrible massacres at Memphis was stimulated by the disloyal press of that city. Judge Hunter states that he has no doubt but that the mob was stimulated by the newspapers. Reverend Mr. Tade says the effect of the press was to incite the riotous proceedings; and expresses the opinion that the Irish have been used as mere cat's-paws; that the papers published there had every day incited them to the deeds of violence which they committed. He states that the Avalanche is the worst, and that the Argus and Ledger are echoes of it. Witness believed that much of the ill-feeling against men of northern birth, entertaining what are called "radical sentiments," is due to the conduct of the press. Out of the seven daily papers there, five were controlled, in a greater or less degree, by men who have been in the rebel army. He states that the Avalanche, which is the most violent, vindictive, and unscrupulous of all the papers there, and which has done the most to exasperate the people against the negroes and northern people, claims to have the largest circulation and the most patronage of any paper in the city, and to most truly represent the sentiments and opinions of the mass of the people. Your committee caused extracts to be made from these papers, which they have carefully read over. Many of the articles were characterized by a bitter hostility to the government, and by appeals to the lowest and basest prejudices against the colored population; by bitter personal attacks upon northern people residing in Memphis ; and, in fact, the whole tenor of the disloyal press was a constant incitation to violence and ill-feeling.

CONDUCT OF THE COLORED SOLDIERS.

As great efforts had been made to justify the massacre of the colored people on account of the conduct of the colored soldiers who have been so long stationed at Fort Pickering, your committee deemed it their duty to take much testimony on this subject in order to satisfy themselves as to the facts in the case. That there was bad conduct on the part of some of the soldiers there can be no doubt, and the riotous and lawless conduct of a portion of them on the evening of the 1st of May is without excuse. General Stoneman, in answer to the question as to how these colored troops compared with white troops under similar circumstances, answered as follows :

"I must say, in justice to the colored troops, that their conduct compared very favorably with that of the same number of white troops under similar circumstances."

Lieutenants Garrett and Hastings, and others, who had been officers in the colored regiment stationed at Fort Pickering, testified as to their general good conduct, and it was testified that there was no disposition on the part of the colored soldiers to maltreat white people, or to attack them in any way, and that whenever it became necessary for them to make arrests of white citizens it was done in an orderly and proper manner.

The testimony of Captain Thomas J. Dornin, of the 16th regular infantry, is referred to as being particularly full and explicit in regard to the character and conduct of the colored soldiers. He was in Fort Pickering with them during the days of the riot, and was in a position to know the facts in regard to which he testified. The behavior of these colored men under the trying circumstances in which they were placed, seeing their families murdered and their dwellings burned, was such as to extort admiration from all the officers in the fort. With the exception of a feeble attempt on the part of a few to seize some arms to defend their families from the butcheries of the mob, there was the most complete subordination among them, although they had been in point of fact mustered out of the service. In answer as to what he had seen in regard to the riotous conduct of these soldiers, Captain Dornin states:

"I never saw any riotous act among them, and one thing I will say for them, that there is no number of white soldiers that I ever saw that could be held in such subjection as they were when their houses were being burned as theirs were. I could not have expected it; never could have believed it could be done."

In speaking of this matter, Captain Dornin, with the instincts which belong to the true soldier, states that he sympathized with the colored people, and was sorry that the men could not get their arms to defend their wives and families. He said he "sympathized with them as things were going, for they could not defend themselves, and it seemed like a brutish slaughter on the part of the mob." Captain D. further states that there were policemen leading the mob and shooting down the colored people, and he himself saw them engaged in carrying off everything they could lay their hands on, and inciting others to do the same.

Captain Allyn, of the sixteenth regular infantry, commanding the post at Memphis, testified before the committee, and gave a very full and detailed account of the riotous proceedings, and the operations of the force under him. His report to the general commanding will be found in the appendix. Captain A. seems to have made the best and most judicious use of the small force under his command. He states, in regard to the conduct of the colored soldiers, that if his own regiment had been there he does not think it would have been possible to keep them from interfering in favor of the negroes with their arms; and if the negroes had been a regiment of regulars, they would have rushed out unless it could have been prevented by previous knowledge, and by placing a heavy guard over it. Speaking his feelings, he said he should not have blamed them.

THE FEELING TOWARD THE GOVERNMENT.

General Stoneman states, in answer to a question as to what was his opinion of the loyalty of the people of Memphis toward the United States, that if the desire to be restored to the Union was considered loyal, he should consider a large majority of the people of Memphis loyal, that far; but if a love of the Union and the flag was considered loyal he would look *upon a large majority of the people of Memphis as not being loyal.* He said there was not that disposition now on the part of the people of Tennessee to recognize existing facts that there was six months previous; that, so far as he could get at it from the press and from the meetings of the people for various purposes, he did not consider them as loyal, if loyalty was to be defined as love for the Union, *as they were six months ago, and that it was growing worse and worse every day.* He states that he knows of only three points where the United States flag is displayed—one at his own headquarters, another at the Freedmen's Bureau, and another is in front of the building used as the printing office for the Memphis Post. He had never seen it displayed at public meetings or places of amusement or theatres, and only sometimes on steamboats coming down the river. Information was conveyed to the general that at the theatre such national airs as "Hail Columbia," "Star-spangled Banner," and "Yankee Doodle" were hissed by the audience, and that rebel airs were received with applause; he was obliged to write to the manager of the theatre that if national airs were to be met with disapprobation, and the "so-called confederate national airs" should be received with applause by the audience, it would compel him to interfere.

Mr. Stanbrough says that he would no more have raised the United States flag over his mill than he would think of putting a match to his property to burn it up; that he would not for his life think of taking the American flag and marching down Main street with it; that if a band should go through the streets playing the national airs it would be received with a hiss and a groan. Everybody residing in Memphis knew the flag of our country was not respected, and that while national airs are hissed, when "Dixie" is struck up there is always a shout, and if played for the twentieth time, for every time there is a shout; but there is no "Yankee Doodle" or "Hail Columbia" in Memphis. He says there is not a bit more love for the laws, the Constitution of the United States, or the Union in Memphis than there was in the hottest days of the rebellion, and that the fires of hate burn as hot and as deep down as ever.

General Runkle, of the Freedmen's Bureau, speaks of having seen pictures of rebel generals in all the shop-windows, but of never having seen those of such men as Lincoln, Grant, Sherman, or Farragut displayed, nor even the picture of Johnson; that there was an academy there called "The Lee Academy," with the name printed in gold letters on the sign-board; that such was the feeling there the people hated the sight of the uniform of a Union officer, and he would not consider it safe for him to be on the streets alone at night in his uniform.

GENERAL CONCLUSIONS.

From the testimony taken by your committee, from personal observation and from what they could learn in regard to the state of feeling in Memphis, and, indeed, through that entire section of the country, they are of opinion that there is but little loyalty to the government and flag. The state of things in the city of Memphis is very much now as it was before the breaking out of the rebellion. Many of the same newspapers published there then are published now, and by many of the same men—by men who, during the war, were in the rebel armies fighting for the overthrow of the government. Professing to accept the situation, they seem inspired with as deadly hatred against the government as ever, and are guilty of the same incitation to violence, persecution, and oppression toward the men holding opinions obnoxious to them, that they were towards the men who were well disposed toward the Union men in 1861. Your committee say, deliberately, that, in their judgment, there will be no safety to loyal men, either white or black, should the troops be withdrawn and no military protection afforded. They believe that the riots and massacres of Memphis are only a specimen of what would take place throughout the entire south, should the government fail to afford adequate military protection. There is everywhere too much envenomed feeling toward the blacks, particularly those who served in the Union armies, and against northern men and Union people generally who love the government, and who desire to see it sustained, its authority vindicated, and who believe that treason is a crime that should be punished. There is no public sentiment in the south sufficiently strong to demand and enforce protection to Union men and colored people. The civil-rights bill, so far as your committee could ascertain, is treated as a dead letter. Attorney General Wallace, in flagrant violation of his oath and duty, whose name has been heretofore alluded to in this report, has, according to the newspapers, proclaimed that he will utterly disregard the law.

The hopes based upon this law that the colored people might find protection under it are likely to prove delusive; for, where there is no public opinion to sustain law, but, on the other hand, that public opinion is so overwhelmingly against it, there is no probability of its being executed. Indeed, your committee believe the sentiment of the south which they observed is not a sentiment of full acquiescence in the results of the war, but that there is among them a lingering hope that their favorite doctrine of secession may yet be vindicated. It is the same idea that Jeff. Davis expressed. When he was seeking safety in flight, a traveller remarked to him that the cause was lost. Davis replied: "*It appears so; but the principle for which we contended is bound to reassert itself, though it may be at another time, and in another form.*" (Pollard's Southern

3

History of the War, vol. 2, page 582.) They believe in the principle and doctrine of secession the same as ever. Though they have been beaten by arms, they assert and maintain that the principle is the same, and hope for its vindication hereafter in some way. Recognizing the friendship to them of what was called the "democratic party" in the north during the war, and acknowledging the aid and comfort they derived from their sympathy and from their efforts to embarrass the government in the prosecution of the war against them, they hope, by combining with them in their political movements, finally to secure by the ballot what they failed to achieve by arms.

The fact that the chosen guardians of the public peace, the sworn executors of the law for the protection of the lives, liberty, and property of the people, and the reliance of the weak and defenceless in time of danger, were found the foremost in the work of murder and pillage, gives a character of infamy to the whole proceeding which is almost without a parallel in all the annals of history. The dreadful massacre of Fort Pillow, which excited the horror of the country and of the civilized world, was attempted to be palliated on the ground that the garrison was taken after the most desperate resistance, and after having been repeatedly summoned to surrender; that the blood of the assailants had been heated to such a degree and their passions so aroused that there was no controlling them, though it is alleged that some of their officers vainly attempted to do so. But no such ground of palliation can be advanced in the case of the Memphis massacres. After the first troubles on the first evening, there was no pretence of any disturbance by the colored people, or any resistance to the mob, calculated to excite their passions, and what subsequently took place was the result of a cool and mature deliberation to murder and destroy the colored people. Like the massacre of St. Bartholomew, the Memphis massacre had the sanction of official authority; and it is no wonder that the mob, finding itself led by officers of the law, butchered miserably and without resistance every negro it could find, and regretting that death had saved their victims from further insult, exercised on their dead bodies all the rage of the most insensate cruelty.

In view of the fact that the state of public sentiment is such in Memphis that it is conceded that no punishment whatever can be meted out to the perpetrators of these outrages by the civil authorities, and in view of the further fact that the city repudiates any liability for the property, both of the government and individuals, destroyed by the mob, your committee believe it to be the duty of the government to arrest, try, and punish the offenders by military authority; and also by the same authority levy a tax upon the citizens of Memphis sufficient to cover the losses for all property destroyed.

THE RESULTS OF THE RIOT.

The resolution of the House directed the committee to ascertain the number of the killed and wounded, the names of the parties engaged in the riot, and the amount and character of the property destroyed. These facts the committee have ascertained in detail, as far as practicable, and present the following proximate results:

THE KILLED.

The number ascertained by the testimony taken by your committee, in common with that taken by General Stoneman's and the Freedmen's Bureau commission, to have been killed, including the white men Dunn and Stevens, is 48, and the names are given as far as known; but there is no doubt in the minds of your committee that many persons were killed whose killing has not been proved. A vast number of colored people had come into Memphis and located in this neighborhood, who were but little known, and who, during the progress of the riot, fled in all directions. Nothing was ascertained from them what portion of their number was killed. The following is a list of the killed, as far as could be ascertained by the committee. The names are given as far as known. A large number were killed whose names are not known:

COLORED PERSONS KILLED.

Joseph Lundy, 3d United States colored heavy artillery	1
Isaac Richardson, 3d United States colored heavy artillery	1
William Withers, 3d United States colored heavy artillery	1
George Cobb, 3d United States colored heavy artillery	1
George Black, 3d United States colored heavy artillery	1
Bob Taylor, 3d United States colored heavy artillery	1
Lewis Robinson	1
Levi Baker	1
George Williams	1
Unknown negroman, at Grady's Hill	1
Unknown negro man, on Mulberry street	1
William Henry, at corner of Henry and McCall streets	1
Unknown negro man, on South street, near Mississippi and Tennessee railroad depot	1
Two colored soldiers, east of the Mississippi and Tennessee railroad depot	2
Colored soldier, on South street, near Rayburn avenue	1
Colored soldier, east of South street bridge	1
George Anderson	1
Old negro man, south side Beale street, near Second	1
Two negroes, in the creek south of South street	2
Unknown negro man, on De Soto street	1
Unknown negro man	1
Freeman Jones	1
Negro boy, on South street, near Causey	1
Negro woman, Emeline, South street	1
Colored soldier, corner of Linden and St. Martin streets	1
Unknown negro man, corner of Shelby and South streets	1
Rachel Hatcher	1
Unknown negro man, near intersection of Rayburn avenue and South street	1
Colored soldier, at negro quarters, south of South street	1
William H. Saunders	1
Colored soldier, on South street	1
Colored soldier	1
John Robinson	1
Two unknown negro men, on road side	2
Unknown negro boy, on road side	1
Charley Wallace	1
Unknown negro man	1
Shade Long	1
Adeline Miller	1
Jackson Goodell	1
Daniel Hawkins	1
Uncle Dick	1
Robert Carlton	1
	46

WHITE PERSONS KILLED.

Stephens, policeman	1
Dunn, fireman	1
	2
Total	48

THE WOUNDED AND MALTREATED.

As near as your committee could ascertain, from their investigations and from the testimony taken by the two commissioners, there were between seventy and eighty persons wounded. Many of them were identified by name, and many were known to be wounded—some severely, some slightly—whose names could not be ascertained, as they had fled from the city. There were some ten or twelve persons in addition to this number who were badly maltreated.

ROBBERIES.

There were one hundred distinct robberies, more or less aggravated. The committee have included in this number the robberies of colored individuals that took place during the entire week in which the riots occurred.

BURNINGS.

As has been stated, four churches and twelve school-houses were burned, and the number of other houses and cabins burnt was in the neighborhood of ninety.

PROPERTY DESTROYED.

It has been difficult to ascertain the precise amount of property destroyed Your committee took much testimony in regard to that subject, but less than that taken by the Freedmen's Bureau commission, whose investigations on this branch of the subject are perhaps fuller than that taken by any other. That commission reports that the loss sustained by the government and the negroes, up to the date of making their report, was $98,319 55; and it was reported that subsequent investigations would increase the amount to at least $120,000. As near as your committee could ascertain from the testimony taken by them and from the other investigations, the amount of government property destroyed was in the neighborhood of $17,000, besides the expenses incurred by General Stoneman, and by the commissary and quartermaster's departments, in the transfer of troops and transportation of persons who left the city in fear of mob violence, amounting in the aggregate to $3,985 41.

RECAPITULATION.

Killed, colored persons.. 46
         white persons.. 2
Wounded.. 75
Rape.. 5
Maltreated... 10
Robberies.. 100
Houses and cabins burned... 91
Churches... 4
School-houses.. 12

VALUE OF PROPERTY DESTROYED.

Individual property, say.................................... $110,000 00
Government property.. 17,000 00
Expenses incurred by General Stoneman and by commissary
    and quartermaster's departments........................ 3,981 41
        Total..................................... $130,981 41

All of which is respectfully submitted.

E. B. WASHBURNE, *Chairman.*
JNO. M. BROOMALL.

VIEWS OF THE MINORITY.

Mr. G. S. SHANKLIN, *from the Select Committee on the Memphis riots, submits the following as his views :*

In obedience to said resolution and appointment, the committee left Washington city on the 17th day of May last, and arrived in Memphis on the 22d. Upon their arrival they had an interview with Major General George Stoneman, United States army, who was then in command of the department of Tennessee, with his headquarters located in the city of Memphis, who stated that he was in Memphis at the time the riot commenced, on the evening of the 1st day of May, and during its continuance, until it was suppressed, on the evening of the 3d day of May, by the military force under his command, and peace and quiet restored to the city.

General Stoneman also informed the committee that shortly after the termination of the riot, to wit, on the 5th of May, he ordered a commission, consisting of five persons, four officers of the army of the United States and one citizen of Memphis, to meet on the 7th of the same month and proceed to investigate and report upon all the facts connected with the recent occurrence and disorder in the city of Memphis, Tennessee, which began on the 1st of May, 1866, &c., &c.; that said commission commenced their labors on the day fixed in the order, and had been some two weeks or more engaged in the investigation, and were then engaged, and had from time to time reported the evidence taken, which was then submitted to the committee by General Stoneman, and afterwards all the evidence which had been taken before said commission was also submitted.

The committee also, at the same time, met Brigadier General Fisk, assistant commissioner of the Freedmen's Bureau for the States of Tennessee and Kentucky, who informed them that he had also appointed a commission of officers of the bureau to investigate said occurrence and disorder, and that the commission appointed by him had completed or were about to complete their investigation, and the evidence taken by said commission was also submitted to the committee for their inspection and information.

The information and evidence developed by the two commissions, and furnished to the committee, aided and facilitated the labors of the committee, and resulted in a much more full and thorough investigation of the facts and details of the occurrence and disorder than could possibly have been made in a reasonable time without their aid.

After obtaining this information, the committee, on the 23d of May, commenced their investigation by the examination of witnesses, and continued it for some sixteen days, during which time they examined about one hundred and seventy witnesses, making a manuscript record of near two thousand pages.

They did not confine their examination to any particular class of persons, but selected them from all classes, both black and white, male and female, from the most intelligent and refined down to the most ignorant and degraded, examining all they could find who knew or pretended to know any circumstance or fact connected with the matter. It will not be attempted in this report to go into the minutiæ of the progress of the riotous proceedings, or the especial acts of savage cruelty, rapacity, and lust of passion that marked the conduct of many who were engaged in it, which would necessarily extend this report to an indefinite and unreasonable length. The testimony exhibits many individual acts that would disgrace the most ferocious savage, and cause civilization and religion to blush and mourn over the depravity of mankind—such acts as have ever characterized all mobs wherever they have occurred, and will wherever they may occur. But it is proposed to present the general and leading features of the occurrence that may be more essential and important in forming a correct conclusion as to the character and causes of this most unfortunate affair.

The testimony of Dr. S. J. Quinby, a northern man, and who had been connected with the United States army as surgeon and assistant surgeon during the war, and then connected with the Freedmen's Bureau in the city of Memphis, proves that, on the first day of May, and about 3 o'clock in the afternoon, two police officers of Memphis arrested a colored man against whom some offence was charged. At the time this arrest was made there was a large crowd of discharged colored soldiers collected at a drinking saloon on South street, and within one block of where the arrest was made, drinking, disorderly, and boisterous. So soon as the discharged soldiers ascertained the arrest had been made they followed the officers and forciby rescued the prisoner. The colored soldiers then returned to the saloon, some forty or fifty of them, quite drunk and noisy. In about an hour after this six police officers returned to the place where these soldiers were collected, and two of them arrested two of the most noisy and boisterous discharged soldiers in a peaceable and orderly way, showing no arms. After the arrest the two officers started off with the prisoners, when they were pursued by a large crowd of colored soldiers, some forty of whom were armed with revolvers, others with stones, clubs, and whatever else they could get, hallooing "Shoot them! Kill them!" &c.

After they had proceeded some distance, the four police officers trying to keep the crowd back, and from the two in charge of the prisoners, some of the colored soldiers fired their revolvers behind the officers in the air; the officers, supposing they were fired at, turned around and commenced firing at the crowd, the colored soldiers returning the fire. In this rencounter one of the police was shot; witness saw him carried off to a grocery. A part of the soldiers then returned, and a part continued the pursuit. In a few moments it was reported to those that had returned that one of their men was killed, when they reloaded their revolvers and armed themselves with whatever they could procure, and again started, much excited, in pursuit of the officers. They soon turned into a different street, and out of sight of the witness, but in about fifteen minutes returned and stated that they had killed one of the police. Two of the soldiers were wounded and bleeding, one of them bringing back with him the club of the policeman, bloody. After this witness went to tea, and upon his return, in about three-quarters of an hour, he heard firing, and saw a crowd of about one hundred and fifty colored soldiers chasing officers in all directions, hallooing to them to "halt," and shooting at them; some fourteen shots were fired at one officer, and some six soldiers chasing another and firing at him. This fight continued until about dark, when the colored soldiers went to Fort Pickering, near by, and did not come out during the night. In these rencounters it is proven that two police officers and some four or five colored soldiers were killed and several others wounded.

The above facts, proven by Dr. S. J. Quinby, give the clearest and most satisfactory history of the commencement of the affray that has been proven by any witness examined by the committee. Indeed, he is the only witness who was examined that gives a full history of the three first rencounters between the colored soldiers and the police. There were several witnesses who prove many of the facts connected with the first day's fight, to wit, Dr. Sharp, W. F. Taylor, Newton Ford, and Tony Cherry, the last named a man of color, and one of the discharged soldiers, and with the crowd engaged in the fight, all corroborating the statements and history given by Dr. Quinby, and none contradicting his statement in any important fact.

Up to this point in the riot there can be but one conclusion or opinion, and that is that the colored soldiers were the aggressors and commenced the fight with the officers of the law in the discharge of their official duty, and that they were guilty of a very high offence and crime against the law. The police officers having conducted themselves with a commendable prudence and firmness in the discharge of their official duty, it is to be greatly regretted that they did not afterwards continue in the same line of conduct. Had they done so, the city of Memphis would have been spared the scenes of savage cruelty, bloodshed, and crime that immediately followed, that cannot be too strongly condemned.

It appears from the testimony of a number of witnesses that about ten o'clock at night, and after the colored soldiers had all retired to Fort Pickering, a posse, numbering about fifty, collected by the sheriff, came down to South street, where the affray had taken place in the evening, and finding all quiet, a portion of them returned, while another portion united with a large police party, who had been engaged in the affray with the colored soldiers in the evening, and others attracted by the disturbance, their passions aroused and excited by what they considered a great outrage committed by the colored soldiers in resisting the law and killing two of their friends in the proper discharge of their official duty, divided themselves into small squads or parties, and commenced an indiscriminate slaughter of innocent, unoffending, and helpless negroes wherever found, and without regard to age, sex, or condition; visiting the humble houses of the colored people under the pretext of searching for arms; breaking open their houses when admission was not speedily granted by the inmates; shooting, beating, and killing them in the most cruel manner without cause or provocation, and in many cases robbing them of the little pittance of money and property they had accumulated by their labor and frugality; in other cases setting fire to their houses and attempting to force the inmates to remain therein until they should be consumed by the flames, or, if they attempted to escape, shooting them down as wild beasts. But, to crown this most disgraceful tragedy, it is proven that some of the colored females were violated by some of these fiends in human shape.

This disorder was continued with more or less violence during the remainder of the night of the 1st of May. On the morning of the 2d quiet was restored to the whole city, and some began to hope that this storm of outrage and passion had exhausted itself and passed; but these hopes were soon dissipated. In the early part of the day squads of police officers, firemen, and quite a number of the lower and disorderly part of the population commenced to collect on South street, in the groceries and drinking saloons, in the neighborhood of the previous night's disorder, and, though restrained somewhat by the presence of small squads of United States soldiers that were patrolling the streets and neighborhood during the morning, again, about nine o'clock, renewed the scenes of the previous night.

The evidence does not satisfactorily explain how or by whom the riot was commenced on the morning of the 2d of May. The evidence is conflicting and contradictory upon this subject, nor is it satisfactory as to the part the discharged colored soldiers took in its commencement on that morning. One witness, D. Upman, who had only resided in Memphis a short time, from the northwest, and once an officer in the United States army, and brevetted major for gallant conduct in the Mexican war. a Union man, and had been during the whole civil war, states that he went down to South street about 9 o'clock of the morning of the 2d and saw a large crowd of several hundred colored people collected near the fort, in front of the fortifications, many of them armed, some with United States muskets, others with pistols; some uniformed, others partly so; some twenty or twenty-five of them were engaged in firing at the people on South street, which was continued about an hour or an hour and a half, when they went back into Fort Pickering. He left shortly after. During this firing by colored soldiers witness saw no firing by white persons.

Tony Cherry, one of the discharged colored soldiers, states that on the morning of the 2d there was firing by colored soldiers at the white people on South street; that four of them had muskets and fired them repeatedly; that they kept up a pretty brisk fire for some time; that they fired a volley at a group on horseback who had hoisted a black flag; that the man who had the flag fell when they fired, and the others moved out of sight, but when they showed themselves they were shot at. Other witnesses speak of two colored soldiers with guns on that morning shooting at some person near the railroad depot, which is situated a short distance from the outer works of Fort Pickering. Other witnesses, and some of them officers of the colored soldiers who had been mustered out of service the day before the riot commenced, numbering about 2,700, state that they were at the fort, and that there was no firing by colored soldiers on that morning near the fort. Taking all the evidence together, there can be no doubt that some of the discharged colored soldiers were, on that morning, engaged in shooting at the groups of police and others on South street from some point near the fort, and also at persons near the railroad depot; but as to the extent of that firing, or how many were engaged in it, or its effect, is altogether uncertain and doubtful, nor can it be determined, with any degree of certainty, whether the firing in the morning by the colored soldiers in the vicinity of the fort commenced before that of the police and mob or not. It is clear that the disgraceful scenes of the night before were renewed between 9 and 10 o'clock of that morning, and continued an hour and a half to two hours, and again at intervals during the evening and night and until the afternoon of the third day of May, when General Stoneman issued his order, directed to the mayor, city council, and all civil authorities of the county of Shelby and city of Memphis, which forbade any persons assembling together, armed or unarmed, white or colored, without authority from headquarters—this order not to interfere with the police force so long as they could be relied on as preservers of the peace, (which order is reported with the testimony of General Stoneman,) and under this order the military took the control of the city, and peace and order were immediately restored.

An abstract has been prepared by the reporter, Mr. Smith, from the testimony, and delivered to the honorable chairman, in which the names of all the killed and wounded, the amount of property destroyed, and its value, are given, as far as the same can be collected from the testimony, and the same is hereby referred to, if filed, and it is supposed that it will be.

General Stoneman, on the first evening of the riot, placed the small military force at the service of the mayor of the city, with the condition that it was not to be called for by the mayor unless it was manifest that the constabulary force under his control was not sufficient for the suppression of the riot.

There seems to be no evidence in this case showing that the mayor at any time during the riot either used or attempted to use the police force under his control to suppress the riot and disorder, or that he again called on the military to do so, but, from the evidence, he appears to have been during the whole time so much intoxicated that he was wholly incapacitated for business or duty of any kind. Several times during the riot small squads of soldiers were brought to the scene of disorder, and upon every occasion their presence had the effect to check and immediately stop disorder without the employment of any force whatever.

Whether the small military force, consisting of about 150 men, (with a large amount of public property to guard,) could have been sooner or differently used, so as to have effectively suppressed the disorder, cannot be determined. It might have been improper and hazardous (with so small a military force) to have sooner attempted to suppress a mob of the numbers then engaged until the passion and fury were somewhat exhausted.

General Stoneman, in whose skill, prudence, and discretion I have great confidence, was upon the ground, and no doubt used all the means at his control to collect the necessary information and facts to form a correct conclusion, and acted thereon according to his own convictions of right and duty.

The several posses summoned by the sheriff, Winters, to aid in suppressing the riot seemed rather to add fuel to the flame than to have accomplished the object for which they were summoned. Whilst he and some of his company made some effort to restore order, much the larger part of his posse joined with the mob. He certainly was unfortunate in the selection of his men. Nor was the city of Memphis less unfortunate in the selection of Recorder Craton for the important office that he holds. If the testimony can be relied on in this case, so far from exerting his official power and influence to suppress the riotous mob and preserve peace and order, it was exerted, by speeches if not by his example, to encourage violence and disorder.

The proof also establishes the fact that many of the firemen of the city, whose especial duty it was to suppress the devouring flames and to preserve and protect the property of all the citizens of the city, instead of employing themselves in this honorable and useful pursuit, for which they are generously paid out of the revenue of the city arising from a tax on the property of the citizens, were criminally engaged with the mob in the destruction of life and property.

It is most conclusively shown by all the testimony in this investigation that this mob was exclusively composed of the police, firemen, rowdy and rabble population of the city of Memphis, the greater part of whom are voters in the city of Memphis, under the franchise law of the State of Tennessee, enacted by what is known and called the " radical Brownlow party," and intended to disfranchise all persons in that State who had in any manner aided, encouraged, or abetted the late rebellion, and thereby place the political and civil power of the State in the hands of and under the control of those they call true loyal men.

It is also most conclusively proven by the testimony reported, that from one-half to two-thirds of the property-holders, men of business, and those regarded as the more orderly part of the population of Memphis, and a large part of the same class of society in the State of Tennessee, are disfranchised and excluded from holding any office or voting in the election of city or State officers; the men engaged in the riot constituting a part of the voters by whom the city officers were elected, against the consent of the masses of the better population of the city. The effect of the franchise law of Tennessee is to exclude from one-half to two-thirds of the men of property, men of business, and that class regarded as the more intelligent and better portion of society in the State, and thereby to place the political power in the hands of and under the control, to a great extent, of the more inferior classes of society, which often results in the selection of officers of little qualification and distasteful to a large majority of the people whose interest is directly affected thereby, and prejudicial to the prosperity, peace, order and security of society. However just, wise or politic some may suppose it to be to disfranchise in the seceded States all who have in any manner participated in the late rebellion, and exclude them from office and suffrage in the election of officers, it is believed by the undersigned, and asserted with confidence, that the franchise law of the State of Tennessee has operated most injuriously to the preservation of order and peace and the security of society in the city of Memphis. The inefficient, disorderly and drunken officers of the city of Memphis, and the vicious and reckless police force and firemen selected and controlled by said officers, are alone indebted to the effect of that law for their success in obtaining the offices they hold and have disgraced, against the consent and wishes of a large majority of the masses of the better class of citizens of the city. No portion or class of citizens kept more entirely aloof and free from the disorder, or condemned its outrages in more decided terms, than those citizens who had been actively engaged in the rebel service, and consequently disfranchised, among them about fifteen hundred paroled confederate or rebel officers and soldiers. Upon the other hand, it appears that a large majority of those engaged in the riot and disorder were registered voters, and, according to the radical test of that law, true, loyal men, and worthy to be intrusted with the high prerogative of office and the dearest and most inestimable right of a freeman—the right to be heard in the selection of those who are to rule over them; and its effects are expected to grow worse so long as that policy is adhered to. No people who have ever enjoyed the blessings of free, republican government will consent long to be governed by a minority, and especially when the masses of that minority are of the more inferior class, the part of that governing class of a higher grade of society, and possessing intelligence, property, morals, or business, being too weak in numbers to control the lower grade.

In the policy of disfranchising a large part of the better classes of society may be found one and a prominent cause of the sad and cruel tragedy of Memphis. Another and perhaps not less active cause of the Memphis riot is to be found in the antagonistic interest and feelings of hostility that exist between the laboring classes of foreign population and the negro race. Both of these classes are numerous in the city of Memphis, arising in part from the peculiar location of the city, midway between the larger cities of the Mississippi valley, and a large immoral and rabble population, both white and black, that collected there during the war, ever ready to engage in rapine and plunder, without character, name, or location. This feeling of hostility and hatred is found mutual, wherever the foreign laborer and negro population are brought in contact, and in no city or place does it more intensely exhibit itself than in Memphis.

No city in the Mississippi valley can claim a more intelligent, cultivated, and refined society, or more active and efficient business men can be found than in the city of Memphis. The growth of the city is rapid, the masses of its population are industrious, orderly, and moral, and with these classes the sentiment of condemnation of the riot is universal; then why should they suffer reproach or condemnation? They were deprived by the law, in the enactment of which most of them had no voice, civil or legal power; they had but recently emerged from military control and government; the military was then present for the purpose of aiding in the enforcement of the law and preventing disorder; and whilst they in a large body offered their services to General Stoneman, and to be under his control, and such officers as he might appoint over them, to aid in suppressing the mob, these proffered services having been declined by General Stoneman, it is fair to presume that they came to the conclusion that it would have been improper for them to interfere in the matter; and in this conclusion no one can say they erred, under all the embarrassing circumstances that surrounded them.

It may be alleged that the people of Memphis had failed, by public expression, to condemn the outrages and acts of cruelty perpetrated by the mob, or to take any steps to bring to punishment the perpetrators of these unlawful acts. But it appears that immediately after the termination of the riot, the commission appointed by General Stoneman, and General Fisk, of the Freedmen's Bureau, commenced their investigations. It also appears from the testimony of Wm. Hunter, the judge of the criminal court of Memphis, and he an extreme Union and loyal man, appointed to office by Governor Brownlow, that the grand jury of his court, whose province and whose duty it was to make said investigation, had been discharged a few days before the riot occurred, and inasmuch as the regular June term of his court would shortly take place, and the military investigations were in progress, he thought it more advisable to take no steps in the matter until the regular term of the court; all of which at least furnishes a good reason, if not a complete justification, for the conduct of the citizens of Memphis.

All of the above stated facts, and conclusions drawn therefrom, are fully sustained by the testimony of General Stoneman, Jno. Hunter, Petser Miller, C. J. Cameron, T. S. Ayres, J. C. Parker, Jno. M. Perkins, Henry G. Smith, W. F. Taylor, W. Foran, M. J. Wright, M. Gridley, J. H. McMahan, L. I. Du Pue, and many more, who are citizens of intelligence, business, and high character, and several of them northern men, who had served as officers of the United States army during the rebellion and then located in Memphis; no witness proving all of the above facts, yet each one of them proving a part of them.

It is also most clearly and conclusively proven by nearly all the above-named witnesses, and many others, that the relations existing between the resident freedmen of Memphis and the masses of the white population are kind, liberal, and just, and especially so between the colored people and those who had formerly been owners of slaves. The same witnesses most satisfactorily prove and establish that the greater body, if not the entire mass of the better classes of the southern people, at least such as are the owners of property and engaged in the business of the country, acquiesce in the results of the war, and in good faith are anxious and desirous that the union of the States shall be restored and peace and harmony once more restored under the Constitution of our fathers; that the prejudice and sentiments of hostility toward persons of northern birth who have settled among them are confined to that class of northern men who hold and advocate the extreme radical doctrines of personal punishment, confiscation of property, disfranchisement of those engaged in rebellion, and political equality for the negro. This is, however, contradicted by some holding these doctrines, or connected with the Freedmen's Bureau, colored schools or churches. They state the feeling of hostility to northern people is general, and hostile to the government of the United States.

Their personal interest and partisan prejudices, as well as their want of familiar association and intercourse with the masses of the people, by which the private opinions and sentiments of a community can be collected, detract much from their testimony and opinion.

That entire harmony, quiet, and peace should immediately follow a bloody and desolating civil war of four years' duration, could not be expected; nor could it be expected that the vanquished should cease to cherish the fondest recollections of their friends who fell on the battle-field, contending for what thousands believed to be a just cause, or that they should cease to mourn over the desolation and ruin that surrounds them, and lies wide-spread over their whole country: such expectations would do injustice to the nobler traits of the human heart and character. Certain it is, that no intelligent man, acquainted with them or their ancestors, will expect it.

The majority of the committee, at the close of the investigation, introduced extracts from several daily newspapers published in the city of Memphis, it is supposed, for the purpose of proving the hostile feelings of the citizens towards the northern population located in the city, and also to prove the sentiments of the people towards the people of the north and the government of the United States. These extracts were carefully collected by Colonel Runkle and several other officers of the Freedmen's Bureau, in which they were several days employed. They were introduced and proven by the officers who got them up, without any notice to the undersigned of an intention to introduce such testimony, or without the slightest knowledge on his part that such testimony would be introduced until it was offered. He had no time then to examine it, nor has he up to this time done so, or had an opportunity so to do. Whether these extracts are taken from the editorials of these papers, or are extracts taken by the Memphis papers from other papers published in other States, or whether the whole articles are extracted or only parts of them, the undersigned has had no opportunity to inform himself, nor does he think any fair or legitimate inference or opinion as to the sentiments of the people among whom the papers are published can be drawn or proven from mere extracts such as these. In order to aid in forming correct opinions upon that subject, it would be necessary to examine the whole tone and sentiment exhibited by the paper, not merely by extracts; and even then public sentiment might not, and would not in a majority of cases, accord with the sentiments of the newspaper. Such testimony is, therefore, deemed unreliable, and protest is hereby entered against its use in this case.

The undersigned has no information as to the views or opinions of the majority of the committee as presented in their report. The honorable chairman has never, at any time, called the committee together for consultation, nor in any manner communicated to the undersigned the contents of said majority report, nor invited his concurrence therein. He was not in the hall at the time the honorable chairman obtained leave to file the majority report, nor had he notice thereof until the next day. But, upon examination of the motion and order, he finds that leave was granted to file a minority report, for which extreme courtesy and consideration the undersigned acknowledges his obligation, and tenders to the honorable chairman his thanks.

Should there be a difference in the statement of facts, or the deductions drawn therefrom, between the majority and minority reports, the undersigned appeals to the evidence taken and submitted to decide that difference. He will, in justice to himself, state that the evidence taken by the committee has been in the possession of the honorable chairman from the time it was closed in the city of Memphis until the last eight or nine days, when, at the request of the undersigned, it was delivered to him, save the newspaper extracts, and also the testimony of some five or six witnesses loaned to him a few days previous.

With such a volume of testimony, and in so short a time, with other duties as a member of the House to attend to, the undersigned has not been able to give the subject that attention and consideration its merits deserve. But he feels confident that his report will be fully sustained by the evidence.

In conclusion, it is suggested that the most certain and quickest practicable mode to guard against a repetition of the Memphis tragedy would be to restore political rights to all from whom they have been taken for their participation in the recent rebellion, or at least to those who have received the Executive pardon. Were this policy adopted, we might hope to see harmony and prosperity restored to a distracted country; the military removed to the frontier and coast; and, above all, the Freedmen's Bureau, the manufacturer of paupers and vagabonds, the fruitful source of strife, vice, and crime, dispensed with, and an exhausted treasury relieved from the burden of its support.

G. S. SHANKLIN.

JOURNAL.

MEMPHIS, TENN., *May 22, 1866.*

The committee met in Parlor No. 398, at Gayosa House.
Present, Mr. E. B. WASHBURNE, *Chairman,*
   Mr. J. M. BROOMALL,
   Mr. G. S. SHANKLIN,
The chairman laid before the committee the following resolutions:

THIRTY-NINTH CONGRESS, FIRST SESSION.

CONGRESS OF THE UNITED STATES,
In the House of Representatives, May 14, 1866.

On motion of Mr. Stevens,
Resolved, That a committee of three members be appointed by the Speaker, whose duty it shall be to proceed, without unnecessary delay, to Memphis, in the State of Tennessee, to make an investigation into all matters connected with the recent bloody riots in that city, which began on the 1st instant, and particularly to inquire into the origin, progress, and termination of the riotous proceedings, the names of the parties engaged in it, the acts of atrocity perpetrated, the number of killed and wounded, the amount and character of the property destroyed, and report all the facts to the House; and the sergeant-at-arms, or his deputy, and the stenographer of the House are directed to accompany the said committee; and that all the expense of this investigation be paid out of the contingent fund of the House. The said committee shall have power to send for persons and papers, and examine witnesses under oath.
The Speaker appointed, to serve as said committee, the following named members:
   Mr. Ellihu B. Washburne, of Illinois; Mr. George S. Boutwell, of Massachusetts; Mr. Francis C. Le Blond, of Ohio.
Attest:

EDWARD McPHERSON, *Clerk.*
By CLINTON LLOYD, *Chief Clerk.*

THIRTY-NINTH CONGRESS, FIRST SESSION.

CONGRESS OF THE UNITED STATES,
In the House of Representatives, May 15, 1866.

The Speaker appointed Mr. John M. Broomall, of Pennsylvania, and Mr. George S. Shanklin, of Kentucky, members of the select committee on the Memphis riots, in place of Mr. George S. Boutwell and Mr. Francis C. Le Blond, excused.
Attest:

EDWARD McPHERSON, *Clerk.*
By ISAAC STROHM, *Assistant Clerk.*

The committee adjourned until to-morrow at 10 o'clock a. m.

WEDNESDAY, *May* 23, 1866.

The committee met pursuant to adjournment.

Present, all the members.

Major General GEORGE STONEMAN and Major General CLINTON B. FISK appeared and were examined as witnesses.

The committee adjourned until to-morrow at 10 o'clock a. m.

THURSDAY, *May* 24, 1866.

Committee met pursuant to adjournment.

Present, all the members.

The following persons appeared and were examined as witnesses:

Col. CHARLES F. JOHNSON,   Mrs. RACHAEL DILTS,
ALBERT HARRIS,   F. H. FINNE.
Mrs. ELLEN DILTS,

The committee adjourned until to-morrow at 10 o'clock a. m.

FRIDAY, *May* 25, 1866.

The committee met pursuant to adjournment.

Present, all the members.

The following persons appeared and were examined as witnesses:

C. M. COOLEY,   JERRY WILLIAMS,
HENRY JACKSON,   T. M. WINTERS,
WM. HUNTER,   F. S. DAVIS,
LAVINIA GOODELL,   JOHN E. MOLLER,
BRANCE HULT,   Rev. EWING O. TADE.

The committee adjourned until to-morrow at 10 o'clock a. m.

SATURDAY, *May* 26, 1866.

The committee met pursuant to adjournment.

Present, all the members.

The following persons appeared and were examined as witnesses:

EWING O. TADE,   JOHN HOLLYHOOD,
TAYLOR HUNT,   AUSTIN COTTON,
WILLIAM COE,   GEORGE JONES,
PERIMUS LANE,   MARGARET GARDNER.
JANE SNEED,

The committee adjourned until Monday next at 10 o'clock a. m.

MONDAY, *May* 28, 1866.

The committee met pursuant to adjournment.

Present, all the members.

The following persons appeared and were examined as witnesses.

Dr. S. J. QUINBY.   FRANCIS ERICKSON,
JANNETTE SWELS,   SOPHIA GAREY,
JOHN BEATTY,   ADAM LOCK,
HENRY ALEXANDER,   SAMUEL DILTS,
WILLIAM H. BRAZIER,   DAVID T. EGBERT,
JOHN OLDRIDGE,   Dr. R. M. CREIGHTON.
J. M. RANDOLPH,

The committee adjourned until to-morrow at 10 o'clock a. m.

TUESDAY, *May* 29, 1866.

The committee met pursuant to adjournment.
Present, all the members.
The following persons appeared and were examined as witnesses:

Dr. ROBERT McGOWAN,
Dr. WM. T. IRWIN,
Mrs. MINERVA E. HEWITT,
JOHN MARTIN,
FRANK LEE,
JOE STICKNEY,
JOSEPH WALKER,
GEORGE W. HAMMOND,
Dr. P. D. BEECHER,
LORENZO JEAN,
JEREMIAH RYAN,
HENRY W. TAYLOR,
Dr. JAMES M. KELLER,
Miss VESTA E. LITTLEFIELD,
A. N. EDMUNDS,
EDMUND LACY,
MITCHELL WHITLOW,
GEORGE HOGAN,
Dr. CHARLES S. LLOYD,
C. W. TURNER,
RHODA JACOBS.

The committe adjourned until to-morrow at 10 o'clock a. m.

WEDNESDAY, *May* 30, 1866.

The committee met pursuant to adjournment.
Present, all the members.
The following persons appeared and were examined as witnesses:

Dr. J. N. SHARP,
Mrs. MARY A. JACKSON,
LUCY TIBBS,
CYNTHIA TOWNSEND,
Dr. WILLIAM H. WHITE,
Dr. JOSEPH E. LYNCH,
H. G. DENT,
HENRY PORTER,
P. G. MARSH,
ANDREW REZZONCO,
DANIEL DAWKINS,
CHARLES W. ANDERSON,
ALLEN SUMMERS,
ANDREW MINTOR,
ABRAM MEANS.

The committee adjourned until to-morrow at 10 o'clock a. m.

THURSDAY, *May* 31, 1866.

The committee met pursuant to adjournment.
Present, all the members.
The following persons appeared and were examined as witnesses:

Dr. ALLEN STERLING,
HARRIET ARMOR,
JAMES H. SWAN,
FRANK WILLIAMS,
MARIA MARSHALL,
JOHN MARSHALL,
Rev. EWING O. TADE,
TONY CHERRY,
MOLLIE HAYES,
MARY GRADY,
J. S. STORMS.

The committee adjourned until to-morrow at 11 o'clock a. m.

FRIDAY, *June* 1, 1866.

The committee met pursuant to adjournment.
Present, all the members.
The following persons appeared and were examined as witnesses:

JOSEPH PIGEON,
J. S. CHAPIN,
HANNAH ROBINSON,
ELVIRA WALKER,
D. UPMAN,
MARY WALKER,
FRANCES THOMPSON,
LUCY SMITH,
W. G. McELVANE,
JAMES E. DONEHUE,
HENRY BOND,
MOLLIE DAVIS,
ELLEN BROWN,
LUCY HUNT,
MARY BLACK,
S. S. GARRET,
JOHN MYERS.

The committee adjourned until to-morrow at 10 o'clock a. m.

SATURDAY, *June* 2, 1866.

The committee met pursuant to adjournment.
Present, all the members.
The following persons appeared and were examined as witnesses :

FREDERICK HASTINGS,
LEWIS R. RICHARDS,
AMBROSE PORTER,
B. F. C. BROOKS,
JAMES E. HELM,
WILLIAM H. PEARCE,
Mrs. COÓPER,
CELIA SIMONDS,

EMMA LANE,
ANTHONY SIMONDS,
SARAH LONG,
BILLY JOHNSON,
THOMAS F. DURNIN,
JOHN HANDY,
ROBERT R. CHURCH.

The committee adjourned until Monday next at 10 o'clock a. m.

MONDAY, *June* 4, 1866.

The committee met pursuant to adjournment.
Present, all the members.
The following persons appeared and were examined as witnesses :

J. T. SANFORD,
G. C. WORSET,
HANNAH GEORGE,
ANN PATRICK AYR,
MARY WARDLAW,
MATT. WARDLAW,
HANNAH SAVAGE,
MARY JORDAN,

GUY THOMAS,
BARBOUR LEWIS,
IRA STANBROUGH,
Capt. E. G. ALLYN,
THOMAS C. SMITH,
Lieut. WALTER CLIFFORD,
M. T. RYDER,
GEORGE TODD.

The committee adjourned until to-morrow at 10 o'clock a. m.

TUESDAY, *June* 5, 1866.

The committee met pursuant to adjournment.
Present, all the members.
The following persons appeared and were examined as witnesses :

PAUL CICALLA,
GINNIE MENARD,
ANN HAYES,
GEORGE WILLIAMS,
ORIN E. WATERS,
Maj. Gen'l GEORGE STONEMAN,

Brig. Gen'l BEN. P. RUNKLE,
PITSER MILLER,
CHARLES S. CAMERON,
TREADWELL S. AYERS,
JOHN C. PARKES,
MARLAND PERKINS.

Mr. Broomall offered the following order :

Ordered, That the sworn testimony taken before the commission organized by Major General Stoneman and that organized by the Freedmen's Bureau, to inquire into the facts connected with the late riots in Memphis, be made a part of the record for the information of the committee, so far as the witnesses giving the same have not been examined by the committee.

Mr. Shanklin objected to the order ; whereupon the roll was called, with the following result :

Yeas—Mr. Washburn, chairman ; Mr. Broomall.   Nay—Mr. Shanklin.
So the order was adopted.
The committee adjourned until to-morrow at 10 o'clock a. m.

WEDNESDAY, *June* 6, 1866.

The committee met pursuant to adjournment.

Present, all the members.

The following persons appeared and were examined as witnesses :

HENRY G. SMITH,	THOMAS BRADSHAW,
W. T. TAYLOR,	JAS. CARROLL MITCHELL,
NEWTON FORD,	ERASTUS CORNELIUS,
MARCUS J. WRIGHT,	Dr. JOSEPH E. LYNCH,
MARTIN GRIDLEY,	CHANNING RICHARDS,
T. H. McMAHON,	DUDLEY D. SAUNDERS,
CHARITY WORMLEY,	Brig. Gen'l B. P. RUNKLE,
L. T. DU PRE,	MARCUS EDWARDS,
JACK HARRIS WALKER,	H. B. BOUDENOT.
PRINCE MOULTRIE,	

Ordered, That the chairman be authorized to examine witnesses to prove the authenticity of the testimony taken before the commissions created by Major General Stoneman and Brevet Major General Fisk to examine into matters connected with the recent riots in Memphis.

Ordered, That the committee adjourn to meet in Washington on call of the chairman.

WASHINGTON, *July* 27, 1866.

The committee met on call of chairman.

Ordered, That the chairman file the report and testimony with the Clerk of the House.

The committee then adjourned *sine die*.

4

TESTIMONY.

Major General GEORGE STONEMAN sworn and examined.

By the CHAIRMAN:

1. Please state your official position. I am colonel of the 3d United States cavalry and major general of volunteers.
2. What is the particular duty to which you are now assigned? I am now in command of the department of the Tennessee, to which I was assigned by the President in June, 1865, with my headquarters at present at this place.
3. How long have you had your headquarters here? Since the 1st day of January, 1866, about the 6th or 7th. I forget the exact date.
4. Have you been here ever since that time? Yes, sir, I have been.
5. And in command? And in command.
6. Please state what knowledge you have, if any, of a riot which recently occurred in this city? On Tuesday afternoon, May 1, Mr. Winters, sheriff of Shelby county, the county in which Memphis is located, with several other persons, came to my office, informed me of riotous proceedings going on in South Memphis, and wanted that I should use the United States troops under my command in quelling it. I asked him if he had made use of the means at his disposal in quelling the riot; if he had summoned a sheriff's posse for that purpose. He told me he had not. I then told him that I had turned the city and this section of the country over to the civil authorities as far as it was possible, and that I held them responsible for the good order and quiet of the city of Memphis. I also remarked to him that the people of Memphis had been exceedingly anxious to get rid of the United States troops, stating that they were perfectly competent and capable of taking care of themselves. I preferred, therefore, that the question should first be tested whether they were capable of taking care of themselves, before the United States troops should be called into requisition; upon that he went off. Subsequently several persons came to me—irresponsible parties, representing themselves as coming from the mayor and aldermen of the city. I told them that if the mayor of the city wanted the use of the troops, or wanted assistance, and would address me a communication to that effect, it would receive due attention; that I could not communicate through irresponsible persons or parties—I wanted it in black and white. In the afternoon of the same day I received from the mayor a communication, of which the following is a copy:

> MAYOR'S OFFICE, CITY OF MEMPHIS, *May* 1, 1860.
>
> GENERAL: There is an uneasiness in the public mind, growing out of the occurrences of to-day, which would be materially calmed if there was an assurance of military co-operation with the civil police in suppressing all disturbances of the public peace. I should be happy to have it in my power to give this assurance at once. It would intimidate the lawless, and serve to allay the apprehensions of the orderly. I therefore request that you will order a force of, say, two hundred men, commanded by discreet officers, to be held ready to co-operate with the constabulary force of the city in case of any further continued lawlessness.
>
> I am, general, very respectfully, your obedient servant,
>
> JOHN PARK, *Mayor.*
>
> Major General STONEMAN,
> *Commanding Department of Tennessee.*

To which I immediately transmitted the following reply:

> HEADQUARTERS DEPARTMENT OF TENNESSEE,
> *Memphis, Tennessee, May* 1, 1866.
>
> DEAR SIR: I am in receipt of yours of this instant. In reply, I have the honor to inform you that the small force of regular infantry stationed at this post, in all not more than one hundred and fifty strong, will be directed to hold itself in readiness to co-operate with the civil authorities of Memphis "in case of further continued lawlessness." This force is in camp at the fort, where you can communicate with the commanding officer in case you shall find that you need his assistance and support. I should prefer that the troops be called upon only in case of an extreme necessity, of which you must be the judge.
>
> I am, very respectfully, your obedient servant,
>
> GEO. STONEMAN,
> *Major General Commanding.*

Hon. JOHN PARK, *Mayor of the City of Memphis.*

It will be perceived that in this communication I so worded it as to indicate to the mayor that the troops would only be used when the civil authorities were unable to protect themselves. And my reply to Sheriff Winters was for the same purpose of testing the question whether they were capable of keeping peace and order themselves, without the interference of the military authorities, as they had asserted in a communication previously made.

The riotous proceedings continued until about the middle of the night of Tuesday, the first instant, when a portion of the regular forces dispersed and scattered the rioters. They went home, and it was hoped no further riotous proceedings would take place. On Wednesday morning Judge Leonard came to me.

7. Who is Judge Leonard? He is judge of the county court for the county of Shelby. He came to me and stated that they were skirmishing down at South Memphis, and made application to me to turn over arms to posses that were being formed of citizens. I told him I had no arms to be used for that purpose, and that if arms were to be used for that purpose they must be under my control. He went away, but returned two or three times. I told him that if I turned over arms to any body, I wanted to be assured that they would be used for proper purposes; that they must be put into the hands of responsible parties, of men who would act under the control of the military authorities. He went off and brought to me a company of men who he said were ready to receive arms. I asked him if he could vouch for them. He told me he thought he could. I took a look at the party, and became satisfied that if he could, I could not; that they were not proper men to put arms into the hands of, and sent them off. I sent instructions to the commanding officer of infantry, that inasmuch as he had a large amount of public property to guard, and his force was small, to double his guard, and with the remaining portion of his forces endeavor to keep the negroes and whites separated; that that was all I could expect him to do under the circumstances, with the men under his disposal, and which he did very effectually. The military were deployed as skirmishers, the negroes sent to their quarters, and the whites disarmed, dispersed, and sent home.

8. In what particular locality was this last affair? In South Memphis. The whole riot took place in South Memphis.

9. Where were the negroes you speak of as being kept separated and apart from the whites? They were nearly all negroes belongining to a regiment which had been mustered out of the service the day previous, and were at that time in the fort.

10. Your instructions to the commanding officer was to keep the negroes in the fort, and the white people out? Yes, to keep them separate.

11. And your command was carried out? Yes, most admirably.

12. Who was the commanding officer there? Captain Allyn, of the regular army. The riot proceeded on Wednesday, the second, and terminated for that day about one o'clock in the afternoon. Nothing more occurred until about ten o'clock that night, when fires began to break out in different parts of South Memphis. The military officers on duty told me it was impossible either to prevent it, or to apprehend the parties who were the incendiaries, as they were going round in packs and on horseback.

On the 3d I received a communication signed by R. C. Brinkley, and directed to me, transmiting copies of resolutions of a meeting of citizens. The following is a copy of the communication and resolutions:

MEMPHIS, TENNESSEE, *May* 3, 1866.

SIR: I am requested by the citizens composing a meeting held this morning at the courtHouse to lay before you the following resolutions, which passed unanimously, and to request from you your co-operation in any measures that may be taken in pursuance thereof.

Respectfully yours,

R. C. BRINKLEY.

RESOLUTIONS.

Resolved, That the mayor of the city and the sheriff of the county, together with the chairman of this meeting, (W. B. Greenlaw,) be authorized to summon a force of citizens of sufficient number to act in connexion with the military, which shall constitute a patrol for the protection of the city, to serve such time as the mayor, sheriff, and chairman of this meeting shall direct.

Resolved, That the chairman, (W. B. Greenlaw,) J. H. McMahan, S. P. Walker, and R. C. Brinkley, be requested to wait upon General Stoneman and inform him of the proceedings of this meeting.

W. B. GREENLAW, *Chairman.*
R. C. BRINKLEY, *Secretary.*

Major General STONEMAN, U. S. A.,
    Commanding Department of Tennessee.

When this resolution was transmitted to me, I told them I had determined to take the thing into my own hands, and that I should have to set all civil authority aside.

13. This was on Wednesday? Yes, sir.

14. At what hour in the day ? In the afternoon; later on in the afternoon, and after having gone through the city myself and ascertained the condition of affairs, I sent this communication :

HEADQUARTERS DEPARTMENT OF TENNESSEE,
Memphis, Tennessee, May 3, 1866.
To the Mayor, City Council and all civil authorities of the county of Shelby, and city of Memphis:

GENTLEMEN : Circumstances compel the undersigned to interfere with civil affairs in the city of Memphis. It is forbidden for any person, without the authority from these headquarters, to assemble together any posse, armed or unarmed, white or colored. This does not include the police force of the city, and will not so long as they can be relied upon as preservers of the peace.

I am, gentlemen, very respectfully, you obedient servant,

GEO. STONEMAN,
Major General Commanding.

I endeavored to communicate through the mayor of the city, but was informed that he was not in a condition to be communicated with, and therefore transmitted it to one of the common council. The parties who had been assembled immediately dispersed and went home.

15. All the rioters ? All the parties who had been assembled by order of the authorities, for any purpose whatever, and quiet was restored. There were no further riotous proceedings in the town after that, although there were apprehensions on the part of many persons that a general conflagration would take place and that the town would be burned down. Several northern people came to me and expressed their fears that measures would be taken to drive all northern people out of the city. I did not share in their fears either that the city would be burned down or the northern people driven out. Teachers of colored schools and preachers for colored churches many of them came to me representing that their churches and school-houses had been burned down, that some of them had been threatened, and others warned, and they came to me for advice. I told them they must be their own judges as to what course they should pursue, but they should have all the assistance I could render them. Some of them asked for a detachment to guard their places. I told them I had not troops enough ; that it would destroy the efficiency of the whole, but that if they would go to the troops they should have protection, and that if they wanted to leave the city I would furnish them transportation to wherever they wanted to go. Many, and in fact nearly all of them, availed themselves of the opportunity and left the city.

16. This was on Thursday that you issued this order ? On Thursday, the 3d.

17. How soon after was order completely restored ? Immediately after that. I put some pickets in town, placed a guard of about thirty men on Main street near the square, and of a few men at two or three other points, with instructions to disperse any party seen or heard of, assembling together for any purpose whatever. This precaution prevented the assembling together of any parties that night, if there was any intention of assembling, which I think, from information subsequently obtained, there was. Some people came over from Arkansas, and some came in from different sections of the country, and I am led to believe there would have been further trouble on Thursday night, had it not been for this precaution.

18. As I understand it, application was first made to you by the sheriff of the county, invoking military assistance, and your objection to that was that the people here had requested the control which you had before exercised over the city to be transferred to the local authorities ? Yes, sir ; they had requested the withdrawal of the troops from the city, stating that they were competent to take care of themselves. I preferred, therefore to, test the question whether they were competent to keep order, and waited for an application in writing from the city authorities before using the troops stationed here to interfere.

19. What reply did the sheriff make to that ? Little or nothing ; he went away apparently not very well satisfied. I understood subsequently that he went through the town, saying that I had refused to assist in quelling the riot and that the people would have to depend on themselves, calling on everybody to assemble.

20. The next application to you was made by Judge Leonard ? The next responsible application was made by the mayor, to which I replied. Judge Leonard came to me the next morning and asked for military assistance.

21. What are the antecedents of this Judge Leonard, as far as you know them ? He is represented to me as being a strong Union man. He represents himself as being very obnoxious to a certain class of people in this country, in consequence of his Tennessee radicalism, which, by the way, is different in some respects from universal Yankee radicalism. A difference is made here among the people.

22. What was the character of the party he brought to your headquarters to be furnished with arms ? It was a heterogeneous mass. Some of them were firemen, some discharged confederate soldiers, and some of them did not belong to anything except the rabble of the town here.

23. How large a number of them was there ? I think some fifty-eight—fifty-five or fifty-eight.

24. What steps, if any, were taken by you, after these riotous proceedings were at an end, for an investigation of the affair ? On the 5th of the month I issued Special Orders No. 89, from which the following is an extract :

[Special Orders No. 89.—Extract.]

HEADQUARTERS DEPARTMENT OF TENNESSEE,
Memphis, Tennessee, May 5, 1866.

I. A commission, to consist of Brevet Brigadier General B. P. Runkle, Captain A. W. Allyn, 16th United States infantry, Captain W. J. Colburn, assistant quartermaster of volunteers, and M. J. Wright, esq., of Memphis, Tennessee, will assemble on the seventh instant, for the purpose of inquiring into and reporting upon all the facts connected with the recent occurrences and disorders in Memphis, Tennessee, which began on the 1st of May, 1866.

The report of the commission will embrace all the facts connected with the origin, progress, and termination of the riotous proceedings, giving the names of those engaged, and the special acts of each as far as can be ascertained; the number and names of those killed and wounded; what property was destroyed, and the value thereof in each case, and who caused the destruction; and, in fact, a complete history of the transaction, it being highly important that the government be fully and correctly informed upon the whole subject.

Captain W. J. Colburn will act as recorder of the commission, and will be furnished with one clerk to assist him in making up the records.

The commission is authorized to send for such persons and papers as may be thought necessary, and to call upon the officers of the different staff departments for statements, showing the expenditures on the part of the United States resulting from the aforementioned disorders.

A copy of its proceedings will be furnished these headquarters from time to time, as the circumstances are developed.

The quartermaster's department will furnish the necessary rooms and facilities to carry out the provisions of the above order.

By command of Major General Stoneman.

W. L. PORTER,
Assistant Adjutant General.

———

The same day I transmitted the following letter to the mayor of the city of Memphis:

HEADQUARTERS DEPARTMENT OF TENNESSEE,
Memphis, Tennessee, May 5, 1866.

SIR: I have the honor to request information upon the following points, viz:

1st. What efforts have been made or steps taken by the civil authorities of the city of Memphis to apprehend and bring to trial and punishment the perpetrators of the outrages which have disgraced the city of Memphis during the past week, and what assurances can be given me that the murderers and incendiaries will be arrested and punished?

2d. What steps or measures have been taken by the civil authorities or the citizens of Memphis to remunerate individuals and the United States government for losses sustained and expenses incurred, caused by the recent riotous proceedings of the people of this city, and are you able to assure me that all claims for such losses and expenses will be promptly paid by the city?

3d. Can, and will you furnish me with a statement showing the sources from which the city derives its revenue, with the amount or amounts derivable from each source?

4th. Are the city authorities able and competent to prohibit and prevent persons, under whatever pretext, from carrying and using arms? I am reliably informed that the city recorder has assured the people of Memphis that they will not hereafter be prohibited from carrying and using fire-arms.

5th. What security can you give me that the rights and privileges of the colored population of this city and surroundings shall be respected and protected, and what disposition has been made of the large number of negroes who have been arrested by the police during the past week?

I have to request that you will do me the favor to give me all the information possible, and such assurances as circumstances warrant, as future action will be based upon your reply to this communication.

In conclusion, I have to assure you, and through you the people of Memphis, that if they cannot govern themselves as a law-abiding and Christian community, they will be governed, and that hereafter it will be my duty and privilege to see that there are no more riotous proceedings or conduct either on the part of the whites or blacks or city authorities.

I am, sir, very respectfully, your obedient servant,

GEORGE STONEMAN,
Major General Commanding.

Hon. JOHN PARK,
Mayor of the city of Memphis.

The mayor on the 6th returned to me the following reply:

MAYOR'S OFFICE, CITY OF MEMPHIS,
Memphis, Tennessee, May 6, 1866.

GENERAL: I have the honor to acknowledge the receipt of your communication of the 5th instant. At the very earliest practicable moment I will furnish you "all the information possible, and such assurances as circumstances warrant," in reply to all the matters referred to.

In this connexion it may be proper to add, that the appointment of a committee to investigate the causes of, and ferret out the participators in, the recent disturbances, had been considered, and would have been acted upon by me had I not received information of your proposed action in the premises, when I then resolved to ask you to associate the law officer of the city, Mr. S. P. Bankhead, with the commission selected by you, and this suggestion would have been made to-morrow, but the occasion presenting itself I submit it now.

I have the honor to be, very respectfully, your obedient servant,

JOHN PARK, *Mayor.*

I responded on the 7th as follows:

HEADQUARTERS DEPARTMENT OF TENNESSEE,
Memphis, Tenn., May 7, 1866.

SIR: I have the honor to acknowledge the receipt of yours of May 6, promising an early reply to mine of the 5th instant, and also suggesting that the law officer of the city of Memphis be associated with the commission appointed by virtue of Special Orders No. 89 from these headquarters.

The object of the order being to ascertain facts, and not to put any one upon trial, I think the interests of all can be subserved as well, if not better, by the law officer presenting to the commission such facts as he may wish brought to the attention of the United States government.

I am, sir, very respectfully, your obedient servant,

GEORGE STONEMAN,
Major General Commanding.

His Honor JOHN PARK,
Mayor of the City of Memphis.

On the 8th the mayor presented me with a long communication, of which the following is a copy:

Reply to the letter of the 5th.

MAYOR'S OFFICE, CITY OF MEMPHIS,
Memphis, Tenn., May 8, 1866.

GENERAL: I have the honor now to reply in detail to the inquiries in your communication of the 5th instant.

"1st. What efforts have been made or steps taken by the civil authorities of the city of Memphis to apprehend and bring to trial and punishment the perpetrators of the outrages which have disgraced the city of Memphis during the past week, and what assurances can be given me that the murderers and incendiaries will be arrested and punished?"

The entire police force of the city, numbering about one hundred and fifty men, were kept on duty night and day until the disorders ceased. The sheriff of the county, the county judge, and the district attorney general, were in charge of different bodies of men. The United States troops at the fort, numbering about one hundred men, rendered very efficient service in suppressing the riot. These different forces, representing different authorities and combining for a common purpose, exerted a moral influence which more effectually checked the negro rioters than did the exercise of physical strength. So far as I know, no arrests were made by either of these forces for offences greater than a simple disturbance of the peace, and for the reason that when arrests for higher offences were attempted the resistance was so obstinate as to result in the death of the malefactors. These preventive measures were persevered in until your order No. — of the — instant relieved me from further anxiety as a public officer, and left the responsibility for the prevention of further crime with yourself, an assumption very agreeable to me, as I felt assured it would not have been made unless within the scope of your authority received from a common superior, the President of the United States. Your announcement of the appointment of a commission to inquire into and report upon all the facts connected with the recent occurrences and disorders, the extraordinary length to which the grand jurors of this district habitually extend their inquisitorial powers, searching into the smallest details of social life for the offender, the known efficiency of the high sheriff of the county in arresting malefactors both great and small, and the recognized zeal and ability of the attorney general in prosecuting to judgment and death, are the assurances which I can confidently give you "that the murderers and incendiaries will be arrested and punished." Of course you are aware that the law of the State—the public law—assigns to various officers of the State government the performance of all the acts embraced in your first inquiry, (and if addressed to them, a more specific answer might be obtained if the occasion was so exigent as to justify their making public the information which is usually retained in their own bosoms,) whilst my duties are restricted by statute, and would scarcely warrant my making assurances which could only be made good by the exercise of an usurped power upheld by military force, with which my constituents, the people of Memphis, have had a long time experience, even unto nausea.

"2d. What steps or measures have been taken by the civil authorities or the citizens of Memphis to remunerate individuals and the United States government for losses sustained and expenses incurred caused by the recent riotous proceedings of the people of this city, and are you able to assure me that all claims for such losses and expenses will be promptly paid by the city?"

The city authorities have taken no steps or measures in the premises, and as I am advised of no statute or law authorizing any such appropriation of money, I take it for granted that no action will be had. I am not advised that a claim "for losses sustained and expenses incurred by the riotous proceedings of the people of Memphis" had been or would be recognized or entertained by any tribunal of competent jurisdiction as constituting a meritorious claim against the civil authorities; and supposing, in my ignorance, that the contrary was the well-established rule in the courts of the country, would have concluded that the inquiry was simply suggestive, and would have acted upon that belief but for the threatening intimation that payment for these claims will be demanded. I can only assure you, then, although their resources have been materially crippled by the war, and would not justify any voluntary assumpsit of unsubstantiated claims, that there has been no disposition evinced by the city authorities to shirk any legal responsibility; and although the city may not be prepared to meet every demand made upon the treasury in cash, she will not seek to avoid their payment by repudiation.

"3d. Can and will you furnish me with a statement showing the sources from which the city derives its revenue, with the amount or amounts derivable from such source?"

I hereto append the report of the city comptroller, marked A, which is believed to be fully responsive to the inquiry.

"4th. Are the city authorities able and competent to prohibit and prevent persons, under whatever pretext, from carrying and using arms? I am reliably informed that the city recorder has assured the people of Memphis that they will not hereafter be prohibited from carrying and using fire-arms!"

Prosecutions for the violations of the State law prohibiting the carrying of concealed weapons have not been and are not of very frequent occurrence, for the reason that offenders are not frequently detected. The city authorities have only the ability and capacity in the premises possessed by the sovereign State of Tennessee; and as she has not been able "to prevent persons, under whatever pretext," from violating the positive enactments of the law, it can hardly be considered culpable that the city authorities have not accomplished more, with only a delegated and limited authority. An affirmative answer to your inquiry would arrogate to the city the right of searching houses and persons "without evidence of the fact committed;" a power which, under the Declaration of Rights of Tennessee, is declared to be "dangerous to liberty, and ought not to be granted." I can assure you, however, that indiscriminate permits "for carrying and using fire-arms" have not been given, and that the city recorder informs me that he has given no such assurance. Where good citizens resided in that part of the town infested with lawless negroes, and other bad characters, permits have been granted them to carry arms for their protection, and to this extent, as I am informed by the recorder, did his assurance go.

"5th. What security can you give me that the rights and privileges of the colored population of this city and surroundings shall be respected and protected, and what disposition has been made of the large number of negroes who have been arrested by the police during the past week?

"I have to request that you will do me the favor to give me all the information possible, and such assurances as circumstances warrant, as further action will be based upon your reply to this communication. In conclusion, I have to assure you, and through you the people of Memphis, that if they cannot govern themselves as a law-abiding and Christian community, that they will be governed, and that hereafter it will be my duty and privilege to see that there is no more riotous proceedings or conduct either on the part of the whites or blacks or city authorities."

A full reply to this would involve a discussion of the results of the emancipation proclamation, the subsequent changes of the fundamental law, and the sincerity of our people in accepting the results of the revolution. You must pardon me if I decline such a task, and rest upon the assurance given you in all sincerity, and speaking for this people, that the rights of the negro are and will be religiously respected, and every allowance and provision made for their altered condition consistent with safety to our persons and property. And allow me to add the expression of an individual opinion, that, as a people, we will be most considerate of those rights and their corresponding obligations, and can better provide for them than can other law-makers: giving to them wholesome and healthful regulations, the result of a practical familiarity with the wants, the capacities, the habits, and the tastes of the negroes, free from the inoculation of a morbid, sickly sentimentalism. In this connexion I refer you to the accompanying report of the station house keeper, marked B, showing that the number of arrests of negroes is smaller than during the latter part of April. The concluding paragraph of your communication reflects so severely and so unjustly, as I believe, upon the civil authorities directly, and upon the whole body of this community indirectly, that, while self-respect might command silence, I nevertheless cannot refrain from giving you the assurance that this people are "a law-abiding and Christian community," ever ready to respect and to obey all laws and orders emanating from all properly constituted legal authorities, and that the recent riotous proceedings can only be regarded as a sporadic effervescence on the part of bad men who infest the best organized societies of the Old and New World. It is confessedly a source of painful regret that a contrary hypothesis should be suggested. But I indulge the hope that if seized upon by the ignorant and malicious to cover us with contumely and shame, as a barbarous people, living outside the pale of morality and law, the facts of the case, as developed by the commission appointed by you, will conclusively vindicate us from any such reproach.

I have the honor to be, very respectfully, your obedient servant,

JOHN PARK, *Mayor.*

A.

COMPTROLLER'S OFFICE, *Memphis, May* 7, 1866.

The revenue of the city government for the ten months ending 1st instant has been as follows, viz:

From privileges	$147,240 00
" wharfage	44,588 35
" city taxes	260,693 47
" market stalls	22,592 02
" fines and forfeitures	30,120 51
" navy yard rents	6,830 25
" other rents	37 50
" freedmen's court	2,723 50
Total	514,825 60

Respectfully,   P. M. DICKINSON, *Comptroller,*
                                                    By BRIDGES.
Hon. JOHN PARK, *Mayor.*

B.

OFFICE OF STATION HOUSE KEEPER, *Memphis, May* 7, 1866.

SIR: In compliance with your request of the 6th instant, I herewith send you the following report with regard to average number of arrests previous and preceding the late unfortunate riot, which are as follows, to wit: I will commence four days previous to the riot, being the four last days in April, and of which there were thirty-four colored arrests made; May 1st and 2d, two days of riot, twenty-three colored arrests were made; four days after riot, thirty colored arrests were made, showing a decrease of four for the same length of time, and I am glad to inform you that everything looks favorable to an early peace and understanding between the most vicious of both classes.

Hoping this report sufficient, I remain, very respectfully, your obedient servant,
                                                    M. H. REILLY,
Gen. BANKHEAD, *City Attorney.*   *Station House Keeper.*

25. What is the present status of the city of Memphis, military or civil? The military control of the city has been withdrawn without any public notification of the fact. The civil authorities exercise their functions the same as before the riot. The Freedmen's Bureau and other military authorities will make such arrests as they see fit, but, generally, I have no control over the city. In fact, to undertake the police control of the city would require a much larger force than I have here at my disposal.

26. Has the commission appointed under the order which you have read entered upon its functions? Yes, sir, it has been in session daily, and has accumulated a large amount of testimony.

27. Have you that testimony with you? I have it made up as far as it has been taken, and lay it before the commission. I will state that I have directed the facts to be sifted out of the mass of testimony, intending to present them in a condensed and intelligible form, to be signed by the members of the commission as the facts elicited by the inquiry.

28. Do you know from your own personal observation the state of feeling among the northern people, teachers, &c., who came to you during the progress of the riot? They were very much frightened.

29. What caused their fright? Fear of their lives.

30. From threats? Some from threats, and others from warnings and intimations from their friends.

31. What were their warnings as you learned them? Sufficient to lead them to believe their lives were in danger. They represented to me that they were not safe here.

32. Did many of them call on you? Yes, nearly all of them.

33. How many of these teachers of schools called on you, if any? Four that I now recollect.

34. Had their school-houses been burned? All except one, I think.

35. Do you know of threats being used towards them? One of the male teachers who called on me said he had been warned the night previous that his school-house would be burned, but that it was saved by a confederate major, who had pecuniary interest in the property, and induced the mob to desist, but that they had intended to return that night.

36. What was that major's name? He did not tell me the major's name; I presume it has been developed by the commission.

By Mr. Shanklin:

37. You speak of the northern population here; do you refer to the whole northern population residing in the city? No, sir; I spoke of a portion of the northern people here—of those, for instance, connected with the "Post" newspaper, and of some who have served in the United States army, or in the federal army, as it is termed here, and after the army was disbanded have settled here in business.

38. Have many northern people settled here in business? Quite a large number.

39. Did the mass of these people express these apprehensions? No, sir; a considerable number of them came to me expressing these apprehensions, in which I did not share. It was entertained by the class of northern people here in business who were obnoxious to the sentiments of the southern people; for instance those connected with the "Post," here; those engaged in instructing negroes; those engaged in preaching to negro churches; and it extended so far as to influence some people who were afraid to live in Memphis because they were radicals. There are a large number of northern people, and I am under the impression a majority of the northern people here, who are not politically what are termed by the newspapers radicals, and these people do not express any fear.

40. What is probably the number of persons here from the north who are engaged in the pursuits you have named? I have no means of ascertaining further than by a communication I received, signed by quite a number of people, stating there were about 1,500 men who had belonged to the federal army, and that there were about 3,000 discharged confederates here. This communication was sent to me asking permission to organize these 3,000 confederates and 1,500 who had been federal soldiers.

41. As a means of keeping down disturbance? Yes. They were to be organized separately.

42. Not as antagonistic forces? Oh, no, sir.

43. What was the object of the proposed organization? To have a moral influence.

44. Was it proposed to place them under your control? Yes, sir.

45. Had these persons who had belonged to the federal army apprehensions of violence to themselves? Some of them had.

By the Chairman:

46. Were these persons who have been soldiers included among those you mentioned as obnoxious to the southern sentiment? A good many of them were, not all of them; some of them belong to the Johnson Club, and are identified with the southern people, more or less. Those who are not so identified are what are termed by the newspapers radicals, and are in favor of the present executive government of Tennessee.

By Mr. Shanklin:

47. Have you any means of forming an opinion as to the proportion of federal soldiers who are connected with the last organization which you have named? No, sir, I have not; it would be a mere guess.

48. Do you think they constitute the larger or smaller portion of discharged soldiers here? I think the larger proportion adhere to the present State government.

49. What was the conduct of the mass of property-holders, the fixed population here, in regard to this riot? Was it to encourage or discourage riotous proceedings? I do not know of a person coming within the class you mention having been engaged in riotous proceedings, unless I should include some of the city officials, such as the chief of police, captains of fire companies, and recorder of the court.

50. I do not allude to those holding office, but to the mass of these citizens? As far as my intercourse with them went, they deprecated the thing very much, but I was thrown with only a very small portion of them. I heard no expression of sympathy with the rioters on the part of what are called the principal men of the town.

51. Was there not, as far as you could learn, a pretty general or universal sentiment among that class of men who are termed prominent citizens, in favor of the restoration of peace and order? There was.

By Mr. BROOMALL:

52. Have you ever seen the property-holders of any city favorable to riots? No, sir.

By Mr. SHANKLIN:

53. Were not the permanent citizens here regularly engaged in business, who were not property-holders, opposed to the riots as far as you could ascertain their feelings? A great many of the rioters were permanently engaged in business. There were among them keepers of grog-shops, hack and dray drivers, keepers of faro banks, and policemen who are permanently engaged in business, and registered voters of the city of Memphis. It was by that class of persons that the depredations to a great extent were committed.

54. Is not that class of people rather transient than permanent? I should presume them to be much less permanent than the well-established merchants and landholders necessarily. The rioters were also composed to a considerable extent of the rabble of the city, and some of them came in from outside. Some of them came in on horseback, armed, tied their horses to the railing of Court square, and stated that they were going to hunt negroes.

55. Did you discover any difference in the sentiment or participation in this matter among prominent citizens, and those having an interest in the city of Memphis, between those who had been engaged in the rebellion and those who had remained at home and were in favor of the Union? I should say, from what I heard and from what I saw, that the paroled confederate soldiers were scrupulous in keeping out of these things. Whenever they were applied to by the civil authorities, by the sheriff or constables, to take up arms to aid in suppressing what was called a negro riot, and which, by the way, was no negro riot, they almost universally said they were under a pledge to obey the laws of the country; that if I called upon them, they would consider themselves released from their paroles, thus far. I am under the impression, from what I heard from Union people and from all sides, that the paroled confederate soldiers were scrupulous in keeping out of the disturbance. It was a matter of pride with them, I think, not to be mixed up with it. A majority of those who committed the murders, the burnings, the maltreatment, and abuse, I am led to believe, were registered voters of the city of Memphis, those who participate in the election of the city officials here.

56. What was the deportment, as far as you know, of the resident black population of Memphis? Their deportment was highly creditable.

57. They evinced no disposition to participate in the riot? Not in the least. Under the circumstances their behavior was highly creditable.

58. Were those who participated in it mostly discharged soldiers? Subsequent to the conflict on the 1st, between the police and negroes, on the corner of South and Main streets, the negroes had nothing to do with the riot, except to be killed and abused. They assembled in no bodies and were engaged in no riotous proceedings.

59. You speak of those being engaged in the riot as registered voters; do you mean under the laws of Tennessee? Yes; the men who vote for city and State officers under the registration laws, and who, as I am informed, number in the city of Memphis about 3,000.

60. Are the citizens here who are property-holders, and regularly engaged in business, generally registered voters? As I understand it, the larger proportion of the property-holders here are not registered voters.

61. Do they attribute the riotous proceedings here as resulting, to any extent, from that fact? That is what they complain of.

62. That they have no power to control the appointment of the civil authorities? That is what they complain of—that they had no control over the city elections, and therefore ought not to be held responsible for the conduct of the city authorities. As far as I am informed, the larger portion of the prominent citizens of Memphis were sympathizers in the rebellion, and are disfranchised under the laws of Tennessee.

63. Since you have been in the city of Memphis, what has been the conduct of the prominent citizens and property-holders here, and what have been their sentiments in regard to the maintenance of peace and good order, and in regard to the government? I can answer generally, that as far as my experience goes, those persons who are pecuniarily interested in the city of Memphis, and who are anxious to have that pecuniary interest increased, are very desirous of seeing peace returned and order restored—to see the original state of affairs, as it existed before the war, brought back.

64. That is the general prevailing sentiment of that class of people, is it not, without regard to political sentiment? That is my impression. There is a class of agitators, writers for newspapers, and men of that class, who have no pecuniary interest in the south at all, and who I look upon as among the worst enemies of the south. They keep up a bad state of feeling among the southern people.

By the CHAIRMAN:

65. You state there are a class of persons who write for and control the newspapers who keep up agitation and bad feeling among the people; do such papers receive the countenance and support of the community? Yes, sir; they claim to have the largest circulation.

66. How do you account for that, if the mass of property-holders and others interested in maintaining the peace of the city are loyal to the government, as it is alleged? These papers

are supported by a class of men who always cheer when they hear "Dixie" played, like a majority of those who cheered yesterday when they heard "Dixie" played, and in my judgment, four out of five of the people of western Tennessee would cheer when that tune is played; and, in my opinion, four-fifths of the people are not property-holders.

67. Then I understand you that a large majority of the people, the men who really control public sentiment are the men who control these newspapers? I mean, those who write for and control them belong to that class of people I term agitators.

68. And what proportion do they bear to the whole community? They constitute a large majority as compared with the property holders or capitalists.

69. Then, does it follow that the class of property-holders and others whom you have referred to as well disposed towards the government, and for the maintenance of law and order, are overruled by the larger class of agitators of whom you now speak? Yes, sir, certainly, as far as their influence in controlling the municipal affairs of the city of Memphis is concerned.

By Mr. Shanklin:

70. Is there not another class of papers taking the opposite extreme which also create bad feeling? Judging from the tenor of the articles I have read in these papers, and from the language used, I do not see much difference between them, taking the two extremes in regard to the exciting influence they have upon the public mind.

By the Chairman:

71. How are the various papers published in Memphis classed in that regard? Adopting their own definitions of each other, there are some papers published here extreme in their fire-eating southern proclivities, and others called extreme radical papers, (using the Tennessee definition of the term,) favorable to disfranchisement as it exists under the present laws of the State. And I wish to be understood, whenever I have spoken of radicalism, as referring to the term as it is used in Tennessee, applying to those who are in favor of disfranchising all persons who had anything to do with the rebellion.

By Mr. Shanklin:

72. And these two classes of persons, wherever they exist, exert their influence to keep up agitation in the public mind? They mutually abuse each other; say pretty much the same things of each other, and both have a bad effect upon the community.

By Mr. Broomall:

73. Did the Post newspaper of Memphis exert an influence in favor of the late riotous proceedings in this city? I think not.

74. Has that paper ever advised or incited violence of any kind? I think not.

75. What other paper of that class or character is there in Memphis? There are none of precisely that character. I do not mean to be understood as saying that any newspaper had anything to do with inciting or getting up the late riot. I only spoke of the influence of the press of Memphis upon the public mind here and in the country contiguous.

76. How are the daily papers of the city classed in that respect, giving the names of each? The Argus and Avalanche are understood to belong to the radical, fire-eating order. The Bulletin and Commercial I have never regarded as belonging exactly to that class.

77. On which side are they radical? They are radical, as I understand, them in catering to this extreme southern sentiment?

78. The negro-hating sentiment? They pretend to be the negroes' best friends.

79. Please name the papers now on the other side? The Post is the only one now published. There was formerly a paper called the Tribune.

80. Have the editorials of the Post been inflammatory in their character for the last five or six months? I mean, have they been of a character calculated to incite public disturbance? I do not think they have more than those of any other paper, if as much.

By the Chairman:

81. Then its influence is bad simply because the doctrines it inculcates are not palatable to the majority of the people here? That is as I understand it.

By Mr. Shanklin:

82. I ask you whether its articles are not denunciatory in their character, and bitter in the extreme? Are they not of that character calculated to arouse, harass, irritate, and annoy men entertaining different political sentiments? In common with those of papers on the other side which pursue the same course, I should say they are.

By the Chairman:

83. Who are the men, so far as you know them, who control these different papers? I do not know who control the papers any further than as I see their names published.

84. Are they men who have been engaged in the war on either side? How, in that respect, is it with those connected with the Post? I understand they were nearly all in the Union army.

85. How is it with those on the other side? I understand they were nearly all sympathizers with the rebellion.

86. Were they not actually in the rebellion? Many of them were, as I understand; and I may remark that they constitute a much better class of people than those who sympathized with the rebellion and kept out of it. As far as my observation goes, the officers and soldiers who have been in the confederate army, not only here, but throughout the south, are embraced in the best class of southern men in the country.

By Mr. SHANKLIN:

87. Did I understand you to divide the newspapers here into three classes; and if so, what is the third class to which you refer? There are some papers that take moderate ground.

88. What principles do they advocate? With the exception of the Post, all the papers in Memphis oppose the present executive of Tennessee. Some of them are more mild in their opposition than others.

89. Are they opposed to the new proposed metropolitan police of Memphis? Some of them are, and some of them are not. I think a majority of the press, so far as I am informed, are in favor of the proposed change. I think a large majority of the reliable and responsible people of Memphis are in favor of the change, and in favor, in fact, of almost anything to get the control out of the hands of the present police.

By Mr. BROOMALL:

90. Please state, if you know, the nationality of the present police force of Memphis? I have been informed that they are principally Irish.

91. Who have recently come to the country, or otherwise? I do not know.

92. Of what nationality is the mayor? I do not know. He has been for quite a long time resident here.

93. How in respect to the recorder? The same. I do not know whether he is an Irishman or not. He has been for a long time a resident here.

By Mr. SHANKLIN:

94. All these policemen, I understand you, have taken the oath required by the franchise law? As I understand, they are all registered voters.

95. And the law requires them to swear that they not only abstained from participation in, but that they have had no sympathy with, the rebellion? I do not recollect the exact language of the law. It requires that they shall have had no participation in the rebellion. I do not know whether it goes further or not.

Major General CLINTON B. FISK sworn and examined.

By the CHAIRMAN:

96. Please state your official position? Brevet major general of volunteers, and assistant commissioner of the Bureau of Refugees, Freedmen, and Abandoned Lands for the States of Kentucky and Tennessee.

97. Where are your headquarters? At Nashville.

98. Have you been at Memphis for any length of time; and if so, at what time or times? I spent about two weeks in Memphis in November and December, 1865, and have been here during the last fifteen days.

99. What knowledge, if any, have you in regard to the recent riots in the city of Memphis? The knowledge I have has been derived chiefly from information received from my own officers, who are on duty here, and from a commission appointed by myself to investigate, which commission is now in session, and will be able to close their report this evening.

100. Were you at the time of the riot? I was not.

101. At what time did you arrive here? On the 7th of the present month.

102. And you constituted your commission immediately afterwards? Before. I ordered Colonel Johnson to make the investigation, I think on the 4th.

103. Have you the order organizing the commission? Colonel Johnson has it. After he commenced his investigation, Major Gilbraith, of Major General Howard's staff, arrived from Washington with orders from General Howard to investigate the same occurrences, and they became associated in the investigation and concluded it jointly.

104. Have you any knowledge of any particular facts connected with the riot outside of this investigation which you instituted? No, sir. I do not know that I have any except that which will appear in this report.

THURSDAY, *May 24, 1866.*

Colonel CHARLES F. JOHNSON sworn and examined.

By the CHAIRMAN:

105. Please state your present official position? Colonel and assistant inspector general for the Freedmen's Bureau for Kentucky and Tennessee. I occupy that position temporarily

106. Where have you been recently stationed? At Washington city.

107. How long have you been at Memphis? I arrived here on the 5th of May.

108. Where from? Direct from Washington—stopping over at Nashville two days on the way.

109. What was the object of your visit here? To investigate the riot in this city, and to co-operate with Brevet Brigadier General Runkle in the discharge of his duties as superintendent of the Freedmen's Bureau for the district of Memphis.

110. Have you proceeded with that examination? I have.

111. Have you the order with you under which you are acting? I have. It is as follows:

[Special Orders No. 76.—Extract.]

BUREAU REFUGEES, FREEDMEN, AND ABANDONED LANDS,
STATES OF KENTUCKY AND TENNESSEE,
ASSISTANT COMMISSIONER'S OFFICE,
Nashville, Tennessee, May 4, 1866.

I. Colonel Charles F. Johnson, Veteran Reserve Corps, having reported at this office, in compliance with Special Orders No, 57. paragraph II, dated War Department, Bureau Refugees, Freedmen, and Abandoned Lands, April 23, 1866, is hereby assigned to temporary duty as assistant inspector general on the staff of the assistant commissioner at Nashville, Tennessee.

II. Colonel Charles F. Johnson, Veteran Reserve Corps, assistant inspector general, is hereby directed to proceed, without delay, to Memphis, Tennessee, to make an inspection, the nature of which will be explained to him in person by the assistant commissioner.

He will remain at Memphis, co-operating with Brevet Brigadier General Runkle, chief superintendent Memphis sub-district, until this duty may be fully completed, when he will return to his station at Nashville, and make full report to this office.

By order of Brevet Major General Clinton B. Fisk, assistant commissioner Kentucky and Tennessee.

H. S. BROWN,
Assistant Adjutant General.

112. Have you, under that order, made that examination by yourself, or with the assistance of others acting with you? On the 11th May Major T. W. Gilbraith, aide-de-camp of Major General O. O. Howard, arrived in the city for the same purpose, and acting under similar orders to mine. The examination, at the suggestion of General Fisk, was conducted jointly after his arrival.

113. Please state how much of an investigation you have made? Not having the power to enforce the attendance of witnesses, we were under the necessity of getting our evidence voluntarily. We have examined two hundred and fifty witnesses, white and black, and approximated the losses as nearly as possible from the examination of these witnesses.

114. Have you the testimony of these witnesses now with you? I have, and now present it to the committee.

115. Does the evidence now presented give all the knowledge which you have on this subject? It does. These affidavits you will find classified according to their character. Those marked "A" relating to the apparent cause of the riot. Those marked "B," to the commencement of the riot; "C," robberies, assaults, and arson; "D," rape; "E," burning alive; "F," killed and wounded; "G," miscellaneous.

116. Do the affidavits on their face show whether the witnesses were white or black? They do not.

117. Do you know how many of each were examined? I do not. I suppose the proportion would be, perhaps, one white out of five.

118. What was the occasion of the difference in the number of white and colored witnesses? The colored ones were the sufferers—they had complaints to make. The whites were the aggressors, and, of course, did not volunteer to come before me. As I have already stated, we had no power to compel the attendance of witnesses.

119. Were these colored witnesses in a position to know the facts to which they testify? I think I can safely say there is not an affidavit in the number presented of a person who was not actually cognizant of the facts stated.

By Mr. SHANKLIN:

120. Who took the affidavits and interrogated the witnesses? Captain Michael Walsh, acting assistant adjutant general and provost marshal.

121. Under whose command? Under the command of the superintendent of the Freedmen's Bureau for the district of Memphis. He received the mass of evidence. Those not received by him were taken by myself.

122. In taking the evidence did you interrogate the witnesses, ascertain what they knew, and then write out the affidavit? or did you write it down from the lips of the witness in his own words? In taking the evidence of the witness I received, I first required the witness to tell me what he knew of the case. I then propounded such questions as I thought necessary to bring out the facts fully; after which I wrote down the answers in the rough as near *ver-*

batim as I could, and make English of it, and the clerk copied it out. After it was copied it was read to the witness, signed and sworn to by him. That was the operation gone through with the ignorant portion of the witnesses.

123. They were not sworn, then, when they made their statements and were interrogated? No; their statements after being written out were read, signed, and sworn to by them.

124. Did you pretend to write down all that was said by the witness, or merely the substance of his statement, as you understood it? I wrote down all the statements of the witnesses having any reference to the riots.

125. Were you under the necessity of correcting many of these affidavits after they were written out and read to the witnesses? I had in several instances to insert a single word, such as "white," when they would give a certain number of names, and the inquiry was made as to whether they were white or black men.

ALBERT HARRIS (colored) sworn and examined.

By the CHAIRMAN:

126. State your age and residence? I am fifty-three years old. I was born and raised in Virginia, but have lived in Memphis about twelve or fourteen years.

127. Have you been a freeman or a slave? A slave.

128. Whose slave? I belonged to J. B. Griffin & Co., of this city, until two or three years ago, when I got tired of living that way, and quit.

129. Have you a family? Yes; a wife. We were raised together, but carried away from each other, and remained until the war, when we met in Memphis.

130. What has been your business recently? Ever since I quit my owners I have been a shoemaker.

131. In what part of the city do you reside? In North Memphis, corner of Winchester and Alabama streets.

132. Have you a shoemaker's shop there? Yes, sir; I have had a shoemaker's shop about three years.

133. In the house where you live? Yes, sir.

134. State what you know about the riot that took place in this city, when it took place, and all you know about it? The riot commenced on Monday night, a little before dark; it commenced at South Memphis. On Tuesday night they came to me and took a gun and all the money I had. I was sitting right down just before supper, when somebody knocked at the door. I said, "Come in." In walks a man who had stood at the corner opposite nearly all day, and some other people with him. Directly he came in he said he had orders to search my house for arms; that he was a detective; that he understood we had arms there; that the neighbors complained about it, and he wanted them. I told him I had a shot-gun, and, of course, if he had orders to take it, it was all right. He said I must get it immediately. When I brought it to him he said, "This is not all." I told him I hadn't any more. He said he would search the house, and if he found any he would hold me responsible. I was afraid he would find some pistols belonging to my boys who were away. They unlocked my trunks, and went searching all over the premises. They found a bowie-knife at the head of the bed, and they took that. They turned my bed all up and everything upside down. At length they opened the trunk where my money was, and I took it out. This man says, "What is that you have got?" I said it was money, and not to take that. He said he had orders to take every cent for having that gun there. He took it, and then said, "Come on, boys. I don't believe they have got any pistols anyhow." They went into the next room, where there was a man very sick, and asked him if he had a pistol there. He was so sick he was hardly able to speak. They said, "Oh, no; he hasn't any pistol." There was another gun there standing in plain view, but they did not seek to get it. One was mine, and the other Henry Johnson's. They took Henry Johnson's gun. I said, "Don't carry my money away; it is all I have got." There were two or three policemen there, and my wife said something to try to get them to interfere. She cried about it. They had a pistol all the time drawn and pointed right at the side of my head. When they started to go I said, "Don't let them carry my money away, it is all I have, and I have worked hard for it." They said, "Go to the Freedmen's Bureau in the morning, and you will get your money." The policemen didn't say anything, and they all went away.

135. Who were the men that came to your house? If you believe me, I do not know the name of either of them. I just knew this man, because he was standing on the corner all that day.

136. Was he a policeman? No, sir; the policemen came with him.

137. How many of them? There were about eight men altogether there.

138. What did this man who was standing on the corner all day appear to be doing? I don't know. Sometimes he would appear to be shaking his head, and looked like he was angry. I noticed him, and others noticed him. There are those who ought to know him.

139. Who is there in your neighborhood who ought to know? I think Mr. Finne, who keeps a grocery on the opposite corner. He was laughing and talking with him the next day.

140. How did you know that any of them at your house were policemen? I just knew them by their stars. Whether they were policemen or not I do not know.

141. Did they appear to be the leaders of the gang? They did not appear to be the leaders, but they appeared to be like they didn't care what happened.

142. Who was it that demanded your arms of you? This same little man who had stood on the corner.

143. Who was it that took the money? The same man.

144. How much money did he take? At the very least he took $350 of my money, $50 belonging to the sick man in my care, and $10 belonging to another man who was away.

145. When you gave this money to the small man you speak of did the others see it? They saw it.

146. Did the policemen see it? I do not know. He knew they had it, for he heard me ask them to not carry it away.

147. What did the policeman say? He did not open his mouth.

148. When they made the pretext of wanting arms did you believe that was what they wanted? I didn't know. They had searched a good many houses about there for arms. I do not know of their taking any money except mine.

149. As soon as they got your money they seemed to be perfectly satisfied? Yes; per-fectly satisfied.

150. Did they make any threats to you or your family at this time? Not particularly, only that they were going to burn up the house we lived in the next night. I understood so. I did not hear them say it.

151. Where did they then go? They went up street; I do not know where. I was afraid to follow them.

152. Do you know anything that took place in the riot after this? The same night a black-smith's shop about fifty yards from me, on Alabama street, was set on fire.

153. Who did it belong to? To Henry Alexander, a colored man.

154. Did they rob him? They burnt up everything he had there. The same night they burnt up a church. I saw that on fire.

By Mr. SHANKLIN:

155. Did I understand you to say they burnt your house? No, sir. I think the reason my house was not burned was that it joined broadsides another man's grocery.

156. Do you know anything of your own personal knowledge with regard to the com-mencement of the fuss on Monday? I do not know anything further than I have said. I staid in my shop working and trying to support my family. I had nothing to do with any-body. I have been as quiet as anybody could be. My former master and mistress will say so to-day. They have not a word against me. They are sorry for me, because I lost every-thing I had.

157. Have you taken any measures to get back your money? No, sir. I do not know any way in the world to get it back. It was all I had. I made it last winter by my work.

158. Who was it said they were going to take your money on account of finding the gun? The very small, little man who stood on the corner all day.

159. Had that little man a badge of any office about him? No, sir. He wore regular citizen's clothes. He was a nice-looking little fellow.

160. You had never seen him before that day? No, sir. I think he was a plump stranger. I do not know who he was.

161. Had he any brogue like a Dutchman or an Irishman? No, sir. I think he was a regular citizen here. He had a little moustache, and walked that night with his pistol right against my head.

162. Of the eight men who were there that night, how many had policemen's badges? Two. One came inside, and the other stood right at the door.

163. Did any of the others have the garb of the military or police on them? No, sir, they did not. When these men came inside the door they said "enough in now." The rest re-mained outside.

164. Did you know any of those outside? I cannot say I did. Some boys told of persons who were there, but I do not know. I was so much concerned about my money that I did not notice if they were there. Mr. Finne came in after me since then and said he was going to take my house away from me for accusing him of having anything to say to that man on the corner that day.

165. Is Mr. Finne a Dutchman? Yes, sir.

166. Did you see Mrs. Finne also talking with the man? Yes, sir; she was laughing and talking with this man all day.

Mrs. ELLEN DILTS, wife of Samuel Dilts, sworn and examined.

By the CHAIRMAN:

167. State your present residence? 152 Causey street, Memphis, Tennessee.

168. How long have you resided in Memphis? Three years.

169. Where did you reside previous to your coming here? In Cincinnati.

170. Have you a family? My husband has been here four years. He has been in the army.

171. Have you any knowledge of the riotous proceedings which occurred in this city in the early part of the present month? Yes; I saw a good deal of it.

172. Be good enough to state when it commenced and what you saw of it? The first I saw of it was on Monday afternoon, the last day of April. There were four policemen walking down the street and met three or four colored men. I do not know what was the matter of the policemen; they seemed to be angry. The negroes turned out for the policemen to pass, when one of the negroes fell down and a policeman fell over him. That appeared to make the policeman mad. I did not hear what they said.

173. How near were you to them? A very short distance; they were almost right across the street. I might have heard what they said. They had some words.

174. How wide is the street there? About as wide as this, (about 60 feet.) After the colored man fell down and the policeman fell over him, as I said, they had some words. They then drew pistols and knives, but they did not shoot.

175. Did the colored men draw pistols and knives? No; the policemen drew them. This colored man then started to go away. One of the policemen ran after him and hit him over the head with his pistol, breaking the breech of the pistol. The other colored men seemed very mad about it, and one of them hit the policeman over the head with a stick; then the policeman hit him on the head with a brick——

176. Another policeman, or the same one? Another policeman. Then, I think, they separated; the colored men going back towards South street, and the policemen in the other direction.

177. Did any one seem to be very badly hurt? The colored man who was struck with a pistol appeared to be considerably hurt; the blood ran from his nostrils and from the side of his head. The blood ran from the back of the head of the one struck with the brick.

178. Did you see anything further at that time? No; that was all there was until about midnight that night, when the policemen seemed to be somewhat excited.

179. Were these same policemen in that neighborhood every night? Yes; that was their beat.

180. How many were there of them? I think seven.

181. Did you have any conversation with them? No; I did not speak to them. I could tell by the way they acted that they were excited. They whispered; I did not hear what they said.

182. What next took place so far as these riotous proceedings were concerned? The next day, on Tuesday, I saw six policemen going very fast down Main street towards South street. They had hardly time to get to South street before I heard a great deal of firing.

183. At what time in the day was this? About noon.

184. Had there been any disturbance that day up to this time? No general disturbance. There had been a good deal of shooting.

185. Did you learn where the shooting you heard about noon was? On South street.

186. How far was it from your residence? Not far; I could not see it.

187. Did you see persons running in that direction? Hundreds of them. The policemen went up and down and gave the alarm, and I should think there were a hundred policemen congregated. There may not have been so many. There were a good many.

188. What led to the firing? I do not know; I only know that the firing commenced.

189. How long after this did you see the crowd of people together? I cannot remember how long. I know that two policemen went up and down the street, and that it was not long, I think not twenty minutes, before hundreds of people came together.

190. What did they do? They had just a battle on South street; they were firing all the time. Once a crowd came running down the street in which I live, and at one time my front room was full of men. They said, "Do not let us be such cowards; let us go back again." The colored men were trying to hide in every place. There was a colored man going along the sidewalk about noon, when a policeman struck him, knocked his head against a post, and swore at him. The negro said, "Don't hit me; I have not done anything; I am just going home from my work." Another colored man ran into a yard; a policeman pointed his pistol at him and told him to come out. I heard a policeman say "Kill every nigger, no matter who, men or women."

191. Do you know that policeman by name? I do not.

192. Did you hear a policeman make use of those words? Yes; I heard him myself.

193. How long did these people remain in your parlor? Only a few minutes.

194. Did they make any excuse for being there? They were frightened; they were afraid the balls would hit them.

195. Who fired the pistols? The policemen and citizens. The policemen were all armed with pistols. Many of the citizens were armed with pistols or clubs.

196. Did you understand there was any firing on them by the colored men? I do not think the colored men had anything to fire.

197. Were the white people firing among themselves? They were firing at the colored people.

198. What were the white people in your parlor afraid of, then? They were afraid the

balls would hit them—not balls fired by colored people; but they were afraid the balls would strike them. That is what they said.

199. How near were any colored men at that time? There were colored men on the side walk and street.

200. How far distant from where you were? But a short distance; I could not tell exactly how far. There was one colored man shot down by the bridge on Elliot street, just a few steps from our house. There was so much firing I did not go out.

201. When was that? The first day of May, about four o'clock in the afternoon.

202. At the time of this firing and general melee, when these people were rushing into your parlor, did you hear of any colored people being in the vicinity and firing on them? No. I do not know of any colored people doing any firing. Every one I saw was trying to get out of the way; some of them were covered with dust and blood, and all were trying to get out of the way.

203. How many of them did you see? I saw them one at a time; I do not know how many I did see. If they would go into any person's yard for protection, the policemen would swear at them and order them out.

204. Did you see colored men at any time make any demonstrations of violence towards the police or towards white citizens? No; I only saw that man on Monday hit the policeman with a stick. The colored people were almost frightened to death.

205. How many colored people did you see beaten or shot at, should you judge? I cannot remember, there was such a crowd.

206. A crowd of colored or white people? A crowd of white people; the white people were the ones who did the shooting. The colored people went by, some bleeding at their heads, some were all covered with dust and blood, as if they had been down in the dust.

207. Did you see any colored man beaten near your house? Yes; one was beaten right at the gate.

208. What was the cause of that? Nothing, except that the man was a negro; he was quietly going home from his work.

209. What was that negro's name? I do not know his name.

210. Do you know whether he was fatally injured? No; I do not think he was very badly injured. You cannot hurt a negro much by hitting him on the head, or else the policeman would have killed the man he struck: the man just staggered under the blow, he did not quite fall down.

By Mr. Broomall:

211. Did any of the crowd of white people you saw collected show any disposition to protect the negroes? No; they were all against the negroes; a great many of them had been in the southern army. I could hear them make remarks that they had, and that they wanted to kill all the negroes.

212. How many persons do you suppose were in the crowd that you saw go by your house? I should think three hundred.

213. And you only saw comparatively few negroes, and they one at a time, running to get out of the way? Yes; all trying to get out of the way. The street was filled with the crowd clear to South street, and as far up the street as I could see. The policemen and citizens went stringing along for about half an hour.

By the Chairman:

214. What number of the men you saw there, do you think, appeared to have been in the rebel army? I do not know. I should think most of them appeared to be southern men; I can generally tell southern men, I think, when I see them.

215. You say you heard some of them say they had been in the southern army? Yes; a good many.

216. How did they express themselves? They said something about the negroes having done them harm in the war by fighting against them, and that they wanted to kill all the negroes.

217. Were you frightened at the time? No; nothing ever frightens me; I have been fired at too many times by rebs.

218. Have you been fired at here in Memphis? No; I have been in Vicksburg once.

219. What countrymen did most of these people appear to be? I think they were almost all of them Irish; a good many of them were.

220. Did you see many who appeared to be Americans? No; I think most of them must have been Irish.

221. Did the men who said they had been in the rebel army appear to be Americans or Irish? They looked like they were all Irish, with kind of red faces; some of them, though, appeared delicate.

222. Do you know anything about the burning of any buildings afterwards? Yes; I saw one man who said he had set a negro school-house on fire on South street.

223. At what time was this? It was about noon on Wednesday, I think.

224. Who was this man who said he had set a negro school-house on fire? I do not know; he was a man who looked like an Irishman, a kind of red-faced man.

5

225. Would you know him again if you were to see him? I might, if he had the same clothes on

226. How came he to make this observation? Some one said to him that he appeared warm. He said he had been at warm work. They asked him what he had been doing. He said he had been setting a nigger school-house on fire.

227. Where were they when you heard this? They were in the street, passing by the door. I then went down Cansey street to see the school-house burn. They set two more of them on fire, and I staid out until the three were burned.

228. Did you hear anything about who set the others on fire? They said it was the firemen.

229. Who said so? The colored people; they said they knew the firemen—that they went round in hacks. I only know in reference to this one man who I heard say he set the first one on fire; all the rest is from hearsay.

230. Did you see any number of negroes together on Tuesday at any time? I do not think I did.

231. There was no crowd at any one time? Not that I remember.

232. You did not see them making any disturbance in any way? No; all that I saw was on Tuesday forenoon—some two or three negroes would be passing along talking together

233. They gave no indications of violence? No. I heard one colored man say he would have given $25 to have been there and thrashed the policemen.

234. Who did this colored man make the remark to? Another colored man.

235. Do you know of any white persons being killed in the riot preceding? No; I did not see any person wounded; I saw one policeman carried by on a cot.

236. Was he wounded? Yes; I think he died.

237. Do you know any of the circumstances which caused his death? No; I do not know who shot him.

238. At what time was that? It was Tuesday, in the evening.

239. What further took place Tuesday night, in your knowledge? Nothing further than that crowds went down street. After a while I saw some white soldiers, and then everything was quiet. The next morning the soldiers went up and came down again; they had not gone down twenty minutes when a drove of policemen came up, and in a few minutes the firing commenced, and they had quite a battle.

240. Who was the battle between? I think it was firing at the negroes over in the fort.

241. Did you see anything of this battle? Yes, sir; I was so far off I could see the crowd, but I could not tell the colored men from the white men; I could see men standing there and firing. I do not know where these policemen were, but they got there so quick after the soldiers went down that they must have been in the saloons watching for them.

242. Did they go down in an organized force apparently, or did they scatter along? There were a good many of them who went together. They were just going down the street without much order; they appeared to be very mad.

243. Were they talking as if they were excited? Yes, they were very busy talking.

244. Did you hear the conversation? Not much. It appeared that they must have been at some place waiting for the soldiers to go off; I think they must have been at a saloon in Grand street; they usually staid there.

245. Do you know who they were firing at? No. I heard they were firing at colored people.

246. Do you know whether the colored people returned the fire? They did not. They had nothing to fire; they had turned over their guns; they tried to get their guns again.

247. Could they be hurt by policemen firing at them from the outside? I do not know; there were a great many colored people killed altogether.

248. Killed in that fight? Yes; I think so. Annie, a colored woman, told me so; she told me there were a good many women killed too, or wounded. They were not shot on purpose, but hit by stray bullets, and some burned to death.

249. Have you any knowledge of any colored women being shot or burned? I did not see them; I saw people who said it was so.

250. How long did this battle last? I should think it lasted until about noon, and then they set the school-houses on fire, two or three buildings; that night they set a great many other houses on fire.

251. Do you know anything particularly about the burning of these school-houses or other houses? No.

251. Then you have no personal knowledge of other matters except those you have stated you saw the first day? No; I have nothing else.

By Mr. SHANKLIN:

252. When you heard this firing on South street could you see the parties engaged in it from where you were? I could see the men; I could not see who was shooting.

253. Could you see the negroes at that time? No; I could not see them.

254. Then you cannot tell whether the negroes were firing, or whether the white people alone were firing, as far as you could see? No; I could not see myself.

255. On Wednesday, when the firing took place, could you see who the parties were from where you were? I should say they were white men, all formed in a line; I could not see them raise their guns and pistols and fire, but I could hear them.

256. Could you tell who they were firing at? No.

257. And you do not know whether the fire was returned by the negroes? I do not.

258. Then all you saw yourself was on Monday forenoon, when the police and negroes were on your street? That was all I saw plainly.

259. So far as the fight on Tuesday and Wednesday was concerned, you were not in a position to see, yourself? No; I only saw the crowd that passed.

260. And all that you have stated about the fighting on those days was from information received from others? That was all.

261. Is your husband now in the army? No; he was mustered out a year ago.

261. What business is he now engaged in? He is not doing anything now; he got hurt last winter.

262. Has he been engaged in business since he was mustered out? Yes, sir, he had a blacksmiths' shop.

263. You are keeping house, are you? Yes.

264. Did your husband have the same knowledge of these facts you have stated? Yes, he was right with me; he did not hear any more than I did, if as much.

265. Was there any white person in the house except yourself and husband? None except the lady now here, in a room adjoining.

266. Did you know any of the white persons who came into your house? I did not.

267. Did you know any of the persons you saw engaged in the affair? No.

268. You took them to be Irish from their appearance, both the police and citizens? Yes, sir.

THURSDAY, *May* 24, 1866.

RACHAEL DILTS, wife of Johnson Dilts, sworn and examined.

By the CHAIRMAN:

269. Please state your residence? I live at 152 Causey street. Memphis?

270. How long have you resided in Memphis? Since the middle of March.

271. Where were you from previously? Fulton county, Illinois.

272. What knowledge have you of the riotous proceedings which have lately taken place in this city? I hardly know how to answer your question. I saw a disturbance on Monday, previous to the 1st of May. It took place in front of my house, between four policemen and two negroes. The negroes were passing up street, when they met the policemen. Some words passed between them, I do not know what. The policemen ran after one of the negroes, and I suppose struck him, for the negro fell and the policeman on top of him. Both got up and went back to the sidewalk. They all used some strong language to each other—the police to the negroes, and the negroes to the police. Finally, the negroes started down street. One of the policemen ran after this negro that fell down and struck him on the head with his pistol. While he was doing that, another negro ran and struck the policeman with a stick. Then the negro stood up and dared the policeman to fight him. The policeman stepped back, and then another policeman threw something at the negroes, I presume a brickbat or stone. They continued talking to each other, and the negroes passed on down the street, while the policeman went back up in the city.

273. Both parties went back the way they came? Yes, sir.

274. Did you hear any of the conversation between the policemen and the negroes? I do not recollect anything more than very hard language used, daring each other to fight.

275. Were the negroes in uniform? They had soldier's clothes on.

276. How many negroes were there? Three negroes and four policemen.

277. Who spoke first? Do you know? I do not know who spoke first.

278. Who turned out from the sidewalk? The negro ran from the sidewalk first, and the policeman after him.

279. Had any violence taken place before the negro left the sidewalk and ran? I do not know; I did not see any; I only heard violent language used.

280. And as he went into the street the policeman followed him? He ran across the street, apparently to get out of the way, and fell, and the policeman running after him fell on the top of the negro in the street. That maddened the policeman and the negro.

281. Then what did you see him do? Then they went back to the sidewalk, and stood and talked to each other, the police and negroes both. Then when the negro started down the street the policeman ran after him and struck him on the head with his pistol.

282. Was there any violence between the policemen and negroes, except what you have stated? Not on that day.

283. You only saw, then, a disturbance between a policeman and one negro? There were two or three of them.

284. Were they all fighting? I do not think one of the three negroes was. I saw two of them engaged in fighting.

285. You have spoken of this one over whom the policeman fell, as being chased afterwards, have you not? I could not say it was the same one; I presume it was. He started down the street, and the policeman struck him with his pistol a very hard blow. It broke the pistol; I saw him pick the pieces up.

286. Where did he strike him ?   On the side of the head.

287. Did the negro fall ?   He did not fall; it stunned him like; he cried out "Oh!" and put his hand to his head; the blood ran freely from his nostrils and the side of his head.

288. What did the other negro do ?   He struck the policeman with a stick.

289. What kind of a stick ?   It was like an old broom-handle.   He appeared to pick it up in the street for the occasion.   The policemen all had pistols, and one of them appeared to have a knife or sword, or something, in his hand, but he did not seem to use it.

290. You state that another negro was struck by a policeman with a brickbat or stone. Did it seem to hurt him much ?   I do not think it did; he did not seem to mind it much.

291. What then took place ?   The negroes and policemen separated and went different ways.

292. Using threatening language towards each other ?   Yes; I cannot exactly remember the words.   The negro dared the policeman to fight—to "come on"—that he was ready for him.   Of course the policeman said come on, but there was no more fighting between them.

293. What next of the riot did you see ?   Nothing further that day.   The next afternoon, I think, between four and five o'clock, I heard firing on Main street, and a crowd passed down toward the south part of the town.   I saw some colored persons, I do not know whether they were soldiers or not, and they all passed down towards the old graveyard, in the south part of the town.   There was firing on both sides; I did not see them; I only heard the firing.   In the course of half an hour I saw some policemen passing up this way; I heard one policeman say to another going the other way not to go down, that there had been two white men shot all to pieces.

294. You say some of these colored men were in this crowd.   What did they appear to be doing ?   They were engaged in fighting; they seemed to be assisting the colored men who were being pursued by the policemen.

295. Then it was a crowd of colored men ?   Yes.

296. How large a crowd of colored men ?   I could not say—from 15 to 20.

297. Where did they come from ?   They came up from across this old graveyard, from towards the fort like.

298. Where did they appear to be going ?   I only saw them run   The first I heard was the firing on Main street, some distance up; I could not tell how far.

299. Do you say that these colored people were in the crowd of policemen that came down ? Yes; they seemed to be running, and the policemen after them.

300. Were there any others except policemen in the crowd ?   I could not see.

301. How large a number was there ?   There was quite a company of them; I could not tell how many.   A great many collected and ran with them.

302. Did the colored people seem to be running, and the crowd after them ?   Yes; they appeared to be running down the street, and the crowd after them.

303. And this other crowd of negroes were coming to the assistance of the negroes being chased ?   Yes; I supposed that to be their object.   They all joined in, and then there was firing on both sides.

304. Were you in a situation where you could see this ?   Yes; I could see it from my window; I could see right over into the street.

305. Were the two crowds mixed together ?   Yes; they were all running.   The colored people were trying to get away from the police; still I think they both fired at each other.

306. When they met the crowd of colored people coming up what did that crowd do ?   They turned and run together, pursued by the police.   They soon got out of sight.

307. Did you see the negro who was hurt opposite your house on Tuesday ?   On Tuesday afternoon, while this crowd was passing down, I think about six o'clock, numbering, I should think, one hundred police, and I do not know how many citizens, I suppose for the purpose of arresting these negroes, all armed with pistols, they met two negroes coming up, I think, from their work, as they had little buckets in their hands.   The policemen struck these negroes.   I saw one right at the gate, holding a negro by the head, and one of the policemen struck him with a pistol.   The negro said he had been doing no harm; that he was just returing from his work.   I saw another negro passing up street after he had been struck.   I did not see him struck.   The blood was running down all over his face.   I do not know by whom he was struck.   He went on up street.

308. Do you know of any others, white or black, being hurt on that day ?   No, sir; not that I saw myself.   There was a negro man shot just below my house.   I did not see it myself.

309. Did you see anything that took place on Tuesday night ?   I only saw the fires.   I saw the flames of buildings that were burning, and heard persons passing in the street.   I think it was on Tuesday night that the buildings were burned.

310. Did there a crowd on Tuesday, in the course of the afternoon, come into your front room ?   That was on Monday night.   One of them pointed out the place where they had been fighting, and wanted his comrades to come up and fight some one; I do not know who. They finally passed down the street.   Some of the others persuaded them to go down the street.   They went on down, and as they went they fired off their pistols.   They seemed to talk very loud.

311. Did they appear to be intoxicated ?   Yes, sir; I think they were.

312. How many of them were there? I could not tell; I should think, probably, eight or ten of them.

313. Were there any white persons in the vicinity with the negroes? No, sir; I think not.

314. Did they fire upon any persons? No; I think they were only a little intoxicated, were feeling pretty well, and making a little noise, to show their courage, or something of this sort.

315. Did you hear anything more of it? No, sir; nothing that night. On Tuesday night I heard considerable firing up the street; I do not know who by.

316. What did you see on Wednesday? On Wednesday morning, I should think about nine o'clock, there was a crowd of citizens and police who went past the house towards the south part of the city.

317. Did you hear any conversation between them? No, sir; not that I remember of.

318. What was their conduct? They seemed to be after the negroes. They passed on south, and I heard considerable firing. I did not see it. That crowd kept on to the old graveyard called the Morris cemetery. I didn't see any one fire that morning. I saw a company of soldiers pass from the "fort." I saw them file off, but they were too far off for me to distinguish who they were.

319. Did you see the policemen arrest anybody? I did not see them arrest anybody. I saw them pass up the street with one colored man.

320. What were they doing with him? He was walking up the street between the policemen. I do not know what they were going to do with him.

321. Do you know any other facts connected with the riots? No, sir. On Tuesday afternoon I saw a man passing up street who seemed to be very warm. He stopped right opposite the house. He said he had been setting a negro school-house on fire

322. To whom did he make this remark? To some gentleman on the street; I do not know who he was.

323. What response did the man make? I do not recollect.

By Mr. SHANKLIN:

324. On Wednesday, when you saw this party coming back to fight, how many men were there in the crowd? I do not know how many: I think eight or ten.

325. There were no policemen near them, you say? No, sir; not that I saw.

326. Was it on Tuesday that the firing commenced? I think so. I cannot state exactly the time.

327. Did you see any policemen in the crowd passing down the street when the negroes were passing up the street before you heard the firing on Tuesday afternoon? Yes; the disturbance that commenced on Main street was before this.

328. Was the crowd you saw going down Main street white men? Yes, with negroes; that was before the crowd which went down in the afternoon. It was a crowd of negroes and whites.

329. Were the first crowd you saw on Main street composed of white and black engaged in fighting? Yes, sir; they were firing.

330. White and black both firing? Yes, sir.

331. Were they all mixed together? Yes, sir; all mixed together, running and firing. The firing commenced on Main street between some negroes and whites, and then some negroes came up the street towards their friends.

332. The firing had commenced, had it, before you saw this company of negroes coming up the street? Yes, sir; I heard the firing some time before I saw them, and then they went down the street firing, and all mingled together.

333. How many negroes do you think were in the crowd after they all mingled together? I could not tell how many negroes or how many white people; there seemed to be quite a large crowd of them.

334. Did you see any fight after that? No, sir; only on Thursday evening, after the crowd passed down. I then saw some men firing, and saw one man fall. I could not say whether he was a colored man or a white man. I saw the smoke of the pistol, and saw the man fall.

335. Where was that? That was in the old graveyard.

336. Could you see the fort? No, sir.

337. You say you saw soldiers coming from the fort on Wednesday morning; were these white soldiers? Yes, sir; they were the regulars.

338. Did you see any negroes in uniform coming from towards the fort? No, sir.

339. Did the firing cease as soon as the soldiers came out? No, sir; not immediately. The soldiers came out and ran very fast. I think there was some firing after they got on to South street. It did not continue long.

340. Did you hear any firing after that on Wednesday morning? No, sir; I do not recollect hearing any after that.

By the CHAIRMAN:

341. You speak of a crowd of white men, policemen, and colored men passing down the street, all fighting together; were the colored men fighting this crowd of white men and

police? Yes, sir; the colored men seemed to be acting on the defensive. The policemen fought them, and they fought back. The policemen were driving them on down the street.

342. What proportion of this crowd were black? I do not know. There were not near so many of them as there were of the whites.

343. Was there one negro to four white men? I could not say. There were not near so many of them.

F. FINNE sworn and examined.

By the CHAIRMAN:

344. Please state your residence. Memphis, corner of Winchester and Alabama streets.

345. How long have you lived there? I have lived on the corner seven years.

346. What do you know of any recent riotous proceedings in this city? I know nothing about them at all, except that I heard about this money being stolen from the colored man Albert Harris.

347. What's your business? I keep a retail grocery.

348. Do you keep liquors? Yes, to sell by the quantity. I do not keep any bar.

349. What do you know about the money being stolen from Albert Harris? It was in the evening. That morning Deputy Sheriff Swayne, I think his name is, came to my store with two other men. The deputy sheriff had some business with me—a man had sued me. I did not know anything about it until Deputy Sheriff Swayne came there that morning with an execution, and he told those two men to stay in the store until further orders. They stayed in the store until the afternoon about five o'clock, when I got released and they went home. Then, the same evening about nine o'clock, those same men, with two soldiers, came to my house and asked for five cents' worth of matches and five cents' worth of candles. At the same time another person came into the house and bought something. I did not wait on them. In about twenty or thirty minutes after this colored man, Albert Harris, came over to my house and said this party had been to his house and taken a double-barrel shot-gun and, I think, something else, and some money. I understood him to state that night that it was $200, but he has since stated it at $300.

350. What were the names of the two men who were placed in your house that day to watch? I do not know.

351. Do you know that those two men who were in your store were the men who robbed Albert Harris's house? I could not say that. They were in my store about half past eight or nine o'clock in the evening with two soldiers. Albert Harris told me that those men, with two soldiers, came into his house and robbed him.

352. Did you see the two men who robbed Albert Harris afterwards? Yes; I saw them the next day, and I saw them about eight days ago on a picnic.

353. And you do not know their names? No, sir.

354. Did not you inquire their names? No, sir; I never inquired their names.

355. Did you not become satisfied they were the same parties who robbed Albert Harris's house? Yes, I thought so.

356. Were the two soldiers who came there dressed in uniform? Yes; one had on a military overcoat, and one had on a military dress-coat.

357. How did you know they were United States soldiers? From their uniform.

358. Did you know from any other reason? No; only by their uniform.

359. Did it excite your suspicions when they bought matches and candles in your store? No, not particularly; there were three or four other men in the store. My little boy gave the matches and candles to one of the citizens. There was, I believe, another man standing outside on the pavement dressed in citizen's clothes. He seemed, like those inside, to recognize the soldiers. I don't know who he was.

360. That made five in the party? Yes; four inside and one outside. When the men came out of Albert Harris's house one of them had something on his shoulder like a gun.

361. Did you see them go into Albert Harris's house? No; I saw them come out.

362. Were they the same crowd who were in your store? I think so.

363. Are you satisfied of that? Yes; I think so on account of Albert, the shoemaker, saying so.

364. Is he a respectable man? Yes; he is a nice man. He staid in my house for about a year, and made right smart of money. His wife made some money, too. They were a very nice family.

365. Describe those citizens. One fellow was about five feet five or six inches high. He was not heavily built. He had dark eyes and black hair. His whole clothing and appearance seemed to me just like a loafer or gambler.

366. Did he have a moustache? No; he did not have any moustache. The other man was five feet two or three inches tall, better dressed, and he had a little bit of a moustache.

367. Did you see him afterwards? I think I saw him four or five days afterwards on the street.

By Mr. SHANKLIN:

368. Were there any policemen at your store? There were two policemen in about that time. I do not think they were there at the same time.

369. Do you know the name of either of them? I know both of them, but I do not know the name of only one; his name is Sullivan.

370. Was he there about the time this party came out of Albert Harris's house? There were two policemen at Albert's house. There are two doors to his house, one in front and the other on the side; it is a corner house. The policemen came out of the side door, I think, about five minutes before those citizens came into my store to purchase matches and candles.

371. Were not those policemen with the four men who came into your store? I think not.

372. How long did this party remain in your house when they came? I think about three or four minutes.

373. How long before you saw them over at Albert's house? About ten minutes after that I saw four men come out of Albert Harris's door.

376. Did you notice whether any person or persons were standing outside when the four men came out? I did not; perhaps there may have been. There were some boys standing about.

377. You are certain there was no policeman who came out of Harris's house with those four men? I am certain they did not. The last time I saw either of them that night was before these four men came into my store. The next night they came in again; they came in every night. But the next night after Sullivan was sent on another beat.

By the CHAIRMAN:

378. Did you have any conversation with either of these policemen the next night? Yes; I said it was a shame that they went over to Albert's house and took his money. They said yes; it had got to be time when a white man did not know when his money was secure, or when they might come in and rob him.

379. Did he make any excuse for permitting it to be done? Oh, no; he said nothing about that.

380. Did he make any response any further than what you have stated? No, sir; after he left, a neighbor of mine came in, and then we talked about street railroads and other matters.

381. Did he appear to defend the act of robbery that had been committed? Oh, no; he did not appear to want to say anything about it.

382. What is the character of the police of Memphis? I do not know; I never inquire anything about the police.

383. Did you have any talk with the other policeman whose name you do not know? No, sir. I remember now another citizen was in my house at the time Albert was robbed, by the name of John Frick.

384. Had John Frick any suspicion of these policemen? No, sir, I think not.

385. If there had been any policemen in at Albert's when the robbery was committed, who would it have been? It must have been these two; there were no others about.

386. Would you believe Albert Harris on oath? I do not know; sometimes he talks a little at random.

387. When he had sworn to tell the truth would you believe him? Yes; when he had sworn to tell the truth I believe he would tell the truth.

FRIDAY, *May* 25, 1866.

C. M. COOLEY sworn and examined.

By the CHAIRMAN:

389. Where do you reside? On Turley street, in Memphis, Tennessee.

390. How long have you resided in this city? Nearly two and a half years.

391. Where did you previously reside? In New York State, where I was raised.

392. Were you here at the time of the riot? I was at my grocery, on Beale street.

393. What knowledge have you of the riot in this city about the first of May? I did not see much. I saw a crowd passing my house composed of policemen and citizens.

394. What day of the week was this? I do not recollect. I think it was the 1st of May.

395. What hour of the day did the crowd pass your house? About three or four o'clock p. m.

396. What was the character of the crowd? It was partly policemen and quite a number of men dressed in citizen's clothing.

397. What was the object of the crowd? I do not know. They said there was a riot on South street. I heard several of them say the negroes had raised a riot.

398. Did you go with the crowd? I did not.

399. Do you know what they did? I do not. I heard others say a number of men were shot, black and white.

400. Did you see any men shot? I did in the evening, just about dusk; I saw one man shot. It was nearly opposite my store, about No. 79 Beale street, I should think.

401. Who was it that was shot, and by whom? It was a negro. It was so dark I could not see by whom.

402. Was he killed? I understood he was.

403. Did you see him shot? Yes, sir, I did.

404. Did he fall? He was down when shot; he was lying down when I last saw him.

405. How long did he lay there? I heard others say he was taken away about eight o'clock, after I left the store to go home.

406. Where was he taken? To the station-house, where he died, as I understood.

407. Did you see any other negroes hurt? I was standing near the store and saw several men cross the bridge over the bayou, and meet a negro in that vicinity; they commenced beating him; he ran into a store; he said he had done nothing; they continued beating him until he managed to get out of the back door, when he ran away. Just as they came out they met another negro; he had, I think, a pan in his hand. I understood he was going to the store for meal for his family.

408. How many times did they strike him? About fifteen or twenty times, I think; any one of the blows would have killed me. They knocked him down in the gutter, when some one shot him twice, or the shots may have been fired by two different parties.

409. Who were these parties? They were white men; I could not say whether they were policemen or not, I was somewhat excited. There were a dozen men near when the beating commenced, and several others afterwards gathered around.

410. What did they do after they had shot the negro? Some of them stood around after the beating, and some walked off.

411. Did you hear any conversation? Nothing more than I heard the negro say he had done nothing.

412. With what did they strike him? Clubs, or something in their hands. It was too dark for me to be able to tell whether they wore stars or not.

413. Did you go to the place where the negro was lying? No, sir.

414. Who took him away? I do not know.

415. How long did he lay there? I was told it was done shortly after I left my store, which was between seven and eight o'clock.

416. When you went away, were there any persons about the body? I believe there were some men there.

417. Did you go near the body? No, sir.

418. Why not? Because I generally keep away when such occurrences are going on; they do not have anything to do with my business.

419. Then you stood in your store and saw him beaten and shot to death without attempting to interfere? I saw him shot down, and, after the first shot, heard him groan; after the second shot I do not know that I heard any noise.

420. Did you see any one in the crowd take the part of the negro? Nobody took the part of the negroes. I did not see any one take their part at all. I made the remark that it was a brutal thing at the time; that it was wrong.

422. What prevented you from going there? I knew I could do no good, and, consequently, I kept away.

By Mr. BROOMALL:

423. Would there have been any danger if you had? I presume there would.

424. Was that what prevented you? I don't know; I seldom go near such occurrences.

425. What became of the negro who was first assaulted? He went out of the back door, and I saw him no more.

426. In whose store did this occur? Either in Mr. Eagan's or Mr. Hollywood's; I think it is either No. 79 or 81.

427. What kind of stores are these, and what is the nativity of the men keeping them? Retail grocery and liquor stores, kept by Irishmen.

428. Did you know the colored person who was killed? I do not.

429. Do you know the names of the persons making the assault upon them? I do not.

430. Do you know any other facts about the riot? I saw a church on the corner of Main and Overton streets burned on the morning of the first, I think, about two o'clock in the morning. I did not dress, or go out; at the time I was living near the church.

431. Are you married? Yes, sir.

432. Were these negroes, who were beaten and shot, interfering with anybody? I do not think they were. I heard them both distinctly say they had done nothing, and cry for mercy.

433. What was said by the ruffians in reply? I cannot say.

434. Were they talking? There was some talking.

435. What countrymen were they? I could not say positively; I was some little distance from them. My store is No. 74, and they were at No. 79, on the opposite side, near the bayou bridge.

436. Have you seen or talked with any of those men you saw that night? No, sir; I do not know that I should recognize them if I was to see them. I should think some of them were policemen. I very seldom speak to the policemen.

437. Why did you think they were policemen? Because I thought they had clubs like policemen.

438. How many had these clubs? I think three or four, perhaps more.

439. Did you see any of these men having clubs strike the negro? Yes, sir; many times.

440. Where? Over the head.

441. Did you see the negro fall? I did; he partly fell after being struck, and they con-

tinued hitting him until he fell to the ground, when some one came up and shot him after he was down.

442. How many shots were fired? Two.

443. How long after these shots were fired did these parties disperse? Some two or three minutes; others remained longer.

444. What was the last you saw of the body of the negro? I did not see it after the crowd dispersed; I do not know how long it remained there. I was told the body was taken to the station-house.

445. You said he had a pan in his hand? Yes, sir, I should think so. I was told the next morning he was going after some cornmeal for his wife, who was sick.

446. Do you know his name? I do not; I have heard it mentioned several times, but have forgotten it.

447. Could you learn it? I expect I could.

448. Did you feel any danger yourself from having witnessed this affair? No, sir.

449. Did you have any threats made against you? Not that I know of; nothing more than against northern men generally.

450. What are they? Nothing, except what I have seen in the papers.

451. What papers? The Avalanche talks very strong against northern men, radicals, and so on.

452. What was the character of the talk? I could not describe it.

453. Was it inciting violence against northern men? No, sir; the general tone of the paper seems to be that northern men have no business here.

455. Where are you from? New York. I moved from there to the west, and remained in Minnesota. I was here in the city some six months before the war.

456. Have you been in the service of the United States? I was employed in the quarter-master's department, and in charge of the tarpaulins on the levee, acting as watchman, generally, under Captain Lyman.

457. Have you any further knowledge of the riot than you have stated? I saw a negro whipped rather severely on the second of May, I think.

458. What day of the week? I could not say; the second day of the riot, I think.

459. Where did you see this? The negro passed my store. It commenced above my store; he whipped the negro nearly a square.

460. Did you know the person who whipped the negro? He was a white man; I knew him only by sight.

461. Does he live in Memphis? I think he does.

462. What did he whip the negro with? A riding whip. The negro was running and trying to get away; he had a basket on his arm, and was crossing the street at the time he was attacked.

463. Did the negro say anything? Not that I heard of.

464. Where did the white man hit him? Over the head and shoulders, probably for two or three minutes; the last I saw of the negro, he went into Main street.

465. Did you see the negro afterwards? I have seen him go past the store.

466. Do you know him? No, sir.

467. Have any steps been taken to punish these offences in your neighborhood? Not that I know of.

HENRY JACKSON (colored) sworn and examined.

By the CHAIRMAN:

468. Where do you live? On the corner of Winchester and Alabama streets.

469. How long have you lived in Memphis? Nine months.

470. Were you here during the recent riots? Certainly, sir.

471. What did you see of the riot? I saw the rioters; one of the policemen struck me.

472. What day was that? Wednesday, 2d day of May.

473. What time in the afternoon? I don't remember the time. I was standing near the barber shop talking to Jerry Williams, when a policeman came along and said, you belong to the party out yonder, and he just struck me and grabbed me by the beard and struck me again until the blood ran down all over my clothes. I said I had not been doing anything, and asked him what was the matter; he raised and struck me again.

474. Where did he strike you? Under the chin.

475. What with? His fist.

476. Did he have a club? I did not see a club; while I was standing there and the policeman holding me, another policeman came up. He struck me two or three times, and would have struck me more had not the other policeman told him to stop.

477. Did you see anything of the robbery of Albert Harris's house? Not exactly; I came along fifteen minutes afterwards, and Brance, the porter at Mr. Myers's said that some people had been and robbed the old man Harris of everything he had.

478. That was the first you knew of it, was it? My daughter told me that one of them was a policeman. I asked if she knew the policeman, and she said no.

479. Was she in the house of Albert Harris at the time? Yes, she was there. She said

they came in to look after guns, but just as soon as they found the money they left. Brance Hutt saw them.

480. Who is Brance Hutt? He is a porter up at Myers's.

481. Do you know anything further of this riot of your own knowledge? I was lying down, and looked out through the window and saw a blacksmith shop close by burned down.

482. Did you see anybody set fire to the shop? No; when I first saw it there was a great blaze. Jerry Williams was in there, and they would not let him come out for a while.

483. Did you see any other violence committed? No; I did not see anything. Jerry Williams can tell you something if you will send for him.

WILLIAM HUNTER sworn and examined.

By the CHAIRMAN:

484. Please state your residence and official position? My residence is Memphis; I am judge of the criminal court of Memphis.

485. How long have you resided here? Between three and four years.

486. How long have you been judge of the criminal court? About six months. I came to Memphis when General Sherman came here in 1862, intending at the time to make this my residence.

487. Were you in the Union service? Yes, sir.

488. For how long a time, and in what capacity? I was in the service as a captain, and was promoted to major and lieutenant colonel after the battle of Shiloh.

489. Were you in the city at the time of the recent riots here? I was.

490. Have you any knowledge in relation to the riots? I have none as to the events. I witnessed none of the outrages or violence perpetrated, and really nothing from my own personal observation.

491. Do you know of acts of violence and outrage being committed? Only by common report and information derived from other persons.

492. Have any steps been taken before your court, or before any proper authority, to your knowledge, to bring the offending parties to justice? There have been no steps taken to my knowledge by the civil authorities; certainly none in my court.

493. Have you heard of any arrests of any parties made by the civil authorities? I have heard of the arrest of no white persons; I believe that some negroes were arrested.

494. How many negroes? I saw myself three or four in charge of the police.

495. Do you know for what they were arrested? It was the first day of the riot; I presume it was for being engaged in it.

496. What day? Tuesday, May 1st.

497. What was done with these negroes? I do not know. I understood they were taken to the police station, and that some were taken there really to protect them from those who were attacking them. I saw two negroes coming in in charge of policemen the first day; one was wounded; the blood was oozing from his right side; two officers had him in charge. He and the other I understood were taken to the police station and kept over night and discharged the next day, not being implicated as having taken any part in the riot; I simply heard that.

498. By whom were they taken? I saw these two men in charge of one or two policemen, and I am confident that two of the sheriff's deputies had one in charge, or that one of the sheriff's deputies was in charge of each of them, I am not positive which. I mentioned it, however, to the deputies next morning, and they said I was mistaken; that they were not there; so that I do not state this positively; I may have been mistaken. I saw them there that day, and I may have been mistaken in regard to their having this man in custody.

499. Will you state the reasons, if you know any, why steps have not been taken to bring the perpetrators of these outrages to justice? In my own court the grand jury have adjourned, and the affair took place only a short time before the final adjournment of the court for the term. No information was filed with me, and no applications made for bench warrants. The question of calling a special grand jury I entertained in my own mind and considered, but hearing that the military were about investigating, I thought they would do it with more thoroughness, and that probably that so late in the term the proceedings of the grand jury would not amount to much. I therefore did not call a grand jury, and did nothing in relation to the matter. No citizen communicated with me upon the subject; I simply thought over the matter without advice or consultation with any one.

500. Have the citizens themselves, so far as you know, taken any steps to bring the perpetrators of these outrages to justice? None that I know of.

501. Is your court a court of full jurisdiction? Yes, criminal jurisdiction for trying all crimes and offences against the State of Tennessee, within the fifth, thirteenth, and fourteenth districts of Shelby county. It only extends to these three districts, which includes the city of Memphis and suburbs.

By Mr. BROOMALL:

502. By whose appointment do you hold your office of judge? By appointment of the Governor of Tennessee.

503. What are the qualifications for jurors under the law as it has existed up to this time? Free white men, white male inhabitants over the age of twenty-one years, citizens, residents of the State for six months, and freeholders within the county.

504. Under that law, is there any disqualification in consequence of being engaged in the late rebellion? No, sir; none under the old law.

505. Please state the change which has been made in the law in that respect? I could not do that; I merely know of the change from newspaper statements.

506. The present law, then, has not gone into operation? No; I understand that a law has been passed within the last ten days, making a radical change in this respect, the provisions of which I am unacquainted with.

507. From your knowledge of the class of persons from whom jurors are taken, what, in your opinion, are the chances for white persons being convicted for outrages committed upon negroes? The chances would be remote. That answer might require some explanation. We have in this city a class of people, intelligent, moral men, who really have participated in the rebellion against the government, but who are above these prejudices. How large that class is I do not pretend to say; they would do justice to the negro as a general thing. There is another class, from whom most of our juries are made up, that would be utterly incapable of doing justice, and enforcing the law with anything like impartiality.

508. What are the antecedents of this latter class? They have all sympathized with, or been engaged in the late rebellion, more or less; they are the ignorant portion of our population—the poor white people of this country, as well as foreigners; of course there are different classes of foreigners. But on the whole, with that explanation, I might say that the chances of conviction would be very remote with the material we have for jurors.

509. Do the judges of your county court select the jurors? They should do it, but they don't attend much to the business, and it generally falls upon the clerk to make out the panel for the term. Under the old law, the panel for the term is hardly ever sufficient for capital cases, and in cases of felony we are obliged usually to issue special *venires.* The regular panel will usually dispose of civil cases, misdemeanors, &c., provided that all who are summoned attend.

510. Is your court the only court which has jurisdiction of these offences, under the State laws? It has exclusive jurisdiction.

511. And, do I understand you, the chance for punishment of the rioters is quite remote? Yes, sir; I believe the same prejudices would extend to the circuit court if it had jurisdiction which would be found before my court.

512. You spoke of a recent enactment, changing the qualification of jurors. Do you consider that an improvement as regards the conviction of whites for offences against negroes? In the form in which I understand it has passed, I consider it very little improvement; whether it goes to the competency of a juror, or whether it is cause of challenge, I have not yet learned. It makes no difference so far as its operation is concerned; though I think it would be better to make it a cause of challenge, because it would give us more jurors. The reason why it would not improve matters in the city of Memphis and in my court is this: It confines jurors for the criminal court to those who are at present voters under the franchise law. Those who are voters under that act can obtain certificates in consequence of voting at the elections of 1864 and the spring of 1865, for the convention for the new constitution, governor, and members of the legislature. That entitles them under the late franchise law to certificates. There were some thirteen hundred votes, more or less, cast at the spring election, and of that thirteen hundred voters I do not think three hundred of them were loyal.

513. Who could have taken the test oath? I don't know whether they could conscientiously have taken it. I doubt whether a majority of them voted at this election from patriotic motives, but rather to put them right upon the record with the military authorities, and agents of the Treasury Department to obtain cotton permits, and other privileges conceded to business men, where it appeared they were sufficiently loyal not to abuse them. Again, a large proportion of the votes cast at this election were by foreigners, who voted, as a matter of habit, as they always do; they have no loyalty, and care nothing about this government; so that that element who are voters, and consequently jurors, would compose about four-fifths of the element under the old as well as under the new law from which we must take our jurors—really worse than the returned soldiers who have been in the rebel army.

By Mr. SHANKLIN:

514. Then your conclusion is that the recent enactment would make no improvement in the qualifications as to loyalty for the persons who are to be selected as jurors? Unless there is another change made by the legislature we will be compelled to resort to that element for jurors. The qualified voters are a worse element than those disfranchised under a strict application of the franchise law.

By Mr. BROOMALL:

515. Have you observed the tone of the public press, and what effect had it upon the riot as a cause of discouragement or otherwise? I have no doubt but what it was stimulated by the press of this city. I think the leading disloyal papers in the city have stimulated it.

Yet there has been a growing prejudice between the police of the city and the negroes, especially the negro soldiers.

516. Do you think there is any civil remedy for the existing evils short of a military force? Practically, I think, there is none that would be efficient.

By the CHAIRMAN:

517. Do you believe that the perpetrators during the riotous proceedings can or will be punished by the civil authorities? They might be partially. I think that with a favorable selection of a grand jury at the next term of the court indictments would be found against many of the parties if the evidence was presented to them, but the chances of a conviction before a traverse jury would, as I said before, be very remote. Convictions might be obtained in some cases.

518. If, as you say, under the recent law for selection of jurors, such selection must be confined to the qualified voters, and the qualified voters being of the class you stated, do you believe it to be possible to have any person convicted for the outrages committed during the late riot? That would depend upon a great many accidents controlling the selection of the jury in each particular case.

519. Would there not, in all probability, be enough selected in every petit jury to prevent conviction being had, in your judgment? Yes, sir.

520. Would it not follow from that, therefore, that no redress could be had from the civil authorities; in other words, although indictments might be found, yet convictions could not be had? Yes, sir.

By Mr. BROOMALL:

521. The district court of the United States for this district selects its jurors from a larger space of country. What would be the chance of a conviction in that court if, as supposed, the civil rights bill gives jurisdiction to that court? It is a question I could not undertake to answer. If jurors in the federal courts are selected from that class of men who throughout the rebellion have been strictly loyal to the government, convictions, of course, could be obtained; but if they are taken indiscriminately from the population in the western district of Tennessee, convictions would be out of the question.

523. It would depend upon the judges and United States marshals in the performance of their duties, would it not? It is not a point I have inquired about. There is a provision of this kind in regard to the United States courts, I believe. It would, of course, depend to some extent on the manner in which they discharged their duties.

524. With care do you believe a jury could be obtained of the loyal and best men of this district before whom convictions in these cases could be had? Oh, yes; I have no doubt of that at all, nor have I any doubt that this federal court could be made a powerful arm for the control of crimes in this part of the State.

525. You have said you saw no remedy short of the military arm of the government; would the proper jurisdiction conferred upon the district courts of the United States be a remedy if proper persons were appointed to fill the judicial and executive positions in these courts? Yes, sir; I have no doubt of that. I have long had that opinion. In my previous testimony I was speaking of the state of things which exist in regard to the State laws. We are confined in our jurisdiction. We must take our jurors from a certain district, and are not allowed to go outside. We must take them as we can get them under the law.

By Mr. SHANKLIN:

526. How long have you resided in this place—ever since the federal possession of the place? I was not here during the whole of the time after I came to the city. I came in 1862, and remained in the military service of the United States really until August, 1863, after the siege of Vicksburg, when I resigned. I had my family in Memphis more than three years ago, while I was yet in the service. They came here, and I was ordered to Vicksburg with the regiments constituting the 4th division. I passed through the siege of Vicksburg, and also the expedition against Jackson under Sherman; returned to Vicksburg, was taken sick, and resigned there August, 1863.

527. On your resignation of your position in the army did you then locate in this place? Yes, sir; and, as I said, my family were here before.

528. And you have been here since August, 1863, as a citizen? Yes, sir, but not continually.

529. What proportion of the time have you resided here? I have been in Memphis continually since February or March, 1864. I have only been out of the city twice since then, and only for a few days.

530. Have you formed, since you have been here, a pretty general acquaintance with the citizens of Memphis, or has your acquaintance been partial? My acquaintance has been as general as any stranger's who was in a new city under the peculiar circumstances that existed here. I am personally acquainted with a very large number of the citizens.

531. Is that acquaintance confined to citizens of one political cast, or is it with all classes? No, sir; it is not confined to those of my own political opinions. I have many personal friends among rebel sympathizers and those who have been in the rebel army.

532. But the larger portion of your acquaintances are of what political complexion? In my intimate acquaintances I am, of course, more intimate with those that are called the loyal men of the city.

533. Before you entered the army where did you reside? At Cairo, Illinois.

534. How long did you reside at Cairo? I resided at Cairo and Mound City between three and four years.

535. Where did you reside previous to your removal to Cairo? Is that the place of your nativity? No, sir; my place of nativity is not in the United States. I am an Irishman by birth—Scotch-Irish.

536. How long have you been in the United States? Since I was two years of age. I have been in the United States forty-seven years.

537. Where was your first residence after reaching the United States? The city of Pittsburg, Pennsylvania.

538. Did you come from Pittsburg to Indiana? No, sir; I went from Pittsburg to Illinois, and remained there for some years.

539. Are the places you have named the only places you have permanently resided in since you have been in the United States? No, sir; I resided at Steubenville, Ohio, and studied law there. I located at De Shocton, Ohio, and commenced the practice of the law there.

540. So far as you could collect the public sentiment of the property-holders and the men who are permanent and fixed in their residence and interest in Memphis relative to this riot, what are their sentiments? Of course, the moral people all condemn it, and so do all men who have respectability, so far as I have learned.

541. Is that class in the city of Memphis large or small? It is large.

542. You spoke about thirteen hundred registered voters under the former law here. What would be the number of voters under the qualifications required by the laws of Tennessee prior to the war in the city of Memphis, I mean *white* male citizens over the age of twenty-one years, who had a residence here? That would be a difficult question to answer, because I have no definite idea what the population of the city is. We have had no census since 1860; to make a loose estimate, we might poll four or five hundred votes. I would not pretend that that estimate was anything like a correct one.

443. Have you had any consultation with that class of persons whom you designate as the better class in Memphis as to the propriety of taking proceedings to bring these offenders to trial and punishment? I have not sought any myself, and have not been approached myself upon the subject.

544. I understood you that when the riot commenced your first grand jury had been discharged, and that you did not summon the second one because the military authorities had taken the matter in hand? And the early approach of the next term.

545. When does the next term commence? The second Monday in June. I thought probably this investigation would gather up the facts more efficiently than if I should convene a grand jury, and that public sentiment would at that time better sustain an indictment found by a grand jury than it would at present.

546. Is that your opinion still? Yes, sir. I still believe my views upon that subject are correct.

By Mr. BROOMALL:

547. You have already said that no steps have been taken to bring these offenders to justice; can you explain why this leading class of persons here, which you describe to be so large, have taken no steps, held no public meetings, and moved in the matter in no way? I could not say what motives may have actuated them in the course they have taken.

548. Have they any power to act except through the courts? Of course not.

LAVINIA GODELL (colored) sworn and examined.

By the CHAIRMAN:

549. Where do you live? In Memphis.

550. Are you married? Yes, sir; I was married. My husband got killed.

551. When did your husband get killed? On Tuesday night, the 1st of May.

552. State your husband's name and business? Jackson Godell. When he was at work he had been out in the country.

553. Did you have a house here? We rented a house of Mr. Moller. When my husband staid in the city he was draying.

554. Now state what you know in reference to his being killed? He came home and said he wanted some supper. I was sick, and said to him that I had nothing in the house to cook him anything from only a little flour, and that if he would get some meal it would be less trouble. He went out of the house to get some meal. In a few minutes after a sister of the church, who lives next me, came in and said, "Sister Lavinia, Jackson is killed." When I went out he was lying and only groaning; I sat with his head in my hand, when some gentleman came along and said, "You had better take him into the house," and that if I would go and get some of my friends, he would stay by Jackson until I came back.

I went and tried to get somebody to take him in, but could not. Some other person then said to me, "You had better go in or they will kill you." I did not know what to do. They told me it would cost me my life if I staid there, and I finally went in. I could not do anything. The next morning when I got up I went to look for him, but he was not there. I took up his hat and carried it in. I did not know where to look for him. Mrs. Hunt, one of the sisters, came in and said, "Don't you know where Jackson is?" I said no. She said that four men came and took him off in a hack, and said they were taking him to a hospital, and that I had better go to the station-house and see what hospital. I went up there, and the old man there, who wears military clothes, stopped me. I asked him to let me go in and see if the dead man who was there was not my husband. He asked me what kind of a man my husband was. I told him he was a low man. He asked me if he had a little bunch of whiskers on his chin. I said yes. He asked me what kind of clothes he had on, and I told him. He said he thought it was my husband lying out yonder, dead, and that I had better not go away. He told me to ask another man he pointed to, to let me go in, which I did, but he would not let me go. I begged him three or four times, but he would not let me. Then another little low Irishman stepped up and said: "Aunty, you wait a little while, and I will see if you cannot go in." After a while he called me, and I went and just peeped through the bars of the window, and saw my husband lying there, dead. They would not allow me to go inside. I went back and said: "That is my husband lying in there, dead." The man asked me how I knew. I told him of course I knew my husband, and asked him what they were going to do with him. He said they picked that man up out of the street. He asked me what my husband's name was. I told him Jackson Godell. He said there was no such man there. He asked me where my husband was killed. I told him on Beal street, almost right at Hollowell's grocery. He said he was there when he was killed; that he was shot dead.

555. What is this man's name? I do not know his name. He is assistant jailer I think. He said he saw the man drag him out of the gutter.

556. What was done with your husband's body? I do not know. I cannot tell you now where he is.

557. Have you asked for it? I did. I said after you have killed him you ought to give me the body. They refused. I do not know where he is any more than you do. I did not see him after I saw him in the station-house.

558. How old was your husband? I reckon he was about twenty-seven years old.

559. Was he a peaceable man? Yes; just as peaceable a man as you could find in the city.

560. Did he belong to the church? No, sir; he attended the Baptist church.

561. Was he a moral man? Yes; he was always talking about religion.

562. Is that all you know about the occurrence? That is all.

563. Do you know of any other outrages committed upon colored persons? No, sir; I do not, because I was sick. I did not see him killed. They called me out.

564. When you went out to see him how did he lie? When I first went out to see him he was laying partly across a log, groaning. I placed my hand to his breast and called him, but he never spoke.

565. Did you see where he was hurt? No, sir.

566. How long did you stay with him? I staid as long as I could, until they told me to go in or I would be killed. They were going to kill every negro they could find.

567. Who told you that? That is what they said on the streets. They said the policemen were going to kill every negro they could catch.

568. Then where did you go? I went into my room and staid there until the next morning.

569. Alone? There was another woman staid with me.

570. Did you go out the next morning? Yes, and found his hat, but he was gone.

571. How far from where you live was he killed? About two doors, on the same side of the street.

By Mr. SHANKLIN:

572. Was there a policeman standing near his body? No; there was no one there when I went out. While I sat there with his head in my hands, there were three who came from this way and went right down Beal street. One of them said: "Here is a damned nigger; if he is not dead we will finish him." Another gentleman then pushed him off, and said: "You have killed him once, what do you want to kill him again for?"

573. Were there any others standing near him? Yes, there were other people, white and black, but I was so badly hurt that he was killed at that time that I did not notice who they were, and do not know.

BRANCE HUTT (colored) sworn and examined.

By the CHAIRMAN:

574. Where do you live? I live in Memphis now; my home is in Missouri.
575. How long have you been living in Memphis? About two months.
576. What is your business? I am a porter in a store.

577. Were you here during the riots? Yes, sir.

578. Did you see any riotous proceedings? I never saw anything, only they came and robbed a man where I was staying.

579. What man was that? The old man Harris, on the corner of Winchester and Alabama streets.

580. Go on now and state when it was, and all you saw? It was on Wednesday, the second day of the riot. I was boarding at this house and had just sat down to eat my supper, when these men came in and said they had been ordered to search for arms. They told the old man to let them search the house. He got up, went in and opened his trunks; he gave them a double-barrel shot-gun. There were two soldiers there and two policemen; one policeman asked him if he had not more guns; he said he had not. As soon as they came to the trunk which had the money, they took the money and went right out. The old man hallooed to them not to take his money, but the soldiers told him to go to the Freedmen's Bureau and get his money.

581. How did you know they were policemen? By their stars.

582. What countrymen were they? They were Irish.

583. How many others were there beside the policemen? Three, making five in all.

684. How were the others dressed? The two citizens were dressed in black clothes; one had long hair; the other was a small-sized man and had a little moustache.

585. How were the soldiers dressed? There was one soldier who had on a blue coat like this man out here, (orderly,) with shoulder straps and a belt with a bayonet to it; he had on a full soldier's rig.

586. Did he take part in the robbery? I suppose he was in it.

587. Was he outside? No, sir; he was inside.

588. Do you know whether there were any additional persons outside? I do not know. There were a great many people out-doors and boys around the house.

589. What was the character of the talk among these people at the time? They said they wanted arms. The soldier told the man with the long hair, whom he called captain, when he came in, to "search the house."

590. Did they carry off all the arms they found? They carried off one gun; there was one gun behind the other door, which they did not take. As soon as they got the money they went out.

591. Did they threaten personal violence to you? No, sir; they did not threaten me.

592. What did they say when Albert Harris asked them to give back his money? They told him to go to the Freedmen's Bureau the next morning and he would get it. They just went right out then and did not say anything else at all.

593. What countryman did this soldier appear to be. He was a German; he had a very red face.

594. Would you know him if you were to see him? Yes, sir; I think I should.

595. Would you know any of the others if you should see them? I think I should know the one that had long hair.

596. Have you seen any of them about since this affair occurred? I do not think I have.

597. Where did they go after they left? They went right on up street.

598. Do you know of any other outrages committed during the riot, of your own knowledge? There was a blacksmith's shop burned up some sixty or seventy yards from the house, the same night.

599. What time in the night? About twelve o'clock.

600. Do you know who set it on fire? It was the police, I think.

601. Why do you think so? There was a colored man in the shop when it was burned who said so.

602. What was his name? I do not know. He was in the shop when they were talking about burning it, and they took his pants and poured coal oil on them, and set it afire.

JERRY WILLIAMS (colored) sworn and examined.

By the CHAIRMAN:

603. State your residence and age? I live in Memphis; am twenty-five years old.

604. How long have you been in Memphis? About a year.

605. Were you in Memphis at the time of the recent riots? Yes; about the first of May.

606. State what you know, if anything, of what took place during the riot? I saw a policeman strike down Henry Jackson, a colored man.

607. Do you know the name of the policeman? Curley McCuen, they call him. Jackson was talking to me. He said he had been down where the skirmishing was and had seen the regulars drive the colored soldiers into the fort. This policeman then just walked up to him, took him by the beard, and commenced beating him.

608. What did he do to you? Nothing to me.

609. Did you see any other person hurt? No, sir.

610. What did he do when the policeman came up to him? Jackson was talking to me, as I said, when the policeman came up. The policeman said to Jackson that he was one of that party. Jackson replied, no, he had nothing to do with it, and the policeman then commenced to beat him.

611. Did he hurt him badly? He blackened his eye and knocked the skin off his face. Another policeman came up and told him not to beat him. He then shoved Jackson off and beat him again, and kicked him.

612. What was the other policeman's name? I do not know the name of the other one.

T. M. WINTERS sworn and examined.

By the CHAIRMAN:

613. State your residence and your official position? I reside in Memphis; I am sheriff of Shelby county.

614. How long have you been sheriff? A little over two years.

615. Were you in Memphis at the time of the recent riots? I was.

616. Please state in a narrative form, and fully, what you saw and heard of the riot? I think it was on the 1st of May. I was summoning a jury, on Adams street, before the criminal court. Mr. Creighton, the city recorder, came up in a buggy and told me the police, a couple of them, had been shot by the negro soldiers on South street. I got into his buggy and went to General Stoneman's headquarters for assistance to go down and quell the riot. When General Stoneman came down, I asked him for some regular soldiers to go down and quell the riot. He told me he had no soldiers to give me; that the people here had petitioned the government to have the troops removed, and I had to go and summon my *posse*. I did so, and went with them as far as Vance street, near Morris's cemetery, and when within about five or six hundred yards of the negroes they fired, and I brought my men back. When we had got about as far as Vance and Linden streets I met a captain with about twenty or thirty regular soldiers. I told him who I was, and asked his assistance to put down any disturbance in that neighborhood. He said he would go with me. It was then about dusk. He went on with his men. There was then a great crowd of men, women and children on the sidewalk, and there was, I expect, about half a dozen shots fired. I got out of the way myself. I didn't know but I might get shot. The captain and his men went on. I went to the corner of Beal and Causey streets and waited until the captain had quieted all the disturbance. I asked him if he would not be so kind as to go down South street and get all the colored people there to go in their houses. He said he would, and I did not see him again that night. Going down Beal street I saw a negro wounded; I took him and put him in a hack. About that time I met six soldiers, two or three of whom had guns, and one appeared to be an orderly. They told me they came from General Stoneman's headquarters, and commenced taking pistols from the few men I had in charge with me. I begged them not to take the pistols away. They said I could get them in the fort. I staid until about ten o'clock that night, and everything was quiet. I told the hack-driver to take this negro to the station-house, where there was a doctor close by, but the orderly said they would take him to the Freedmen's Bureau hospital, I think. I did not know that there was a hospital attached to the bureau, but they took him away; I do not know which way they went. These five or six soldiers acted very badly, as I thought. I went to the station-house and found a negro dead there. I do not know whether this was the one I had put in the hack, or whether this orderly took him to the Freedmen's Bureau hospital, as he said he was going to. In the mean time Captain Garrett, chief of police, with the police, was ahead of me about half an hour before I got there. I saw very few police. I took with me my own *posse*. This was on the first day. The next day, about nine o'clock, I was in my office, when word came up that the negroes had come out of the fort and were killing everybody. Judge Leonard ordered me to go and summon a *posse* of five hundred men.

617. Who is Judge Leonard? Judge of the county court. I summoned as many as I could, and put myself and deputies at the head of them. I sent Deputy Sheriff Lamfort down ahead, and told him to arrest black and white, everybody who was making a disturbance. He went down, but I believe the mayor, chief of police, and police were there ahead of him. They were shooting at the time he got there, and he left. The men with him had no fire-arms. He came back and told me he could do nothing. In the mean time I had an interview with Captain Allyn, who had charge of the regulars down at the fort, and who agreed to meet me with thirty or forty regulars on Beal street. I then went down to South street. When I got there a very large crowd had assembled. The first thing I saw was two white men, one a policeman and the other a citizen, taking a negro dressed in federal uniform towards the crowd. I got ahead of the crowd and told them not to interfere with the negro; that I came down there to protect black and white; that I was there as an officer of the peace, and would arrest any man who made disturbance. I took the negro, I expect, about fifty yards and put him in his cabin. The mayor and chief of police then took their police force away. By the time I had returned from putting the negro in his cabin, General Wallace, the attorney general, came down with about forty men armed with double-barrel shot-guns. I took charge of them, and directed General Wallace to take charge of another party of about forty men armed with pistols. I dispersed the crowd at that point and went on as far as the Hernando road, where I found another crowd. They had four negroes in the middle of them, and one of the negroes was being beat. I rode up as quick as I could and told them not to hurt the negroes. I sent two of my *posse* with the four negroes to the edge of the wood the other side of the Hernando road with orders to there turn them loose,

which I waited to see them do. I expect those negroes did not stop running till night. If I had not been there I expect they would have been killed by a parcel of lawless white men who were prowling round there to burn up everybody's house, to rob and steal. This was the second day of the riot. About one o'clock on Wednesday everything was peaceable, and I summoned my *posse* to meet me at my office between six and seven. I was afraid there might be some disturbance and was determined to patrol the south part of the city that night. I started from my office about eight o'clock that evening and went to South street. I did not see a negro, man, woman or child, that night from eight o'clock until about one. All the crowds I came across were these lawless, drinking fellows; thieves, in fact, some of them. I dispersed every crowd I came across. I came up as far as Adams street and went down to the station-house about eleven o'clock that night pretty well tired out. I heard the bells ringing for fire and started back again the same route I had come. There was a fire at the corner of Hernando and Pontitoc streets, where there was a negro school-house. When I got as far as Beal street I met the fire-engines coming back. They had not gone down as far as the fire. I proceeded as far as the fire and turned down Vance street, and waited until the fire was over. It had proceeded so far before my arrival that I could not do anything to control the fire. I met this same captain that evening down about the fire with twenty-five or thirty regular soldiers. There were some of the soldiers who behaved very badly. They had no guns, but merely belts around them with bayonets. They were round with some lawless white men—in fact, thieves. These soldiers were, as I supposed, regulars; they were dressed in full uniform. It seemed as if they came just to get at the negroes with this other lawless crowd. Some of them were half drunk. I left Hernando street about twelve o'clock that night, came up Adams street as far as Beale, and saw a crowd coming over where there were a great many negro cabins, about the corner of Gayosa and Linden streets. I expect they were the same crowd I had seen about Washington and Beal streets. I remained here about half an hour, and it was one o'clock at night when I got to my office. Everything was then perfectly quiet. I discharged my men, but when I had gone as far as Washington street I saw a fire again at the corner of Main and Overton streets. That was the last I saw of the riot.

618. Did the riot close on Wednesday night? I think it did.

619. Was there no further violence committed? No, sir, I think not.

620. I understand you to say that you went on Tuesday afternoon, between five and six o'clock, to General Stoneman's; how far had the riot progressed at that time? I did not know anything about it; I was summoning a jury on Adams street when I received this information.

621. State particularly the reasons which General Stoneman gave for not furnishing assistance? He said he had very few troops here to guard the public property; and he said, further, the people here had petitioned the government to have the troops removed from here, and that I had to summon my *posse.*

622. Was that all the conversation that occurred? I think it was.

623. How soon after that did you summon this *posse* you speak of? I got as far as the corner of Adams and Second streets, where I expected to meet the police, but they had gone. There was nobody there, and I then went down to Jefferson street and summoned everybody I came across.

624. Were there a good many in the streets? Not many until I got down as far as Monroe street.

625. What sort of men did you summon? Good men, but very few of them went.

626. Were they armed? Not one with guns; some of them may have had pistols.

627. Where did you go then? With about twenty men I had collected I went on to Beal street, through St. Martin to this Morris cemetery, where some shots were fired by a few negroes. I then met this federal officer with a few troops.

628. When you got to this point, which you speak of as being a rise of ground, you say there was a crowd of people? No, sir; no crowd.

629. Were there any people in the vicinity? The police force was there.

630. How large a police force? I have no idea.

631. At what time in the evening did you get down to this place? A little before dusk.

632. And the negroes, you said, fired? Yes; I expect two or three shots.

633. Did you see them? I could not tell whether they were negroes or white men, but from what I heard I expect they were negroes who fired over. I did not remain but about a minute.

634. Did you see the force at all? Yes; I did not see over three or four men.

635. Then you are not able to swear from your own knowledge whether they were black or white men? I could not tell; it was a little duskish. I then went down to Vance and Linden streets and met this captain.

636. Was that Captain Allyn? No, sir; I do not remember his name at this moment. He was an army officer, with a force of from twenty to twenty-five men.

637. What was he doing there with his force? He heard the shooting and came out; he said he came from the fort. I told him who I was, and asked him if there was any disturbance to assist me in putting it down. He said he would. In my conversation with him as we were together at the corner of Linden and Vance street, the firing commenced down about

Linden and Causey. He put his men at double-quick, and as the shooting was rapid I got out of the way.

638. Where did this firing come from? From the neighborhood. There were a great many negroes living on that street.

639. Did I understand you that this firing was indiscriminate between the different parties? I do not know. I suppose one of the police was shot, and his friends were there shooting at the negroes. I cannot say of my own knowledge. I heard the shooting and got out of the way, for I had not even a pistol with me.

640. What became of this regular force? They staid there to quell the riot; I did not see them after the firing had ceased.

640. Did you see, during all the troubles, any negro making an attack upon white people? No, sir, I did not, for the fight in every instance was over before I got there, except this shooting on Causey street quelled by Captain Smythe, who was the officer whose name I could not recollect.

641. Was that all you saw on Tuesday night? That was all, except as I told you of these half-dozen white soldiers, some of whom had guns.

642. Did you take them to be soldiers still in the service, or discharged soldiers? I took them to be soldiers belonging to the regulars. I was alongside one of them in the crowd.

643. Did he appear to be a rioter? He appeared to be one of the crowd.

644. Did he have any kindly observations towards the colored people? His observation towards them was exhibited by his licking one of them.

645. What was the provocation? He was about half drunk; I do not think the negro gave any provocation whatever.

656. Did you attempt to arrest this white soldier for that? No, I had no right to arrest him.

647. What was the character of the remarks made by these soldiers in respect to the negro? I heard nothing except this soldier calling a negro a G—d d—n son of a bitch, and then made a lick at him.

648. How badly was the negro hurt? He was not hurt at all. The soldier attempted to pull his bayonet out afterwards.

649. How came the negro there? I do not know anything about it; I think he was coming from his work. There is another matter I forgot to state. On the first night of the riot, on the corner of Adams and Main streets I believe it was, it appeared there were a lot of boys calling themselves the "mackerel brigade" got after a negro; I happened to be going up the sidewalk and saw them. These boys are a set of little thieves; I crossed over, took the negro and gave him to a man by the name of Jim Coons, and sent him to the station-house for protection. He was taken there and turned out in the morning. He was not injured, although he would have been but for my interference.

650. What was the age of these boys? From eight to twelve or thirteen years of age.

651. Of what nativity? Pretty much all born in this country.

652. Of what parentage? Almost every description. They are a very bad set of boys, some with Jewish parents, some with Irish, and so on. I arrested six of them when I was chief of police for robbing a bank of five or six hundred dollars.

653. I understood you to speak in your first statement of four negroes who were cornered. Is that the same affair you now speak of? No, sir; that was on Wednesday. In that case I took a negro and put him in his cabin, and after I sent that first negro off, and Captain Allyn came there, I did not see another negro at all. There was no demonstration made by the crowd toward the negro, but I was afraid if he did come up there he would be killed. Some of the police were very much excited; I told them that the first one who interfered I would put in jail. I took the negro away about fifty rods, and by that time General Wallace came up with his *posse* armed with double-barrel shot-guns, which I took possession of. Then the taking of these four negroes from the boys was about the last of the matter that day, except that two men by the names of Gallager and Kelley, who attacked an old negro in my office and said that he drew a pistol. There were a few excited men gathering round there, and they went and swore out a warrant for the negro for drawing a pistol on this man Kelley, and they put the man in jail. He had an examination before Squire Hall; I do not know what became of him.

654. How many negroes did you see on Wednesday mixed up in these riotous proceedings? I never saw a negro except those I spoke of.

655. What was the riot about? The riot was all over by the time I got there.

656. What time did Captain Allyn get there with his forces? He and I got there together.

657. Did General Stoneman, at any time after the occasion you mention, attempt to interfere to prevent the riot? I think he did; I think he did all he could afterwards.

658. Do you know how much this military force under Captain Allyn did to suppress the riots? They did everything he and his men could. There was no fighting after they got there; there was a large crowd there, which he dispersed.

659. Was the crowd very much excited at this time? They had nothing to be excited at; there was not a negro in sight.

660. What was the crowd there for? I heard that some negroes were shot and killed; I do not know.

661. You speak of some negroes coming out of the fort? That is what I heard in the morning; as there was a very small force down there, I thought they had broken out in spite of the soldiers.

662. Did you meet many of the police at this time? The police were all in one batch when Captain Allyn and I got there.

663. Did the police afford you any assistance in suppressing the riot? There were probably ten or fifteen the first evening when I went down there, accompanied by their chief of police.

664. Did they assist you? They did everything they could.

665. What did they do? Nothing at that time; there was no disturbance.

666. You spoke of a fire which took place on Wednesday night, and about the fire-engines being on their way back? Yes, sir; I went up there about eleven o'clock, pretty much jaded out, having been all over the city of Memphis. I was at the station-house probably about twenty minutes when the fire bells rung. I came out and found there was a fire at the place I had left; I sent my *posse* back again up Main street and down as far as Jefferson. I went to the chief of the fire department to know where the fire was, but found no one there. When I got as far as Beal and Main streets I met one of these fire-engines coming back. I proceeded to the fire as quick as I could, but it had gone so far I could have no control over it.

667. Have you arrested or known of the arrest of any of the parties engaged in these riots except this negro man? No, sir. That is the only arrest I know of; and these men, Gallagher and Kelley, arrested him. I do not know anything about what he did except what they said.

668. Are you charged with the execution of the laws against breaches of the peace? Yes.

669. Have no warrants been placed in your hands by any person for the arrest of parties engaged in the riots? No, sir.

670. What is the idea, as far as you know, of the people in relation to these rioters? I not know.

671. Do they propose to punish any of the parties? If they are convicted, it is a hanging offence.

672. Have any measures, looking in that direction, been taken by any parties? Not in relation to these riots.

673. Did you see the recorder of the city during these riots, other than the occasion you have spoken of? Yes, sir; I believe I met him about eleven o'clock on the night of the fires at the station-house. He came there about the time we were there and went down to the fires.

674. Did you see him before this? No, sir, not that night; I saw him down there the first night.

675. What was he doing the first evening? He was pretty much helping me all the time, though the shooting was over when I got there, as I have told you.

676. How many negroes in all do you think you saw during these riots in any way connected with the riots? I did not see any, for everything was over when I got there.

677. You spoke of seeing a dead negro at the station-house. What was done with the body of that negro? The city buried him, I think.

678. You do not know who he was? No, I do not.

679. Do you know the number of persons killed in all this fray? I do not know; I never saw but one killed and one wounded.

By Mr. BROOMALL:

680. As far as you saw, who were the rioters? In my travels I saw no shooting except on Causey street, and then I got out of the way.

681. Who were the parties assembled together proposing to do mischief? They were all white that I saw; they were very much excited. They said two or three of the police had been shot and some of them wounded, and they raised a good deal of excitement towards the negro.

682. Did you hear the conversation of these parties who were together in this state of excitement? No, sir; I did not.

683. Did you hear what they talked about, and how they talked? It was excitement towards the negroes who had killed the police; I heard them speaking about that; I did not know but that at any moment I might be shot down by these men.

684. Do you know of shooting done by any negroes? I did not see any.

685. What part did the police take in the matter as far as you saw? I did not see any other policemen than those with me, and they were under the chief of the police.

686. Did you see any policemen with any lawless white man? No, sir. There were about fifteen police with me; I expect there were about twenty negro cabins in the neighborhood where I went. There was a great feeling against the negroes, and I went there for their protection.

687. When you were going towards this burning building, and met the firemen returning without going there, did they give you any reason for not going? I did not ask them; I thought the chief of the police department knew his business.

688. Did you see the recorder on any occasion present in the crowd and speaking to them?

I heard him make the remark that during this riot he would not fine any one for carrying concealed weapons.

689. Who did he tell that to ? I did not notice who it was to ; it was about the time we were sending this man to the station-house. His brother in a buggy told me that he saw the negro shoot this man Stephens.

690. Did you ever find out whether that was true ? I did not. When the fire first commenced, there was a white driver and a negro driver that run their vehicles together. They commenced whipping one another with their whips until some party run after the police. There were some negroes who came to the assistance of one of these boys. The police went there to arrest the parties, and it was in that way the shooting commenced.

691. Do you know of any parties who saw this transaction ? Not certainly ; I think Captain Smythe saw it.

692. Do you know of any instance, in your own knowledge, where a white man was hurt by a negro ? I did not see any.

693. Was any application made for the body of this man in the station-house by his wife or family that you know of ? I think I heard something of that at the station-house, but I do not know anything about it.

694. Do you know of any reason why it was not given up if application was made ? I do not.

F. S. DAVIS sworn and examined.

By the CHAIRMAN :

695. State your residence and business ? I reside in the city of Memphis, and am president of the First National Bank.

696. How long have you resided in Memphis ? A little over two years.

697. Were you here at the time of the recent riots ? I was.

698. Have you any knowledge of what took place during the riots ? Nothing except hearsay, with the exception of seeing the fires.

699. You were not then in the vicinity of the disturbance ? Yes ; I was quite near them, near enough to hear the reports of the pistols and guns.

700. What day was this ? The first day of the riot.

701. Where was it ? It was in front of my residence, on Bank street.

702. Please state the character of that crowd ? I saw no crowd, although I heard the report of fire-arms ; I was at the time taking my dinner. Probably an hour afterwards I was informed by a servant that a man had been shot in front of the house, and that the crowd were fighting there, but before I went to the front door the crowd had dispersed.

703. Who was the man shot ? It was a negro, I understood ; I did not see him. He was killed in the afternoon. After that my coachman, who is a negro boy about seventeen years of age, stated that he was going home through a back alley, about one o'clock, when he was met by two persons, one of them a policeman, and that a policeman drew a pistol and shot him in the head. The next morning he was very weak and his garments were all covered with blood.

704. Has he recovered ? He has nearly recovered.

705. Is he a boy whose testimony can be believed ? I should think so ; he is a very ignorant boy.

706. What is his name ? Taylor Hunt.

707. Do you know anything further in relation to the riot ? I cannot say that I do : I thought it advisable to keep in the house at that time.

708. Why did you think it was advisable ? I thought every man who was known to be a loyal man might not be entirely safe on the streets at that time.

709. Why did you have that feeling ? From the fact that our newspapers are continually giving us to believe that we are not wanted or needed here ; that we are intruders upon their rights.

710. Have any threats been made against you or against Union men ? Not that I am aware of ; but I know that when the passions of men are heated by a mob, people can be very easily put out of the way without knowing who the parties are.

711. Have any measures been taken, as far as you know, to bring the perpetrators of these outrages to justice ? No, sir ; none that I know of.

712. How do you account for it ? I can hardly account for it, unless it is that they do not care to have the facts exposed.

713. What has been the general sentiment of the city, so far as you have observed it, with respect to this riot ? Judging from expressions, they have denounced it. I have never heard a person speak of it except in that manner, but the papers which are the organs of the southern people only show one side of the question, making it appear that the negroes were the only ones to blame in the matter. For that reason I believe the people who are the patrons of these papers have something of the same feeling. Yet every expression I have heard uttered on the subject has been to denounce it.

714. But they have taken no measures to bring to punishment the parties engaged in it ? No, sir ; none at all.

715. What papers have the most patronage here, the loyal or disloyal? I think disloyal. The Avalanche has the largest circulation.

716. Which paper is the most violent? The Avalanche is most violent. The Argus has been nearly as much so since this occurrence. My impression is that since the course they have pursued in reference to this matter their patronage has been very much greater than prior to that time. They have denounced Union men and denounced negroes as being the cause of the riots.

717. Do you think these extreme papers represent the sentiment of the city? I should think of about two-thirds of the citizens.

718. How in reference to the other one-third? I think about one-third of the citizens here are loyal; the other two-thirds I consider disloyal, or, in other words, they would prefer two confederacies to the present state of affairs.

By Mr. BROOMALL:

719. Is this division you speak of carried into politics? Yes, sir.

720. What are the political names of the divisions you speak of? The extreme southern party, the two-thirds, call the other party radicals, and themselves conservatives. The so-called radicals call themselves Union men, and the others secessionists.

By Mr. SHANKLIN:

721. Where were you from before you lived here in Memphis? From Cincinnati, and previous to that from Vermont. I am a native of Vermont.

722. Have you been in your present occupation ever since you arrived? I have.

723. You came here for the purpose of going into the banking business? Yes, sir.

724. You speak of one-third the population here being loyal; are these men who are loyal voters? Yes, sir.

725. And these two-thirds of the population you speak of as being disloyal are not voting population, many of them, are they? They are not voting at present. They consider themselves disfranchised. Some of them, however, do vote.

726. Has the loyal portion of the population here taken any steps to have these men guilty of the outrages during the riot punished? No, sir: thinking that a military commission would reveal the truth in the matter. That is the reason I have never suggested it myself, and I believe that is the reason why others have not.

727. Then you considered it a prudent, discreet course to wait until the military were through with their investigations? I thought that was the most advisable course.

728. The only mode citizens have of punishing offenders in this country is through the courts, is it not? Yes, sir.

729. And it was therefore the common understanding, so far as you know, to wait until the military were through with their investigations before prosecutions were commenced by citizens? I presume that is the reason. I have never considered it necessary for citizens to take any action in regard to the matter, feeling that the military commissions appointed would deal out justice in the matter. Furthermore, it is, I have no doubt, true that any committee appointed by loyal citizens would be regarded by the disloyal element as showing impartiality, and the Union people would, of course, feel the same way if a disloyal committee were appointed.

730. You speak of the tone of the public press here as being calculated to arouse a feeling of excitement. Is there not at least one paper here which advocates the proscription of persons who have sympathized or engaged in the rebellion? Yes, sir; I think there is.

731. Have articles been pretty frequent in this paper, urging that policy? Yes, sir.

732. Do you think these articles have grated upon the feelings of men who labor under that disability, or do you think they were calculated to appease their feelings and quiet them? I presume the tendency would be to arouse them.

733. You then think the public press here, representing both extremes of sentiment, have had the effect of rousing and exciting the public mind? They both would probably have that effect; not so much, however, upon the part of Union papers as that of the others.

734. You think that articles proposing to disfranchise an element of population which is the largest here would be less calculated to excite them than the articles of the southern papers would the Union people? I hardly know which would be the most excitable. I think any one, almost, would have his feelings aroused by articles of that kind.

735. If peace, good order, and quiet are the objects to be attained, do you think the articles in the papers here, representing either extreme of sentiment, would be calculated to effect that object? No, sir; but I think the first articles of that nature were published by the so-called southern papers; and then, in vindication of the rights of the freedmen. the Union papers perhaps went further than they otherwise would have done.

736. You offer that as an excuse or an apology for the course of the Union paper here, as you call it? Yes, sir, as an explanation of its course.

737. And you think even with that excuse its course has been such as was calculated to arouse excitement in the public mind? Perhaps so, to some extent.

By the CHAIRMAN:

738. You speak of the papers on both sides. Please name the papers you refer to on both sides? There is but one paper on the Union side; that is the Post. There are two that are very extreme on the southern side, the Avalanche and Argus, morning papers, and one little evening paper. There are two others not so extreme, although regarded as strong southern papers—that is, strongly in favor of southern rights. There are five papers that may be termed southern-rights papers.

739. You have named the character of the articles appearing in these papers. Have you ever noticed an article in the Union paper calculated to excite attacks or violence upon southern men? No, sir; not that I know of.

740. What has been the character of the articles in that paper to which you allude? The character of the articles has been to show that the negroes were not to blame in the recent riots.

741. Were you not under that impression yourself? No, sir. I thought the negroes were some to blame on the first day. After that, I do not think they were.

742. From what circumstances do you get your information? From hearsay; that when the difficulty first commenced, it occurred in consequence of the conduct of the negroes who had been discharged from a regiment, and who were drunk and quarrelling. That is merely hearsay.

743. Who did you hear this from, negroes or white men? White men.

744. You did not hear the negro side of the story? No, sir.

745. Then the cause of offence upon the part of the Post was, that it suggested the negroes were not to blame for the riot? Yes, sir.

By Mr. SHANKLIN:

746. Was there any article in any of these so-called southern papers previous to the riot which advised any sort of violence? I think not, that advised it; yet there were articles having a tendency or effect to cause violent action.

747. What were the articles tending to have that effect? Could you give their purport or character? No, sir; I could not, specifically. They are continually speaking of the worthlessness of the negro. Articles of that kind I refer to, which would have the effect to lead the ignorant class to suppose public sentiment would sustain them in acts of violence against the negroes.

748. These are the kind of articles which you refer to as calculated to excite the public mind? Not only that, but they set forth all depredations committed by the negroes, while they make no reference to depredations committed by white men, and white men of the lower class would be led to suppose that public sentiment would be much more lenient with them for acts of violence committed against negroes than against white men.

749. What is the character of the other papers you refer to? The Appeal and Commercial may be considered as more conservative.

750. Do the Appeal and Commercial advise restoration of the Union and obedience to the laws and Constitution of the United States? Yes, sir; I think they are rather advising it, and are in favor of it; at the same time they speak of southern rights, or the rights of the southern people, and the infringement of their rights by northern people. Then there is still another paper here, called the Bulletin; I cannot tell much about; it is one way one day, and another way another.

751. Do not all the papers you speak of profess to acquiesce in the policy of the President? They do, I believe.

JOHN E. MOLLER sworn and examined.

By the CHAIRMAN:

752. Please state your residence and business? I reside in Memphis, and keep a retail family grocery.

753. How long have you been in Memphis? Nine years, pretty nearly.

754. Were you here during the recent riot? Yes, sir.

755. Do you know anything about it personally? If so, what? There was a colored man who lived in the basement of my house; he was a very quiet, still, sensible man, by the name of Jackson. On the afternoon of Tuesday, the 1st of May, he was coming home. I do not believe he knew anything about the riot. He started to come into my store, as I understand, to get some cornmeal. As he was just by the door three men (two of them were watchmen) came out of a grocery next door and followed him with revolvers. He slipped through the house, and they knocked him on the head. He got a little damaged, but not very much. He slipped through the house, went round and came out at the other door. They saw him; caught him; called him a d—d rascal; knocked him down, with his head in the gutter; fired two shots at him, and went off.

756. What was the name of this man? His name was Jackson. His widow was here this morning. I believe his name was Jackson Godell.

757. Was Jackson a quiet, good man? Yes.

758. Do you know the names of the parties who knocked him down and shot him? I think I could identify two of them. I do not remember their names.

759. The two policemen? One was a policeman, and the other a fireman, I think.

760. After they knocked this man down and shot him what did they do? They went off, saying they were going to shoot every d—d nigger. I heard some of them, too, say that the Jews and Germans ought to be killed, because they make the negroes free.

761. Did you understand that to apply to you? In general I did. I think it was intended for me somewhat. I stood just in the door, where they could see me very well, and they know me to be as black a republican as any man.

762. Did they say they were going to drive out every d—d abolitionist? Yes: they and the Germans; they said that.

763. Where did they go to after shooting the man? They went up Main street, and then I heard shooting on Beal street, a little further up.

764. Did you see any acts of violence other than the one you have stated? Yes; I saw them knock down a little negro boy just on the opposite side of the street.

765. This same crowd? No; some others. Then there was a policeman on horseback—a lieutenant or sergeant, or whatever he was; he said, "Kill them all together."

766. Did you hear him say that? Yes.

767. Do you know this policeman? No; I do not know his name; I might know him by sight.

768. What did the boy do? He did not do anything but cry. He hallooed to them to let him alone.

769. What was their precise language, as far as you can recollect it? That the God d—d niggers ought to be killed all together—no matter—the small and the big ones.

770. Where did this last crowd that beat the boy go to? They went down Beal street, in the same direction of the crowd that killed Jackson.

771. How long did the body of Jackson remain there? He lay until night. He looked as if quite dead, but I understood that he was not. They took him to the station-house, and the rumor is that they killed him there afterwards. I do not know whether it was true ro not. I did not see anything of it.

772. Were there any persons about the body while it remained there? It laid out there, half on the pavement and half in the ditch; some took notice of it, but could not do anything for fear of danger to themselves. I told his wife myself that she should keep quiet and should not do anything. I was afraid they would go in there and maltreat her and set the house on fire. The riot was nothing else than a well-appointed thing that they had been working on for a long time.

773. Why do you think that? You recollect, perhaps, that the Memphis papers said early in the winter that there was going to be a riot by the negroes about Christmas. At the same time I heard very much talking from just such men as I have seen engaged in this riot—the strongest rebels you can find, guerillas and such, talking in favor of the negroes—that the riot ought to break out, etc. One morning, about three weeks before Christmas, I was coming up Main street—there is an alley there with two saloons in it—there were some negroes there, and a man I have known for a half a dozen years, but do not know his name; he was a gambler, guerilla, and so on. I heard him saying, "You're the boys that saved the country." I was standing on the corner, just as if I was looking into a jewelry store. I heard him say to one of them who was a non-commissioned officer in a colored regiment, the others, one of them being in civilian's dress, and the other in the uniform of a private: "You're what saved the country, and you ought to have just as much privileges as white men; if they do not give it to you, you ought to take them; you can take Port Hudson, and you can take your rights, too." He was just trying to work them up, but the negroes were sensible enough not to think of such things. The negroes never had any intention to harm the white man—never. And these watchmen here are nothing more than a set of lawless thieves. The whole city government is Irish, and about the same character. The riot began in this way, as I heard from a man who was on South street and saw the commencement of this whole affair. A negro had been talking loud, and was drunk a little perhaps: a policeman goes among the negroes to arrest some of them; two or three negroes asked him what he wanted to arrest them for, they had done nothing; he then shoots right among them.

774. What reasons, other than those you have stated, have you for saying this was a well-planned scheme? The way the watchmen treat the negroes; they like to come in conflict with them all the time. Then there is a certain class of these rebels who are seeking to place obstacles in the way of the policy of this government. They will be polite to you; they will deprecate any violence, but they use these low-lived Irish rascals as their tools. These men who have come in from the country and offered their services to the general for the purpose of keeping order have done it for nothing else than to get a chance to arm themselves.

By Mr. SHANKLIN:

775. Do you know any of this last class you have mentioned who are so hypocritical? Yes.

776. Can you name them? McGiveney and Greenlaw are among them; they are rebels, real strong, and will never be anything else unless they are hung, and then they will be something else.

777. What are the men you speak of about here engaged in? Greenlaw is a rich man, building houses and living from his rent. McGiveney was a rebel colonel, and has come back for his place as book-keeper. He is one of those who belonged to the vigilance committee during the first of the war.

778. Are they all engaged in this sort of business? They are all rebels, and will be rebels; they try to make it possible for a riot to break out again; that is my opinion. That is the tendency I see in the articles in the Avalanche and Argus.

779. How many do you know of this sort? I know a good many; Memphis is full of them; I know them when I see them in Memphis.

780. You think this whole rebel population are doing this thing? Yes.

781. How long have you been here? Nine years.

782. Where did you come from? I lived in Richmond two years before I came here.

783. From what place did you go to Richmond? New York.

784. How long did you live in New York? I lived in New York two years; then at Morrisanna three years; then in Richmond.

785. Were you born in Germany? Yes.

786. How many years have you lived in the United States? Sixteen years.

787. How old were you when you came to the United States? Thirty-eight.

788. What is your business here? I keep a family grocery.

789. Do you keep liquor? No; I do not like that part.

790. Are you a voter here? Yes, sir.

791. Are all the voters here loyal men? No, sir; not a sixth part of them. I would not like to say a tenth are.

792. Are not a great many prevented from voting because they are not loyal? No; they are not prevented; they come up and vote because there is no authority to keep them away.

793. Does anybody vote who are not registered? I guess there has been enough voting by those who have not been registered; they will say they have left their papers at home, and the Irish at the polls will say they know the man, and let them vote without seeing the certificate.

794. Do you speak of what you know to be the fact? It is a fact; I have seen men who are not registered vote in that way. I have known more votes to be polled in this city than there were voters registered.

795. Have you had any personal difficulties or quarrels with these men lately? No, sir; not lately. I used to have some difficulty with them in war times.

796. What was the reason of your difficulties in war times? I was against the war.

797. Did you remain here while the rebels had possession? Yes, sir.

798. Did they interrupt you in any way? They tried two or three times to mob me.

799. Did they ever imprison you? No.

799½. You still carried on your business? No. I closed my business at that time, until the federals came here.

Rev. EWING O. TADE sworn and examined.

By the CHAIRMAN:

800. Please state your present residence and occupation? My residence is Memphis; I am a clergyman.

801. How long have you lived at Memphis? I came here last March a year ago.

802. Where from? Iowa.

803. What part of Iowa? Washington county.

804. Were you in Memphis during the recent riots? Yes, sir.

805. Please state fully what personal knowledge you have of the riots? The riot broke out Tuesday, the first day of May. I did not see the commencement of it. The first I saw of it, I was going from my residence down Court square; I came along on Second street, near where the Freedmen's Bureau is, when I met a crowd, just before, near the market. As I came along there were two hackmen who had collided, and some fuss followed; quite a crowd gathered about them. When I met this crowd on Second street I supposed they were going there. I spoke to some of them, and told them that the fuss was all over; but they ran right on. They were a mixed multitude, armed, some of them with unsheathed daggers in their hands, others with revolvers in plain sight, and others with them attached to their belts, holding them to keep them from flapping against their hips; one or two, perhaps, had shot-guns or something of that kind. This was on Tuesday evening, about six o'clock.

806. In reference to this collision, did you see it yourself? Yes, I saw them as they were being separated; this affair had nothing to do with the crowd, as I supposed it had at the time. I think the hackmen were two colored men; I merely referred to it as an explanation as to what I supposed this crowd was.

807. Can you state of your own knowledge that both of these hackmen were colored men? I cannot say; I was of the impression they were.

808. Were they off their hacks? Yes, and seemed to have been down arranging things; one of them may have been a white man.

809. Did you go down with the crowd? No; I passed right along; my wife was with me, and for a little while the crowd was so thick we stepped aside to let them pass. A colored man stood very near me—a few feet off. We were both standing on the outside of the walk. He was simply standing there, not knowing, I believe, what the crowd was about, when a man came along dressed in policeman's uniform, seized the colored man and commenced pounding him over the head—jammed him up against the wall on the other side of the sidewalk—drew out his revolver, and commenced to swear most furiously. I looked at him pretty straight, and he let him go and left in the crowd.

810. Was the negro hurt? No; I think not seriously; he pounded him with his fist; he swore he would blow his brains out and shoot him through.

811. Did you hear menaces and threats used against colored people? Yes, I did; terrible threats.

812. What were these threats, as near as you can recollect? One of them was, "You damned niggers ought to be shot." "You ought to be all driven out of the place. He talked very fast, and he looked very threatening—anything but what a policeman ought to say and do, I presume.

813. Did anybody intercede for the negro? No, sir; the crowd simply passed on. I only looked at the policeman, and did not speak to him. I kept my eye on him very straight, and he watched me to some extent at least. He let him go and ran right on. I then went on down Court square, and in half an hour afterwards I met a part of this crowd, apparently, at any rate a crowd coming back. We were walking along, and just ahead of us were three colored men walking along in single file on the outside of the walk. This crowd I do not think was as large as the one which went out; there were two men dressed in citizen's attire walking along side by side. Just as the last of the negroes passed along, these two men caught the hindmost one, and the three started on a run. The white man nearest the inside of the walk pulled out a dagger, I think fully a foot long, and started after them, hitting the hindmost one on the back. It seems he could not get close enough to stab the negro, so he struck him that way, the effects of the blow I did not learn. Then I went on about a block further, and came on a dying colored man who had been set upon, his wife, who was holding his head, told me, by four men, he having been out of the house but a few minutes to go to market. It was then getting dusk, but from the appearance of the man, as I saw him, he had been very severely wounded. He had been shot through the chest and through the head. I did not press my finger in to see if there was a hole, but it looked to me as if the brain was oozing out. He was in a dying condition. There was nobody there to take care of him but two colored women. I did not learn his name. I tried to get some colored men to carry him away, but they were afraid. These were all the acts of violence I saw that day. I then went on home. The next morning I went out and took my stand on a high lookout, so as to be able to see the movements of a large crowd near the fort. I could not see who they were, but I stood there to watch their movements. This was on Wednesday between 9 and 10 o'clock in the morning. I could see a few colored soldiers walking backwards and forwards on the parapet of the fort, apparently on guard duty. I heard a good deal of talking. This crowd seemed to sway backwards and forwards at the west end of South street. There was an occasional shot fired, apparently not from the crowd, but from persons straying round among the shanties. I could not see the persons discharging the pistols, but could see the smoke and hear the discharge. There were quite a number of persons standing about. One Irishman near me was very bitter in his denunciations of the colored people. He said they were idle vagrants; that if there was any disturbance anywhere you would find fifty or a hundred of them collected together. He was in favor of driving them all out. He used other threats in regard to them and in regard to those who sympathized with them, who taught them to be insolent, &c.

814. What did he propose to do with this latter class of people? He was in favor of killing them, or of not allowing one of them to stay in the place. This was said to a little crowd on the spot where I stood. I said nothing, and they said nothing to me. They did not know who I was.

815. Did you know the speaker? No; I think I would know him if I were so see him; he was rather well dressed, and I should think rather up for that class of people—probably the owner of drays or something of that sort. After standing there until 11 o'clock, perhaps, there came two squads that seemed to bring up this crowd on the west end of South street; they came down to opposite where I stood. The first squad were nearly all Irish; it contained one or two policemen, but was composed mostly of citizens. They were armed with shot-guns and other guns, and some were armed with revolvers, which they carried, some on their shoulders, and others had them swinging from their belts. I should think there were seventy in this crowd. They filed off into a vacant lot or street, and went through some army expressions, such as presenting arms, and other movements of the army drill. Presently the company nearly broke up, and ran across the street to a grocery to get something to drink. Then there came along in a few minutes another crowd, led, as they told me, by General Wallace. When he came up, I recognized him as the attorney general; he was acting as captain. That was more of a citizen crowd; there were several on horseback, some of them were drunk; they came up and filed off; presently some of them ran off south, behind a house; I am not sure whether it belongs to colored or white

people. Back of this house there were shanties near the bayou; presently I heard two or three shots in that direction, and there were shouts of "Kill him, shoot him." When they came back they said, "There are two damned niggers out of the way." I did not go to see them. In a few minutes I noticed two shanties on fire. I saw the smoke coming out, and very soon they were all in flames. Quite a number of this same squad went into this same grocery and called for something to drink; then most of them came down Hernando street, but several of them ran off in another direction, as though they were chasing some one, and very soon I heard shots fired in that direction. I staid there until that crowd left the neighborhood.

816. Did you see any negroes in this melee? There was not a colored man to be seen. There were some colored children, and one of them was one of my scholars, a boy about fourteen years old; his mother had heard that her husband had got killed, and sent the boy to look for him. He was the largest colored person I saw.

817. What did the mob seem to be driving at? They seemed, from their actions and words, everything taken together, to be hunting colored people, to drive them out; they were ready to shoot any colored man that came along. My impression is, that they drove the negroes out of their shanties when they could, and if they started to run they were shot down indiscriminately. That was the spirit of it, judging from actions and words.

By Mr. SHANKLIN:

818. Were these men with Mr. Wallace, the attorney general? They were his men who ran back of the house and set these two shanties on fire.

819. Was Mr. Wallace with them all the while? He was up there; he did not go around the house.

820. Where was he at the time; was he in sight? Yes, sir.

821. Do you think he saw the shooting and setting the shanties on fire? I do not think he could help seeing it. They stood for five or ten minutes drawn up in double file, as though for inspection, when. by and by, they commenced to scatter away, a part of them going to the grocery, but the larger part, I think, remaining with General Wallace.

By Mr. BROOMALL:

822. Is this Mr. Wallace the attorney general for the State? Yes, sir.

823. How long has he been in office? I do not know; he was appointed by Governor Brownlow. There has been another man appointed in his place now; he has been removed since this occurrence.

824. Do you know any instance when a white man or woman was shot or wounded in any way by a negro during the three days' riot? No, sir; I do not.

825. Did you see during the three days any crowd of negroes congregated together and having a threatening aspect? Nothing except what I saw from a distance from the fort. On Tuesday night the colored people in that part of the city went inside the fort for safety. Outside the fort I saw no crowd of colored people at all. I might, perhaps, have said that on Wednesday morning before I went out to this place, and. learning that a crowd very early that morning went out in the vicinity of the fort to see if the colored people had risen in force, a man connected with the Post newspaper—at least he had a bundle of Posts in his hand—told me that he went out very early; that when the crowd came near the fort a colored soldier came down with a flag of truce; that they respected it. He said to them, "Gentlemen, you are not wanted; we want no disturbance, and if you will go away all will be quiet." The colored man said this to the crowd, and then went back; they marched on, as though they would follow him up. A party on the earthworks of colored men, who had guns, fired. The balls struck a little ways short of the crowd, knocking up the dust. Then the crowd broke and run with all their might, their revolvers sticking out behind. They came down Main street, crying out, "The negroes have risen, and are going to take Memphis." This was on Wednesday morning, between seven and eight o'clock.

826. What do you think would have been the consequence if these negroes had not sought and obtained protection in the fort? I think they would have been murdered by scores right in that neighborhood.

827. What do you think the object of that crowd was, so far you can judge from their actions and words? They were full of fury and vengeance, in consequence of a policeman that had been killed and another wounded. Those who went out early in the morning went out breathing threatenings and slaughter, and they carried out their threats as far as they could find victims. This crowd that went out in the morning, when there was nobody to be found except men who were about their business, and who had been told to remain at their work and they would not be disturbed, and shot them down.

828. What is your judgment, from your knowledge of what you saw and heard, as to the origin and cause of the riot? My judgment of the matter is, that the cause of the riot, or one of the leading causes at least, was the feeling that exists between the Irish and the negroes. The Irish have an intense hatred for the negroes, because they are afraid they will take away their work. They have combinations here now to drive out colored draymen and hackmen. The Irish and others, I know, are in league now, having regular organizations for the purpose of suppressing colored labor. The circumstances of this immediate outbreak, as I was

informed by a colored man who was present, are these: there were some colored soldiers on the street who had been evidently drinking some, but were making no disturbance, simply enjoying themselves, and the police undertook to arrest them. This was on Tuesday.

829. Was this feeling of which you speak between the Irish and negroes fostered in any other way by any other class of citizens? I think it has been fostered by other citizens to the best of their ability; I mean by those who are known in the community as "southern men." I think it has been fostered by nine-tenths of the citizens here, although they profess to be opposed to it. In talking freely with them I find a great majority of those who have been slaveholders and southern men have a spirit of almost desperate hate towards the colored man, and towards any man who has anything to do with him for his good. I have talked very freely and plainly with southern men, two or three of whom I know here well. I had a talk with a southern man who owned slaves on the Tuesday before the riot; of course it had no reference to the events that followed. He was blaming northern people for their sentiments. The real subject that brought us to understand each other was a statement the Avalanche had made in reference to two or three of the northern merchants of the city. I said to him I did not approve of that; I thought it was all wrong; that every man had a right to his political opinions, and nobody else had the right to brand him for entertaining them. I said to him, "Mr. Dent, I am in your parlor; I have my opinion; you have yours. I do not think any the less of you for your opinions; I look at them and take them for what they are worth, and give you credit for them." "Now," said I, referring to the article in the Avalanche, "that is not the way to do things; it is not right; it is not fair. You would not say it was fair if the case were transferred to Chicago, and the persons proscribed were southern men; but it would be no worse. Suppose these men do think it would be right to disfranchise those who have been connected with the rebel army. I think so, not because I am from the north; and I will give you an instance to show you that the opinion is a correct one. Missouri has tried it, and there is no southern State flourishing as Missouri is financially. Land is coming up, and society is improving. There is no southern State so safe to live in, with the exception of, perhaps, Eastern Tennessee. What is the reason? Because the party called radical are in power, and they are disfranchising the rebels. Another reason is that, as was said by Andy Johnson, treason must be made disreputable, or this thing will have to be gone over again. You know just as well as I do that in Memphis there is a very different feeling among the southern people to-day from the feeling immediately after Lee's surrender. Rebel soldiers returning then talked to me like this: 'I have only half a head on my shoulders, and that is due to the mercy of the government.' I was then acting for the Christian Commission, and carried books and papers to the rebel soldiers as they came pouring in here. That is the way they talked; that they deserved to be hung. They were ready to accept anything. If I had my way about it, I would have hung half a dozen rebels in every State, sent a dozen or more to the penitentiary, banish thirty or forty more from the State, and disfranchise them all, and then the south would be reconstructed upon a proper basis."

830. Was this Mr. Dent, to whom you said this, a southern rebel? He is a southerner, strong and bitter in his feelings.

831. Did this man approve these attacks of the Avalanche on these Memphis merchants? Yes; he said if they had these opinions, they ought to keep them themselves.

832. What effect has the press here in Memphis had in exciting these riotous proceedings? I think it has been immense. I think these Irish have been used as mere cat's-paws, and that these papers, published here every day, have incited them to the deeds they have commited.

833. What particular papers in Memphis do you refer to? The Avalanche is the worst; the Argus is an echo of the Avalanche. The Evening Ledger is another echo. The Appeal is more manly. The Bulletin is switching round, and to-day contains the most sensible article I have seen in any southern paper. To resume my narrative: I left that stand-point shortly after the crowd dispersed, and returned home, thinking it might be prudent for me to remain about home and get things as much in readiness as possible. I removed most of my effects and scattered them round with different persons, so that if my house should be burned I might not lose everything.

834. What made you fear being burned out? Threats that were made.

834½. Made by whom and when? I was told by Rev. Mr. Bailey that he had been informed by a German in the northern part of the city who was a friend of mine, (he keeps a grocery,) who pretended to be a friend of these southerners, and so got into their secret conclave. And he said that on Thursday night, after the burning of Wednesday night, the next move was to be made on the teachers and negro preachers. He advised me by all means to go away.

835. Is this Mr. Bailey living in the city? No, sir. He went away.

835½. What did he leave for? He left in fear of his life. He had a wife and two daughters who were engaged in teaching.

836. Do you know where he is now living? I think it is in Saco, Maine. I am not sure. On this Wednesday night, about ten o'clock, we had just retired, but had not gone to sleep when a tremendous light broke in on our back window. The barracks on the Hernando road were on fire. It led me to feel a little uneasy, and I did not go to sleep that night. I saw the men, seven or eight in number, who were engaged in the work. When the fire was under full headway, so that there was no chance of saving the barracks, these men got on their horses and rode away in a westerly direction. Very soon afterwards a light began

to show itself in the direction of Pontotoc and Hernando streets. Then, in twenty minutes after, the same horses, and I suppose the same men, appeared at a point—I do not remember the name of the street—where five houses built by colored people were standing, and they were set on fire. I saw the colored people running and leaving the houses and carrying what little things they could save out of the way. A few minutes after I heard a great pounding. I did not know what it meant. Presently I began to see the light coming through the roof of three other houses belonging to white people, but in which colored people lived. They burned down pretty quick. About twelve or fifteen feet from the last one there stood another house, and before the fire got very hot they ran on to the roof, covered it with quilts and blankets, and kept throwing water on it until it became so hot that I could distinctly see the steam rise as it was thrown on. There was no effort whatever made to stop the fire in the other houses, but the colored people carried away what they could. When the party came back the second time there was with them a man with the full uniform of a private soldier. I do not know whether he was a soldier or not. Soon afterwards I saw lights in the northern part of the city, about one o'clock. I think a young man came and called at my door and asked me if I had been over to see "Lincoln chapel." I had been previously looking from my back window, but this called me to the front door, when I found the barracks on Bank street were all on fire.

837. United States barracks? Yes; with a large lot of government stores in them. I told the young man that I had not been to the chapel, and would not go; that if they had not already set it on fire they would not do it that night.

838. What is Lincoln chapel? It is a chapel built mostly by my own hands as a place for preaching to the colored people.

839. Was it burned down? Yes. I went over about three o'clock and saw the chapel, with the school-rooms in the rear, in ashes.

840. What amount did you lose by this burning? I do not remember what I put in. I handed in a bill to General Stoneman's commission. I think I claimed damages for the whole thing in the neighborhood of $3,000, covering the building, books, stationery, apparatus, and everything.

841. After whom was this chapel named? After Abraham Lincoln. It was dedicated on the first day of January, 1866, in that name. A vast crowd gathered on the occasion; more than sufficient to fill three such churches. On Thursday morning we had a very considerable crowd there of those who felt an especial interest over the ashes.

842. What led to this destruction? It was all done by this mob. We had a very orderly school there. There has never been the least disturbance or objection raised. The only crowds which we have ever had about have been composed by southern people themselves stopping in front of our door to hear the children sing. Our children have gone quietly and peaceably home. There has never been even an obscene word written on the front of the house, although it stood perfectly exposed. I think so far as any objection being made to the management of the schools, I could now rent a lot of a secesh neighbor to rebuild it on.

843. Have you ever had any difficulty with those whom you call secesh? Not a word since the school has been started. There was a gentleman who has preached twenty years in Memphis called about the time I was finishing it, and undertook to tell me how to preach to negroes. I remember saying to him that he understood the subject a great deal better than I did; that I did not know his negroes; that when they came together on the Sabbath I could only preach to them as dying men; that I could not know even that they were negroes. That is about the sharpest word I ever said to any man. He wanted to know why I called the place Lincoln chapel. I said to him that they had here their Asbury chapels, their Wesley chapels, and I did not know but what Lincoln was as good a saint as any of them.

844. Have you written any statement of this affair? I have; and directed it to the secretary of the American Missionary Association, by which I am employed. I will furnish the committee a copy of it if they desire.

SATURDAY, *May* 26, 1866.

Rev. EWING O. TADE appeared, and his examination was continued as follows:

By Mr. SHANKLIN:

845. What has been your occupation since your arrival in Memphis up to the present time? The first part of the time, up to September last, I was the agent of the Christian Commission in this place. I visited the soldiers in hospitals, camps, forts, gunboats, and prisons, with books and papers, and sometimes with sanitary stores in the shape of clothes and things to eat, especially for the sick in hospital and prison. That was the general character of my work.

846. Was the distribution of papers and books and reading matter exclusively of a religious character, or was it religious and political? It was not wholly religious; we had many secular papers, but the great bulk was religious.

847. Of what description were the secular papers generally? Those known as radical papers? I do not know that they were wholly of that kind. There were papers among them of that kind. We had the Missouri Republican, the Missouri Democrat, a few copies sent, I suppose, by those who had friends here. We also had the Chicago Tribune. I do

not remember whether we had other papers or not; I could not be certain now that we had more than these three of a political cast.

848. Had you no papers from New York, Philadelphia, or Boston of a political cast? No, sir; I think not. We had papers from all those cities, but they were of a religious character.

849. Had they no politics in them? It is hard work to tell what you call politics.

850. Have not most of the papers professing to be religious journals mixed up very much religion and politics for the past four years? I suppose I am to answer that as I understand it. I think the best class of papers, and in fact all religious papers, have had more or less politics in them, but only as they touch upon the great moral questions.

851. In which we are all interested? That is as I regard it. Of course there are exceptions. I speak of the general rule in respect to the best religious periodicals in Philadelphia, New York, and Boston.

852. And these were the papers you distributed mostly? We had the leading papers of the principal cities, and many small publications from different localities were sent here by those who had friends in this locality.

853. What was your mode of employment after you ceased that occupation? Have you been engaged in any other employment since you have been in Memphis? Not, except as missionary for the American Missionary Association. My labors began as missionary of that association in September, 1865.

854. What have been your duties in that operation? They have been to visit and labor among the colored people, especially in the way of distributing clothing and the necessaries of life as they were needed. I usually go armed with a large copy of the psalms under my arm and read and pray with them.

855. Do you distribute these copies? I have distributed a great many copies, but not that. That is a peculiar copy; a very large one; there is none like it in the city. I carry it for my own use.

856. Had you a regular place of worship for these people? Yes, sir; after I built it. We met for a while in the barracks, but one interruption after another forced the conviction upon me that I could not do much as a missionary without a regular place of meeting.

857. And that was the Lincoln chapel? Yes, sir; the Lincoln chapel. I built it myself.

858. You spoke of some schools being connected with the chapel. Yes; I had a day school and a Sabbath school.

859. You were a teacher in these schools? I was superintendent of the Sabbath school, and had general charge of the day school. I did not teach there.

860. How many assistants did you employ in the day school? Three most of the time.

861. Were they male or female? They were mostly female. A part of the time I had a male teacher.

862. What were the places of nativity of these teachers as far as you know? One was born in Ireland, one in Pennsylvania, and the other in Ohio. I was born myself in Illinois. I am a "Sucker."

863. In your intercourse with the colored population did you talk to them about their civil and political rights, and instruct them what their rights were? Very little. I had very little occasion for that.

864. Did you do anything in that way in your intercourse with them? Did you advise them what they ought to claim, assert, or were entitled to? No, sir; I do not remember anything of that kind in my private intercourse. I have spoken sometimes in their literary societies to young men, and made allusions to what might be, or ought to be, their privileges, and what they would be eventually if they took the stand they ought to, worked and improved themselves as they had the opportunity to.

865. Did you advise them what stand they ought to take, or what would be proper for them to take? My main advice and my main subject of conversation and instructions has been as to their present duties, not in reference to their civil or political standing, but especially to deport themselves quietly, peaceably, and industriously, and save what they have to educate their children, and abide the results that will be worked out. That has been the general theme on all occasions.

866. When you alluded to these other subjects, as I understand you did occasionally, what did you advise? I presume I have told them—I do not recollect positively about it—that, in sight of justice and God, they had a right to vote, unless it was a right only that belonged to a certain class; that if man, as man, had a right to vote, they had that right; and that if they educated and fitted themselves for it, I had no doubt they would enjoy that right ultimately. I said that I was in favor of a limited suffrage; that I was in favor of a suffrage that should be equal to all, without distinction of color.

By the CHAIRMAN:

867. You would be in favor of such a proposition as President Johnson announced in his letter to Governor Sharkey, that all those who had borne arms, had property to the amount of $250, and could read and write, should have the right of suffrage? Yes, sir; I should be heartily in favor of that.

868. Then you and President Johnson would agree upon that? Yes. That is the only way I have spoken upon that.

By Mr. SHANKLIN:

569. Has that been the doctrine you have taught when you have touched upon that subject? Yes, sir; I have always put it in that shape. My object has been to bring to bear upon them every consideration I could to encourage them in improving themselves.

560. During your residence in Memphis have you also had frequent intercourse with white persons? Yes, with some; not with as many as I would like to have had.

561. You spoke yesterday of expressing your individual opinion as to what the policy of the government should be; in favor of punishing a certain number in each State by death, some by imprisonment, some by exile, and of depriving all who had been engaged in the rebellion of their franchise and political rights. Have you frequently spoken these sentiments and opinions? No, sir; I never carried them out in conversation except with but one real southern man.

862. Then you have stated it to no class other than the black population? I have not stated it to the black population. When I am with those I know to be of my own mind I talk freely upon all subjects.

863. Then you have inculcated that doctrine among those who you regarded being of your mind? Yes, we have talked the matter over.

864. Have you been in the habit of writing articles on the subject for publication, either in Memphis or other places? No, sir; I never have. My will has been good enough, but I never had the time.

865. You have not, then, been one of the letter-writers upon this subject? No, sir.

866. Do you think, from your intercourse with the people here, and the knowledge you have of the sentiment of the mass of the people on the subject of the rights of the colored population, that an expression of the sentiments you gave yesterday as having expressed in a conversation with a gentleman would be calculated to promote peace and quiet in the temper of the people, or to harass and annoy them? You may judge, perhaps, what my views would be from the fact that it has been my policy, in conversation with southern men, not to volunteer my opinions. In this instance this man gave me his views, and wanted to know mine. I very frankly and kindly told him what were my political sentiments; that I held them in all good conscience, and only asked the same respect to myself, personally, for them as I would be willing to accord to him for his. My impression is that, as things are, it would not be advisable to preach them on the corners of the streets.

867. You think it would have a bad effect? It would with a certain class without doubt. I think there is a better way. There is a certain class who would be very much irritated by them, especially those who are secessionists, and did not go into the southern army, but remained on our side of the lines or staid at home.

868. Is not the right of suffrage in the State of Tennessee and in the municipal elections of the city of Memphis confined alone to those who are required to swear they never have given aid or assistance to the rebellion in any way? That is as I understand the recent enactment.

869. Has not that been the rule in the elections that have hitherto taken place since you have been here, or have you not inquired into the subject? I could not say what the distinction has been. There is a recent enactment I know that is considered more stringent. I remember something of the oath I had to take under the old law to get a certificate as a voter.

870. What was the substance of that oath? As I remember, it was that I had not given any aid or comfort to the enemies of the country, or any voluntary assistance to the recent rebellion.

871. Then if that law is executed, it would exclude all those who had given aid or assistance any way in the rebellion from the right of suffrage? Yes; unless with the exception of those who had been pardoned. I am not sufficiently advised to speak certain about that.

872. Do not you know it to be a fact that two-thirds of the people of this city are disfranchised under the law as it has heretofore existed? I think not, and for some reason I do not exactly understand. My impression is, from the number of votes given, I do not remember how many, that they were a very fair proportion for a place of this size. That I remember was my impression of the result of the last election. It was a puzzle to me how there came to be so many voters under the oath I had taken.

873. Have you any idea what the white population of Memphis is? I should think in the neighborhood of 40,000.

874. Have you any knowledge of the number of votes that were cast out of that population at the last election? The number does not now occur to me. I only remember the impression made upon my mind in reading the account of the election. I wondered how so many voters could be found under the oath I had taken, and which I supposed everybody else had taken who voted.

875. I ask you whether there is not a newspaper published in Memphis that has been daily advocating pretty much the doctrines you have expressed as having entertained yourself in relation to the course of policy that ought to be pursued towards the rebels? I suppose there is one whose views and teachings I sympathize with to some extent.

876. Is that the Post? Yes, sir.

877. A daily paper? Yes, daily and weekly. There is also another paper more radical than that—the Republican. That is a weekly paper, and published by southern men, however.

878. Is that paper now published? Yes, I think it is. Mr. Brooks, the editor, handed me a copy some few weeks ago.

879. Are either or both these papers largely patronized in this community? My impression is that the Republican is not very widely circulated. I do not speak positively, of course, as I have not seen the list. The Post, I think, has a very fair circulation in the city.

880. Did you give testimony before the military commission ordered by General Stoneman for the investigation of the recent riot in Memphis? I was before that commission as a witness.

881. Did you read your testimony after it was written out? It was read to me, and some corrections made where there was a misunderstanding by the reporter.

By Mr. BROOMALL:

882. You have spoken of the advice you gave to the negroes of Memphis. Do you know whether they have followed that advice in the main, and behaved quietly and well? Yes, as far as I know they have done very well.

By the CHAIRMAN:

863. You have spoken about a newspaper. Is there anything in the Constitution or laws of the United States, or in the Constitution and laws of Tennessee, which prevents a newspaper from being published here and expressing its opinions? Not that I am aware of.

864. Do you know who are connected with this paper called the Post? I am acquainted with two or three of the principal men.

865. Do you know if any of them have been in the army, and if so, on which side? Yes, they have on the loyal side.

866. Do you know what parties are connected with the other papers, and in which army they have been? I know some of them have been in the rebel army. I do not know that they all have been.

877. Have you seen in the Post any incitation to mob violence? Not a word.

878. Has it in any way justified the killing of these negroes by the mob? No, sir.

879. Has it incited violence against the rebels who have fought against the country? Not as such.

880. In what respect has this paper been blamable in the manner in which it has been conducted? That is for every one who has read it to decide for himself. In my opinion, it is just a little bit too tender—too afraid to meet right square in open daylight the issues that must be met before they are settled.

881. When it is spoken of as a paper tending to incite bad feeling among the people here, do you mean to be understood that any paper published by loyal men, advocating loyal doctrines, tends to excite ill feeling? My opinion is that the purer, more honest, and true any paper started here would be, the greater disturber it would be regarded by the other city papers.

878. What was the conduct of the colored people after the riot, and particularly your congregation and your school? Those who worked as draymen, day laborers, &c., thought it would be the safest to stick right to their places, as if nothing had happened; but I think, perhaps, a majority of the working class were afraid to be seen, and hid themselves. The children and women were greatly alarmed, and some of them hid themselves, while others left the place by cars and boats. General Stoneman furnished transportation to all the families of the colored regiment then mustered out up or down the river, if they desired it.

879. Did you hear threats of vengeance or retaliation among the colored people with whom you associated? I never heard anything of that kind.

880. What became of your little flock that worshipped in Lincoln chapel? Some of them have gone away and have not come back.

881. Have you had any place of worship since that? I went out on Thursday morning after the burning to the ruins of the chapel. Quite a number of the parents came out, and a large number of the children. They seemed to be very much troubled on account of it, expressed strong feelings of attachment, and so on.

882. What was the spirit in which they received this thing? The spirit was great sorrow and depression.

883. Was it a feeling mingled with one of vengeance and retaliation, or was it a Christian feeling? There was not a word, or look, or expression of envy or hatred. I told them not to be discouraged—*that there were ashes enough there to build another Lincoln chapel.* I told them we would meet the next Sabbath morning on the opposite side of the street in the shade of some cottonwood trees.

884. Did your church meet there? No, sir: during the week I secured other rooms, and on Sabbath morning I went round over the hills where some of them lived, called some of them by name and told them to meet me at a certain place. They followed me to this place, perhaps 100 strong, and we had services there as usual. And we have had services there since that time.

By Mr. SHANKLIN:

885. You have spoken of loyalty. Is there not a difference in the opinion of men as to what constitutes loyalty, or do all men agree as far as you know in their definition of it? I do not think they do.

886. According to your views of loyalty do you consider a man devotedly attached to the principles of the Constitution of the United States, as expounded by the courts, giving to that Constitution as expounded a hearty support, but opposed to all effort to change those principles on one side or the other—would you consider such a man a loyal or disloyal one? He might be loyal and he might not, it seems to me, in that case. I do not know that there is anything in the Constitution necessarily unchangeable or that would brand a man for wishing to change it.

887. But for a person who adhered to the principles of the Constitution, as expounded by the courts, and is opposed to a change by any possible means—would you consider such a man loyal or disloyal? I should not think he was necessarily either.

888. Suppose you briefly give your opinion of what loyalty consists in? My idea of loyalty is to defend the government and the whole country against all attempts of treason.

889. I would like to know what you mean by "attempts of treason?" One attempt is to make war against the government just as this rebellion has. For anybody who would seek to apologize for this rebellion, or to aid or comfort the enemy, directly or indirectly, I should feel very doubtful about his loyalty.

890. Would you, according to your opinions of loyalty and political duty, consider it disloyal or wrong, if a proposition is made to effect a change in the Constitution, for a man to oppose that change in public speeches or fair debate? No, sir; not necessarily. I am in favor of such things; I am in favor of free discussion, and just as much on one side as the other.

891. If a man opposed in a legal and constitutional way a change of the Constitution of the United States, would you consider that a disloyal act? No, sir; not necessarily. I can conceive of a man being loyal to his government and yet have what I conceived to be very wrong opinions on that subject.

892. Then he might have wrong opinions without being disloyal? Yes; that is, opinions which I believe to be wrong.

By the CHAIRMAN:

893. Suppose one man is fighting in the Union army and another one in the rebel army—which is loyal and which disloyal according to your judgment? If the man was in the Union army I should regard the indications as being in favor of his loyalty, and if in the rebel army the indications as of his being disloyal. There may be exceptions. I found a man when I was at work for the Christian Commission who had on the confederate gray, and I took him to be a rebel soldier, but as soon as he found I was a loyal man, he told me he was imprisoned in Mobile and had made his way through woods and swamps, befriended by loyal white people and black people. He was heartily ashamed of the gray. I have no doubt there were a great many Union men in the rebel army, and there may have been rebels in the Union army.

894. Do you know of any colored women being shot during the riot? Only from what was told me by a gentleman with whom I was conversing.

895. What was that gentleman's name? His name is Rankin. He is a colored man.

896. You do not know anything further except from this hearsay? I know that she was killed; I know nothing about her murder.

897. Do you know of any one in this city who is cognizant of the facts? I do not.

898. Did you hear any conversation with a man who had been in the rebel army, who is connected with one of the papers here, with regard to the burning? Yes, sir; I heard a man who is one of the editors in chief here.

899. Who was he? I cannot tell his name. He was a general in the rebel army. I was passing along Main street coming up this way, and as I passed by a door at the corner of Madison and Main, I think, there was a tall gentleman with black hair and black whiskers standing talking with two ladies. He asked the question, as far as I remember, "How did you enjoy the illumination last night?" They made some reply I could not catch. Then he said "Certainly, it was a brilliant affair," and they all burst out laughing among themselves. I passed on a few doors and stopped, and this same man came by. A gentleman who was one of the proprietors where I was standing said, "there is one of the ringleaders, General so-and-so." Then I told him what I had heard.

900. What paper is he the editor of? I am not sure whether it is the Argus or Avalanche. I think it is one of them.

PRIMUS LANE (colored) sworn and examined.

By the CHAIRMAN:

901. State your age and residence? I am between fifty-nine and sixty years old. I live in Memphis.

902. What is your business? I have been tending to a brewery.

903. Have you been a slave? Yes, sir.

904. When were you made free? I was made free by Massa Lincoln.

905. Were you in Memphis at the time of the recent riots? Yes, sir; I was here.

906. State what you know about it? I did not know anything about it until Wednesday morning. The colored people came there and asked me if I knew about the fuss; I told them

I did not. They said that down in South Memphis they were killing colored people and shooting them severely. I said I didn't know anything about it. On Wednesday night they came to my house just about midnight; there were six together; I do not know who they were; I think they were, probably, Irish.

907. Did you see any man among them who had a policeman's star on? If they did, I did not see it.

908. What was your first knowledge of their coming? They came in there to the old colored man's house and said "Get up; get up; Mason, get up." Mason says, "There is no man in here except myself and wife." They said, "Mason, you are all right." Then they came in at the door. I told them I would get up as quick as I could. They said, "Make a light—make a light damn quick." I said I would as quick as I could. I didn't know whether I had a candle in the house; I lighted a match, and they looked round and found a piece of a candle. Then they looked round under the bed and everywhere; I did not know what they were looking for. I started as if I would go out, and three of them, with guns, said, "If you go out we will put daylight through you." By this time they had set the house afire and it had begun to burn up pretty severely. The fire frightened me and I went back to get out my trunk; I ran back and got two bed quilts and carried them away. Everything else I had was burned up.

909. What became of these men? I do not know; they did not ask for anything at all. They heard some money jingling in my wife's hand, and they just grabbed it. Another said, "Don't touch the money; we didn't come here for money"; but they took it and went away. My wife was afraid they would come and take the money any how, and she had it in her hand. It was silver money, and they heard it; my wife said, "Gentlemen, do not take what little money I have." The man said, "God damn you, hush," and struck her on the head. One of them said, "Gentlemen, give her the money back." They gave me a part of it back; what became of the rest I do not know; I never found but $4; there was $7 in all. They came back right down street; they said they had a hack, but I did not see any hack.

910. Why did they not disturb the other colored man in your house? I do not know; they told him, "You are all right, Mason."

911. What did their object appear to be—to rob you and burn your house? I allowed they wanted to burn me up in the house; I took it for granted that was what they wanted.

912. Why did you suppose that? Because they said they did not want the money, and they set the house afire, and it was all burning on the sides and top before they would let me go out.

913. How far had the fire progressed before they left? All across the little shanty and on top. They set the room on fire inside and on the outside.

914. What did they tell you not to go out for? I could not tell you; they kept me in and would not let me go out.

915. What language did they use? They said damn me, I could not go out, and they didn't let me go until the fire got so strong they could not stay there, and then I ran out, and told my wife to come out.

916. Did you get burned any? I got burnt some in going back and trying to get my clothes and things out.

917. Did they hurt your wife? They struck her; they didn't hurt her very much.

918. Was she in bed? Yes; both of us were in bed. When we came out I was in my shirt-tail, and she was in her chemise. I ran in and got my old pantaloons and a dress for my wife. That was all we had left at the time.

919. Do you know anything else that happened of your own knowledge? I do not; I have not been round any; I have been steady working ever since.

920. Cannot you describe these men; have you no idea who they were? I have not.

921. Have you had any trouble with any of these men? No, sir; not since that night.

922. Did you give them no cause for burning your house? No, sir; I never gave any cause to any one since I have been here.

923. What do you suppose they came to disturb you for? I will tell you as near as I can. I had a son in the army and my son came there; there was a grocery right opposite. They came to that store, and they must have let them know about my boy, and they came over after him, I think.

924. Where is your son now? He was away; he went out into the country to work. They disturbed a great many who were discharged from the army, and I told him he had better go away.

925. Who is this man who told them about your son? The people over there to the store; I think it must be them.

926. White people? Yes, sir.

927. Irish? Yes, sir.

928. Do you think they knew anything about this? I cannot say positively; I heard several people say that they went there the night before and got some whiskey.

929. Did they disturb any other colored people in your neighborhood? I heard that they disturbed a good many; I do not know of my own knowledge.

930. How much property did you lose by this burning? I lost all I had, and I had a good deal for me to lose. I had a couple of hogs that weighed 200, that they burned up; they

7

burned about twenty chickens and the little stuff that was in the cabin. I had right smart of garden stuff there too, and all that was destroyed.

931. Have you ever been dependent on any one? Did you get any help from the Freedmen's Bureau? No, sir; not during the rebellion or since; I always depended on myself.

932. You have had no difficulty with anybody? Never since I have been a man.

MARGARET GARDNER sworn and examined.

By the CHAIRMAN:

933. Do you live in Memphis? Yes, sir.

934. How long have you lived here? Ever since the rebellion.

935. Were you a slave? Yes, sir.

936. Do you know anything about the riot that took place the first of the month? Yes, sir; I saw a man who had a soldier on a dray, and saw some policemen carrying him along.

937. What day was this? I think it was on Monday evening, but I am not certain; I know it was done, because I saw it when they were going with the man on the dray. He was not dead, but he was struggling. Every time he struggled they would rise up and strike him with the clubs they had. There was another policeman by the name of Carroll who walked by the side of the dray, and would keep throwing the man's arms up.

938. What were they taking this man away for? I do not know what they were taking him for. They said they got into a fuss about drinking, and after the soldier gave up, they all got on to him and beat him, and then they put him on a dray and beat him all the way to the station-house. That was the first of the fuss.

939. Was seeing this negro man being carried away all you saw of it? Yes; and I do not know what they were carrying him away for only that he had been drinking, and after he gave up they undertook to kill him. They knocked him down on South street, and carried him by where I lived. I did not see it, but a woman said she was walking by the man and the man was not doing anything at all when the policemen came up.

940. Who was the woman? I do not know her name.

941. At what time in the day was this? In the evening; I could not tell the hour.

942. Did you see any one else hurt? No, sir; nobody but that man.

943. Were you disturbed yourself? No, sir; only I was in trouble seeing the fight. While the fuss was going on all the people, white and black, were out seeing what was going on.

944. Did you know any other black people who were set upon by white men? No, sir; I did not see any others.

945. How many policemen were there with this man? There were four of them; one was on the dray.

946. You do not know who the policemen were? I did not know but one.

947. Did you see them strike the negro man? One of them struck him, and one threw up his arms. They were going very fast, the horse was running; the black people were after them. Some of the soldiers said they were going to have a fuss because they treated the man so, and they run the horse.

948. How far up did the black people follow the dray? A right smart chance; they went out of sight from where I was.

949. What did the black people do? They were all running, and said they were going to give the policemen a trial if they caught up.

950. Did they catch up? No; but I believe the policemen killed the man before they got to the station-house. I asked some of them I saw coming back if they caught up with the dray; they said no, they could not catch up.

951. You do not know who this man on the dray was? No, sir.

952. Do you know any of the crowd of colored people who followed them up? No, sir; I did not know a single one of them.

953. How many of them were there? I do not know; the streets were full of men and women running. The women were running to see what they were going to do.

954. What did this woman who was with the colored man when he was arrested say? She said he was merely talking to her.

955. Do you know who this colored woman was? I do not know her name, and do not know that I could find her, they have scattered so much since the fuss.

956. You saw nothing else? No, sir; they said there was one woman burnt up.

957. Who was she? I do not know; I know her sister.

958. Do you know anything about the murder of Uncle Dick? No, sir; only that he was killed. A colored man was telling me about it.

JANE SNEED (colored) sworn and examined.

By the CHAIRMAN:

959. Where do you live? In Memphis, not very far from the fort.

960. How long have you lived in Memphis? Going on four years.

961. How old are you? About thirty-eight years old.

962. Are you married? Yes, sir.

963. Have you been a slave? Yes, sir.

964. Do you know anything of the riot that took place the first of the month? Yes, sir; I know this much about it: when it first commenced, it began among the soldiers and policemen on Monday evening. A colored soldier came up from a little ways where I live, and got into a fuss. When I saw him there were six policemen there; one was a great big, heavy, whiskered man, I knew by sight, I did not know his name; the others I did not know, They took him across the street and knocked him down with a club; then one of them called for a dray and they put him on it. My daughter, the one that was shot, went up and saw it. On Tuesday afternoon they commenced again on Main street; after a while they went on down to South street. There were a great many colored soldiers; there were not any of them I knew. The policemen kept firing and shooting at them, and one policeman was shot and taken into a saloon. They then went up town, and the policemen and white citizens just shot everybody they found. They came down back to my house, took a man out and carried him down to the bridge and shot him. On Wednesday they came into my house and searched for arms; we told them we had not any: they searched all around, and not finding any went away. They did not come back again for some time, and before they came to my house they went to Adam Lock's house, right along side of mine. Then with Rachael, my daughter, I went out to help get the things out of his house. Some people hallooed out, "You had better go in or you will get shot." We went back and watched these white men; a great many of them were there; some of them had guns, and some had not. In a few minutes Rachael said to me again, "Let us go and help get the things out of Adam Lock's house." I told her I thought we had better try and save ourselves. By that time the house had been set on fire and was burning. There was a man in the house they had shot that night in the hand, asleep, and some of the people asked me to go and wake him up or he would get burned up. I went and knocked on the door, but it had been opened and the man had got out. When I went back I walked upon the body of Rachael; she was dead and the blood running out of her mouth. I turned and ran down to my house the back way; it scared me more than I had ever been in my life; I started back and called to my husband to let me in; I knew my house would get on fire from the one that was burning. Mr. Callahan, who lives at the corner of Causey and South street, came and pushed open the door where I was standing, with the biggest pistol in his hand I ever saw in my life. He asked, "Who is in here?" I told him nobody but me and my husband. He said, "Come out," and asked me if we had any arms. He said to my husband, "Come over here till I shoot you." I begged him hard not to shoot my husband. At this time there came up two of the regulars and told us to go to the fort. We went, and were gone about half an hour when two ladies told me that this Mr. Callahan took my bed-clothes and chickens, and everything he wanted, and then set fire to the house.

965. What became of Rachael? She lay there; I never went back any more. When they set the house on fire her clothes caught fire, I suppose. Some of the people told me that her clothes were all burned off from her. She had been complaining two days.

966. Have you seen anything of her since? I have found it since where she was buried, and seen her name on the headboard.

967. Who put it on? I do not know; I only knew where she was buried by seeing her name.

968. Was she killed at the time she was shot? Yes; she was shot dead.

969. What knowledge have you that she was burned? Several people who saw her told me that she was; and I know she was, because I went back and found a part of her clothes lying in the yard. I found a part of her dress and underclothes, and a woman on Causey street had some of her clothes the next Sunday evening.

970. How old was your daughter? About fourteen years old.

971. Have you any reasons, other than those you have stated, for believing she was burned? Yes, sir; Dr. Quimby, the surgeon of the sixty-first regiment, saw her, and said it was the awfullest sight he ever saw. There were a plenty of people who saw her burnt.

972. Who were the white ladies you spoke of? Mrs. Swels and Mrs. Garey.

973. You stated something about regular soldiers that came up? Yes; they made the men let us alone. The men wanted to shoot us. Mr. Callahan did not attempt to shoot, but this other man did. He pointed his pistol at us three times; he was right close to us; as close as I am to you.

975. What language did he use? He said to my husband, "Come out, God damn you, until I shoot you." Callahan said to him, "Let them alone; do you want to kill everybody?" He said, "Yes, I will shoot you; God damn you, come out."

976. Was this man a policeman? No, sir.

977. Were there any other people there except these? I do not know; it was so dark I could not see.

978. What is this Mr. Callahan's business? He is a grocery-keeper, and staying in his grocery right now.

979. Do you know who it was that shot your daughter? I understood since it was Mr. Callahan; I do not know; I did not see anybody shoot her.

980. Did you lose everything you had? I lost everything I had except what I had on my back.

981. What time of night was this? About half an hour before daybreak.

982. What first gave you the alarm? The fire; they had been setting the houses on fire all around us.

983. Did you see any other acts of violence? No, sir.

984. Did you see any other colored persons that had been hurt? No, sir; not that night at all.

985. Was your husband sick at the time? He has been sick now for nine months. He has been a soldier, and had been sick before he came out of the sixty-first regiment.

986. Was he a peaceable man? Yes; Dr. Quimby will tell you all about my husband and family; he has been in the regiment ever since it was formed.

987. You are certain that Callahan was one of the men? Yes, he was one of the men that came out to our house. I have known him for six months, and traded with him often.

988. Have you ever given him any cause to have ill feeling towards you? None in the world. I was tending to my own business. I was sending my daughter Rachael to school.

By Mr. SHANKLIN:

989. Have you seen anybody who saw your daughter shot? Yes, Johnny Romey saw her. Did he know who shot her? He said Callahan was the man; and Billy Allen said he saw the man come right down the steps and shoot her.

JOHN HOLLYWOOD sworn and examined.

By the CHAIRMAN:

990. Where do you reside? In Memphis. How long have you lived here? It will be three years in June. Were you here in Memphis during the recent riots? Yes, sir.

991. Did you see any portion of them? I saw something; I could not help it; there was a man stabbed right before my house.

992. State what you saw? On Tuesday, the first day of the riots, there was a great excitement in the streets. I staid in my house, and did not shut up. Some of the neighbors told me not to shut up, that it would look bad. I said I did not want to do anything that would look bad. As the mob was returning, before dusk, a negro came running through my house and back into the yard; he lived back of my house, and used to come in and trade. I kept a little grocery. As he got into the door, three or four men got hold of him and were licking him with pistols. I begged them to have some mercy on him, and asked them not to kill the man in my own house. He got away from them, and got away through the back part of the house.

993. What was the name of this negro? Austin; he lives in the house back in my yard. I knew him well; he was a very good boy, and I hated to see him abused

994. Who were the parties that abused him? I do not know, they were all strangers to me.

995. Was this negro doing anything to provoke these men? I do not know; he came into my door, and I believe if I had not been there he would have been killed, judging from the excitement the men appeared to be under. I went back to see if he was able to get home, but he made good tracks to his own house. As I came back there was a still larger mob opposite my door, and they had another negro down there. I did not go out; I was so excited I did not know what to do. When the crowd had ceased and gone off, (it was all the work of a minute,) I went out, and there was still life in the negro. There were some colored women there, and I asked them to bring him into the house. This man's name was Jackson Goddell, as I understand.

996. Do you know anything further, of your own knowledge, of the riots? No, sir, I do not.

997. When you came back and found a crowd around this last colored man, did you know any of the parties? I did not know them; they were all strangers to me.

998. Were any of these parties those who first came into your store? There were some of these parties.

999. What countrymen were they? I could not say; there might have been Irishmen among them; I could not recognize them. I think there were as many Irishmen as any other class, as I could not identify one of them.

1000. Have you seen any persons who admitted to you that they participated in the assault upon Austin or Jackson? I have not.

TAYLOR HUNT (colored) sworn and examined.

By the CHAIRMAN:

1001. How old are you? As near as I can guess, I am sixteen.

1002. Where do you live? I live with Mr. Davis, upon Bank street, Memphis; I am his coachman.

1003. State to the committee if you have been beaten or assailed recently? I was shot.

1004. When were you shot? On Tuesday, I think it was the first of the month, about eight o'clock.

1005. State the circumstances under which you were shot? I was going home to my mother's, and when I had got to Brown avenue and De Soto streets, I met two men, one was a policeman, I do not know who the other was; the policeman shot me in the head.

1006. What were you doing? Nothing but going home. After he had shot me, he asked me if I was a soldier. I said no. He said it was a good thing I was not, and he then went along.

1007. Did he strike you? No, he just shot me.

1008. How far were you from him when he shot you? About as far as across this room.

1009. Where did the ball strike you? On the side of the head.

1010. Did it hurt you much? It did not hurt me until about midnight; it made me weak for about two days, but it did not stop me from work.

1011. Did he say anything more to you? No.

1012. Could you tell this policeman if you were to see him? No, sir.

1013. Had you been in any crowd of colored persons that day? No, sir.

1014. Did you see any colored people beaten? There was one beaten; I did not see him exactly, or know him, but he was beaten very badly.

1015. What was his name? Ike Reed, they said; I heard them say he was beaten by the firemen.

1016. Do you know where this Isaac is? No, sir. I reckon I could find him; he goes home at night most of the time.

1017. Did you give the policeman any reason for firing at you? No, sir.

1018. Had you spoken to him? No, sir; I was not close enough to speak to him.

1019. Did he say anything to you? No, he did not say anything.

1020. What was the first indication you had that he was going to shoot you? The first thing I knew was when I felt the ball strike me; he walked up to me very fast, and asked me if I was a soldier. He said it was a damned good thing that I was not.

1021. Did you understand that if you had been a soldier that he was going to kill you? I do not know; that was all he said.

By Mr. BROOMALL:

1022. Do you know whether he was aware that he had hit you? Yes, because I commenced bleeding right fast.

1023. Did you tell him that he had shot you? No, sir; I just put my hand to my head.

AUSTIN COTTON (colored) sworn and examined.

By the CHAIRMAN:

1024. Where do you live? In Memphis.

1025. How old are you? About twenty-nine years old.

1026. Have you been a slave? Oh, yes, sir.

1027. Were you here during the first days of the riot? Oh, yes, sir.

1028. What did you see at the riot? I did not see anything, but as I came from my work—I am a carpenter—I saw some people on the street talking; I do not know what they were talking about. After I had passed them they cried halt, and came running down toward me, when a citizen grabbed me and held me, while a policeman pounded me over the head; this was at Mr. Hollywood's grocery.

1029. Who was it grabbed hold of you? I do not know; they came on me so suddenly that I could not tell who they were.

1030. How did he take hold of you? He took me by the waist; I attempted to break away; he hung on to me, and they kept beating me over the head.

1031. How many men were beating you? Two men.

1032. What did they beat you with? They beat me with pistols.

1033. How did you know they were policemen? I saw the stars they wore; I looked back and saw the policemen; I knew I had done nothing, and started to run; I could have got away, if this man had not caught me. The policeman said "Halt! you damned nigger, or we will knock you on the head.

1034. How did you get away? I at last broke away and went through the store, the back way.

1035. Did they knock you down? No; they whirled me round until they saw another man at the door, when they knocked him down and shot him.

1036. Was that Jackson Godell? Yes, that was the same man.

1037. How badly did they hurt you? I have not worked a day since; my head hurts me very badly; I lost the use of my arm partially.

1038. Where did you go then? I went right to my house and staid there; I was so crippled that I could not get out; I have staid there ever since.

1039. Have you ever had any difficulty with any of these policemen, or anybody else? If you can bring a colored man or a white man that will say that I have spoken a cross word in eight years, you may take me out and hang me to-day; I have not had any disturbance since I have been in Memphis.

1040. What was the reason they assailed you? I suppose they could not get satisfaction from the soldiers, and they came up here and knocked down every colored man they saw.

1041. Do you know of anybody else being hurt except Jackson? No, sir; I saw numbers of them at headquarters, but I did not know them. I did not know that I could do anything, and I just left my party in the hands of the Lord, and let it go. They had all the upper hand of us, and we could do nothing. I belong to the church, and I believe the Lord will take care of us.

1042. What church do you belong to? The Baptist church.

Were any of the members of the church beside yourself hurt? I do not know whether there was or not; I kept myself so scarce that I did not know who got hurt.

1043. Were you in great fear of further violence? The next night they were going on in the same way. I kept watch; I wanted to save myself, if I could not save my house; if I saw them coming I had made arrangements to get out of the way.

1044. Were any houses burnt in your neighborhood? No, sir. I live on St. Martin and Beal streets, and that is pretty well up town.

By Mr. SHANKLIN:

1045. How long since you have been a freedman? Since you all got here. I was run down below, but in three or four months the man gave me up, and sent me home. I have been here ever since.

1046. What has been the general treatment of the citizens of Memphis during the riot to you? Did any of them abuse you or maltreat you? No; no one abused me; it was because I was humble as a slave almost. I have heard them say to me, "You are right, Uncle; you are humble just like a slave." The colored people do not have any rights; if one of them lifts his finger he will be fined five dollars, when he would not have been if he had been a slave.

1047. Do they employ you to work? Yes, sir.

1048. And pay you a fair price? Yes, sir, they always paid me a fair price. I have never said anything about price, when I have been employed to work. I have been with one man three years, and he has dealt fairly and honestly with me. After I was hurt he told me to come around to his grocery and get what I wanted.

WILLIAM COE (colored) sworn and examined.

By the CHAIRMAN:

1049. Where do you live? In Memphis.

1050. How old are you, and what is your business? I cannot exactly tell my age; my business is blacksmithing.

1051. How long have you been in Memphis? I have been here many years, and cannot say how long; I came here with my master from Virginia.

1052. Were you here during the disturbance at the first of the present month? Yes, sir.

1053. What do you know, if anything, about that disturbance? I was up at my shop on Alabama street; there were a couple of men who staid at Mr. Finne's grocery store all day and night. I asked one of Mr. Finne's boys who they were; they said they did not know. At night Mr. Finne's boy, Frank, gave these men a candle and some matches to go over to Albert Harris's house to search it. The next night they burnt my shop up; they came there about 12 o'clock in the night; there were three men I saw slipping into the shop, and they set it on fire.

1054. Have you a family? I used to have one, but have not now.

1055. Who was in the shop with you? There was another man in there with me; he was in one room and I in another.

1056. What was the first alarm you had? I was lying down, and heard the men come and knock at my door once, and said "Open the door." Nobody in the shop spoke, and one of them said, "Break down the door, John," and they done so; as they broke down the door, and came into the room where I was, they had a can of coal oil with them; they found a tin on a bench, and turned the oil out into that. I said, "Gentlemen, don't trouble that tin; there's something in it. They said "What are you doing in here? Go out, or I'll blow your brains out." I started to go out, and they wouldn't let me go. I said, "Gentlemen, what's the matter? I've not done anything." They told me they wouldn't hurt me, if I'd go out. I said I'd get my shoes and go out. They said no, they would not let me get my shoes, and were going to burn up everything I had. Then they let me go out, and I saw them pour the oil around, and set the shop on fire. One man there seemed to know me, and said I was a mighty good boy, and not to hurt me; that I had done a job of work for him, and he didn't want me hurt.

1057. Did you see any policemen? No, sir, I did not. I didn't know who they were. It was very dark, and I could not distinguish them.

1058. Could you not see them when the shop was on fire? Yes, sir; but they were running away then.

1059. What became of the other man in the shop? While they were talking to me he got away, and they never saw him at all.

1060. Did they inflict any violence on you? No, sir; they did not do anything to me. I suppose they would have done but for the one who said I had done some work for him, and told them not to hurt me; otherwise I suppose they would have shot me. Two of them stood close to me while the other one set fire to the building.

1061. Did you own the shop? No, sir. Alexander and George Jones owned the shop. I was working there.

1062. Have you had any disturbance with white people? No, sir; never.

1063. What took place the next night? I could not say any more than that there were plenty of fires going on. There was nothing that I know anything of myself.

1064. How much damage was there done to you by burning up the shop? There were some few tools I had there and all the other clothes I had—both bed and wearing. They took them, spread them out, poured oil over them, and set them on fire.

1065. What had you on when you left? I had on nothing but a pair of pants, and I came near not getting my shoes, but they finally had the consideration to let me get my shoes, and I went back for them, and I pulled down this old coat and my hat.

1066. Did you believe Mr. Finne's boy when he said he didn't know who those two men were that were at his father's store the other day? No, sir. I believe he did.

1067. How old are Mr. Finne's boys? I do not know how old they are. Mr. Bostwick's son said Frank Finne gave them the candle and matches.

1068. Who is Bostwick? He is a white man who lives close where I am.

By Mr. BROOMALL:

1069. Were the men who burnt your shop the same men you saw at Mr. Finne's during the day? I do not know. I tried to see who they were, but I could not.

1070. Do you think they were the same men you saw at Mr. Finne's? They looked like them. To tell the truth I do not know whether they were or not.

1071. What did they talk about all this time? They did not talk at all, and did not call each other by name. I thought they wanted to kill me and were going to burn me up.

1072. Did they say what they were going to do anywhere else? No, sir; the tall one said, "He has done some work for me; don't hurt him."

1073. Did they say anything about shooting you? Yes, sir. They said if I knew them they would blow my brains out. They told me to go out; I started to go, and they would not let me go out; finally one of them said, "He's a good fellow," and let me go out.

By Mr. SHANKLIN:

1074. How have the citizens of Memphis treated you; well or badly? They have treated me pretty badly. I've had pretty bad luck myself; this makes four times I've lost everything I had.

1075. What were your other losses? They were my clothes and money. That was last year. They robbed me.

1076. White men? Yes. They just came in and took from me a new suit of clothes I had just bought.

1077. How do the citizens who own property about town treat you? They have been pretty rash all the time.

1078. They have employed you to work, have they not? I am now working for a butcher. He treats me pretty well. After they set fire to the shop that night I ran up and told him, and he came down to see about it.

1079. Have these men of property you have had dealings with dealt fairly by you? The ones I lived with before treated me mighty bad about paying me. I didn't get one-third of what was due me. I've tried to get it, but they have put me off in such a way that I didn't like to say much, hoping they would do something for me.

1080. Have your dealings here been with the foreign population, Irish and Dutch, or American people? With American people.

1081. And they have all treated you badly? Yes, sir.

1082. Did you live here when the war broke out? Yes. I've always remained here.

1083. Have they treated you better since you've been a freedman than they did before? No; they've tried to treat me worse.

By the CHAIRMAN:

1084. How do you account for that? I thought I'd been treated bad enough before then but everybody seems to try to get the advantage of me, and not against me alone, but against every colored person.

GEORGE JONES (colored) sworn and examined.

By the CHAIRMAN:

1085. What is your age and business? About 50. I've been working at a wagon shop going on three years.

1086. Where do you live? In Memphis.

1087. Were you here at the time of the riots? Yes, sir.

1088. State what you know, if anything, that took place? The shop belongs to a man named Alexander; he's a blacksmith. I was out working, but I had some tools in the shop and a good deal of property there.

1089. What was done with the shop? It was burnt up.

1090. When? I think it was on Wednesday night, the second night of the riot.

1091. Were you in the shop at the time? No, sir. I was away about three-quarters of a mile on Poplar street.

1092. What was the value of your property destroyed? I do not know. I took a statement of it on paper and carried it to the provost marshal on Monday last.

1093. Who burnt it? I do not know. It was done the same night they burnt these churches and school-houses.

1094. Did you see any violence inflicted on any person? No, sir; I saw nothing.

1095. And you have no knowledge of who burnt the shop? No, sir; I do not know. I was not in the shop. William Coe was in the shop.

MONDAY, *May* 28, 1866.

Dr. S. J. QUIMBY sworn and examined.

By the CHAIRMAN:

1096. What is your residence and profession? I reside in Memphis, and am a physician.

1097. How long have you resided in Memphis? About five months.

1098. Were you in Memphis during the recent riots? I was.

1099. Have you any, and if so, what personal knowledge of anything that took place during the riots? The colored troops in the fort had been mustered out of service and were waiting their payments. On Tuesday afternoon some hundred of them were out on a drunk; there was a grocery near my store where they seemed to be getting most of their whiskey. There were, I should judge, about fifty of them who were pretty drunk. Along in the afternoon, about three o'clock, I heard up on Main street, which is only about one block from where they were, great cheering. I stepped out to inquire the cause; they said the officers had been up there arresting a man and the soldiers had rescued him. There was at that time no other fight. About four o'clock in the afternoon, perhaps an hour after this, while I was standing in my office-door there came by in the direction of Causey street six police officers; four of them stopped next door to me, and the other two went along to the crowd. There were two soldiers who were very boisterous in the crowd and the two officers arrested them, showing at the time no arms that I saw, but made the arrests in a perfectly orderly manner. As the police officers took the men along, the soldiers began to gather around them from all over the street, and began to call out, "Stone them, club them, shoot them," and all sorts of expressions that an excited body of men would use; they were all colored. The officers took the men and started down in the direction of Causey street; the other four officers joined in a little distance behind and attempted to keep the crowd off. Before they got to the first bayou, which is about fifty yards from my office, the soldiers began to fire their revolvers in the air; from what I saw I should judge there were about forty of them armed with revolvers, and the rest had stones, clubs, and whatever else they could get hold of. As they began firing in the air the officers seemed to think that they were firing at them, turned round and began firing at the crowd. Then, at once, I saw the crowd firing at them, and heard one of the crowd sing out, "One of them," meaning an officer, "was shot." I saw him carried into a grocery; then a part of the crowd went on and a part came back. In the course of some six or eight minutes I heard one of the colored soldiers speak back to the crowd, making the remark, "They have killed one of our men." At that all this crowd that had come back reloaded their revolvers, or took whatever they could get in their hands to fight with, and ran back towards the police, very much excited; they turned down Causey street, so that I saw no more of them until they came back. They returned in about a quarter of an hour, and remarked that they had killed one of the officers. I saw two soldiers come back who were wounded, and one of them had a policeman's club. Everything quieted down for about three-quarters of an hour; I went up at that time to tea. About two squares from there, over on Shelby street, as I was coming back I heard firing; on looking over towards Main street I saw about one hundred and fifty colored soldiers; they were chasing officers in all directions; they chased two right down by me; there were about six men after the two; they were calling out to the policemen, "Halt," and firing after them all the time. There were at least fourteen shots fired at one of the officers. As they came down into Shelby street I saw a black man come up, armed with a Spencer rifle, who called out to the officers, "Halt, you white son of a bitch," and fired at him. The officer kept on; this was about dark; the soldiers went at once into the fort and were not out during the night again. About ten o'clock at night there came up into the street about two hundred men, policemen and posse; they came and patrolled up and down the streets, but found nobody or any force to oppose them. Then they broke up into small squads and went among the colored people's houses. I did not see anything at that time, but heard firing. The next morning early I was called out to see several that were wounded. They went into the house of one man and asked him if he had any arms; he said not. They then went into his house and searched it, and took everything valuable in the shape of watches and jewelry. They asked him if he had been out that day. He told them no; that he was in government service; they then shot him through the head. At one house where I was called they came hunting for a man. They called up his wife, put a revolver to her head and told her to get a light quick; they then searched the house for a man, but did not find him; then they threatened to shoot a woman who was at the time lying in bed with a child. She said to them, "Don't shoot me; I'm not a man;" but one of them as he was going out fired into the bed; the ball passed through her arm; raising her hand at the time, cut off one of her fingers and lodged in her breast. At another place they came and shot a man, in the first place in the head, then shot him in the abdomen, and *then* asked him if he had any arms; he told them he had none; then they went to work and searched his house and took everything they could find of any value; this was on Tuesday night.

On Wednesday morning at 8 o'clock the street was as quiet as any time on Sunday that I ever saw. I do not think there were ten soldiers to be seen on the street anywhere, and there was not a man armed. A posse came up, about fifty of them. I know I spoke in a laughing way to some one, wondering what they were to fight. By and by they commenced to scatter off among the houses. I at once heard firing like skirmishing. I went out, and in a short time there were four men shot dead, who I am certain had not had anything to do with the affair; they were at the time unarmed, and did not belong to, or had not had anything to do with, the army. Two of them were men who had been out to work; one man was coming from his work, across the railroad, when a man who had something to do with the train ordered him to "halt;" the colored man had no arms and replied that he was about his own business, and went on; the white man came down from the engine and shot him; this white man was employed by the Mississippi and Tennessee Railroad Company, and had something to do with the train; that was all I saw at that time. I saw this girl Rachael Hatcher, who was shot and burned up afterwards, the next morning; she was shot in the mouth.

1100. Was the shot immediately fatal, or was she burned alive? The shot was fatal; she was on the outside of the house; a house was burning a few feet off, and she went to put the fire out; some one went up the steps and shot her, and she fell partly under her own house.

1101. What was her mother's name? She called herself Sneed; the mother had married the second time, but the daughter's name was Hatcher; she was shot, and fell right under the house, as I said, and the house burned up over her; the shot, however, was immediately fatal; it went directly into her mouth; she was shot some time in the night; her clothes were all burned off, except her shoes and stockings; on the lower part of her body her flesh was burned very badly, and a portion of the upper part was also burned very badly; her face was very much burned; there was a stream of blood running out of her mouth in front of her, it seemed to me there must have been four quarts of it—a stream of blood a foot and a half long, and six or eight inches wide. This man who was shot through the head walked up to the fort and back the next day; the ball passed through the back of his head, below the brain, and just in front of the spinal column.

1102. How large a crowd was this on Tuesday afternoon? About one hundred men.

1103. Did they appear to have been drinking much? Yes, sir; they did.

1104. Were they merely cheering and drinking, or did they appear to be quarrelsome? They appeared to be on a regular spree, and did not do any harm.

1105. At whose grocery was it they got their liquor? There were two or three bars in the neighborhood, and one kept by a colored man, a freedman; I forget his name.

1106. What was it that led to the attempt at arrest by the police in the first instance? There was a colored man who had been committing some offence; there had been a ball the evening before in which there had been some fuss, and this man had been cutting up; this I only heard. A complaint had been made of him to the officers, and they came up to arrest him; they did arrest him and were carrying him away in a perfectly orderly manner at the time.

1107. Was this colored man a soldier? No, sir; but this crowd of drunken soldiers were less than a block off; the soldiers had a spite against the officers and went and took the man away.

1108. How many policemen arrested this man? Two.

1109. Were there no other policemen about? No, sir.

1110. How long before these other policemen came back? About an hour.

1112. Did this colored crowd remain around there during this time? Yes.

1113. When these six policemen came back what did they undertake to do first? Four of them stopped, and two went down to the crowd of negroes, who were cutting up pretty badly.

1114. What were they doing? Just hallooing and carrying on in a boisterous manner.

1115. They were not fighting? No; there had been no fighting in the street at that time.

1116. Then what took place after these policemen got into the crowd? The crowd began to gather around them; some were calling out, "Kill him," and "stone him;" there was no firing at that time. The police arrested the two men and came out; they started with them down towards Causey street.

1117. Where were they carrying them to? To the station-house in town; they were going by the way of Causey street.

1118. Where did the firing commence? They had come up within about five rods of my office—a crowd of, I should think, a hundred men following them. The four policemen who had remained behind staid back to keep the crowd behind; the colored men then, as I said, fired in the air, and the police turned and fired at them.

1119. How far were the police and colored soldiers apart when the police commenced firing? About fifteen feet.

1120. Are you certain the colored men fired in the air? I am certain, for they were right close by me, and the officers at once turned and fired on them. The officers thought they had been fired on.

1121. Were there any persons in the crowd injured by the shots the policemen fired? No; at that time I do not think there was a man hit. The crowd then began to fire at the policemen, and one of the police was shot through the thigh at the first fire; some of the crowd sung out, "He is shot," and in the course of three or four minutes I saw them carry him into a saloon on the corner.

1122. Who carried him, the other policeman? I could hardly tell; there was a part of the crowd there.

1123. They were not colored men who were carrying him in? I could not tell for certain.

1124. Who shot this officer? The firing was from the crowd at the officers; then I heard the colored people sing out that an officer was shot.

1125. Shot by them, or shot accidentally by the police? I inferred he was shot by the crowd. They were firing at the police and doing their best to hit them. At the first fire, I heard them say he was shot. They then fired backwards and forwards for six or eight minutes; it seemed just the same as a fight.

1126. What was the result of the fight? The officers went on; I did not see any of them hit after that. They turned down Causey street, and the crowd came back. I heard them say one soldier had been killed, and then the crowd turned down Causey again after the officers.

1127. Was the soldier killed very soon after the policeman was shot? Very soon. They sung out, "They've killed one of our men." That proved to be a mistake; he was only wounded in the arm. When the crowd went back, an officer was the first one killed; he was shot through the head.

1128. What officer? One of the policemen who had charge of the men arrested.

1129. Then there were two policemen shot, one wounded and one killed? Yes; when they got down Causey street one policeman was shot dead.

1130. By whom was he shot? By one of the colored soldiers.

1131. Do you know who he was? No, sir.

1132. Do you *know* the fact that it was a colored soldier who shot him? Only by hearsay; they all said so. I saw one of them bring back his club, and the club was bloody. I saw two soldiers coming back, one shot in the hand and the other in the arm; they were both bleeding as they came back. They said, "We have killed one of them." I asked them how he was shot. They said through the head.

1133. This was what you heard from others? Yes, from the soldiers who came back bringing the bloody club and saying they had killed an officer.

1134. Were there any other policemen killed in the skirmish? Not at that time.

1135. How badly was the policeman who was wounded hurt? He died afterwards.

1136. Did you see either of them afterwards? No.

1137. You did not examine the bodies of either of them? No; all that I saw was the carrying of this first man off.

1138. How many soldiers were there wounded in this skirmish? There were three that I saw at that time.

1139. How badly wounded? Two of them were wounded in the arm and one in the hand, not seriously.

1140. Was that the end of the affair? No, sir; the officers went back, got a re-enforcement of fifty men and returned about six o'clock. I was at tea when they came back, and saw nothing of what took place at first. I was told they had a fight there for about twenty minutes; that the soldiers were driven back in the first place, but afterwards rallied and drove the policemen back; then the police drove them as far as Main street, where the soldiers again rallied in larger force, ran the policemen into town, and scattered them in every direction.

1141. At what time did these soldiers get back to the fort? About dark. That seemed to be the end of the affair that night as far as the soldiers were concerned.

1142. Was it quiet all Tuesday night? Yes, with the exception of this crowd that came up from town. If it had not been for them, it would have been as quiet as it ever was. The police were there and their posse. This was after everything was through and the soldiers were all at the fort. There came up two hundred men, all armed. They patrolled up and down the street by fours, and when they found there were no soldiers there they scattered around in small squads and went among the shanties, "hunting for arms," they said. They were breaking open houses, and killed four men that I knew.

1143. Please state the names of the killed, and the circumstances under which they were killed? The name of the girl shot in bed was Rhoda Jacobs; they called at the house where she was, put a revolver at her mother's head and told her to strike a light quickly. They searched the house for her father, but could not find him, and then turned around and shot her in bed; there was in the same bed a child.

1144. How old was Rhoda Jacobs? In the neighborhood of twenty.

1145. Was the child in bed her child? I do not know.

1146. Was she killed? No, sir; the bullet lodged in her breast. I believe she has recovered. The next was John Manson, shot through the head and his house robbed; he was abed and asleep. They woke him up and shot him. The ball passed through his head, but he is still alive. The next was Joseph Walker, who was shot in the shoulder with a charge of buckshot. He was standing at the time at his gate watching the police go by. He did not say anything to them, or they to him; they just fired at him. The name of the other man I don't know; he was shot in the afternoon.

1147. Now, please state the condition of things on Wednesday morning—was there a riot or any negroes on the street? Nothing at all; it was just as quiet as on a Sunday; there did not appear to be the least thing going on. There were very few soldiers on the street, and none with arms; there could not have been ten men on the streets at the time. Apparently all the disturbance was over. I told persons with whom I was talking the storm was over.

1148. At what hour did the policemen come down? About nine or ten o'clock.

1149. Did you see them when they came down? Yes, sir.

1150. Did you hear any talk? No, sir; they came down from Causey street, coming by twos, some four or five of them were on horses, before they got to the bayou bridge, and then began to scatter off among the negro cabins.

1151. What party was this? The sheriff and his posse.

1152. Did you see Sheriff Winters with the policemen at that time? I am not acquainted with him; they told me it was his posse. They scattered among the houses, and I heard firing, the same as skirmishing.

1153. Who was that firing by? The firing was by them.

1154. Who were they firing at? They were firing at unarmed freedmen wherever they found them. There was one man by the name of Fayette Dickerson, who had formerly been a soldier in the fifteenth colored infantry; he was standing by his house; two men came up and struck him over the head with a stick; they then shot him in the head, a glancing shot; they then shot him in the abdomen, and then asked him if he had any arms about himself or in the house.

1155. Are you making this statement from your own observation? No; but the man himself told me this.

1156. You saw the wounds of the man who told you this? Yes, sir.

1157. Was he living? He lived for six days after he was wounded. After that I did not attend him. I think he died.

1158. Had he been engaged in the riot? No; he was a perfectly peaceable man. I was well acquainted with him. He had been a soldier during the war; he after that was at home and worked hard; he was a man about forty years old. The next man I was called to see was Joseph Walker; he was the man I saw shot on the railroad.

1159. How badly was he wounded? He was wounded through the hip so he could not attend work for a week or two. A corporal of my old regiment was hit, I think, in the breast. He was killed instantly.

1160. By whom? By the men who came up with the posse.

1161. Was it the posse or the mob, or was the posse the mob? They were all a mob at the time. At that time there were only the fifty men who came up with the sheriff who were doing any firing. This was in the forenoon, about nine or half past nine. This corporal was either going to or coming from some work he was doing. He was unarmed, but he had on at that time blue pants.

1162. Was he a peaceable man? Perfectly so. He was walking along peaceably and quietly. They said their orders were to shoot every man wearing blue clothes.

1163. Ordered by whom? I suppose by the sheriff.

1164. Do you know that these orders were given? I only know because the posse said so.

1165. Did any of them say so to you? Yes, sir, but who I cannot tell; it was the common talk among the crowd.

1166. Did all the parties who were shot have blue clothes on? Every one who was shot on purpose did. There were quite a number shot by accident, I suppose. I could not say anything about that.

1167. Did they say anything to you about being ordered to rob only those who had blue clothes on? They did not say anything about that. There were two others shot within half an hour. I did not see them shot, and do not know their names. They were shot dead.

1168. Had they blue clothes on? Yes, sir; they had been in the army.

1169. You do not know the circumstances under which they were shot? No, I simply saw them dead upon the streets.

1170. Where was it that you saw those? It was when I came back from the grocery; it was about one block from where I saw the posse go among the houses. I saw one body lie further up across the bayou, on the bank.

1171. Have you stated all the acts of violence you saw? I think so. There was a man named Lorenzo Jean who saw all I did not see.

1172. Do you know the names of any of these parties who committed the murders? No; I only know from what I've heard.

By Mr. SHANKLIN:

1173. What State are you from? I was from Centre Harbor, Michigan.

1174. What connexion did you have with the army? I entered the army in 1862, and was detailed with the forty-eighth Ohio infantry. In July of the same year I was ordered to the forty-sixth, as acting assistant surgeon. In November of the same year I was ordered to the one hundredth Indiana infantry, in the same capacity. In April, 1863, I was ordered to assist in raising the fifty-ninth colored infantry. In September, 1863, I was appointed surgeon of the sixty-first colored infantry, and was mustered out on December 31, 1865. Since that time I've been practicing here.

1175. Have you told us all you know about this riot, and of all the outrages you saw committed by white or black? Yes, sir; there was one circumstance back of it with regard to the spite the soldiers hold against the policemen. I did not see it myself; the name of the man who saw it and told me was Frank Lee, on South street, or it may have been Mitchell Whitlow.

Mr. SHANKLIN. You need not tell what you heard.

FRANCIS ERICKSON sworn and examined.

By the CHAIRMAN:

1176. What is your residence and official position? I am the coroner of Shelby county.

1177. How long have you resided in Memphis? Since the fore part of 1864.

1178. How long have you held the position of coroner? Since last July.

1179. From whom did you receive your appointment? From the county court.

1180. Where did you reside ere you came here? At Somerville, Tennessee.

1181. Are you a native of Tennessee? No, sir; I am a native of New Jersey. I have lived twenty-one years in Tennessee: I have lived in the State just half of my life.

1182. Were you here during the recent riots? Yes, sir.

1183. State what circumstances you know attending them? I have no knowledge of it myself, except by rumor.

1184. Have you held inquests upon the bodies of any alleged to have been killed during the late riots? I did, on ten bodies in the neighborhood of South street, and three others not in that neighborhood, alleged to have been killed in the riot. I held inquests altogether at that time on thirteen colored persons and one white man.

1185. Have you the findings of the inquests in all those cases? I have them here.

1186. Are they the original papers? They are; I present them to the committee.

1187. Did you summon the jury? I did.

1188. Of how many did they consist? Seven—the number required by law.

1189. Were they freeholders? They were citizens here.

1190. Did they examine the witnesses? Yes; we took all the evidence we could get. I summoned the men up here in the city and went down on Thursday, the 3d of this month. At first I could not get any information, or find where the bodies were, from the people; they looked as if they were scared to death, and would not tell me anything; finally I got some names from some little colored boys.

1190. Did you hold an inquest on the body of a girl named Rachael? Yes, sir; she had been shot through the back of her head; she was badly burned, her clothes being nearly burnt off of her.

1191. Where did you find her body? On South street, near where a building had been burnt the night before.

1192. Had the body been moved? I do not know; it was lying right where the fire had been.

1193. Was there any crowd around there? Not that I remember.

1194. You know nothing of the circumstances under which these parties were killed? No; I only found out the bodies and had them buried.

1195. Do you know of bodies being found upon which inquests had not been held? Not of my own knowledge; I saw a body on St. Martin street, but when I went there to hold an inquest it had been carried off.

1196. At whose instance did you summon a jury and hold an inquest? Of myself; I heard the bodies were there, and deemed it my duty to do so.

1197. Who was this white man? I forget his name; he was killed on Centre alley, near a drinking establishment; he was killed for simply talking to a black man. The proof was, that he was standing talking to the negro man, when a fireman came up and said "This is no time to be talking to niggers." He turned round and said, "This is no bad man; I've known him for years." The fireman said, "By God, this is no time to be talking to niggers," and shot him.

By Mr. SHANKLIN:

1198. Did you hold an inquest upon the bodies of any negro soldiers? The bodies of all the negroes were dressed in soldiers' clothes; whether or not they were soldiers I do not know.

1199. What was the character of the wounds generally? Nearly all had been shot and some of them stabbed. One man, I recollect, whose body we found in a house, had been shot and stabbed.

1200. Was there any other person in the house when you found his body? No; he had a little place fixed up where he kept soda-water, cigars, &c. He was an elderly man, and was sitting there when he was shot; he was cut on both sides.

1201. Did you state that the colored people down there were so much frightened that you couldn't get any information from them? Yes; they appeared to want to shun me; finally some old women and boys told me the names. After they found what we were after they did not appear to be so shy.

By the CHAIRMAN:

1202. What did you do with the bodies? I had them all picked up, put into coffins and buried by Thomas Smith, undertaker, as they bury all paupers. I went round with him and saw them all put in coffins.

1203. Do you know whether any of the relatives of these parties had any opportunities of paying the last rites to them? I do not know; I never saw anybody claim to be relatives.

1204. How long had they apparently been killed? There were three of them who were said to have been killed the first day of the riot; they were lying near the bayou.

1205. Had they lain there ever since? Yes, sir; from the 1st to the 3d; they had every appearance of having been killed forty-eight hours.

1206. Had they become decomposed? They were quite offensive; decomposition had commenced.

The following are the verdicts of the coroner's jury, referred to by witness in his testimony:

STATE OF TENNESSEE, *Shelby County:*

An inquisition holden at the corner of Main and Mill streets, in the city of Memphis, State and county aforesaid, this the 4th day of May, 1866, before F. Erickson, coroner of said county, upon the body of Henry Williams, colored, aged about twenty-five years, there lying dead, whose names are hereunto subscribed, who, upon their oaths, do say that the said Henry Williams came to his death on 3d instant, from various wounds on the body inflicted by some persons unknown to the jury.

JOHN DILLON.
S. C. PENDERGRAST.
JAMES HOSEY.
WILLIAM FLYNN.
MICHAEL CUNNINGHAM.
L. E. STOCKS.
E. D. EVANS.

MEMPHIS, *May* 2, 1866.

At an inquest holden at the house known as Frank's saloon, Bank alley, between Madison and Monroe streets, in the city of Memphis, this day, before F. Erickson, coroner of Shelby county, upon the body of B. Dennis, aged about forty years, the jury, whose names are hereunto annexed, certify that the said Dennis came to his death by a pistol shot in the region of the heart from the hand of some (man) person unknown to the jury.

J. B. MOWLEY.
F. M. COPELAND.
D. JAMESON.
JOHN H. TEMPLE.
C. PATTERSON.
THADEUS CARMICHAEL.
JOHN D. GOODE.

Witness:
JOHN MYERS.
D. COBB.

STATE OF TENNESSEE, *Shelby County :*

An inquisition holden at the rear of 326 Main street, Memphis. Tennessee, this the 4th day of May, 1866, before Frank Erickson, coroner of said county, upon the body of William Saunders, colored, age about thirty years, there lying dead, by the jurors whose names are hereto subscribed, who, upon their oath, do say that the said William Saunders came to his death on the night of the 3d instant, from a pistol ball shot through the head, inflicted by some person unknown to the jury.

J. C. HOLST,
J. C. MILLS,
R. G. CRAIG,
E. JONES,
D. BRISKE,
JAMES NORTH,
ED. CROW,
Jurors.

STATE OF TENNESSEE, *Shelby County :*

An inquisition holden on Causey street near the bridge, on this the 3d day of May, 1866, before F. Erickson, coroner of said county, upon the body of Richard, colored, there lying dead, aged forty years, by the jurors whose names are hereunto subscribed, who, upon their oaths, say that the said Richard, colored, came to his death on the night of the 2d instant from a shot inflicted by some person unknown to the jurors.

A. T. CLARK,
H. L. MATTINGLY,
PAT. JONES,
GEO. E. JONES,
J. N. SMITH,
SAM. DAVIS,
S. LEE,
Jurors.

STATE OF TENNESSEE, *Shelby County :*

An inquisition holden near the Mississippi and Tennessee railroad, on this the 3d day ot May, 1866, before F. Erickson, coroner of said county, upon the body of James Hare, colored, aged twenty-four years, there lying dead, by the jurors whose names are hereunto subscribed, who, upon their oaths, do say that the said J. Hare came to his death on the morning of the 2d instant, by a shot inflicted by some person unknown to the jury.

A. T. CLARK,
H. L. MATTINGLY,
PAT. JONES,
GEO. E. JONES,
J. N. SMITH,
SAM. DAVIS,
S. LEE,
Jurors.

STATE OF TENNESSEE, *Shelby County, ss :*

An inquisition holden on the bayou, south of South street, this the 3d day of May, 1866, before F. Erickson, coroner of said county, upon the body of Bill, (colored,) aged thirty-eight years, there lying dead, by the jurors whose names are hereunto subscribed, who, upon their oaths, do say that the said Bill (colored) came to his death by a gunshot wound inflicted on the evening of the 1st instant by some person unknown to the jury.

A. T. CLARK,
H. L. MATTINGLY,
PAT. JONES,
GEO. E. JONES,
J. N. SMITH,
SAM. DAVIS,
S. LEE,
Jurors.

STATE OF TENNESSEE, *Shelby County, ss :*

An inquisition holden on South and Causey streets, upon the body of Rachael, (colored,) aged about twenty-five years, there lying dead, before F. Erickson, coroner of said county, this 3d day of May, 1866, by the jurors, who, upon their oath, do say that the said Rachael (colored) came to her death on the night of the 2d instant from a shot wound, inflicted by some person unknown to the jury.

A. T. CLARK,
H. L. MATTINGLY,
PAT. JONES,
GEO. E. JONES,
J. N. SMITH,
SAM. DAVIS,
S. LEE,
Jurors.

STATE OF TENNESSEE, *Shelby County, ss :*

An inquisition holden on the bayou, south of South street, this the 3d day of May, 1866, before Frank Erickson, coroner of said county, upon the body of Robert Collins, (colored,) there lying dead, by the jurors whose names are hereunto affixed, who, upon their oaths, do say that the said Robert Collins came to his death on the morning of the 2d instant from a gunshot wound, inflicted by some person unknown to the jury.

A. T. CLARK,
H. L. MATTINGLY,
PAT. JONES,
GEO. E. JONES,
J. N. SMITH,
SAM. DAVIS,
S. LEE,
Jurors.

STATE OF TENNESSEE, *Shelby County, ss :*

An inquisition holden at a shanty near South street and Raven avenue, this the 3d day of May, 1866, before F. Erickson, coroner of said county, upon the body of Jack Robertson, (colored,) aged twenty-five years, there lying dead, by the jurors whose names are hereunto subscribed, who, upon their oaths, do say that the said Jack Robertson came to his death on the evening of the first of May from a shot inflicted by some person unknown to the jurors.

A. T. CLARK,
H. L. MATTINGLY,
PAT. JONES,
GEO. E. JONES,
J. N. SMITH,
SAM. DAVIS,
S. LEE,
Jurors.

STATE OF TENNESSEE, *Shelby County, ss :*

An inquisition holden on this 3d day of May, 1866, near the corner of Webster and Raven avenues, before Frank Erickson, coroner of said county, upon the body of an unknown negro man, there lying dead, aged about thirty-five years, by the jurors whose names are hereunto subscribed, who, upon their oaths, do say that the said unknown colored man came to his death by a shot wound, inflicted by some person unknown to the jury.

A. T. CLARK,
H. L. MATTINGLY,
PAT. JONES,
GEO. E. JONES,
J. N. SMITH,
SAM. DAVIS,
S. LEE,
Jurors.

STATE OF TENNESSEE, *Shelby County, ss :*

An inquisition holden on Clay street, near Raven avenue, on this the 3d day of May, 1866, before Frank Erickson, coroner of said county, upon the body of an unknown colored man, aged about twenty-two years, there lying dead, by the jurors whose names are hereto subscribed, who, upon their oaths, do say that the said unknown colored man came to his death on the 2d instant from a shot wound, inflicted by some person unknown to the jury.

> A. T. CLARK,
> H. L. MATTINGLY
> PAT. JONES,
> GEO. E. JONES,
> J. N. SMITH,
> SAM. DAVIS,
> S. LEE,
> *Jurors*

STATE OF TENNESSEE, *Shelby County, ss :*

An inquisition holden near the corner of Avery and South streets, this the 3d day of May, 1866, before F. Erickson, coroner of said county, upon the body of William, (colored,) there lying dead, aged thirty years, by the jury whose names are hereunto subscribed, who, upon their oaths, do say that the said William (colored) came to his death on the night of the 1st instant from a gunshot wound, inflicted by some person unknown to the jurors.

> A. T. CLARK,
> H. L. MATTINGLY,
> PAT. JONES,
> GEO. E. JONES,
> J. N. SMITH,
> SAM. DAVIS,
> S. LEE,
> *Jurors.*

STATE OF TENNESSEE, *Shelby County, ss :*

An inquisition holden on the bayou, south of South street, this the 3d day of May, 1866, before Frank Erickson, coroner of said county, upon the body of Daniel Hawkins, (colored,) aged thirty-five years, there lying dead, by the jurors whose names are hereunto subscribed, who, upon their oaths, do say that the said Daniel Hawkins came to his death on the morning of the 2d day of May, 1866, from a gunshot wound, inflicted by some person unknown to the jury.

> A. T. CLARK,
> H. L. MATTINGLY,
> PAT. JONES,
> GEO. E. JONES,
> J. N. SMITH,
> SAM. DAVIS,
> S. LEE,
> *Jurors.*

STATE OF TENNESSEE, *Shelby County, ss :*

An inquisition holden at No. 133 Beal street, city of Memphis, State and county aforesaid, this 3d day of May, 1866, before F. Erickson, coroner of said county, upon the body of an unknown colored man, there lying dead, aged about forty years, by the jurors whose names are hereto subscribed, who, upon their oaths, do say that the said unknown colored man came to his death on the night of the 2d instant by a pistol shot in the neck on the left side, inflicted by some unknown person.

> M. T. SUMMERS,
> JOHN HEINRICH,
> A. M. FERGUSON,
> S. LEVY,
> S. PATTON,
> FRANK KROOS,
> AUGUSTUS CROWE,
> *Jurors.*

Mrs. JENNETTE SWELLS sworn and examined

By the CHAIRMAN:

1207. Where do you live? In Memphis.
1208. How long have you lived here? About six months.
1209. Where did you live before you came here? In England; I am a Scotch woman.
1210. Were you here at the time of the riot? Yes, sir; I was on South street.
1211. State what you saw and heard? On Tuesday night, the first night of the fires, I saw John Callahan come across the street from the place where they burned the girl up. He had a colored woman's bed on one arm and a pistol in the other hand. I said to him: "Are you going to give me that bed?" I was frightened at the time. My husband was standing beside me. Mr. Callahan made no answer. He went straight down to his house and did not come back. The name of this girl who was burned was Rachael.
1212. How old a girl was Rachael? I should think between 14 and 15. She appeared to be a real nice girl.
1213. Was she entirely black? No, sir; she was more like a yellow girl. Indeed, I never took any particular notice. I never knew one from the other.
1214. Where did they live from you? Right opposite.
1215. Did they seem to be peaceable? Yes; very peaceable, quiet people.
1216. Did you see Adam Lock's house burned? Yes; and Rachael's father's, both. He came out and begged them to let him go. He is a very sickly man; has not been well since Christmas. He begged hard to get away, and finally did get away and his wife also, but Rachael was shot.
1217. Did you see anything further? I saw a man taking things away from the same house on horseback. I do not know what his name was. The things were all gathered up and taken away.
1218. Do you know the name of any other man who carried away any of the things, except Callahan? I saw George McGinn carry away beds and things. I heard Mrs. Adam Lock three or four times call George McGinn to come and help her, and every time she called he fired at her. We were going to build a little place on Causey street. I kept a dressmaker's shop. They came over, and I heard them say: "Let us get in here; they have got money. They are going to build next week." We got out of the house and went into an Italian's, the next door. They did not come in. I think if they had they would have killed myself and husband both.
1219. At what time was it? I think between 2 and 3, or 3 and 4 o'clock in the morning. We opened the door and saw these men coming down the hill from where the houses had been burned with the things.
1220. What does George McGinn do? I believe he was a cooper at one time down on the levee, but he keeps a kind of grocery on Mulberry street now.
1221. Is that all you know about this matter? Yes, sir.
1222. You did not see any further violence? We saw the policemen running and firing at every one. I did not know any of them by name. There was one ball that struck the house where I was. It struck the porch. I do not know where it came from.
1223. Did you see any other person wounded that day? I saw a soldier lying upon the bridge. I believe he was killed. They said he was killed. They threw him down into the water. They buried these folks the next day. I saw him lying on the bridge for above an hour.
1224. Was he a white man or a negro? A negro.
1225. Had he a soldier's clothes on? Yes; he had soldier's clothes on.

By Mr. SHANKLIN:

1226. Did you see anything of the fight between the negro soldiers and white men? When the fuss commenced they said there was a fuss on Main street. We saw the policemen running that way and the civilians going to help them. There was a man came into my house with a policeman on Tuesday and asked my husband for his gun. My husband asked him his name. The policeman said: "If he does not bring the gun back again I will give you the money for it."
1227. Were the colored people engaged in that fight? Yes, sir; the colored soldiers were.
1228. Were colored soldiers engaged in fighting with policemen on Wednesday? There were no colored soldiers fighting and no policemen at first in the morning. I do not think the policemen would have gone into it if there had been no one but them. Two gentlemen drove past in a buggy together. The policemen were standing back. These men said they would go and report them for not standing up to their duty. They went up then.
1229. At what time was this? This was about 3 o'clock on Tuesday.
1230. Did you see firing on both sides? Yes; I saw firing all round. These civilians were all firing.

By Mr. BROOMALL:

1231. Did the crowd you saw on Tuesday night consist altogether of white men? Yes, sir. There were no negroes to be seen. They said they would shoot every negro they could catch, and the negroes did not come out.

8

1232. How many were there? I should think between forty and fifty.

1233. Were there any policemen among them? I saw some policemen. I could not tell who they were. I do not know any of the policemen's names. They said the policemen were just as bad as Callahan and the others were; that they would just shoot down any negro they saw, as these civilians did.

MRS. SOPHIA GAREY sworn and examined.

By the CHAIRMAN:

1234. Are you a married woman? Yes, sir.

1235. Where do you live? In Memphis.

1236. What is the occupation of your husband? He is a confectioner.

1237. How long have you lived in Memphis? Three months.

1238. Where had you lived before? In Cincinnati.

1239. What countryman is your husband? He is an Italian.

1240. Are you an Italian? No, sir; I am a German.

1241. Were you in the city of Memphis during the recent troubles? Yes, sir.

1242. Do you live near Mrs. Swells? Right next door.

1243. What did you see on Tuesday night, May 1? It was not at night. It was in the morning. I kept in my house and was afraid to look out.

1244. What did you see in the morning? I saw Mr. Callahan and Mr. McGinn and another young man, whose name I did not know, coming down the hill from where the houses had been burned. Mr. Callahan had a feather bed on one arm and a pistol in the other hand. The young man had on the hoop skirt and the Balmoral skirt of the girl who had been shot the night before. When Callahan came past with the bed I asked him if he was going to give it to me. He made no answer. He went away down to his house and took it into his house. Then came McGinn with a lot of things in his arm looking like bedclothes, and went into Callahan's house. There were others coming from the same direction whose names I did not know. Some men on horseback had chickens and ducks they were carrying away. They appeared like police. I saw them knock the chickens and ducks on the head and take them off.

1245. Did you see anything of the burning? No. In the morning we moved away. We were afraid to stay there. My husband kept a saloon and we moved away everything we had. A colored man lived next door, and they had shot a colored girl in his house. Who did it I do not know. We heard the report of a pistol and heard Rhoda say, "I am shot right in my breast." That scared us, and we ran away up on the hill. It was daylight then.

1246. What day was this? I think it was on Wednesday morning.

1247. Do you know what the young man's name was who took off the hoop skirts? No, sir; it was a right young man, who looked as if he was 19 or 20 years old.

1248. Did he say anything? He made some remark; I did not hear what it was. He had the skirts on him, and they were dragging along. They all ran into Callahan's store. I saw, I should think, two hundred people right at Callahan's store. He came out with bottles and commenced treating them.

1249. Did you hear the crowd say anything? They said they would shoot them all. They said the next night they wanted to kill "these damned Yankee niggers." They called us "Yankee niggers." Some of them came and sat on our door-steps, and we heard them talk. They said the next night would be our turn; so we left the next mórning early. That morning, about 7 o'clock, Callahan had a pistol. There was nobody on the street making any disturbance, but he shot at everybody who came along. He said he wanted to kill the owner of that bar, (that was my brother-in-law,) and three or four more, and then he would be willing to die. A colored man came along to see a place that had been burned. He started to fire at him, but his brother took hold of him and took him in the house. He slept all that day and did not go out again.

1250. Why did they call you Yankee niggers? I do not know why they called us that way.

1251. Who was this colored girl they shot next door? A colored girl about twenty years old. They wanted to shoot her father. We gave them the key, so if the house was entered from the front they could get out the back door, and her father got away. They hunted under the bed and everywhere for a man. The woman said "there is no man here." He pointed the pistol at the mother first, and then drawed off and shot the girl. They knocked at the door first, and nobody answered. In a few minutes they broke in the door and then shot the girl.

1252. Did the girl say who they were? The girl said it looked like a policeman; one had a club in his hand.

1253. Where is this girl now? Up on Main street, about four squares from us.

By Mr. BROOMALL:

1254. Who were they that called you Yankee niggers? I do not know. They said we came from the north, and that we were no better than the niggers themselves; so my husband said we would move away.

1255. What was the reason of your moving? Because we were afraid. They said they wanted to kill my brother-in-law, the owner of the bar.

1256. Had you ever done them any harm? No, sir; we had only been here three months.

1257. Was it simply because you came from the north? My brother-in-law rents his saloon from Mr. Callahan, and Mr. Callahan does not like any one who came from the north.

1258. Is Callahan an Irishman? Yes.

1259. Do you know how long he has been here? I do not know. I guess he has been here a good while.

JOHN BEATTY sworn and examined.

By the CHAIRMAN:

1260. State your name. My name is John Beatty. They usually call me John Rommay.

1261. Why do they call you John Rommay? Because I came from Rome, I suppose. I am an Italian.

1262. How long have you been here? About seven months.

1263. Where did you live before you came here? I was discharged from the army. I have been in the 6th Illinois cavalry. I served three years and was discharged on account of wounds.

1264. Were you in Memphis during the riots? Yes, sir.

1265. What did you see of the riot? The first I knew of it I heard some hallooing on Main street. At that time there were some policemen just in front of my house. I kept a saloon on South street. At the time Recorder Creighton passed by in a buggy with another man. He ordered the policeman to see what was up. The policeman allowed that that did not belong to his beat. The recorder says, "I do not care a damn whether it is your beat or not, I want you to go there." They went on. As they passed by my house I heard a pistol fired; I could not say who it was. This was on the first of this month.

1266. Did you see anybody hurt that day? I saw some colored people. About half an hour after the beginning of the disturbance I saw a colored boy about fourteen years old hurt. His name is Joe Strickney. He was shot about one hundred yards from my house.

1267. Do you know any other case? After the boy was shot a large crowd from up town came down there. There were a good many policemen in it, as I could see by their stars, and they were shooting everybody. They seemed to be firing at random. They did not seem to be particular to see whether they were shooting the wrong man or not. I saw two soldiers shot; I do not know who they were; one was shot right on the bridge, about one hundred yards from my house, about the same place where I saw the boy. The other they shot right back about fifty yards from the bridge.

1268. Do you know who shot them? I do not. I saw a good many policemen and Irish, as I understood by their talking. I saw a good many, too, in rebel uniform.

1269. What was this crowd saying when they passed by? Nothing but hallooing, shooting, and going after the colored people.

By Mr. SHANKLIN:

1210. What time was that? When the fight began it was about 5 o'clock. I should say it was between 5 and 6 o'clock in the evening. I recollect the next night, when they set fire to a house right in front of my saloon, they shot through my door.

1211. What for? I do not know, unless it was because I had been in the United States army. They did not give us any chance to look out. My brother-in-law, the bar-tender and myself were bound to stay in the house. My sister-in-law and Mrs. Geary saw something, I believe. I heard them talking outside as if they were going to come in and rob me.

ADAM LOCK (colored) sworn and examined.

By the CHAIRMAN:

1212. How old are you? About sixty-seven.

1213. Where do you live? In Memphis.

1214. How long have you lived in Memphis? The last time I came here was about three or four years ago.

1215. What is your business? I do plastering or anything of that sort.

1216. Have you been a slave? I have.

1217. How long have you been free? You may say since the rebellion broke out. In fact, I hired myself out several years before.

1218. Had you a house in this city? Yes, I had four or five that I had put up myself.

1219. Where were you living at the time of the riot? On South street.

1220. Do you know anything of the mob in this city at that time; and, if so, state what you know of it? I know pretty much the beginning of it. I saw four policemen on Tuesday afternoon between 1 and 2 o'clock. These four policemen came on from towards sunrise, going towards sunset, on South street. There was a company of soldiers at the fort who came out and went down South street by the graveyard, keeping up a mighty racket. There was a great quantity of the crowd, some sixty or seventy altogether. They clustered up around the police, and were some considerable time talking and going on. I was some one hundred yards from them, standing and looking at them. The old man, Carroll, one of the policemen rather bore off, and took one of these soldiers and led him on back. They crossed the bridge down on South street, when one of the soldiers shot up, when one of the policemen whirled round and shot into the crowd of soldiers. These colored soldiers then fired at the policemen, struck one and he fell; I saw that. One colored man and two policemen picked him up and carried him into a saloon close by. In ten or fifteen minutes, it may be more than that, one policeman came across the street and met another soldier. What was said I do not know; but in a moment he was clubbing him and beating him over the head. He then turned him loose and shot him. He did not kill him. Shortly after that there was a crowd of these colored soldiers ran back and shot this policeman right at the next bridge. They killed that policeman. It was but very few minutes from the time the racket began when this second man was shot. I turned right back, went into my store and staid there considerable time. In an hour or an hour and a half a crowd came down out of town, and they shot and cut down colored men mightily. I saw them shoot one boy, I should think not more than twelve or thirteen years old. The boy came over and staid in my house an hour or such matter. In the time this boy was there the crowd came up the street, and pretty much clustered round my house. My son-in-law was in my house; he and I had been out whitewashing. These men came in my house and asked me what I was doing. I said I was not doing anything. They looked round and saw my son was lying across the bed. They snatched him out of bed, and said what are you doing? He said I am lying down. They said come out here. They snatched him out and took him into a cluster of white men. Some wanted to hit him on the head, some wanted to kill him, and some ordered them not to strike him.

1221. What is your son-in-law's name? Abram Means. They took him out on the same bridge where they shot the first policeman. They then let Abram go, and he came back.

1222. Who was it shot the white man? I saw a black man shoot him. I do not know who he was.

1223. Was he a soldier? He had on soldier's clothes.

1224. Did he shoot him with a pistol or gun? With a pistol; then for a while everything was silent. I thought they were through labor for that evening; there was no more disturbance that night. The next morning, from about ten to eleven o'clock, they were shooting and going on as bad as the night before.

1225. What was done at that time? There were several colored men, perhaps a dozen, I know more than half a dozen colored men, were shot and fell.

1226. What were they doing when they were shot? They were struggling to get out of the way.

1227. Who were they shot by? By white citizens; I do not think any were shot by policemen; the policemen seemed to be, at this time, behind. On Wednesday night they were firing houses, and my house was fired. About three o'clock in the afternoon they fired a school-house within eight or ten feet of my house; I had to knock off that side of my house. My son and some other colored men and some white men knocked it off, and the women drew water and turned on until the fire got too hot for them to stand it. There were four men on top of my house; the roof was burnt pretty well, but I saved my house that night. After the school-house was burned down, I had my house fixed up again that same evening. After a while some gentleman came there and I asked him if he thought it was safe for us to stay there that night. I had my things all carried out into the yard. Said he, "Old man, I do not think there will be any more trouble, you had better put your things back in the house." I put my things back, but tied them up in blankets and sheets. All through the course of the night there were fires burning all around us. There was a room in the house I had rented to a colored soldier in the fort; his wife had left and gone to her husband in the fort between eleven and twelve o'clock. That room was broken open, and about a dozen times they were passing back and forwards in it. By-and-by I heard some one tramping outside; they piled up some planks and stuff against my house and set it on fire; when I looked out it was blazing up as high as my head, as high as I could reach. I went out and threw a bucket of water on the fire, and they shot right against the place where I was standing. I went round the house and it was nothing but one shooting right against my house all the while, I then went in, got my things and carried them away about thirty yards from the house; when I saw a man put fire to my house and kindle it a second time. Said he, "Old man, pull off your hat and lie down or they will kill you." Said I, "Massa George, what is the reason you are burning my house down? I want to live where I am living as well as anybody else." This was George McGinn. Said he, "I am ordered to do it, and I must or they will shoot me." I said to him that he was one of the men doing it for himself, and that I had some valuable things for a colored man, and I wanted to go there and get them. "No" said he, "stay right where you are." In about a couple of minutes a man walked up to us and said, "Leave there, damn quick." There were about half a dozen standing around; we went off about one hundred yards, and had not been standing there ten minutes, when they broke open my trunk and took out the things.

1228. Who were they? George McGinn, Mr. Callahan, and several others; I do not know their names.

By Mr. SHANKLIN:

1229. Were any of these policemen? No; there were no policemen in the crowd.
1230. Were they Irishmen? Yes, sir; they lived right in the near neighborhood.
1231. How are they employed? George McGinn has a little grocery, and Mr. Callahan has a grocery store, a large building.
1232. Do you know anything about a colored girl being shot? Yes, sir; she was shot in my yard between my house and her mother's house; my own son Abram saw her fall. In a minute three or four shots were fired right against the door. She had been shot half an hour or more before the fire came near enough to catch her clothes.
1233. Was she alive? No, sir; she never moved after she was shot. This Callahan, shortly before the girl was shot, came and proposed to take away her father and mother, and sister and sister's husband—as much as to take them out of trouble. Then they came back and plundered the house and set it on fire. The fire from her mother's house first caught a white handkerchief she had round her face, then her clothes caught on fire, but she never moved.
1234. What was she doing when she was shot? She was going from my house to her mother's house; she had been to my house to help me get out my things.
1234. When they were firing at your house was it for the purpose of shooting you all in it? I thought they meant to burn us all up in it.
1235. How did you get out? I had a door that had been nailed up, and chopped it open.
1236. Was your house surrounded by people that were firing? Pretty much.
1237. Do you think if you had not got out the people there would have let you burn? I have no doubt about it.
1238. How large was the crowd about your house? Some four or five apparently were on the front side and four on the other side.
1239. Can you say who they were? No more than that Callahan on one side appeared to command the company, and George McGinn on the other.
1240. Have you had any difficulty with them before? No, sir; except that about four years ago Mr. Callahan and me differed. He got me to haul about sixteen cords of wood; he measured it before it was hauled, and measured it again after it was hauled, and said it did not hold out. He would not pay me, and I went to the provost marshal and made him pay me. After that he struck me in the back part of the head and knocked me down; he was brought up for that; since that time I have worked for him time and time again and never had any other difficulty.
1241. Do you know of any other acts of violence that took place? There was a fellow I rented a room to by the name of Minter; I do not know his other name; they shot him in bed, rolled him about there, and took everything of value in his house.
1242. How badly did they shoot him? They shot him about the hand somewhere and then cut him in the side with a knife.

By Mr. SHANKLIN:

1242. Were you present when the shooting of Minter was done? I was not present, but I was right close by so as to hear the shooting.
1243. Do you know whether Minter knew who did it? He said this same man, John Callahan; that he pulled open the window and he came in.
1244. How soon did you see him after he was shot? I saw him in ten or fifteen minutes afterwards.
1245. How much did you lose? I could not say how much; I had put up two snug little buildings there, about twelve by thirteen, since Christmas, and I had put up three others; they have all been burned. I think my little buildings and other stuff was richly worth $1,500. I am now left without anything, with a family of one child of my own; my wife also has a child, and my daughter has a child.

HENRY ALEXANDER (colored) sworn and examined.

By the CHAIRMAN:

1246. Where do you live? In Memphis.
1247. How old are you? About thirty-six.
1248. What is your business? I am a blacksmith.
1249. Were you in Memphis at the time of the riots? Yes, sir.
1250. Did you see anything of them? No, sir; I did not see anything at all.
1251. Did you lose any property? Yes; my shop on Alabama street was burnt.
1252. What were the circumstances of its being burned? I do not know; I only know it was burned; I was at home, in bed and asleep.
1253. Who burned it, and what was it burned for? I do not know.
1254. How much did you lose? I do not know exactly; me and my partner I think lost $400 or $500; in fact I would not have taken $300 for my part.
1255. Who is your partner? George Jones.
1256. Was he in the shop? No; he was at home.

1257. Who were in the shop ?   Two colored men, Billy Coe and Billy Fuzzle.
1258. Did they get out without difficulty ?   Billy Fuzzle got out without their seeing him. Billy Coe had a talk with them.

SAMUEL DILTS sworn and examined.

By the CHAIRMAN :

1259. Where is your residence ?   Memphis.
1260. How long have you resided here ?   Over four years.
1261. Where did you live before you came here ?   I was in the army ; I went into the army from Illinois, and was out four months.
1262. Were you in Memphis at the time of the recent riots ?   Yes, sir.
1263. Did you see anything of them ; and if so, state what you saw ?   The first knowledge I had of it was on Tuesday, when I saw men running down Main street to the old cemetery.
1264. Had you seen any trouble before on Tuesday ?   On Monday I saw some trouble right across the street from my house.   I saw three or four negroes coming towards Causey street ; four policemen were there on the street ; they had some little talk ; the negroes were going south, and some difficulty occurred between them.   Then I noticed a policeman pick up the barrel of his pistol, and I saw that he had the butt of it in his hand.   The women said he had struck the negro over his head ; I did not see it, but I saw the negro going off with his head bleeding.   The first I saw on Tuesday was some men coming down Main street ; I did not know what the trouble was.   In the course of a short time I saw a policeman come up Causey street, that I knew.   I asked him what was the trouble down there.   The policeman said no matter ; I had better go up and keep in the house, and said something about the damned niggers—I could not understand.   In about an hour there came down a crowd of citizens armed with guns, pistols, and other weapons.   I should judge there were about all the policemen in town, and a good many citizens of what I call the lower class ; a majority of them certainly were.   When they were about opposite my house, they said there goes a damned nigger ; shoot him ; they shot him down.   I got up and went out ; by the time I got to where the street turns, the shots came up my way pretty thick, and I said to myself it is hardly worth while to set myself up as a target, and went back to the house.   The shots came from policemen and white citizens ; the negroes were running in every direction.
1265. Did you see any one killed ?   I do not know of any one being killed ; I saw one man shot and lying there ; several men went up to him.

By Mr. SHANKLIN :

1266. What time in the evening was that ?   It was between four and five o'clock, or somewhere along there.   It was not earlier than three nor later than five o'clock ; there was a great deal of shooting, but I saw no one shot.
1267. What became of this negro ?   I do not know ; I did not go to him.
1268. Was he left there long ?   I do not know how long ; he was there a few minutes. The crowd was so strong that I kept out of the way.
1269. What was the character of the conversation of this crowd ?   It was, "Kill every damn nigger, shoot him."   I saw right opposite my house one old negro who, I think, is a preacher ; he was coming along and meeting a crowd started to go down to a stable right opposite to my house.   He came to an alley and turned right into the crowd.   A policeman halted him and said, "You damned black nigger, come out, come out."   The old man walked out to the middle of the street and the crowd passed him.   At the same time he was coming out, I saw a negro in employ at a government stable ; he was through his day's work and was coming home, terribly scared.   He saw me at the gate and called to me, "Let me in, let me in," and passed me.   A policeman pointed his pistol to him and said, "Go in there and stay there, or I will blow your God damned brains out."   The pistol was pointed right at my face, although he was talking to the negro.   I could not help noticing the fact, that on one side of the street the men had their pistols cocked and pointed at a man to prevent him from going into an alley, while this one was doing the same thing to keep a man from coming out.   Then I could hear them say, "There goes a damned nigger, shoot him."   That was about all I heard.
1270. Did you hear them use any threats against white people ?   No, I do not think they did ; I did not hear it from my house.   I could hear shots fired and bullets hitting houses close by.   I saw them running through the bayous, where the negroes were, in almost every direction.

WILLIAM H. BRAZIER sworn and examined.

By the CHAIRMAN :

1271. What is your residence and business ?   My residence is Memphis ; I am in the Ætna insurance business.
1272. How long have you been in Memphis ?   Only since January.
1273. From what part of the country did you come ?   From southern Illinois latterly, formerly from Chicago.

1274. Were you in Memphis at the time of the recent riots ? Yes, sir.

1275. Have you any personal knowledge of the facts, and, if so, what ? I was personally on the ground on the evening of the first day, I think it was Tuesday, about six o'clock. I was standing on the corner of South and Causey streets. There was a great deal of commotion and a great deal of shooting all around in every direction.

1276. Shooting by whom ? The shooting was by white persons, all that I saw.

1277. Were the white persons suppressing a mob ? They professed to be suppressing a mob. It was reported that the negroes were armed in large numbers and were about to make a charge upon the whites, and I retreated ; but I recovered myself and went back to the ground. When I got back I heard considerable firing. I saw a negro lying there and was informed that he had been shot within two or three minutes.

1278. Was he killed ? He was dead when I left him. He was in a dying condition when I saw him. Do not know what his name was. He was a federal soldier, as his uniform indicated. He denied vigorously having anything to do with the riot.

1279. What did the crowd say ? I heard such remarks as "It is good enough for you, you God damned son of a bitch." It was charged that he was one of the instigators of the riot. He denied it vigorously.

1280. Do you know how long he lived ? Only a few minutes. He had one shot through the head and one through the breast.

1281. Did you see any other man shot, or any acts of violence ? Immediately after hearing these remarks in reference to this dying man, they called a hackman to take his hack down a few squares below to get a policeman who they said had been wounded. The hackman went down there, and I followed on. They got the wounded policeman and put him in the hack. They arrested a negro there having the federal uniform on and attempted to put him in the hack, but some one said, " Don't put the God damned nigger in, he will murder him." Then they pushed him back and attempted to shoot him, but there was such a crowd they could not do it with safety, and they carried him to the station-house.

1282. Did you say he had a federal uniform on ? He had on blue pants ; whether he had on a blue coat I do not recollect. This was on Tuesday evening, between six and seven o'clock.

1283. Did you see the wounded policeman in the hack ? I saw them carry him away. I was then within, perhaps, twenty steps of him. That was all I saw that evening. The next morning I went down to the corner of South and Main streets, and was on the ground there some time. There was a large crowd congregated, citizens and police. The city mayor was there. There was a good deal of disturbance. The negroes down there had gathered together in the neighborhood of the fort, perhaps some little distance outside the fort. They appeared to be drawn up there. I was standing on the ground some time, and there was considerable firing in all directions in the neighborhood of South street.

1284. By whom was this firing ? It was mostly by white persons.

1285. Who were they firing at ? I do not know. I supposed they were firing at random and indiscriminately, and at negroes in the neighborhood.

1286. Were the negroes in the neighborhood of the fort negro soldiers ? I supposed they were ; I could not tell at that distance whether they were soldiers or not. This was about ten o'clock in the morning.

1287. What further took place ? There appeared to be three or four shots fired from the direction of the fort, one of which struck close by me and one whistled past close to my head. The crowd remained there until noon, doing nothing apparently, but appeared to be very much excited. There were various reports about the soldiers in the fort, that they had given up their arms to the negroes, and many appeared to believe that was the case. I saw a man who came out of the fort, and he told me himself the white soldiers had given up their arms.

1288. What did this crowd do ? Their determination seemed to be to get hold of negroes and kill them. That appeared to be, apparently, their only object. There was a little negro boy about fifty or sixty yards from the corner of South and Main streets ; I saw a white man bring him out, shoving him ahead right in front of him. The crowd cried out, " Shoot him." The negro threw up his hand and said something I did not hear, The man having hold of him started back, apparently with the intention of shooting at him. The negro ran in the direction of a shanty and was shot at a dozen times before he reached it. I do not know whether he was hit at all, though by the way he ran I thought he was wounded. He went out of sight, they running after him ; and I suppose he was killed, for it was impossible for him to get away.

1289. What was the character of this crowd you speak of ? It was a mixed crowd of citizens. The Irish element seemed to predominate.

1290. Was it what is called a posse ? I do not know ; the mayor was there.

1291. What was the mayor doing ? He was standing there inactive ; he did not seem to have any conception of what the condition of things was.

1292. What was his condition ? I do not know just at that time ; I saw him a few hours before, as I thought, very badly intoxicated.

1293. Did you see any mob except the police and posse ? It all seemed to be in the nature of a mob more than anything else.

1294. Did you see any negroes except those at the fort? Yes, occasionally I would see some negroes going apparently about their own business.

1295. Were they orderly, or were they kicking up a disturbance? I saw nothing hostile upon the part of the negroes at all from first to last. Immediately after, there was another man brought out of some of the huts down there; there were four or five persons, apparently, bringing him out. I saw one man take him by the back of the neck and push him forward; another strike him with the breech of his gun and knock him down on his face; there were then some five or six shots fired at him after he was down.

1296. Where did the crowd then go? I do not know; I left very soon after I saw this last murder. I left before the crowd did. I had business in the town, and saw nothing further.

1297. Can you identify any policeman who was committing acts of violence or outrage? I do not think I could. There was one man I have seen in the last three weeks. I do not know whether he was a policeman or not I know he was with the crowd, and I think, certainly, that he was the man who knocked the negro in the back of the head.

1298. Do you know his name? No, I do not; he is an Irishman.

1299. Did you hear any speeches made to the crowd at that time? No; I did not.

1300. Did you see Recorder Creighton? I saw him on the ground somewhere, but I forget whether it was Wednesday or Tuesday evening.

1301. What was he doing? He was quiet when I saw him; I think this was on Wednesday morning. I think if there had been no hostility on the part of the whites there would have been none that day. There was quite a crowd, perhaps 1,500 people there. The negroes were then a quarter of a mile off.

By Mr. SHANKLIN:

1302. You only saw the conclusion of the fight on Tuesday evening as I understand? I did not see the first part of it.

1303. Did you see any negroes on Tuesday evening shooting towards the police or anybody else? No, sir.

1304. On Wednesday morning when you saw the negroes outside the fort, apparently drawn up in a line, how many shots were fired from that direction in the direction of the crowd? There were three or four shots from that direction.

1305. Do you know whether it was negroes or white men who fired these shots? I do not.

1306. Did you see any white men in this crowd? The distance was so great I could not have distinguished them if there had been any. The shots came from that direction. I do not think there were more than four shots.

1307. Did you see more than one white man wounded on Tuesday or Wednesday? No, sir; not that I know.

1308. How many negroes did you see that had been wounded or killed? I suppose I saw a dozen on Tuesday afternoon.

1309. Were you near the parties when they were shooting at these negroes, any of them? I was within twenty steps, perhaps, where one of the parties was shot.

1310. Did you make any effort to prevent him from being shot? No, I did not. I made the remark that it was damned barbarous to shoot a man in that way. There were two or three men standing near by, who looked round very savagely at me and remarked "It is right," or something of that kind. This reminded me of the fact that I had better take my own personal safety into consideration, and I did not make any further remarks.

1311. How many persons do you think were in the mob on Tuesday afternoon? It would be mere guess-work. They were strung along over a large distance. There were a thousand or more.

1312. Were all the persons you saw there taking part in the disturbance? No, sir; many were looking on.

1313. How many do you suppose were taking part in the violence and outrage? I do not know; it would be mere guess-work. The whole crowd seemed to be encouraging those who were acting, or seemed to be indorsing their proceeding. At least I came to that conclusion from the remarks I heard all around me.

1314. On Wednesday what do you think was the extent of white persons participating in the acts of violence and outrage? I should think, perhaps, there was a thousand or fifteen hundred gathered about South street. The most of them were mere lookers-on. The idea seemed to be that they all had one purpose in view, referring to the blacks down at the fort.

1315. How many do you think there were of these blacks on Wednesday congregated at the fort? It looked to me as though there were four or five hundred.

1316. Were they all armed? I could not see whether any of them were armed at that distance.

1317. Did they continue there the whole time this crowd you speak of remained on the ground? Yes, sir.

1318. They did not attempt to approach the crowd, or the crowd them? No, sir; no attempt was made to bring on a collision.

By Mr. BROOMALL:

1319. What has been the behavior here of the negroes for the past few months? I never have seen any bad behavior on the part of the blacks. My business has been in every part of the city. I have met negroes drunk and sober, but I have never seen any bad behavior. I have been in localities where there was nothing but blacks, but I have never seen a negro who did not give me the sidewalk, or who offered any offensive remarks at all.

DAVID T. EGBERT sworn and examined.

By the CHAIRMAN:

1320. State your residence and business? I have been living in Memphis for the last six months. I was keeping a saloon at the time of the riots. I then closed up my saloon, and have since been working at my trade as a carpenter.
1321. Where did you live before the war? In Fulton county, Illinois.
1322. Have you been in the army? I have—as sutler.
1323. Were you here at the time of the riots? I was.
1324. State what you know, if anything, that took place? On the morning of Tuesday a large crowd of citizens went down St. Martin street and went by my saloon. I closed up and went down as far as Vance and St. Martin streets. The crowd of police and citizens were running back with pistols, shot-guns, and other things. After the crowd got by, I stopped some one on the corner and asked what was the matter. They said if I'd go up there I'd see what was the matter; that the negroes were shooting everybody. I did not see any negroes at all. They said I must know something about it. I told them I did not think there was any danger; that I was not afraid to go up there. One of them said to me, "You are a damned abolition son-of-a-bitch." I said I am not; I have just come up here to see what was going on. One person who wore gray clothes hauled out his pistol—an army or navy revolver. I did not say anything. They kept on cursing me for a while and then went up Main street. My landlord and some other citizens remarked to me about noon that they looked every moment for my head to be shot off.
1325. What was the language they used towards you? I have stated about the substance of it; they abused me as an abolitionist.
1326. Did they say anything as to what was going to be done with the abolitionists? No. After cursing me a little they said they were going up Main street where the fight was going on.
1327. Did they say they were going to clean out the Yankees? They said they were going to clean out the negroes, but said nothing at all about the Yankees. My landlord said they were going to clean the negroes all out; that they would clean them all out by the next day. This was on Wednesday, I think. At all events, it was on the next day after the commencement. The policemen had some fuss on South street that day.
1328. What did these men seem to have against you? Nothing more than what I remarked. The only thing I said was, that I was not afraid to go up there; that I did not think there was any danger.
1329. Did these men you saw in gray appear to be rebel soldiers? I think they were. I saw one of them the other day. The other one, who had two pistols, I did not know at all. I was going to meet the crowd when these policemen and citizens met the crowd going down.
1330. Did you see any acts of violence committed on anybody? I saw one black man shortly after he was shot on Beal street near Main.
1331. Who shot him? I do not know. A large crowd of policemen and citizens had passed up a short time before.
1332. Do you know who the black man was? I do not.
1333. Do you know anything else connected with the riots? Only that my landlord remarked that they had threatened me, and did not want me in his building; that he did not want his building burnt. I asked him what I had done. He said no matter; that he had it from pretty good authority that it was not safe for me to remain there.
1334. What was your landlord's name? A. N. Edmonds. A grocery keeper opposite warned me not to get any more goods in. He said I had better not stop in that neighborhood; that they had me spotted, and it wouldn't be safe for me to remain. His name was John Metcalf.
1335. Was this said in a friendly spirit? Yes, sir; I think it was in a friendly spirit. I remained for about three-quarters of an hour, and went up towards Main street shortly after the crowd had left. In the course of the night I heard some one at my saloon door say "Hisht." I did not make any reply. The next morning I was over to the grocery store, and the man asked me if I had heard anything during the night. I told him I did. He said that was him; that he came there to warn me to keep out of the way; that these parties were at his house. He asked me if I saw anybody around there. I told him I did not. Mr. Edmonds said I had a good deal of negro trade, and that was the reason why I was in danger. I did not open my saloon after that.

By Mr. SHANKLIN:

1336. Was this conversation by the crowd the next day after the shooting? Yes, sir.

1337. Was it the evening of the first burning? Yes, sir; there had been no burning up to that time. It was the morning after the policeman was shot.

1338. Had you been in the habit of selling liquor to negroes in that saloon? Yes, sir. Since the latter part of January I have sold to black and white, but I did not begin to have the liquor trade that others in the neighborhood had; they sold at 10 cents a drink; I sold at 15 cents.

By Mr. BROOMALL:

1339. Have you ever seen any disorder on the part of the negroes here? No, sir; I have never seen anything of the kind to my knowledge.

JOHN OLDRIDGE sworn and examined.

By the CHAIRMAN:

1340. State your residence and business. I live in Memphis, and have no business at present.

1341. How long have you lived in Memphis? Since the beginning of 1858.

1342. Where did you live before you came here? I came from Iowa.

1343. Were you here during the rebellion? I was here all through.

1344. Were you conscripted? No; I managed to wriggle out of it.

1345. Were you in Memphis during the recent riot? Yes, sir.

1346. Did you see any of the disturbances? Yes, sir. On Tuesday afternoon, on the 1st of May, my attention was called to several shots being fired close to my neighborhood, a short distance from me. I think about five o'clock I saw Mr. Creighton, the recorder, and Mr. Hays, a lieutenant colonel of a Fenian regiment, right by my house, very much excited. Shortly after that a son of the Rev. Mr. Pearne came into my house and said he came right from South street and the negroes were being killed there. About six o'clock in the same evening I went down to South street, walked around a good deal, and staid some time at the corner of South and Main streets. I saw a negro lying dead on the sidewalk. I knew him well; his name was Eli—a yellow man—a well-behaved, inoffensive man. An Irishwoman told me he was shot close to his own door. I understood that a policeman shot him, but I have no proof of the fact. I went on through the old graveyard. I met Colonel Ryder, United States marshal, and we went around together. I saw two other bodies lying in the vicinity of the graveyard. It became dark and I went home. On Wednesday morning at about eleven o'clock, as I was going up town with my wife, I saw a great excitement on Main street, and thought it prudent to take my wife back, which I did. I then went down by the fort, and the first thing I met a policeman I know very well, drunk, with a revolver in his hand; his star shone out very conspicuously. I heard him say that, if he could get twenty men as good as he, he would go to the fort and take every damned nigger in the crowd. He was the most disorderly man I saw. Shortly after that I met John Park, the mayor, making an ass of himself, and drunk. He was going to straighten out the whole thing, but he did not make any effort to do it. He was telling the people to let it alone; that he would make it all right; but he didn't make any effort to make it right.

1347. Who did Park appear to be with; with policemen and posse? With Charles S. Cameron, a lawyer here.

1348. What was Mr. Cameron doing? He was just like Park, both about three-fourths drunk.

1349. How many people were there about at this time? There was a great crowd; I really could not give an estimate of their numbers.

1350. What was the crowd composed of? They were generally citizens looking on. I think the greater part of them, like myself, were drawn there by curiosity to see what was going on. On going away from there my attention was drawn to a negro man lying dead near the railroad, who had been shot in five or six places. Henry W. Taylor, a painter, told me he saw the man shot, and there was never a more deliberate murder; that the man was doing nothing.

1351. How many acts of violence did you see committed? I saw no acts of violence such as shooting, as it had all been done before I got there.

1352. How many did you see engaged in acts of violence? I saw none Wednesday morning because it was all done before I got there. Wednesday night when the burning took place I took a walk with the Rev. Mr. Pearne, who was boarding with me, and as we passed the corner of Hernando and Vance streets I saw a negro church which had been set on fire. A fire at that time on Echols street was burning very brilliantly. We left and went over on Echols street, but by the time we got there the building was nearly all consumed. When we came back near Grace church—a negro church there—it was also nearly consumed. I saw there Sheriff Winters with a lot of ragamuffins, some of them boys, with a lot of shot-guns. Mr. Creighton and others were there, and all appeared to be drunk, with the exception of Winters. I believe he was the only sober man in the crowd. His posse appeared to be very drunk and excited. There was no attempt made to put the fire out; the whole crowd appeared to be having a regular jubilee. A great many knew me, and I thought at the time it was not safe for me to be there. There was a man there by the name of O'Hearn, a constable, who made a proposition to me in 1861 to take an oath to the southern confederacy. I refused, and never did, and the result was that nearly all my goods were taken away from me in August, 1861. This O'Hearn took them.

1353. Was Creighton in this last crowd? Yes, sir; he was blowing around there, and appeared to be three parts drunk.

1354. Did you see Charles Cameron again? I did not see him that night, nor any time, except Wednesday morning, when he was with the mayor; they were going around arm in arm together. I came back down Hernando street and walked up Vance street to my house on Shelby street. We passed some negro quarters on the corner of Vance and Main. I remarked that I would bet any money they would be burnt up that night. I went in my house, lit my pipe, and came down the street near twelve o'clock. I met two of Sheriff Winters's posse on Vance, between Shelby and Main; one of them was formerly a police officer; I know him well; he halted me on Vance, between Shelby and Main; when they saw me they said, "Oh! is this you, Mr. Oldridge?" I remarked, "Is that you, Kane?" I said it was an outrage to destroy property that way, and that I didn't know where it would stop. I took the ground that if a negro was to blame he should be punished, but that to shoot men down and burn property was a devilish outrage. He took the opposite ground, and argued the point. The crowd came up. He told me I'd better not go away alone; that the crowd might halt me. My impression was, and always will be, that this man came up with the crowd and was with them in what they were doing. I came along down and met O'Hearn with sixteen others; none of them had guns or rifles, but every man was armed with one or more revolvers. O'Hearn knew me; he came up and spoke to me. I kept very quiet; I had a pistol in my pocket, but I did not wish for the necessity of using it. I saw O'Hearn call off three or four of the party, and, after some consultation in the street, he went with two others to the northeast corner of that negro school-house. I saw him pile up some matter and strike a match; when he struck the match I saw the reflection on his face as plain as I see you now. I waited until it burnt up. The first fire went out. The noise of the crowd drew the attention of a man who lived in a cottage adjoining; he came out and begged them not to put fire to the building; that it would burn his cottage. O'Hearn called out, "Shoot the God damn son of a bitch; if he comes out I'll shoot him myself." The man then went back towards his cottage. O'Hearn called out, "If they burn your property we will pay for it; keep in your cottage." Then O'Hearn and three or four others set fire to the building the second time. Two regulars then came down Main street; one, I think, was a tall man and the other short; the shorter one, I think, remarked, "Here's a fire; it's a damn shame to burn a fine building like that." Said he, "I'll just go and kick it out," and started to go and do it. An Irishman in the crowd called him back. Fires were then burning very brightly down Main street. Said he, "You see those fires there? You just go there and let us manage this." They went out Vance street, and no attempts were made to put out the fire. One end of it was on fire. I saw them go two-thirds down the building, beat in a window, throw in some matter from the outside, and set it on fire. The partition was also broken down to allow free vent, and the whole building was soon in flames. While it was burning, a policeman, a tall man, an Irishman, named John Mickey, had on a federal overcoat, and had a revolver in his hand. I heard him say, "May the mon that sit that on fire niver be sick. God bless him," said he, "that is the only place I've had to say me prayers for the last three months, and divil the place have I now; I'll have to say me prayers on the sidewalk."

1355. O'Hearn belonged to Sheriff Winters's posse, did he? I could not say whether he belonged to the posse or not; he took a very active part; and I should say that he belonged to the posse.

1356. Did this man attempt to keep the peace, or did he belong to the posse? My impression is that Kane and the other man I met, armed with shot-guns, were the advance guard, to clear the way in firing buildings. I may remark, that when this church was burned, and this man came out of his cottage and asked them not to burn the church, because his cottage would be burned, the owners of the cottage drew water to save it. I walked around, near by, and recognized a great many boys, and one young man, named Dare, who has since been shot. It is supposed he was shot by negroes, on Madison street. I saw him draw water and throw over this man's cottage; he appeared to take an active part in endeavoring to save it. With Wm. O'Hearn, and his Irish crowd, I saw no American. Sydney Dare took no part with them.

1357. What further took place? I do not know anything further. I waited there until the whole building was burned, and saw no effort made to save it.

1358. Do you know the names of any of these parties, except O'Hearn? No, sir; I did not know many: several of them had their faces dirtied and blackened up for the occasion; they appeared to be regularly organized. O'Hearn called out, "No. Ones! fall in." As I heard their conversation, I understood they were going to burn Caldwell Hall. I heard them say they were going to burn "every nigger building, every nigger church, and every God damn son of a bitch that taught a nigger." The question was asked, who was the editor of the Post; and somebody said Joe Clouston, who lives in South Memphis; another said it was a damned lie; but if they had the editor of the Post there they would put him in the middle of the fire.

1359. What were they going to burn Caldwell Hall for? Because it was used as a negro church and school.

1360. Did you hear any threats of burning the Post building? Nothing more than I have said.

By Mr. SHANKLIN:

1361. How many were there in the crowd with O'Hearn? There were sixteen with his party.

1362. Did you say they appeared to be organized? Yes, thoroughly organized; when O'Hearn called out, "No. Ones, fall in," they did so as orderly as possible.

By Mr. BROOMALL:

1363. Have you observed the behavior of the negroes for the past three months, and if so, what has it been? I have; it has been peaceable unless they have had too much whiskey aboard.

1364. They have shown no disposition to be disorderly? No, sir; none other but peaceable.

By Mr. SHANKLIN:

1365. Has there not been for some time a bad feeling between the rabble of Memphis and the negroes? There has been to some extent; I do not think it has been as bad as represented; I have not seen it.

Dr. R. W. CREIGHTON sworn and examined.

By the CHAIRMAN:

1366. Please state your residence and profession? I live in Memphis, and am a physician and surgeon.

1367. How long have you lived in Memphis? About twenty years.

1368. Have you been here during the war? Yes, sir; I've been practicing my profession all the time, serving in the Union hospitals since the federal occupation of the city. I gave my services gratuitously.

1369. Were you here during the recent riots? Yes, sir.

1370. Have you any knowledge of what took place? I have of their consequences; I saw but little of the riot. I dressed the wounds of four men in my office. I think it was on the first of May, in the evening, that I was in my back office socially, when a hack drove up and two policemen came running in with their pistols cocked. They told me there had been, as they expressed it, "a hell of a fight on South street," with the niggers. One of them said his cousin had been killed, and, said he, I have brought him here for you to doctor him. Said I, "I thought you said he was killed." He said "no," and brought him in. He had a little bit of a flesh wound on his finger and was making great lamentations and complaints. The man was very much excited; I told him to uncock his pistol; he seemed to be perfectly frenzied, and said, "I'm going out to kill a nigger." He ran out, cocked his pistol, and shot at the first negro he saw. I called Dr. Irwin who was there to see it, and remarked "it was an outrage." I was very sorry I did not take his number.

1371. Who was the man he shot? He was a quiet fellow just returning from his day's work as I supposed; he had all the implements of the whitewashing business about him.

1372. Was the man killed? No, he was not hurt, but the policeman shot at him; there were ten or twelve policemen around my office. In the mean time three more hacks came up and two more wounded policemen came into my office, and two citizens who were accidentally wounded. The name of one of the policemen was Slatterly; he was carried into my office by four policemen, apparently badly wounded in both thighs; there were two wounds, one in each thigh. I examined the wounds, found they were merely flesh wounds, and told him to go home, giving directions how to care for the wounds. He was carried into my office, but walked out of it on my assurance that he was not badly wounded. The policemen were very much excited, and they would have killed any negro man they saw.

1373. What became of Slatterly? He was carried home and got well. I was called upon that night in a consultation with Dr. Irwin and Dr. Keller to see a policemen by the name of Stevens, who was mortally wounded. He was shot in the upper third of the thigh, the course of the ball having been backwards and downwards. My impression was, and has been since I saw him, that he was not shot by a negro, nor by anybody else but himself. We asked him how far he was from the crowd firing at him; he said about thirty yards; that he fell through a bridge and was shot at exactly that time. From the direction of the wound, it could not have been fired except from a vertical position. I named it to the gentlemen with me in consultation. Dr. Irwin agreed with me; Dr. Keller thought he was shot by a negro It made no difference, however, in the man's life, the wound was fatal. We could not find the ball, but in putting my finger into the wound I had to follow it longitudinally; the ball could not have taken that course without having been fired from a vertical position; another reason I had was that the wound seemed to be powder-marked.

1374. Did you call the attention of Dr. Keller to that fact? Yes; the doctor said the man was an Irishman, and so dirty that you could not tell whether the portion blackened was caused by powder or not: it was the only black spot on his leg, and was just such as would be made by a powder burn.

1375. How was Slatterly shot? They said he was shot from the fort; he must have been shot at long range. I dressed the wounds of a fourth man, one of the lookers-on; he was just kicked by a horse.

1376. Did you dress the wounds of any colored man? No, sir; I did not see any colored wounded; I heard divers rumors about the colored wounded and killed; they were so contradictory that I placed very little reliance upon them. The next day I heard a policeman remark, who I thought would be likely to know how many were killed, that he counted, on a single acre, forty dead negroes. I asked him if he was telling the truth; just at that time a man came along, and the policeman asked him how many negroes he saw dead. The man said he had been all over the field and only saw two. The policeman told him he was a damned liar, and drew his pistol. I told him I didn't want any such conduct in my presence.

1377. Did you believe him when he told you he saw forty? I did not; though at the time I believed he had more information than any outsider could be possessed of. When this man told me he had surveyed the entire ground and had counted forty, I presumed he had seen them, although I thought there must have been a pretty big skirmish to have forty men left on a single acre.

1378. You saw no acts of violence yourself? None at all; except what I've mentioned, seeing the policeman shoot this negro.

J. M. RANDOLPH sworn and examined.

By the CHAIRMAN:

1379. What's your residence and business? My residence is Memphis; I am a photograph operator, though not following my occupation at the present time.

1380. Were you here during the time of the riots? Yes, sir.

1381. State what you know in relation thereto? I do not know a great deal; I saw a great deal generally, but I do not know the names of persons. I saw some policemen shot down, and one colored man; several shot the colored man after he was down; one policeman went up and shot him in the back as he lay on his face.

1382. What was the negro doing? He was running, a great crowd after him crying "Shoot him, shoot him;" he was running down South street. I saw him at the time he fell, and I saw him a few seconds after, moving as if in the agonies of death. Another policeman came up, turned him over and shot him in the back.

1383. How near to him did you go? I did not go nearer than twenty yards from him; I thought I might get into a fuss myself; the whole crowd seemed to be running that way. Occasionally a policeman would catch a little darkey and jerk him across the sidewalk. Then as I came back on Beal street, below Second, there was a colored man in a store; the crowd gathered round him as he came out; he was trying to get them to let him go; he said he had done nothing; they were beating him over the head. I knew well enough they were going to shoot him and turned my face away; they did shoot him a moment afterwards. One of the persons beating him was a policeman; I do not know whether the other was or not, as there are a great many police who do not wear the badge.

1384. Did you hear the mob make any threats to anybody? I did not.

1385. Did you see any other negroes shot or maltreated? I saw none shot, but a good many maltreated.

1386. Maltreated in what way? Such as catching them by the head or throat and jerking them off the sidewalk.

1387. Were the negroes misbehaving? No; they were going along quietly, and seemed to be entirely innocent. The negro I saw in the store, I think they said, was a working man.

TUESDAY, *May* 29, 1866.

Dr. ROBERT McGOWAN sworn and examined.

By the CHAIRMAN:

1388. State your residence and profession? I live in Memphis and keep a drug store.

1389. How long have you lived in Memphis? About twelve months.

1390. Have you been in the United States service? Yes, sir.

1391. How long? Since I came to the country from the north of Ireland, which is about three and a half years.

1392. Were you in Memphis during the recent riots. I was.

1393. Did you see anything of it, and if so, state what you saw? I heard shots fired as I was sitting in my store on the first of May. I saw a crowd of colored soldiers there, and saw some police running after them; the police were coming across the bridge when one of them was shot down. Another policeman was shot on Causey street. I was called upon to attend this policeman who was shot, and went down and saw him. He was carried into a house on Causey street; he had been shot through the leg.

1394. Was he afterwards taken to Dr. Creighton's office? I think he was taken home; he died subsequently.

1395. Did you see his wounds? Yes: he had a compound fracture of the thigh-bone. About the time I was dressing his wounds, the policemen came back again, a whole lot of them, accompanied by citizens, and commenced an indiscriminate slaughter of all they could find on the streets. I saw a colored soldier killed on the bridge by a policeman.

1396. Did the policemen and posse make an assault upon the colored soldiers drawn up and in arms or inoffensive citizens? They were innocent people; they made an indiscriminate charge on all men, women, and children they could see who were colored.

1397. When the policemen, posse, and mob came back again, was there any riotous conduct on the part of any one there? No, sir.

1398. Would you have seen it if there had been? I should have seen it, as I was standing in my own door; all the colored people I saw were walking along quietly attending to their own business.

1399. What other acts of violence did you see? I saw two or three murdered, that was all.

1400. Under what circumstances were they murdered? The policemen and mob fell upon them, no matter where they were, fired at them and beat them over the head with pistols.

1401. How many did you see murdered in that way? I saw two, and I saw others lying dead. I saw the police and this mob run up to one on the bridge, shoot him down and beat him to death. I saw another man in the bayou; they shot him down and beat him afterwards.

1402. How many others did you see lying dead? I cannot exactly state the number. I saw three or four, any way. It then settled down quietly until after dark. A darkey came into my office and asked me if he could stay there until an ambulance came to gather up the dead and wounded. I said "Certainly." A man came in and said, "You damned nigger, what are you doing here?" I said, "Let him alone, he is here waiting for an ambulance to gather up the dead and wounded;" the man then spoke to me and said, "You damned Yankee son of a bitch! you can't live down here." I believe he added the expression, or somebody did, "We'll burn you out."

1403. Who was it? He was a citizen. I was told that his name was Porter, and that he was a butcher.

1404. Was he an American? Yes, sir. Then he went out and told the mob that "Here was a damned abolitionist." The crowd came up round the door and shouted "Bring him out." I thought better to go out, and went; the captain of police came up and told the mob "to let him alone, I know him." They let me go, and then I shut up my place; next morning I went down and found the place opened. I was told some person had fired in; but I don't think it was the fact. I found no traces of it. I then closed up the place and did not open it again for eight days.

1405. What was the character of the mob in the street? They were all white and composed of citizens—men, boys, and policemen.

1406. How large was the crowd? I suppose fifty or sixty, and perhaps more.

1407. What was the nature of their conversation when you came out? The man who said, "Here's a damned abolitionist," brought me out.

1408. What would have been your fate if the captain of police had not interfered to protect you? I supposed they were going to take me up to the station-house, but was told afterwards they intended to shoot me.

1409. Did you see anything that took place afterwards? On Wednesday morning I had a patient to see in that neighborhood. I saw a negro soldier lying dead, who had just been killed by a policeman, as I was informed. I know nothing further of my own personal knowledge than what I have stated.

1410. Did you give this crowd any cause of offence? No, sir; not a word, except that I told a man not to touch this black boy; to "let him alone."

1411. Did you hear any threats made about driving abolitionists out of the city? They told me I could not live there; that I was a damned Yankee *son of a bitch*, and could not live down there; and some person added, "We'll burn you out." I don't know who said it.

By Mr. BROOMALL:

1412. Can you name any of the policemen you saw in the crowd? Yes; the man who ran up the street to bring down the crowd, as I supposed, was named Carroll.

1413. Was he an Irishman? I think not. I think he was a Virginian; there was one policeman who treated me very well. I believe he protected me considerably; his name was Clark; I do not know any of the others.

1414. What has been the behavior of the blacks in Memphis for the last few months? I think the negro soldiers have not acted very properly several times; the citizen negroes acted very well.

1415. Was it the citizen blacks of Memphis or the soldiers that the attack was made upon? Citizens and soldiers indiscriminately.

By Mr. SHANKLIN:

1416. What time was it on Tuesday afternoon that you saw the first difficulty? I do not know exactly the hour; it must have been between three and four o'clock. I took no observation of the particular time.

1417. If I understand you, when you first saw the difficulty you saw some police retreating from the negro soldiery? I saw three.

1418. How many negroes were pursuing them? They were not pursuing when I saw them; they were firing indiscriminately.

1419. How many do you think there were? I could form no idea; they were a good distance off; I judge about 50 or 60.

1420. Firing towards the police? Yes, and the police retreating from them.

1421. You do not know how the difficulty commenced? I do not.

1422. Were these negro soldiers drunk? I do not know; they were at a distance from me; I just went to my door and looked at them.

1423. What were they firing with, muskets or pistols? I think they were pistols, from what I saw.

1424. Were they much excited? I presume they were. I heard them shooting and firing.

1425. You stated that one policeman was shot down on the bridge. Did you learn his name? I have since learned his name was Stevens.

1426. He was not brought up to the city? No, sir; he was taken to his own house, as I understood, and died afterwards. I loaned them a stretcher and told them to bring him up to the city hospital, but was afterwards told they took him to his own home.

1427. Was his house in the locality where he received the wound? I believe his house is in Gayoso street, near Second.

1428. Did you see any other police who were wounded on that occasion? No, sir, I did not.

1429. After that, I understand you, there was a cessation of hostilities. How long did that last? I went down to see this man, and it was during the time I was dressing his wound that the police came back—probably twenty minutes.

1430. When the policemen returned with a force of 50 or 60, as you state, had these negro soldiers left the neighborhood they were in during the first firing? They had.

1431. Where had they gone? I do not know; they had probably scattered around among the houses and some had gone to the fort.

1432. When the mob came back in force, was it a mob of negro soldiers and citizens mixed up indiscriminately? It seemed to be.

1433. You say there was no resistance made by the negroes in any way? The negroes avoided everything of that kind, or seemed to do so.

1434. How long did the riot again continue before there was another cessation? I did not see any more riotous proceedings until that night when the policeman and crowd came down there. That was the third time the policeman came there.

1435. How many were in the crowd that came down that night? I cannot exactly say, sir; but I should think about 100 policemen and a large crowd of citizens.

1436. Did they commence shooting indiscriminately all negroes whom they met? I do not know. I was in my house, but heard some firing. I don't know who was firing and who they were firing at.

1437. Tell us what description of people these several mobs were composed of—what class of citizens, as far as you could judge? I could not form any opinion as to that. I believe they were generally of a very low class.

1438. It was not participated in by the quiet and orderly citizens of the place? I do not think it was.

1439. Was it not composed principally of police, hackmen, draymen, wharf hands, and persons of that class? Principally by police and others of that class of people, which, I should suppose, might have those occupations.

1440. Are not those police, hackmen, draymen, wharf hands, &c., generally composed of foreigners—Irishmen and Dutchmen? I understand they are Irishmen, principally.

1441. You stated you did not think the negro soldiers were engaged in the riot. Will you state what had been the course of the soldiers previous to the riots? They would get drunk sometimes; and I have heard them shout at the policemen; their language sometimes being abominable.

1442. Will you repeat what you have heard them say on the streets? I have heard them use very filthy language; calling them "damn sons of bitches," telling about being in whorehouses, and such language as that.

1443. Was it a common thing before the riots? It was an every-day occurrence for some time previous.

1444. Were not negro soldiers walking along the streets often rude and insolent to persons whom they met? To a certain class they were, I believe; to the police and Irishmen they were especially rude.

1445. Elbowing them out of the way? Yes; more particularly if they happened to be on a drunk.

1446. How long had this course of conduct on the part of the negro soldiers been pursued before the riots? From the time I came to live here, in February last, it had been their constant habit as far as I could learn; the citizen negroes behaved pretty well, but the soldier negroes outdid them all.

1447. Were there many negroes on the street? A great many of them.

1448. Frequenting drinking saloons and getting drunk? Yes, sir.

1449. Howling and cursing? Yes; shouting, cursing, and blackguarding one another.

1450. Were the men who came into your drug store in liquor? They did not seem to be under the influence of liquor; they were excited under the knowledge of what had occurred.

1451. Were they of the same description of persons you have described as constituting the mob? Yes, sir.

By the CHAIRMAN:

1452. You speak of the return of this mob the second time, and of their firing indiscriminately at the negroes. Did I understand you that there were any negro soldiers down there that you saw? There were none that I saw that night; I was not outside, however; the crowd came down and patrolled the streets, and fired shots, as I said.

1453. You speak of the mob being composed of the lower class of citizens. Did you see any of the better class of citizens attempt to suppress this mob of policemen and others? I did not see any attempt to suppress it; they seemed to have full sway.

1454. Do you know of any efforts being made by the so-called better class of citizens to suppress the mob that night? If there was I have not heard of it.

1455. Do you know whether this better class of citizens have taken any measures to denounce the perpetrators of these crimes and barbarities and bring them to justice? Not of my own knowledge. I have not heard of any.

1456. You speak of the disorderly character of these soldiers before the riots. How many of them have you seen in the streets together guilty of disorderly conduct? I have seen them in squads of three or four.

1457. Drunk or sober? Generally drunk.

1458. Have you seen white people disorderly or drunk at the same time? No, sir; I have not.

1459. Is drunkenness exclusively confined to colored soldiers? I speak exclusively of colored soldiers now.

1460. Do you know of any of the parties killed who were guilty of disorderly conduct or drunkenness? Those of them that I saw were very quiet, and attacked by the mob without provocation.

By Mr. SHANKLIN:

1461. Would it have been safe for you or any other quiet citizen, or even a number of you, to have interfered or undertaken to have stopped the operations of the mob? That would have depended upon who the man was. I think the authorities could have stopped it without any difficulty, but a private party would have had no chance, and I think he would have endangered his life.

1462. You speak of not seeing any negro soldiers when the attack was made that night; there were two attacks or difficulties before that, during the day, were there not? The soldiers first attacked the policemen; the policemen then went off, got re-enforcements, and attacked the negroes indiscriminately.

1463. After the policemen got back, were there negro soldiers mixed with citizens? There were; it was a soldier who was killed on the bridge; at least he had soldier's clothes on.

By Mr. BROOMALL:

1464. Who were the rioters during those three nights? They were the policemen and the lower class of white citizens, such as hackmen, draymen, &c.

1465. How large was this mob at any time? There were probably 100 or 150 together at one time.

1466. You speak of its being impossible for private citizens to interfere; if the mob were composed of 100 such men as you have described, could not a force of 200 private citizens of a better order have suppressed it, if they had attempted? I think if they had gone out and patrolled the streets it would have prevented trouble.

1467. Suppose some of your distinguished men here had gone out and spoken to the mob, could not they have stopped it? I think they could.

1468. You heard of no such attempts? No, sir; I did not.

HENRY W. TAYLOR sworn and examined.

By the CHAIRMAN:

1469. State your residence and business. I reside in Memphis; am a painter.

1470. How long have you lived in Memphis? Since August, 1863.

1471. Were you here during the recent riots? Yes, sir.

1472. State what you know, if anything, in relation thereto. On the first day of the riot I was standing in my shop door and saw a crowd of people going to South Memphis. This was on Tuesday afternoon. I followed the crowd. I asked those who were running, as I was, what was the matter; they said there had been some disturbance between the negroes and the police. I went down as far as the bridge on South street, and remained there standing and looking on. I took no part in it whatever, but was merely a spectator, as thousands of others probably were that day. I stood there probably half or three-quarters of an hour and then went home.

1473. What did you see there? That day I saw no one shot. I saw two negroes that had been shot; one was killed and the other wounded.

1474. By whom? That I could not say.

1475. What was the talk you heard in the crowd? The general talk seemed to be principally among the police—that they were going "to shoot down the damned niggers." It appeared that they had killed some policemen, and the police were going to have revenge. I paid no attention to it. I was not mixed with the crowd, except those who were looking on. I had no arms, and did not propose to have any. The same evening, as I was going up Vance street. I saw a fireman who had been shot; he was standing in the door of a grocery at the corner of Vance street, and I do not recollect the name of the other street.

1476. What was the name of the fireman? I do not know his name. The next day, Wednesday, I believe it was, in the morning, I was standing in my shop door and saw a crowd running past. I asked them what was the matter; they said there was more shooting going on below. As before, I followed with the crowd. The only person I saw shot that day was by the blacksmith's shop, near the depot.

1477. Who was he? That I do not know; he was a colored man.

1478. What conversation did you hear in the crowd? It was a regular mob; it was hard to tell what they were saying or doing.

1479. Who headed the mob? There was a company got up by the sheriff to suppress the mob, and I suppose they did as much as possible to quell the riot.

1480. Was this crowd gotten up by the sheriff a part of the mob? No; they were more by themselves. The principal crowd that I saw was standing at the corner of South and Shelby streets. This company, got up by the sheriff, was marching all around and trying to quell the disturbance as much as possible; they were trying their best to put a stop to it.

1481. Did you mix any in the mob and hear what was said? Yes; it was all mixed up. There seemed to be a very strong animosity shown against the negroes.

1482. Was there any strong animosity shown towards the abolitionists or Yankee negroes? No, sir.

1483. Where did you reside before you came here? At St. Louis. I was born and raised there.

1484. Have you any further knowledge in reference to the riots? I have not. I may state the impression made upon my mind, that this shooting I saw was the most cool-blooded murder I ever saw. The negroes all seemed to be perfectly quiet, and did not know what was the matter. They tried to keep out of the way. I did not see a colored man on the route who had any weapons at all, or who was trying to defend himself. There was one shot that came over the heads of the crowd that appeared to come from the direction of the negroes in the fort. It may have been a colored man who shot it, or it may have been a white man; I only know it came from that direction.

By Mr. SHANKLIN:

1485. What time was it when you first went down where this difficulty was going on the first day? About five o'clock in the afternoon.

1486. How many do you suppose were in the company with which you went down? There were several thousand, I should judge—quite a crowd.

1487. How many out of this crowd was participating in this indiscriminate shooting? It seemed to be general among the police.

1488. Then a large portion of the crowd were like yourself—spectators, and not participating in it one way or the other. Yes, sir.

1489. Do you think there were as many as fifty men engaged in acts of violence, as far as you could see? I should think there were just about that many. There were at least that number.

1490. If there were more, state how many more, in your opinion. It would be mere guess-work. I should say fifty would be a very fair average, police and citizens.

1491. At the time you first went there, five o'clock, were there any colored soldiers in uniform in the neighborhood where they were shooting? Not in full uniform; I may have seen one or two in full uniform—coat, pants, and vest. A majority of them seemed to have United States pants on without a uniform coat or vest; some of them had the coat on without the pants—it went to show that they had been in the United States service, and had some portion of their uniform left.

1492. After you got there you saw no shooting or acts of violence. The only acts of violence I saw were towards the negroes by the mob.

1493. How long did that riot continue? I staid there probably half or three-quarters of an hour.

1494. Had it pretty much ceased when you left? No, sir; it was still going on.

1495. The next day when you got there you say the sheriff's posse was going about for some time. Did you see any of that posse engaged in shooting or doing violence? I did not.

1496. Did you see the sheriff himself? No, sir; I did not. I did not see the posse from the time they left the court-house, where they were organizing when I passed, till they got

9

to South street; they then went off in another direction, and I saw nothing of the posse again until I went to town—that was on Wednesday.

1497. You did not see them so as to be able to tell whether they were aiding the rioters, or attempting to suppress the riots? No, sir; I did not.

1498. Did you see this fireman who had been shot? I did.

1499. Was he a white man? He was.

1500. Where was he when he was shot? I do not know.

1501. Where was he when you saw him? He was standing at a grocery or saloon on the corner of Vance street; I do not recollect the other street. He was standing there with another man.

1502. Where was he shot? I do not know; I merely asked if he had been shot. He said he had. A couple of men were holding him up.

1503. Did you afterwards ascertain the name of the man who had died? I have heard his name; he was a fireman of engine No. 2 or 3; I paid no attention to it.

1504. Have you been in the army? I have been in the quartermaster's department, in Benton barracks. Since I've been in Memphis I've been captain of company C, Memphis enrolled militia.

1505. Have you noticed the conduct of these colored soldiers in Memphis previous to this last riot? I have.

1506. What was their deportment on the streets; quiet and orderly, or disorderly and riotous? As a general thing, when they've had whiskey in them, they've certainly been very boisterous. I've once been shoved, myself, off the sidewalk by a negro in United States uniform, for the simple reason that he did not wish to get into the mud.

1507. Have you seen them treat other white men in the same way? I have not noticed them particularly.

1508. Have you seen them drunk and disorderly? Very frequently.

1509. Have you heard them use obscene and vulgar language? I have.

1510. Have you ever heard them use taunting language, as regards the police? No, sir; not as regards the police.

1511. Have you to citizens? I've heard them use very obscene language to citizens.

1512. What have you heard them say? I've heard them use every description of obscene language to citizens. I've seen them push citizens off the sidewalk, using language not fit to be used by white or black.

1513. Give us a specimen of that language? I do not know that I could repeat the language used. It is enough to say that it was not at all proper.

1514. Was this a frequent occurrence? Not very frequent, occasional.

1515. Were the resident negroes in the city quiet, peaceable, and orderly? Yes, sir, as far as I noticed. I've had a good many of them in my employ, and never had occasion to find any fault with them.

1516. But the soldiers you have found the other way? That was only when they were intoxicated.

1517. Was that of frequent occurrence? Not very frequent. I've never seen them more than two or three times so.

By the CHAIRMAN:

1518. Then, as I understand what you have said is, that since the 1st of January you have on two or three occasions seen disorderly conduct on the part of the soldiers? I refer to two or three years back.

1519. Then within that time you have seen colored soldiers using improper language on two or three occasions? Yes, sir.

1520. How many instances have you seen, within that time, of white people drunken, and using improper language? More frequently than negroes.

1521. You spoke of the conduct of resident negroes; from your knowledge and information, what proportion of resident negroes were killed? That I could not say, for the reason that I saw but one, and he was partly dressed in uniform.

By Mr BROOMALL:

1522. Were the brutal murders of which you speak in your testimony committed on resident negroes here? I alluded to but that one instance. I saw no one killed directly but that one.

1523. Did you see any of the killed? He is the only dead man I recollect seeing. I saw one or two wounded, but they went off again.

Dr. WILLIAM F. IRWIN sworn and examined.

By the CHAIRMAN:

1524. Please state your residence and profession? I have lived in Memphis for sixteen years; am a physician.

1525. Were you in Memphis during the recent riot? I was.

1526. Have you any personal knowledge of the riot? If so, please state what you know? I know nothing about the riotous proceedings. I attended a good many of the wounded.

1527. Whose wounds did you dress? I assisted in dressing the wounds of Stevens; and Nally, I think his name was, a policeman; also another policeman who had his finger or thumb shot off. The next morning I assisted in dressing the broken arm of a negro, broken by a shot, and of another negro man who had been cut—that was all.

1528. State the nature of the wounds of the white men? One of them, I think his name is Nally; I am not sure, but think he is a brother-in-law of the recorder, John C. Creighton. He was shot in both legs, the bullet in each case passing through the leg and making a flesh wound. We sent him home. I was called in consultation to see the other man, Stevens. He died. He was shot in the upper third of the thigh. It was a pistol ball: it passed through the bone, shattering it above and below. The intention was when I was first brought in consultation to amputate the limb, but the surgeons concluded to give him a chance to save his leg. He was himself very much opposed to having his leg taken off.

1529. How did the wound appear to have been given? I do not know. I probed the wound; he remarked that he fell through a bridge just as he was shot. I made the suggestion that his own pistol might have caused the wound. I practice surgery very little, except in consultation.

1530. Was there any powder mark about the wound? It would have been as well upon the clothing as upon the wound. There was a black mark around the wound that is not usual for a gunshot wound.

1531. Then you do not give any opinion yourself as to the way the wound was inflicted? It went almost directly through the bone, shattering it in every direction. Dr. Keller performed the surgical operation of dressing the wound. The other white man had his finger shot off—the end of it; he made more complaint of it than either of the others. One of the negroes had his arm fractured, and the other had some cuts upon his face and on the back of his head.

1532. How were the cuts made? He said he was just out of his house, and was struck with a stone and club. I saw another white man, an engineer of No. 5 company; he was evidently dying; he was attended by others, and I made no examination of his wounds.

By Mr. SHANKLIN:

1533. Did you ascertain the name of the fireman who was shot and killed? I have heard his name. I think it was Dunn; I am not certain.

1534. Where was his wound? In the back of the head.

1535. You state you have been living here for some time. What has been the deportment of the negro soldiers on the streets of the city previous to this riot? They have been rather rude when they were not on duty. They have been in the habit of taking most of the sidewalk.

1536. Were they rude to white persons? They have never been so to me. I have seen them when they evidently felt above their position in that way. I never had any difficulty at all with them myself.

1537. Have you seen them intoxicated upon the streets making a noise? Yes, sir; I have seen them swearing and making a noise, but that is usual both to whites and blacks when they get in that condition.

1538. Have you heard them using obscene language upon the streets? Yes, sir; I have.

1539. Have you heard them use taunting language towards the police? I do not know that I have. I have never seen any conflict between them and the police at all.

1540. But you think their conduct upon the streets has been indecorous? I do not think it has been general, but I have seen instances of it. When they were on duty I think their conduct was correct; it was only when they got off by themselves that they behaved improperly.

1541. Have they frequently been off by themselves? I have seen them frequently, or at least, negroes having uniforms on; probably many of them have worn the uniform after they have been discharged.

1542. What have been the feelings and sentiments of the better class of the citizens in regard to this riot, so far as you have been informed? It was a matter of regret with them—every one, so far as I know—that anything of this kind should have occurred. I think they would have taken every means in their power to have stopped it. I think the riot originated between the lower class of whites and these negroes.

1543. Was it confined to the lower class? Yes, sir; I think so, entirely. I do not know of one respectable person engaged in it at all, unless it was the sheriff, who summoned a posse to go down and quell it.

1544. And so far as you know, has been universally condemned by them? Yes, sir, it has.

1545. Has any encouragement whatever been given to it, as far as you know, by the better class of people here? So far as I know there has not.

1546. Did you regard it as an accidental occurrence, or as premeditated? I have had no means of forming any opinion on the subject. The rumor was various ways; that it was premeditated, and that it happened accidentally by a row that occurred; both parties being drawn into it as they came on the ground. I had no reason to know or suppose anything about it; it was unexpected to almost everybody. There had been several collisions between the negro soldiers and the police. I recollect one several months ago down on Beal street.

1547. Has there not been some feeling of jealousy and hostility existing between what you term the lower classes and the negro population for some time? I cannot say there has been. I think it more than likely there has been some feeling of the sort. I do not think the negroes who have been inhabitants here have ever borne any other than a good reputation among the citizens of this town.

1548. What have been the feelings and sentiments of the people of the city, so far as you have been able to ascertain, towards the resident negroes? Have they been unkind, or have they been perfectly kind? Perfectly kind—and I think the negroes will say so themselves—both before the riots and since. I owned eleven or twelve before the war, and during the riot they came—all of them—and staid at my house for protection.

1549. Those white persons who are engaged in draying, hack-driving, working upon the wharves, jobbing, and occupations of that sort, are, I understand, principally foreigners. Has there not been some hostility exhibited between them and the negroes engaged in the same occupation? Yes, sir, I think it has been a kind of a competition of labor.

1550. So far as the citizens of Memphis—owning property and engaged in regular business, employing hands—are concerned, are they as much inclined to employ negroes as white men? Fully, and I think more so.

By Mr. BROOMALL:

1551. You have spoken of some instances of rude behavior on the part of negro soldiers. Will you tell me, if you can remember it, how many instances you have seen within the last year? I could not tell you. I've seen them going along the streets cursing and swearing and behaving themselves very badly, especially when they were a little drunk. But a few days before the riot I saw two persons walking along the street who were met by several men in uniform. As they passed, I saw one of the negroes place his arms a-kimbo and put his hand to his pistol. I think I've seen a thousand instances on the streets of noise and bad behavior on their part.

1552. What was the conduct of the negro soldiers as compared with white soldiers when equally drunk? I don't know of any difference between them.

1553. You have said that the behavior of the resident blacks has been good for years. Do you know whether the attacks of the mob were made on resident blacks? I do not know anything about it. I am not accustomed to passing down that street.

1554. You have said that the public sentiment among the better class of citizens has always been against riotous proceedings and mob violence? Yes, entirely. I've heard frequent expressions that while this thing was commenced by the negroes, it was carried on by the mob to an unjustifiable point.

1555. Was there not here, however, a public sentiment, not among the better sort, but among active, noisy, and busy politicians—Irish recorders and mayors, and that sort of people—that would sustain the mob in what they have done? I think not. I have mixed, however, very little among that class of people.

1556. Is there not among the Irish policemen and their friends a public feeling that would sustain the mob? I think it has grown up by the frequent quarrels they have had with each other.

1557. As I understand it, almost all the officers here are not native Americans? No, sir; they are almost all Irishmen.

1558. Those who elect them are of course the ruling population of Memphis at this time; and of course those who are elected will be of the class who elect them? I could not say. Most of our elections for the last few years have been very slender. The voice of the respectable people here has not been heard. The elections have been controlled by the Irish.

1559. How do you account for the fact that no public proceedings have been taken in respect to the riots; that there has been no preaching against them, no public demonstrations of any shape to discountenance them, and no efforts to relieve the wants of the sufferers? I do not know whether there was any public demonstration or not. If I recollect aright, a letter was written to General Stoneman and a commission appointed by him.

By Mr. SHANKLIN:

1560. Why is it that these elections have been under the control of the Irish and lower order of people here? I do not know, except that recently by the franchise law many men have not been able to vote. Then the Irish are a people that band and clan together more than any other people in the world. They were always nearly able to control our elections in olden times.

1561. Are not the better class of your people disfranchised by the laws of the State? Yes, sir; particularly by the present law.

1562. Were they not by the previous franchise law? The previous law disfranchised a good many, but not near so many as the late law.

By the CHAIRMAN:

1563. On what grounds were they disfranchised? I presume because they were disloyal at that time.

1564. Was not that their own fault, or was it the fault of other parties? I presume it was their own fault.

1565. You have spoken of the present character of the city government resulting from the fact that the better portion of the population were disfranchised; is that your opinion? Yes. I think if they had been allowed to vote the officers who would have been elected would have been of a higher tone

1566. Who is the present mayor of the city? His name is Park.

1567. Who was mayor of the city at the breaking out of the war, when this better class voted? Park was then mayor of the city. It was his first term of office. The mayoralty has never been an office that a good man could afford to have. The salary has been so small that the better class of men could not be induced to take the office at all.

1568. If these colored people of whom you speak are peaceable, well-behaved, and respectable, and so well thought of by the better class of the people of Memphis, what was the cause of some thirty or forty of them being murdered in cold blood? I do not know that they were. I saw one down here at the door who was killed. He was the servant of a gentleman down town. I presume he heard of the row by night and ventured out. He had a pistol buckled around his waist.

1569. Was there any reason for shooting him? No, sir. But when a mob of that description gets under way it is no easy matter to stop it.

1570. What was the character of the rumors you heard that the riot was premeditated? The rumor was that the negroes intended to have a row, and they had it. Others thought the affair grew simply out of an accident and was not premeditated by anybody.

1571. You have spoken of there being a universal regret by the citizens of Memphis that the riot should have taken place. How has that found expression among the better classes? By the conversation of everybody.

1572. Has it found expression through the public press? I think it has.

1573. Has it by public meetings? I do not know of any.

1574. Has it found expression through the pulpits? I do not know whether it has been spoken of in the pulpits or not.

By Mr. SHANKLIN:

1575. I ask you whether General Stoneman when he proclaimed martial law in this city did not forbid the collection or assembling of the people for any purpose in the city of Memphis? He did, undoubtedly.

By Mr. BROOMALL:

1576. How long did that last? It has lasted until this time, I believe; I have not heard of its being revoked.

1577. Was he asked to give permission for a public meeting to be held? I do not know that he was.

Dr. J. M. KELLER sworn and examined.

By the CHAIRMAN:

1578. Please state your residence and profession? My residence is in Memphis. I am a physician.

1579. How long have you resided here? Not including the time of the war, when I was absent, ten years.

1580. Where were you during the war? In the confederate service as a surgeon.

1581. Were you here at the time of the riot? Yes, sir.

1582. Have you any knowledge of the riotous proceedings? None except professionally.

1583. What professional knowledge have you? I had just rode to the stable to put my buggy and horse up. I was summoned by the sheriff to assist him in putting down the riot. I told him I was a physician, and did not obey the summons of a sheriff; that he had no right to command my time. He said to me, "Your professional services are needed, as I understand a number are wounded." Said I, "That being the case, I will go." I went down to the corner of St. Martin and Pontotoc streets The first wounded man I saw was a negro, who had been wounded by a rock thrown by a boy. I believe a policeman had him, taking him to the station-house. There was a large number of boys following, hallooing "kill him." I was on the opposite side of the street. I went over immediately, and said "Stop! you shall not kill him." The policemen had him and had their pistols drawn at the time. They desisted for a moment. The chief of police, Captain Garrett, came up, ordered them to desist and take the boy off. Just at that time I was approached by a gentleman, who asked me to go and see a policeman that was shot. From a slight examination of this negro, I did not think he had been wounded by anything more than a rock thrown at him. I went to see the policeman Stevens, who had been shot in the thigh—a very bad fracture extending up and down about eight inches. It had been dressed by Dr. McGowan; he had applied a bandage. He was a brother-in-law to a gentleman who asked me to go and see him. I had a consultation with Drs. Irwin and Creighton the next morning, and I found that death would inevitably ensue, which it did soon afterwards.

1584. Were you called in reference to any other wound? I was trying to think. I believe I saw one man who came into Dr. Creighton's office who was wounded in the leg.

1585. What was the character of this wound in the thigh of this policeman, Stevens? It was evidently done by a large-sized pistol ball, which shattered the shaft of the bone at least eight inches, I think.

1586. How did the wound seem to have been given, as far as you could judge? There was no exit of the ball; it entered the right leg about the upper third of the thigh. Where the ball went to I was never enabled to ascertain, friends of the party objecting to a search after death. I made an incision eight inches long to get out pieces of the bone.

1587. Have you any idea of the direction from which the ball came? It must have been from diagonally in front.

1588. What was the direction of the wound? It was straight through, as far as I could judge by running my finger in it. It was evidently anterior; it was not shot from the posterior.

1589. Was there any suggestion made as to how the wound was received—whether from his own pistol or that of anybody else? None at all; it evidently was done by a second party; it could not, I imagine, have been done by himself; the shot must have been almost horizontal.

1590. Do you know what his position was when the wound was received? Only from the statement of his friends.

By Mr. SHANKLIN:

1591. Where did you come from? Alabama is my native State. I married in Kentucky, near Louisville. I received my education at the university at Louisville; ten years ago I came to this place.

1592. From your relations, professionally and otherwise, I presume you have had pretty free interchange of sentiments between yourself and the citizens of Memphis. What have been the feelings and sentiments of the people so far as you could collect them, men of business and property here, in regard to the negro population? Has it been kind or unkind, in your estimation? I can only judge from my own personal observation and intercourse, and I presume, what I state in regard to myself, will accord with the experience of others here. When I left this place I believe I left thirty-three negroes, belonging to my mother's estate; since I came back they have borne the same relationship they formerly did, and I believe that is true in respect to all faithful negroes; the only difficulty I have ever had is with one rascally boy, a boy about my age, who had been gambling and drinking all his life—he induced the soldiers to be impudent to me sometimes

1593. What has been the deportment or general conduct of the resident negroes in the city, peaceable? Very, indeed; I cannot see any difference between now and before they were free.

1594. Has the treatment of the whites towards these people been generally kind and considerate? Yes, sir, it has.

1595. Have their relations been friendly and agreeable? Yes, sir; I believe that in many instances, if possible, they have shown more disinterested kindness towards the negroes.

1596. What, so far as you have observed it, has been the deportment of these colored soldiers in passing about the streets? Unfortunately, they have pushed me off the sidewalk once or twice, and pushed some ladies off in my presence, and I knocked several of them over. I would not allow a white man to do it in my presence. It was only when there were bands or crowds together that they would do such things.

1597. Have they been frequently in the habit of appearing on the streets in a state of intoxication or in liquor? On outer streets of the city I have seen them frequently in large crowds, drunk.

1598. Were they generally noisy and boisterous when drunk? They were impertinent, excessively so—disposed to curse every white man they saw as a "son of a bitch," if you will pardon the expression.

By the CHAIRMAN:

1599. You say the conduct and deportment of the negroes, except the colored soldiers of whom you speak, was respectful and obedient to law? Indolence is the only complaint I could make against them.

1600. Have you known of their being insolent, or committing any crime against the law, particularly? Nothing except indolence and vagrancy.

1601. Are there not some white people who are indolent and vagrant? Yes; a great many of them. I know of no impertinence from negroes not soldiers. I, myself, have never been subjected to any.

1602. But you state that these colored soldiers, when under the influence of liquor, have been impertinent oftentimes? I do not know whether they have been under the influence of liquor or not, they have been impertinent to me once or twice.

1603. For how long a period has this extended back? I think the last occurrence of the sort was under these circumstances: I had been sent for to see an old gentleman, three miles in the country. His son came for me and took me out in a hack. It was night when I came back; the hackman stopped on South street to light his lamps; I had fallen asleep from fatigue; when the hack stopped I found about a dozen negro soldiers around the hack; it excited me naturally; one of the soldiers was a boy I had known since the war; said he, "That is Dr. Keller, let him alone ;" the others had hold of the horses. I paid no attention to it, but I felt satisfied that my having known this boy prevented trouble. The afternoon before that I was walking on Main street, between Monroe and Madison. Next before me was a lady I did not know. I saw a negro soldier, holding his head down, intentionally shove her off of the pavement; my first impulse was to knock him down, which I did. If he had been a white man I would have done the same thing. There were two Illinois soldiers present at the time, cavalrymen, I think, who took my part, and would have killed the negro if I had not interfered.

1604. Was the driver of the hack a white man or a negro? A white man.

1605. Have you seen instances of disorderly conduct among the white people? Yes; I see white people drunk nearly every day.

1606. Are they boisterous and obstreperous also? Yes, sir.

1607. Did you learn of a large number of these colored citizens being killed in the riot? Yes, sir; I believe I heard a hundred reports about it. I did see one dead man; this was a policeman. I have no doubt there were a number killed.

1608. Of that number what proportion were of this class you have spoken of as obedient? I have no idea, because I did not see them.

1609. What justification was there—I ask you as a southern man, as a man who has been in the confederate service—for killing that class of people? I presume you must account for it on the same principle you do for the proceedings of all mobs or riots. The sides collect, one against the other, against law and order, and murder will ensue.

1610. What was the particular motive the mob had in killing these innocent people? I do not know how many innocent people were killed. I heard a number of shots fired. I believe the negroes were not armed, and excepting some of the soldiers, as far as my knowledge extends, have been respectful. I have no idea what the motive was for killing soldiers or private negroes. I presume it is a conceded point that the sons of Erin do not like the sons of Ham, particularly when they come in conflict in their wages. That may have had something to do with it.

MAY 29, 1866.

Mrs. MINERVA E. HEWITT sworn and examined.

By the CHAIRMAN:

1610. Where do you reside? In Memphis.

1611. What is your occupation? Only a housekeeper; I have no occupation particularly.

1612. Have you a husband? Yes, sir, I have.

1613. How long have you resided in Memphis? Eleven years.

1614. Were you here during the riots? Yes, sir, I was.

1615. Did you see anything in connexion with it? If so, state what you saw? I saw them on Tuesday running by my house. I walked out to the gate to see them. Most of them were policemen armed; a few citizens had shot-guns. I did not know one of them at all. A colored man came by, going home. He had no arms. A white man came along with a pistol in his hand and ordered the negro off the sidewalk. I thought he was going to strike him, but he did not. The negro had a hatchet in his hand which the man took from him. Just then a policeman started out and called on him to shoot the son of a bitch. That frightened this man and he started to run. A gentleman said, "Don't run, boys, for God's sake." He started on, and just as I got in I heard a pistol fired. I do not know whether they hit the man or not. I was told they had shot a black man out there, but whether it was the man they took the hatchet from, or another man, I don't know. The next day I did not see anything at all.

1616. What language did the citizen use towards the negro who had the hatchet? He did not curse him at all; he just told him to halt and surrender.

1617. You do not know, of your own knowledge, whether this negro was killed or not? No, sir; I do not think he was. I think it must have been another colored man I saw in the street with a ham on his shoulder.

By Mr. SHANKLIN:

1618. How long have you been living in the town of Memphis? Several years.

1619. Have you ever seen many soldiers passing by your house? Very few passed my house; they were further south.

1620. So far as you have seen of the negro soldiers passing by your house, have they been quiet and orderly? More so than other soldiers. I've never been molested or seen any one molested by them at all. Every one I've seen has been respectful; always been so to myself and family.

VESTA E. LITTLEFIELD sworn and examined.

By the CHAIRMAN:

1621. How long have you lived in Memphis? Very nearly three years.

1622. Were you here when the recent riots took place? Yes, sir.

1623. State what you saw, if anything, that took place in relative thereto. I saw a negro shot. I could not tell who it was done by. There was a wagon between him and me.

1624. Was it a negro who ran out of a house? I think not. I think the negro I saw shot was on the other side of the street.

1625. Did this negro have a ham or anything on his shoulder? Nothing at all; he was walking quietly along the street. The ball struck him on the top of his head, but did not kill him. He walked along, and some of the mob caught him. I saw him fall. He fell right in the gutter. He was not injured seriously, but got up and walked along.

1626. Was the mob composed of white men? Yes, sir; I think mostly of policemen and Irishmen.

1627. What was the mob saying? I could not hear what they were saying, there was so much excitement. I would not be able to identify a single person there.

JOHN MARTIN sworn and examined.

By the CHAIRMAN:

1628. Please state your residence and business? I live in Memphis. I have been engaged in the practice of law for some time.

1629. How long have you lived in Memphis? Twenty-four years; with the exception of two or three years, all the time.

1630. Where were those two or three years spent? On a plantation below Helena, Arkansas. I sold out my plantation in 1852 to General Pillow. I came back in 1851.

1631. Were you here during the recent riots? I was at Nashville. I left Nashville on the evening the riot commenced and got here the next evening.

1632. Did you see any of the riotous proceedings? If so, please state what you saw. I believe not, of my own knowledge. There was a little trouble in Chelsea, in my immediate neighborhood, on Friday afternoon. I reached home before it had entirely subsided. It did not amount to much. There had been a picnic out in that neighborhood. In the afternoon about five o'clock a parcel of drunken Irishmen came along there and shot at some negroes in the neighborhood close to my house. I suppose it was just the result of the bad state of feeling existing between that class of people and the negroes. They got excited about the riot and did not feel that it was over entirely. There was no cause whatever for their conduct. I had a negro who was a brick-maker, and two or three negro men were employed with him. They commenced shooting among them, and passed down to a little negro settlement below and shot two or three negroes there.

1633. Who were the negroes shot? I do not know them personally. None of them were badly hurt. One of them was shot through the arm. The other was shot through the leg. I did not see them.

1634. Were there any steps taken to arrest these men? None at all that I heard of. A battalion of regular soldiers of the 16th infantry came into my neighborhood, reaching there on Saturday night. On Sunday morning I went over to see the commanding officer, and told him about this thing. While there a Mr. Anderson, in the neighborhood, came over and asked him if he had any power to take testimony in a case of this kind. He said he had not. He referred him to General Stoneman. Mr. Anderson remarked that he knew of parties engaged in this thing.

1635. Can you state the reasons why any measures have not been taken by the civil authorities to bring these men who shot the negroes to justice? I do not know of any reason particularly. I know this: there was an effort made by some citizens here, and I co-operated with them, to make an investigation of this thing. We applied to General Stoneman to co-operate with us, but he ignored us entirely. He said he would attend to this thing himself. He forbid by proclamation any assemblage of citizens at all for the purpose of investigating this matter.

1636. Was application made to General Stoneman for permission to hold a public meeting to investigate this riot and bring the offending parties to justice; and did he refuse to permit such a meeting to be held? No, sir; I did not say that. I said this: There was a deputation of citizens who waited on General Stoneman, who offered their co-operation, with a view of stopping any further riotous proceedings, and that General Stoneman issued his proclamation, refusing to have anything to do with citizens.

1637. Who was that deputation composed of? The mayor co-operated with them—Colonel McMahon, editor of the Appeal, R. C. Brinkley, and others.

1638. Was the communication of these gentlemen of whom you speak for the purpose of investigating this matter, or for raising a force to co-operate with the United States authorities in order to put down any further resistance to laws? It was for the purpose of co-operating with General Stoneman to stop further riotous proceedings, and not for the purpose of investigation.

1639. Then, did I understand you correctly that General Stoneman refused to permit citizens to hold any meeting? No; General Stoneman answered the communication addressed to him prohibiting any organization of citizens for any purpose whatever. The police, however, were to be permitted to go on and perform their duties.

1640. Did you understand the purport of that proclamation to be to prevent citizens of the own from co-operating together to denounce these proceedings and bring the perpetrators of these outrages to justice? I understood it to be this: that General Stoneman had taken charge of the affairs of the city so far as they were connected with the riot; that he would manage them himself, and did not want citizens to interfere in it in any way whatever.

1641. Was that the proclamation itself, or your inference from it? It was directly in his proclamation that they should not organize for any purpose whatever.

1642. Is that the reason why the citizens here have taken no measures to bring the perpetrators of these outrages to justice? I think this in regard to the better class of the citizens of Memphis—that they opposed this thing and deprecated it; but when General Stoneman issued that order, they felt they were not privileged to investigate that matter any further; that it was in his hands; that he was an officer of the United States army and would attend to it himself. He appointed a committee to investigate the matter, composed of General Runkle, Marcus J. Wright, who was a general of the confederate army, and others; and the citizens felt that they were not permitted to have anything further to do with it.

1643. Did you understand that they prohibited the citizens from having the men who committed the murders, burning, and ravishing during the riot arrested and bound over to answer the indictments that might be found against them? No, sir; I did not understand it in that way. We have had some civil law. We have an attorney general and a criminal court, whose duty it is to convene a grand jury and investigate the matter.

1644. Is it not the duty of every citizen, when he knows the perpetration of crime, to take measures to bring the perpetrators to justice? It is, unquestionably.

1645. Has that duty been performed by the citizens of this place, so far as you know? I do not know of anybody who has been arrested in the case. There were some men arrested here, as I understood, when this commission of General Runkle was organized. I do not know it of my own knowledge.

By Mr. SHANKLIN:

1646. I ask you whether the citizens of the city and State have any means of bringing violators of law and order to justice other than through the courts and public officers? No other that I know of. We have here in the city of Memphis a criminal court embracing four sub-districts, including Memphis and suburbs.

1647 Did not you understand the proclamation of General Stoneman as declaring martial law in the city of Memphis, and prohibiting any assemblage or concert of action on the part of the citizens in relation to this matter? I did.

1648. Then if the citizens had no right under that proclamation to act in concert, could any such measures as you have been inquired about been taken? I think not.

1649. That proclamation, however, did not prevent the legal authorities from the discharge of their duties? I should think not.

By Mr. BROOMALL:

1650. Did you offer to combine for the purpose of bringing these offenders to justice or to prevent further outrages? To prevent further outrages. It devolved upon our criminal court to bring these offenders to justice. It is the duty of the criminal judge to charge the grand jury to search out all violators of the law.

1651. But that is on initiatory steps taken by the action of individuals, is it not? No, sir. It is their duty to, whether complaints are made or not.

1652. In the case of an ordinary murder you do not wait for the grand jury, do you, before steps are taken to arrest the offender? No, sir. He is arrested and imprisoned or bound over.

1653. You spoke of General Stoneman declaring martial law. Did his proclamation declare martial law? I do not know.

1654. Was not martial law already in existence here? It has been a condition of *quasi* martial law all the time, I believe. It was our understanding, however, that he took entire charge of the city for the time being.

1655. What is the probability of any of these offenders being brought to justice from your knowledge of the people, courts, magistrates, police, mayor and other authorities here? I think from the general bearing and temper of the people of the city, the citizens would be glad to see brought to trial and punishment the perpetrators of any outrages committed, that were not justified by the action of the negroes at the time the riot broke out. And in connexion with that I may say I have not seen any respectable gentleman who did not deprecate this thing.

1656. You speak of this being the feeling of the best citizens. Is there not a class here powerful enough to keep in office riotous policemen and a drunken mayor who would, to a certain extent, justify these riotous proceedings? I may answer that in this way: There is an antagonism, undoubtedly, and has been ever since I have known this town, (and I have been here twenty-four years,) between the negroes and Irish. The present mayor, who is understood to be a drunken mayor, was first elected in 1861. He was not then a drunken mayor. He was considered a very fine business man, and is now, when sober, probably the best mayor Memphis has had. He was elected then under the patronage of the Irish, and was sustained by good citizens for the purpose of ridding ourselves of a mayor who was incompetent for the position. After that he continued to be elected, probably by the Irish vote, for a majority of the voting population had gone south into the war, leaving the Irish population at home. At the last election the legislature of Tennessee had passed a franchise bill that prevented a great many from voting who would have voted against this man. The Irish having remained home during the war, elected him again.

1657. Your jurors are made up to quite an extent, are they not, out of this disorderly class? I do not know that you can properly term them disorderly.

1658. I refer to the class that has this antagonistic feeling towards the negroes? No, sir; I do not think there is a very large class of that description here.

1659. Would there not be likely to be at least one on every jury of that class? Yes; I suppose three or four.

1660. Would it be possible, then, through your courts, under their present organization, to punish the perpetrators of outrages such as have been committed here during the recent riots? I cannot answer that, for I do not know what estimate these men place upon the value of their oaths.

1661. The noisy public sentiment, then, does not emanate from the best citizens? Does it not come from a class below them, such as the police is taken from? That class are evidently in control here in elections and things of that kind, to a certain extent.

1662. And from that class your jurors are taken? Well, we have jurors from all classes; our grand juries are usually composed of the best citizens in town. For the petit juries there is a class of people who hang about the court-house looking for a chance to get a dollar, and the sheriff summons them very often as jurors.

1663. As a general rule how impartial would they be in the trial of an outrage committed by a white man on a negro? I am satisfied you could get men here who would punish such outrages.

1664. But I am now speaking of the chances or probability of conviction, supposing one man of that class to be on the jury? He hangs the jury for that term, of course.

By Mr SHANKLIN:

1665. Have you remained during the war in the city of Memphis? All the time; I was here during the confederate rule. I remained when the town was captured by the federal authorities, and I have been here ever since.

1666. I understand the reason given by you for the exclusion of the orderly and better portion from the elections is, that, under the laws of the State, they have been prescribed? They have been disfranchised; yes, sir. A law was passed by the legislature of Tennessee requiring certain conditions before a man could exercise the elective franchise which prevented a great many of our people from voting who would vote right in our elections if they had a chance.

1667. Have you been disfranchised? No, sir; I have not. I was here and voted in the election for President, and governor; probably that gave me the right to vote in all elections under the franchise law. The recent franchise law would disfranchise me; they require an oath I could not take. While I have been as good a Union man, probably, as any in Tennessee, yet every relation I had in the world, except my own immediate family, was involved in the rebellion, and I could not come forward and swear I had no sympathy with that people. I had no sympathy for rebellion.

1668. Does the oath under the recent law go that far? I think so.

1669. What is the feeling on the part of the orderly portion of the people of Memphis toward the freed people here who have been residents of Memphis? I can tell you that I know, probably, as much about that thing as anybody here. My business has thrown me a great deal among the negro population here, the old barbers, draymen, and all that class of negroes. I have heard the expression of opinion upon the part of these negroes and on the part of the citizens toward them. I have observed the conduct of the older and better class of citizens here, and I know they acquiesce in the present condition of things. They have nothing but the kindest feelings for these negroes, and the negroes have nothing but the kindest feelings towards them. To illustrate the feeling on the part of the negroes: I was a candidate for attorney general of the criminal court at the election the other day; we held an election in violation of that franchise law, because we believed it to be unconstitutional. I have no doubt myself that it is unconstitutional; at any rate it is to be tested. Some four or five of us ran a race in that election; the old negroes of this town came to me and said they had a certain influence they desired to exert, and I am satisfied they worked for me in that election. There is certainly a kind feeling existing here between the negroes and the old citizens; we prefer to employ them; we keep them in our families; and there is nothing but the best feelings existing.

1670. What has been the conduct of the negroes here? First-rate.

1671. What has been the conduct and behavior of those colored soldiers who have been about the streets of the city for the past four or five months? Has it been orderly, peaceable and quiet, or has it been disorderly and rude? Of my own personal knowledge I have never seen anything, even upon the part of negro soldiers, that was not orderly and quiet; I have heard of turbulence and drunkenness on the part of a few. I knew a good many of the negro soldiers who were from the city, and I never met one who was not respectful to me; I have always treated them kindly. I know of some instances where they really did not go into the army voluntarily; they were rather forced into it. Down about the fortifications where this riot commenced and where whiskey shops gave them every opportunity to obtain liquor, the general understanding was, that some of them would get drunk, and I think this whole riot, probably, commenced from some disorderly conduct on the part of some drunken negro soldiers.

1672. If the population of Memphis could vote as they did before the rebellion, is it your opinion, from your knowledge of the character of the people here, that you would have city authorities here who would be able to maintain order, quiet, and peace ? The population of Memphis is greatly changed since the war. There is a very large element in here now that did not exist before the war ; but I think myself, candidly, that if the elective franchise was thrown open to every man who under the laws of Tennessee was entitled to vote before the war, we could elect a mayor, city council, and police, who would preserve order.

1673. Under the present franchise law you have some doubt, however, whether you can do it or not ? Yes, sir ; I have very great doubt. For instance, there is a large foreign element that remained here during the war, laboring Irish, Germans, &c., who voted under the old franchise law, and will have no trouble in getting their certificates again. There are a great many of the same general class of people who would have no scruple about taking the oath, whatever may have been their sympathies or action during the war. I think as the law now stands there is very little hope of any improvement in our elections. If the law should be decided to be constitutional, which I am very confident it will not be, it is certainly very unfortunate for Memphis that it should ever have been passed.

By Mr. BROOMALL :

1674. What kind of a judge of a good white man is a negro ? You will find a great many intelligent, shrewd negroes, who will judge of a man pretty well.

1675. Suppose you were to have a mayor chosen by the Irish and that class of men who control your elections here, or one chosen by the resident negroes ; which do you think you would prefer to trust your life and property under? I will answer that question frankly, though not directly. I will state that I am very anxious myself, candidly, that the negro should be intrusted, under proper limitations, with the elective franchise. I am well satisfied we have a large negro population here that would vote very intelligently and understanding-ly—with quite as much understanding, and probably more than some of our white men entitled to the franchise. And, gentlemen, I say to you this—that while a majority of what we understand to be radicals in Tennessee—I mean in Eastern Tennessee—will not permit the negro to have any show, so far as I am concerned, I hope to see the day very soon when the negro will be educated and permitted to vote.

By Mr. SHANKLIN :

1676. In the present condition of the negro as to morals and education, would you regard it as safe or advisable that the elective franchise should be extended to them indiscriminately as to white men, that is, to all male citizens over twenty-one years of age, with residence ? I think it would be a great deal better for the elective franchise to be extended to the negro with limitation.

1677. In the present condition of the negro, would you consider it safe or prudent to extend indiscriminate franchise to him ? I have been an old-line whig all my life, and have seen too much of a franchise any how among white people. To answer the question directly, I do not believe it would. I think to give them a limited franchise, and educate them up to it, would be the best course.

By Mr. BROOMALL :

1678. Would you not think it best to have some limitation as to white population also ? I always thought that.

1679. You would then make impartial suffrage based upon education? Education, I suppose, would be the only practicable limitation ; I always thought, myself, that a property qualification would be best when it could be reached in that way.

A. N. EDMUNDS sworn and examined.

By the CHAIRMAN :

1680. State your residence and business ? Memphis ; I am in the commission business.

1681. How long have you resided in Memphis ? Twenty-one years next July.

1682. Were you here during the recent riots ? Yes, sir.

1683. Do you know anything of the riotous proceedings that took place ? Nothing of my own knowledge.

1684. Did you have a store rented to a man by the name of Egbert? Yes, sir.

1685. Do you know of any threats of violence against him ? All I know is this : I heard some talk across the street ; I did not hear any words. This man, Egbert, rented a store over across on St. Martin street ; I thought he was a gentleman when I rented to him. He had a lady with him I supposed to be his wife. Some months afterward this lady left him, went up to Illinois, and has never returned. He took a negro woman with him, and she was there all the time after his wife left. He rented a room in the house to her without my knowledge or consent; his lease from me forbid him to sub-let. Since his wife left him, he has been sleeping in her room with her, staying all the while. The crowd went there one night to burn up the house during the riot. I went down to make some inquiry about it, but I could not find out anything about it, and I just told this man he had to leave my house. The next day the county clerk notified me that he would hold my house responsible for the taxes; that this man was holding the house and carrying on business without paying any license. He sent an officer down and closed up the house; I got clear of him in that way, although he was in my debt forty or fifty dollars. During the time of the riot I was standing on the corner of Pontotoc street; I saw this same man on the corner of Vance street, fifty yards away, and another man talking with him; I could not hear what passed between them. I saw the man draw a pistol on him, and expected he would shoot him; he did not shoot. Egbert came back making some pretty heavy threats of what he was going to do.

1686. Did he do anything? Nothing that I saw.

1687. Was your property threatened by the mob? Not that I heard, only by the common talk—that a man who lived there with negroes would not be safe.

1688. Who threatened all these houses in that neighborhood? It was just the common talk. The negroes were just running and saying they were all going to be burned out that night. I paid no attention to it. There was a woman who came up and said she heard they were going to burn her house. I told her if she observed any signs to come up and tell me, and I would guard her house. There was a man who rented some houses of me over on Market street; he said he heard his houses were going to be burned because he rented one to a negro; but there was no attempt made to burn them.

1689. Did you see any houses burned that night? I saw some burning down on the Overton settlement, in our neighborhood.

1690. Had you any fears, at any time, that your property would be burned? I have not had any fears that have caused me to set up nights, or to lose any sleep. I saw the chief of police, Ben. Garrett, and asked him about it. He said there would be no fires, and I would not be in any danger at all. I had confidence in what he told me, went to bed, and did not give myself any trouble about it.

1691. Do you know of any buildings being burnt in the city of Memphis during the riots? Not in my own neighborhood; I have heard of their being burnt elsewhere.

1692. Did you give as a reason for Egbert leaving your house that you were afraid he would be burned out? If Egbert had staid there, paid his rent, and minded his promises, he would not have been interfered with.

1693. Did you have any fears of it at all? Only for the reason that he was trading with the negroes, and selling liquor to the negroes all the while. I had my fears about it for that reason, and for nothing else. I have seen him sell liquor to negroes.

1694. Have you seen other people selling liquor to negroes? I do not know that I ever saw liquor sold to negroes by white men elsewhere.

1695. Have you seen negroes drink in his house? Yes, sir; when I have been there collecting my rents, I have seen negroes drink there, both men and women.

By Mr. SHANKLIN:

1696. It was, then, the character of the house kept by this man Egbert that aroused your apprehensions? Yes, sir. I understood he had left town, but I went down there last night and he was there with this same woman. This morning I went down, and saw him again, just before I was summoned to this committee. A black woman, who lives in the other end of the house, told me this man, Egbert, had been coming back and sleeping with this yellow woman every night.

1697. You are an old citizen here, and are familiar, I presume, with the sentiments of the people; is there any unkind or hostile feeling existing, so far as you know, between the resident population of the city, white and black? None in the world between southerners and the negroes. I think there is a more kindly feeling between Americans, southerners, and negroes, than there is between the negroes and the northern class of people that come here. I think the negroes would go to the southerners quicker for a favor, to ask for money, than they would to any of these foreigners.

1698. Has there been some feeling between laborers, such as white draymen, hackmen, and hands about the wharf, and the negro population engaged in the same business? That is my opinion, so far as I have had the opportunity of observing. So far as any hostile feeling exists between the two nations, I think it is between the Irish and negroes. I think the negro population here look upon the old residents—southerners—as their best friends, and would like to have their protection if they were to get into any trouble with the Irish population.

By the CHAIRMAN:

1699. When they got into difficulty with this Irish population did these old citizens protect them? Every old citizen I heard speak on the subject said only one portion of the negroes were to be blamed at all: they were the negro soldiers who had been mustered out, had money, went to these groceries and saloons round town, got drunk and raised a fuss. Then the innocent negroes, who had nothing to do with it at all, suffered from the mob.

1700. Did these old citizens, who are so friendly to the negro, attempt to protect the negroes who suffered from the riot? Yes, sir; all the time.

1701. What did they do? They tried to keep these men where they would not be hurt, and to protect them as much as possible.

1702. Did they have any concerted movement to stop this murdering, burning, robbing and ravishing of these innocent men, women, and children? I could not say as to that; I do not know how it was. I know that a generality of the citizens were in favor of stopping the riot.

1703. Has this generality of citizens taken any measures to bring these parties to justice? I do not know anything about that.

1704. What have the people you speak of, as a body, done to vindicate the laws, vindicate justice, and vindicate the reputation of the city of Memphis? I could not say, of my own knowledge, that they had done anything.

1705. What, then, was their good will worth? It was only for the present; for instance, a negro would come along the street and the crowd would halt him; they would step up and excuse the negro, and induce the crowd to let him go.

1706. How many cases of that kind did you see? I did not see more than two or three; I got my information from Mr. Ferguson, who lives in the neighborhood, and who told me how the whole thing started.

1707. Were you here during the war? Yes, sir; all the time.

1708. Are you a registered voter in this city? I do not know that I can say whether I am or not. I did not get a certificate, but the officers who received the votes knew me all the time; knew that I was entitled to vote, and received my vote.

FRANK LEE (colored) sworn and examined.

By the CHAIRMAN:

1709. State where you live? In Memphis.

1710. How old are you? I do not know exactly my age; between 23 and 24, I believe.

1711. Have you been a slave? Yes, sir.

1712. How long have you been free? Since the war.

1713. What have you been doing in Memphis? I have worked on brick buildings, carrying hod.

1714. Were you here during the riots? Yes, sir.

1715. What do you know about them? I do not know much of anything. I was sick at the time. I saw them shooting at colored men, and the colored men running from them. I was put out of the colored woman's house I was in; I had the small-pox at the time.

1716. Did the mob do it? They did not do anything. A lady had me put out of the house. She said she would have the house torn down over my head, and said she would have me put out by the policemen if I did not go. She did tear one side of the house down.

1717. What did she have you put out for? I do not know. She came three times and said if I did not go she would send a policeman. She was a white woman who lived near the house where I was. She said one day she was going after a policeman, and I left the house.

1718. What was the name of this woman? Mrs. Diggins; she was an Irish woman.

1719. Did she use any violence? No, sir.

1720. Do you know of any violence used toward any one else during the riots? Yes, sir; an old man, " Billy," was shot through the bowels.

1721. Did it kill him? No, sir; he is living yet.

1722. Who shot him? I do not know; he was at work; he saw some men coming, and ran under the house. They shot him while he was under the house.

1723. Do you know of any other cases of violence? I do not, except of this Irish woman putting me out of the house when I had the small-pox.

1724. Where did you go then? The lady I had lived with, and who got me this place when I had the small-pox, after I was turned out got me another place with white people. She was afraid, if I lived with colored people, I should be killed.

EDMUND LACEY (colored) sworn and examined.

By the CHAIRMAN:

1725. Where do you live? I have been staying here at the hospital in Memphis.

1726. How long have you been in Memphis? About three years.

1727. How old are you? About twenty years.

1728. Have you been a soldier? Yes, sir.

1729. In what regiment were you? Third United States colored heavy artillery.

1730. When were you discharged? When they discharged the regiment and mustered the soldiers out lately.

1731. Were you here during the recent riots? I was here; I was not in that, but I was shot afterwards.

1732. Where were you shot? I went out where the 59th were. A couple of men came out and shot me. They asked me if I had been in the fort with the soldiers. I gave them my money and then they shot me. I ran away.

1733. Who were they? One of them had a wooden leg and the other man had not.

1734. Were they rebel soldiers? The one with the wooden leg had jean clothes on; that was all I knew.

1735. What language did he use towards you? What I said was all he said. I denied being a soldier to him.

1736. What did you deny that for? I thought it would be best for me; he had a pistol in his hand.

1737. Were you away from any person's house? I was right close to a colored woman's house.

1738. How much money did you give him? All I had; I do not know how much.

1739. Where did they shoot you? Right here in my shoulder.

1740. Was it a bad wound? I do not know; I can use my shoulder right smart; it was bad.

1741. Did you see anything of the riot? No, sir; when it was going on I never went out of the fort.

1742. Did you see these colored people commit any outrages? No, sir.

1743. Did you see them commit any violence upon white people in any way? No, sir; I did not go out of the fort.

1744. What did you hear them say? I heard them say they were fighting; I never pestered my head about it the whole time.

1745. What day and what time in the day was it you were robbed? It was Saturday, and a little after 11 o'clock.

1746. Where did they go to? I do not know. They got my money, shot me, and then run off. I never paid any attention where they went.

1747. You speak of one man being in jean clothes and having a wooden leg; who was the other man? I could not tell; both had pistols.

1748. Who dressed your wounds? Dr. Beecher.

1749. Where did this affair take place? Right out of town where the 59th are encamped.

1750. Was any person in sight? There was a colored lady there in her yard right in sight.

JOE STRICKNEY (colored) sworn and examined.

By the CHAIRMAN:

1751. Do you know how old you are? About twelve years old.

1752. Where were you born? In Mississippi.

1753. What county in Mississippi? I do not know what county.

1754. Have you been abused by anybody lately? Yes, sir; by white men and policemen. I was wounded that day of the fight. One of them came up to me and shot me on the hip. (Witness here exhibited marks of the wound.)

1755. Who shot you? A policeman.

1756. Where? On South street; I was playing there, when he run up and shot me. I do not know what he shot me for.

1757. What did you say? I did not say anything to him. He just came up and shot me. I staid in a black woman's house that night, and the next morning my mother came after me. They fought all night. A black woman took me into her house close by where I was shot.

1758. What were you doing that made him shoot you? I was doing nothing but playing with some boys when he shot me.

1759. White boys or black boys? White boys and black boys too.

MITCHELL WHITLOW (colored) sworn and examined.

By the CHAIRMAN:

1760. How old are you? About thirty-eight.

1761. Where do you live? In Memphis.

1762. Where did you live before you came here? I was born and bred in Middle Tennessee.

1763. How long have you been in Memphis? I have been in the 61st colored regiment. I joined in May, 1863, and served up to January last. I have been living here since that time.

1764. Were you in Memphis at the time of the recent riot? Yes, sir.

1765. What did you see? It occurred while I was at work. There was a noise raised up in town; I thought it was a fire; it was late Monday afternoon between four and five o'clock. I was at work at the bench on South street. A couple of men were at work with me. They told me to put up my tools and come down and see the fire.

1766. Colored men? One colored man and one white man. I put up my tools, and saw the folks coming back.

1767. Was this on Monday evening or Tuesday evening? I remember now it was on Tuesday evening; we stopped there and saw the folks coming back; there were two or three policemen close where I was, fifty or sixty others, and a lot of soldiers. They came right along the road ; some of them were cheering; I supposed they had just got out of the service ; the policemen did not take much notice of them ; we stood talking, and the policemen went on down street ; as soon as they turned the corner to the left hand they commenced firing.

1768. Who commenced firing? I suppose the policemen from the balls coming toward the house; several of the balls struck the house; I could not tell who shot them; the crowd then commenced falling back; they said two men were shot ; I did not see them; about an hour after that I went home.

1769. Did you see any man shot during the whole riot? I did not.

1770. Do you know any man who was shot? I saw one man who was shot, a drayman; I did not speak to him; there was such a crowd round him that I did not go to him.

1771. Who was round him? Some soldiers and citizens.

1772. Was there any violence exhibited by any of the people looking at them? No, sir; they appeared to be very sad; I went straight home; when about half way home, on Elliot street, I saw a large number of men fighting right smart; my wife was with me ; I went right on through; nobody said anything to us.

1773. Who was doing the shooting? White people. There was a lot of police and citizens, some forty or fifty; I could not tell who they were, nor could I see what they were doing, except they were running and shooting; one woman was shot close by me; she was in a window, and I suppose the balls were flying around so thick she was hit accidentally; I have seen her since walking about and holding her arm.

1774. Did you see anybody else shot? No, sir; I kept in all that evening and did not go out again for a day or two ; I did not see this woman shot, but I saw her soon after she was shot.

JOSEPH WALKER (colored) sworn and examined.

By the CHAIRMAN:

1775. How old are you? Twenty-three years old the coming March.

1776. Where do you reside? In Memphis.

1777. How long have you lived in Memphis? I lived here about fifteen years ago, and I have been here now since the north took Memphis.

1778. What have you been doing? I helped build the breastworks, and then I was in the camp guard for a year.

1779. Have you been a soldier? No, sir; no more than to be in the camp guard.

1780. Were you here during the recent riots? Yes, sir.

1781. What did you see of the disturbances? While it was going on, I was going home from my work one day; I saw the police and citizens coming down South street; I dodged round to get out of their way by the Tennessee and Mississippi depot, when a fellow got down from the cars and ordered me to halt; I would not halt and he shot me.

1782. Who was he? He was the depot agent, I believe.

1783. Do you know his name? His name was Palmer, depot agent of the Tennessee and Mississippi depot.

1784. What did he say to you? He did not say anything, except to order me to halt. His brother was on the top of the car, and called out "shoot the damned son of a bitch." He then pulled out a pistol and shot at me twice as I went off, only one hitting me.

1785. What was you doing? Nothing.

1786. Did you give him any words? Not a word.

1787. Where did the shot hit you? They fired three times at me altogether, but one hit me. The doctor could not get the ball out and it is in there yet.

1788. Are you getting well now? I am getting better.

1789. Have you a family? Yes; I have a mother, wife, sister, brother, and one child.

1790. Do you have to take care of them all? Yes, sir.

1791. Have you been able to work any since you were wounded? No, sir.

1792. What did this man say to you after he had shot you? He did not say a word. He went back to the depot, and then they got after another black man. That is the reason they let me go. When they shot me I ran off, and they could not catch me. They saw another soldier dodging around the bayou. This man got after him, shot him and killed him. My wife saw him when he was shot.

1793. This same man, Palmer? Yes, sir.

1794. Do you know anything else about the riots? No, sir; nothing else.

1795. Do you know what reason the Palmers had for shooting you? They did not have any reason at all.

1796. Have you had any difficulty with them? I did not know them at all; never saw them before that I know. I was just walking along quietly; the engine was standing on the track ; he jumped down and ordered me to halt.

By Mr. SHANKLIN:

1797. Are the Palmers employed about the depot? Yes; a colored man about the depot told me they were depot agents and staid there all the time.

1798. Are they Irishmen?   I do not think they are.

Were they engaged in the mob at the time they shot you, or standing there by themselves? Standing by themselves at the time.   I did not see whether they were in the crowd at all or not.

Dr. D. P. BEECHER sworn and examined.

By the CHAIRMAN:

1799. Where do you reside and what is your occupation?   My residence is Memphis; am now in the employ of the Freedmen's Bureau as surgeon in charge of Freedmen's Bureau dispensary.

1800. How long have you resided here?   I've been in the city three and one-half years.

1801. Were you here at the time of the riots? Yes, sir.

1802. State what, if anything, you saw in relation to it?   I did not happen to see a gun fired or anything of that kind, although my residence is within a block of where it took place.   I've seen quite a number of the wounded who were taken to the hospital; I was in charge of six or eight that were brought to the hospital.

1803. What were the nature of the wounds?   All had gunshot wounds, and some of them were stabbed also.

1804. Can you state the names of the persons who were brought to your hospital wounded, and give a description of the wounds?   I do not remember the names; I can obtain them if you desire it.   There were two wounded in the hospital.   They were sitting outside late in the afternoon, about sundown, and while they were sitting there some policemen and citizens fired a volley right among them, wounding these two.   One of them was a boy whose limbs had been paralyzed for two years; he was shot in the shoulder; the other one was wounded in the calf of the leg.

1805. In civilized warfare is it allowable to fire into a hospital?   It is not.   There was no one taking refuge there who had been engaged in the affair at all, as I was informed by parties.

1806. What offence had the parties shot committed?   None at all; they were merely sitting there quietly.

1807. Did these policemen and citizens do anything further than to wound these two men? No; the policemen were falling back at the time they fired, retreating before the negro soldiers.   This was a little before sundown.   I did not see it myself; I learned what had taken place from the patients in the hospital.   One of my nurses came down to see me; a policeman arrested him, took him to the city jail, and kept him over night.

1808. You know nothing, then, of your own knowledge of these parties being driven back? No, sir.

1809. Was there a boy in the crowd who was wounded and whose wound you dressed? No, sir.   Dr. Sharp was with me and may know some circumstances that did not come within my knowledge.

1810. What was the character of these wounds; were they severe?   Some of them were, but none were mortal.

1811. What was the character of the wounds that were severe?   The wounds were near the spine and in the vicinity of the bowels.

1812. Have you any knowledge of the circumstances under which these men were wounded?   Only from their own statements.

1813. Were they citizen negroes or soldiers?   Every one was a citizen negro except one; he was a soldier, and had been stabbed as well as shot.   Before I let any of them leave the hospital I reported them to General Runkle, so that he could get their testimony.   I dressed the wound, on the second day morning, of a colored man living with a neighbor of mine; he was shot through the arm.

1814. Have you had much to do with these colored people?   I have.

1815. In what capacity?   As surgeon in charge of them.   Detachments of them have been under my charge at various times.

1816. Have you any knowledge of this regiment recently mustered out?   I have.

1817. What has been the character of these citizens and soldiers; have they been peaceable and orderly or otherwise?   Some of them have been very bad men.

1818. Soldiers or citizens?   Mostly soldiers; in fact about all.

1819. What was the character of their conduct?   They have been inclined to pilfer and steal, particularly when they have been in crowds, in open daylight as well as night.

1820. Have they been addicted to drunkenness?   Yes, sir, somewhat, though not as much as the same number of whites would have been under similar circumstances.

1821. Have they been guilty of disorderly conduct at times, when drunk or sober?   Yes, sir; though I should say mostly when sober.

1822. What has been the character of their conduct?   Their great difficulty seems to have been a want of something to live on, or something of that kind.   They more or less have wives or women whom they live with.   Some time during last winter, about the Christmas holidays and along there, they did not receive their pay for a good while.   They said their families were suffering, and they were more prone to steal on that account.   I had my own house entered once; I do not know of my own knowledge whether by negroes or white men. I think there have been a great many robberies committed by whites that have been charged to negroes, but there have been a great many robberies, no doubt. committed by negroes.

1823. Has the conduct of the negro soldiers generally been worse than that of the same number of white soldiers? Generally, I would not say it had. I might qualify that in this way: a white soldier will pass through the street without ever having a taunting remark thrown out about his being in the army, which the colored soldier will hear, and they have more provocation sometimes for that reason.

1824. Have the colored soldiers been the subjects of insults and taunts by the citizens of Memphis? They have to a great extent—that is my opinion.

1825. You think they have been excited and influenced by these taunts and insults heaped upon them? I can give an answer to that by stating my own opinion of what led to this riot. Three or four weeks previous to the riot the policemen of the city had been making very unnecessary arrests. They annoyed these colored soldiers, and irritated them; in a good many instances using unnecessary violence. I think that is what brought on the difficulty. A week before the riot I heard of the case of a colored man who was arrested for some trifling occurrence, and pounded with a pistol until his brains came out; they killed him. I was satisfied from that, and from what I saw every day, from the conduct of the policemen, that that was what led to the killing of this man Dunn, and then to the fight that ensued; he was the first man killed that evening. Five soldiers shot him in the back, as I am informed. I believe he was the man who made the arrest the week before. I think the colored men, excited as they were, would have killed that man any way, whether there had been a riot or not.

1826. Do you know that he was the one who had been guilty of killing the negro the week before? Only by hearsay.

1827. But you know that the feelings of the colored soldiers were very bitter? Yes, and I have frequently heard the policemen talking about them.

1828. What have you heard them say? The character of it was, that they wished every "damned nigger" was killed, and soldiers particularly.

1829. Did they threaten to kill them? No; they did not do that, except with some qualification.

1830. Have you ever heard policemen or citizens make threats not against colored people, but those whose opinions were not in accordance with their own? No, I have not; though I am satisfied that was the way some of them felt.

1831. Why were you satisfied of that, if you had heard no expressions? I am a northern man; have lived here about two and a half years. I bought considerable property here at the time of the United States tax sales. Last fall I had two anonymous letters threatening my life if I did not settle.

1832. Did you settle? No, sir; I did not. The evening after the fires here, an Irishman, whom I had protected the week before when he was visited by the marshal, by explaining that he could not legally take the man's property—this man came to my house that evening as a friend; he brought a man with him to stay with me, and said if there was any trouble he could bring forty Irishmen to protect me. This was the day when it was said northern men were going to be cleaned out. I had no particular fears. I had my pistols ready, and was prepared to defend myself if there was any difficulty. But as there was some excitement, and the friend this man brought was one that I had known before, I allowed him to remain with me.

1833. What protection did you suppose they would give—the protection the wolf gives the lamb? Oh, no, sir; I suppose he thought I was obnoxious to a certain class of southern inhabitants, and he came to assist me.

1834. Do I understand you that this man came to you in good faith? Yes, sir; certainly, on account of the favor I had done him some time before.

1835. Then did you infer that he understood you would be likely to be attacked? I did, and it was for that reason that he desired his friend to stay with me.

1836. Was there any disturbance at all that night? No, sir.

1837. There has been none since? There has been none since.

1838. Have you ever heard threats against northern men? I have against the more radical portion.

1839. What were they? That they ought to be driven away from here—not that there would be violence used to drive them. Articles have appeared in our papers calculated to have that tendency.

1840. Do you know of any person or persons who have left on account of these threats? On the evening I refer to, which was the third day, there were some of the more radical men, one I recollect particularly, by the name of Chapin, an insurance agent, from the State of Wisconsin, came to me to consult as to what they had better do. Mr. Chapin asked me if he had not better send his wife and daughter to Cairo. I told him I did not think there would be any further trouble, but that it might be advisable to prepare for it; that I did not think I would send my wife and daughter away. He told me he was satisfied there was more feeling than I supposed there was. Upon the strength of that I went out to make some inquiries. I knew three or four families who had been in the Irving block when I had charge of it, and

I knew I could find it out if there was any disposition to trouble us. I got into a social conversation with them, took three or four out and treated them, with a view of being still more sociable and finding out what they knew; I became satisfied that if there was any such thing in contemplation they did not know it. Two of them, who had been in the rebel service, remarked that they did not care if the negroes did clean out some of the rebel citizens here, who had been the means of driving them into the rebel army. Mr. Chapin also consulted me in regard to the Rev. Mr. Bliss, as to whether he had not better take the boat that evening. I told him I thought he had better go out into the country three or four miles, and remain until the excitement had subsided; but for my own family I should have gone over there that night.

1841. Why was it that Mr. Chapin felt in danger? He said that from what he had heard that day, though I do not know that he mentioned any particular person or remark, that he had fears, and was alarmed for the result. I began to think that perhaps I had underrated the probability that there might be a further difficulty, though I had not had any fears at all until he came and talked to me that evening.

1842. Did he consider his opinions obnoxious to the people here? Simply from his being in the habit of visiting and carrying tracts to the colored people on Sabbath day.

1843. Is that considered a good cause of offence with the southern people? It is; he told me that one day he came into a store with a bundle of tracts under his arm, and made a remark to a man whom he had insured the day before, indicating what they were. The man told him that if he had known he was peddling tracts to colored people he would not have insured with him.

1844. What is the character of Mr. Chapin as a man? He is a Christian man.

1845. Where are you from? From Illinois, one hundred miles south of Chicago. I have always been considered at home a copperhead, but I have become one here of the Brownlow stripe; it is because I have always belonged to that party that I can get the opinions here of the extreme type. I am conversant with their feelings and opinions. I am more or less intimate with a good many who have sympathized with the rebel cause. I told them plainly that if it was their disposition to turn out northern men because they were northern men, I was with the negroes, or any body else, from this time on.

1846. Has there been a disposition here, as far as you have been able to ascertain, to drive out northern men who hold opinions at variance with a large majority here? Yes, sir; I am satisfied that while, perhaps, no violence will be used to drive northern men away, yet the feeling with a great majority here is not to encourage northern men. That has been the feeling here since a month or two after the surrender, when there was a change in the tone of public sentiment.

1847. Is such a feeling prevalent now? Yes, I think so.

1848. Has that feeling been fed and fostered by the press here? It has been to a great extent. I attribute it to that as much as to prejudice against the north.

1849. Have northern men, who hold what are considered to be the opinions of what are called radicals, been held up by any newspapers here as men to be shunned and avoided? Yes, sir; that has been to a great extent so. The character of the press here, except the "Post," editorially has all tended that way.

By Mr. SHANKLIN:

1850. While you were in the army were you connected with it as surgeon of a colored regiment? Yes, sir; my duties have been various. I have never been examined as a surgeon, but have acted under contract up to this time. My first assignment was to the 9th Illinois cavalry. I was then a short time in charge of the post hospital in Lagrange; from there to Corinth; from there I was ordered here in charge of the dismounted cavalry camp. I was then ordered as surgeon on the staff of General Hurlbut, and from that time until within a short time I have had charge of headquarters here.

1851. This fort has been garrisoned until within a short time back entirely by negro soldiers, has it not? Yes, sir, it has.

1852. And you have been surgeon of the post? There have been two colored batteries here until January that I had charge of for a time.

1853. You spoke of a prejudice in the public mind here against northern men. Is not that prejudice, or whatever you may call it, against northern men entertained only against those who hold very extreme views, and speak of them pretty freely? Including those who bought property at this government tax sale. I am satisfied I have no enemies, politically, here.

1854. Then I understand you to state that the hostility to northern men, so far as you know, is confined to men entertaining extreme radical views, and who talk pretty freely about those views, and men who bought property at the government tax sales? Yes, sir.

1855. I ask you whether that property sold for anything approximating to its value, or whether it did not sell for a very small percentage of its value? It sold for a very small percentage of its value, probably from ten to fifteen per cent.

1856. And you think there is some feeling against such persons as purchased said property at such rates? I know there is. I've heard time and time again that we would not be allowed to remain there.

1857. Have there not been some northern men here who have been somewhat noisy and forward in promulgating their sentiments with the freedmen, regarding emancipation, &c., speaking the extreme radical views? Yes, sir.

1858. Was that promulgation of their views, entertained politically by them, tending to harass and annoy persons in this section of the country who entertained different political views? It would probably have that effect.

1859. I ask you whether there are not many northern men here who have gone into business, and against whom there is no sort of prejudice or feeling that you know? There is no prejudice or feeling against them. But I know this to be the fact, because I've talked to a good many of them, and made the remark to citizens here that they would sooner southern citizens should succeed than northern ones, and their general course has been to encourage that feeling.

1860. Then it is a mere question whether they will give their patronage to southern men rather than northern men? Yes, sir, it is.

1861. You think they exercise that preference more liberally in favor of southern men than northern men? Yes, sir.

1862. You spoke of the feelings on the part of the police towards these colored soldiers. I ask you whether you have heard any expression of hostility of the southern soldiers against the police? Yes, sir, I have.

1863. What have you heard them say about the police? The expressions would generally refer to some real or supposed wrong they had suffered at the hands of the police.

1864. What would they say—would they make any threats against them? Yes, sir. Not to threaten life, or anything of that kind, but that they would not care if the police were all cleaned out of the city, or expressions of that character.

1865. Have you noticed the deportment of the colored soldiers in going about the city under the influence of liquor; and if so, what has been their deportment towards the citizens and police? Not worse than with intoxicated white men.

1866. Do you think it would be as bad? I do not think they would go as far with it, because what a white soldier would do a citizen would overlook sooner than he would if the same thing would be done by a negro.

1867. Still, you think their conduct, when under the influence of liquor, has been a little disorderly and offensive? Yes, sir.

1868. Were they not frequently straggling about the city in little groups of three, four, or five together? Yes, sir.

1869. They had no difficulty in getting liquor in the city? Only in certain classes of saloons, I do not think they ever have had. There have always been a plenty of saloons where they could get liquor.

1870. You have frequently seen them in liquor? I have; both white and black.

1871. You have known of the existence of this feeling between the police and negro soldiers for some time back? I have.

1872. Did not the feeling against the soldiers also extend to white draymen, hack drivers, and persons of that class, and also against black men engaged in those occupations? Yes, sir.

1873. And that feeling so existing was one of the causes which led to the riot? Yes, sir.

1874. So far as you have seen the general feeling and deportment of the quiet and orderly people here towards the resident colored population, who are orderly and quiet, have they been friendly or hostile? They have been friendly.

1875. This unkind feeling and jealousy is, then, confined to disorderly white men and disorderly black men, and that is what has led to these disturbances? I also understand you to say that if there has been any unkind feeling, it has been to wish that the negroes were out of the country, or something of that kind, and that it has not extended to any active hostility? There is a prejudice, of course, since the colored people became free, against their being here at all; but it would never result in anything unfriendly as long as they were here, or against those who were industrious.

1876. Do people employ as laborers colored people? They have to depend upon them in a great measure. The labor, I think, would be given to white men in preference, if they were here.

1877. That is a matter of opinion on your part, as I understand? I have had a little experience, in connexion with a partner here, in running drays; he spoke of the propriety of changing from black to white drivers; we made the change and found the difference in favor of the whites. I give my opinion from that circumstance. I have had no difficulty with colored people at all.

1878. Was that because persons who wanted to employ a dray would prefer a white man to a black? Yes, sir.

1879. As far as you have observed, which are the most careful operatives, white or black? White.

1880. Do men who employ laborers, employ the most competent as a general rule? Yes, sir.

By the CHAIRMAN:

1881. Is there such a good state of feeling here towards the quiet and well-behaved colored citizens on the part of the people of Memphis? There is no such good feeling; they wish them out of the country, but it is not such a feeling as would lead to the perpetration or sanction of such outrages as have been committed.

1882. Do you know anything further in regard to this whole matter than what you have stated? I was a little prepared for that trouble that afternoon, although I did not suppose it would lead to such a thing. I was in the hospital about five o'clock; there were about thirty or forty colored soldiers came across Main street to Shelby street, near where the hospital stands; they were singing and cheering. I started towards South street, and was satisfied there would be trouble if they got down there. I then cautioned my nurses to keep the patients all in the hospital; that there would probably be trouble. I supposed there would be nothing more than a drunken row, or something of that kind.

By Mr. SHANKLIN:

1883. Did these people seem to be under the influence of liquor? I could not say they were, not being close enough to observe them.

1884. But you thought, from their deportment, there was danger of some difficulty? Yes, sir; I knew there was a good deal of feeling on the part of soldiers, and when I saw thirty,or forty of them going away cheering and hallooing, I felt very sure there would be trouble.

By the CHAIRMAN:

1885. Is this hospital that was fired into generally known to be a hospital? Yes, sir.

1886. Have you any idea that the parties firing knew it was a hospital? That is a matter of opinion. I think they had; they were firing indiscriminately at men, women, and children, and I do not suppose they would have hesitated to fire into a hospital.

The witness subsequently presented the following memorandum of cases coming under his personal attention during the riots:

Case 1st. ALLEN SUMNER, discharged soldier; Gunshot wound through right shoulder; ball extracted after admittance into hospital.

Case 2d. ROBERT DAVIS, patient in the hospital; has lost the use of lower limbs; shot through right shoulder while sitting in hospital door.

Case 3d. LARRY SUMMERS, patient; gunshot wound through the calf of the leg; shot while sitting in the door of the hospital.

Case 4th. LOUIS BENNET, citizen negro; fracture of arm; lives in Arkansas; came to the city on evening of the riot; met near the Gayoso house two policemen, about dark; one struck him with a club on the arm, afterwards again over the head, taking from him a watch and fifty dollars in money.

Case 5th. CATHERINE FLETCHER; shot in the back while walking along in Main street; ball lies under shoulder blade; does not know who shot her.

Case 6th. ROBERT THORNTON, citizen negro; gunshot wound in right thigh, on the morning of 2d May, on Poplar street; was going to the baker's after bread; a citizen shot him.

Case 7th. HENRY BAINE, citizen negro, a blacksmith; was going home from his shop on the evening of May 1st; was shot by some one in a crowd of policemen and citizens, from behind him; was then, while down, hit over the head with a club and robbed of forty-five dollars.

Case 8th. JAMES JONES, citizen negro; was shot through the arm, while standing in the yard of his employer, by a white man.

Case 9th. ROBERT SMITH, citizen negro; knocked down with a gun by a citizen, and robbed; wound over forehead.

Case 10th. JAMES MOORE, citizen negro; knocked down with a gun in the hands of two citizens and robbed of twenty dollars; first was fired at, and then ordered to halt.

GEORGE HOGAN sworn and examined.

By the CHAIRMAN:

1887. State your residence and business? I am first sergeant company G, second battalion of sixteenth United States infantry, at present stationed in Memphis.

1888. How long have you been stationed in Memphis? Since the 13th of April, 1866.

1889. Were you here at any time during the riot? Yes, sir.

1890. What did you see in reference to it? We were suddenly called upon about 7 o'clock on the evening of the 1st of May. We went out in the city and found crowds of citizens everywhere assembled. I could see very few colored people. We had not any particular orders of any kind except to quell disturbances; everywhere we appeared all disturbance at once ceased. The next day we were ordered out again in the forenoon; we heard reports of fire-arms in the vicinity known as South Memphis. There were crowds of people down there, policemen, the head marshal, and sheriff; but I saw no colored people whatever having arms. We marched up street and then deployed as skirmishers, going through all the streets and alleys in that portion of the city. We searched all colored people for arms, and took their arms away if they had them.

1891. Did you have any order to take arms away from white people? No, sir; no orders to take arms away from white people at all. They all had arms and were careering around in every direction, hooting, hallooing, and shouting. I considered them a great deal more to blame, in fact, than colored people.

1892. Who gave you orders to disarm all the colored people? I received my orders from Lieutenant Clifford, and I presume he received his instructions from the commanding officer, Captain Allyn.

1893. Did you find any colored people armed? Very few.

1894. Did you arrest any? No, sir; I arrested none.

1895. What was the proportion of white people to colored people in the crowd? About one to fifty.

1896. What were the colored people doing? They were doing nothing at all except to find shelter.

1897. What were the white people doing? They were running hither and thither, calling out to shoot the damn niggers, and the action of the troops seemed to be rather to sustain the citizens in what they were doing.

1898. Who was in command of the squad you were with? The squad I was in when this was occurring was in the immediate command of Lieutenant Clifford.

1899. What was the conduct of Lieutenant Clifford? After we had skirmished up and down, we assembled, halted, and remained there, sending out different parties to hunt up colored men who had lately been in the third colored heavy artillery, bring them back into the fort, and prevent their going out. There were no orders given to disperse white people or prevent them from committing breeches of the peace.

1900. What conversation of the mob did you hear about the colored and other people? They wanted every "God damned nigger to be cut off from the face of the earth," massacred, burned out, &c. They were very glad the white troops had come there, for the insolence of the colored people had got to be unbearable; They thought the white troops would take the matter into their own hands and settle it.

1901. What did the white troops say or do? They had nothing to say or do except to stay and listen to their scoffs and jeers; for my own part, whenever citizens came around me talking in that way I ordered them off. They were a class of people who were in the habit of treating troops to intoxicating liquors for the purpose of inducing them to commit acts of violence, and as soon as their backs were turned they would commence swearing at the vile Yankee uniform.

1902. What language did they use? I've heard them say they had better make friends with the white soldiers, as they wanted their help to put down the niggers.

1903. Did they say anything of how they would serve white citizens, northern people, Yankees, and abolitionists? Yes; they spoke of Yankees, abolitionists, and in fact the whole northern people, as nothing but a pack of fire-eaters and hell-hounds. They said the events of the war compelled them to acquiesce now, but that there were better times coming, and they discussed their plans of bloodshed, vengeance, and so forth.

1904. What were these plans? To watch their opportunities until they could get together in sufficient numbers to overcome the troops and carry things with a high hand. The next morning a proclamation was issued by Major General Stoneman, forbidding the assembling of any people for any purpose. If that had been done in the first place, and we had been allowed to disperse these graceless scamps, there would have been no trouble. As it was, the troops were so widely dispersed that they could have been of but little assistance to each other in case of a collision. On Wednesday night the fires were looming up in every direction; before we were ordered out, the fires were under full headway, and it was impossible to prevent the buildings from burning down. We went down to South street and strung out in a line, by order of Captain Smyth, with directions to let no one through; but we found the line so long for the small force we had as not to be able to accomplish anything. After that, as we saw a fire looming up, we would go to it, and then see another looming up somewhere else.

1905. Who started these fires? This mob of white citizens who were roaming through the streets everywhere.

1906. Were there policemen among them? There were police all through the crowd.

1907. What did they appear to be doing? They did not appear to be doing anything but running round with the rest of the crowd; all their desire seemed to be to get hold of the colored people.

1908. Did you see any colored people to get hold of? Not with my own eyes; we were kept running about until I got tired. At my suggestion I was allowed to take a squad of five or six men and go about for the purpose of arresting parties who were setting these buildings on fire. We saw parties prowling about, but the moment they heard the tramp of my squad they would scamper off and disappear in the dark. It was so dark we could not see twenty yards in any direction. However, it had a good effect; for many of them got to have the impression that there were secret patrols of soldiers going about, and that they would be likely to be shot if they were caught setting buildings on fire; consequently there were no more fires after that.

1909. Do you think this military force which was out on Wednesday night prevented further burning and riotous proceedings? I think it prevented them from doing further damage.

150 MEMPHIS RIOTS AND MASSACRES.

GEORGE W. HAMMOND sworn and examined.

By the CHAIRMAN:

1910. What is your rank and position? Sergeant of company G, second batallion, sixteenth United States infantry:

1911. How long have you been in the service? Six years.

1912. Were you here during the riots? Yes, sir.

1913. What did you see? I saw most all of it going on; I was in it most every night; I helped disperse negroes and citizens when they had collected together.

1914. Where did you disperse negroes or citizens? It was on Tuesday night; I saw a building burning and no one trying to save it. The next evening after the fire I was at the National Theatre; Charley Morningstar, proprietor of the theatre, came and asked me how I liked the fire. He made some remark that it was a good thing; that they ought not to be allowed to stay in this place. He spoke of a church down on the corner of Main and some street. He said, "I was not there myself when it was set on fire, but I got a man to go in my stead; my business was urgent and I could not go."

1915. Got a man to go for what? I understood to help burn the building.

1916. Who is Charley Morningstar? Is that his proper name? I think that is his proper name. He is proprietor of the National Theatre.

1917. Is he an American? No, sir; I think an Irishman. He said "it was a good fire,' and laughed and joked about the affair.

1918. Did you see any violence committed? No, sir.

1919. Did you see anybody set fire to any building? No, sir; I do not know that I did; the streets were crowded.

1920. Did you hear any conversation of the mob? No, sir.

1921. Then you know nothing except the conversation you had with Charley Morningstar? I saw some men—I would know them if I were to see them again—having a bucket with them which they hid behind a post as we came along. One of them said, "That is some of the sixteenth, and we will get away from here." I know they were connected with the burning from what I heard and saw of them; I heard one man say there were plenty in it; that there were several different parties in it. I had no orders to arrest any man unless I saw him actually engaged in setting fire, and therefore made no arrests.

1922. What orders had you? If I saw men trying to set fire to buildings to arrest them, or if I saw men assembled together to disperse them.

1923. Did not your orders cover such a case as this? No, sir.

1924. Do you know anything further? No, sir; I should know these men if I should see them again. I know they are in business here in town.

1925. What countrymen are they? One is a Dutchman; the other an Irishman.

Dr. CHARLES S. LLOYD affirmed and was examined.

By the CHAIRMAN:

1972. State your residence and profession? My residence is Memphis; I have lived here about three years. I am a physician

1973. Where did you reside before you came here? I came from Canada.

1974. Were you here during the riots? Yes, sir.

1975. State what, if anything, you saw in relation to them? The first evening I saw nothing of it; the next morning I went down South street with Dr. McGowan. It was perfectly quiet that morning, although I heard there had been some little disturbance early in the morning a little distance from there, and that Dr. Sharp, perhaps, had been out dressing some wounds. Directly afterwards I saw a crowd looking up the black men shot the night before, and I left and went up there; after that I saw a great posse going up South street. Directly they started a darkey or two and all of them commenced firing away; who they killed I could not see. I saw no disturbance among the colored men; I saw one or two of them about. There was no crowd of them together; they were just hunting up these men; some were running one way, and some another. One of the men they started after ran through Main street, and came round quite close to the mob; they hallooed "halt;" he ran right on, and they turned and shot him.

1976. You do not know who he was? I do not know; he died afterwards, I understood.

1977. What did the crowd say? Mr. Garrett went up and remarked to some policemen, "By God, men, this shooting must be stopped." The policemen said, "This is a man who has been shooting us." I said that such was not the case. About that time another man stepped up to me and said there might be men there who did not know me, and I had better not say anything about that.

1978. Who was it said that? I do not know; I was introduced to him, but do not remember his name.

1979. You inferred, then, did you, that you were getting into trouble yourself? Yes.

1980. Did you see any other acts of violence? I saw some parties burning houses.

1981. Was this in the night? No, sir; this was in the afternoon of the first day of the riot. There were some houses close along the railroad, and I saw some parties go there. I asked what was up now? Some one remarked there was a white woman down there living with a negro ; the crowd came along directly, commenced breaking up the furniture and then set fire to the house. I was standing by the old grave yard, within thirty rods of the house.

1982. Did you see anything further ? I saw a great many chasing the darkies ; I saw them looking under shanties and everywhere, and when they started a darkey they shot him ; they would kill them and then burn them out.

1983. Did that apply to anybody but negroes ? After I went back, the first thing I saw was this crowd of policemen standing around Dr. McGowan's drug store. The night before there had been some fuss with the doctor, as I understood. When I got there Dr. McGowan was away, and a partner of his was in the store. A policeman was there who had the partner by the shoulder shoving him around very rudely. Another policeman drew up his gun three or four times to shoot this partner, but it was each time knocked down by others. Finally Captain Garrett came up and lectured them ; he said to them we came here to keep the peace and you are not doing it. They finally went away, and I got him to lock up his door, fearing he would be hurt. Parties came back three or four times and proposed to break through the door, and I believe some one did shoot through the door.

1984. Were there any threatenings against northerners, Yankees or abolitionists ? These men talked about that store being a place that harbored negroes, instigated riots, &c.

1985. Was it such a place ? Oh, no ; Dr. McGowan is very much of a gentleman in all his relations. Having a little store down there on South street, it would be natural that he should have a good many negro customers.

1986. You do not know of his inciting negroes to riot ? No, sir ; he was never that kind of a man at all.

1987. Do you know anything further ? That is all I can say personally ; there was a man shot right close to my door as he was going from his work ; I did not see him.

1988. Did you see his body ? No ; my landlord saw the body ; I heard Mr. Woolmer say he saw it. The darkie had been pulling down a little stable on Main street, and was going home ; the firemen were going home from the fires, apparently, and shot this black man.

D. W. TURNER sworn and examined.

By the CHAIRMAN :

1989. State your residence and business ? I live in Memphis ; I keep a family grocery.

1990. How long have you resided in Memphis ? About five years.

1991. From what place did you come here ? From Mississippi.

1992. Were you here during the rebellion ? Yes, sir ; all through the rebellion.

1993. Are you a qualified voter ? I am ; I am a native of the State of New York ; I came to this country ten or twelve years ago.

1994. Were you here during the recent riots ? Yes, sir.

1995. State what, if anything, you saw in relation thereto ? I saw some firing going on in South street during the early portion of the riot. I do not know any of the parties, however, firing the shots ; I saw one or two negroes shot, and one killed.

1996. State under what circumstances and by whom ? The persons shot I do not know. One of them I think has a store on Beal street. Some of those engaged in shooting I judge to be firemen, though I do not know any one of them.

1997. What did the negro that was killed appear to be doing ? He appeared to be running.

1998. Did you go to him ? I did not ; he lay there twenty-four hours ; in fact, I saw several negroes lying in the bayou, who, I was told, had laid there thirty hours.

1999. How about the man who was wounded ? That was on South street. He was a negro boy, about fifteen or sixteen years old. I was quite a distance from him. I think he was playing with some children, or going along ; they called on him to halt ; he started to run ; a policeman fired and shot him in the leg.

2000. What was done with the boy afterwards ? I do not know ; I saw him go up the street.

2001. Are these all the facts you know ? All that I know on that day. The next day I was on Main, near the corner of South street ; I saw the same men pursuing a negro there ; they were a policeman and a fireman ; they ran him down South street till he fell. The sheriff of the county was down there, and there was quite a commotion about that time. Several policemen went down to this man, to make an attack on him. The sheriff and chief of police both went down and took this negro man and led him off towards the fort, until he was away from the crowd, then turned him loose and told him to go to the fort. I know the sheriff and chief of police, both, had some difficulty in keeping the crowd from abusing this man.

2002. Had these colored people you saw shot given any cause of offence ? None that I saw. I saw a negro man, the first day, pass by my house and run into a house occupied by Mr. Merriweather, chief engineer of the Mississippi and Tennessee railroad. As I passed there I saw a negro man lying in the room. Mrs. Merriweather called to me to get a surgeon to extract the ball from his arm. I started out and met my friend Dr. Beecher coming along ; I called on him to extract the ball. The man stated that he was shot by a policeman while attempting to pass from a steamboat to the house.

2003. Did you see any cause of offence on the part of the negroes ? No, sir ; none at all.

By Mr. BROOMALL:

2004. Were they dressed in soldiers' clothes, or otherwise? The one I saw wounded was not; the one who was killed had soldier's clothes on.

2005. How were the three bodies you saw dressed? They all had on soldiers' uniforms.

By Mr. SHANKLIN:

2006. At what time, on Tuesday afternoon, did you see the first difficulty? I think it was about three or four o'clock.

2007. Were negroes engaged in shooting, when you first saw them? I could not tell you. The first firing I heard was in the vicinity of Elliot and Avery streets; I live on Avery, within about one hundred yards of Elliot. As I went down there, I saw firing on the part of the whites and negroes. This was the first I had known of there being a riot.

2008. Were there many soldiers around those streets? Not a great many.

2009. Did you see any of them with weapons? I did not.

2010. Did you go down South street, where the firing was? I went down there until the bullets whistled by me pretty close, and, as it was not *my fight*, I went home.

2011. Where did the bullets come from? I have no idea whether they were fired by white men or black.

2012. Did you see any negroes armed during the whole time? No, sir, I did not.

LORENZO JEAN sworn and examined.

By the CHAIRMAN:

2013. What is your residence and business? I am living in Memphis; am a carpenter by trade.

2014. How long have you lived here? About five months.

2015. From what place did you come when you came here? I formerly lived in Indiana.

2016. Were you here during the riot? Yes, sir.

2017. State what, if anything, you saw in relation to it? The first evening of the riot, I heard some firing close to my house; I looked out and saw ten or fifteen white men firing at a negro, running. The colored man ran around my house; they kept on firing at him; shot at him ten or twelve times, but did not hit him; they went off and left him. This was the first day of the riot, between sundown and dark.

2018. Was the negro a soldier? No, sir; he was a citizen. On the second day, a man by the name of Dennis came up to my house; he had some goods on South street he wished to move. I went down the next morning, with my wife and two children, and was helping him pack up his goods; I looked out and saw fifty or seventy-five men collected together near by, on South street; nearly all of them had arms, some revolvers and some shot-guns.

2019. Was this crowd composed of white and black? Of white citizens, in the first place, as I supposed. I told him I thought he had better get out of the way, as I apprehended trouble. Just as we came out of the house a colored man came running past, and just as he came opposite us they shot him in the arm.

2020. How near was he to you? He was so near as to touch my wife. I stopped to look, and she was three or four steps in advance, and the ball came right past, within a foot of her, striking the colored man in the arm; he ran on to get out of the way; we came off up into the town. Previous to that, I heard a shot fired; I looked out, and some one had shot a negro; I do not know who it was, and did not make any inquiry; I came back and went to work. I brought my family into town and staid till late in the evening, when I came back home. Everything was quiet until about 8 o'clock, when the burning commenced close to my house. I was up stairs and saw some one come up and fire the barracks occupied as a school-house; he fired them and went off. In a few minutes there were two or three more houses fired below.

2021. Do you know who fired these houses? I do not; I did not go out of my house at all. The first night of the riot, there was a colored man who lived about twenty steps from my house; he had been sick three or four weeks; I was personally acquainted with the man; he was a very good, quiet man. They came into his house that night, took him out of bed, made him stand up against the door casing, shot him, and left him lying dead right inside his own door. I heard the shot, saw the crowd, and went in and saw him dead.

2022. Who lived with him in his cabin? His wife, daughter, and, I believe, two or three others. It had very lately been an old stable, and was made into cabins.

2023. Where were his wife and daughter? In the room. I heard them beat and break down the door as I was standing in my house.

2024. You only know from hearsay of his being made to stand up, and of his being shot? His family told me.

2025. Where are his family? They are in the country; they moved out the next day.

2026. Was the house burned afterwards? No, sir; the house was not burned.

2027. You say the door was broken down? The door into the stable was broken down; he was lying in the door.

2028. What was the name of the colored man killed? His name was Shedd.

2029. Was he a peaceable man? One of the best colored men I ever saw in my life.
2030. Had he been a soldier? I think not; not that I ever heard of.

RHODA JACOBS (colored) sworn and examined.

By the CHAIRMAN:

2031. Where do you live, and what are you doing? I live in Memphis. I've not been doing anything since I got wounded, three or four weeks ago.

2032. When were you wounded, and where? It was on the Thursday night of the riot, I think. I cannot say for certain. I cannot tell who shot me; the man came to the door, knocking and banging away at it, and my mother opened the door. I was lying in bed. He asked my mother if there was a man in there. My mother said there was no man there. He told her it was a damned lie, there was a man in there. He pulled out his pistol and told her, God damn her, if she didn't light the candle quick he'd shoot her brains out. She lit the lamp, and there were five or six men came in at the same time. I could not tell how many there were outside. When my mother lit the lamp one pulled out my mother's bed, another turned around and saw me in the bed behind the door, and, before he had said, "There's nothing in there but children"—but he saw me looking large, I suppose, and I said, "I'm a woman, don't shoot!"—he just fired his pistol at me, and walked right out of the house.

2033. Where did he shoot you? The ball came into my arm between my elbow and shoulder, went through my arm, grazed two of my fingers, went through between the lips of my little sister lying in bed with me, entered my breast, and the bullet is right there now. The next day I moved away from there, and went into the fort with my mother and step-father. He was in the house at the time the men came, but he ran out the back door.

2034. How old was your little sister in bed with you? She was going on eight years old. I generally sleep on the floor, but I was so scared that night that I said I would sleep with my clothes on.

2035. Do you know the man who shot you, or any of the others who were in the house? No, sir; I never looked at his face, I looked at the pistol. I was afraid they would shoot my mother; I was not thinking about myself at all. He had his pistol at my mother's head, and had it cocked.

2036. Were they white men? Yes, sir; all white men.

2037. Had any of them a star on, such as the policemen wear? I do not know; I think my mother said some of them had clubs; they banged at the door, but whether it was with a club or a pistol I do not know.

2038. At what time of the night was this? I think about 3 or 4 o'clock in the morning.

2039. Were you asleep when they came to the house? I was. I snored so loud that my mother woke me up when they knocked at the door. She said I snored so loud that the folks could hear me on the street.

2040. What did you say, when they saw you and pointed the pistol at you? I said, "Oh, I am a woman! I am a woman! don't shoot!" One man said, "John, don't shoot, they are only children in that bed." We should not have noticed that the ball passed through my little sister's lips, if she had not said in the morning, "The man struck me right across my lips;" and then we saw that her lips were swollen. She was lying by my side, pretty nearly under me.

By Mr. SHANKLIN:

2041. What is your step-father's name? Anthony Simmons.
2042. How old are you? My mother says I'm about twenty.
2043. What else did you hear these people say? When I woke up all I could hear was their knocking at the door; then I heard a man call Anthony Simmons, and say, "Where is Anthony Simmons; ain't he in there? Open this door." If they said anything else I cannot remember it.
2044. Did your mother wait until she was dressed before she opened the door? She had on her dress; she had not taken it off that night.

JEREMIAH RYAN sworn and examined.

By the CHAIRMAN:

2045. Where do you live? In Memphis.
2046. How long have you lived here? About nine years.
2047. Were you here during the war? Yes, sir.
2048. What were you doing? Following my trade. I'm a wagon-maker.
2049. Were you here during the riot? Yes, sir.
2050. What did you see? I had been up town the day the riot occurred. I was going down Causey street coming home. I was crossing Vance street over into Main street, when I heard some hallooing. I did not know what it was: there was very much excitement. I turned around and went down Elliott street. There was a white man who came right against me, running. I've understood since that it was a policeman. He passed me on the

sidewalk. In a moment there was another man came up riding on horseback; then I saw a crowd of negro women on South street. Then I saw the man on horseback come riding up to the man who was running and stop him there. In a few minutes three citizens came up, and they shot this white man in the back, and he fell dead. Then I turned around and went home.

2051. Do you know who shot him; a white or black man? It was a black man.
2052. Did he shoot him with a pistol or gun? With a pistol.
2052½. How many black men were together? Three.
2053. How many white men? Only the one.
2054. How far was it from South street? The next block.
2055. Did they kill that white man? I do not know whether they did or not; I expected they had killed him. I understood afterwards that he recovered, and I also heard that he was dead. I do not know what his name was.

WEDNESDAY, *May* 30, 1866.

Dr. J. N. SHARP sworn and examined.

By the CHAIRMAN:

2056. What is your residence and business? My residence is Memphis. I have been a surgeon in the army most of the time, and am now acting assistant surgeon United States volunteers connected with the Freedmen's Bureau. When the riot occurred I had been out of the service a couple of months.
2057. Where did you reside before you came here? I came from Iowa. I have been here since August, 1863, except three weeks in Arkansas.
2058. Did you go up to Arkansas to remain? No; I went on business.
2059. What was the cause of your leaving there? I had a business house there in which my partner remained, and I returned to Memphis and opened an office here. I have been practicing some little since then. My time now is mostly engaged in connexion with the Freedmen's Bureau.
2060. Do you know anything connected with the late riots here? Yes, sir. On the evening of the 1st I was down town, and went home, I think, about four o'clock. As I went up Vance street I saw a large crowd near Vance and Causey. I did not go there. I saw a policeman I was acquainted with, who told me there was an outbreak of the negroes. The crowd went out South street. As I followed along I saw them firing and shooting every negro they met. When I came to the Bayou bridge I saw another negro in the bayou being chased. There were, I should think, thirty shots fired at him. He run up right among the crowd, and I saw several policemen shooting at him and beating him with their pistols and clubs. I then went round the corner and met a negro running, the crowd firing at him. I jumped over into a back yard and went through in front on to Avery street. There was a negro lying there who had been shot through the shoulder. I went up to him. I heard that a number of citizens shot him, making the remark that they hoped every one of them would be killed. I saw my wife standing out on the street where we live, and went up and stood by her. About half an hour afterwards I saw another person go along there and kick him several times in the face. He then stepped back, pulled out his pistol, came up again, put it right over his breast, and fired. I went down shortly afterwards and rolled the negro over. I found that he was pretty badly hurt. He was in the 3d heavy artillery last winter, and I knew him when I was at the post hospital. I got a negro to carry him down home and I dressed his wounds. I went up and was standing in Dr. McGowan's office. A citizen came in there and said he hoped every negro would be cleaned out. I told him that was riot, and that I thought it was the duty of every good citizen to discountenance such things. There was a negro boy, who had been left there by Dr. Hood while he went to take care of the wounded. A burly Irishman came into the door half drunk and walked round this boy two or three times. Said he, "You damned nigger, what are you doing here? Why are you not out shooting round the corner like the rest of them?" Dr. McGowan said, "Let that negro alone, I know him; he is a good boy." He turned to Dr. McGowan and called him a "low, dirty Yankee;" said that he was harboring "damned black scoundrels who were murdering white men." He swore "by God" that they did not want any damned Yankees here, and he be damned if they should stay in the country. I did not say anything, and Dr. McGowan said not another word. There was a large crowd around the door, and I knew if anything was said they would kill us. He called Dr. McGowan a liar, and abused him as an excited, drunken man would. This was after dark on Tuesday night. I started out and had gone about one hundred feet from the door, when somebody with a pistol halted me. I stopped. He said they wanted me; that they were not done with me yet. This was a citizen. He said to two policemen as they came up, "This is one of the men; I know him, by God." The same Irishman who was in the store put his pistol to my breast and said he would kill me. He pushed his pistol against my breast several times. A policeman, who had me by the arm, shoved him off. I appealed to him for protection, and asked him if he was going to stand still and see me murdered right under his eyes. He commenced hallooing for the captain of police. He came and ordered the policeman to let me go, and to let Dr. McGowan and the rest of them alone. I told him that I had not been connected with the mob at all, and, in

fact, I had said very little. He told me to go along home. I told him I would not go un less he would give me protection; that I was afraid I would be shot in the back. He told a policeman to see me out of the crowd. The policeman went along with me for some distance. I then went home and staid at home.

2061. Do you believe it was the intention of the mob to kill you? Yes, sir. I believe if the captain of police had not been there I would have been killed. I told Dr. McGowan not to open his mouth; that there were fifty men round the door, and that I had no doubt they intended to kill us. A policeman came to the door and said, "Come here. There is a God damned low Yankee who harbors the negroes that are out shooting." Carter, the clerk, told him that McGowan had done no such thing. The policeman said, "You are a damned dirty liar; I will shoot you," and drew his pistol to shoot him.

2062. Do you know by whom the pistol was presented to you? By an Irishman; I do not know whether he was a policeman or not.

2063. Have you ever seen that Irishman since? No, sir; I do not know him at all.

2064. Whose wound had you been dressing? Allen Summers's.

2065. How badly was he shot? He was shot in the right shoulder. I thought he had been shot in the breast. He stated that a man stood right over him and shot him. There was a wound about the seventh rib, but when I came to examine it I found it was a stab.

2066. Was there any injury about his head? He was struck over the eye, seemingly, by a policeman's club. The blow was a pretty severe one, and stunned him. He lay for about half an hour before he came to. I dressed the wounds that evening of several colored people. There was one man came to my office—I do not remember his name—who lived out in the country, and had come to town to do business for his employer. He ran into the mob before he knew it. There were two negroes together, and as a policeman ran between the two he shot this negro just below the knee. I have not seen him since that afternoon. I went also to see a colored woman the next morning who lived round on South street. The mob came to her house about midnight, kicked in the door, and asked if there was any man there. She said no. They ordered her to get up and get a light, and while she was doing so some one— her daughter told me it was a policeman—stabbed her twice. I dressed her wounds. They told me the crowd were going round hunting colored men, and were going to "kill every damned nigger" they found. The next night when I went down to see her she was gone, and I have not seen her since.

2067. State the nature of the stabs? The stab in front was just below the bulge of the short ribs and penetrated the cavity. The stab behind was about an inch from the spine.

2068. Was that fatal? I think not; although she was suffering a great deal of pain. I think she was bleeding inwardly, although I did not consider her dangerous when she left. The incision was a small one, not more than a quarter of an inch wide, perhaps made by a pocket knife.

2069. How old was she? She must have been about fifty years of age.

2070. What else did she say they did? I believe that was all. They went from there to other houses. I asked her if she could identify the man who stabbed her. She said not. Her daughter thought she identified the policeman, but she did not strike a light, and could not see him distinctly. While I was standing near the corner of Elliott and Avery streets, perhaps two hundred yards from South street, a crowd of police and citizens passed. I saw a little negro boy, I should think from his looks about twelve years old, come running down an alley to see what was going on. He stood about ten feet from the sidewalk, when a po- liceman came along, put out his pistol and shot. I saw the smoke of the pistol, saw the boy fall, and heard him cry out. He lay there a little bit, but finally got up and went off up the alley. I did not see or hear anything of him afterwards.

2071. Where was he shot? I thought it was through the hips, judging from the range of the pistol and his walk when he went off.

2072. You do not know the boy's name, or the name of the man who shot him? No, sir.

2073. Was he playing with other boys? No, sir; he appeared to be running down the street to see what was going on.

2074. You have spoken of the wounds you dressed. Were there any others? There were quite a number in the freedmen's hospital, at the head of Main street, I attended to.

2075. Was Dr. Beecher with you? Yes.

2076. Were they the same parties whose wounds Dr. Beecher saw? Yes.

2077. Then you know nothing of any other cases Dr. Beecher could not testify to? No, sir. I may perhaps remark that this Allen Summers was brought to the hospital.

2078. What did you see the next day? The next morning I started down town, went by the hospital and saw Dr. Beecher. I saw citizens running up street. They said there was a mob up Causey street. From there the crowd went over to what they call "Lickskittle," on the Overton property, where there were a great many negro shanties. They then came around on to and up Main street. I did not go anywhere near them at all; I kept out of the way of them that day. I did not leave my house. I stood at my door sometimes and could see them firing on Main street. I could see the smoke of the pistols and could see the men, but it was too far off to identify anything.

2079. Are you a surgeon of colored troops? No, sir; I have been for two years in the general hospitals of this city, until last winter, when I was ordered out to the post hospitals at Fort Pickering, where were colored soldiers.

2080. While you were in the fort, and the colored regiment was there, what was their conduct there? Very good.

2081. Do you mean inside the fort or outside? I mean inside.

2082. Do you know how it was outside? I do not. I have heard some complaints of soldiers thieving, but I never saw anything out of the way. They were always polite and gentlemanly towards me.

2083. Do you know of their being riotous or being boisterous towards citizens? I have never seen any of it since I have been in the city, and never saw any difficulty in reference to them until that morning, and then I saw no negroes fighting or shooting at all. All that I saw were running or trying to get out of the way.

2084. From your knowledge, living here in Memphis and having opportunities to know, will you state what has been the conduct of the colored people in Memphis, those who are soldiers and those who are not soldiers? As far as my knowledge goes it has been very good indeed.

2085. You have known, I suppose, of isolated instances of bad conduct on the part of negroes? Not more than you would find among the whites. You will now and then find a negro who will get drunk, steal, break into houses, &c., be arrested and punished, but generally they will be very quiet and peaceable.

2086. What has been the conduct of the people towards colored persons? I have not mixed much with the citizens, and know very little except what I have seen in the streets. When the police arrested a colored man they were generally very brutal towards him. I have seen one or two arrested for the slightest offence, and instead of taking the man quietly to the lock-up, as officers should, I have seen them beat him senseless and throw him into a cart.

2087. How many instances of this kind have you seen? I saw one on South street about a week before the mob. I was at Dr. McGowan's drug store. I saw five of the police walking rapidly past. I went to the door and saw a negro standing on the bridge. He had his arm up over a colored woman. I did not see that he was doing anything. I went back, and in a moment Dr. McGowan called me to the door. They had hold of the negro pulling him along. The negro was talking to them and wanting to know what they had arrested him for. They took him along right in front of the drug store, and one of the policemen went up and struck him over the head from behind. They took him along as far as Causey street, when he began to pull back. A policeman came up again, struck him over the head and knocked him down with his mouth in the mud. He lay there some time, just quivering, in the mud. They called a dray and put him on. That was the first time I heard any threats on the part of the colored soldiers. They said the man had just come out of the fort, and had not done anything. If they had had the opportunity, I think they would have used some violence. I advised them to keep quiet and let the police officers alone, for I had heard the negroes say if ever the police came up again and arrested a negro in that way they would resent it. It was about a week afterwards that the police came up and arrested this negro that created the riot.

2088. Who was the negro who created the riot? I do not know, except what I have seen in the papers. I do not know how the thing was started at all. I have heard that a negro was arrested, and that the negro soldiers got after him and killed him.

2089. Did you see or hear any other acts of violence committed on the negroes? No, sir; nothing more. I have dressed the heads of a good many.

2090. How many negroes' heads have you dressed? When I was in the Gayoso hospital two soldiers came in, one shot through the shoulder and the other struck over the head by a policeman. There was a case last winter, when I was in the post hospital, of a negro who was shot; I do not remember whether he got well or not; and another case of a negro who had served in the rebel army, and who had been shot by a policemen on Front street. He was shot through the brain, and another shot through the heart, and another through the back of the neck, breaking his spine—all three shots fatal.

2091. Do you know under what circumstances he was shot? The negro was employed on the bluff here by some men who owned cotton. After working all day he had gathered up a sack full of loose cotton, which his employer told him to take to his house. A policeman saw him out the way and accused him of stealing the cotton. The negro explained how it was, but the policeman arrested him and commenced dragging him along and abusing him. He resisted the policeman, who pulled out his revolver and shot him. The first shot was fatal, and he fell instantly, but the policeman fired two other shots after he was down. The policeman was arrested, tried by a military commission, and, I think, sentenced to the penitentiary at Nashville for five years.

2092. How many of these cases altogether have you seen? These five are all that I know of, or which have come immediately under my own observation. There are a great many many others I have heard of. I could give you no idea how many. There has been a great deal of it going on for the last two or three years.

2093. What has been understood to be the conduct of the police towards the negroes generally? Very brutal.

2094. Have you known the city authorities to punish a policeman found guilty of murder, assassination, or brutality towards a negro? No, sir; I do not know of an instance where they have taken any action in reference to this riot, so far. There have been no arrests made by the city or municipal authorities.

By Mr. SHANKLIN:

2095. You spoke of having been engaged in business over in Arkansas—what kind of business have you been engaged in? Mercantile and general supply business at Cotton Plant, Woodruff county.

2096. You spoke of an instance of what you conceived to be cruelty to a negro by a policeman who arrested him about a week before the riot—will you state whether the negro resisted the policeman in any way before he was struck? Nothing more than to pull back. There were five policemen who had hold of him. They were pulling him along, and of course he pulled back. He was hallooing and talking very loud. I heard the policemen tell him several times to keep quiet, but he still kept pulling back, when the policeman who was behind him struck him.

2097. Then the cause was that he was resisting, and they were compelled by force to drag him along? He did not resist all the time; he would walk along ten or fifteen steps and then stop and want to talk; he would want them to explain why he was arrested; then they would commence dragging him again. One policeman had him by the collar, dragging him when they struck him over the head.

2098. I ask you whether the soldiers in the fort have not been in the habit of coming down into the city in small groups of three or four, or more? Yes, sir, very often.

2099. Will you state whether many of them have not been in the habit of frequenting drinking houses on South street and in that portion of Memphis? I could not give you an opinion, from the fact that I do not think I was ever on South street before this riot.

2100. Have you seen them about drinking establishments in the city? Very seldom. I have seen negro soldiers quite drunk.

2101. Have they been, generally, when drunk, noisy and boisterous, talking loud and cutting up on the streets? I have never seen a negro on the streets drunk or boisterous. When they got drunk they would generally be arrested and brought back to the fort. It is very seldom you will see one on Main street drunk. They are generally to be found, when drunk, on the back street sand alleys, where I do not often go. Last winter there were soldiers round all the time patrolling the streets, and when they would find one under the influence of liquor they would bring him in.

2102. Were there many brought in that way? No, sir, not many.

2103. You spoke of threats being made by some negro soldiers who saw this one arrested and brutally treated by the police—will you now state what language you then heard used? I will tell you just as nearly as I can remember. When they started off with the negro on the dray or cart, there were, perhaps, twenty-five negroes standing there on the corner, and perhaps half of them negro soldiers. As I came back I heard a negro say that the police never came up on that street to arrest a negro without arresting him in about that style—that they must fall upon him and beat him senseless before they could carry him away. As I remember, he said, "That is about played out," or something similar. Said he, "By God, if I catch a policeman arresting one of our men in that way again I will resist him." The man's name is Posey. I said to him "You had better mind your own business. These men are officers of the law, and they have arrested that man for something you do not know anything about." I counselled them to let the police alone.

2104. What reply did they make? I do not know that they made any reply. I went off and went on home. There was considerable excitement among them at the time. They were talking on the corners pretty loud, as negroes will, denouncing these things, &c.

2105. Do I understand you to say you have never seen these negroes upon the streets act rudely or discourteously towards the police or anybody else? I never have. I have been here three years, and have never had a negro insult me or crowd me off the sidewalk. They invariably get out of the way when I come along. I have never had a rude word from one of them.

2106. Have you never seen anybody else crowded off the sidewalk by them? I never have. I think they have received credit for things they have never done. There has never been a robbery, theft, or burning, where the parties were not known, that has not been charged to the negro soldiers here.

2107. Has there never been any charges of that kind made against white men in the papers? Yes, sometimes, but that was where the parties were known. Arrests have been made of white men for stealing, murder, and drunkenness, but wherever there were houses burned or broken into at night, and the parties were not known, the negroes had to bear the blame.

2108. Will you give me a description of the material the mob you have spoken of was composed of; what sort of people were in it? The mob was principally composed of Irish police, Irish citizens, and firemen. There were a good many other citizens mixed up among them, but there were none I was acquainted with. I do not know as I can identify a man in the crowd. There was but one policeman I knew. He was a German, who had been in some way connected with the United States army.

2109. Were there not many citizens there mere lookers-on who were taking no part in the disturbance? Yes, the principal part of them were lookers-on, the same as myself; but a good many of them came out with pistols, which they loaded and handed to the police as fast as they fired them off.

2110. How many citizens and police would you think were actively engaged with the mob, using violence? I could not say how many—several hundred, I should think. There was quite a large crowd, and they were scattered over a large portion of country. I was not with the mob the first day. There was quite a large crowd I could see. I should think at least two or three hundred in it, and I should say thirty or forty leaders, who went ahead and did the firing. Then there were a good many citizens who stood back, but would run up and hand pistols to those who were shooting, and a good many others who seemed to be mere lookers-on.

By Mr. BROOMALL:

2111. You have spoken of the manner in which the negroes have been arrested by the police. Do you know whether any efforts have been made upon the part of citizens here to prevent that brutality? I have never heard of any.

2112. Is there any public sentiment that would warrant citizens so disposed from interfering to prevent such brutality? I do not think there is.

2113. Do you think it would be safe for any one who witnessed an outrage of that sort to be active in bringing police officers to punishment? No, sir; I would not want my name known if there was not military protection here.

2114. You have spoken of the manner in which the mob of firemen, policemen, and citizens acted—could that mob have acted as they did without a public sentiment to back them? No, sir; if the mayor of the city had said quit, they would have quit at any time.

2115. Where is the public sentiment? In what sort of people? It is confined to the southern people; not only to such people as the mob was composed of, but to such as the Argus and Avalanche people.

2116. Do you know whether any of the papers here that represented the great mass of people here have ever denounced this conduct of the police in arresting negroes in a brutal manner? No, sir. Some of our papers did, in effect, advocate it. Along last fall for two months they made the citizens believe that the negroes were all going to rise before Christmas, and advising citizens, if they did, to clean them out. They were constantly stirring up the people in this way. I was among the negroes of the 3d heavy artillery at that time, and I never heard a breath of such a thing from them.

2117. Has there been any behavior on the part of the negro soldiers or resident negroes to warrant any suspicion that they intended mischief? No, sir, not to my knowledge.

By the CHAIRMAN:

2118. What was the object of these continued predictions of insurrection about Christmas? I do not know, unless it was to get up just such a mob as was raised about the first of this month. I was talking with a man in reference to this very matter. He swore that the citizens of Memphis ought to "clean out every God damned negro in the city." I said to him that will not do. The negroes must have protection as well as the whites. He replied they might as well do it now as at any other time; "we will have to do it eventually." I told him we had no right to do anything of that sort; that we had law, and I thought all law-abiding citizens ought to discountenance all such proceedings. This was on the evening of the first day of the riot. He said that as soon as the soldiers were away they would have to do it, and he thought the people of Memphis might as well rise up and clean them out now as at any time.

2119. What is your opinion, from what you saw and heard, in regard to their cleaning out certain obnoxious white men as well as negroes? I have heard nothing, except the single remark I stated a while ago, made by an Irishman when drunk.

By Mr. SHANKLIN:

2120. Was he the same man who was advising citizens to rise up and clean out the negroes? No. He was the man I spoke of in the drug store. I think he brought this crowd to the door in the first place.

2121. What sort of men were those you heard make use of this language? The one who thought the citizens ought to rise up was an old gray-headed man, a citizen here.

2122. Was he an Irishman? I do not think he was. I think he was a native-born citizen.

2123. Have you ever heard any threats or intimations of this sort from the better class of the citizens of Memphis? I have not. The persons I have named belonged to the lower class of society.

2124. You stated you thought the tone of certain newspapers here gave encouragement to mobs by publishing articles stating there was danger of the negroes rising. Do you know what information those papers had on which the articles were based? I do not.

2125. If they had information on which they could reasonably rely that such was the intention of the negroes, would you have considered it wrong in them to publish it? No, sir. I know that among Union men no such information existed. I know that the publications in the papers so excited the people that many of them really thought that there would be an outbreak. General Stoneman even went so far as to require every officer stationed at the fort to remain there and not go out for nearly all the week of Christmas; but the thing passed over quietly, and there was no insurrection after all.

2126. Then all you can say as to the truth of these articles is, that you were not able to obtain such information? I was not, and I thought I had a pretty good opportunity. I questioned a good many negroes and was among them all the time. I was acquainted with two or three negroes who were educated, and with one who was employed by General Stoneman to ferret the thing out, if it existed at the fort. He was busily employed among negroes at the fort for two weeks, and he said that no such thing existed—that they never dreamed of such a thing.

2127. Do you think you had sufficiently the confidence of the negroes, or with that portion of them who would be likely to be engaged in a thing of that sort, to have induced them to confide it to you if they had such an intention? I think I could have got it from them at least as soon as the editors of these papers.

2128. Do you think they would have been as likely to communicate it to you as to any one else? Yes, for the reason that I was among them all the time, and the excitement ran so high that I took it upon myself to question them very closely.

2129. If there were negroes who contemplated such a thing, do you think they would have been likely to communicate it even to the better class of negroes? If such a plot existed, I think some of them would have known it and given information to the authorities. The better class of negroes certainly would have not countenanced it in any way.

MARY A. JACKSON sworn and examined.

By the CHAIRMAN:

2130. Where do you reside? In Memphis.

2131. Are you married; and if so, what is your husband's business? I am. He is a harness maker, and at present a paper carrier for the Argus.

2132. How long have you lived in Memphis? Five years. I came from New York city here.

2133. Were you here during the recent riots? Yes, sir.

2134. State what, if anything, you saw going on. I was in front of my house and saw one black man killed.

2135. What was his name? I do not know. I heard he was a stranger in the city.

2136. Do you know who killed him? I think they were white citizens. I am not sure whether there were any policemen among them or not. This was the second day of the riot, about 10 o'clock in the morning.

2137. What was the negro doing when he was killed? I do not know. They chased him across the bayou from the back of my house to the front, and there shot him. He laid there all night. His body was taken away the next day.

2138. Did you hear the crowd say what they shot him for, or make any remarks? I heard a lot of white people calling out, "Shoot him, kill him;" that he had shot at a white man on a horse, not hitting the man, but killing the horse.

2139. Who were the parties that said this? I do not know the parties. I heard them talking about it the next day. I heard them say the black man had just come in from the country the day before with some hay, or to get some hay, and that he joined some black men in the neighborhood aiming to do some mischief.

2140. Did you see a black man chasing white men at any time? No, sir; I only saw white men chasing negroes. I saw negroes running towards the fort. I saw one black man running, and heard him say he would take the life of one white man in that neighborhood. This was on Thursday, the next day after the riot.

2141. Was there a party of colored persons together? There were six or seven together, and they were all talking. One of them swore by the Almighty that he would take the life of a certain man who had burned down his house.

2142. Did you hear of the life of any such white man being taken after that? No, sir.

2143. Where were these negroes? On the same avenue I live on. I only saw them fighting on the second day of the riot. On the first day I only saw a negro shoot down a white man from a distance. I could see it from my back yard. The man fell; but whether he was killed instantly or not I could not tell at that distance. After that I saw two white men chase the negro, who shot him over back on the other side of the bayou. I do not know whether they killed the negro or not.

2144. Did you see any other shots fired by parties? No, sir.

2145. How far were you from where the white man was shot? About as far as that little shantie over yonder, (about one hundred yards.)

2146. How could you distinguish whether it was a white man or a black man at that distance? The white man was running away from the black man when the black man fired. I could see them distinctly. I do not know how badly the man was wounded.

2147. And you do not know whether the colored man was afterwards wounded or killed? No, sir. This was on Tuesday afternoon, when the riot first commenced.

2148. Did you hear white men making any threats against colored men? No, sir.

2149. Did you hear any threats made during the riot by colored men against the white? No, sir, only by the negro after the riot.

LUCY TIBBS (colored) sworn and examined.

By the CHAIRMAN:

2150. Where do you live? I have lived in Memphis very nearly three years.

2151. How old are you? I do not know exactly. I suppose about twenty-four.

2152. Have you a husband? Yes; my husband is on a steamboat. We came here from Jackson, Arkansas, when the rebellion broke out.

2153. Were you here during the riots? Yes, sir.

2154. State what you saw? Where I am living is where they had the best part of the fight. On Tuesday afternoon, when I first started on South street, I did not see it. When I saw the crowd they broke and run in every direction, boys and men, with pistols, firing at every black man and black boy they could see. They shot them down as fast as they could come to them.

2155. How many did you see shot down on Tuesday? I saw two. I knew one of them very well; he was a sergeant at the fort. Both of them belonged to the fort. They were killed dead about ten rods apart.

2156. By whom were they killed? The first was killed by John Pendergrast.

2157. Is he a policeman? No, sir; he keeps a grocery right there by my house. I was looking right at him when he shot the man. The soldier made an effort to get up the bayou. Mr. Pendergrast went to a policeman and got another pistol and shot him in his mouth.

2158. How near was he? As near as you are to me. I saw him put his pistol right to his head. I cried out, "Look here; see John Pendergrast shooting down innocent men in that way." By this time another man came in sight, about one hundred yards off. They beat him and kept him down until they could load their pistols. They shot him three times, burst his head open, and killed him.

2159. How far were you from this? About one hundred yards off.

2160. Were you near enough to see distinctly? Yes, sir: I was near enough to know him. This Pendergrast is such a notable man I could not help but know him.

2161. Who killed the second man? There were so many round I could not tell who killed him. Pendergrast was there. A colored man saw him fall over his dog in trying to get to him. I could not say who it was that killed him.

2162. What did they do after they left this second man? They just broke back to South street, shooting at every colored man they saw.

2163. How many other soldiers did you see them shoot at? I could not tell exactly. Every man they saw they went after, and the men would get behind other houses and out of sight. I do not know whether they killed any more at that time or not. There were plenty of them killed on South street; but I did not see them killed.

2164. How many dead colored people did you see on South street altogether? There were four who laid about two hundred yards from my house two days and nights. There was a colored girl burned up just a little way from my house. Her name was Rachael Hatcher.

2165. Did the four you mention include the two you saw shot? Yes, sir; four in all. I saw Rachael when they shot her, and I saw her when she was burned up.

2166. What were the circumstances under which she was burned? They burned down the school-house that day, and at night they set the houses on fire. They barred up all the doors, then surrounded the houses and told the folks to stay in there.

2167. Is that what they told you? Yes, sir; but I saw them surround the houses. The old man Pendergrast and his son set them on fire. I saw them when they set the houses on fire. When the fire got very hot I saw men, women, and children break out and run to the bayou. They shot at them as fast as they could while they were running. They wounded some of them, but did not kill any except that girl. When the house she was in was on fire she ran out, and just as she turned the corner they shot her in the mouth. She fell down between two houses, and both houses were burned. I saw her body the next day, and they took it away the same evening.

2168. Who took these bodies away finally? They said the citizens took them away. I know the wagons went round that evening and took them up. It was white men that took them away.

2169. How long did the bodies remain before they took them away? Some of them lay from Tuesday afternoon until Thursday or Friday before they were taken up. I took no notice of the date.

2170. Were there any threats made against you? Mr. Pendergrast's boy, the one that has since run off, said to a yellow woman that if I said he killed the man across the bayou he would kill me.

2171. Who is this Pendergrast? This young man run off about three weeks ago, but he dodges back and forth. The old man is still there, and one of his sons.

2172. Was it the young man or the old man you saw shoot? It was the young man who run off. I saw the old man and his youngest son both in the crowd there.

2173. Did the old man have pistols? The old man and his son both had pistols. Just where I live, when the greatest fight was going on Wednesday morning, there were, I should think, four hundred persons in the crowd. They were just firing at every colored man and boy they could see. They killed a colored soldier just above my house on Wednesday morning, about 9 o'clock. The policeman Roach shot this man and wounded him in the leg. A man by the name of Galloway, a white drayman, was there. The policeman said, "Galloway, there is a damned rascal who was in the fray yesterday afternoon." There were two soldiers together; one of them ran and got away. They surrounded the other and kept him there. He said to them, "I was not in it at all; please don't kill me." They said, "Yes you were," and policeman Roach fired and shot him in the leg. At this time he was rather leaning over a gate. Galloway walked up to him, put a pistol to his head and shot him down. He died before anybody could get to him. After Mr. Cash shot Charley Wallace, and they had searched his pockets, some women came up and bathed his head in water. He belonged to the 59th regiment. I do not know the name of the other colored man who was shot.

2174. Where does this Mr. Cash live? He is staying at Pendergrast's now.

2175. What does he do? He is not doing anything. He got burned out some two months ago. I understood he bought another place a few days ago.

2176. I understand you to say, then, you saw four men killed under the circumstances tated, and that you know in addition of two others being killed, and that then you saw the dead body of this girl Rachael? Yes, sir; and my brother got killed on Tuesday afternoon; who killed him I do not know.

2177. What was his name? His name was Bob Taylor. He had been a member of the 59th regiment, but was out of the service. On Tuesday afternoon when they were firing and going from house to house, I told him to try and get away if he could. He started to run away, but was found dead the next morning by the bayou just back of my house. He was older than I am. They robbed me that night of $300 of his money.

2178. Did they come into your house? Yes; a crowd of men came in that night; I do not know who they were. They just broke the door open and asked me where was my husband; I replied he was gone; they said I was a liar; I said, "Please do not do anything to me; I am just here with two little children."

2179. Did they do anything to you? They done a very bad act.

2180. Did they ravish you? Yes, sir.

2181. How many of them? There was but one that did it. Another man said, "Let that woman alone—that she was not in any situation to be doing that." They went to my trunk, burst it open, and took this money that belonged to my brother.

2182. Did they violate your person against your consent? Yes, sir; I had just to give up to them. They said they would kill me if I did not. They put me on the bed, and the other men were plundering the house while this man was carrying on.

2183. Were any of them policemen? I do not know; I was so scared I could not tell whether they were policemen or not; I think there were folks that knew all about me, who knew that my brother had not been long out of the army and had money.

2184. Where were your children? In bed.

2185. Were you dressed or undressed when these men came to you? I was dressed.

2186. Did you make any resistance? No, sir; the house was full of men. I thought they would kill me; they had stabbed a woman near by the night before.

2187. How old are your children? One of them will soon be five, and the other will be two years old in August.

2188. What did they mean by saying you was not in a condition to be doing that? I have been in the family way ever since Christmas.

2189. Who was this woman stabbed the night before? I do not know. I heard a woman and a man who went over there and saw her talking about it.

2190. Was she violated too? I suppose she was; they said she was. The next night they burned all those shanties down. Where they went to I could not tell.

2191. How many houses did they burn down? Three or four.

2192. Would you know this man who committed violence upon you if you should see him? I do not think I would.

2193. What countryman was he? I could not tell.

2194. What countrymen did the crowd appear to be? They appeard to be like Irishmen.

2195. How many rooms were there in your house? Only one.

2196. And this took place in the presence of all these men? Yes, sir.

2197. Have you stated everything you know? They killed a woman's husband who lives next house to me. He lived a week. She was gone to the fort. The next day he said he would stay close in the house, and he did not think they would trouble him. They called him outside the house and shot him down. There was a crowd about, and I could not tell who shot him. They shot him three times, and one of them said, "Damn you, that will show you how to leave your old mistress and master." They took $25 from his pocket. I saw them when they shot him on Wednesday morning. His name is Fayette Dickerson.

2198. Then that makes five you saw killed? Yes, sir.

2199. Did you know any one in this last crowd? The old man Pendergrast and his three sons were all in the crowd. Mr. Cash was there and Charley Toler.

2200. Who is Charley Toler? He is a young white boy, very nearly grown, who lives right there. I could not identify any of the others, except Charley Smith; I did not see him kill anybody or do anything. He said he had been in the Union army; he had been teaching school; I had been to school to him. I asked him if he would not come and stay at my house and protect it. He said he could not and could not tell me anything about it; that he was out with his gun the night before with thirty or forty others, and he did not know what they were going to do—that the negroes started it, and that he would be ready for them. I believe he was put in jail.

2201. What for? A woman who washed his clothes made complaint against him. His clothes were all bloody, and she supposed he brought a dead man's clothes there for her to wash. They were clothes he had never brought before.

2202. Do you know who he was arrested by? He was arrested by the bureau and is confined at the fort.

By Mr. SHANKLIN:

2203. Did you see the commencement of the fight, or had you heard shooting before you saw anything? I did not see the commencement; I heard the first firing.

2204. Where is your house located? Just the other side of South street, on Rayburn avenue.

2205. What time was it in the evening when you saw the first fighting? I suppose about six o'clock, perhaps half an hour before sundown, when I saw the first man killed. I had heard shooting before that.

2206. How far from where you live was the first firing that afternoon? It was right in sight of my house. I could not tell you how far. I suppose about two blocks.

CYNTHIA TOWNSEND (colored) sworn and examined.

By the CHAIRMAN:

2207. Where do you live? On Rayburn avenue, Memphis.

2208. How long have you been in Memphis? About eighteen years.

2209. Have you been a slave? Yes; but I worked and bought myself. I finished paying for myself a few days before they took this place.

2210. Were you here at the time of the riot; if so, state what you saw? Yes. It was right before my door; I do not believe I could express what I saw. On Tuesday evening, the first of May, the riot began. I saw shooting and firing. On Wednesday morning I saw a man by the name of Roach, a policeman, shoot a negro man; he was driving a dray. Mr. Roach ran up and shot him right in the side of his head. I saw Mr. Cash on Wednesday morning when he shot a man by the name of Charley Wallace. Charley ran down to the bayou; came back; and as he turned the corner of my house, Mr. Cash shot him in the back part of the head. They went up to him, turned him over, turned his pocket inside-out, and took out his pocket-book.

2211. Where were the policemen? I do not know the policemen only by the star they wear. I know Mr. Cash. I did not see any other men killed. When the old man Pendergrast was burning up the houses there, I saw them shoot a young girl; I could not say who did it. She fell right between two houses standing close together, and the houses were burned down right over her. I saw the Pendergrasts burning and plundering until broad day-light. The colored people were trying to get out of the houses. They told them that if they came out they would kill them. They fired into one house at a woman. She said, "Please, master, let me out." He said, "If you don't go back I'll blow your damned brains out." She went back. They set the house on fire. She just broke right out, and they all fired at her as fast as they could. I saw Mr. Pendergrast's son Pat fire at her as soon as she came in sight. This girl Rachael who was shot and burned was a nice, smart girl; I could not tell you how old she was; she was quite a young woman.

2212. How many shots did they fire at this woman when she came out? I could not tell how many shots—a great many.

2213. Did you see them firing at other people who were coming out of the houses? Be sure and state only what you saw. Yes, sir; I am telling you the truth, and I know I have got to give an account of it. There were little children coming out of the houses, and they fired at them. I saw four or five come out at one time. Little children, old people, and women seemed to be all coming out together, and they just fired right at them. I did not see it, but they said they shot one little child's arm off.

2214. Where did these people go when they came out of the house? Some of them ran into my house. I do not know what has become of them since.

2215. Have you a husband? Yes. My husband and son are about seven miles in the country at work. I sent word to them not to come back until this fuss was over.

2216. Do you know the names of the family you saw come out of this house? No, sir; I do not. One woman came running up and said she liked to have been burned in her house. Mr. Pendergrast had shot at her. She said she got down on her knees and prayed the man to let her out; that she had a little son in there with her. He told her if she did not go back he would kill her. This man McGinn was in the crowd. He seemed to know this woman, and said, "That is a very good woman; it is a pity to burn her up; let her come out." She came out and her little boy with her. The boy had blue clothes on. They pushed him back, and said, "Go back, you damned son of a bitch." She fell on her knees and begged them to let the child out; that it was the only child she had. McGinn told her that she might take some of her things out, which she did; and I saw them take the things from her and burn them up. They let her little boy out afterwards. There was a man broke into my yard while they were shooting. They followed him and shot him down, right in my yard. His name is Dickerson. They did not kill him then. He was just as clever a man as ever I saw.

2217. Are you a member of the church? Yes; a member of the Baptist church. I saw Mr. Pendergrast go into his grocery, and give ammunition to a policeman to load his pistols with. Then they started out again, firing and shooting. They started a negro man, who ran up the bayou. They told him to come up to them. He came up, and one of them put his pistol to the man's mouth, and shot his tongue out, and killed him dead. His name was Lewis Robertson.

2218. Did you see that? No, sir; but I saw him directly afterwards, when he was kicking and struggling in death. His tongue was out; they opened his mouth and said his tongue was shot off; they shot him twice, once through the head and once through the thigh. The lady who lives next door was looking out, and said, "Just look at that man, John Pendergrast, shooting and killing that negro;" and this Pendergrast was a man the colored folks thought so much of, too, and had done so much for him I sent for the old man to ask him about it. He said, "Aunt Cynthia, I am the man that fetched this mob out here, and they will do just what I tell them; I know you are good old people here." I said, "Mr. Pender, will you please take my house and keep it for your own, and let me go away until this fuss is over?" He said he would not advise me to go away; that it was all done with now.

2219. Did they rob your house? Yes; they took my clothes, and fifty dollars in money, but I did not consider that much. They came in my house and took what they pleased; they took out some quilts that I had, too, but I never said a word about it.

2220. Who did the money belong to? It belonged to my son who was in the army, Frank King.

2221. Do you know of any violence being committed on the women in your neighborhood? Yes, sir; I know of some very bad acts.

2222. State what you saw? I could not tell you what I saw; I could have seen it if I had been a mind to.

2223. State the circumstances? There is a woman who lives near me by the name of Harriet; Merriweather was her name before she was married; I do not know what her husband's name is. There were as many as three or four men at a time had connexion with her; she was lying there by herself. They all had connexion with her in turn around, and then one of them tried to use her mouth.

2224. Was this during the riot? Yes, sir; it was on Monday evening.

2225. Did you see these men go in the house? Yes; I saw them going into the house and saw them coming out, and afterwards she came out and said they made her do what I told you they did; she has sometimes been a little deranged since then, her husband left her for it. When he came out of the fort, and found what had been done, he said he would not have anything to do with her any more. They drew their pistols before her and made her submit. There were white people right there who knew what was going on. One woman called me to go and look in and see what they were doing; that was when this thing was going on. She is the woman who came and made a complaint to Charley Smith; she is a very nice woman.

2226. Did she make complaint against Charley Smith for having a hand in this outrage? No; she complained to him; he was not in the house.

2227. What was the name of this woman? I cannot tell you; there are two of them who live on Webster street.

By Mr. BROOMALL:

2228. How many houses did you see burnt? I do not know that I could tell you; the first one I saw burnt was right close to my house. There was a square which had a school-house on it, and I could not tell you how many little cottages; I suppose there were as many as twenty cottages burned on that square.

By Mr. SHANKLIN:

2229. Did you see with your own eyes any portion of the difficulty on the evening of the first fight? Yes, sir; I did see a good deal; I saw a policeman shoot a soldier on Causey street. From that these black soldiers gathered, and a lieutenant at the fort shot the policeman who shot the soldier.

2230. Did you see colored soldiers shoot? Yes; I saw them shooting; I did not see them hit any one.

2231. How many colored soldiers were there shooting? I could not tell; they had given up their guns, and had nothing but their pistols.

2232. How many white men did you see engaged in shooting on Tuesday evening? I do not know; I never saw so many together, they gathered from every direction.

2233. Do you know the man who shot the policeman? He was a lieutenant in the colored regiment, a white man; I do not know his name.

2234. He was with the colored men shooting at the police, was he? Yes, sir; I do not know how the fuss began, though I was within two hundred yards of it when it began. I do not know that it amounted to anything, I only heard the report that the policeman was shot.

By the CHAIRMAN:

2235. Who was killed first, the colored man or the policeman? The colored man, one or two of them; then the soldiers came down South street, and went after the policemen as fast as they could.

Dr. ROBERT WHITE sworn and examined.

By the CHAIRMAN:

2236. State your residence and profession? I have been living in Memphis about two years, and have practiced medicine.

2237. Where did you reside before you came here? In the State of Iowa.

2238. Were you here at the time of the mob? I was, but saw nothing of it at all.

2239. Were you called upon to dress any wounds? I was not; and know nothing whatever about the affair, from my own knowledge.

2240. What have you heard said about the cause of the riot? I have no doubt it originated from a feeling which has existed here for a long time between the colored people and the police. It is very questionable in my mind whether it was not caused by over-anxiety on the part of the police to do their duty in arresting colored people.

By Mr. SHANKLIN:

2241. Do you know of any fact which led to the creation of this feeling between the police and colored people? I cannot say I know any particular fact. Several difficulties occurred long before, in which our police, I think, showed at least a want of good government. It is well known that our present police, as a body, are exceedingly poor. It is made up mostly of the poorer sort of Irish, whose prejudices against the negro are very strong. I will say for the people here, although I am a northern man, that I do not believe the better class of citizens either knew of or had anything to do with the riot in its inception. I mean the better class of southern gentlemen whom I have met here. Those I have conversed with have regretted very much what has occurred. I do not mean to include in my remark the mayor of the city or some of the common council, by any means.

2242. Have you noticed the deportment of the negro soldiers here on the streets since Christmas, or about that time? I have; they have been very orderly and quiet. Previous to General Stoneman's coming here there was cause of complaint; since he came we have had perfect order. He broke up the practice of allowing negro soldiers to walk through the streets with their arms when not on duty.

2243. What was the deportment, previous to that, of these negro soldiers when on the street? Sometimes as good as it could be, and sometimes a little ugly.

2244. Have you seen them drunk at any time? Yes; I saw a collision one day between a gentleman and some soldiers right in front of my office. I think the gentleman was as much to blame as they were. They happened to hit against him as they passed. He turned and cursed them, until finally the negroes drew their pistols, and I thought they were going to fire, but they did not.

By Mr. BROOMALL:

2245. You have spoken of violent arrests upon the part of the police, or of arrests in which the police used more violence than was necessary: can you state any instances of such violence? I recollect one instance that occurred as I was going down from my dinner. I think two negroes were shot. The police were after them and seemed to fire indiscriminately; in fact, everybody in the neighborhood was in danger. If you had lived here two or three months ago you would have come to the conclusion that you were in more danger from the police than anybody else. One of the parties shot, I believe, was struck in the shoulder, but he was not killed. I do not know where the other was wounded.

2246. You have stated that the better sort of people here deprecated these recent occurrences; is there not a public sentiment here, more noisy than that of the better class of people, which justifies it? I think there is. I think there is a sentiment of that sort among the lower class of Irish and other citizens that would justify almost anything, simply because they do not stop to reflect at all.

2247. If the better class of citizens were to exert their full influence upon this lower class, is it not your opinion that the difficulty might be remedied? I will tell you how I think it could be remedied. There are two sorts of papers here—one is doing all it can to harmonize the feeling among the people, and the other is going just as far in the opposite direction.

2248. What papers do you refer to? I should include the Avalanche and Argus in the latter class.

2249. What has been the feeling of the people towards the negroes here? There is a class of persons here who are under the impression that the negro was born to steal and lie. I think most of them, however, are inclined to treat the negroes well.

By Mr. SHANKLIN:

2250. I ask you whether the better class of people, under the laws of Tennessee, have any control over the elections of the city officers, or the appointment of the police? No, sir. Our present organization is exceedingly bad. I am in hopes our new police commission will give us a better class of men.

2251. Would it not be dangerous for any citizen here, whatever his standing, personally to interfere with these police, or remonstrate very earnestly against their proceedings? A person might be in danger.

Dr. JOSEPH E. LYNCH sworn and examined.

By the CHAIRMAN:

2252. State your residence and profession? I live in Memphis, and have been practicing medicine and surgery for the last year. I enlisted in the United States service in New York city, and came here in charge of the government hospital.

2253. Were you here at the time of the recent riots? Yes, sir.

2254. What, if anything, did you see of them? I was coming in from the orphan asylum late in the afternoon, about dark, and about Vance and Hernando streets saw a crowd of, I should think, one hundred and fifty policemen running out. I asked them where they were going. They said there was a big fight in South Memphis. They did not know what it was, but said they were ordered out there by the mayor. I was in a buggy, drove out there rapidly, and got there before the firing commenced on the corner of Causey and South streets. When the police came up there was considerable firing on both sides. My horse got frightened and broke his harness, and I had to get out. The police were firing pretty rapidly. I gave my horse in charge of a servant. At that time there was a negro shot right in front of my horse, on the bridge. I met Dr. McGowan, a friend of mine, standing over a policeman who had been shot. He examined his wounds, had him put on a stretcher, and conveyed back into the city. The policeman, I believe, had been shot in the hip. I remained with Dr. McGowan a little while, until the fight was all over, and then drove back into the city. As I went down Hernando street I saw another negro killed on Beal street, close to the bridge. I do not know how the fuss commenced. They were beating him on the head when I first saw them. The negro got away from them, over on to the pavement, when some one hit him with a billet of wood and knocked him down. About that time one of the party engaged in beating him shot him once, walked back four or five steps, came up and shot him again. I supposed he was killed. That evening, after tea, I went to a drug store to see a man who was dying. At the same time I had been told there was a man round at my office dangerously wounded. I saw the man was evidently dying, and did not stop to make any examination. His name, I believe, was Dunn, an engineer of the fire department. He died, as I understood, in about twenty minutes. When I got to my office the man who had been there waiting had been taken away. I believe he was a policeman, and had Dr. Keller to attend him.

2255. Were there any policemen in the crowd on Beal street that killed this negro man? I do not know the policemen of this town. Half of them do not wear their uniform. They were white men.

By Mr. SHANKLIN:

2256. When you got down there, were white men doing the shooting, or was it being done by white men and negroes both? I could not say; I saw one or two white men shooting, and there were a great many of the police flying round. I did not know where the shots came from. I know I came very near getting shot myself, though I do not suppose any one intended it. I do not think I saw any negroes engaged in shooting.

2257. What was the character of the mob down there as far as you can state it? It was composed of citizens and policemen, mostly not in uniform.

2258. Were the citizens engaged in shooting? I did not see them shooting; they were up there, I suppose, prepared to shoot; most of them had arms.

2259. Were they orderly citizens, or composed of the rabble? They were rather of the rabble of the city. I did not see a respectable man among them.

H. G. DENT sworn and examined.

By the CHAIRMAN:

2260. State your residence and occupation? I have lived in Memphis about twenty-five years; am a real-estate broker at this time.

2261 Were you here all the time during the war? Yes, sir.

2262. Were you here during the late riots? Yes, sir.

2263. State what, if any, knowledge you have of what occurred? I cannot say that I have any knowledge of what occurred, although I live within a square of where it is said to have originated. I went down home and found there was some excitement. About a square off I found a negro lying, who seemed to be badly wounded. I inquired how it originated, and was told. I came back in the course of half an hour, saw a crowd of white men and negroes, who seemed to be shooting; that was about as much as I could see.

2264. Were you out that night or the next night? I was round my premises at home. I saw no violence myself. On Wednesday, when I left my office, there was a good deal of excitement, and I saw white men shooting at negroes.

2265. Did you see any negroes shooting? No, sir; I did not. I presume it was about nine or ten o'clock when I got back. The report at my office was, that the negroes had killed somebody, and that the fight began in that way. On the street below me, Calhoun street, which runs east and west, I saw them run out to the Overton tract, where there are a good many negro cabins. I saw them running and shooting at negroes. There was no firing near me, with the exception of the one man wounded, as I have said. About noon there was a squad of men came along. The militia had been called out, as I understood, and just been disbanded. I saw a negro come along; one of the squad pushed him, and told him to run, and fired at him; he told him to run again, and fired again; he told him to run the third time, and fired again. He walked on, and none of the balls seemed to take effect. It he had started to run, I have no doubt he would have been killed. I had understood in some way that they were going to set some buildings on fire that night. I had some property in danger; went down alone, and was out until two o'clock. I met squads of white men passing and repassing. They seemed to be Irish nearly altogether. Until Wednesday, after the militia were called out, I saw some respectable gentlemen in the crowd; after that I did not see one of that class. At night it seemed to be Irish and police, I supposed a great number of them were extra policemen; they were men of the same class; they were just passing from one block to another, and fires would break out; the military also were out. It seemed to me that fifty men might have put out all the fires. There did not seem to be any excitement at all.

2266. Were there any attempts made to put the fires out? None at all. I saw them on Overton street kindling fires. I saw military pass by, and the police standing by, neither of which seemed to be making any effort to put the fires out. I saw two or three fires I could have put out with a bucket of water.

2267. Did you have any conversation with the crowd? No, sir; I walked up sometimes near enough to hear them talking and cursing the negroes. It seemed to me it was the negroes against the Irish. The negroes have always behaved themselves better than the Irish. Within the last four or five months the negroes in South Memphis have been very annoying, firing off pistols at all hours of the day and night. I have seen a storm brewing between the negroes and Irish for a long time.

2268. Do you know of any negroes committing violence? No, sir; and there were no negroes on the street the night of the fires; I scarcely saw one.

2269. Did you see negroes doing anything to the Irish? Nothing that night; it all originated before that. I suppose there was some cause of difficulty between them and the police; I only heard so; did not see anything. The Irish and thieves had been wanting an excuse to get into a riot with the negroes.

By Mr. SHANKLIN:

2270. Have you seen any disturbance on the street with the negro soldiers previous to the riot? Yes, sir, I have seen a great deal of it.

2271. State what you have seen of their conduct? I have seen them drunk on the street, carrying weapons, and cursing everybody who did not get out of their way, especially in our part of the town, South Memphis.

2272. Was that a frequent occurrence? Yes, sir.

2273. How long had it continued before this riot? It continued three or four months; I know that parties applied to the authorities to have something done to stop it. The negro soldiers up town would get liquor, and come down late in the evening, get to firing off their pistols, and people would have to keep out of their way and dodge them.

2274. How many would go at a time? I have seen at times as high as twenty or thirty. About a week before the riot I saw about twenty or thirty going right by my house, firing in every direction, and the policemen had to get out of the way. I understood there had been a ball or something broken up. They came firing and cursing, and everybody had to get out of the way. Many of them were drunk, and they could get liquor if they desired it anywhere in that region. I suppose there was hardly a square in that part of the town where they could not get liquor in a dozen places from low-down sort of people.

2275. So far as you could judge of this mob from what you saw of it, was it composed of these Irish police and rowdy population of the city? Entirely; as I remarked awhile ago, I do not think I saw a respectable citizen after Wednesday, when the militia were called out; before that I had seen good citizens.

2276. Did you see any of these good citizens participate in the riots in any way? Not one. It seemed to be Irish police and thieves. I do not know how it is in other cities. There are persons here pointed out on the street, whom the police seem to know perfectly well as thieves, but who are never arrested, because, I suppose, never caught in the act of stealing.

HENRY PORTER (colored) sworn and examined.

By the CHAIRMAN:

2277. What is your residence and occupation? My residence is Memphis. I have been a barber. I am now keeping a little grocery store. I have lived in Memphis since ten days before the fall of Vicksburg. Before that I came from Alton, Illinois.

2278. Were you here during the time of the riot? Yes, sir.

2279. State what, if anything, you saw. On Tuesday evening, when the riot commenced, I saw people at a distance, running to and fro. I was at home, on Rayburn street, near the graveyard, which extends into Main street, and I only saw the crowd at a long distance.

2280. Then you know nothing of what took place on Tuesday night? Nothing more than seeing people passing and repassing. On Wednesday morning I saw between seventeen and eighteen colored soldiers pass up between Mr. Pendergrast's store and his dwelling. The space between the two was about as much as the width of this room. He was standing on the portico of his store. They made some remarks to him—I do not know what; to which he replied, "You had better go on and get in your holes." They went on three or four hundred yards, more or less, across the branch, where some soldiers who had been killed on Tuesday evening were lying. While they were over there looking about, Mr. Pendergrast's mother came and called him to breakfast. I saw him when he went to the house and saw his mother come and take charge of the store. While he was at breakfast these men returned back again from where they had been to see the soldiers. Apparently there were two or three of them who had revolvers in their hands; they raised their revolvers, and I heard them say, "You have murdered our soldiers, and we intend to get you." He was not in the store, and they passed right on. I believe if he had been there they would have shot him, because they understood he shot a man out on the hill. They were gone but a few minutes when another colored soldier came up. Policeman Roach and drayman Galloway were there. They walked up and Roach pulled out his pistol and shot the man in the leg; then this drayman put his pistol right to the man's head, shot the man, and walked on. That was all I saw then. I went to breakfast, came back and found a cluster of soldiers gathered about my shop. I understood that the general over in the fort had given arms to the people in the fort to protect themselves with. I did not want any man to come up and take my life, and I started, and all of them went with me to the fort. I was over there for half an hour, and saw my mother, my wife and little daughter coming over in great haste. By that time the Irish people had come from the cars right up Main street. They met the crowd coming from town, and the firing and shooting commenced. This was on Wednesday evening. Mother asked me would I venture down to Mr. Pendergrast's to see him. I started to go down there, but met three gentlemen besides Mr. Pendergrast coming up with revolvers in their hands. They went into Mr. Pendergrast's store to load their pistols, and I went in. I went back to my little grocery and picked up a camphene can as an excuse for speaking to him. I said, "Good evening," and then I said, "There's hell to pay around here," just as if we were in favor of it. He said, "Yes, they were going to kill every nigger." Presently the other men went off, and Mr. Pendergrast told me what he had done that morning. Said I, "Do you suppose there is any danger of burning us out?" He said "No; I am the ringleader of the mob out this morning, and you will not be disturbed. I saved you myself last night." I asked him to go up and see mother. He went up, and she asked him about the same questions that I did. He said she need not be alarmed; that he would not allow them to burn her house. "But," I said, "you are not everywhere the crowd is, and they may burn down the house when you are away." He replied, "You shall not be hurt." We stayed and watched the house all night. They commenced the burning that night with a house right opposite Mr. Pendergrast's store. I could see Mr. Pendergrast, and his son they called Pat, as well as the other son, all at work. The white soldiers were out there on patrol and were keeping the fires up, just as much as any one else.

2281. Were the soldiers helping the mob? Yes, sir; I saw that myself. We watched all night. There must have been five or six in the party I saw firing the houses. As a general thing they were boys, from ten to fifteen, or it may be twenty years old. I saw them go and strike a light, in the morning just before daylight, about as far as from me across the street, at the old school-house, and it was burned down. This was in the fore part of Wednesday. There were women and children in some of the houses, and they fastened them in when they set the houses on fire. I could hear the screams of the children fastened up in the houses. By the time the houses were pretty well blazing all around, they commenced bursting the doors open. As soon as they came out, the parties outside commenced shooting at them.

2282. How many persons altogether did you see shot? I only saw one, Rachael Hatcher.

2283. Did you see any other children fired at? Yes, sir; to the best of my knowledge

I saw three or four children fired at; children ten or twelve years old, and from that up There were also one woman and two men in the party. They ran towards the bayou, which is very deep and crooked. Mr. Pendergrast came up with his pistol, pointed it toward them and snapped it, but the cap did not go off, and by the time he was ready to fire again they had raised the opposite bank. The old man Pendergrast was the only one I saw shoot at this woman. He shot the girl Rachael in the mouth.

2284. Who did you see fire at the other children? Pat Pendergrast. He ran down the bank where they were.

2285. Was this house set on fire when that family, husband, mother, and children were in it? Yes, sir; I saw it. It was as light as day with the fires that were burning around.

2286. Were there armed men around the house when it was set on fire? Yes, sir; there were a lot of men round the house, and the people inside were begging to come out.

2287. What response did they make outside? I could hear talking, but could not tell what they said.

2288. Who occupied this house that was set on fire? I do not know.

2289. Are you certain the house was shut up after it was set on fire? I know it was. I heard the screaming inside.

2290. Did the mob outside appear to be keeping the people inside until they were burnt up? Yes, sir; that must have been their object, for they were firing at the house. There was a boy shot through the arm, as I understood, as he was running across to the bayou. and they shot Rachael and killed her, between the two houses. In the morning, after daylight, the old man Pendergrast and his son were the last persons who left the fire. There was one woman and a child down there, and she came across to my house with her little boy about twelve years old; they were in that house the night before. I asked her how she got out. She said some men came up and begged to let her out, and that when she was permitted to come out; but when her little boy, who had blue clothes on, started to come out, they said "Put him back; put him back." Some one said "Don't burn the boy; he isn't to blame for having blue clothes on," and they let him out finally.

2291. Have a great many of these people who were burned out run off? Yes, sir; I do not know where they have gone.

2292. Do you know of any person actually burned, except this Rachael? I heard of other cases, but I do not know who they were.

2293. Do you know of any acts of violence committed on women? I did not know it to see it, but it was done close by our house.

2294. Who was the woman? Harriet, I believe is her name. Some three or four or five men had to do with her, and afterwards made her suck them.

2295. Do you know Lucy Tibbs? Yes, sir.

2296. Do you know anything about violence being committed on her? I have heard something about it.

2297. Was it understood that this was going on with Harriet on the outside? Yes, sir. I learned it from a colored man. He told me they were in there with the colored woman.

2298. Were you robbed? No, sir; only two white soldiers stopped me and took my pistol from me.

2299. What did they take your pistol away for? That is more than I know. It was a common thing during the riot.

2300. Did they search your house for pistols? They said they were ordered to come and take them.

Were they at the same time taking pistols away from white people? Not as I know of.

2301. State what the regular soldiers did in your presence? I saw two soldiers when they came into the house next door to me, down in a place they call Jack's lot, where there is a lot of dissipated women, and they robbed all along there. Then they came right in front of my house. Some of them broke a picket off the fence and went through. And they were not so long as I am talking to you smashing up the glass in a saloon close by. They could not find any pistols, I suppose, and so they smashed up the glass. They came up to me then and asked me if I had any money. I said no. They asked me if I had any pistols, and I said yes. They said they were ordered to take pistols away from everybody. I know of two men they met on the street and robbed twice.

By Mr. SHANKLIN:

2302. Who was engaged in that fight on that first Tuesday afternoon? The colored men and white men were shooting at each other. That was on Tuesday evening, between four and five o'clock.

2303. How long did the shooting continue at that time? Along until about dark, and about half an hour after dark it commenced again. It commenced down about the South street bridge, in Rayburn street, about a block and a half from me. I did not go near them.

2304. On Wednesday morning, after you saw those seventeen soldiers pass by Mr. Pendergrast's house, you say you went to the fort? Yes, sir; and I remained there until eleven or twelve o'clock, until the general that stays in the fort came there and told the soldiers all to remain in the fort.

2305. At any time on Wednesday, while you were at the fort, were there any of those discharged soldiers formed outside, in view of where the mob were? There were numbers of them on the breastworks, and some of them outside, near by.

2306. Were any of them shooting towards the mob? There were three or four of the soldiers, to the best of my recollection, who were shooting. One came to the fort with a gun in his hand. There were two or three who joined them. The man who had the gun shot twice and came back to the fort again. That is all the shooting I saw done while I was there.

2307. On the first day of the difficulty, did you see a collection of soldiers down about South street, drinking and carousing? I did not. I had not been away from home that day.

2308. Were there many of them passing and repassing along on South street that day? Not more than any other day.

P. G. MARSH sworn and examined.

By the CHAIRMAN:

2309. State your residence and occupation? I live in Memphis, and am a plasterer.

2310. Were you here during the late riots; and if so, state what you saw? I was; and everything I saw of the whole affair was right back of me. A negro man was knocked down. I saw him fall, and then saw some men pounding him. What was done with him I do not know.

2311. Did they kill him? I think the negro died. I went and saw him afterwards. He had been stabbed in the breast two or three times.

2312. Do you think he died from the stabs? I think either one would have killed him.

2313. How many were round him? Six or eight.

2314. Were there any police around him? I did not see any. They were all white men.

By Mr. SHANKLIN:

2315. When was this? It was the first day of the riot, between 6 and 7 o'clock.

2316. How long have you been in Memphis? About 15 years.

2317. Where did you live before you came here? I was born and raised in Lexington, Kentucky.

2318. Have you discovered any feeling of hostility existing between the better class of people in the city of Memphis and the colored people here for some months previous to the riot? I will just tell you how I am situated. I have taken no hand in this matter, and paid no attention to it, and listened to no talk by anybody. I think if we had the right sort of policemen in the city we would have had no trouble. I have heard drunken negro soldiers talk about doing this and that, and I have heard drunken white men talk the same way.

2319. Was this previous to the riot? Yes; there has been a pretty general riot here since the war closed.

2320. Do you state that the government here has been under the control of the better order of people? I shall not brag about it.

2321. I ask you whether, under the laws of Tennessee, the most quiet and orderly portion of your citizens are not disfranchised and allowed no control of your city elections? I believe they are disfranchised.

2322. And they have no legal mode of controlling these authorities? None in the world.

2323. What has been the behavior of the resident blacks? I have heard no cause of complaint of them. I have two or three working for me.

ANDREW REYYONCO sworn and examined.

By Mr. BROOMALL:

2324. How long have you lived in Memphis? About seven months. I came here from Toronto, Canada West.

2325. Were you here during the riots; if so, state what you saw? I was. The first evening the riot began I was standing on Second street, near Jefferson, when I saw a crowd of people going to the south part of the town. There were policemen with them. I have some men living on South street, and I generally go down there three or four times a week. In the afternoon of that day I was down there. Three or four days before, I saw five policemen down there. They took a negro soldier on South street. I do not know what the negro soldier had done, but the policemen arrested him and started off with him, one on each side and one behind. One policeman took a club and knocked the negro soldier on the head. I ran up to the corner of Causey street, and the policemen and soldier were coming towards Causey street. The man was making a noise, but he was not drunk. He was begging the policemen to let him alone. When about twenty feet from the corner of Causey and South streets, one of the policemen went behind, and with a club knocked him down, so that he was more dead than alive. There was a large crowd of policemen around there, and some soldiers standing near the corner. The soldiers grumbled about it a good deal. They said that was not the way to knock a man down, colored or not. They ran to the fort to get assistance. They were gone some ten or fifteen minutes, and instead of coming back right to the spot, they came up the road. In the mean time the policemen had hired a dray and taken the negro away. Some of the soldiers wanted to follow them, but others said it was no use; they could not overtake the police. My opinion was that evening that if the colored soldiers had come in time they would have killed some of the policemen. This Tuesday evening I thought it was something between the police and negro soldiers, and I went down as quick as I could where the disturbance was. When I reached the corner of Causey and Main streets there was a great crowd of white people, all armed. There were a couple of carriages coming back from South street carrying wounded persons.' I did not go down to South street then, because it was getting dark and I thought it was dangerous. I saw a white man drunk. He got a pistol and was trying to go after the crowd. Captain Garrett ordered some of the police to stop him. I came up to the corner of Vine and St. Marten streets. There were three or four white men who got hold of a negro soldier, began to knock him in the head and damn him. One struck him on the head with a brick and knocked him down, and then these men kicked him and tramped him in the face three or four times. Three or four citizens standing on the corner said it was a brutal affair. After the crowd had gone away I saw the same man lying on his back on the same spot. He seemed to have been stabbed in the face, in three or four places, with a knife. The next morning I went down on South street, and everything was quiet. A friend of mine said he would show me where two persons were killed. I went over, and saw two negroes lying dead.

2326. Were they soldiers? No, citizens. In another place I saw a soldier lying dead. I was informed that he had been killed that morning. When I was coming away, about 10 o'clock, I saw a crowd coming down South street.

2327. How many bodies did you see in all? Eight in all.

2328. Was the mob composed of all white men? I did not see any colored people in it.

DANIEL DAWKINS (colored) sworn and examined.

By the CHAIRMAN:

2329. State your residence and business? I came from Monroe county, Mississippi. I have been in Memphis a little over two years. I stay at Dr. McGowan's drug store.

2330. What do you know about this riot? On Tuesday evening I was on the street, when a policeman came along and knocked me off the street. He had been beating a colored soldier. There was a young fellow named Charley Toler, who knocked a man over the head with his pistol. This Charley drew back and shot the young man. I was about five steps from him.

2331. What was the black man's name. I do not know. This was about 5 o'clock on Tuesday evening. I did not see anything else that evening. The doctor put me in a room and told me not to go out of it. I have a scar on my head here where I was struck by a policeman. I do not know who he was. He got killed about five minutes afterwards.

2332. What were you doing? I was not doing anything. He just drew up and struck me, and passed right on down the street. Some colored soldiers ran after and caught him. He struck me at the corner of Causey and South streets.

2333. Where was the policeman shot? Right through the breast; so Dr. McGowan told me.

2334. Is that all you know? I saw, away across of the bridge from me, near twenty beating a black man. They killed him. He lay there the whole night. I do not know what his name was.

2335. Do you know the names of any of the parties who beat him? They were all police. They shot the loads out of their pistols, and then took their pistols and beat him over the head.

2336. How many shots did they fire? I suppose more than forty.

CHARLES W. ANDERSON sworn and examined.

By the CHAIRMAN:

2337. State your residence and occupation? I live in Chelsea, the northern precinct of Memphis. I am a manufacturer of soda water.

2338. Do you know anything about a row up there in Chelsea; and if so, state when and what it was? It was about the winding up day of the riot, or the day after, about the second or third day of the month. I was in my house and heard firing. I came out and could see a negro running, who appeared to be wounded. There were men pursuing him, and they fired a good many shots at the negro very rapidly. I went into my house and got my revolver and came out, and these men were in drinking at the corner grocery. Nobody in the neighborhood seemed to be taking any interest in the matter. I thought it was the better part of discretion to go back. I started and met a gentleman who used to live there, Mr. Chettain. I returned with him to the corner. These men had then left the grocery and were shooting some more negroes. I said this was horrible, for people to be shot down that way; that we ought to take some action. But it appeared the tongues of the people were glued to their mouths. I could get no response. I went out and met two negroes who had been hit. The shots fired at the negroes had also been aimed directly towards me. A great portion of the party were on horseback. I told this black man which way to run to get out of the way. The grocery man, and in fact all the Americans I saw there, whether late confederates or federals, deprecated the conduct of these foreigners, for they were principally Irish. That night we met, about eight or ten of us—I believe a majority of the party were late confede rates—formed a patrol, and saw that everything was quiet. These men shot the negroes down without the least provocation. It was the most inhuman thing I ever saw in my life.

2339. How many men were shot? I could not tell; they were firing indiscriminately. I saw these two shot. The first one appeared to be hit. They kept on firing as they advanced towards " Pinch," an Irish settlement.

2340. Were any measures taken to bring the offenders to justice? I must say that there have been no steps whatever taken to ferret out these matters. I stepped up to one of the parties on horseback and 'said, " This is an unrighteous piece of business. The God of battles is just, and he is still in Memphis." I see that man about town yet.

2341. What response did he make to your remark? I could hardly tell; it was vague. He was loose from his party, and there were two of us.

2342. Do you know anything about the riot that took place in Memphis the first and second of May? I passed through that part of the country with soda water. I saw the negroes fleeing; I saw the crowd collected; I saw white men with implements of destruction hunting and pursuing negroes.

2343. Did you talk with any persons who admitted they had any knowledge of these riotous proceedings? Yes.

2344. Did you talk with a man by the name of McMahon? Yes. He told me that Mr. Creighton, the recorder, came to his house to see if the building in the rear could be burned down without interfering with his house.

2345. Was that building burned? It was not. He said this: that there were two federal soldiers with a party who came out, and they had no money. They went out, and when they came back they had $30 or $40 apiece and fine shot-guns. They had also several revolvers.

ALLEN SUMMERS (colored) sworn and examined.

By the CHAIRMAN:

2346. State your residence and occupation? I live in Memphis. I have been a soldier. Did you see anything of the riots? Just on the day this thing occurred I was at home, about twenty yards from Second street bridge. I borrowed $25 from a man to go to the store and get some things. Before I got there I met some men coming up with guns right ahead of me. I turned and run; got into my house and under the bed. A great big policeman, with a big, heavy moustache, came in and pulled me out. I got away from them and run about two hundred yards before they could hit me. They were shooting in every direction. This big policeman snapped his pistol once before it went off, and then fired right through my shoulder. This great big red Irishman knocked me down; a policeman came up and struck me with a stick. The Irishman then stabbed me, put his hand in my pocket, and got my $25. They allowed they "were going to kill the God damned nigger soldiers who were fighting here against their rights—the black sons of bitches." Then he commenced tramping on me, and this Dr. Sharp came up and asked them if it was right to persecute a man after he was dead. They left me for dead, and at that time they saw another soldier and took off after him. Dr. Sharp came up to me and asked me if I could walk. I told him I could if they would leave me. A colored man came and took me by one arm and the doctor by the other. They carried me to my house, took off my clothes and dressed my wounds, sent to the fort for an ambulance, and took me to the hospital.

2347. Have you got well? No, sir; I cannot do anything now. I was shot in the arm and stabbed in the abdomen, and then they knocked me on the head.

ANDREW MINTER (colored) sworn and examined.

By the CHAIRMAN:

2348. Where do you live? I have been living in Memphis ever since May. Before that time I had been away for two years in the naval service. Since then I have been running on the river.

2349. Were you here when the riot took place? I came here about that time. I got in at 4 o'clock in the afternoon. I did not know anything about the trouble until I got to South street, where they were shooting and fighting.

2350. Did you see anybody shot? I saw, I think, as many as fifty men shot, and got shot myself.

2351. What kind of a fight was it? The evening it first started the black soldiers and white men were all fighting, but when I was there the colored soldiers were all running and trying to save themselves, every one I saw, and the white people were chasing them.

2352. How many white men did you see shot? There were three or four white men. I counted eight colored men shot within three hundred yards of one another.

2353. Were they all killed? Yes, sir; every one was killed. I went right by them. They all had soldiers' clothes on. This was on Tuesday night. I did not see any more. I staid at home that night. On Wednesday morning I was afraid to go back down to the boat. The first thing I knew a crowd came up out of town with guns. I was in the house. I just heard them shooting. The soldiers were all out in their houses. They were not in the fort. I saw a man run up right before Mr. Callahan's door. A white man there stopped him and shot the soldier right down. What was the name of the soldier I do not know.

2354. Do you know the name of the man who shot him? I do not. It was a citizen on his horse. He shot him so dead he did not kick. He lay there until the next day, until near 12 o'clock. Then they shot two or three soldiers in the lot where I was. They broke and run out. The white men run after them, and would shoot them and beat them in the head. It was about 8 o'clock when they came out, and until near 12 o'clock they were shooting around there.

2355. Did you count the men who were killed? No, sir; but they did count them around there, and they said there were forty or fifty.

2356. Who counted them? White men counted them and told me so. A white man who keeps a saloon right close by told me there were over fifty killed.

2357. How many did you see dead? I could not tell the number.

2358. When were you shot? It was on Wednesday night. It was about 2 o'clock in the night.

2359. Who shot you? Mr. Callahan.

2360. Who is he? An Irishman who has a grocery on the corner of South and Causey streets.

2361. What did he shoot you for? I do not know. I had traded with him often. I had bought more than $100 worth of provisions of him. He always appeared to be very friendly to me. That night he tried to burst the door open, but I had it barred. He then came round and burst the window open. I jumped up in the bed just at that moment, and he pointed the pistol right in my face. The revolver went off and hit me through the fingers. I was certain he would hit me in the head, but it did not. He came right in at the window and said, "The damned son of a bitch, we will kill him. I know he has got money. He has always got money." He came up on the bed and just put his knife right in my side. I never flinched, but lay as if I was dead. I had $25 in my belt. He knew where it was. He unbuttoned it and took the money from me. Said he, "God damn him, I have got his money, but he has got some good clothes." They just smashed my trunk, took out my clothes, and went away. They were not gone long before they returned, and Callahan said, "Now we will burn the damn son of a bitch up." I was in the house then, and in a moment it was in a light blaze. There was a room adjoining where a woman was packing up some things. I just put a quilt over my head and went out that way. They did not know me from a woman and let me go. I went a little ways and fell right down, and a woman threw some things over me. I remained until daylight, and that was the way I escaped.

2362. What is Callahan's first name? John—John Callahan.

2363. Did you see any other people maltreated that night? No, sir; I never saw any one but myself that night.

2364. Were there any other houses around you burned? Yes, sir; there were houses all around me as thick as they could be, and they burned them up, always with all the clothes of the people, nearly every one of them. Neither my wife nor I saved a thing but what we had on our backs. I had about fifty dollars and a good many provisions laid in.

2365. How much do you think you lost in everything including money? The value of everything in my house was worth about $1,000.

2366. What sort of a house was it? A shanty or a frame house; a good frame house with two rooms in it. When I came out of the navy I had a good deal of money and I put it in a house. After I came out of the service I did not stop a week, but went right to work. I was getting fifty dollars a month. My wife was a good seamstress, and was all the time making dresses. I started with $500 in the first place.

2367. Is your wound getting well? Yes, it is getting pretty well.

2368. At what time in the night was this affair in your house? It was about 12 o'clock, I think.

2369. What first awakened you? Knocking at the door to see if anybody was in there. The night before they were going round and knocking at people's doors, and as soon as a man would open the door they would shoot him down, so I would not answer. Then Callahan said, "The damned son of a bitch is in there, I know; come round to the window, and you can burst that open." The window was only tied by a little bit of a string and they burst it open.

ABRAM MEANS (colored) sworn and examined.

By the CHAIRMAN:

2370. Where do you live? At Adam Lock's, South Memphis.

2371. Were you there when his house was burned? Yes, sir; Mr. McGinn and Mr. Callahan set fire to it, as far as I could see. I was in the house and saw the m there. When I came out Mr. Callahan never said anything. I asked McGinn what made him set our house on fire. He said he was ordered to set colored people's houses on fire.

2372. Was this Adam Lock's house? Yes, sir. I am his son-in-law; I am living with him.

2373. Did they rob you of any money? No, sir; I did not have much money.

2374. What did you have in the house? All the bed clothes and clothes I had, and I had right smart of them, and right smart of provisions.

2375. What was the value of your bed clothes, clothing, and provisions? I should think about $100, or more.

2376. Did they fire at you? Yes, sir; I do not know who it was. They told us to leave our clothing; we were carrying them out. I was stiff and fell; when I jumped up they did not hit me.

2377. Did they fire at your wife? No, sir.

2378. What did they say to you after they shot? They told us to leave, and then they set the house on fire.

2379. Did you see anybody else shot? Yes; I saw Rachael shot. I was standing in the door when she was shot, and saw her fall.

2380. Who shot her? I do not know; I did not see the man; I heard the gun and saw her fall.

2381. Did you see any other houses burned? Yes, sir.

2382. Was there anybody burned in the houses, that you know of? No, sir; not that I know of.

2383. Was there anybody in the houses when they were set on fire? Yes, sir; this man who just went out was one

2384. Did you see anybody shot? Yes; I saw five men shot dead.

2385. Do you know their names? I do not; there were four soldiers and one citizen. I do not know who shot them; it was somebody from town. They were shot right up the bayou, south of us. I saw a man shot on the bridge when the fuss first commenced.

2386. Do you know the man who shot him? I do not.

2387. Do you know whether a white man was shot before the colored man was shot? Yes; there was a white man shot when the fuss commenced. I saw them carrying a white man, wounded, across the bridge; two negroes were carrying him. One of the soldiers pointed up his pistol and fired, and then one of the policemen turned round and shot the colored soldier. Then the fuss commenced. I never saw anything further after that; I just kept close at home.

2388. Were you a slave? Yes, sir; in Marshal county, Mississippi.

MEMPHIS, *May* 31, 1866.

Dr. ALLEN STERLING sworn and examined.

By the CHAIRMAN:

State your residence and profession? I have resided in Memphis since 1862. I am a physician.

2389. Were you in Memphis at the time of the recent riots? Yes, sir.

2390. State what, if any, knowledge you have in relation to the riots? I did not see a great deal except the excitement. I do not think I saw any acts of violence.

2391. Were you with the crowd? I was the first evening. I went down Union street and met John Creighton. He said he had just come up from South street, where they were fighting policemen and citizens.

2392. Who is John Creighton? The recorder of the city. He said that he was riding along there, and that there were a lot of drunken soldiers. That he ordered the policemen to disperse these soldiers, as they were blocking up the street there near the corner of Causey. He said that was the commencement of the riot.

2393. Did he say what he had to do with it? No; he said he had the right to order the policemen to disperse the crowd, and that that was what he did. I think he said two policemen had been shot.

2394. Did you hear any threats of what was to be done? Not by him; no, sir.

By Mr. SHANKLIN:

2395. Where did you come from when you came to Memphis? I came here in the army, and came from Corinth. I entered the army in New York city.

2396. And you are now practising your profession in this city, are you? Yes, sir; I have been in private practice nearly two years. I resigned in the autumn of 1864.

2397. Were you a surgeon in the army? Yes, sir; assistant surgeon.

What, so far as you have been able to learn from your intercourse with the people of Memphis, is the feeling between the better class of citizens, of property-holders, and men permanently in business, and the resident colored population of Memphis? I think, generally speaking, the feeling is a good one. I know in regard to this riot all the people I talked with were down on the way in which the thing had been carried on—in the indiscriminate slaughter which took place. I have not talked with a prominent citizen or a southern citizen here who does not regret it.

2398. Do you discover any difference in the sentiment of those who appear to be unconditional Union men and the southern men so far as the treatment of the colored people is concerned? I do not think there is any particular difference. I think a great majority of the old citizens are disposed to treat the colored people fairly. I believe the policemen trea the negroes worse than anybody else.

2399. And the policemen are made up of what class? Of Irish, almost every one of them.

2400. Is there not in this city, as in almost all other commercial cities, a rabble population who have no fixed place of abode and no particular business? Yes, sir.

2401. How is the feeling between that sort of people and the resident negro population? I hardly know how to answer that question. I suppose under excitement this rabble or floating population would be very hard on them, including pretty nearly all the Irish beyond a doubt.

2402. So far as you could discover in any of the crowds you saw what class of citizens was the mob actually engaged in the riot composed of? First, of policemen, and they of course brought their particular friends; and there were federal soldiers, who were just as bad. Then there was a class of people ready for anything, who, if they could catch a colored boy, would shoot him if they could do it safely. All the colored people I saw were down upon it.

By Mr. BROOMALL:

2403. Did this better class of people you speak of take any measures to prevent the riot? The only thing I know of was to meet together and organize a force.

2404. Do you mean the posse who were armed and joined the mob? No; I refer to a meeting held afterwards in which they proposed to arm the better class of citizens and to pick out the men; that is what I understand.

2405. Have they taken any measures since to bring the guilty parties to justice? I have not heard of any.

2406. Were you at the tournament the other day? I was not.

2407. Do you think the public feeling among the better class of people would allow a tournament to be held to raise monuments over the bodies of Union soldiers? I think it would. It might not be patronized as well. I think there would be some who would not go, but I do not believe there would be any trouble to prevent it. I am meeting and conversing with confederates every day. Of course there are some who are very bitter, but it is confined to a few of them.

By the CHAIRMAN:

2408. Do you think that during the riot the better class of people with whom you talked were all opposed to it? They thought it was all foolishness, this indiscriminate slaughter which took place.

2409. Then foolishness was all? Yes; of course there was a great deal of anxiety. They said it was all unnecessary. If the sheriff and his posse had not gone there, I do not believe there would have been any fuss at all.

2410. Then, as far as you could understand, these men were opposed to it on the ground that it was foolish alone? Yes; they thought it was nothing more than a row between the policemen and negro soldiers, which they have had, more or less, for the last two years.

2811. Did not this riot progress for two days? It commenced on Tuesday. On Wednesday night they burned the churches and school-houses, which was about the winding up of the thing.

2412. During all this time, while this thing was progressing, when these colored people were being killed and their churches and school-houses were being burned, what efforts were made by this better class of people of whom you speak to suppress the riotous proceedings and restore tranquillity? I do not know of any except the meeting of the citizens, in which they petitioned General Stoneman to be allowed to form a guard, and which the general declined. Judge Leonard and the sheriff also raised a posse which did more harm than good.

2413. What did they do? I think they only helped to keep the excitement up.

2414. Do you think they participated in the riots in any way? I think some of them did: I think if they had not been there that night the churches, &c., would not have been burned. I do not know it; that is my private opinion.

2415. This is your private opinion, is it, that the posse which went out to put down the mob became a part of the mob? Yes, sir; more or less.

2416. Have these citizens since the riot taken any measures to express their feelings of disapprobation by public meetings or anything of that sort? No, sir; not that I know of.

By Mr. BROOMALL:

2417. As I understand you, the citizens you term the better class embrace the wealthy Yes, sir, those who own land, real estate, &c.

2418. Have they taken any steps to rebuild these churches and school-houses which were burned? No, sir; I think not.

2419. And are not likely to do it? I presume not; I do not know.

2420. It is in evidence that poor people—black people—have been robbed of everything they had, and burned out of house and home: do you think the wealthy people have done anything to relieve them? Not that I am aware of.

2421. And are not likely to do it? I presume not. If they were asked, they might give two or three dollars; I do not know.

2422. But are not likely to take any active measures for their relief? I presume not.

By Mr. SHANKLIN:

2423. Will you state whether martial law was not proclaimed in the city by General Stoneman? It was, on Wednesday evening.

2424. In that proclamation were not citizens forbidden to congregate or collect for any purpose whatever?

Mr. BROOMALL said it had been asserted in the committee on several occasions that General Stoneman had proclaimed martial law, and witnesses had been asked to state what the effect of the proclamation was. He objected to the question on the ground that the proclamation itself should be produced, so that the committttee could judge for themselves as to what it was, and that witnesses should not be asked to construe it.

Mr. SHANKLIN replied that the committee had not so far on any occasion confined itself to the strict legal rules of evidence. If they would do so in other cases he would be perfectly content; but considering the latitude which had been allowed, he thought it was perfectly competent to show why citizens had not assembled to adopt any measures in reference to the riots, as the proclamation, as he understood, forbid the assembling of citizens for any purpose whatever.

The CHAIRMAN remarked that while the exception taken by Mr. Broomall would be good in a court of law, this committee had adopted a wider range of investigation, in order to ascertain all the facts. He would consider any question tending to an elucidation of the facts in the case proper to this investigation; and as the question asked was of that character, he would direct the witness to answer.

WITNESS: They were forbidden to assemble for any purpose.

2425. And the military force ordered to disperse them if they did? Yes, sir.

2426. Has that proclamation up to this time, as far as you know, been revoked? I think not; if it had been I would have seen it in the newspapers.

2427. Upon the subject of remuneration to these colored people who had suffered in the riot, I understand you to state there have been no contributions for that purpose as far as you know—do you mean there have been no private contributions? I mean there have been no public meetings for such purpose, so far as I know. There may have been citizens who have contributed fifty or a hundred dollars apiece privately, for anything I know.

2428. Then you do not say there have not been contributions to aid these people? Not at all; there may have been; all those I have talked with have spoken of the disturbance as foolish and wrong.

2429. What do you mean by foolish? I mean the burning of churches and anything of that sort. It may have been that some of the colored soldiers were drunk, but most of the colored people had nothing to do with it, and that it was wrong therefore to burn their churches and school-houses.

2430. Had private citizens any means of stopping this riot, except through the military, as far as you know? No, sir; if there is a riot here, all the means they have are in the mayor, city council, and police; if they want more assistance it is their duty to call it out.

2431. But you think the effort made by the sheriff and other authorities rather aggravated the difficulties than otherwise? It had that effect in my judgment. They thought they were doing what was best, I presume, but with the state of feeling existing I do not think they accomplished any good.

2432. What was proposed to be accomplished by the organization of citizens of which you have spoken? The object was to form a guard of good, reliable men, and to guarantee the character of the men who should be connected with it.

2433. Was that proposition approved of, as far as you know, by the civil authorities here? I think so. There were some who thought General Stoneman ought to have taken the thing in hand on Tuesday night. In reply to the proposition made, General Stoneman sent an order back issuing his proclamation.

By Mr. BROOMALL:

2434. Did you see General Stoneman issue a proclamation of any kind? No; I told you when I commenced I did not know anything personally.

2435. Did you hear these people make the proposition to General Stoneman which you have mentioned? No, sir; it was a public meeting.

2436. Then, all you know about the proclamation and about the proposition made is from hearsay? Yes, sir, and through the press.

2437. Do you think this proclamation was to prevent the citizens of Memphis from meeting anywhere, or for any purpose? Yes, sir.

2438. Did it prevent them from meeting in the theatres and churches? No, sir; they still met.

2439. Might they not have taken measures to repair this damage at their theatres and churches? In other words, would the proclamation take hold of a meeting of fifty citizens, assembled for the purpose of contributing from their own means to the relief of those negroes who have lost everything? I do not think it would, as I construe it?

2440. The proclamation did not prevent the tournament, did it? No, sir; it did not prevent any meeting of that sort. The object, as I understand it, was to prevent persons who were inciting the riots from assembling and organizing.

2441. In other words, to prevent the mob? No, sir, to prevent assemblages generally.

2442. As far as the citizens had assembled and were permitted to organize and go armed into the streets, they were of the mob, and with the parties who burned down the houses, were they not? I do not know who burned down the houses on Wednesday night. I think they did more harm than good by adding to the excitement.

By the CHAIRMAN:

2443. Do you know of General Stoneman's having given any order, either in writing or verbal, forbidding the citizens of Memphis from assembling for the purpose of expressing their abhorence and detestation of the crimes that had been committed in this city during the riots, of taking measures to vindicate the character of the city, to repair damages, &c.? No, sir; I do not. I do not presume General Stoneman would have any objections to that.

2444. Did the proclamation he issued, of which you have spoken, go to the extent of forbidding assemblages of that kind? I think not; I may be wrong, but I think not.

2445. On the other hand, was not the object of the proclamation simply to prevent all riotous bodies of citizens? I should construe it differently from that, whether right or not.

2446. What was it for? The way I understood the proclamation of General Stoneman was this, that he thought it would be better for the military to take charge of the city, and put down the riot at once without citizens meeting together. He did not know but their meetings might lead to something else. They did not seem to have done much good; and he thought the soldiers would settle the matter if everybody else would keep quiet.

2447. Then I understand you that you do not mean to state that General Stoneman has issued any order or proclamation forbidding citizens of Memphis, or this better class, from meeting to give expression of their opinion in regard to the riots? No, sir; I do not think so.

HARRIET ARMOUR (colored) sworn and examined.

By the CHAIRMAN:

2448. Are you married? Yes, sir.

2449. Where is your husband? He went up the river after he came out of the fort.

2450. When was he discharged? It has been about a month since; it was just after they got sort of quiet, after the riot.

2451. How long have you been in Memphis? Six or eight years. Mr. Merriweather brought me here about eight years ago. I came from McMinnville ten years ago.

2452. Were you here during the riot? Yes, sir.

2453. Did you see any portion of the disturbances? Yes, sir; I saw right smart of them. They commenced the first day of May, down on South street; they were fighting and shooting—the soldiers and policemen. I saw five black men lying dead down there. That was not the beginning of what was killed, but that was all I saw.

2454. What took place on Tuesday night, the first night of the riot? There was not any fuss that night I saw.

2455. What took place on Wednesday morning? There were some gentlemen came round the next morning hunting for arms. They said the name of one of them was Dunn.

2456. Who was he? He was dressed in citizens' clothes. They came up the hill on the south side of the street, and said they came after arms. They came into my room.

2457. Who? Mr. Dunn and another gentleman.

2458. What did they do in your room? Mr. Dunn had to do with me twice, and the other gentleman once. And then Mr. Dunn tried to make me suck him. I cried. He asked me what I was crying about, and tried to make me suck it. I have not got well since my husband went away.

2459. When they commenced on you what did they tell you? They just told me I had to do it. They barred up the door, and I knew I could not help myself.

2460. What did he do with the window? I could not have got out of the window; there were two slats before it.

2461. And you made no resistance? No; they had barred the door. I could not get out, and I could not help myself.

2462. Did they get any arms? No, sir. There was a black man who had an old gun on the side of the house, and he went up there and got it.

2463. Why did you tell him where it was? He asked me, and I did not know whether to tell him or not. I was a little excited.

2464. Do you know of anything else that took place on Wednesday night; did any one else come to your room? No, sir; not to my room. The guards were around, and went to all the rooms in that neighborhood, they said, looking for arms.

2465. Did anybody offer you violence after that? No, sir.

2466. Who is this Dum? He lives on South street. I have not seen him since, and do not know where he is now.

2467. Did they rob you of anything? They looked in my trunk, under the bed, and all about, but they did not take anything.

By Mr. BROOMALL:

2468. After they left you who did you tell this to first? I told it to a woman who lives in a house near by. I think, perhaps, I told it the very first to a family of white people who lived right next door. They knew about as much about it as I did. Molly Hayes knew that it was going on.

2469. How do you know that? It was an open shanty, and they could see right in.

2470. Did Molly Hayes see it? She said she did not see it.

2471. Did I understand you that you did not try to prevent them from doing these things to you? No, sir; I did not know what to do. I was there alone, was weak and sick, and I thought I would rather let them do it than to be hurt or punished.

2472. Then you gave up to them from fear? Yes, sir; I knew I could not do anything with two men.

2473. Could not the people outside have come to help you? Yes, sir; but I should have been afraid to call to them.

2474. What were you afraid of? They had revolvers with them.

2475. Did they both have revolvers? I do not know; Dunn had. He had his revolver, and he just as much as said I must do it, and I thought I had just better give up freely; I did not like to do it, but I thought it would be best for me.

2476. Do you recollect what language he used when he threatened you with his revolver? He just told me right down that I had to do it; that I need not try to get around it, for I just had to do it.

2477. Did he say anything else? No, sir; he did not make any heavy threats with the revolver at all.

2478. Were there only two men in the room? Only two; but Mr. Dunn had to do with me twice and the other man once, which was the same as three.

2479. What kind of a looking man is Dum? He is a young looking man. He would be a very nice man, but I do not call him nice now.

2480. Is he an Irishman? No, sir; I think they were both Americans. I never saw him before nor since. He did not look to be more than twenty years old.

By Mr. SHANKLIN:

2481. Did you see this difficulty when it first commenced between the colored soldiers and the police? Yes; I could see it from where I was. I was just a little piece away from it, not further than from here to the bank of the river. After it had commenced they ran out right by the house I was in.

2482. How many policemen were there in the crowd you saw? I did not see only three.

2483. How many colored soldiers were there? I should think there were a dozen of them.

2484. Who commenced the shooting, the colored soldiers or the police? They fired one after the other; I do not know which fired first.

Which gave back first? The police ran the soldiers.

2485. Then did the soldiers make the police give back? No, sir; they did not make them give back any more. We understood there were two white men and one black man dead before we knew anything of it. They were killed before we got a sense of it.

JAMES H. SWAN sworn and examined.

By the CHAIRMAN:

2487. State your residence and occupation. I reside in Memphis; I am deputy sheriff of Shelby county.

2488. Have you recently had an execution against a man by the name of Finnee? Yes, sir; I levied the execution on some goods in his store. I left two men there in charge of them until Mr. Finnee came down and replevined them.

2489. What were their names? I do not recollect the names. I can ascertain them, and will furnish them to the committee. (Witness subsequently appeared, and gave the names referred to as Wilson and Tyler.)

2490. Were you in the city at the time of the riots? Yes, sir.

2491. State what, if any, personal knowledge you have in relation thereto. I know less than anybody occupying my position you could possibly find. I never saw anything like violence on either side during the whole time. There was an order sent by the sheriff to raise a *posse* of men to put down this riot, but at the time I was away on other business, and had nothing to do with it.

By Mr. SHANKLIN:

2492. You did not command any of the *posses* that went down to suppress the riot? No, sir. After the riot was over I went down there by myself, and met large crowds coming

12

back. At the junction of South street and Main a little crowd of twenty or thirty were stand
ing, but just as I got there a federal officer brought up a man or two with arms and inquired
for the sheriff. I recognized them as men who had been armed by the sheriff. I told him
the sheriff had armed these men for the purpose of putting down the riot. He released them
and I sent the men home. I staid there twenty or thirty minutes, and as they brought in others
I sent them home. I told the officer wherever he found them to fetch them up to me, and I
would send them home.

2493. Are you familiar with the sentiment of the people of Memphis towards the colored
population? I do not know as I am familiar with it fully; there is a variety of sentiment.

2494. I would like to hear from you, so far as you have been able to collect it in your
intercourse with the white citizens and negroes of Memphis, what the public sentiment of all
classes and grades of society here is in reference to the colored population? I think a majority of the people of Memphis are favorably disposed towards them. There are a few exceptions, however, especially among policemen with whom they have had some difficulty. My
impression is that a large majority of the old citizens are favorably disposed towards the
colored population.

2495. And disposed to treat them kindly? Yes, sir.

2496. What is the sentiment and feeling of that class of people to which the police belongs?
I do not know as I could explain that to your satisfaction. We have had little riots and
difficulties before. As a matter of course they have engendered feelings on both sides it is
difficult to explain.

2497. There is, however, a feeling of hostility existing on the part of that class of people?
I think so. Certainly with several of the policemen. They are probably not all open to the
charge, but I think the feeling exists with a good many of them.

2498. Have the policemen engaged in this riot been discharged? I think they have, some
of them.

2499. Were the policemen here of the same class of people as the draymen, hackmen,
porters, and hands on the wharf, &c.? Yes; and I think that class of white laborers, when
they come in competition with colored laborers, are not very friendly.

2500. Do all the policemen belong to that class of people? No, sir; they do not all belong to that class of people. They seem to assume to themselves an authority which has
come in continual conflict with that of the colored guards. There has seemed to be a competition which should excel in authority. The policemen did not want to give up to them,
and the colored guards did not want to give up to the police. I am, however, very little
acquainted with the present police of Memphis.

2501. Were not these police generally registered voters here? I do not know whether
they are or are not.

2502. Are these city officials registered voters? I do not even know that.

2503. Does it require the same qualification for a man to hold office that it does to vote?
I should think so; but whether the city authorities paid any attention to that generally I
do not know. They had the power to put any one in the police they chose.

2504. I ask you whether that population of the city of Memphis, known as rebels, who
participated in the rebellion, are not denied the right of suffrage? I think they are. They
had no hand in the elections whatever.

2505. Have you discovered any difference in the sentiment of these people who are known
as rebels and southern sympathizers from the better class of those who are known as Union
men in the city? As far as I have been able to take notice of them, I think those who were in
the rebel army, and those who were rebels had less to do with the riots here than any other
class. I have heard it frequently spoken of that the rebels had nothing to do with it, and that
the negroes and police might fight it out. As a matter of course there may be exceptions.
You can expect nothing else of a rebel, but that he will take sides against the army. I do
not think that they are generally disposed to do it. They are all paroled, and their honor
holds them from it. They are pretty sensitive upon that subject, many of them; I am more
disposed to think the whole thing grew out of a feeling of spite between the police and
negroes. One was not disposed to submit to the other.

2506. And that feeling had existed for some time before this riot? Yes; it has been gradually growing up. I have heard it remarked that it would ultimately come to a riot, the way
the thing was going on. They would meet every few days and have a fuss. I think the
quiet part of the people of the city were opposed to it.

2507. I suppose you are a pretty good judge of the population here, and I believe they
have, as in all river cities, a rabble population, with no fixed place of abode, or permanent
occupation. Is not that the fact? Yes, sir; that is so. A considerable portion of our population is not fixed upon anything and care little about anything.

2508. And who neither regard law, order, right nor justice? No, sir; they are a kind of
floating population that has gathered in from every part of the world, and they do not care
what becomes of themselves or any one else. It has been the case for several years—not
only since the war, but before. They create a great deal of trouble here.

FRANK WILLIAMS (colored) sworn and examined.

By the CHAIRMAN:

2509. Where do you live? On Main street, in Memphis. I have lived here about three years. I was in the service two years.

2510. Were you here during the riots? and, if so. state what, if anything you saw. I was on Adams street when the fuss first started. I went down home, and went to find out what the fuss was. I found that down in the neighborhood of South street, they were gathering up to go down and fight. I heard them say they would kill every damned one who had blue clothes on. I knew that I was a soldier and had blue clothes on, and I made haste to get to my quarters. Before I got there, they had been down and were coming back on Main street. I saw them shoot two fellows One belonged to the same regiment I did. He was on his horse. His name was Joe Lundy.

2511. Who shot him? Policemen and citizens, all in a crowd. I saw a policeman when he shot one; I suppose he was a policeman; I saw his star. The man shot was a citizen negro. He shot him dead. The negro's name was Baker.

2512. Did they kill both of them? Joe Lundy was not killed dead at the time; he died afterwards; the other one was.

2513. How many shots did they fire? Three or four shots. The negroes were not doing anything at all. I went through Shelby street, on my way to the fort, and stopped to look at them good, and they were just knocking over every colored person they saw on the street.

2514. Did they shoot you? No, sir; I did not give them a chance. They shot two fellows right before me. This was late Tuesday afternoon, the first day it started.

2515. Was there a large crowd round there? No, sir; only a crowd of people who were looking out, and stopping on the sidewalk to see what was going on. After a while the policemen came running back this way up town.

2516. Did the policemen shoot these two men as they were coming back? Yes, sir.

2517. Were there any colored men fighting them? No; I never saw a colored man, except those they were chasing. I suppose when they went down there were a good many of them.

2518. At the time the policemen shot these two colored men, were the colored men chasing them up into town? I did not see them chasing them.

2519. You saw no colored people making any hostile demonstration? No, sir; none at all.

2520. Did you see any of them have arms? No, sir.

2521. Did those you saw killed have arms? The citizen had not. I disremember whether the soldier had or not.

2522. Did you hear them say anything? I heard them say. kill the damned son of a bitch. I did not hear anything further they said. The policeman who shot the last fellow I would know if I should see him again.

By Mr. SHANKLIN:

2523. When you got round on Shelby street, where you could see them, were there any colored soldiers then on South street? No, sir. There was a great quantity of policemen and citizens who looked like they were shooting every woman and child almost.

2524. Where were the soldiers then? The regulars came on out then.

2525. How many soldiers did you see going from South street toward the fort? Some six or seven. Some of them had pistols. Do not know whether they had been engaged in fighting or not. I was the first one who ran in and reported to the captain of the regulars that they were killing the men over there. I knew I was a soldier. that I had nothing to do with this thing, and so I went right to the fort and reported.

2526. Did you hear the soldiers say anything about it? I heard one soldier say they were killing every soldier they found, and those who had nothing to do with the fuss.

2527. You had no talk with them as to what they had done? No, sir.

MARIA MARSHALL (colored) sworn and examined.

By the CHAIRMAN:

2528. Where do you live? I have been living for about six months in Memphis. I came here from Natchez.

2529. Were you here during the riots? if so, state what you saw. I was. They killed a colored man right by the side of me. I believe they said it was on Wednesday night. It was just before they set the houses on fire that he was killed. He had been sick about two weeks, and had not been out of his bed until the very evening they shot him. Some white men shot him. I do not know their names. The name of the man killed was Shadrach Garrett. He had been hauling out wood and selling it.

2530. What did they kill him for? I never could find out what it was done for. That was all I saw that night. They shot my husband the next night.

2531. What did you see the next morning? I did not see anything. I went out there and looked at the man they had killed the night before. He laid just at his room door.

2532. Who was in his room? Nobody but his wife and children.

2533. Had they taken any steps to have his body buried? I do not know. I was not there when they took him away.

2534. What became of his wife? She went out where her folks were.

2535. Did they offer any violence to her or her children? No, sir, not that I heard of.

2536. What did they say when they shot this man? They asked him had he been a soldier. He said no. He was in his bed. They told him to get up and come out of his room. He told them he was not able to come out. They dragged him out, stood him up against a post, and shot him. I do not know who it was. When they first came there they chopped down the front door with hatchets; then they went in and called him. It was in the night, about twelve o'clock. They woke him up by chopping down his door. I got up and went out. Two or three of them stood and looked at me, but did not say anything to me.

2537. Did they put his clothes on? He was already dressed and lying by the side of his door. They stood him up against a post and shot him three times.

2538. How long did they make him stand before they shot him? They shot him just as quick as they stood him up. They said they were going to kill him, but did not say what for. I saw him when he fell, when they shot him the first time. He made a struggle as if to get up, and they shot him again.

2539. When was his body taken away? It was taken away and buried the next evening. There were two or three families who assisted his wife in taking him away.

2540. Did they commit any robbery? Yes, sir, they broke open his trunk, stole his fine clothes and his money. His wife said she never could find out exactly how much money. They said the next night they were coming to set the house on fire.

2541. Did they? No, sir.

2542. Did you see anybody killed during Wednesday? No, sir.

2543. What happened on Wednesday night? I do not know; I went away.

2544. When was your husband shot? He was helping to put out a fire, they said, on Echols street. He was shot by some man who set the house on fire. His name was Joe Marshall. He was a carpenter, but had been in the army. He had not been gone from the house long when he was shot.

2545. What did they shoot him for? Because he was helping to put out a fire. They had set on fire a little grocery or saloon belonging to two colored men in Echols street.

2546. Did you see the first part of the riot on Thursday? Yes, sir, I saw them run two colored soldiers over into a bayou.

2547. Did you see any white man shot? No, sir, I did not.

2548. Do you know what occasioned the riot? No, sir.

2549. Were these men in the bayou being fired at? The white men were firing at every one.

By Mr. BROOMALL:

2550. Did you see any colored men firing? No, sir, I did not.

2551. Do you know what became of those colored soldiers who ran into the bayou? No, sir, I do not.

2552. How many men were driving them into the bayou? There were a good many after them. I did not stop to count them. It scared me very badly. I thought I might be killed, and my husband too. A part of them were the police, and all white people.

2553. Did they rob you or offer violence? No, sir, they did not trouble me at all, because I remained in the house, and did not go out among them. They were in the yard that night when they had shot that man. They called several other white men and told them that "here was the place where they shot that nigger." The others told them to "come on, they did not want to have anything to do with him."

2554. Did you see many colored soldiers going about that first evening? No, sir, I did not see more than three or four.

2555. Did you see any colored persons misbehaving that evening? No, sir, I did not.

JOHN MARSHALL (colored) sworn and examined.

By Mr. BROOMALL:

2556. How long have you lived in Memphis? I came here in 1861.

2557. Were you here during the riots? and if so, state what you saw, beginning at the beginning. I was awaked at night by hearing them cutting the door down in the house adjoining. I jumped up and opened the door. There was a man standing right in front of the door with a pistol in his hand. He stood there about fifteen or twenty minutes, when another man said, "Charley, come here, we don't want anything in that house." I stood and looked through the cracks while they were dragging a man out of the house. They stood him up with his back to the door, and a white man shot him right in his mouth. The man fell, and when he was getting up another man walked up to him, kicked him over, and shot him again. Said he, "God damn you, you will never be free again."

2558. Did you know any of these men? No, sir. Some of them had on dark clothes. I could not tell whether they were policemen or not. I think they had on citizens' clothes.

2559. How many did you see? There were three that I saw. They broke two trunks open and took some women's things. That is about all I know that they took.

2560. What next did you see? That was all I saw on Wednesday night. My wife was so scared she would not stay at home, and we went over to my uncle's. While we were lying there they set a saloon on fire that a fellow-servant of mine kept. I went up with three or four men to help to put the fire out. Some man below shot me in the hip, and called out, "Get away, you damned son of a bitch, and let that fire alone."

2561. How many were there that shot at you? I do not know. There were some persons lying down by the fence. I suppose there were five or six white men.

2562. Were there any policemen among them? I do not know; I did not see any.

2563. How badly were you wounded? I was wounded very badly. I have hardly been able to work since.

By Mr. SHANKLIN:

2564. Did you see anything that Tuesday afternoon when the riot commenced? Yes, sir; I was close down where it commenced. I was on the top of a house at work. I saw some white men run two black men down. I heard some shooting, and would not go out for fear they might shoot me. There was a colored man I saw a little ways from me. Some women told him he had better run, as they were killing all the colored men they could find. He jumped and ran out of the house, and ran down right where the crowd were. They shot him at least twenty-five times—policemen and citizens. I was not more than twenty-five yards from him. They caught another colored man about the same time, and beat him over the head with a pistol. I think they were citizens. I saw Policeman Roach keep one man from shooting; I saw that myself.

2565. You did not see the fight when it commenced between the soldiers and colored people? No, sir.

2566. How far was the house you were at work on from South street? It was at the corner of Echols and Vance, a block or more from South street. I could not see down on South street, and do not know what was going on down there of my own knowledge.

Rev. EWING O. TADE recalled and examined.

By the CHAIRMAN:

2567. Have you ascertained the name of the rebel general whom you saw in the street that day? Yes, sir; it was General Dearing.

2568. What is his business? He is editor of the Appeal.

2569. Do you know the number of colored schools there were in the city at the time of the riot, and the number of scholars? I do not. There were colored schools kept that were not interrupted. There was one kept in this Gayoso House building, for instance. It was the bureau schools that I had more knowledge of.

2570. How long were these schools interrupted? The first one was reopened on Monday last, I believe. I am not certain but that one was opened a few days before.

2571. State how many churches were burned down? Four, including the Lincoln chapel, used exclusively for churches. There is another building near by, on Gayoso street, in which religious services were held, which was set fire to but not burned down.

2572. Was there any provision made, after these churches were burned, by the people of Memphis for the worship of the colored people? No, sir; not a single step taken by anybody.

2573. Were any of the churches here opened for their worship? No sir; I do not think they dared to open them. The best church burned was owned by the Methodist southern conference. They are pretty wealthy, and have several churches here, but were afraid to offer them to that congregation. Mr. Collins, after whom the church burned was named, preached occasionally for the colored people himself.

2574. Then no churches were opened for the colored people at all? No, sir; none that I could hear of. In fact, the colored people were afraid to go out. I rented the old botanic college on Saturday, and have taken charge of it for the purposes of these colored people.

By Mr. SHANKLIN:

2575. Why were they afraid to open their churches to the colored people? The reason given was that they were afraid of violence from some men engaged in the mob.

2576. That was the cause, was it, why some of the churches were not opened? Yes; I presume there were some of the churches that might have been extended to these people but for that. There are but two of the white churches in town that even have colored Sunday schools. They all stand idle in the afternoon, and if they were disposed to evince a brotherly spirit, I think they would have permitted a mission colored Sunday school at least to have been held in some of the churches.

TONY CHERRY (colored) sworn and examined.

By the CHAIRMAN:

2577. State your residence and occupation? I live on Main street, in this city, and have been for the last two weeks at work shelling corn on the levee.

2578. How old are you? Going on nineteen.

2579. Were you in Memphis at the time of the riots? Yes, sir.

2580. Did you take any part in them? I was amongst it both days down on South street.

2581. State what you saw and heard? The first day, when the fuss began, there was one of our boys on Shelby street who was shot six times by a policeman then he broke and run. When we went on South street there were four or five of them came down there. The colored men had been drinking right smartly, and some of them hallooing "Hurrah for Abe Lincoln," and so on. A policeman came along and told them to hush, and not be hallooing in that way, and another policeman said, "Your old father, Abe Lincoln, is dead and damned." The boys had got into a quarrel with this policeman the day before. He had taken one of them and beat him right smart, and this fellow they had taken up and beaten was in the crowd then. He saw the policeman, and wanted to hit him, but the boys would not let him. The policemen stepped off about forty steps. I followed them slowly. They went up as far as the bridge, drew their revolvers, and fired. As quick as it could be done (and, indeed, I do not know which fired first) our boys fired. The shots were all fired almost right together.

2582. Did you see any white man fall? Yes, sir; I was standing behind a little wagon when one of the policemen fell on the bridge.

2583. Did any colored man fall at the same time? No, sir; later on I saw them shoot down one of our boys.

2584. Have you been a soldier? Yes, sir; I was in company H, 3d colored heavy artillery. I was discharged on the 17th of April, but did not get my pay until directly after the riot.

2585. Then you were with these soldier boys at the time of the riot? Yes, sir; but as soon as the fuss commenced and I saw how things were going, I went out to camp, and staid there. They shot one of our boys right behind me, and they shot through my cap twice.

2586. Did you have any arms? No, sir; I did not have anything at all. I tried to keep the boys still; but they had been drinking. There were about thirty or forty of them when the fuss began. There were several saloons in the neighborhood where they got liquor. They were not very drunk; but you know what soldiers are when they get mustered out. There were four policemen who came up there first. One of the policemen who came up knew one of the boys of the regiment, and asked him what the boys were doing. He said, "They were just drinking and going on." The policeman said, "This will not do." He was a great big fat fellow with red whiskers. Another came up, and the boys began to cheer for Abe Lincoln. The policeman cursed them, and told them their old father was dead. Then the fourth one came up and drew his revolver. He did not say anything that I heard, but stood there. There were two of them doing the talking; the others stood there with their revolvers drawn. The boys, some of them, told them to leave. This one they had taken to the station-house the day before could hardly be kept off.

2587. What did they take him to the station-house for? There was a house burned down, and they suspected him, but he did not have anything to do with it. A citizen said he thought the man had something to do with it. They just took him, beat him, put him on a dray, and took him to the station-house. He was turned out the next morning. He knew the policeman that took him up. He cursed him, and wanted to hit him, but the boys would not let him. I kept him from hitting the policeman once. That boy's name was Charles Nelson.

2588. How soon after that did the shooting commence? In about five minutes. As soon as they could walk thirty or forty yards they turned round and fired. One of the policemen seemed to be drunk. He was cursing the boys, and drew his revolver. One of the boys then drew his revolver. Then the policemen all took out their revolvers. Then our boys all took theirs out. There were twenty or thirty of our boys who had revolvers. Then they all commenced shooting.

2589. As the policemen retreated did the boys follow them up? No, sir; the boys just staid there.

2590. Then did the policemen, when they commenced to fire, return towards your boys? Yes, sir; and commenced firing. I was going along right behind the policemen, and I jumped behind a little wagon to keep them from shooting me.

2591. Then did the policemen fire into the crowd of colored soldiers? Yes, sir.

2592. And then the colored people fired again? They all fired pretty much together. The first man shot was a policeman. Then this big one went on to town, as I heard, to get more men. The other two took up the one that had fallen, put him on a dray, and one of them went off with him. The other started round as I understood, to shoot some of our boys. I believe some of our boys followed him and shot him. So I heard them say. He had fired, and was loading his pistol when they shot him.

2593. What did the boys do then, remain there in a crowd, or disperse? Some of them stood there, some went back to the fort, and some went along the street with me. As soon as I saw the policemen coming back I jumped and run. They had scattered all around, and I had to go right through them. Richardson, a boy belonging to the same company I did, was killed. I guess he was about twenty yards behind me.

2594. What did they say when they killed him? I do not know. I was running. I did not hear anything. I saw one other boy shot that evening. I got up on the hill, and stopped there and rested. The next morning I came out about daylight, with another boy belonging to the same company I did.

2595. What did you go out so early for? I thought it was all over. Sergeant William Withers was out there, too, to see about one of the boys who had been shot, belonging to my company.

2596. Who shot him? I think a policeman shot him. There were people about who were getting sort of restless, and I told the sergeant I was going away. He said there was no danger. I went out on a hill to a house they burned down afterwards, belonging to some colored woman. I heard them firing. I looked back and saw a colored boy standing upon a knoll. The sergeant I had left was just ahead of him. Some policemen ran by him after the sergeant to kill him, but they could not catch him. One of the policemen dropped his revolver, and stopped to pick it up. The sergeant stood and cursed him. They then turned back to this colored boy, who was still standing there, shot him five or six times, and beat him for twenty or thirty steps before he fell.

2597. Where did you go then? I went to the fort, and stood on the breastworks, and saw them shooting the boys.

2598. At any time during that morning was there any crowd of colored people standing there together? No, sir; I did not see more than two together at any one time.

2599. Did the colored people shoot at white men that morning? No, sir; the boys did not fire that morning for a long time, until they had killed a good many of our boys. Then some of them went out on South street and fired a few shots. The white people came out like cavalry, on horses, and shot our men down like dogs.

2600. Did the boys arm themselves at the fort, and go out to meet the white men? No, sir. Some of them had old shot guns they had got out of houses, which they used.

2601. Were they afraid the crowd would break into the fort? Yes, sir; the boys were scared.

2602. How many boys got together on this second day with arms, and fired? I did not see but four of them go. They had four old muskets, and fired as hard as they could at the policemen.

2603. How far were they apart? At one place, down by the Mississippi depot, they were not more than fifty yards. On South street I guess they were three hundred yards off. The men down at the depot, belonging to the train, were shooting just as much as anybody else.

2604. Who did they shoot at? At our men on the hill.

2605. Did your boys shoot anybody? I do not know. I heard them say one man fell.

2606. Did any of your boys get killed by the firing at this long distance? No, sir.

2607. What did they go out of the fort and fire for? They were killing our boys everywhere. We saw them shot down like beasts, and it was pretty hard to remain quiet, for those who had arms, without trying to do something to stop it. One of our boys was killed on Mulberry street. He could have got away, but he would not. Finally some citizens took him, carried him up Mulberry street, and stabbed him. I was told this by some women who saw him. I went up and saw him lying there. His name was George Cobb.

2608. How many colored people do you know of being killed, or did you see dead, that day? I saw five of our men killed—William Willers, George Black, George Cobb, Ike Richardson; the name of the other I do not remember.

2609. Do you know of any other having been killed besides these? I do not know of any other. I saw another that was killed. I do not know his name. He belonged to company M.

2610. Do you know, of your own knowledge, of any robberies having been committed? No sir.

2611. Do you know of any acts of violence committed on the person of any colored women or others? No, sir.

By Mr. SHANKLIN:

2612. At what time of the evening on the day of the first fight was it that these colored soldiers were called together with pistols? I think the sun was about an hour and a half high. I did not notice particularly.

2613. When the four policemen first started away from the crowd of colored soldiers, did they attempt to carry off any of the soldiers with them? No, sir.

2614. You say you walked behind the policemen when they started off. How many of the other boys walked on behind them? There were not any of them exactly walking with me. There were two or three on the other side of the street. I do not know whether they were with the crowd or not. There was nobody who followed right after them but me. I thought it was all done.

2615. How far did the policemen go before there was any pistol fired? I guess about forty yards.

2616. When the policemen got on the bridge, how near were the nearest soldiers to them? The nearest I should think was about thirty yards off, but he was not following them. I was closer to them than that—about twenty yards off.

2617. When they commenced firing, you say they all fired together, and that there were four policemen who were firing at the soldiers. How many of the colored soldiers were firing at the policemen? From the reports of the pistols I should think there were about twenty.

2618. You say one policeman was shot at that time on the bridge. Was there a colored man shot about the same time? I did not see any hurt. I heard shortly afterwards that one had a little mark on the back of his neck.

2619. Did you know the policeman who was shot and fell on the bridge? I did not.

2620. Did these policemen remain long there after the firing ceased, or did they go directly away? About the time we saw the pistols drawn, and the man was shot on the bridge, they all went away but one, who stayed to assist the policeman. One went on up town to get assistance; the other went round the corner. Some of our boys went round to meet him, and when they came back they said that they had killed that policeman.

2621. Which one was it who claimed to have killed the policeman? I do not know the man's name. I know he belonged to the regiment.

2622. How long after this was it before the police came back with a crowd? It was not more than about half an hour.

2623. Then, I understand you, your boys were still on the street, and the policemen and your boys commenced shooting again? The policemen and citizens commenced shooting everybody they saw who had a blue rag on them.

2624. Did the colored people shoot too? Yes, sir, some of them did.

2625. How long after the police came back before your boys commenced shooting? As soon as the policemen struck South street they commenced shooting. Then some of our boys commenced shooting towards them.

2626. How long did that shooting between the colored soldiers and policemen continue that evening before they were separated? I guess until about eight o'clock; any way, the sun was down, and it was getting dark before the firing stopped that evening.

2627. Which do you think shot the oftener that evening, the colored soldiers or the policemen? The policemen shot oftenest; they had the most arms.

2628. But your boys were shooting as often as they could? They were doing the best they could; but they had hardly anything to fight with; a good many of them who had pistols had no ammunition.

2629. They shot as long as they had ammunition? Yes, sir.

2630. What did they do then? They went on the hill and would stay there until somebody would give them ammunition, and then they would go back again.

2631. Then, Wednesday morning you saw some of them come out with guns on South street before the firing commenced? No, sir; they were on the hill in front of the fort. The policemen and citizens were on horses down on South street firing at every colored boy who had blue clothes on. They had a black flag, and our boys shot at the flag. The man who had the flag fell, and the flag fell. I do not know whether the man was killed or not.

2632. The black flag was not raised any more? No, sir; I did not see it any more.

2633. Were the policemen with the man who had the black flag? I think so. They were on horses, just the same as cavalry. I was on the fort then.

2634. How many of your boys were engaged in shooting policemen and citizens on the street? I saw four of our boys who were firing.

2635. There were more than four on the hill, in front of the fort, were there not? Yes, sir. There were more firing down by the depot.

2636. How many were firing down by the depot? I could not say exactly. I could see boys coming round the corners of houses and getting a shot occasionally.

2637. You could tell that there were a good many down there shooting, could you not? There were not any of our boys shooting then. The four of our boys who were shooting were on the hill.

2638. Did not all of your boys that had arms continue to shoot as long as their ammunition lasted? Not all. Some of them did not go out at all, although they had revolvers with them.

2639. But those who were out remained shooting as long as they had ammunition? Yes, sir. We had been mustered out, but had not been paid, and were allowed to go down into the city whenever we pleased—so they got back in time for their pay, and they were scattered all around town.

2640. Did the soldiers have any difficulty in getting liquor down on South street? I never saw any one refused there yet.

2641. Which were the saloons at which the colored people got their liquor? They did not generally get it themselves. They would take a canteen and get a woman to fill it for them. The saloons were allowed to sell to women.

2642. Who kept the saloons where the colored boys got their liquor? I do not know their names. They were all up and down South street.

2643. Who was keeping the saloon where they had all collected and were enjoying themselves when the difficulty first commenced? It belonged to two of the sergeants of my company.

2644. They would sell to the soldiers themselves, would they not? Yes, sir; they kept beer, whiskey, apples, cakes, &c. They were in the service, and would sell to any of the boys.

2645. Was that the saloon that the greater number of the colored soldiers went to? A good many of them would go there, but they would go to other saloons too. A grocery kept by a white man, as a general thing, would get more trade from the colored men than if it had been kept by a colored man. I do not know why.

2646. Where did you come from? Savannah, Tennessee. I have been here three years.

2647. Have you a wife here? No, sir; my family are in Illinois.

By the CHAIRMAN:

2648. How many colored men did you see or hear firing their pistols after the police had returned to the scene of the fight on the first (Tuesday) night? I could not exactly tell the number of pistols. There were some of them out there who fired a good many times.

2649. How many rounds? The first time I think there were about twenty pistols fired, six times apiece.

2650. Were they fired at the police? Every one of them.

2651. How many volleys were fired by the policemen? There was one policeman, I think, who only shot twice. I do not think the one who was shot fired but once.

2652. How many colored men were killed in all? I cannot exactly tell you. I heard somebody say there were twenty-five killed.

2653. When did you first see this black flag? I saw it the second day, along about ten o'clock in the morning, just as the fuss began on that day.

2654. Who was the flag carried by? I do not know. I was on the breastworks. I could see it distinctly. I guess it was carried by a white man, though it was in a crowd of citizens.

2655. Are you certain it was a black flag? Yes, sir.

2656. Were you near enough to distinguish? Yes, sir; I was on the breastworks.

2657. What did you suppose it meant? It meant to kill them all, I allowed.

2658. Was the man who carried the flag on horseback? He was on his feet when he was shot down. There were horses all around them.

2659. How many men on horseback were there? I suppose sixty or seventy.

2660. Did the man who carried the black flag appear to have been on horseback? I could not say. He was on the ground when I saw him. Some of the boys in our regiment fired a volley at the man who had the flag, and he fell. I could not tell whether he dodged the ball, or whether he was shot.

2661. What took place then? They all got on their horses and went around the hill, so that the boys who fired towards them could not see them. The boys would occasionally see one of them, and shoot at him. Then the firing commenced at the depot, and our boys fired back on them there.

2662. Could you identify the man who carried the black flag? No, sir; I was too far off.

2663. What was the general opinion of the colored troops when they saw the flag raised? It was that it meant, "Show no quarter."

2664. What did they expect? They thought they had either to fight or run. The boys thought they were going to make a charge on the fort.

2665. How many of your boys had arms at this time? I only saw the three or four muskets.

2666. How many were there in the white crowd altogether, of men on horseback and men on foot? I should think there were near a hundred and fifty of them altogether near the graveyard.

2667. Did the policemen and crowd retreat at any time? Yes, sir. When the boys commenced firing they scattered off behind houses and hills.

2668. Then did the colored boys advance on them? No, sir; there was not enough of them for that.

2669. Were there any of the colored boys who had pistols? Yes, sir; there were plenty of them had pistols, but they had no ammunition. They expected they were going to charge and kill everybody who had pistols in the fort.

2670. Were you scared? No, sir. I was on guard before two pieces of artillery.

2671. Did you load them? Yes, sir.

2672. What for? If they came in there to shoot them. I was not very much scared, but the boys at camp were very much scared.

2673. When did you intend firing off the artillery? When they made the charge, if they made it.

2674. Did you fire the artillery? No, sir.

2675. Did you intend to fire it unless they made a charge? No, sir. We had a captain over us in the fort. He was going to defend the fort against the mob.

By Mr. SHANKLIN:

2676. Did the colored boys make any attempt to get arms from the arsenal or fort the night after the fight commenced? The boys went up to the ordnance house to try and get some. The soldiers on guard told them they could not get them. The boys told them they would go down and see the colonel about it. They did not try to get them by force.

2677. Did they talk about making a charge upon the arsenal so as to get the arms? Some of the boys wanted to do it, but they could not all have the same opinion, and they did not do anything. Four or five of the boys went up to the ordnance house, but the guard fired at them and they did not go any further.

2678. How many of them do you suppose wanted to take the guns by force? They tried three or four times to get up a squad, but when they got as high as ten or fifteen they could get no further.

By the CHAIRMAN:

2379. What did you want these arms for? To defend ourselves.

By Mr. SHANKLIN:

2680. Was this a white man who had charge of the artillery guns you have referred to? Yes, sir. He was a captain in the fort.

Mrs. MOLLY HAYES sworn and examined.

By the CHAIRMAN:

2681. Where do you live? On South street, Memphis.
2682. How long have lived there? About three months. I came here from Georgia.
2683. Were you here at the time of the riots? Yes, sir.
2684. State what, if anything, you saw of them? I saw right smart of it, though I never saw anybody killed; I saw them firing, but did not see anybody fall.
2685. Did you see anybody commit acts of violence? No, sir; I staid in my house.
2686. Do you know of any committed in houses occupied by colored people? Yes, sir; right next door to me.
2687. Did you see houses broken into? One. It was the house of a colored woman they called Sallie. I did not know her other name.
2688. Does a woman by the name of Harriet live near you? Harriet lives right adjoining me. My mother-in-law and two children live with me.
2689. Did any persons break into Harriet's house? No, sir; I did not see them break in. There were two men who came there and asked her where her husband was. She said he was in the fort. They said, "Is he a soldier?" She said, "Yes." They asked her if that was her trunk. She said yes. They told her to open it, and I reckon she did. Further than this I do not know anything about it. The last word I heard him say was, "Shut the door." I do not know what he done. I stepped out.
2690. Do you know how many men were in there? She said there were two. I do not know.
2691. Do you know whether she was robbed? I do not know; I allowed that she opened her trunk, and I suppose it was for the purpose of robbing it.
2692. How long did they remain in there? I do not know. I heard them go out and then come back again.
2693. Did she make any complaint of these men? Sometime afterwards she told me they acted very bad. I never asked her what. I took her word for it.
2694. Did you understand they were committing acts of violence upon her? She told me so.
2695. Did she say it was through fear? She said so. I never heard them make any threats. I might have heard more if I had staid in the house.
2696. Did you see anything more of the riots? I saw houses on fire. I do not know who burned them. They were a right smart distance off.
2697. Did you know this woman Harriet? Yes. We lived in adjoining houses.
2698. Was Sallie's house robbed? I do not know. I saw them burst open the window and go in. I do not know what they went in for or what they did.
2699. Did you see any people, besides the men you have mentioned, around her house afterwards? Yes; I saw two more men go there. One man came up and called out to a colored man to halt. The man stopped and gave up his pistol. I was scared. He had his pistol pointed right towards my house. He came into my house and dropped his knife. Then he came again and asked where his knife was. I did not know anything about his knife. He told me if I did not tell him where his knife was he would burn up the whole "shebang." That was the last word he said.
2700. Was the man drunk? Yes, sir.
2701. Did you see when the riot commenced? I was standing out and saw the fight, and did not know who done it. I just saw the fight between the colored people and the police. It was on Tuesday afternoon, I believe. I do not know who commenced it. I heard that there was a policeman shot, but did not know who commenced it.

Mrs. MARY GRADY sworn and examined.

By the CHAIRMAN:

2702. Where do you reside? I reside in South Memphis.
2703. What is your husband's name? Patrick Grady.
2704. Were you in Memphis at the time of the recent riots? Yes, sir.
2705. Did you see anything of them? If so, state what you saw. The first afternoon of the riot, before dark, a black man started out of my yard for South street, riding on a horse.

I told him he must not go; that the watchmen and citizens were shooting on South street. He started over there; the moment he got there they dismounted him, took away his horse, and commenced beating him with their pistols. They took him to the old graveyard, but the firing had commenced—by the people at the fort or some one else. He started to go back. They shot him through the back and killed him. That night my husband was in the yard with another man who lived on the same lot, whose name was David Smith. Thirty or forty policemen and citizens got hold of this man and began to abuse him. Said I, "For God's sake, don't kill him'; he has lived in my lot for four years, and I would not have him killed for anything in the world; if you kill him, you have got to kill me first," and I stood between him and them. Seven of them had their revolvers drawn. They said they wanted to kill the "dog-goned nigger." One of them knew me and called out, "You must let Mrs. Grady alone." Pat. Penders (Pendergrast) came in and said that no man should hurt anybody in this house; if they did, he would shoot him. He said that Dave should not be hurt. They did not do any further damage at that time. Before morning, however, a parcel of men came to my door and broke it down; one of them pointed to me and said, "Halt!" I was lying down and said, "I am halted." He said, "Here is that nigger resort; you keep a nigger ball-room, and I am going to kill you." I said, "You can kill me; I have but one life to live." They went behind the counter and took from a little box two hundred (200) dollars; they abused me, and told me if I said a word they would blow my infernal brains out. Then they went into the back room where my little girl and a black woman were in bed, and asked if there were any arms in there. The black woman said there were not. They then felt of her and wanted to get into bed with her. She told them they would have to kill her before they got into bed with her. Then they wanted my little girl, nine or ten years old, to kiss them. She said no, she would not kiss anybody. Then they tried to feel of her. My husband then called to three or four discharged Union soldiers who were sleeping in the back part of the house, to get up and come down quick, that they were doing Mary mighty wrong. The boys got up out of bed, and the party, hearing them, left. There were six or seven of them who said before this, "If you do not shut your mouth, we'll burn your house down in five minutes; you harbor niggers." I told them I did not harbor niggers any more than anybody else did, and that it was none of their business.

2706. State, if you know, who these men were who went into the room where your little girl was. I do not know.

2707. Was your little girl sleeping? Yes, sir, she was sleeping behind the black woman.

2708. Did these men attempt any violence to the black girl? They attempted to get into bed with her; put their hands under the clothes, and were feeling of her.

2709. What did they say to her? They abused her. I do not know that I heard all they said.

2710. What did they do to the little girl? They were wanting her to kiss them, and feeling of her. They did not do anything further. When they found that white men were asleep in the back part of the house they broke and run. I did not see them any more. These men in the back part of the house were laboring men who were just boarding with us.

2711. Have you been harboring colored people there? I have been renting rooms to them, and they had been trading in the grocery, the same as they do in other groceries in the neighborhood.

2712. Did you see anything which took place on Wednesday? On Wednesday morning the fuss commenced again. I saw a black man run out of a shanty and run towards the bayou. The people followed and shot at him twenty times, but did not kill him; then they took a gun and killed him and let him lie there by the railroad. I saw them burning houses close to me that night. The first house they burnt was that of a black man who had married a white woman. I saw a citizen set the house on fire. Henry Bankins is the name of the man whose house was burned. His wife came there, but they would not allow her to take one thing out of the house; everything was burned in it.

2713. Is she a full white woman? Yes, sir, she is a full white woman and an American woman. She came from Arkansas. I know the man who set the house on fire well by sight. I thought they would probably burn my house down. I went to the sheriff about it. He told me I need not be afraid. But even now I am a little afraid, for there is nothing but secesh down there. I have never been secesh in my life, and never intend to be. I have seen a plenty of secesh, and I tell you there are not many old residents about here who are not secesh. On Wednesday night there was a little shanty, belonging to a Mrs. Black, right close to me. I saw four people sitting out on the steps there watching my house. When they saw me they ran back and commenced breaking Ann Black's furniture and everything else in the house.

2714. Was she a black woman? Yes.

2715. State the value of all you lost. They only took two hundred dollars in money, and they broke up and destroyed about ninety dollars' worth of groceries.

By Mr. SHANKLIN:

2716. What sort of a house were you keeping? I kept a little family grocery.

2717. What do you keep in your grocery? All sorts of things to eat and drink, and everything else, just like any other little grocery.

2718. Did you retail out liquor to be drunk in the house? I had done it, but I have quit now about two months ago.

2719. At the time of the riot, had you any liquor in the house? I had none at all, except about a quart or half gallon, and that was for my husband and the men who boarded in the house.

2720. What kind of groceries did they break up? Such as green teas and other articles which they carried off.

2721. Did you keep an eating-house at the time of the riot? Yes, sir.

2722. Did the black people go there to eat and drink? They used to buy from me, but not to eat in the house; such as cakes and anything they want to eat or drink. A great many carried it out, but those who wanted to, could eat or drink there.

2723. White or black? Yes, sir.

2724. Is your house patronized by black people pretty freely? Yes, there are a great many blacks who come there to trade, and that is the reason they wanted to kill me. There were a great many colored people who thought a heap of us, and they would come there often.

2725. What liquors did you keep to drink? There was wine, soda water, brandy peaches, and such as you would find in any little shebang.

J. S. STORMS sworn and examined.

By the CHAIRMAN:

2726. State your residence and occupation. I reside in Memphis, and am in the grocery business; I have a small store on corner of Hernando and Elliot streets.

2727. Were you here at the time of the riot? If so, state what you know, if anything, in relation to it. It was right in my neighborhood. I do not know that I saw any one who was hurt on Tuesday. I saw them chasing colored people about the streets and shooting at them. · On Tuesday night, soon after the commencement of the riot, they ran up into our neighborhood and were firing at any colored men in front of my store they could start. I did not see any one who was shot. There was a man came to the store who was wounded and wanted his wound dressed. He was a colored man. I did not get his name. He said it was a policeman who shot him. He said it was an accident; that they were not shooting at him, but at another man who was passing him. He was shot in the leg. On Wednesday morning it was quiet until about nine or ten o'clock, when policemen and citizens came down in this part of the town.

2728. What did they come for? To put down the riot, they said.

2729. Was there any riot? Not that I saw; there was no disturbance until they got down there.

2730. Did they make any disturbance? The first I saw was after they went down there, when the firing commenced. All the colored people I saw in my neighborhood were running and trying to get away. The crowd seemed to be all citizens, and there seemed to be one or two hundred of them.

2731. Under whose lead did they seem to be? I did not know the man who had charge of them. I supposed the sheriff was on the street. I understood he was in charge of the posse.

2732. Did he seem to be exercising any acts of command? I do not know whether he gave any orders. I understood he was in command.

2733. Were there any other riotous proceedings except what was effected by this crowd? No, sir.

2734. Were there any negroes engaged in riotous proceedings? No, sir. On Tuesday and Wednesday night there was hardly a negro to be seen. They kept back out of the way. They were afraid.

2735. Was there any number of negroes together in your neighborhood on Wednesday morning when this posse came down? No, sir.

2736. Did you see any negro armed, or any making any resistance? No, sir.

2737. Were they burning any buildings at this time? I think there were one or two burned just across South street. I do not remember the time of day. I think it was just in the afternoon. On Wednesday night I saw fires. I did not go to them. I thought it best to stay by my own building. On Wednesday night, when I was on the street, there was a posse on the street; some of them were constables, and some of them were sent out, I suppose, as extra policemen. They were walking about, and a good many of them seemed to be drunk.

2738. Were they suppressing the riot? I saw no riot to suppress. They were creating more disturbance than anybody else, and they were, I think, the rioters. There were no black people on the street at all. There was a small building set on fire right next to my store. I went outside and heard one of this posse say, "It is about time for that fire, let us go down." They followed me right over to my store and stopped there. The fire had been put out. The black people said they were the same parties who set it on fire.

2739. Do you think when these men said "it was about time for that fire," they were waiting for the building to burn? I have no doubt of it. These were policemen. I entered into conversation with one of these men after the crowd had left the store. I said I hoped they would not set fire to any building close by me. He said they knew where to fire, that it was all arranged beforehand. He said it was a sort of a Fenian movement.

MATILDA HOWLEY (colored) sworn and examined.

By the CHAIRMAN:

2740. Are you a married woman? Yes, sir.

2741. Where is your husband? He is working on the railroad now. He has not been long out of the service.

2742. Were you here in the city at the time of the riot? Yes, sir; and I saw a good deal of it.

2743. State what you saw. The riot commenced on Tuesday afternoon, the first day of May. The first I saw was some colored soldiers and police quarrelling. They were cursing each other. I did not pay very much attention at the time. After that I heard shooting. I went away when they got to quarrelling. When I heard shooting I went round again, and saw one policeman shot down. The soldiers were all running. The police went off up town. After awhile fifty or sixty of the police and citizens came from up town; many of them were on horses. The police and citizens commenced running and firing. They shot a soldier right by me. His name was Charley. I do not know what his other name was.

2744. Who shot him? The police shot him. Then they all retreated, and after awhile more white men came back, and they all had a regular fight. I saw two men shot. My husband was in my house sick. I was afraid they would kill him, and I staid out on the street all the time. I saw a colored man by the name of George Howard, who had had the small-pox, with four white men, going about. They came to the house of an old man they call Uncle Dick, and shot somebody there. I heard the man groan. They walked down past my house, and one of the men said, "George! O, George Howard!" The colored man answered, and he said, "Let us fire these houses." Another man said, "No; we promised not to disturb these." George Howard said, "Let us go in here and kill them while they are asleep." He said, "No; wait till we see what they are doing round here."

2745. What further did you see? I think they came back and struck a light. It may have been a light from the fires that were burning, however. All of them went in, and I heard them knocking around there. After that they went away.

2746. Did they rob Uncle Dick? I do not know. I guess they did. The next morning I went in there and saw him sitting up dead in his bed as stiff as could be.

2747. Did you see them kill any one else? No, sir. The next morning I saw some people they had killed that night. I did not see them when they were killed.

2748. Were they colored people? Yes, sir; there was a girl named Rachael. I think she was burned after she was shot. I saw a couple of colored soldiers lying dead as I was going to the fort. I saw them shooting and killing, but I did not see who was killed.

2749. Who was this George Howard? I have seen him passing. I had never known him before that night. He stays over in a yard next to mine, I believe. He rents a house from a policeman named Day.

2750. Did the colored people generally understand that he was with the white men and against the colored people? Oh yes, they all know him. They know he has no use for colored people at all.

By Mr. SHANKLIN:

2751. Have you ever been a slave? Yes, sir. I have been free about three years.

2752. Who did you belong to before you were free? To Welland Jones, of Marshall county, Mississippi. I was the child of a white woman and a black man. I was stolen after I got to be a big girl. Afterwards my mother married a white man.

2753. Were you born in Mississippi? No, sir; I was born in Christian county, Kentucky.

2754. How old were you when you went to Mississippi? I do not know.

2755. Did you see the commencement of the fuss on Tuesday afternoon? Yes, sir. I saw three or four police and four or five colored men quarrelling. There were three or four citizens standing there. I do not know whether the citizens had any hand in it or not.

2756. How many colored soldiers do you think you saw shooting that afternoon? It looked as if there were twenty-five or thirty.

FRIDAY, *June* 1, 1866.

JOSEPH PIGEON sworn and examined.

By the CHAIRMAN:

2757. State your residence and occupation. I live in Memphis, and keep a bakery.

2758. How long have you resided in Memphis? Since the federals took this place. I came here from Rochester, New York.

2759. Have you ever been in the Union army? No, sir, not in the army; I have been in the militia.

2760. Were you in Memphis at the time of the riot? and if so, state what you saw in reference to it. I was. On the day the riot commenced I went to the corner of Gayoso and De Soto streets to collect some money. I saw a great crowd running, and went back. I saw very little in the way of acts of violence. I saw one or two shot. One negro was shot dead, and one was shot in the neck, but not killed. I do not know the circumstances under which the man was killed. Somebody told us a negro had been killed, and I went over and saw him lying in a gutter against some timber. I saw another running, who had just come from work. He had been shot in the arm.

2761. Do you know his name? No, sir. He lives there somewhere in that neighborhood. I do not know who shot him. There was quite a crowd running. We asked a fellow we met what was the matter. He said they were shooting and killing negroes. That is all I know of the matter on Tuesday afternoon. On Tuesday night, as quick as I came home after we closed up, there were five or six colored men who worked for us; we were afraid they would be molested, and we put them in the cellar and hid them. At night we saw a good many fires. I did not go away from home. I believe, also, I saw a few fires on Wednesday night. I heard some firing on Wednesday and firing on Tuesday night, all round, but I saw no acts of violence.

2762. By whom was the firing; by negroes or white men? I could not tell you anything about it.

2763. Why did you fear the negroes employed by you would be harmed? Because there was a crowd going round shooting negroes. There were a lot of drunken men, and the policemen were pretty near as bad as the citizens.

2764. How long did you keep them hid in your cellar? All that afternoon. At night they came out for supper, and then I put them back in the cellar and locked them in. On Wednesday they went to work until night, when I put them in the cellar again. One of them did not go in with the others. He went home and got knocked down.

2765. At what time did you give them their liberty? I think it was on Thursday morning.

2766. Do you know anything further? I do not, except that once in awhile I could hear men talking and making their brags that they had shot so many negroes, &c. I do not know who they were. I did not listen to them. I would, once in awhile, catch a word as persons were going by.

By Mr. SHANKLIN:

2767. Were you born in the United States? No, sir. I came here when I was about ten years old. I was born in Canada. My father was born in France.

J. S. CHAPIN sworn and examined.

By the CHAIRMAN:

2768. State your name, occupation, and residence? J. S. Chapin; I reside in Memphis, and am an insurance agent.

2769. How long have you resided here? I came here with my family in November last, from Jamesville, Wisconsin.

2770. Were you in the city during the recent riots? Yes, sir; and saw considerable of the riots on the first evening.

2771. What day was that? That was Tuesday evening, May 1, when it commenced.

2772. State what you saw and what you know of your own knowledge of the riots? As I stood on the corner of Elliot and Hernando streets I saw some men on horseback and some on foot chasing the negroes and firing at them. This was about half-past six, as I was going home to tea. When I got to Beal Street market I saw the extra force which was being sent down. I saw men on horseback riding as fast as they could after the negroes, and I saw several at once firing at them. As soon as they saw a negro he was shot at with their revolvers.

2773. How long did you remain there? I staid there some ten to fifteen minutes seeing the shooting, coming north from South street on Hernando, and going east to Elliot. I then walked to my house, near South street, and I saw shooting and running of the same kind on South street. I heard remarks made by some of these men, "We'll kill every damned nigger that we find."

2774. Who were the persons shooting, and who said this? Some were police, and some were citizens; white citizens.

2775. Did you see any colored person fire? I did not see a negro fire a gun or revolver, or armed. On the same evening I saw a negro who was a porter in a store on Hernando street; a white man came along and struck him with a pistol.

2776. What else did you see? About nine o'clock I went into South street, which was only about a couple of rods from my door. Hearing some disturbance, I went out, and saw a *posse* of, I should think, forty or fifty men. I think they said there were twenty policemen who were on guard on South street that night; the rest were citizens. Almost all who were there were armed with guns. I went among them in my shirt sleeves, and without my hat, that they might see I belonged right there, and asked them what they were there for. They said they came to keep the peace, and some said they were going to kill every damned nigger they could find, and burn up every shanty there was on South street. I then left, not feeling safe among them, and returned to my house. I heard them passing my house in the night, but I saw nothing more of them.

2777. What, if anything, did you see next day? I left my house between eight and nine in the morning, and went into South street, near to Main street. I did not see a dozen colored men, and but few white men, and all was quiet. I returned home in the afternoon about four o'clock, for I was unwell, and going down Main street to South street I saw Mr. Rankin's church and one or two other buildings close by that had been burned by the mob.

2778. Who constituted the mob? I mean the policemen and the citizens who were helping, as they said, to keep the peace.

2779. Did you see anything else? That evening and that night there were three if not four fires on the block below me—that is, on the block west of Hernando and south of South street.

2780. Did you see any building set on fire? I saw the buildings while they were on fire.

2781. Did you see if the mob—that is, the policemen and citizens—did anything to prevent the fire or anything to assist in putting it out? They did not do a thing. I went out twice on the opposite side to the fire, and found the police sitting there, and both times I found white citizens there looking on, but doing nothing to put it out.

2782. Did you see any negroes about that evening? Very few, and very seldom. Once in a while I did, when I told them to go home.

2783. What did you tell them to go home for? Because I considered their lives were in danger from the policemen and citizens constituting the mob.

2784. Did you see any assaults upon any of these negroes that evening? No, sir; I did not. I was up most of the night, at fires from school-houses and churches in different directions. This was Wednesday night.

2785. State what you saw on Thursday? Thursday morning I went to Beal Street market, where I saw a colored man that had been shot lying on the sidewalk. I did not hear his name.

2786. Did you see the sheriff at any time during those days? I saw him on Tuesday afternoon or evening. I saw him first in Beal Street market getting a *posse* to go down to help the police.

2787. What were the police doing? They were fighting negroes.

2788. Did you see the sheriff any more? I do not remember seeing him afterwards.

2789. Did you see the recorder during those days? I do not know that I did.

2790. Did you see the mayor during that time? I do not know the mayor.

2791. Did you see the deputy sheriff or attorney general? I might have seen them in the city, but not down where the fighting was. On Wednesday, the day of the burning of Mr. Rankin's school-house, I saw a man on horseback, who said he was ordered by the mayor to collect as large a *posse* as he could to go down and quiet the negroes. I did not know the man. He was an Irishman, and I heard him order several, who also were Irishmen, to go down with arms. He was dressed in citizen's clothes.

By Mr. SHANKLIN:

2792. Did you ascertain if there had been any fighting between the police and the negro soldiers before you saw anything of the fighting or rioting on Tuesday evening? I heard so on Beal street as the *posse* was going down there. It was about half-past six before I saw anything.

2793. Will you state what class of people, and of what nationality they were, who composed this mob? I think those I saw were, almost without exception, Irishmen.

2794. Did you see any of the orderly citizens mixing up with that mob or taking any part in it? I saw none of our merchants or business men. Those I saw were laboring men, judging by their appearance.

2795. Were they that class of men usually employed in draying, and hauling, and driving hacks, or employed upon the wharf? Partly that class and partly the frequenters and those found around the saloons; the class of idle men I should call loafers.

By Mr. BROOMALL:

2796. You have said that the better class of citizens—the merchants, and business men, and property holders, for instance—were not in this mob? I did not see any such participate.

2797. Do you know if that class of citizens usually participate in the doings of mobs? I suppose that they do not?

2798. Would you not suppose that that class of persons would be adverse to the destruction of property? My impression at the time was that a great portion of the people were indifferent to the rioting, for, as some said to me, they did not care which whipped, whether the Irish killed off all the niggers, or the niggers killed off all the Irish. That expression was made to me by business men.

2799. If public sentiment among the better class of people, such as professional and business men, had been in favor of protecting the negroes, could a mob have gone on for several days destroying property and killing them as they did? I have no idea that they could.

2800. Do I understand that you saw none of this orderly class of citizens trying to stop the mob either by advice, preaching, teaching, or anything else? I did not see anything of the kind.

2801. What has been the behavior of the resident negroes during the past few months? As far as I know it has been as good as that of the lower class of Irish, and I have had pretty good opportunities of knowing.

2802. What has been the conduct of the colored soldiers, I mean their general behavior, as compared with that of the same number of white soldiers under the same circumstances? I should, perhaps, make this distinction: The Eighth Iowa infantry patrolled the city a year ago last winter. They were, I think, a better class of soldiers, and generally better behaved men than the colored soldiers, taken as a class. Our citizens here objected to colored men patrolling the city, and there was brought here a regiment of Missouri men, and they were as much worse than the negroes as the negroes were worse than the Iowa soldiers.

By Mr. SHANKLIN :

2803. What was the deportment of the negro soldiers on the street, for some two or three months previous to the rioting ; was it orderly and quiet, or the reverse? It was as orderly and quiet as white soldiers. In three instances, I think, I saw some colored soldiers in liquor. I once saw them racing horses on Main street. At another time I saw perhaps a dozen boys, colored soldiers, under the influence of liquor; they were noisy, having sport, and having "a good time" generally, but entirely among themselves. They were troubling no one.

2804. Have you ever heard them using obscene language on the street? I do not know that I ever have. I have heard them using profane language, but not much.

2805. Have you ever seen them forcing citizens who were passing to leave the sidewalk? I never have. And I should add that I never saw colored soldiers so drunk but once that I could not go up to them and talk to them as a Christian man and stop their noise at once. That once I went up to a crowd, and one of them was so drunk that he came up to me, and put his arms right round me to hug me.

2806. Did you see any of these colored soldiers down on South street just previous to this difficulty, collecting about the drinking saloons there in pretty large companies? I am seldom in South street except on the Sabbath, when I would sometimes see a company of ten or fifteen together.

2807. Have you seen them under the influence of liquor? Never on the Sabbath, nor at other times so as to make them noisy, or to make a disturbance.

2808. You said you thought if the citizens had desired to stop this rioting and to protect the negroes they could have done so. Did you make any effort to protect them? I did, at the time the shooting was going on, among the policemen and citizens.

2809. What success had you? I cannot say that I did any good. My wife and daughter came to me, thinking I was exposing my life. It was the first time I had ever seen life sacrificed in that way, and I expressed myself strongly, and I thought it had some influence with them ; it seemed to quiet them down somewhat.

2810. But you finally gave up the job and left them? Yes, sir.

2811. Why did you suppose other citizens could have done better? Because I am little known, and have but little influence, while there are others who are better known and have much influence.

2812. Then you thought it was a dangerous thing for a citizen to undertake to control that mob? I did for myself, for I am a northern man, and known as such.

2813. Did you suppose the better class of southern people were the enemies of the negroes? Some of them, I know, are decidedly opposed to the negroes being educated. I know very many southern people who have good feelings toward the negroes, and are interested in their welfare.

2814. Does that kindly feeling extend to the negroes, or is there a feeling of hatred and hostility against the southern people? I have seen no manifestations of it.

2815. As a general thing, have the manifestations of feeling on the part of the old citizens of Memphis—leaving out the Irish population—towards the negroes been kind or unkind? Some I know have warm and tender feelings towards the negroes, while others have not. But my acquaintance is too limited to enable me to speak positively on that point.

2816. Have you ever known an instance in which a quiet, orderly negro, one who attended to his business, has been been unkindly treated by any of the class of citizens I have mentioned? No, sir? I have not.

2816. Do they not still employ them? Yes, sir ; they are the class they employ almost altogether.

2817. Do you know if those who formerly owned slaves give a preference to negroes over white men? I do not know, to speak positively ; my impression is that they would give the preference to those whom they used to employ.

2818. Is not that preference one of the causes which has excited this ill-feeling on the part of the Irish towards the negro population? My impression is that there is an inherent antipathy between the two classes. It has always been so in New York, and it is so here.

2819. How does the negro regard the Irishman, as a class? About as well as the Irishmen regard the negroes.

2820. Then you think it is in Memphis as it is in other places? Yes, sir; except that here the Irish rule.

2821. How is it that they have control of the city? I was not here at the last election, but I know, at least it is generally so understood, that the Irish here are in authority.

2822. Do you know that the right of franchise has been taken away in consequence of their participation in the recent riots? I do not so understand.

HANNAH ROBINSON (colored) sworn and examined.

By the CHAIRMAN:

2823. State your name, age, and where you live? Hannah Robinson; I shall be forty years old at Christmas; I live on Gayoso street, Memphis; I have lived here three years come next July; I came here from Mississippi, Yallabusha county. I have been a slave.

2824. Were you here when the riots took place? Yes, sir. They came into my house on Wednesday night, the 2d of May, and when they came up to the door, which was bolted, they broke it open. There were about twenty men. Directly they came in they said, "Och, here's a chance to be killed." My daughter was sick at the time; she is seventeen years old. There were four colored ladies sitting up with her. There were no men folks in the room except my husband and my son-in-law. The men came in in such a frightening and blustering way, that the women all squatted down and tried to hide as much as they could. They said, "Get up, you God damned niggers, and give us your arms." I said, "We have no arms." With that they knocked me down. They then broke open my trunk, and threw everything out, and took twenty-five dollars that I had there, and all my things they scattered on the floor and trampled over them. They then went to my husband and said, "God damn you, give up your arms." He told them he had no arms. They said, "God damn you, come out and we will search you." They searched his pockets, and took his pocketbook and his pocket-knife. Then they went to the bed where my daughter was lying, and just broke down the bed so that my daughter was squashed right down, and she was frightened very much. I then ran to my bed and took my baby, for I thought they were going to kill us all.

2825. Did you notice any who were in this crowd? I saw Mr. Chambers in the squad, and the policeman Dave Roach. These were all I knew. Mr. Chambers came to me on Tuesday morning, when I paid him my house rent; on Wednesday night he was with the squad that came to my house. I afterwards heard him say that he came with them to keep them from burning up the house.

2826. Was your daughter injured? She died on Saturday evening of the same week, about three o'clock in the afternoon. She was getting better at the time the men came, but she was so much frightened that she did not get over it.

2827. Were they armed? They all had pistols except Mr. Chambers. I did not see any in his hands. Dave Roach was the man that pulled out the trunk from under the bed and commenced throwing out the things.

2828. What was the amount of your property destroyed? The damage that they did, together with the money they stole, would be as much as $100.

2829. How many policemen did you see there? I think I saw four. This was about nine o'clock in the evening of Wednesday. They did not strike my husband, but just robbed him. Next night they came down and fired a colored person's house near us. My son has been a United States soldier. I am a seamstress. There were about twenty in the crowd. I knew some of them were policemen from their having slung-shots or clubs. When they left Dave Roach said, "Close up, close up; right shoulder shift. It is white man's day now." I understood by this that the colored people had been free, but that they had now gained the day back, and we thought they meant they were going to return us into slavery again. I was not afraid of being made a slave, for I felt certain that we should all be killed. When they asked my son-in-law to give up his arms, then they knocked him down.

By Mr. SHANKLIN:

2830. Did Mr. Chambers say anything? Mr. Chambers did not say anything; he neither encouraged nor discouraged. He was standing close to my son-in-law when he fell. He did not say anything when he saw my son-in-law knocked down.

ELVIRA WALKER (colored) sworn and examined.

By the CHAIRMAN:

2831. State your name and where you live? My name is Elvira Walker.
2832. What is your age? I shall be twenty-seven next fall.
2833. Have you been a slave? I have been a slave.
2834. Were you in Memphis at the time of the riots? I was here in Memphis at the time.
2835. What work do you do? I do washing.

13

2836. Are you married? A man boards with me: he is not my husband; he sleeps in the same room.

2837. State what you saw of the late riots here? On Thursday night about ten o'clock, I was entirely alone; some men came and knocked at my door. They came in, and said they were hunting for weapons.

2838. What did they do? They looked into my trunk and searched everywhere. One of them put his hands into my bosom. I tried to stop him, and he knocked down my hands with his pistol and did it again. He may have been searching for money. He then said there was $5 forfeit money, and that I must come to the station-house with him.

2839. Did they rob you? They took my watch. It was the best kind of silver watch, and was worth $45. There was a chain, but it was a common one, and not gold; both were presents to me; they took both.

2840. What else did they do? They then went to Mr. and Mrs. Bloom's; they are colored people; they live in the adjoining room.

2841. Do you know what they did in Mr. Bloom's? I did not see anything. I heard her say, "Quit, and leave me alone." A man said if she did not hush he would shoot her.

2842. Did Mrs. Bloom afterward tell you what had happened? Mrs. Bloom was kind of bashful about it afterwards, but she told us what they did, that they had ravished her. She did not say whether more than one had violated her. This was while Mr. Bloom was out of the house. He had been away, perhaps, for nearly half an hour to get the $5 for the forfeit, and he paid this $5 to the men when he came back.

2843. Do you know if they took anything else? They took a locket from Mrs. Bloom, and they also took Mr. Bloom's razors. He is a barber.

D. UPMAN sworn and examined.

By the CHAIRMAN:

2844. State your name, residence, and occupation? D. Upman; I reside in Memphis, and keep a restaurant.

2845. How long have you lived here? I came here in July last, from Chicago, where I kept a hotel on Randolph street.

2846. State if you were here at the time of the riots? Yes, sir; I was.

2847. Did you see anything of them? Yes, sir; I think it was on the evening of the 1st of May, there came a report that there had been a riot. On the 2d day there came a report that there had been a fight. So, on Wednesday morning about nine o'clock, the second of May, I walked slowly along Main street down to South street, where I found the people collecting, but, from what I saw, I thought there could be nothing serious. I have been an officer in the United States army. I had no arms with me. At Fort Pickering I saw a multitude of black people—some uniformed, and some half uniformed; and firing was going on pretty briskly from the colored troops. They were troops that were mustered out, but had not been paid. They were firing at the people.

2848. Who were the people they were firing at? I think they were northern men, some Irishmen and policemen.

2849. Were the Irishmen and policemen firing at the negroes? No, sir; they were not. At one time there was a white man who caught a colored man by the throat; the colored man had a uniform on and had been firing. The chief of police then said, "Don't fire, don't fire; stop that." The black man then got up and ran off.

2850. How near to the fort were you? I was pretty near—near enough to see.

2851. How much of a crowd of white people were there at that time? There were different groups; there must have been in all several hundred.

2852. What were they doing? They appeared to be observing, as I was.

2853. Were there any policemen there? Yes, sir; Ben Garrett was there. They were all standing under the shelter of the building and were not doing anything at that time. At last the mayor of the city, John Park, Cameron, and a man by the name of Shelby, came up towards me and said, "Let us walk up towards the fort." In the mean time Colonel Kappner, the lieutenant colonel, and a lieutenant, came up in a buggy; the lieutenant was on horseback. I used to see these officers in my place, and I knew them. The mayor talked with the colonel and said, "I want to know if you have any control over your men, and if the firing will be stopped or not?" He said he did not know if he had, but he would try. Mayor Park said, "That will not do; you must go there and stop this; I cannot keep the people back unless you stop this." I suppose he meant he could not stop the people from turning out in the city. The colonel said he was going up to do all he could.

2854. What took place then? The colonel went up, and the firing stopped. In the mean time there was a small squad of some twenty to twenty-five of the sixteenth infantry came up, under command of an officer, who, spreading themselves out in skirmishing order, drove all the negroes back into the fort

2855. What became of the white people who had collected there? Most of them went home.

2856. What time was this? It was about 11 or 12 o'clock.

2857. How many discharges of muskets or pistols did you hear—that is, from the colored men? A good many; they stood behind a fence, and with an opera glass, which I had, I could see them plainly. They were loading United States muskets, and kept on firing.

2858. Who were they firing at? At the groups of people there.

2859. Was there any firing by the white people there? Not at that time.

2860. What else do you know? In the evening the trouble broke out again, but I did not see that.

2861. What time did you leave the ground in the morning? About 12 o'clock. I was on the ground about two or two and a half hours.

2862. Did the balance of the crowd leave when you did? Most of them did.

2863. Did you see anybody killed or hurt? No, sir; I did not. There was no firing from the white people; the firing was from the blacks, so I could not see if any of the whites were hurt. I went up towards the fort, for I wanted to see if it was an organization.

2864. What did you see there? It did not look like an organization.

2865. Was the firing done to defend themselves? It did not look to me so. There were no crowds of white people advancing on them. There were reports that a drunken soldier had been killed on South street. The white people said that three or four colored people had been killed.

2866. Were you called upon to go down to suppress the rioting? No, sir. When I saw the United States soldiers skirmishing, I thought it was all over, and the negroes were driven into the fort.

By Mr. SHANKLIN:

2867. How long did you live in Chicago? Three years.

2868. Where did you live before that? In Milwaukee, where I lived about three years.

2869. And where did you reside before that? In Minnesota, where I was a register of the United States land office for six years under the administration of James K. Polk.

2870. What did you do before that? Before that I was in the United States army. I was appointed second lieutenant, and rose to captain and was brevetted major for gallant conduct at the battle of Chepultepec.

2871. Where do you live in this city? 81 Jefferson street, opposite the Memphis theatre.

2872. Do I understand that you were in the neighborhood of the rioting about ten o'clock on the second of May? Yes, sir; most of the crowd were there with me.

2873. You say, do you not, that you heard and saw firing from the direction of the fort? Yes, sir; and when I got to within 100 yards or so, I saw there were colored people who were firing.

2874. And some of them were uniformed and some partly uniformed? Yes, sir.

2875. How many colored people were there in that group? There were a multitude—several hundred; perhaps 300, 400, or 500. I was somewhat scared, as I thought they might make a charge.

2876. How many out of this number were engaged in shooting? I did not take particular notice. I should say 20 to 25; but I do not know for certain.

2877. Were those you saw firing using United States muskets? Some were using United States muskets and some pistols.

2878. How many muskets do you think they had employed in shooting? I do not know that I could give a correct answer. I could safely say I saw a dozen.

2879. How long did they continue to shoot from these muskets and pistols? It must have been from one to one and a half hour.

2880. Did they continue to shoot till this colonel and lieutenant colonel had an interview with Mayor Park? Yes, sir. They ceased firing when the colonel, the lieutenant colonel, a captain, and a lieutenant went there to stop them, and at the same time the United States troops came up.

2881. Were these officers you speak of the men who had been in command of these negro troops before they were mustered out? Yes, sir.

2882. During the time you were there, while these negroes were firing upon those groups in the direction of South street, did you see any white person shooting towards those groups of negroes? No, sir.

2883. Did you see these colored soldiers you speak of shooting towards some persons in the direction of the railway depot? That is the direction they were shooting at.

2884. Did you see these same colored soldiers shooting in the direction of South street? They shot in several directions. I was north of South street. They had been shooting towards South street, and all at once they commenced firing at us. Balls were whistling close by us. I then walked alone, as I thought there would not be so much danger as there would be in a group.

2885. You say, do you not, that you were on the ground about two hours? I arrived there about 10 and left about 12.

2886. Were these negro soldiers, or groups of negroes, engaged in firing when you first got sight of them? Yes, sir.

2887. How long did you remain there after they ceased to fire? Not very long; perhaps not more than twenty minutes.

2888. Did you see any one killed or wounded while you were on the ground? No, sir.

2889. So far as the resident negroes were concerned, did you see any participation in the riot by them? No, sir. Some of the resident negroes stood in the groups, and they ran back with the white people with whom they were mixed up. I noticed this, for it seemed it was not a negro fight, but with the colored people that were in the army; so it appeared to me. I saw no violence on the streets. The negroes mingled with the white people, and there did not seem any hard feeling on either side.

2890. Have you been engaged in the recent rebellion, on either side? No, sir. I kept a hotel, and could not go unless I made a great sacrifice—besides, I am getting old, being nearly 61 years of age.

2891. Have you been in sentiment and feeling on the side of the general government? I have always been a Union man. I could have cried almost when I heard that Sumter had been fired on.

2892. How long have you been in this country? I have been here some 32 years.

2893. Of what country are you a native? I am a Hanoverian by birth.

By the CHAIRMAN:

2894. Do I understand you to belong to the Union party? I am no politician.

2895. Were you not a politician when you held office under Polk? No, sir.

2896. Where were you in the land office? In Winona.

2897. What party did you act with? None, sir. I am a democrat—that is, a Union democrat, but no politician.

MARY WALKER (colored) sworn and examined.

By the CHAIRMAN:

2898. State your name and where you live. I live in Memphis.

2899. Have you been a slave? I have; but have been free for four years.

2900. Were you in Memphis at the time of the riots? I was here at the time. Joseph Walker, who testified before the committee. is my husband.

2901. State what you know of the rioting. On Wednesday morning my husband, who is a levee hand, was coming home from the Mississippi depot. I was standing at my door looking at him, when I saw a white gentleman jump from behind the engine and shoot off his pistol.

2902. Do you know the name of the man? There were two of them; they were brothers; and their name was Palmer.

2903. Did they shoot your husband? When they shot at my husband they missed him, and another colored man commenced to run; they followed him and shot him dead. I saw him fall into the bayou, and I saw he did not get up.

2904. Did you see anything else? I saw other white men firing at colored men, but I do not know their names.

2905. Did you hear them say anything? When the man Palmer shot at the colored man and killed him, I heard him say, "Kill the damned son of a bitch." My husband was afterwards shot. That was between 8 and 9 o'clock Wednesday morning.

FRANCES THOMPSON (colored) sworn and examined.

By the CHAIRMAN:

2906. State your name and residence. My name is Frances Thompson; I live in Gayoso street, here in Memphis.

2907. What is your occupation? I sew and take in washing and ironing.

2908. Have you been a slave? Yes, sir.

2909. Where were you raised? I was raised in Maryland. All our people but mistress got killed in the rebel army.

2910. Have you been injured? I am a cripple. (The witness used crutches.) I have a cancer in my foot.

2911. Were you here during the late riots? Yes, sir.

2912. State what you know or saw of the rioting. Between one and two o'clock Tuesday night seven men, two of whom were policemen, came to my house. I know they were policemen by their stars. They were all Irishmen. They said they must have supper, and asked me what I had, and said they must have some eggs, and ham, and biscuit. I made them some biscuit and some strong coffee, and they all sat down and ate. A girl lives with me; her name is Lucy Smith; she is about 16 years old. When they had eaten supper, they said they wanted some woman to sleep with. I said we were not that sort of women, and they must go. They said "that didn't make a damned bit of difference." One of them then laid hold of me and hit me on the side of my face, and, holding my throat, choked me. Lucy tried to get out of the window, when one of them knocked her down and choked her. They drew their pistols and said they would shoot us and fire the house if we did not let them have their way with us. All seven of the men violated us two. Four of them had to do with me, and the rest with Lucy.

2913. Were you injured? I was sick for two weeks. I lay for three days with a hot, burning fever.

2914. Did any one attend you? I had a cold before, and Dr. Rambert attended me after this.

2915. Were you robbed? After they got through with us they just robbed the house. They took the clothes out of my trunk and took one hundred dollars that I had in greenbacks belonging to me, and two hundred dollars that belonged to a colored woman, that was left with me to keep safe for her.

2916. Did they take anything else? They took three silk dresses of mine and a right nice one of Lucy's. They put the things into two pillow slips and took them away.

2917. How long did these men stay? They were there, perhaps, for nearly four hours; it was near getting day when they left.

2918. Did they say anything? They said they intended to "burn up the last God damned nigger."

2919. Do you know any of them? They were all Irishmen; there was not an American among them.

2920. Did anything else take place? There were some quilts about that we had been making. They asked us what they were made for. When we told them we made them for the soldiers they swore at us, and said the soldiers would never have them on their beds, and they took them away with the rest of the things. They said they would drive all the Yankees out of the town, and then there would be only some rebel niggers and butternuts left. I thought all the time they would burn the house down, but they didn't.

LUCY SMITH (colored) sworn and examined.

By the CHAIRMAN:

2921. State your name and how old you are. Lucy Smith; I am going on 17 years of age.

2922. Have you been a slave? I have been a slave girl, and have been free four years come July next.

2923. Do you live in this city? I live in Memphis, and was raised here.

2924. Were you here at the time of the riots? I was living with Frances Thompson at the time of the riots.

2925. State what you know of the late riots. On Tuesday, the first night of the riots, some men came to our house. We were in bed. They told us to get up and get some supper for them. We got up, and made a fire, and got them supper.

2926. What else took place? What was left of the sugar, and coffee, and ham they threw into the bayou.

2927. How many men were there? There were seven of them; but I was so scared I could not be certain.

2928. Did they rob you? We had two trunks. They did not unlock them, but just jerked them open. They took $100 belonging to Frances, and $200 belonging to a friend of Frances, given to her to take care of. They took all the money and clothes and carried them off.

2929. Did you know any of the men? There were two policemen with the men; I saw their stars.

2930. What else took place? They tried to take advantage of me, and did. I told them I did not do such things, and would not. One of them said he would make me, and choked me by the neck. My neck was swollen up next day, and for two weeks I could not talk to any one. After the first man had connexion with me, another got hold of me and tried to violate me, but I was so bad he did not. He gave me a lick with his fist and said I was so damned near dead he would not have anything to do with me.

2931. Were you injured? I bled from what the first man had done to me. The man said, "Oh, she is so near dead I won't have anything to do with her." I was injured right smart, and kept my bed for two weeks after.

2932. Did they do anything else? We had some quilts in the room that we had been quilting red, white, and blue. They asked us if we had made them before or after the Yankees came. We said after. They said, "You niggers have a mighty liking for the damned Yankees, but we will kill you, and you will have no liking for any one then." There were some pictures in the room: we had General Hooker and some other Union officers, and they said they would not have hurt us so bad if it had not been for these pictures. They were in the house a good while after they hurt me, but I lay down on the bed, for I thought they had killed me; it was mostly from the choking and the lick on the side of my head.

2933. Did any one attend you? Dr. Riley, a colored doctor, afterwards examined me. I was in bed two weeks after.

W. G. McELVANE sworn and examined.

By the CHAIRMAN:

2934. State your name, residence, and occupation. W. G. McElvane; I am assistant station-house keeper; I live in Memphis.

2935. Were you here during the rioting? Yes, sir.

2936. Were any persons arrested during the riots? I do not recollect of any persons being brought to the station-house for participation in the riots; not during my presence there.

2937. Were there any colored persons arrested? There were two or three colored men brought there during the night, who were arrested on suspicion of being concerned in the riot; they were released without any examination.

2938. And was there no person arrested during or after the riot? The day after the riot there was a man brought to the station-house by the name of Woods. He said he was acting deputy constable. He could not tell under what charge he was there; he said people hallooed, "Catch him." He was held some five or ten minutes, and no person preferring any charge, he was released. He was a white man, and an American.

2939. Was he not arrested for killing a man who had taken the part of a negro? I do not know.

2940. Did you not hear that he had "only killed a damned nigger?" I do not recollect anybody saying, "He has only killed a damned nigger."

2941. Did you understand that he had killed a man? I understood that he was the man who had killed Dennis.

2942. Who was Dennis? He was an old citizen of this place. He has been here at least eight or ten years, and has always been regarded as a peaceable man. He was an ex-rebel soldier. He came out of the army a year after he went in.

2943. What was he killed for? I could not tell you.

2944. Was he not shot for taking the part of a negro man? I so understood it. I understood he made the remark that this negro was as good as any white man; and being asked to repeat it, he did, and was killed on the spot.

2945. Has any complaint been lodged against any of the negroes who were brought to the station-house by the police? There were three or four brought there under suspicion of having been concerned in bringing on the riots, but they were released from the fact that nothing was found against them.

2946. Do you know anything about a wounded colored man named Goodell being brought to the station-house? As I was going home, when near the Beal street bridge, there was a dense crowd, and I heard two pistols fired. When I got a little further, a merchant who keeps a clothing store touched me and asked me what I was going to do with that boy, pointing to a colored boy lying in the road. I could not render him any assistance except pulling him out of the gutter. There was a piece of timber there on which I laid his head, for he appeared to be in spasms and dying. Next morning a colored woman came to the station-house to see the colored boy, who was brought to the station-house in the night. She did not get to see him then, for we were very busy; there were two courts going on there. She afterwards got to see him, whether through the bars or not I do not know; but she said it was her husband, and that he was dead.

2947. Who is your city recorder? John C. Creighton.

2948. Is he an elected officer? Yes, sir; and is a magistrate by virtue of his office.

2949. What is his character and conduct? I have known him for eight or nine years. He has always had the character of being a clever, upright man.

2950. Has he not had several difficulties with citizens? Yes, sir. He is in the habit of drinking a good deal, and will sometimes knock a man down and fight a little.

2951. Has he ever killed anybody? I believe he did kill a man here about six months ago.

2952. What was done with him? He was discharged by Judge Hunter, judge of the criminal court, before whom he had a trial, and it was found justifiable homicide.

2953. Did this take place while Mr. Creighton was recorder? Yes, sir.

2954. What is your official position? I am assistant station-house keeper, and have police powers.

By Mr. SHANKLIN:

2955. From what State are you? I came here in 1840 from Pennsylvania, my native State.

2956. How long have you held your present office? I have held it since September, 1862. It is an office appointed by the board of mayor and city council, and is held during good behavior.

JAMES E. DONAHUE (colored) sworn and examined.

By the CHAIRMAN:

2957. State your name and where you live. James E. Donahue. I have lived in Memphis nearly three years.

2958. Have you been a slave? Yes, sir; but became free 31st July, 1863. It was said the proclamation of Mr. Lincoln freed us.

2959. Did you see anything of the late riots here? I saw some of it. There were a great many citizens, and I saw three policemen among them on the first night of the rioting. I was in an alley way. I saw three shots fired, and I believe they were fired by the policemen, at a house where there were some women and children, who made back into the house.

2960. What did you see or hear? I heard them say that they were going to kill every damned nigger in Memphis. There were some three or four families in a building when they shot at the women and children who were there. I saw the policemen have three colored men in custody the night the riot broke out. There was a policeman on each side and one behind each colored man, and they seemed to be badly beaten and used up.

2961. Did the colored men resist the officers? The colored men made no resistance, but walked along in silence.

2962. What trade do you follow? I am a house carpenter, and worked at my trade during the riots, and was not disturbed. No person gave me a cross word during the riots.

By Mr. SHANKLIN:

2963. What State do you come from? I was raised in North Carolina, and was in Macon, Tennessee, when the war broke out.

2964. How long have you been here? I came here in 1863, and have been here ever since in business.

2965. Have you been a slave? Yes, sir; but for ten years before the war broke out my master allowed me to do my own business, make my own contracts, collect the money, and pay it over to him.

2966. Do you make good wages here? Yes, sir: I make pretty good wages.

2967. Do the citizens treat you kindly? Yes, sir. I have heard a good deal of complaining among colored people that they could not get their money, but I never had any trouble except with one man. I built him a house, and gave him up the key on the 31st day of January last. He was to pay me cash, but he owes me about $100. Some of those who complain are industrious and prudent, and some are of the other sort, but a colored man has to be humble to get along.

2968. What has been the feeling of the colored people towards the police of the city? There has been a good deal of trouble between the Irish police and the colored people, and I have sometimes fought (blamed) both parties; sometimes the colored people were inclined to be dull, and cut up, and do things they ought not to do, and that would create difficulties between them and the police. Then sometimes the police would arrest a colored soldier when he had no right to. But one thing I noticed that I did not like. Whenever a policeman arrested a colored man, the first thing he did was to strike him. I did not know whether that was right for him or not, but it did not seem to me to be right. I have seen, perhaps, as many as a hundred colored people arrested here, and I do not remember ten who were not struck by policemen. It was that that made me careful to keep out of scrapes.

By Mr. BROOMALL:

2969. Have colored people been generally paid for their labor by the citizens? The most common complaint against white folks by colored people has been refusing to pay them for their labor. But I think the bureau has settled that very nicely among them.

HENRY BOND (colored) sworn and examined.

By the CHAIRMAN:

2970. State your name and where you live. Henry Bond; I live in Memphis.

2971. Have you been a slave? Yes, sir, but have been free since the war.

2972. What is your occupation? I live by draying.

2973. Were you here at the time of the riots? Yes, sir.

2974. What did you see of them? Nothing was done to me, but I saw a good deal done to other men.

2975. State what you saw. On the first day the riot broke out, Willis Jones, the blacksmith, was shot in the eye by a policeman. It did not kill him, and he is alive yet. I was standing near my stable, and he was not twenty steps from me when he was shot.

2976. Do you know who shot him? I do not know the policeman's name, but I know him when I see him.

2977. Where was this? This was on Talbot and Mulberry streets.

2978. What else did you see? The next I saw shot was a colored soldier. It was about sundown on the first day. There were, I suppose, about a hundred men, and two policemen had the colored soldier, each by one arm. The constable, Bill O'Hern, came up, riding a pony. "Gentlemen," said he, "let me shoot that fellow," and he out with his pistol and shot him in the neck. Then the colored man broke and came running through the yard, trying to save himself, but a white man pushed him back, and he ran round the house to the corner of Mulberry street and Brown's avenue, and there they finished him.

2979. Did you see anything else? The third man I saw shot was Eli. He was shot by a policeman. I was well acquainted with Eli; he was a peaceable man. He was standing on the street as I was, and a policeman came along and up with his pistol and shot him. I was not a hundred yards from him when he was shot.

2980. When was this? It was on Tuesday afternoon.

2981. Did you hear any expressions from the crowd? Yes, sir; they said they were going to "kill every damned nigger they came across." I do not know how it was that they ran by me when they had as good a chance to kill me as anybody else.

2982. What did you see the next day? Next day I saw another colored man beaten by the crowd; they gave him, perhaps, 200 or 250 licks with a stick. A policeman commenced beating him, and a citizen went on whipping him till another citizen took him away. He was beat awfully, and tried to get out of the way.

2983. What had this colored man done? He was doing nothing when they set upon him

2984. Were the colored people armed? None of them were armed that I saw.

2985. Were you hurt? I did not get a scratch, but they came very near burning my mule.

2986. How was that? When they set the government barracks on fire, and burned the stables, the sparks blew on my stable, and it would have all been burned down had it not been for one of my colored friends.

2987. What was the size of the government barracks? It was about 100 feet long. It was fired by the citizens.

2988. What was the government barracks used for? The colored schools and the colored church were kept there.

2989. By whom was this rioting and shooting done? All the shooting was done by white men; there was not a negro seen on the street at night.

MOLLIE DAVIS (colored) sworn and examined.

By the CHAIRMAN:

2990. State your name and where you live. Mollie Davis; I have lived in Memphis since 1861.

2991. Have you been a slave? I used to belong to Dr. Davis.

2992. How long have you lived here? I came here with the doctor's wife during the war.

2993. Were you here during the riot? Yes, sir.

2994. State what you saw of it. On Thursday night my house was burned down. They told me that it was done by John Egan and his crowd.

2995. What did you lose? I had nice clothes. The furniture and clothes they burned were worth $550. The bedstead and mattress and two sets of pillows cost sixty-five dollars.

2996. Who is John Egan? He is a policeman. He is mad with me because I had him arrested. John Egan arrested me, and I had to put up fifty dollars forfeit money. Egan had to pay me back the fifty dollars forfeit, and he had to pay twenty dollars costs, and he was turned off for getting this money under false pretences. This is what he was mad about. During the riot I kept close, for I knew John Egan would kill me if he saw me. John Egan has a partner; his name is Clarke.

2997. Are you married? I am not a married woman. My friend is a white man. He is a Kentuckian, and I have had him for six years.

ELLEN BROWN (colored) sworn and examined.

By the CHAIRMAN:

2998. State your name and where you live?˙ Ellen Brown; I live in Memphis; I live with Mollie Davis.

2999. What do you know of the late riots in this place? John Egan, who is a policeman, came to our door and knocked, and asked me to open it. He cursed, and as I did not open the door, I heard him say, "By God, let us burn it down." After a while he peeped through the window, and I saw it was Egan. After a while he went away. That was the first night of the riot. We were told by Mat. Wardlaw that Mr. Clark, who was a policeman of the 5th ward, said they were coming down the next night to burn us out. The house was burned down and everything in it.

LUCY HUNT (colored) sworn and examined.

By the CHAIRMAN:

3000. State your name and where you live? Lucy Hunt; I live on the south side of the hill, here in Memphis.

3001. Have you been a slave? I have, but have been free three years.

3002. Were you here at the time of the riots? Yes, sir; I was.

3003. State what you saw? I saw Mrs. Black's house burned up. My house, too, caught fire, but we put it out. Five or six men came to my house. Chris. Pigeon, who lives on the railroad by the depot, was one of them. He is an Irishman, and keeps a grocery; there were three or four others and one colored man who was with them. They knocked at the door, and I heard them say, "He is in here." I said there is no one here but me and my husband. I think they were looking for a colored soldier. They said if we can't get him we will burn you. They set fire to my things and pushed me back three or four times into the fire. One of them caught hold of my throat and said, "I am going to burn you up." When they pushed me into the fire it burned my dress behind. When the girls hallooed that the regulars were coming they ran off as fast as they could. I believe they would have burned me up if the soldiers had not come.

3004. How much property did you lose? They broke open my trunk; I had $325 in it.

3005. Where did you get all that money? I had been at the fort and had done cooking for company D for sixteen months. All my money was in greenbacks.

3006. What was the value of your clothes? They were worth $100. My wearing clothes were burned, and my sheets and counterpanes which I had bought and laid up in the fort.

3007. Did you see anything else? I saw Joe Lundy shot; and I saw one shot by the railroad; he was shot six times and killed. When he was down they knocked him on the head.

3008. When was your house burned? It was on Tuesday night.

By Mr. BROOMALL:

3009. Did these men say anything to you? When I hallooed out they told me to hush and not to make any fuss. Then my sister called to me, "Come away, Lucy." But they were all around me, and one of them put his gun right to my cheek and said, "God damn you, if you leave I will shoot you." When they saw the regulars they ran off.

MARY BLACK (colored) sworn and examined.

By the CHAIRMAN:

3009½. State your name and where you live? Mary Black; I live on the south of Memphis.

3010. Were you in Memphis at the time of the riots? Yes, sir; I was.

3011. What did you see? They came to our house between nine and ten o'clock Wednesday night. They called to us first to open the door. There were none of us asleep. They called three or four times, but none of us answered. Then we opened the door and they told me to get a candle; if I didn't they would kill me.

3012. What else did they do? One of them took a match out of his pocket and said he would have a fire directly; and after that they got two chunks that were on fire and put them right into the middle of the bed.

3013. Did you know any of these parties? No, sir; but the old lady who lived with me said one of them was Mr. Pigeon.

3014. Who was living with you at the time? The old lady, Maria Scott, and my daughter, twelve years old.

3015. What else did they do? They did not rob me, but just burned up all in my house. They broke up the chairs and put them on the fire. Mr. Pigeon stood at the outside. One of them said to Mr. Pigeon, "Shall we pour turpentine on it?" and he said, "Yes." They then poured turpentine on the bed, and it flamed up to the ceiling. They asked me where my husband was, and I said I did not know where he was. I said "he went off this morning."

3016. Was your husband a soldier? He was in the fifty-fifth regiment, and had been discharged about two or three months before Christmas.

3017. Was your house burned down? They burned up all in my house, but they ran off when the regulars were coming. That is how we got out. Before the regulars came these men were keeping us in the house.

3018. How far had the fire progressed when you heard the soldiers were coming? All one side of my house was falling in. We had three rooms that they burned down.

3019. Did you make any effort, you and your daughter, to get out? We asked them to let us out, and they said they meant to burn us up, and I believe they would if it had not been for the soldiers coming down.

3020. Did you try to get out while the house was burning? I was so scared I could do nothing. I would as soon be burned out as shot. The old lady tried to get out.

3021. Where were the men? The men who burned us out stood at the door.

3022. How much did they burn up? They burned up everything except my feather bed. There were two beds in the room. I saved one and some of my clothes. I had right smart of furniture, and the house was mine. My husband paid $25 in money for it. It was a plank shanty, and we had $100 worth of furniture and clothes. I had besides a barrel of flour, and a barrel of meal, and a keg of meat, and it was all burned.

3023. Did you see any one shot? I saw them shoot one man, but I do not know his name. I saw him fall; there were as many as ten or fifteen or twenty shots fired at him. He ran into the bayou; then they brought him up and one man knocked him down with his gun-barrel, and they fired five or six times after he was down. I saw a good many dead bodies: I know I saw four besides this first one.

3024. How long did the dead bodies remain unburied? I think they were taken up Friday or Saturday.

By Mr. SHANKLIN:

3025. Do you know how much money Lucy Hunt had? No, sir, I do not; but her husband had just been paid off.

By Mr. BROOMALL:

3026. Where does Lucy Hunt live? Not far from my house.

3027. Did you see them try to fire her house? No, sir; but I heard them there; I heard them running in and about her house.

3028. Do you know of Lucy Hunt's clothes being burned? I did not notice.

3029. What do you know of her? She is an industrious woman. She has been living in the fort.

S. S. GARRETT sworn and examined.

By the CHAIRMAN:

3030. State your name, residence, and occupation. S. S. Garrett; I reside in Memphis, and have been here for the past three years; I am now employed at the Freedmen's Bureau.

3031. Have you been in the service of the United States? I was 1st lieutenant in the 3d United States colored heavy artillery.

3032. State if you were in Memphis at the time of the riots; and if so, what you know of your own knowledge? I was stationed at Fort Pickering. I had no command, but was with the regiment. I know nothing of the beginning of the riot on the first day. I saw the beginning of the riot on the second day.

3033. Be good enough to state what you know. I rode out from the fort on the second day of the riots, at about half-past eight o'clock, to South Memphis, the scene of the riot of the previous night. I saw a couple of colored soldiers there that had been shot. I knew their names at the time, but do not recollect them now. The gentleman who was with me, Mr. Sample, recognized them. There was no trouble, nor any appearance of any, at the time. We left the bodies and rode towards the post office. About an hour after we saw perhaps 40 or 50 policemen, in squads, going in the direction of South Memphis. They were followed by some citizens preceded by some four or five men on horseback. I followed the crowd till I reached South street. The policemen halted at South street for a short time. There was some difficulty at a drug-store there. They then marched across the street to a little eminence towards the negro quarters. I hurried to a point where I could see what was going on, and I saw different policemen pointing and saying, "There's one," "there's another." I then saw that they were pointing out men who had on the United States uniform, and then they commenced shooting at them. I saw one man shot who was running towards them, seemingly for the purpose of surrendering. I saw another shot down who was in his shirt sleeves trying to get away. The balls whistled round there rather lively. My attention was then directed to the disarmed soldiers of my regiment. Their attention had been attracted by the firing, and I could see them on the parapet. This was about half-past nine o'clock. I thought they might perhaps come down out of the fort. I therefore rode round to a little eminence on the Tennessee and Mississippi railroad, and was urging them to go back. I told them it was no good their coming out. As it was, I think none of them got out. While I was there a ball passed in close proximity to my head, though I know not by whom it was fired. I think not by the colored people. It was not from the soldiers I was urging into the fort.

3034. Did you see any firing by the colored people? I did not see any shots from the colored party. I think there were none. After that I went into the fort.

3035. If there had been any firing by the colored people, would you have known it? There might have been firing by the colored people that I should not have known of.

3036. Was there any large number of colored people about the fort who were firing at the white people coming up towards it? No, sir.

3037. Could there have been any such firing without your knowledge? No, sir.

3038. Did you see any firing at all by the soldiers who were on the parapet, or who were a little outside? No, sir. There could not have been any firing by the soldiers, from the fact that they were disarmed. Their arms had been turned over.

3039. Do you know that to have been the fact? Yes, sir, I do.

3040. Are there any others who know of that fact? Yes, sir; every officer here knows it. None of them could have had muskets unless they stole them.

3041. Could as many as a dozen have been there firing muskets, and 40 or 50 others firing pistols, without your knowing it? No, sir; not at the fort.

3042. Did you see a mob of policemen and citizens approaching the fort at any time? No, sir.

3043. Did you see any hostile demonstrations of persons who were on the parapet towards the mob coming up? I know nothing of a mob of policemen and citizens, except those that went down to South street, and I saw no collision whatever.

3044. What did the policemen and citizens go down to South street for? I do not know.

3045. Did you see any rioting? I was there an hour before, and I saw nothing, nor was there any rioting when the police arrived there.

3046. How near together were the police and citizens and the colored soldiers at any time? There might have been some colored soldiers out there, but those I speak of were not nearer than a quarter of a mile.

3047. Were there any others, except those you speak of, who were nearer than that? Not that I know of. There were some colored citizens in United States uniform that were shot at; these were outside the fort.

3048. What were they doing? They were running away from the crowd, and I saw one of them shot down.

3049. What time did you go into the fort? It was between half-past nine andten o'clock.

3050. Do I understand you to say that if there had been any firing, such as I have described from colored soldiers or colored men, you must have heard it? Yes, sir; I was in a position that I could not have helped hearing.

3051. What has been the conduct of these colored soldiers since you have been in command, and what has been their recent conduct? The regiment was organized here and has remained here all the time, nearly three years. There have been some acts of vandalism on the part of these men.

3051. Describe the acts you refer to? There have been some acts of robbery and house-breaking, though it has not always been fastened on that regiment.

3052. How many cases have there been which have been fastened on the regiment? I do not know that I could say; not more than three or four.

3053. What has been the general conduct of these troops? The general conduct has been very good.

3054. How has it been as compared with white troops? It would compare favorably.

3055. What was their conduct after they were mustered out, and when waiting for their pay? I did not see anything wrong in their conduct. They remained in the fort, as a rule, though some of them went out, I presume, but not many of them.

3056. Did they keep sober when they went out? I saw none of them drunk.

3057. Was there any disposition, when any crimes were committed, to throw it upon the colored soldiers? The press has done a good deal in that way.

3058. What has been the feeling of the people here towards this regiment of colored soldiers? It has not been favorable.

3059. Have any of these colored soldiers been arrested by the police, and, if so, under what circumstances, and what has been the treatment of the soldiers so arrested by the police? There has been an antipathy existing between the police and the colored soldiers, and when they made any arrests they did it in a very cruel manner.

3060. Have the soldiers resented this way of being arrested—that is, the maltreatment? Not to my knowledge; they have borne it in a manner no other people would, probably. Their disposition is to cause them to endure bad treatment. I have myself witnessed several brutal arrests. I saw one arrested about six weeks ago; I do not know for what cause. The policeman struck him on the head with his pistol and knocked him down. The colored soldier was then put upon a dray and hauled off to the station-house. I have heard numerous complaints of this same kind of treatment.

3061. Did the soldier resist the policeman? I saw nothing of the kind.

3062. Did you hear of anything of the kind? I did not.

3063. Was the soldier disabled when he was knocked down? He was. I saw them put him on a dray and haul him off.

3064. Have you heard any threats made by colored soldiers against the police? I have not.

3065. Have you heard any threats made by the police force of Memphis against colored soldiers? No, sir.

3066. What was the conduct of the colored soldiers in the fort on the first day of the riot? They wanted to go out, but the officers dissuaded them from going out. They would get together in little knots and discuss the matter, and they would seem ready to go out till an officer would go and induce them to come back. They seemed to have an idea that their people were being murdered and misused by the police force, and they wanted to go out and defend them.

3067. Were they afraid that this force would get into the fort and capture them? No, sir; I did not hear any fear of the kind expressed. Many of the soldiers had homes in South Memphis; their wives and children were there and what little they possessed of personal property.

3068. Did you see any acts of violence committed by the crowd more than you have described? I saw nothing but the shooting of these inoffensive people.

3069. Were those two negroes who were shot creating a riot? They were not doing anything.

3070. Was there any riot? None whatever.

3071. What did you suppose the police force was down there for? My supposition was that they went down to have revenge for some acts that had been committed by some colored people prior to that time.

3072. Then it was not to subdue a riot? No, sir; from the fact that there was no riot to subdue.

3073. Do you know what took place on Wednesday evening? That was the evening on which the burning of the colored people's houses took place. I saw the fires from the fort. I was up till one o'clock, but know nothing of the parties who were engaged in it.

3074. Were there any regular troops at the fort at that time? Yes, sir; they were under the command of Captain Allyn.

3075. Was he in the fort all the time you were there? My impression is that he was, though I was not with him.

3076. If there had been this large number of colored people at the fort with the number of arms I have mentioned, Captain Allyn would have known it, would he not? Yes, sir.

By Mr. BROOMALL:

3077. You say that about half past nine or ten you induced the colored soldiers to go inside the fort? Yes, sir.

3078. Do you know if any colored soldiers left the fort after that? I did not know of any.

3079. Had any considerable numbers left the fort would you have known it? I think I should.

3080. Had there been as many as a dozen, would you have known it? There might possibly have been that number leave without my knowing it. It is a long line of works, perhaps a mile or a mile and a half long.

3081. Have you any idea how many of the colored soldiers had wives and families in the south part of the town? I think probably a majority of them had wives and children there.

3082. When these groups of colored soldiers were collecting together and talking and wishing to go out, did they state their object? My understanding was that it was to defend their wives and families.

3083. Was this talk from those who had families? Some of them to my own knowledge had.

By Mr. SHANKLIN:

3084. Were you connected with the army before you became an officer in this colored regiment? Yes, sir; I was a private in the 55th Illinois. David Stewart was the colonel.

3085. In what capacity did you enter the colored regiment? I entered the colored regiment as quartermaster's sergeant; from that I was promoted to sergeant major; then to second lieutenant; then to first lieutenant.

3086. What is the extent of the fort? It is about 10,000 feet from the river round to the river; perhaps nearly two miles.

3087. In what portion of the fort were you? In the central portion.

3088. If a company had been collected outside of the outer lines of the fort and within fifty or sixty yards of the railway depot, how far would you have been from it? It certainly would not have exceeded a quarter of a mile.

3089. Might there not have been a company shooting down in the neighborhood of the depot without you seeing it from the point where you stood? I think not, sir.

3090. If there had been could you have seen it? Yes, sir.

3091. Was there any shooting from the parapet? None at all, that I saw.

3092. When you went into the fort did you leave any colored persons outside of the fortifications? I think not, sir; some were on the parapet.

3093. Did you see any with muskets? No, sir.

3094. Were there many of those soldiers who had been mustered out who had revolvers? There were none who had to my knowledge.

3095. Do you know if any of the negro soldiers were engaged in the disturbances that took place on Tuesday evening? I know nothing of my own knowledge, though I heard there were some of them there.

3096. Do I understand you to say that, as far as you know, none of the colored soldiers were engaged in the firing that took place on Wednesday? I did not see any firing done at that time by colored men.

3097. Will you state if the cannon that was at the fort was loaded sometime on Wednesday? To my knowledge there was no cannon loaded at the fort. There were, I know, two pieces taken to the camp of the 16th infantry, but that was under the direction of the officer commanding there.

3098. Did any of the negro soldiers get control of the cannon? I believe not.

3099. Was any effort, to your knowledge, made by any of the colored soldiers on Wednesday to raise a squad to make an assault upon the arsenal and get possession of the arms? I heard something of the kind from the officers, but I saw no demonstrations. I know that the men wanted their arms. I heard the expression that they would like to have their arms, and they thought the government ought not to have taken their arms from them; that they could not defend themselves.

3100. You say, do you not, that you saw no colored man who had been a soldier fire a gun or pistol? I did not see one fire.

3101. And you saw no company engaged in shooting? No, sir; at no time during the riot.

3102. Do you you know anything about the colored soldiers leaving the fort and going out to procure arms and ammunition? No, sir; I neither saw nor heard of it.

3103. Where were the colonel and lieutenant colonel of that regiment during the riots? They were at their quarters.

3104. Where are they now? The colonel commanding that regiment is now in Cuba. I do not know where the lieutenant colonel is; he has left this city.

By the CHAIRMAN:

3105. State if the colonel and lieutenant colonel were at the fort that day. Yes, sir; except when the colonel went down to see General Stoneman. He may have gone out more than once. I saw him in his buggy riding backwards and forwards.

3106. What was the name of the lieutenant colonel? His name is Wiley. Lieutenant Helm was also there; also Lieutenant Hastings. I saw them all together, and they saw what was going on.

JOHN MYERS sworn and examined.

By the CHAIRMAN:

3107. State your name, residence, and occupation. John Myers;-I live in Memphis, and keep a saloon and restaurant here. It is called the Frank saloon.
3108. Of what country are you? I am a German-Swiss.
3109. Was there not a man shot in your saloon? Yes, sir.
3110. What day was it? I do not know what day it was; it was the day after the negroes were "raising hell."
3111. What was the name of the man who was shot? It was Ben Dennis.
3112. Did you know him? Yes, sir. Some time he was on a steamboat.
3113. What was he in your saloon for? I suppose to get a drink.
3114. What was he doing when he was shot? Nothing.
3115. State the circumstance as far as you know. There was a negro passing by; I know him long time; his name is Reub; he keeps a barber's shop; sometimes he does something for me; I called him in to get a drink; then Ben Dennis stepped in and was talking to the negro; I did not hear what it was, and paid no attention. It was dinner time. A fireman was there eating his dinner. When he heard what Ben Dennis said, he jumped up and said, "What do you say?" and at the same time shot him.
3116. Who was it that shot Dennis? He was a fireman, but I do not know his name.
3117. Had you seen him before? He had eaten two or three meals there.
3118. What was the conversation between Ben Dennis and the colored man? I paid no attention to it. When the fireman came out he said, "What did you say?" and Ben Dennis said, "I did not mean any harm;" and then was shot.
3119. Did this fireman, or any one else, coming out of the dining-room, say, "You are taking the part of a damned nigger?" I do not know. I did not hear more than I have said.
3120. Did Ben Dennis speak after he was shot? He said, "John, I am shot;" that is all. He did not live ten minutes.
3121. What became of the man who shot him? He ran away, of course; he was scared.
3122. Was he not arrested? Two citizens arrested him and took him to the station-house, but they did not know what had happened. They said there had been some difficulty, but nobody knew, and he got loose, and nobody has seen him since.
3123. Where is this colored man? His name is Reuben; he keeps a barber's shop on Jefferson street, between Main and Front Row.
3124. Was Ben Dennis shot because he was talking to the negro? I do not know, and I did not hear what was said more than I have told.

MEMPHIS, TENN., *June* 2, 1866.

FREDERICK HASTINGS sworn and examined.

By the CHAIRMAN:

3125. State your name and residence, and what has been your occupation of late? Frederick Hastings. For the past five years I have been a soldier; for three years I have been first lieutenant; two years before that I was a private soldier. I was first lieutenant of the 3d United States colored heavy artillery, stationed at Fort Pickering, Memphis, and have been on duty here as ordnance officer for the past three years.
3126. State if you were at the fort on the 1st and 2d of May last. Yes, sir, I was.
3127. What was the condition and position of the regiment at that time? A few days before that they turned over their arms to me, with the exception of two companies, who retained their arms for camp duty; and a day or two before the riot they turned over their arms to me.
3128. Had all the companies turned over their arms to you before the riot? Yes, sir; they had.
3129. Did you see what took place on the first day of the riot? About 3 or 4, possibly 5 o'clock on the first day of the riot, I was on Shelby street, in a buggy, coming towards the fort, when the first pistol shot was fired. On the corner of South and Main there was quite a gathering. A few minutes after many shots were fired, but as that was common I paid no attention to it. About two hours after that I went down street towards the fort, and there seemed to be great excitement among the negroes.
3130. Do you know by whom those first shots were fired? I do not know.
3131. Continue your narrative as to what took place. Previous to this there had been several difficulties between the police and the negro soldiers—indeed, it was a rather common occurrence; but I never before heard so much firing as at that time; it seemed more like a

skirmish. The men in the fort were very much excited. The colonel sent for the officers to prevent the men from turning out. It was reported among the colored soldiers that their houses were being burned down. Many of them had their families in that portion of the town. Many of the men went out on the first evening of the riot—probably one hundred went out; they all broke out at once; it was when they heard this firing. I was standing on the parapet trying to prevent them.

3132. Did you see what led to the first breaking out of the riot? No, sir, I did not.

3133. Did you see any acts of violence committed on Tuesday? I saw two cases after they were shot. There was a man working for me whose wife was shot. He said it was a soldier belonging to the 16th who shot her. She was brought into the fort; it was only a flesh wound. That is all I know of Tuesday.

3134. State what you saw on Wednesday. On Wednesday morning, about ten o'clock, there was a great deal of fighting going on, when the mayor and his staff came riding up to the fort asking for the commanding officer of the fort. The colonel and lieutenant colonel rode out to confer with the mayor, who guaranteed there would be no trouble if the colonel kept his men in the fort. During this time one of those with the mayor pointed his rifle at Major Smyth, who was riding in uniform, but another person put it down with his hand. The man who pointed the rifle was drunk. The colonel said to the mayor that the men's houses were burning, and if the men got that idea it would be impossible to keep them in. When the colonel came back he told the men they must stay in the fort; that their houses would not be burned, nor their wives or children molested. This was between 10 and 11 o'clock that this speech was made to the men; and they did keep in.

3135. What was the rioting that was going on at this time? All that I saw were some horsemen who were running round and firing. They were the ones, as far as I could see, that did all the shooting, and it was colored men that they were shooting at.

3136. Did you see any number of colored people together at this time? No, sir; I did not, except in the fort.

3137. Of whom was the crowd outside composed? I could not tell you.

3138. How large was the crowd? They were in squads of eight or ten, and I saw three or four different squads. Most of them were on horseback.

3139. Were any of them policemen? There was Sheriff Winters and his *posse*.

3140. What were they doing? They were galloping round and firing, and their object was, I understood, to take the arms away from the negroes.

3141. Did you hear them make any remarks? No, sir; I did not.

3142. Were you in a position from 10 to 12 o'clock on Wednesday morning to see what the colored soldiers of your regiment, inside and outside of your fort, were doing? Inside the fort they were standing round in groups talking and in their quarters.

3143. Were there any considerable numbers of this colored regiment outside of the fort from early in the morning up to 12 o'clock? I asked the adjutant, who had the roll called, and he said there were some two hundred absent.

3144. Where were they? In the city somewhere.

3145. Were they collected together in any numbers outside the fort? Not to my knowledge; I did not see fifty people together.

3146. Had men been collected in a body outside the fort would you have seen them? Yes, sir.

3147. Was there any firing by colored men at these squads of white men that you saw? Not that I saw. I saw one shot fired from the parapet. There were some cavalry, and one of the men, having a rifle, fired, and an officer sent and took the gun away from him.

3148. Had there been any other firing from the parapet or from outside would you have known it; that is, firing on the crowd outside? Yes, sir; I should, for I was in a position where I could not but have seen it.

3149. Were you in a position that, had there been ten, twenty-five, or fifty colored men near the fort firing, you would have seen them? Yes, sir; I should.

3150. Was there any firing at the fort except that you have spoken of? No, sir. There was a great deal of firing further up South street, but there was no firing at all in the fort.

3151. Was there any considerable number of colored people who were armed, either with pistols or guns, outside the fort, and facing these squads of white men, and firing? I saw nothing of the kind.

3152. A witness who has been before this committee testifies that when he got to within one hundred yards of the fort he saw colored people firing; and in answer to a question he says: "I saw a multitude of black people." * * * "There must have been several hundred—three, four, or five hundred." Is that correct? I am positive it is not. I was in the fort all the time. I was afraid the men would get their arms, and I put extra guards to prevent it.

3153. Did they make any attempt? On the first evening, Tuesday, there was a squad of twenty or thirty who started to get their arms, but the guards halted them and fired, and they rushed back. That was all the attempt there was to get possession of their arms.

3154. What did they want their arms for? They wanted to get outside.

3155. For what purpose? I suppose to use them. Many of them had wives and children outside.

3156. Was this attempt to get their arms made by those who had wives and children outside? Some of them, I know, had.

3157. This witness (quoting from D. Upman) further says that out of this number—three, four, or five hundred—"I should say there were from twenty to twenty-five who were shooting." Could that have been so? No, sir; it could not have been so, and I was there all day.

3158. Were you in a position where you must have seen it had it occurred? I was, sir.

3159. Could you, from your position at the fort, have seen it had it taken place between the fort and the depot? Yes, sir.

3160. This witness from whose testimony I have read is asked, "How long did they continue to shoot from these muskets and pistols?" and his reply is, "It must have been from one to one and a half hours." Did any such firing as that take place? There was shooting going on further down South street, but there was none going on at the fort.

3161. What time was it that Colonel Kappner and the lieutenant colonel and Captain Riley rode out of the fort? It must have been between 9 and 10 o'clock. They went out to meet the mayor. The mayor said he was afraid to come into the fort. They held their parley with the mayor probably about 10 o'clock.

3162. Where was Colonel Kappner after that up to 12 o'clock? I think he rode into the city in a buggy, but I will not be positive. I saw him a number of times after 10 o'clock.

3163. How long did Colonel Kappner remain at the fort after he made that speech to the men? I do not know. He went after that to his headquarters, and I saw him go out with Colonel Wiley in his buggy, and I saw him several times during the day afterwards.

3164. Had Colonel Kappner, to your knowledge, any parley with the colored people outside the fort? No, sir; he had none that I know anything of.

3165. Would you have been likely to know it had he done so? I cannot say that I should.

3166. What was the character of the speech made to the men by Colonel Kappner? It was calculated to allay their feelings. He told them to keep quiet; that they had no arms, and could do no good if they had and went out, and he therefore advised them to keep quiet and remain in their quarters, for if they went out it would probably make things worse, and they might themselves get shot down. Some of the men spoke out and said that reports were coming in that they were burning their houses and murdering their wives and children, and that they wanted to go out to protect them. I suppose there were one hundred families that had moved into the fort for protection.

3167. Did Colonel Kappner tell them of the pledges he had received from the mayor? Yes, sir. He said the mayor had guaranteed that there should be no further violence, and he told them that he stood pledged to the mayor that they should stay in the fort. Some of the men said that the crowd had promised to come into the fort and clear them out. The colonel promised them there would be no further trouble if they would keep quiet.

3168. What is the character of Colonel Kappner as an officer? I consider it very good. He is very strict. I have always thought he had the best colored regiment that was ever here.

3169. What was the character of this regiment? It was good.

3170. What had been the general conduct of the men before and after being mustered out? Very good. There were some bad men in it, but the conduct of the generality was good.

3171. What was the conduct of the regiment after it was mustered out and waiting to be paid off? Both inside and outside the fort they were very orderly.

3172. Do you know of any cases of drunkenness outside? I only saw one case of a drunken soldier. He had a pistol on, and I had him sent back to the fort. I saw no other.

3173. Were many of the families of the soldiers living in the vicinity of the fort? Yes, sir; great numbers. I know I had many detailed from different companies who had families living there; I should say one-third of them had.

3174. Did their families live in those shanties where the riots had been going on? Yes, sir.

3175. Were any of those shanties burned? Yes, sir; some of them were.

3176. Did you see any persons killed during the riots, either white or black? No, sir.

By Mr. SHANKLIN:

3177. I understand you to say that about 3 or 4 o'clock on Tuesday evening, as you were going out to the fort from the city, you heard firing; on what street was that? The pistol shot I heard fired was on Main street. Going up further, I heard another shot, and I noticed perhaps half a dozen men running; there were others that seemed to be gathering. In half a mile I heard fifteen to twenty shots. After that I heard no more of it till it was nearly dark.

3178. Do you know who fired those shots? I could not say.

3179. When you heard what you described as skirmishing do you know by whom that shooting was done? No, sir; I do not.

3180. Were there any of these colored soldiers who had been mustered out on South street when this firing commenced? I was not along South street that evening.

3181. State if these colored soldiers had not been frequently going about the streets previous to that time? Yes, sir; there were four out of each company allowed passes daily.

3182. Is that the whole number that were allowed to go out daily after they were mustered out? I think there was no limit after they were mustered out, though I will not be positive, but before that there were four only from each company. There were twelve companies.

3183. Do you know what the conduct of the colored soldiers had been on the street before they were mustered out? With one or two exceptions they behaved very orderly. I saw one or two at different times swaggering along and acting very insolently.

3184. Were there not a good many in the regiment who were in the habit of drinking freely and becoming intoxicated? I know two or three men who worked for me who would occasionally get drunk.

3185. Did you see the colored soldiers on Tuesday evening, after you heard this firing and between sundown and dark, coming into the fort in considerable numbers? No, sir. Just at dark there were, perhaps, a hundred. This was inside the fort. I asked if any one was killed; they said three or four were, and among them Joe Lundy, who had been working for me. They said he was trying to get two drunken men into the fort, and was shot while doing that.

3186. Were there many of those men in these squads that seemed to be under the influence of liquor? No, sir; I did not see a single drunken man, and they did not seem to be much excited.

3187. Were you down on South street after that time that evening? No, sir.

3188. On Wednesday morning do you know how many belonging to the heavy artillery were absent from the fort from eight to twelve o'clock? No, sir. I asked the adjutant, but I am not positive when it was—it may have been in the morning—and he said there were two hundred absent. The colonel had ordered roll-call.

3189. During that morning, did you at any time between breakfast and twelve o'clock see groups of those soldiers collecting on the parapet, or outside the parapet? Yes, sir; there were, about nine o'clock, a great number standing around, till Captain Deering told them to keep down. There were not half a dozen outside the parapet. It was reported that these men on the parapet had guns, and Captain Deering ordered them down.

3190. Did you see any guns in the hands of these colored men about the parapet on Tuesday? Only two, and these were taken from them.

3191. What kind of guns were they? One of them was a Springfield rifle.

3192. Did you see any pistols in possession of those soldiers who were in the fort that morning, or who were outside the parapet? No, sir; I did not.

3193. Then you only saw one colored soldier who shot off his gun that morning? That is all. The other colored soldier was attempting to shoot, when Major Smyth or some one took the gun away. He was attempting to fire at a party of horsemen who were eight hundred to one thousand yards away.

3194. How far were you from this colored man at the time? Probably one hundred feet.

3195. How many men were there in that group of which you have spoken? Probably fifty, possibly seventy-five, standing down behind the parapet, although when ordered all left the parapet at once for the camp, which is, perhaps, six or eight hundred yards distant.

3196. Then you say the parapet and the front of it at that time was clear of colored soldiers? Yes, sir.

3197. What is the distance from the parapet to the railroad depot? It is a quarter of a mile from the angle of the fort to the depot. The ground is somewhat broken, but I could see clear up beyond those shanties, except under the bluff of the bank, which is about one-fourth of a mile from where I stood. That bank is near the depot; about fifty yards distant.

3198. Might there not have been a collection of colored people under this bluff, and not within your view? Yes, sir; but there was no fighting of any consequence, or I should have heard it.

3199. From this point under the bluff, towards the depot, would that point have been in range of South street? It would have been in view possibly six or eight hundred yards.

3200. You spoke of an effort being made by twenty to twenty-five colored soldiers on Tuesday to get possession of their arms: had they previous to that time asked for their arms? No, sir; not that I know of. I heard of the men grumbling among themselves that their arms had been taken away from them.

3201. When they made the effort to get them, did they go up on the run? No, sir; when they were ordered to halt and did not the sergeant fired, when they all left.

3202. Were there not, during the night and next morning, groups of them discussing the possibility of getting their arms? No, sir. There were teams sent there the second day to take out the arms, and I expected there might have been some little difficulty when the men saw the arms going outside, that they might probably try to get them, but there was no attempt and no disturbance.

3203. Were there not one or two pieces of cannon taken possession of by the colored soldiers, and were they not loaded? Yes, sir; and I think the cannon were loaded.

3204. When was that? It was, I think, the day after the riot. I had orders, and my instructions were if I heard any volley firing to bring out the pieces and put them in position. On Thursday night it was reported that they were coming to take the fort. Captain Allyn ordered these pieces out, and they were officered by a captain from our company. They were got out on Wednesday night and on Thursday they were manned.

3205. Was there any firing in South Memphis when that cannon was taken there and loaded? Yes, sir; there was firing and burning. The long roll had beat, and the regulars had turned out.

3206. Can you state where the colonel and lieutenant colonel were on Wednesday, the second day of the riot, between eight and twelve o'clock? They went out in the morning to meet the mayor; they then came back and were in the fort the most of Wednesday. They were out twice to meet the mayor, but were not gone more than twenty minutes.

3207. Was either of the other officers out with the colonel and lieutenant colonel? I think Major Smyth was, but neither of the others.

3208. Where are the colonel and lieutenant colonel now? The colonel is in Cuba; Lieutenant Colonel Wiley is somewhere in Illinois; Major Smyth is in Cincinnati; Major Williams is at Richardson's landing, and Major Atwood is here at the fort.

3209. Did you discover any pistols in possession of those discharged soldiers on Wednesday morning? No, sir.

By Mr. BROOMALL:

3210. You say that where you stood commanded all the ground except under the bluff. Was there room for three hundred men to stand between the bluff and the depot? Yes, sir, I should think so.

3211. Could three hundred men stand behind that bluff and fire at groups of white men between them and the depot, or in the direction of the depot? No, sir. It is only fifty or sixty feet; it would have been impossible.

3212. A person, then, on South street could not see three hundred men hidden from you by the bluff firing at groups of men towards the depot? I think it could not be.

3213. What was the behavior of the police towards the colored soldiers previous to this difficulty? They treated them very badly.

3214. State how. In unnecessary abuse of them. I have heard of it all through.

3215. Was there any time when the city was patrolled by negro soldiers? Yes, sir; there were certain streets patrolled by colored soldiers, who were ordered to arrest all colored men found out.

3216. The colored soldiers, then, had been accustomed to be a police to themselves? Yes, sir.

3217. What was the treatment of the negroes towards the police? I never saw a colored soldier arrest a policeman.

3218. Did you ever see a colored soldier arrest a white man? No, sir, and never heard of an instance of that sort.

By Mr. SHANKLIN:

3219. Did you continue to occupy the same position in the fort on Wednesday, the second day of the riot, say from ten to twelve o'clock, or were you changing to different positions? During the firing I occupied the same position. When it quieted down I went down to the camp, which is about eight hundred yards from where I stood.

LEWIS R. RICHARDS sworn and examined.

By the CHAIRMAN:

3220. State your name, occupation, and residence. Lewis R. Richards. I live in Memphis, and occupy the position of city registrar.

3221. How long have you occupied that position? Since 1847, with one year's intermission.

3222. Have you a list of the duly elected and appointed officers of the city of Memphis, who were in service of this city in the months of April and May last? I have made it out, but it is not quite completed. The captain of the night police has not rendered his report. I will complete it so that it may be attached to my testimony.

3223. How long has John Park been mayor of your city? Three years.

3224. Was he mayor at the time of the breaking out of the war? Yes, sir.

3225. Did all the people vote for him? Yes, sir.

3226. When was he next elected? He has been successively elected ever since.

3227. When was the last time he was elected? Last June, a year ago.

3228. Was there not a disfranchising law in existence at the time? There was some qualification required, but I do not know what it was.

3229. Do you know how large a vote was cast? I do not.

3230. I wish you to ascertain and attach to your report the number of votes cast at all the elections when Mr Park was elected mayor. I will do so.

3231. Of what nationality is Mr. Park? He is an Irishman.

3232. Is the police force now of about the same nationality as they have been for some years past? Yes, sir, for the past two years; before that we had a pretty fair division, but since that it has been a very much one-sided business. Four-fifths now are foreigners by birth.

3233. How do you hold your office? By election of the board of aldermen.

3234. When was the present board of aldermen elected? June, a year ago.

3235. What proportion of the population who had been voters before that time were allowed to vote when the present city government was elected? I am not prepared to answer that fully, but I suppose not more than one-quarter of those who had voted previously.

3236. Were they prohibited by any law? Some were prohibited, and some from not feeling that sort of interest I think they should have done. They were not in favor of any of the candidates, and I myself felt somewhat indifferent about it, from the fact that none of the men were precisely of that sort that should have filled that position.

3237. What portion of those who had previously voted were disqualified by any law of the State? I do not know.

3238. Do you know what the qualifications of the voter were a year ago? That he should not be a sympathizer with what is termed the rebellion—the southern branch of it. Some understand it in one way and some in another, but it was more in consequence of their indifference than on account of disqualification or being prohibited by law.

3239. Were there not a great many who were voters, but who did not vote on account of their being absent in the rebel army? I think they were mostly at home, though they had been absent.

3240. Who is your present city recorder? John C. Creighton.

Mr. SHANKLIN:

3241. Will you state what were the habits of Mayor Park when he was first elected; whether he was then a sober, sensible business man or not. He was occasionally seen drunk, but he was considered a sober, sensible man of business.

3242. Will you state whether those habits of intemperance have been growing upon him from that time to the present? That is my honest opinion, sir.

3243. Do you consider him in habits the same man he was in 1861? By no means.

3244. At the time of the last election, was he not a different man from what he was in 1861? So far as my observation extended that is the case.

3245. About the recorder—was he not different in his habits when he was first elected? By no means. I have always regarded him as a very improper man to fill such a position or any such position, and I have known him from a boy.

3246. Is the police force appointed by the board of aldermen? Yes, sir. There is a police committee who selects them, and they are then recommended to the board, by whom their nomination is confirmed.

3247. What is the nationality of the present board of aldermen? It consists of sixteen: nine are Irishmen, one is a German, and six are Americans.

3248. Under the franchise of the State of Tennessee, which was in force at the time of the last election of city officers, what proportion of the property holders and men engaged in business would, in your opinion, have been disfranchised by that law? I do not think it would have been one-half, but their inertness and want of interest in the matter was such that they did not care to qualify themselves. Several of my particular friends who could have qualified themselves failed to do so.

3249. Do you think there was less than a majority of that description of citizens who have not actively participated in the rebellion, or given aid and assistance to the rebellion in some way or other? Perhaps a majority of them have, and that under the law would disqualify them. What I meant to convey was that not perhaps one-half of those who might have voted did so.

3250. Has not your population been rapidly changed during the war, and at the same time been increasing? Yes, sir.

3251. Do you know what the population of Memphis is at the present time? It is estimated to be about fifty thousand. It has always been a very fluctuating population.

3252. Do you know what the voting population would be, provided all were permitted to vote who voted before the war? I do not know.

3253. What proportion of the fifty thousand are colored persons? I include the whole population, and there has been a considerable increase of the colored population, greater perhaps than the increase of the white population, but I could not state the proportion of the colored.

3254. Will you state what has been the state of feeling between the citizens of Memphis—those who have been in the rebellion, as well as those opposed to it—towards the negro population? My honest opinion is that there is a kindly feeling existing between those who have been raised and have grown up with the negro population and the negro, decidedly better than there is between the Irish population and the negroes. The general feeling is a kindly disposition towards the negro here.

3255. What is the feeling on the part of the negroes towards the white population of the city, leaving out the Irish? It is decidedly kind and social.

3256. How does the feeling on the part of your citizens towards the negro compare with that of the northern population who have come here? I have found the greater proportion kind to the negro.

Is it more liberal and kind than that exercised by other citizens who were slaveholders? I think not more so.

By Mr. BROOMALL:

3257. Among those resident citizens of Memphis, is it popular to teach the negroes? Yes, sir, they seem disposed to teach them. I know some families where they are teaching their negro servants, but a great many of the negroes are capable of reading and writing, having been taught by their masters and mistresses.

3258. During the late riots there have been some half dozen school-houses burned: will they be likely to be rebuilt by the old residents? I understand it is in contemplation to tax the city for that.

3259. Is it likely to be done? The law will compel them to do it. Under the statutes of the State of Tennessee, the city is liable for the damage done by rioting.

3260. In what manner has this good feeling of which you have spoken manifested itself towards the negroes since the riots? In general kindness.

3261. Have there been any demonstrations of that kindness? Have those who were burned out been aided by the old citizens of Memphis? None of the rioting occurred at my end of the town, but I know that during the progress of the riot many negroes were taken care of. One I know slept in my room for many nights.

3262. Do you know if any provision has been made for those who were burned out and their furniture destroyed? I do not know of any such.

By the CHAIRMAN:

3263. You say that under the statute law of the State of Tennessee, the city is liable for all the damage which has been occasioned by the mob: has the city of Memphis taken any measures to carry out that law? No, sir, not yet; but the present board is just about going out, and it is in contemplation that the next board will levy a tax to do it. It is the duty of this board to assess the value of the property destroyed.

3264. By whom is it assessed? By the board, composed of the mayor and aldermen.

3265. Of whom is the board composed? Of Mr. Taylor, Mr. Tye, Mr. Gyon, and Mr. N. S. Lawrence, clerk.

AMBROSE PORTER sworn and examined.

By the CHAIRMAN:

3266. State your name and residence. Ambrose Porter; I live in this place.

3267. Have you been in the service? Yes, sir; I was a soldier up to the 30th April last. I was first lieutenant of the 3d United States colored heavy artillery.

3268. Were you connected with that regiment at the time of the riot here? Yes, sir: the regiment was mustered out, but not paid off at the time.

3269. Did you see anything of the riot? Some little.

3270. State what you saw, and the hour of the day. I believe it was on Tuesday evening, the first of May; I heard the first row on South street; I was at the time in camp. I and some of the other officers walked on the breastworks and noticed it a little, and then two of us concluded to walk down towards it, as we thought we might do some good. We went down South street, where there was a great crowd. We found one colored man on the bridge, shot, but not dead. We had him taken into a house; his name was Richardson, I believe, of company H. We came back on to Shelby street, and there was a colored woman who had been shot; I do not know her name. It was now getting dark, and we went down on Main street, where Joe Lundy, wagonmaster of the regiment, had been shot. He was in the grocery. I then went back to camp, and saw nothing further that night.

3271. State what you saw on Wednesday morning. Wednesday morning I was not at camp. I believe I was in with the company.

3272. What were they doing? They were in the fort waiting to be paid off.

3273. Did you stay any considerable part of that day in the fort? I could not say that I did.

3274. Were you in position to see if there had been any considerable number of colored people on the parapet, or just outside, at any time? No, sir. I was right in camp all the time. I saw quite a crowd at sallyport No. 3, inside, on the works. I did not notice any on Tuesday.

3275. Did you hear any firing by the colored people? Yes, sir; but I could not say which side it was on.

3276. Was there much firing? Yes, sir; there was considerable.

3277. At any time of the firing, had you an idea whether it was by white or colored people? No, sir.

3278. Did you get up on the parapet during this time? I do not think I was on the parapet any time on Wednesday.

3279. Did you see any of the soldiers firing from the breastwork? No, sir.

3279½. Were you in a position to see, if there had been any firing? Yes, sir.

3280. Might there not have been some firing from the parapets without your knowing of it? I do not think there was any firing from the parapet that day.

3281. A witness testifies that on this morning between 10 and 12 o'clock there was a multitude; several hundreds—perhaps three hundred, four hundred, or five hundred—collected together in a group, and from twenty to twenty-five of them were firing, and that the firing continued for an hour or an hour and a half: could such a state of things have taken place without your knowing it? It could have taken place without my knowing it, as I was much in the office; but I think I should have known something of it if there had been such firing, and it had continued for that length of time.

3282. Did you hear of any such large company being outside of the fort? I did not, and I think should have heard of it had there been.

By Mr. SHANKLIN:

3283. When the firing first commenced on South street, do you know who commenced it, or who engaged in it? No, sir; I did not see any parties engaged in firing, but I heard they were firing on both sides; policemen and citizens on one side and colored people on the other. I was in the fort when the firing commenced.

3284. What time did you go down on South street? I started down before the firing had ceased.

3285. Did you meet with any colored soldiers? Yes, sir; and I told them to go to the fort.

3286. How many did you meet? I guess I must have passed one hundred, or rather I saw that number.

3287. Had any of these colored soldiers you met arms of any kind? I did not notice any; if they had any they were concealed. I told them that the best place for them was in the fort.

3288. Did you understand that they had been firing upon the police? No, sir.

3289. Did you understand that they had had a fight with the police? Nothing more than that there had been fighting down on South street, and I inferred that the soldiers and the policemen had been fighting.

3290. Did you understand that they had killed any policemen? When I was down on South street, I understood that they had killed one, and wounded one or two; but I saw nothing of it.

3291. On Wednesday morning, might there not have been a collection of persons, between 10 and 12 o'clock, of soldiers and other colored persons, outside the parapet, and between the depot and South street, without your being able to see them? Yes, sir.

3292. You state you heard some firing on Wednesday morning; state whether it seemed to be on South street, or in front of the fort, or between the fort and the depot. The firing seemed apparently on South street, in the neighborhood of the depot; but I do not know who it was firing there.

3293. Were not the colored soldiers, who had been mustered out a day or two before, passing in and out of the fort on Wednesday morning, and up to 12 o'clock? I was not in a position to see.

3294. Could not the colored soldiers have passed over the parapet at almost any point where there was not a crowd? Yes, sir.

By Mr. BROOMALL:

3295. Where could those soldiers have got a dozen muskets from, if they had turned over their arms? I could not say.

3296. Would it have been possible for three hundred, four hundred, or five hundred soldiers to go out with a dozen muskets and some revolvers, and firing them off for an hour or an hour and a half, without you knowing it? I do not think they got any muskets from inside the fort that day.

3297. Do you know of their getting any on Tuesday? No, sir; not to my knowledge.

3298. One witness speaks of a group of three hundred, four hundred, or five hundred soldiers, a dozen of them with muskets, and many of them with pistols, firing at groups of white people, between 10 and 12 that morning; please to state if such a thing could or could not have taken place without your knowledge. I heard a few shots, but I did not see any person outside the works, but I could not have seen them had they been there at that time.

3299. Were you in the fort when the mayor rode up towards the fort? I was in the fort with the company.

3300. Were you in a position to know whether three hundred to five hundred men in a body, for an hour, or an hour and a half, were near the fort, or towards the depot firing at groups of white people? I do not think that could have been without my knowing something about it.

B. F. C. BROOKS sworn and examined.

By the CHAIRMAN:

3301. Please to state your name, occupation, and address? B. F. C. Brooks; I live at No. 149 Jefferson street, in this city, and am the editor and publisher of the Republican, a weekly paper printed here.

3302. How long have you lived in Memphis? I came here in December, 1854.

3303. Where did you reside before that? I spent ten years in Mississippi as a doctor.

3304. Were you here during the rebellion? I was here through the little skirmish we had, though part of the time I was lying out. Unfortunately for me I was one of the small party here who voted against secession.

3305. Were you here during the recent riots? I was, sir.

3306. Have you any personal knowledge of what took place at that time? Yes, sir; of some things that transpired at that time.

3307. Please to state what you saw. I saw quite a number of persons collected on the streets, and making for South street. This was Wednesday morning. I saw a number of persons with arms, as if seeking for a fight.

3308. Did you see any one hurt? I did not.

3309. Did you see any acts of violence committed by any of these parties? I know of threats made against many persons, and of threats that the Republican office and my residence should be burned.

3310. How far down did you go with the crowd? As far as Union street. I saw the crowd going down. On Wednesday morning, I think it was, Dr. Carr and myself were standing together when a man by the name of McElmore came along and asked me how many niggers I had killed. I told him that was not my business; he replied, "By God, I have killed five," and thrusting his hand into his pocket he pulled out some buckshot, and, said he, "This is the kind of balls I do it with."

3311. Who is this McElmore? He is a citizen here; a man of rather a desperate character.

3312. What else did he say? He said he was going to kill some more of them.

3313. State anything else you saw in connexion with the rioting. On Sunday, before the riots commenced, I was going down Madison street when a man met me, and said, "How are you, Colonel?" I told him I was well. He said, "I've just got up, but I am ready for action." He added, "I have got a regiment, and, by God, I am going to kill these damned niggers."

3314. Who was this man? I do not know the man's name, though I have seen him here frequently. He was an Irishman. At the time I thought it was only some of his blowing, but when the rioting broke out on Tuesday, it revived the cirumstance, which otherwise I might have forgotten. During the riots I was asked by several persons if I was not in for killing the negroes. My reply was that killing was not my profession, but to try to cure. I objected to such a course and denounced it. On Wednesday morning I heard two old citizens talking of the matter. One of them had been sent out of the lines by the military. The other who had remained here, I do not know his name. remarked, as I passed, "By God, I have no regrets for anything I have done; the only regrets I have are that it was not some of the damned Yankees."

3315. Who was this other old citizen? L. V. Dixon. He was sent out of the lines for disloyalty.

3316. What did you understand him to refer to? I understood him to refer to the difficulties that had occurred the night before.

3317. Who is this Dixon? He is a number one lawyer here. He had property here at the time he was ordered away by General Washburn, and he made a sacrifice of it

3318. Did you hear any other conversations at that time or before, having relation to the recent riotous proceedings? My tenants, who were colored persons, were threatened. They threatened to burn out "that damned abolition hell," and some parties came about there seemingly with this intention.

3319. What were they going to burn you out for? Because I had some negro tenants, and was publishing a republican newspaper. My residence and office are together.

3320. What was the objection to your paper? The objection is that it is radical. The serious offence, I suppose, was that I had hoisted Thad. Stevens for President, and Brownlow for Vice-President. They were abusing Stevens a good deal, and saying all the hard things they could of him, so I came out squarely for him as President in 1868.

3321. Did you press his claim for the presidency in a respectful manner? I certainly did when I first announced it. I spoke of him in just such terms as I felt. I felt I was in the same ranks, and I felt like defending Mr. Stevens and doing justice to his merits.

3322. Was it for those reasons that it was proposed to mob you and burn down your establishment? It was in consequence of that, and of my having so many colored tenants. I have had some seventeen or eighteen at once.

3323. Is there anything in the statutes of Tennessee against letting tenements to colored people? No, sir; there is not.

3324. Had you been guilty of any unlawful acts at the time? No, sir.

3325. What was the general feeling at the time towards the colored people? There was considerable ill feeling towards them, and also towards the radicals

3326. Who were understood to be the radicals? Those who were in favor of the franchise law. Every man who is in favor of our State franchise law is said to be a radical.

3327. Did the prejudice extend to that class of men? Yes, sir; I think there was as much prejudice against them as against the negro. Such, in fact, is the prejudice that were it not for the federal troops I would not stay here.

3328. Why would you not stay here? Because my life and property would not be safe.

3329. In your judgment, would the lives and property of other persons holding like sentiments to yours be safe? No, sir.

3330. State the reasons why you do not think they would be safe? There are, perhaps, nine-tenths of this population who have been connected with the rebel army, or with the rebellion in some way or other; and there have been congregated here from every portion of the southern confederacy, men whose conduct during the rebellion has been such that they dare not return to their former homes.   Missouri has sent her hordes here, and many of them cannot go back; and the same is true of Mississippi and Alabama and every other southern State.   There are men here from all these States, whose conduct during the rebellion has been such towards Union people in their own States that they are ashamed to meet them there.   So they come here, bringing with them all their bitter feelings towards the United States government and its friends, in addition to the mortification they feel at having to leave their homes.   I have heard these men say that there would come a time when there would not be a damned Yankee or nigger here.   I have heard the remark again and again, "By God, we'll clean you all out.   Just get the troops away, and we'll show you, when we get things into our own hands."

3331. Mention any one from whom you have heard such sentiments.   Colonel Saffrons.

3332. Has he not recently been elected to office here?   Yes, sir; judge of the county court. He added something to the effect, "we shall some time get things into our own hands.   True, we cannnot vote now, but we have friends who can, and we will soon get you fellows out of here, and then we will take things into our own hands."

3334. Do you think he represents the sentiments of a large number of the citizens here? Yes, sir; he represents the sentiments of a large number of the people of Tennessee.   I frequently hear such remarks upon the cars.

3335. Do you think his sentiments represent those entertained by the majority of the people of Memphis?   I think the majority of the people entertain that feeling, and I believe that if the troops were away all northern men participating in what are considered objectionable opinions would have to leave.   In fact, I am so firmly convinced that this is the case that I would not stay.

3336. What do you think would be the result of the taking away of the troops?   Mr. Merryman said to me one day, (and I believe it is the sentiment of a very considerable number of northern Union men here,) said he, "As soon as I can I will sell my property; I am going to leave.   I believe that Johnson is going to manage so that we will not have any troops here, and that being the case, I am going to try to arrange my business so as to leave when they leave; for though I have lived here almost all my life, I find it would not be safe for me to be here if the troops were withdrawn."   And such are the expressions and sentiments of perhaps nineteen out of twenty Union men here.

3337. Is this feeling of prejudice against northern men you speak of participated in by the press of the city?   That is so plain that it is hardly worth while for me to say so.

3338. What has been the character and tone of the press in this respect?   The character and conduct of the press, through their editorials, at least of a portion of the press, has been to excite a feeling of hostility to people entertaining these radical sentiments.   They have advised placing the sign of "small-pox" over their doors; they have advised the people not to patronize them, and have endeavored, by every kind of ingenuity that the editors could devise, to bring contempt upon northern men, simply because they were northern men, or because they were friends of the present Congress of the United States—I will not say of the present administration.

3339. State if you have read the leading articles of the various papers published here; and if so, what was their general tone and sentiment towards the negro population—that is, before the recent riot here?   Some of the papers here have labored to produce a kindly feeling and course of conduct that would be christian-like towards the negro, while others of them have spoken of the negroes as outlaws and savages, &c.   The articles in the Avalanche have been inflammatory from the beginning.   Even since the riot, speaking of the action of the State legislature, the editor advised his friends to entertain and to treasure up eternal hate, fire, and faggot for the advocates of the franchise law, i. e. the law by which rebels are excluded from voting.   That is a specimen of their teachings.

3340. Are you not a southern man?   I was born in Alabama.   I was born and raised a southern man, and have never been further north than Cincinnati.

3341. What has been your status during the war?   I do not think there is a man here who will say I am not a Union man.   I was here at the breaking out of the rebellion, and was one of five men who voted against secession in 1861.   During that year I had to leave the city, and for three months I was travelling around buying goods.   A man by the name of Loony represented that I was obtaining recruits for his company—he was raising a company for Tennessee—while I was really buying goods for Dr. Fulk and S. P. Walker.   During that three or four months I found but one man that wanted to join the confederate army, and I conducted him to Looney's company and he joined it.   That much I have done, and I have bought some things and sold them to parties engaged in the confederate cause.   But this I did on compulsion; as it were, and to avoid being compelled to do worse.   This was in the latter part of '61, when the rebels had Memphis.   In three or four days after the Union men got possession of Memphis, in June of '62, Dr. Pulaski, myself, and another went to work, and in August we had a battalion raised, and I went with those troops to Nashville as their surgeon, turned them over to the authorities there, and when I got back here assisted in various ways with the Union forces, and finally was assigned to duty as assistant surgeon in the Gayoso hospital.

3342. What was the state of feeling here against northern men, or Union men, or quasi Union men, at the time the rebels had possession of the city?   It was intensely bitter.   I have seen an express wagon going through the streets of Memphis, containing a man with his head shaved, and a label on him directed to "Old Abe." He was sent up here from Mississippi.

3343. What became of him? He was sent on to Columbus labelled in that way.

3344. Were any threats of violence made against you? Yes, sir. I voted on Saturday. On Monday my wife came to me almost frightened to death. She said I must leave immediately; that there was a crowd hunting for me, intending, if they caught me, to hang me. Mr. Chandler came to me and requested me to leave immediately. I told him I was not prepared to leave; that I had not the money. He pulled out his pocket-book and told me to take what I needed, but for God's sake to leave immediately. I said I wanted my wife to go with me. However, I thought it well to follow his advice, and with a single shirt rolled up and thrust into my bosom I left, went by the graveyard, where but a few days before my only daughter had been buried; went out by the Memphis and Ohio railroad, intending to go to the first station and buy a ticket and get away. In short, I left, and I was compelled to leave to save my life; but I hate, gentlemen, to talk of these things.

3345. Do you know of any other acts of violence? There was a vigilance committee here, whose object was to arrest and try persons suspected of what they called treason. Every man suspected of being loyal to the United States government was arrested. The president of that committee was a man by the name of Fraser Titus, an old resident here, and their purpose was to sit in judgment upon any man suspected of being disloyal to the southern confederacy.

By Mr. SHANKLIN:

9346. I understand, Doctor, you are the editor of the Republican, a weekly paper published here? Yes, sir.

3347. Has it a pretty large circulation? No, sir; nearly a thousand.

3348. Is its circulation confined to Memphis? About five hundred are circulated in the city of Memphis.

3349. What general policy of the government towards those who sympathized with the rebellion have you advocated in your paper? That they should be held to a rigid account and punished according to the heinousness of their crime; in other words, that the leaders should be hung.

3350. You have advocated confining to the penitentiary of some and the banishment of others. I have advocated the hanging of some, the expatriating of others, and the disfranchisement of all engaged in the rebellion. I have endorsed everything that has been done by the republicans in Congress, except, perhaps, some technical quibble, and I have uniformly urged that the course of Congress should be supported by the people.

3360. Have you not published some articles that have been somewhat severe against the President of the United States and his policy? I have sir. After the speech of the 22d of February I came out with some pretty severe articles.

3361. And from that time up to the present have you not continued to denounce the President and his policy? Yes, sir; and the Johnson club.

3362. I suppose your feelings are pretty bitter towards the mass of the people of Memphis, are they not? Personally not so; but towards the political sentiments of the mass of the people here I am opposed.

3363. Is the feeling of hostility towards northern people of which you have spoken, generally entertained by the people of Memphis? I believe it is entertained against all northern people here who are true friends of the government.

3364. You say you were, under restraint or coercion, recruiting for the army of Tennessee? Yes, sir; but that was before they were turned over to the southern confederacy.

3365. What were you buying when you were ostensibly engaged in recruiting? Domestics, boots, shoes, woollen goods, &c. I was buying them of country merchants, and paying them, at wholesale, their retail prices.

3366. Were these goods intended for the southern army? They were to sell to any person who wanted to buy.

3367. Were you engaged in the purchase of any other articles, such as provisions? No, sir. I did, on one occasion, buy a few guns and sold them to parties who sold them to the southern confederacy.

3368. Did you know when you sold them that they were to be sold to the southern confederacy? I did not know; though, tied up as I was, I had to make a living for my family.

3369. After you were connected with the federal army, had you any contract for the government? No, sir; I was not engaged in any sort of trade, either on my own account or that of anybody else.

3370. Are you still in the United States service? I am still retained, though I have not received any pay for eight or ten months.

3371. But you still feel you are entitled to pay? No, sir; I do not feel I am entitled to it, as I have rendered no service of late. I have endeavored to get relieved, but have not succeeded.

3372. Have you made any efforts to dispose of your property with a view to leaving? Not since the federal occupation of the city till since this rioting. My property is now for sale. I want to be in East Tennessee, where I think I could breathe more freely than I can here.

By Mr. BROOMALL:

3373. The parties who are now disfranchised here are the ones that had control of things here in '61, are they not? Yes, sir.

3374. They had no franchise law here then, had they? No, sir, beyond issuing a proclamation that men should vote only a certain way, and those who did not vote that way should be hung to the first lamp-post. The proposition was that they were to vote with a ticket printed on red paper and that the ticket should be open, and the clerk was to spot every man who did not vote that way. That was the proclamation of the citizens.

JAMES E. HELM sworn and examined.

By the CHAIRMAN:

3375. State your name and residence. James E. Helm; I live in Memphis.

3376. Have you been in the United States service? I was first lieutenant in the third United States colored heavy artillery at the time the regiment was mustered out.

3377. Where were you on the first and second of May? I was at the fort and around the town.

3378. Did you see anything of the disturbances here? Yes, sir, I did.

3379. State what you saw on the first day. I was in the fort all day Tuesday, and did not know of the riot till evening, when it was said that the colored men and the policemen had had a fuss. When it was pretty nearly dark I came out of the fort, and there was a great deal of shooting on South street. This shooting was done by policemen and citizens—white men—on negroes, who seemed to be trying to get out of the way.

3380. Did you see any wounded or killed? When I came back I saw one or two wounded men running into the fort for protection.

3381. What did you see the next day? I remained in town that night, and I saw two or three colored men that had been killed. One of them was a man who had been with me three years. His name was Joe Lundy. When I had been there for an hour news came that the negroes had risen again. I went down about 10 o'clock. The negroes had pretty well run into the fort for protection. I saw a great many citizens who wanted, seemingly, to get at them.

3382. What time did you go into the fort Wednesday morning? When I came down the mayor was trying to disperse the people. I got into the fort about half-past 11 o'clock. When I got into the fort I saw as quiet a set of men as I ever wish to see anywhere.

3383. Between 10 and half-past 11 were there a large number of colored people outside of the fort, many of whom were firing at the crowd? I saw nothing of the kind, but I was not in a position to see it.

3384. How long were you with the regiment? Ever since it was organized.

3385. What has been its general character? I think it had the best name of any regiment I ever saw.

3386. Was it under good discipline? It was; and kept under good discipline until it was discharged.

3387. Did you hear of these colored soldiers before they were discharged being guilty of turbulent and disorderly conduct in the city? Yes, sir.

3388. Were those charges correct? Three or four times I have heard of our men robbing stores, but it was the same with white troops.

3389. In an equal degree? I think white troops stole quite as much as colored troops.

3390. What was the conduct of these colored soldiers as compared with the white troops? As good as any white troops I have ever known.

3391. What was the conduct of the colored troops after being discharged and before receiving their pay? As soon as they were discharged this rioting commenced. They were in the fort perfectly quiet, and I could not see that they wanted to get into any muss.

3392. Were any down town on Tuesday afternoon? Some few were, and did considerable shooting; that is, from what others say, but the general conduct of the regiment was orderly. I think it was a very small proportion that had anything to do with the fuss.

3393. Was your regiment detailed as patrol in the city? Yes, sir.

3393½. How did they demean themselves? I cannot speak from personal knowledge; I was quartermaster of the regiment.

3394. Do you know of their having arrested and maltreated white men while on duty? No, sir.

3395. Do you know of their being arrested and maltreated by the police? I heard of a great many instances, but I do not know of any personally.

By Mr. SHANKLIN:

3396. I understand you to say that you were lieutenant in the 3d United States colored regiment? Yes, sir; I usually had about twenty men detailed to me for driving teams.

3397. Were you in the fort when the firing commenced on Tuesday? Yes, sir.

3398. And after the firing had progressed some time you came down into the town? Yes, sir.

3399. As you came down you met soldiers going towards the fort, and occasionally turning round and shooting? I probably saw twenty shoot back. This was on Tuesday evening.

3400. When you got down to South street did you find many soldiers there? I could not say. I found it was promiscuous firing, and I kept away.

3401. Between whom was this firing? Between colored and white people; and it continued until it was quite dark.

3402. Did you see any colored people shooting on Wednesday morning? Two or three.

3403. Where were they? They stood between the fort and South street.

3404. How far from the fort were they? Half way from the fort and the Mississippi and Tennessee depot.

3405. What were they shooting with? Revolvers. I did not see any with anything but revolvers.

3406. Were they colored soldiers? I do not think they were; they were colored people. I saw one or two different men fire two or three shots each. They were firing and running towards the fort. At the same time there were white men shooting at them.

3407. Were there many persons outside the fort? They were mostly in the fort, or passing in; a very few were passing out. There were some in the fort who had families, who would not go out for fear.

3408. How many of the soldiers of this colored regiment had revolvers? Probably one hundred and fifty or two hundred—perhaps more; but where it was known they were taken away from them.

3409. What disposition was made of them? I do not know.

3410. Did you see them make any exhibition of their weapons? I never saw them with any weapons in their hands in the fort.

3411. Did you see any attempt made by the negroes, Tuesday or Wednesday, to take possession of the arsenal to get their guns? I heard from Major Williams that some of the boys had attempted to break into the depot, but were prevented.

WILLIAM H. PEARCE sworn and examined.

By the CHAIRMAN:

3412. State your name and residence. William H. Pearce; I reside in Memphis.

3413. Have you been in the United States service? Yes, sir; I was captain in the third United States colored heavy artillery.

3414. Were you here during the riots? Yes, sir; in Fort Pickering.

3415. Did you see the commencement of the riots? Yes, sir.

3416. State what you saw. I heard firing outside the fort and disturbance, and men were running into the fort. I was requested by the commanding officer to remain with my company.

3417. Did you see any colored men wounded or killed? I saw persons who were wounded, and four men of my company were killed on Tuesday evening.

3418. Do you remember their names? George Cobb, Isaac Richardson, William Weathers and George Black.

3419. By whom were they killed? They were killed by policemen and citizens here in the city.

3420. Do you know the circumstances under which they were killed? They had no arms when they were shot down, as I learned from the quartermaster sergeant, who was there. Black was killed in the field; they pounded him to death. George Cobb was taken out from under a bed, where he had concealed himself, in the house where he had eaten his breakfast with Alfred Tinnon. Tinnon was shot through the arm. Both were taken out of the house and arrested by the police. Cobb was beaten to death by clubs. He was so beaten that you could not recognize him. Everybody that came by gave him a kick. As far as I know these four men were just as innocent and inoffensive men as there were in the regiment. They were good soldiers and did their duty to the United States government in every respect. Richardson, I think, was a volunteer from the State of Illinois.

3421. State what you saw on Wednesday morning. I was in the fort, and was in a position to see what was going on inside and outside the fort: I was at my quarters down on the parapet.

3422. Do you remember any number of colored soldiers in a group, outside the fort; and if so, what were they doing? There was no such group.

3423. Are you certain of that? Yes, sir.

3424. Were you in a position to observe it, had there been such an assemblage? Yes, sir; and there was nothing there of the kind.

3425. A witness has testified that between 10 and 12 o'clock on Tuesday morning there were a multitude, several hundreds, three, four, or five hundred, and he states he was somewhat scared for fear they should make a charge. State if that is true? There were only women and children who had run from their homes to seek protection at the fort; there were no soldiers there.

3426. Did you see among this crowd twenty to twenty-five colored men or soldiers engaged in shooting? There was no such thing.

3427. Were you in a situation to know? I was, sir.

3428. Could such a thing have been without your knowing it? No, sir.

3429. Did you see any colored people having muskets outside the fort? No, sir; there was not a musket in the regiment; I am certain of that. There might have been one in forty who had a revolver, but he kept it concealed. I had my quarters searched every day, and if any revolvers were found they were taken away from the men.

3430. This witness from whom I have quoted further states that this crowd of colored persons kept firing for one or one and a half hours. Could any such thing have taken place without your knowing it? It is false, every bit of it.

3431. What has been the conduct of these colored soldiers? Their conduct has been soldierly and, in general, excellent. I have never had any trouble with my men. I had over one hundred and fifty men under my command at a time, and they were obedient to orders, well disciplined and respectful.

3432. Did they use to come into the town occasionally? Yes, sir.

3433. Under what regulations? Generally from two to four from each company per day, to be selected by the company commander or the first sergeant.

3434. What was the conduct of these soldiers when they were out of the fort? Orderly and good.

3435. Did you know of any instance of insolence towards or maltreatment of white people? No, sir; but I know this much, that the police of this town have felt very much hatred against the colored people, and colored soldiers especially. They did not like to see them wearing the United States uniform and carrying a musket. I have seen a man on duty here, carrying his gun right shoulder shift, and a policeman has come along and said "good evening," and the next instant hit the man over the head. He then tried to get his gun, but the darkey was too smart for him. The gun was not loaded, or it might have been all the worse for the policeman. The soldier then ran and tried to get away, when the policeman fired on him. The policeman was arrested. I do not remember how it was settled, but the policeman, I know, was not punished.

3436. Had the soldier been guilty of any crime which justified his arrest? No, sir; he was walking along quietly by orders of his officer.

3437. Do you know of any of these colored troops arresting white people and maltreating them? No, sir; and I know of their making no arrests without orders.

3438. When they had orders were they unnecessarily rough in their treatment of the parties arrested? No, sir; not that I know.

3439. What has been the treatment of colored soldiers when they have been arrested by the police? When they were arrested they were generally afraid to be guilty of much maltreatment, but as soon as they found out that the colored soldiers were disarmed, they broke out on them.

3440. Do you think they had been waiting for the opportunity to carry out any feelings of revenge? That is just what it is. When they found that the arms of the regiment were given up they took occasion to have their revenge.

3441. Do you know of any rioting here on the part of the colored people? There was no such thing.

3442. Did you hear anything or see any disposition on the part of the colored people to maltreat or attack white people in any way? No, sir; nothing of the kind. On Wednesday morning when they were rushing on the colored people and driving them from their houses, defenceless men, women and children—when the colored soldiers saw them running and crying murder, then they came up and demanded something to protect themselves with. They wanted the colonel to devise some means by which they could get some protection for their families, who they thought were all being murdered. On Tuesday, I think it was, they got an idea that the mob was about making an attack on them, when a rush was made for the arsenal, but they were halted and sent back to their quarters.

3443. What is the character of the colonel of your regiment? He is a good officer and a strict disciplinarian.

3444. Did he have any talk with the regiment on Wednesday morning? Yes, sir; he counselled the men to be quiet and wait, and he would do all he could to protect their wives and families, and advised them to do nothing without orders.

By Mr. SHANKLIN:

3445. Were you in the fort during the whole time of the riot? Yes, sir.

3446. You speak of seeing a crowd of citizens who sought protection at the fort on Wednesday morning; how many were there in that crowd? Perhaps two hundred.

3447. Were there any soldiers mixed up in that crowd? There might have been a few, but not to any extent; perhaps half a dozen.

3448. Were there any soldiers in that crowd about that time engaged in any shooting with any weapons? No, sir.

3449. How far were you from them? Probably three hundred to four hundred yards; they were running up towards the fort for protection.

3450. Did you see any colored persons with pistols when the riot was going on? I did not see any colored man shoot during the whole riot, though I have no doubt there were some who had pistols and who used them down on South street at the commencement of the riot.

3451. Do you know what portion of the colored soldiers had fire-arms in their possession? Very few of them, and those who had them had them concealed, because the officers had strict orders not to allow them to have arms in their possession.

3452. Do you know what portion of the colored soldiers were out of the fort when the riot commenced on Tuesday evening? Possibly forty or fifty. I judge not more.

3453. You think then there were no shots fired from the neighborhood of the fort on Wednesday morning? I know there were not, to any extent, either on Tuesday or Wednesday. All the shooting there was by either party was down on South street or main street. Whenever they saw a colored man down there they chased him, hunted him down, and generally shot him.

3454. At any time during the riot were there any pistols or guns fired in the neighborhood of the fort, or between the fort and South street, or between the fort and the depot? There were shots fired between the depot and South street, but none between that and the fort. The firing was on South street and on the corner of Shelby street, but round the fort I did not see or hear any firing.

3455. Did you see any colored soldiers coming up towards the fort. and occasionally turning round and shooting back? No, sir; I did not.

3456. Did you, at any time, see any sort of shooting of that kind done? No, sir; I did not.

3457. Was there, or not, a good deal of hostility existing between the colored soldiers on the one side and the policemen on the other, previous to the riot? Yes, sir; and I think the police had considerable hard feelings towards the colored soldiers and citizens.

3458. Had the colored people any hostile feelings towards the police? No, sir; I think not.

Mrs. S. COOPER sworn and examined.

By the CHAIRMAN:

3459. State your name and where you live. Mrs. Cooper: I live on Gayoso street.

3460. Are you a married woman? Yes, sir; my husband lives here in Memphis.

3461. Were you here during the recent riots? Yes, sir.

3462. State what you saw and what you know of the rioting. We had only been on Gayoso street two days when it commenced. My husband had bought one of the government barracks when it was sold, and had taken it down to Gayoso street, and had put it up to rent it out to colored people. It was on Wednesday I heard shooting above the bridge, and I sat there, trembling, with my four children. I noticed that the woman who lived next door, an Irishwoman, was moving her children out. I then summoned courage to go to the men I saw collected at the bridge and ask them what they were going to do. They were white men, policemen and citizens. "What are you about?" I said. "I have done nothing to you, nor have my children." They said they were not going to harm me or my children, but if they laid hold of my husband or Mr. Glasgow they would kill them. They said they would have no abolitionists in the south. Mr. Glasgow, who has been in the federal army, has been teaching a colored school here, and has been working with my husband on the building, helping to get it ready, for two months.

3463. How had your husband become obnoxious to the mob? He is a shoemaker by trade, but they called us abolitionists because we were living among the colored people.

3464. Where did you come from? We came here from Pennsylvania.

3465. Has your husband ever made himself busy in attacking or insulting the people in any way? My husband is a sober, steady man: he speaks for the right, and wants to see the right thing done to every man, and they all thought he was doing too much for the colored people; he spoke occasionally in their chapel. Mr. Shirving, who is, I think, a policeman, and who was at the head of the gang, said, "I suppose you are Mrs. Cooper, and it is your husband who gets up and talks to the colored people, and tells them that they are as good as white men." I said, "I do not know what my husband says, but we came here to live peaceably and quiet;" but they said they would kill him if they found him. I said, "If you injure my husband you injure me." They said, "You intend to rent your place to colored people." I said, "I do not know how you will live if you drive the colored people away, for one-half you get you get out of the colored people." They said they lived before the colored people came here. And while they were telling me they would not injure me, the place was set on fire. My husband and Mr. Glasgow tried to put it out, and while they were doing that they fired at them several times.

3466. Who set fire to the building? I do not know; there were four of them, but I think Shirving was the man; he lives just above us. The next day, Thursday, he came by our house, swinging a large revolver by his side, as if looking for somebody. I thought it very hard of them that they should set fire to the house while my four children were in it, and telling me they should not set it on fire, while it was their intention to burn us up. They chased a negro man and he took refuge in my house; he said they were after him to kill him; his name was Dick. When he came to my house I told him to creep under the bed, and he lay there all night, while I was there alone with my children. He was secreted there at the time of firing my house.

3467. Was your stock burned? We heard of their threats, and next day, Wednesday, we had our boots and shoes sent into the town to be auctioned off; we thought it better to save a little than to lose all; they burned all our furniture. The next day my husband went up the river for fear they would kill him.   Mr. Glasgow was in danger of losing his life, but he did not leave.   I had no place to be in the next day, and one house where I thought they were our friends, they would not take us in, for, said she, the policemen said she must not have us there.   I did not know till afterwards of my husband having to leave for fear his life would be taken, and I heard nothing of him for three or four days, and I was about searching for him, not knowing but he had been killed.   My husband took sick of the chills and fever and has not been well since; he has been unquiet in his mind and cannot rest.

3468. How much did your loss amount to?   We lost, except what we got for the boots and shoes, all we had.   Our loss on the boots and shoes and the furniture, at the least, would be $1,000.   The building would bring us in $50 a month.   Mr. Glasgow had a share in the rent.

By Mr. SHANKLIN:

3469. Where did you originally come from?   From Bolton, England.   We were in Pennsylvania seven years before coming here.

3470. Had you any connexion with the colored school?   No, sir.   Mr. Glasgow has been teaching the colored school.   He has been boarding with a colored man in the same building, and has been a partner with my husband in the building.

3471. Were your boots and shoes taken by the mob?   No, sir; they were taken to the auction rooms and sold at a great sacrifice.

3472. How much did they bring?   Five hundred and fifty-five dollars.

3473. How much was your furniture worth?   Our furniture was worth $500.

3474. What sort of a house was it that the mob set on fire?   It was one of the government barracks.

3475. How much did it cost you?   My husband gave $280 for it, and moved it down there, and we intended to let it out in rooms.

3477. What were you expecting to rent the rooms for?   Some for $10, some at $8, some at $6, and some at $5 per month.

3478. How large were the rooms?   Some were about 20 feet by 13 feet.

3479. How many of them were occupied?   I think five of them were occupied; but they have been moved about so much they have not been able to pay their rent.

3480. What are you engaged in now?   I am now keeping a grocery in front of the building which I attend to.

3481. Do you keep liquor for sale?   We only keep whiskey in bottles; we sell bottled porter and soda-water; but we do not sell liquor to be drank on the premises.

CELIA SIMMONS (colored) sworn and examined.

By the CHAIRMAN:

3482. State your name and where you live.   Celia Simmonds; I live on the end of Main street, Memphis.

3483. How old are you?   I don't know; I guess I have a child about 19.

3484. Are you married?   Yes, I am married.

3485. Have you been a slave?   Yes, sir.

3486. Were you here during the riots? if so, tell us what you saw.   I was here in the midst of the riots.   I saw shooting and burning on Tuesday evening.

3487. Who shot first?   I could not tell; they were coming down South street, and the people were advancing to the colored people.   I saw one man fall about one hundred yards from where I was.   He was a policeman; a white man.   I saw a colored man who was killed a little further on.

3488. What else did you see?   On the second day the people came down South street, a great many of them; but they did not interfere with me that day.   The white people just shot at every colored person they saw.   I did not see any killed, but I heard there were.

3489. Did they rob you?   They came in and shot my daughter in bed.

3490. How old is your daughter?   She is going on 20.   Her name is Rhoda Jacobs.   She and the two children were lying together, and I and my babe were lying together.   They came to the door and knocked.   After they knocked they stopped and talked.   Then I jumped out of bed, and my daughter said, "Hush, ma; don't say anything."   Then they knocked again, and I said, "Who is there?"   They said open the door, and I went to the door and opened it.   One of them had a pistol in his hand, and it appeared he was going to shoot at the children, when one of them said "Don't shoot, John."   I said, "Oh, don't shoot, Johnny; that's the children."   They said, "Get a light damned quick."   As I was trying to light the match, they said, "Where is that damned nigger?"   I could scarcely speak.   They raised up my bed, but did not see anything.   Then one of them just raised his pistol and shot, and said, "Lord, I've shot a woman."   Then they went out.   I looked at my daughter and thought death was upon her.   The ball had gone through her arm, had hit her fingers, and shot into her breast; and, what I did not see till afterwards, the ball had glanced the child's lips.   I fixed up my daughter's wounds by the light of the burning house on the other side of the street, and put them all to bed.   I put out my lamp for fear they would come back again.   It was a fuss all the time, and I dared not put my head out.

EMMA LANE (colored) sworn and examined.

By the CHAIRMAN:

3491. Tell us your name and where you live. I guess I am about 20 or 25.

3492. Have you been a slave? I have been a slave all the days of my life until last June.

3493. Where were you raised? In Alabama. I have been here nearly a year.

3494. Are you married? I was married a year ago.

3495. Were you here at the time of the riot? Yes, sir, I was.

3496. Tell us what you saw of the rioting. It was on Wednesday night, the 2d of May, between 11 and 12 o'clock, they came to our door and knocked. My husband was asleep. His name is Richard Lane. They said, "God damn you, open the door;" and as I could not get up soon enough, they burst it open.

·3497. Do you know who those persons were? One was Mike Colton, L. D. Young, another was Billy Barber, and another was a policeman. They belong to No. 7 engine. They then told us to raise a light. I ran behind the counter to get a match. We kept a saloon. My husband went to screw up the wick. By the time I lighted the match, and while it was burning in my hand, they asked my husband for his arms. My husband said he had no arms. They said, "God damn you, give us your pistol," and six of them shot over the counter; and as they were going out one of them shot my little girl through the right arm.

3498. How old is your little girl? She is two and a half years old. They shot my husband. The ball went in on his shoulder, and was cut out below in his back.

3499. Will your daughter lose the use of her arm? I do not know; the bandages are not yet taken off. She screamed dreadfully and bled awfully, and looked just as though she had been dipped in a tub of blood.

3500. Did you have the wound dressed? I did not send for a doctor till morning; we durst not.

3501. What did you do, then? I could not do a thing but keep cold-water cloths on it.

3502. Did they rob you? No, sir.

3503. Did they disturb you any more? They came there Tuesday night; they told us to open the door, but getting no answer, went away.

3504. Do you know who it was that shot your daughter? I do not know.

3505. Was the shot aimed at her? I do not know that it was aimed at her; the match was out, and there was no light at all. When I looked at my husband and my child, I commenced screaming, when they broke and ran up the hill. They only disturbed my family about there.

ANTHONY SIMMONS (colored) sworn and examined.

By the CHAIRMAN:

3506. State your name, and where you live. Anthony Simmons; I am the husband of Celia Simmons; I live in Memphis.

3507. Have you been a slave? Yes, sir; I have lived in Memphis sixteen years.

3508. Did you see anything of the riots? A white man kept me locked up in his house all day Wednesday. On Wednesday night he gave me the key and told me how to get out. I saw them shoot down five soldiers. I was standing within my door, and every once in a while I would peep out. I saw the dead bodies of these five colored soldiers. Wednesday night, when aunt Jane's daughter Rachel was shot, they ran in calling for Anthony Simmons. I ran out; they shouted for me to come back. I said I would not come back, as they would only kill me. They shot my wife and daughter. My daughter was shot in the lip. I was robbed of $200.

3509. State the circumstances. They tried to catch me, but did not till Thursday morning. One of those who robbed me was a policeman. I could not get his number to save my life. The others were citizens. On Thursday they came across me on South street, and I had to run. They were hunting down everybody and stopping them. They said, "You damned old nigger son of a bitch, we know you have got some money." I pulled out my pocket-book, and was going to take out my money, when one of them said, "Damn you, don't be so kind;" and taking my pocket-book, and taking all the money out, they handed me back my empty book. Then they searched the handkerchief tied round my head. There was a policeman and four other gentlemen. They searched all my clothes. I had my money tied round my ankle, in a handkerchief. When they put their hands on my leg and searched down, then my heart began to flutter, for I knew when they pulled up my breeches they would see the handkerchief. While they did this, two of them held pistols to my head, and damned me, and said if I did but grunt, they would shoot me. I had $165, which they took. There were five of them that robbed me; all white men.

3510. Have you been a soldier? No, sir.

3511. How did you make all this money? I do plastering, and I earned the money by working.

3512. Did you see anything more of the rioting? I saw them catch one discharged soldier and take away his discharge paper, which they tore up, and his money, $25.

3513. Do you know the man's name? I do not, gentlemen.

SARAH LONG (colored) sworn and examined.

By the CHAIRMAN:

3514. State your name and where you live. Sarah Long. I live about five miles from here.

3515. Were you in Memphis at the time of the riots? Yes, sir; I was.

3516. How old are you? I am between twenty and thirty.

3517. Have you been a slave? I have been a slave.

3518. What did you see of the rioting? I saw them kill my husband; it was on Tuesday night, between ten and eleven o'clock; he was shot in the head while he was in bed, sick.

3519. Who shot him? I do not know; there were between twenty and thirty men who came to the house; when they first came, they hallooed to us to open the doors; my husband was sick in bed and could not get up; he had been sick in bed two weeks; he had the jaundice; I lay there, I was so scared; we have two children who were with us. They broke the outside doors open: I staid in the bed till they came in; the inside door was open; they came into the room and asked if we had any pistols or shot guns in the house; my husband said he had one, but it was only a rusty pistol, that his little boy had found; it was fit for nothing but the child to play with; then they told my husband to get up and get it; he got up and gave it to them. I then lighted a lamp after they got the pistol; they told my husband to get up and come out, that they were going to shoot him; they made him get up and go out of doors; he told them he was very sick; they said they did not care a damn; they took him out of doors and told him if he had anything to say to say it quick, for they were going to kill him; if he said anything, I did not hear it. He stood outside, perhaps, a quarter of an hour; they asked him if he had been a soldier; he said he never had been. One of them said, "You are a damned liar; you have been in the government service for the last twelve or fourteen months." "Yes," said he, "I have been in the government service, but not as a soldier." Then another said, 'Why did you not tell us that at first?" Then one stepped back and shot him as quick as he said that; he was not a yard from him; he put the pistol to his head and shot him three times; this was between ten and eleven o'clock; when my husband fell he scuffled about a little, and looked as if he tried to get back into the house; then they told him that if he did not make haste and die, they would shoot him again. Then one of them kicked him, and another shot him again when he was down; they shot him through the head every time, as far as I could see. He never spoke after he fell. They then went running right off and did not come back again.

3520. Did you remain in the house? I staid there there till morning.

3521. Did they rob you? Yes, sir; they robbed me. They took fifty five dollars in paper money and thirteen dollars in silver; that was all we had; they took all his clothes, but they did not take my clothes. They took everything before they killed him; they took all the money we had except seven dollars, which he had in his pocket; the money they robbed us of was in the trunk, which they broke open.

3522. Did they say anything further to you? They said they came round to kill everybody who had pistols and shot in the house. They said they were policemen. The pistol they took from us was one my little boy had found, but it was worth nothing; but when they asked if we had any pistols I gave them that. When I found my husband was dead, I staid there till next day about three o'clock in the afternoon.

3523. Was your husband taken away? I was trying to get somebody to bury him, but they were scared to death, and so he remained where he was shot till next day, when he was buried.

BILLY JOHNSON (colored) sworn and examined.

By the CHAIRMAN:

3524. State your name and where you live. Billy Johnson. I live in Memphis.

3525. How old are you? I am about twenty years old.

3526. Have you been a slave? I have been. I came from St. Louis here.

3527. How long have you lived in Memphis? About three months.

3528. Were you here during the riots? I just got here before they commenced.

3529. What did you see of them? I saw David Roach shoot the colored soldier, Jem. I saw him shoot another colored man just as he was coming out of his mother's yard. He shot at him three times, and killed him dead.

3530. What else did you see? They stopped me on South street and asked me where I was going, when Tom Harris kicked me, beat me, and searched me.

3231. Who is Tom Harris? He is a fireman belonging to No. 5.

3532. Did he rob you? He did not find any money on me. He then let me go, and called me a damned Yankee son of a bitch.

THOMAS J. DURNIN sworn and examined.

By the CHAIRMAN:

3533. State your name and present residence. Thomas J. Durnin. I am at present stationed in Memphis.

3534. What is your position in the service? I am captain of the sixteenth United States infantry.

3535. How long have you been in the service? I have been in the army as private soldier and officer for eleven years.

3536. Have you risen from the ranks? Yes, sir.

3537. Were you in Memphis at the time of the riots? Yes, sir.

3537. State what you saw of them? I was in command of the troops here from about ten o clock on the first of May to the return of Captain Allyn, about one o'clock.

3538. Did you see anything of the riots preceding the first of May? I was at supper about six o'clock in Fort Pickering, when sergeant of company A, second battalion, came in and reported that there was a great deal of shooting going on. I was rather used up, for I had been suffering from rheumatism, but I went out and turned the command out, and told Mr. Clifford to take what men he pleased with him, and go at once. Captain Smith gave him twenty-five men with three sergeants. Major Smith went out with the second command, and the rioting was stopped.

3539. State what you saw of the rioting. I saw the shooting at the commencement. I saw policemen and mounted men, that I afterwards learned were called the Mississippi regulators. I was told they called themselves so. I went over the parapet and saw considerable shooting by the policemen and regulators, as they were called. On that night I had been appointed by General Stoneman ordnance officer of the post, and on the 29th of April I had received the arms of the third regiment of United States colored heavy artillery, which were all turned in. After they had been fighting for some time, and after I had sent out these two parties of the sixteenth United States infantry, many of the colored soldiers in the barracks wanted their arms. I heard them say we must have our arms. Immediately after some twelve or fifteen of the colored soldiers made a rush on the building where the arms were stored. I gave orders to fire. The men had their bayonets fixed, but the colored soldiers retreated at the first fire.

3540. Were any shot? I gave orders to fire high.

3541. What did they want their arms for? They wanted them to defend themselves against the policemen of the city. The police were shooting them down.

3542. Do you know the origin of the riot? Major Smith told me that they made an arrest of one colored man who was shooting, but who seemed to be defending himself. He was arrested, and the police were taking him away, and I understood that this man was shot down before he got to the police station.

3543. State what you saw on Tuesday night. I saw the policemen in South Memphis, on the south side of the bayou. There were some colored men on the other side. Some were running and some were firing pistols, but they were discharged at such a distance from the white crowd that they would hurt no one. I think I saw one black man fall, but am not certain.

3544. State what you saw on Wednesday morning. Captain Allyn was in command of the fort and had about fifty men. The rioting opened by about twenty-five or thirty men mounted and a large number on foot, who were shooting down the darkies. These parties came from the city down to South Memphis, and as far as I could see they were shooting down all the colored men they could see. I was standing on the parapet of the fort, and was awaiting the return of the guard somewhat anxiously, for I was afraid the mob would get into the fort. I was at the time standing with my field-glass in my hand. About ten or ten and one-half o'clock the mayor with his aids and some fifteen or twenty men on foot came towards the fort; the colonel drove out in his buggy to meet them.

3545. Did you notice the time? We marked time by hour calls, and I remember looking at my watch.

3546. At the time you refer to were you on the parapet? Yes, sir.

3547. Was there any number of colored soldiers on the parapet? The colored men had gathered on the parapet and I saw them congregating outside of the fort, and I sent to Major Smith to have them sent back into their quarters. It made me a little anxious, as I had no white troops there.

3548. Did you observe any of the colored men armed with muskets? There were two men who had muskets. They were at first outside, but they fell back into the parapets.

3549. What were the colored soldiers doing on the parapet? They were cheering those two men who were on the outside.

3550. How many men were there on the outside of the fort? There were perhaps nine colored men outside.

3551. What were they doing? They were using arms against the policemen.

3552. How many men do you think there were on the parapet? There must have been four hundred or five hundred men on the parapet. They were standing right along by the side of me. As I noticed they were attracting attention, and having no troops to defend myself, I ordered Major Smith to take two men with him. They were unarmed, and they sent the men into their quarters. Every man of them went back.

3553. What time was this? It was about 11 o'clock.

3554. How long did those colored men remain on the parapet? It was about three-fourths of an hour from the time when I first noticed them till they left it.

3555. How many colored men, armed and unarmed, were there outside the parapet from the time you went on the parapet yourself till 12 o'clock? I counted nine, and some of them were firing pistols.

3556. Did you see any firing with guns? I only saw two with long arms. One was armed with an Enfield rifle and the other with a Springfield. I ordered them to be disarmed.

3557. How many men with arms did you see in the fort? I saw no men there: only a number of women and children.

3558. Did you see some colored men behind a fence in this neighborhood, loading and firing United States muskets? I did not.

3559. Were you in a position to have seen, had anything of the kind taken place between 10 and 12 o'clock? I could, everything that was going on between the parties. My field-glass gave me a perfect view of all that was taking place.

3560. A witness states that there was a multitude, some three, four, or five hundred colored men near the fort, and he states that he was somewhat scared for fear they would make a charge. Do you know anything of that? I suppose he means the men I ordered to have sent back to their quarters. I found them very much excited, and begging to have their arms that they might defend the women and children.

3561. Were these men outside of the fort? No, sir; they were not; they were inside all the time, and not over the parapet—there were only nine over the parapet—those I have spoken of. If the statement refers to persons outside the fort, it is false.

3562. The witness further states: "I did not take particular notice; I should say twenty to twenty-five" were armed with muskets and pistols, and shooting at the policemen and citizens. Was there any group in which there were twenty or twenty-five men armed, and shooting at white people? That is not true; there were nine men; at first I could not see them; I only saw the smoke of the pistols; but finally, they were driven up to the top of the hill, back by the fence in the front of two white houses, and when they came up there the men on the parapet raised a cheer; two of them came over the parapet, and I had both of them disarmed.

3563. Did you see anything that looked like a charge on the part of the colored people? No, sir. The only demonstration they made was when these men inside raised a cheer at the nine men I have spoken of; there was no such thing as a charge by the three or four hundred soldiers within the fort during that time; there was not at any one time as many as twenty colored soldiers together to do anything.

3564. How long did those who had arms continue to shoot? Perhaps fifteen minutes after the troops passed through the sally-port.

3565. The witness states that the firing must have continued from one to one and a half hours. Is that correct? The firing commenced before our men turned out, but whether it was by negro soldiers I could not tell. The troops left the fort at about 10½ o'clock, and it was not more than fifteen to twenty minutes when all the firing ceased, and there was not another shot fired.

3566. How long have you been in Fort Pickering? From the 13th of April before the colored troops were mustered out; I saw their last two parades.

3567. Did you see enough, and were you there long enough, to form some judgment of the character of the regiment? My judgment was, that the men were under bad discipline; that their officers had not control of them, and did not seem to take the trouble to control them.

3568. How did they behave? They behaved very well indeed; only at nights they would go round, and the pistols they had bought they would fire indiscriminately.

3569. How did they behave after they were mustered out? After they were mustered out they behaved very well; better than before.

3570. What was their general behavior? The night before the riot there were about seven or eight pistol shots fired, and I sent Mr. Clifford out to stop it, and he did so; and the day before the riot there was no trouble. All the men of the colored regiment who were employed up there behaved themselves well.

3571. State any other circumstances you saw. When I stood on the parapet on Wednesday morning, a boy came running up, and saying that one of the men's wives had been shot. That created a great deal of excitement, of course. But as soon as I told them to go to their quarters, they went right off; there was no trouble at all. They were very obedient to my orders, though out of service. Some of them had been paid off.

3572. Do you know of their having been riotous, boisterous, or disorderly after they were mustered out, and before they were paid off? I think there was more subordination after they were mustered out than I saw before.

3573. What seemed to be the character of the men? Were they vicious generally, or well behaved? About the common run of men.

3574. Did you see any riotous acts on the part of these colored people at any time, further than in self-defence? I never saw any riotous act among them. And one thing I will say for them, that there is no number of white soldiers that I ever saw that could be held in such subjection as they were, when their houses were being burned as theirs were. I could not have expected it; never could have believed it could be done.

By Mr. SHANKLIN:

3575. I understand you to say that on Tuesday evening you saw little or nothing of the difficulty on South street between the colored soldiers and the police? I held the balance of the command under arms; and on Wednesday morning, about 10 o'clock, I went on to the parapet overlooking the whole of South Memphis, and I stood there probably till a little after 12. When I first went out I saw about nine colored men; some of the others I think were not soldiers, but defending themselves. The two that I spoke of were colored soldiers; these nine formed a sort of skirmish line.

3576. How far were they in front of the parapet? Five or six hundred yards from it, right in the opposite direction from South street; they were about as far from the fort as from South street.

3577. At that time, how many colored soldiers were on the parapet, and congregated near where you were? I should say between four and five hundred.

3578. Were those persons under much excitement at that time? They were pretty well excited, and regretted that they had returned their arms and could not defend their homes.

3579. How long was it after you reached the parapet, those on the parapet cheered those nine men? It might have been ten minutes. It was while I stood on the parapet I received an order from General Stoneman to keep the men in their barracks. At the time this cheer was given, those nine men who had been shooting retreated back towards the parapet.

3580. How near had these nine colored men, who had been shooting, got to you at the time the cheer was given? Between five and six hundred yards from the nearest point of the parapet. They came up the hill and then turned round and fired. When the cheer was given they started down again, and went in the direction of a large party who had been standing there, and in a few minutes two of them came running up the hill, and those I disarmed.

3581. Could there have been a collection of men under the hill without your seeing them? No, sir, unless they were on the other side of the railroad.

3582. Do you know of any effort or demonstration on the part of the colored soldiers in the fort on Tuesday morning towards making an assault on the arsenal to recover their arms? Yes, sir; I heard one of them say we must get our arms to-night. This created some suspicion in my mind, and it was this that made me double the guard. Some twelve of them made an attempt, but at the first fire they all stopped. There was no demonstration after that.

3583. You say, do you not, from what you saw, they were not under good discipline? It was not what I call good discipline; it might have been considered passable discipline. The officers did not seem to have control of the men, nor did they give that attention to discipline which I had been accustomed to.

3584. Had you seen any of these colored soldiers when off duty, on the streets of Memphis, passing about in groups? Yes, sir, in groups of four or five, going out and coming in.

3585. Did you see them frequently under the influence of liquor? I did not; I never saw but two or three of them all the time I was there, under the influence of liquor.

3586. Did you at any time see them congregating on South street, or other points in that neighborhood? I frequently passed that way for my meals for the first four or five days at all times, and never saw any disorderly conduct on the part of the colored troops.

3587. Were there many of the colored soldiers in the fort who had revolvers? I know there were some who had pistols, because as they would go along they would fire them in the air, but you could expect nothing better of them; but this was after they passed the second draw-bridge.

3588. Did you see anything further on Wednesday? As soon as our squads made their appearance everything was quiet: there was no further shooting that day till night, when they commenced burning.

3589. Were your troops on duty in the city when the buildings were fired? Yes, sir; Captain Allyn told me that he wrote a communication to the mayor to the effect that he would keep South Memphis all right, if he would keep his police away from there. The first building I noticed burning was a school-house. This was between two and three o'clock Wednesday. There was no general fight after the troops went out that day. I confess that I sympathized with the colored people, and I was sorry that the men could not get arms with which to defend their wives and families. I sympathized with them as things were going, for they could not defend themselves, for it seemed like a brutish slaughter on the part of the mob.

3590. Could you tell the character of the men who seemed to be shooting down the negroes in South Memphis? No further than that I saw there were policemen among them and leading them in the shooting down of colored people, and I myself saw them engaged in carrying off everything they could lay their hands on and inciting others to do the same. From that I could not but judge of the character of the men.

3591. What was the character of the men who were assisting the police in these riotous proceedings? I should say they were the lowest class of men to be found in the city; they were men who seemed to be willing to do anything.

15

3592. Did you see any colored men, as they retreated from South street to the fort on Tuesday, turning and firing back on the crowd? No, sir; to the best of my belief there was no shooting done by the colored men on Tuesday evening after the first ten minutes that Mr. Clifford went out; that was about half-past six, before sundown.

JOHN HANDY (colored) sworn and examined.

By the CHAIRMAN:

3593. State your name and where you live. John Handy. I live in Memphis.
3594. Have you been a slave? Yes, sir; I have, but I was freed by Massa Lincoln.
3595. Were you here during the riots? Yes, sir; I was.
3596. State what you saw of the rioting. It was on Tuesday evening as I was coming home from my work, I saw them shooting colored people. My wife said to me "You had better come into the house." At that time I saw them fire at a man in a doorway; he ran off. Then they fired at me twice and hit me once. I was lame for a week; the shot went clear through my leg.
3597. Who was it shot you? Jerry was the name of the man who shot me; he was on horseback; he rode a light bay horse.
3598. What did they shoot you for? I do not know; I had nothing against them. There were three men that tried to kill me with an axe; they said they would kill every one of you damned niggers. They cut me in three or four places with their pistols.
3599. What was the name of the other colored man that was shot? His name is Harry Towns. He was shot right through his shoulder.
3600. Do you know who shot him? It was the same lot of white men that shot. When three of them struck me he ran into a stable; then they went after him and shot him.
3601. Did you see anything else? They also shot at Joe Davis.
3602. Do you know anything further of the rioting? They broke open my house.
3603. When was it Joe Davis was shot? It was Tuesday evening, about six o'clock. He was in bed sick when they struck him; they said damn him, they would do for him.

By Mr. SHANKLIN:

3604. Have you been in the United States service? I was on the gunboat Tuscumbia three or four years ago.
3605. Have you been a slave? Yes, sir; when the war broke out they carried me back to Louisiana.
3606. How long was you in the United States service? I went as soldier at James's Landing, and was in the service eight or nine months. I took sick and was discharged.
3607. Have you had any difficulty with the old citizens of Memphis? No, sir; not one. When the citizens heard I was shot I was told they said that if there was one colored man in Memphis that ought not to have been hurt it was myself, John Handy. I never had any difficulty with the people at all; they always paid me what was right. No, indeed, I never had any difficulty with anybody except Mr. Davis. I chopped five cords of wood for him, and he never paid me. All the rest have treated me very kindly.

ROBERT R. CHURCH (colored) sworn and examined.

By the CHAIRMAN:

3608. State your name and residence. Robert R. Church, 132 Monroe street, Memphis. I have had a saloon on De Soto street.
3609. Were you born in this place? I was born and raised here.
3610. Were you in the city at the time of the recent riots? Yes, sir.
3611. State what you saw of the rioting. On the first of May, between five and six o'clock, as I was standing in front of my house, with fifteen or twenty other persons, some policemen came along with pistols in their hands; there was a great excitement on the street, and an old colored man was knocked down, and he was beaten badly, but he jumped over the fence and got away. On Wednesday I saw a great many men go down the street with shot guns and pistols, but I did not see anybody disturbed; on Wednesday evening, about nine o'clock, a crowd came by me, when they got hold of a colored man and beat him unmercifully; they ordered me to shut up my house; they fired at me and struck me in the neck; another ball glanced past me, and another ball struck me; in all they shot twelve to fifteen shots at me; they broke into the saloon, drank all the whiskey, broke open the money drawers; they took out two hundred and forty dollars in big bills and about fifty dollars in small change, making two hundred and ninety dollars in all.
3612. What do you think was the extent of your loss? I do not know the exact amount; it was between four and five hundred dollars, besides the money. My whole loss is over seven hundred and fifty dollars. They drank all the whiskey they wanted, and the balance they turned off.
3613. Did you know any of the rioters? One of the policemen who shot at me was Dave Roach.
3614. Do you know where he is now? He is lounging about the streets yet.

3615. Do you know the names of any of the others? I do not know their names; most of them were policemen that came into my place. The men that committed the robbery were all policemen.

3616. Are you a registered voter? No, sir.

3616. How much of a colored man are you? I do not know—very little; my father is a white man; my mother is as white as I am. Captain Church is my father; he used to have a packet line. My father owned my mother.

3617. Were you a slave? Yes, sir; but my father always gave me everything I wanted, although he does not openly recognize me.

MEMPHIS, TENNESSEE, *June* 4, 1866.

J. T. LANFORD sworn and examined.

By the CHAIRMAN:

3618. State your name, residence, and occupation. J. T. Lanford; I live in Memphis, and am deputy sheriff.

3619. Were you in Memphis at the time of the riots? Yes, sir.

3620. Have you any personal knowledge of what took place during the riots? Very little; I never saw anything till Wednesday, and then I saw nothing of the rioting. Tuesday night I went down South street; I saw two wounded men, one black, the other white, but I do not know their names.

3621. Was the white man a policeman? Yes, sir.

3622. Where was he wounded? He was wounded in the side.

3623. State what you saw on Wednesday morning. There was considerable excitement in town, and Mr. Winters gave orders to get ready a posse of men, and told me to assist him. I summoned probably about one hundred and fifty.

3624. What orders did he give you? He told me to go down South street and arrest every one, black or white, that was making any disturbance and bring them to the court-house.

3625. State what you did. I went down town, but I saw nothing. I saw some few squads of people standing and talking; I saw one old negro; I was, perhaps, two hundred yards from him; it seemed he came running from under a house, and there were a great many who took after him. I saw several shots fired at him, and I saw him fall. I said I was not there to suffer that, and that I should go back and get more men, and that I would arrest every one that did anything of that kind; I came back to town and reported that they were not doing exactly what it was intended they should do.

3626. Was this the posse that went down? No, sir; it was the crowd that was there before.

3627. Did the crowd appear to be under any one's direction? They appeared to be led by men on horseback; there were four of them.

3628. Who were they? I do not know who they were, though I inquired.

3629. Were the men on horseback the principal ones who made the disturbance? They were the only ones I saw firing.

3630. Did other parties participate in the firing? There was a good deal of excitement and a good deal of firing, and they gave expression to such sentiments as "kill all the damned niggers."

3631. How many men had you with you? I think I had about one hundred and fifty.

3632. How large was the other crowd? There must have been rising two hundred.

3633. Were not the men who fired at the negroes a part of these two hundred of whom you speak? Yes, sir.

3634. Had you not force enough to arrest any of these men who were guilty of these outrages? Yes, sir; though I saw nobody guilty of anything of this kind except those on horseback.

3635. Were not those other people who were not on horseback part of this crowd and sympathizing with them? I suppose so.

3636. And did you suppose they were all of one gang? That was my feeling.

3637. And did you take no steps at that time, being under command of the sheriff, to arrest anybody engaged in these lawless outrages; did you make any efforts to arrest them? Yes, sir.

3638. With what success? We arrested some, but they just said "We have done nothing; if you can show we have committed any outrages or fired a shot we are perfectly willing to be arrested.

3639. You said, did you not, that these men were part and parcel of the crowd? They seemed to be of the same crowd, though I saw them do nothing.

3640. What was done after you had seen this firing, but without making any arrests of the parties except what you have stated? I tried to arrest these men on horseback, but they rode off south over the track, and I could not get near them at all.

3641. What did you do then? I told the men that I would have to get a greater force, and would then arrest every one who committed a disturbance.

3642. Were your men armed? The party I went with had only pistols; I then met General Wallace, who had forty-five men, and Mr. Winters, who had quite a crowd, and I told them that the men out there had a stronger force than we had; then we turned round and all went down, I with one party, and Mr. Winters with another.

3643. What did you do then? Mr. Winters went towards the fort, and I went the other way; I did not see anything.

3644. Did you arrest anybody? No, sir.

3645. Did you see any cases of violence? No, sir.

3646. How long did you remain there? Till nearly one o'clock.

3647. Then what was done? Nothing was done; we all came back to the town then.

3648. Did the men who went down with you mingle with the men who were there? No, sir; we made two separate companies.

3649. What was the talk you heard? I was not in a position to hear any talk except of the party I went down with, and they were as much opposed to disturbance as any one.

3650. Were any arrests made? Not that I heard of.

3651. Did you know of houses being burned down and property destroyed? None that day; I saw some at night, but most of the fires I saw were at a distance.

3652. What time did you leave South street the second time? About dinner time.

3653. Where were you the rest of the day? At the office.

3654. What did you do at night? Patrol the town from one end to the other.

3655. Did you see any fires? Yes, sir.

3656. Where? One or two in South Memphis, one east, and one in Chelsea.

3657. Did you go to the fires? Yes, sir.

3658. Were there any efforts made to put them out? They were all in full blast when we got there; we could not put them out. The captain of the regulars got there earlier than we did; he said he came there to see if he could make any arrests. I and Mr. Winters, with our squads, then went to another fire, but it was in full blast when we got there.

3659. What buildings were there? I saw two school-houses on fire.

3660. Who set them on fire? I have not the most remote idea.

3661. Then you did not make any arrests during all these troubles? No, sir.

3662. How do you account for that, in a riot where there were forty or fifty persons killed, one hundred wounded and 100,000 dollars worth of property destroyed? I do not know, gentlemen; but I saw no one to arrest, unless I arrested everybody that was out; all that I saw at the fires seemed to be only looking on, but doing nothing; we could bring no charges against them except that they were standing and looking at the fire.

3663. What was the object of organizing the posse on Wednesday morning? It was to suppress any rioting and to keep the peace; we heard there was a riot in South street.

3664. Did you find a riot there when you got down? No, sir.

3665. What did you see there? There were a great many people scattered round on the hills.

3666. What time did you get there? About ten o'clock.

3667. Did you see a large number of colored people there at that time? No, sir.

3668. Was there any riotous proceedings among the colored people? No, sir; I saw no demonstration of any kind.

3669. From the position you occupied could you see up towards the fort? Yes, sir.

3670. Were you about the crossing of South street and causeway? The nearest place was Morris's cemetery.

3671. Did you see a large number of negroes congregated outside the fort? I saw some.

3672. How many? It looked to me there were about fifty negroes.

3673. What were they doing? They were standing there looking on at the crowd below.

3674. Did you see or hear any firing by this crowd of negroes? No, sir; I saw two negroes about three hundred yards from us firing from muskets.

3675. Did you see any other firing? I did not. I did not know whether they intended to shoot any one or not; they were a long ways above, but I heard them distinctly.

3676. How long have you resided in Memphis? About one year.

3677. Where did you come from? From Huntsville, Alabama.

3678. Are you a registered voter here? No, sir.

3679. Is it because you could not take the oath? I have not applied for it; I could not be a voter under the late franchise law.

3680. Were you in the southern army? Yes, sir.

3681. You would not be eligible for want of sufficient residence? No, sir.

By Mr. BROOMALL:

3682. Do you know whether any persons were seen committing these depredations? No, sir.

3683. Have you made any inquiry to find out whether there were any seen committing depredations, or not? Yes, sir; and I have not heard a man say that he saw anything done.

3684. Have you inquired among the negroes whether any of them saw any acts of violence done? Only one; I saw one, and he said he went into his house and locked himself up and did not see anything at all; he is the only negro I have inquired of.

3685. Why did you not inquire further of the negroes? I have no particular reason for it.

3686. Had you not reason to believe that they knew, if anybody did, inasmuch as they were the parties injured? Yes, sir.

3687. Why did you not inquire of them then? I did not know I had authority to investigate these matters myself; and I did not think it devolved upon me.

3688. What is the usual course for an officer to pursue if a murder should be committed in the night? If the parties are pointed out to the officer he is bound to arrest.

3689. Is not the officer to make inquiry? Yes, sir.

3690. Does the officer wait till the parties are pointed out before they make inquiry? It is their duty to make inquiry.

3691. Did you make inquiry? I made inquiry of several white gentlemen and one negro.

3692. Was the negro one of the parties injured? No, sir.

3693. Then you did not make inquiry of any of the parties injured? No, sir.

3694. Did you make any effort to find persons who had been injured or robbed, by way of getting at the offenders? No, sir.

3695. Do you not usually make such inquiries when disturbances take place? That is the duty of the sheriff, Mr. Winters; it is his work.

3696. Do you know if any inquiries have been made by him? Mr. Winters told me that he had made some inquiries, and he told me that Mr. Garrett had also done so.

3697. But you have not found a single person who witnessed the offences? No, sir.

By the CHAIRMAN:

3698. What was your position in the confederate army? I went out as private; was then orderly-sergeant, and then clerk in the commissary department.

G. C. WORSET sworn and examined.

By the CHAIRMAN:

3699. State your name, occupation, and residence. G. C. Worset, 133 Unicn street, Memphis. I was part proprietor of the Southern Loyalist, a newspaper. I am not at present engaged in any business.

3700. What State did you come from? Originally from Ohio, latterly from Iowa.

3701. How long have you been in Memphis? Four years in November.

3702. Have you been in the United States service? I served three years in the twenty-seventh Iowa.

3703. Were you in Memphis at the time of the recent riots? Yes, sir.

3704. Did you see any of the disturbance? I saw the murder of one colored man, and I saw two or three others after they had been killed.

3705. When was this? This was on Wednesday morning the 2d of May. I was standing in front of General Runkle's headquarters when I heard that the riots had been renewed. This was about ten o'clock. After the mob had got to the south of South street and the head of Causey street, they commenced an indiscriminate firing. I went down and found one colored man had been shot. In the meantime the crowd had left. I then assisted the colored man who had been shot, and got some water for him, and I told them to go for a surgeon. In the mean time another colored man, named Charlie Watkins, had been knocked down. I then came to the head of Main street on South, where I heard more firing in the little ravine across which the railroad track runs. I was told that the mob were in pursuit of a colored man who had escaped into a house, or behind the railroad cars. Presently they got him out.

3706. What was the character of the crowd? Some were mounted on horseback, others on foot, all armed, and headed by the police.

3707. What else did you see? While I was standing on the track I saw a policeman shoot this colored man, and afterwards knock him down, with various oaths. They were all policemen.

3708. Do you know the names of any of them? I was afterwards told that the policeman's name was McCormick, who rushed at the colored man and struck him with his carbine, and broke it in three pieces with the blow. After the man was down, they shot into him half a dozen times. After that McCormick received the congratulations of his brother policemen, and was looked to as leader.

3709. What did you see on Wednesday night? I saw a good many buildings burned. I was stopping then at the Freedmen's Teacher's Home. We were up all night guarding our own premises. Part of the time I was called to guard the school barracks, which was set on fire at three o'clock.

3710. Did the building belong to the government? Yes, sir.

3711. What was it worth? The barracks itself was not worth much; but General Runkle told me that there was a large quantity of quartermaster's stores in it; all of which were burned.

3712. Why did you think it necessary to guard this building? I made up my mind to guard this building because I knew it was in danger. I knew they had burned the rest.

3713. What did they do it for? They were incited by hatred towards the negroes and towards the negro teachers. I knew that, for I had seen enough of their doings.

3714. Did you see any of the city officials there ?   I saw Recorder Creighton there.

3715. What was he doing ?   He was there looking on at the fire.

3716. When was this ?   It was about half-past one on Thursday morning.

3717. Was he making any effort to put it out ?   No, sir ; he was merely looking on.   No outsider took any part in it at all.   They usually leave fires to the firemen, but it was too late then, when it was nearly burned down.

3718. What was the character of the crowd you went down with ?   It was composed of Irish policemen, with a fair sprinkling of the old secesh here.   I should say nine-tenths of the crowd were inspired by hatred of the negro.

3719. State any other proceedings you saw.   Right after this man was killed, and they were looking out for other victims, a company of the sixteenth regulars came up and deployed on either side of the crowd as skirmishers.   Then they went down South street through the negro quarters.   They searched through the negro cabins and wood-piles, and anywhere else where they thought negroes were lying concealed.

3720. Did they find any negroes ?   I do not know that they did.

3721. What did they go there for ?   I think they went there to find out if any of the negroes were armed or in any way connected with the disturbances.   I could not see that they had anything to do, but I could not see that they were protecting the negroes in any way.   I am not inspired with any great sympathy for the negro myself, but I would like to see justice done to all.

3722. Then you think these regulars, instead of making headway against the mob, went through the negro quarters merely to find arms or armed negroes ?   Yes, sir.

3723. Who was in command ?   I think a lieutenant.   As far as I was capable of judging, the policy of that company should have been to surround the mob and disarm them.   The mob who had been engaged in rioting met with no opposition.   The regulars went to the left or east side, and part of them came up on the left flank of the mob and deployed, while the rest came on the west or right hand and deployed, and all went south ; and of course the mob had nothing more to do ; the skirmishers were between them and the negroes.

3724. Was it not the object of the regulars to get the negroes into the fort and out of the way of the mob ?   It may have been : I do not know what their motives were.   I know they took the work the mob had been doing out of their hands—that is, shooting down colored men, insulting them, and searching through their cabins without any cause, as far as I could see ; and I could not see that they met with any opposition.

3725. You say they took the work of the mob out of their hands ; did they shoot down colored men and rob their cabins ?   I did not see any instances of the kind.

3726. How then did they take the work of the mob out of their hands ?   By giving the negroes no defence.   I thought the easiest way the colored people could have been protected would have been to have surrounded that mob, deprived them of their arms, and driven them back to the town.   There was no disturbance in South Memphis till the mob went down.

3727. Do you know who was in command of these regulars ?   He was a commissioned officer.

3728. What time was this ?   It was about 12 o'clock.

3729. What was the spirit of the mob ?   It was highly inflamed with liquor and with hatred against the negroes and all their sympathizers, and with a malicious spirit to "clean out," as they expressed it, "all the damned niggers."

3730. Who did you understand was meant by those who sympathized with the negro ? The colored teachers here ; those who were connected with the Freedmen's Bureau, and those who are called radicals.

3731. Did you hear any threats made against these parties by the mob ?   It was a constant jabber all the while.   I did not pay any particular attention to what any one person said.   I know there was a great deal of swearing.

3732. Have you seen the policeman McCormick since ?   Yes, sir ; about a week after this occurred.   I saw him on duty.   I was going along by Union church, and I saw him go up to a painter and ask him a question.   I afterwards went up to the painter and asked what he had inquired about.   The painter told me that McCormick had inquired whether it was a white or a colored church.   When he was told that it was a white church, McCormick said it was all right.

3733. Could you swear that McCormick was the murderer of the colored man of whom you spoke ?   Yes, sir.

3734. Do you know if McCormick is on duty now ?   I have not seen him for some time.

3735. Do you know of any other acts of violence ?   None about which I could swear positively.

3736. Do you publish the paper called the Southern Loyalist yet ?   No, sir ; it was published three months.   It failed about two months ago.

3737. What were the politics of your paper ?   The kind of paper we published did not suit this climate.   It was a radical paper, and was the first attempt in this city to establish a paper of this kind.   There were seven large daily copperhead papers against it.   We started our paper as an experiment and failed.

By Mr. SHANKLIN :·

3738. What are you engaged in now? I have not been doing anything for the last two months, since our paper ceased.

3739. Have you a family here? I am stopping with Mr. Connelly, my former partner; we worked some sixteen or eighteen hours a day on our paper, and I was pretty well played out.

3740. Was your connexion with that paper the only business you were engaged in? I was a soldier for three years, and was in charge of the government printing. I was discharged last summer, and I made up my mind there was work for me to do here in a moral point of view. When I started the paper I was a compositor. I believed there was to be a leavening of this section of the south by northern enterprise and northern loyalty.

3741. I understand, then, that you have been attempting somewhat to improve the morals of the country as well as fulfilling the duties of a soldier? Yes, sir; I sacrificed my time and means in establishing a loyal paper in Memphis. Though I failed in that, I mean to stay here.

3742. Do you think your efforts have improved the loyalty and morality of the people? The efforts of one man are of but little avail.

3743. As far as the paper was concerned, do you think your efforts improved the people? Yes, sir; the paper was conducted with a good deal of tact in the editorial department.

3744. Was it conducted upon political or moral principles? Both.

3745. You were then attempting to improve the political as well as the moral atmosphere of the South? Yes, sir; we combined both.

3746. What was the character of the morals you were teaching? That is a pretty general question; the policy that we marked out and pursued was to let by-gones be by-gones, provided that nobody talked treason now, or interfered with the right policy of reconstruction; we did not care what a man had been provided he was all right now. I believe we had the good will and support of the radicals here. They looked upon our paper as their organ, and we had the sympathy of a large number of the old rebel sympathizers.

3747. What was your policy of reconstruction? Of course that had to be developed as events progressed.

3748. As far as you went what did you develop? Up to the time our paper closed there was no great difference of opinion between the President and Congress, but we did not say so much about politics; what we attempted to inculcate was social and moral progress, and inducing people to go to work to repair their losses. The papers published here, from the course they pursued, only stirred up the bad passions of the southern people and retarded their progress; we thought they should leave the powers that be to take care of reconstruction.

3749. You say you advocated the doctrine of letting by-gones be by-gones, provided they talked no further treason; do I understand you to mean that if they adopted your policy you would be willing to forgive them? We held that the great masses of the northern people were not inspired by hatred in attempting to crush the rebellion, and that we were willing to accept the issue on good terms.

3750. What issues do you mean? Abolition of slavery, &c. Our paper was just such a one which, if published north, would be called radical or republican.

3751. Did you advocate the policy of banishing some, imprisoning others, and disfranchising all? We never got quite that far.

3752. You spoke of the regulars going out on Wednesday morning and deploying and separating the mob from the negroes, and you say, do you not, that you thought the course pursued by the regulars was rather to take up the work of the mob than to restore peace and order? That is how I regarded it.

3753. Was there any more disturbance after these regulars got down there? Did not their presence and the plans they adopted restore peace and quiet by separating the negroes and the mob? It had that effect.

3754. If that was the object for which they came there, to restore peace and order, they adopted the right means to secure those results, did they not? It is a question with me whether it had not about ceased its operation before the regulars took it out of their hands. The regulars had come out of Fort Pickering before this crime of McCormick knocking the negro down, and if the regulars had been deployed as skirmishers before that they might have saved that man's life.

3755. There was a difference of opinion, then, as to what course should have been taken? Yes, sir.

3756. And military men, I suppose, like doctors, sometimes differ on matters of that sort? Yes, sir; and they, having the longest pole, knocked down the persimmons.

HANNAH GEORGE (colored) sworn and examined.

By the CHAIRMAN:

3757. State your name, residence, and occupation. Hannah George; I live on South street, Memphis; my business is sewing, washing, and ironing.

3758. What is your age? I am twenty-nine years old.

3759. How long have you lived in Memphis? I have been here three years.

3760. Were you here at the time of the riots? Yes, sir.

3761. Did you see anything? if so, state what you saw. I was standing in Mrs. Ryan's door; she is an Irish lady, and her husband keeps a grocery; this was the first evening, Tuesday. There were four policemen who were taking two colored soldiers who had been ripping round there. The colored soldiers followed them and drove them up towards Causey street; then the policemen fired at the negroes: before that the negroes had fired, but they shot over the policemen, just to scare them. The next time they fired they shot a policeman, and they took him to the grocery, where I saw him on the bed. There was another policeman shot, and three colored men were shot down; one was hit in his breast, and another in his head, and another of them was dead. It did not look as if any of them would get over it. Then they commenced shooting faster, and I turned round and went home.

3762. Who was it you saw fire first? It was the police who fired first.

3763. Do you know if there had been any trouble between the police and colored people before that? No, sir; not that I know.

3764. How many people did you see shot? I saw three colored men and two policemen.

3765. Did you see any other violence? No more that night.

3766. What do you know, of your own knowledge, of what happened on Wednesday morning? The next morning I saw colored people coming out of the fort; they seemed to think the trouble was over.

3767. How many did you see coming from the fort? I saw a dozen or two colored soldiers in squads; presently they came running back, policemen, citizens, and country people firing at them, and I saw four of them shot on the hill. I saw them from my door; it was right on the hill at the corner.

3768. Do you know their names? No, sir.

3769. Who were they shot by? By policemen.

3770. What else did you see? I saw several small boys carrying arms.

3771. What became of those men who were shot? They were lying there late that evening.

3772. What else did you see? On the morning that they set the church on fire there were many colored people living close by, and I saw the crowd take out their things, chairs and other things, and throw them into the church to burn up.

3773. Did you see them commit any other acts of violence on the colored people? I saw them shoot Rachel Hatcher.

3774. Did you know her? Yes, sir. She was about 16 or 17 years old. She went to school, and was a right smart girl; she was the head of the class.

3775. Do you know who shot her? I do not know who shot her; a good many fired at her.

3776. What was she doing when they shot her? She was running away from the flames. She had been helping a neighbor to move his things. When they shot at her her mother commenced hallooing, and they shot at her and her father.

3777. Did you see colored people come outside of the fort on Wednesday? No, sir, I did not.

3778. Could you see the fort from where you live? No, sir.

3779. Were you robbed? No, sir.

3780. Do you know of any persons being robbed? Some colored people in the yard where I live had their things taken away.

ANN PATRICK AYR (colored) sworn and examined.

By the CHAIRMAN:

3781. State your name and where you live. Ann Patrick Ayr. I live on Gayoso street, Memphis.

3782. How old are you? I do not know. I have lived here seventeen years.

3783. Were you in Memphis at the time of the riots? Yes, sir.

3784. Have you been a slave? I was a slave to Mr. Patrick for seventeen years. I am now free.

3785. What did you see of the rioting? I only saw them when they shot into my windows.

3786. Who were they who shot? White people.

3787. What did they shoot into your window for? They were shooting everywhere.

3788. Who were in your house? There were five of us in all, with my two children and my eldest boy?

3789. How many shots did they fire into your room? They fired five times.

3790. Did they hit any one? They did not hit any of us, but came very near.

3791. What else took place? They came into our house and robbed us.

3792. What did they take? They stole a dozen shirts, two pair of drawers, a suit of clothes belonging to my husband, and his hat, and many other things.

3793. Did they take any money? I had none for them to take.

3794. Do you know who they were who robbed you? I could not tell who they were.

3795. When was this? About twelve o'clock on Thursday night.

3796. Was your husband at home? No, sir; he was at Mound City.
3797. Do you know of their robbing any body else? Yes; they robbed my next door neighbor. That is all I know about the riots.

MARY WARDLAW (colored) sworn and examined.

By the CHAIRMAN:

3798. State your name and residence. Mary Wardlaw; I live in Memphis.
3799. How old are you? I am thirty-seven years old.
3800. Have you been a slave? I have been, but am free now.
3801. Are you a married woman? Yes, sir.
3802. Were you here at the time of the riots? Yes, sir.
3803. State what you saw of them. On Wednesday night they came to my house and knocked at my door, and swore that they had a great mind to burn my house up. They were white people. On Thursday they came and said, "It's a damned old house and we will burn it up." About one o'clock they set our house on fire.
3804. What did you lose? We lost a wardrobe, bureau, and a trunk of clothes, a wash-stand, a carpet on my floor, and a great deal of clothing.
3805. Did you lose any money? No, sir.
3806. How much was the value of what you have lost? I think five hundred dollars would not pay for it.
3807. Would six hundred dollars be a fair estimate? I do not know what would be the value of what we have lost, but I don't think one thousand dollars would pay for it. They even burned up the old man's ploughing gear and harness.
3808. Do you own the house? No, sir; some colored people had bought it for a church.
3809. Why did they threaten to burn your house up? I do not know. I heard them say, "We will burn up the damned old house."

MAT. WARDLAW (colored) sworn and examined.

By the CHAIRMAN:

3810. State your name and where you live. Mat. Wardlaw; I live in Memphis.
3811. Have you been a slave? I have.
3812. How old are you? I am forty-seven years old.
3813. Were you here at the time of the riots; and if so, did you see any acts of violence? I saw some shooting, but did not see any killing; that was on the first day.
3814. Whereabouts was this? It was between South street and Beal street.
3815. Who did the shooting? Irish policemen; and they were shooting at every colored person they saw.
3816. Did they shoot at you? I did not give them a chance; they shot at a man near me, when I broke and made my way home.
3817. Did you know his name? I saw the man who was killed next day, but I do not know his name.
3817½. Did you see the first start of the riot on Tuesday afternoon? No, sir.
3818. Did they do you any damage? They burned my property on Gayoso street; the colored society bought it for a Methodist church.
3819. Do you know if that was the reason why they destroyed it? Yes, sir; because it was a colored church. Old man Ford's house, who lives close by, was not burned.
3820. Is he a colored man? No, sir; he is an Irishman.
3821. Did not the burning of your house expose his? It would have been burned, but the fire engines saved his while they burned mine.
3822. What has been your loss? I lost about 1,600 or 1,700 dollars; they even burned up my dray harness. I run three drays, and have run four.
3823. Have you reckoned up your loss? I gave in an account to the Freedmen's Bureau, and they told me to get a white man to write out a statement of my losses; so I got William Green, but he would not make out nearly as much as I lost; he did not think I ought to get anything.
3824. How much did Wm. Green make out your loss to be? He would not tell me, and he would not add it up after he made it out.
3825. Did you add it up afterwards yourself? No, sir; I could not.
3826. How do you know, then, it was worth 1,600 or 1,700 dollars? I would not have taken less than that for what I lost.
3827. Have you been a slave? Yes, sir; but I have been free four years. I was Miss Wardlaw's slave.
3828. Have you accumulated this property since you became free? I had the best part of it before. I always had a good chance. I ran on the railroad nine years as fireman and train hand. I hired my own time.
3829. Did you see any other acts of violence? On the first night, (Tuesday,) when they had a fuss down South Memphis, a whole string of police were shooting everybody. The police shot Bob George not far from my house.

3830. Did you see anybody else killed? I saw two colored soldiers killed next day, but I do not know their names. I heard Clark and Egan say that the "damned niggers ought to be hung."

3831. Have any measures been taken to pay you for the property you lost? No, sir; I thought you were going to pay us.

By Mr. SHANKLIN:

3832. How have you made your money here? I made it by draying. It was nothing for a man to make ten dollars a day, and I have made fifty dollars a day; and I bought loose cotton at fifty and sixty cents.

3833. Were you trading with white men? Yes, sir.

3834. In your draying who did you work for, white men or colored men? I did not allow my draymen to haul for colored men, because it would get them into difficulty. Colored people are mighty tricky.

3835. Did those who employed you deal fairly with you? Yes, sir, generally. In the city there are fixed charges, but outside the corporation you could have what you pleased to charge. At the commencement of the war I would charge twenty dollars for a job and get it easy.

3836. Were you here before the war? Yes, sir.

HANNAH SAVAGE (colored) sworn and examined.

By the CHAIRMAN:

3837. State your name and residence. Hannah Savage: I live on Gayoso street, Memphis.

3838. How old are you? I am twenty-three.

3839. Are you married? Yes, sir. My husband is a blacksmith and lives in this town.

3840. Have you been a slave? Yes, sir.

3841. Were you here when the riots took place? Yes, sir.

3842. State what you saw of them. They run me out of my house.

3843. When was this? State the circumstances. My house faces Mat Wardlaw's house. They set his house on fire; I saw them do it.

3844. Who was it that did it? There were six of them; I do not know their names.

3845. When was this? It was about one or two o'clock at night, Thursday night.

3846. State what you know of the rioting. They came to my house, and my husband he jumped out at the door, he was so frightened. They shot at him, but did not hit him. When he ran, one of the men said "There goes a damned nigger," and shot at him. I took my little boy, five years old, and jumped out of the window, and ran with him to the bridge. I there met my husband.

3847. Were you robbed? They took my pillow slips, pillows, and blankets from my bed, five skirts, my linen and clothes, and $120 from my bureau drawer.

3848. Did they set fire to your house? No, sir; they just robbed us of everything.

3849. Was the money yours? It belonged to my husband.

3850. What was the value of your clothes that were stolen? I do not know exactly.

3851. Do you think it would be worth $200? I reckon it would.

3852. Did you hear these men talking? I was so scared I could not tell what they said, except I remember when my husband got away they said "There goes a damned nigger."

3853. What did you do when you escaped? We hid ourselves till day. Mr. Parry a captain of the police, told us we had better go away. He said they would kill us if they found us there.

3854. When were you told this? It was when we came back to our house that Mr. Parry told us this.

3855. Did you know this Mr. Parry? I have known him for two years.

3856. What countryman is he? He is an Irishman.

3857. Was he one of the party that robbed you? I could not tell. He was at Mat Wardlaw's house; I saw him have hold of the hose.

By Mr. BROOMALL:

3858. Was your husband dressed in soldier clothes? No, sir.

3859. Has he been in government service? Yes, sir; he has been a government blacksmith.

MARY JORDAN (colored) sworn and examined.

By the CHAIRMAN:

3860. State your name and where you live. Mary Jordan; I live in Memphis.

3861. How old are you? I am thirty-three years old.

3862. Are you married? Yes, sir; but my husband is dead.

3863. Have you been a slave? Yes, sir.

3864. Were you here when the rioting took place? Yes, sir; I lived on Aiken street.

3865. What did you see them do? There was a man came down on Wednesday eve. He began talking about the mob. He said, "You have now found out what your Yankee friends will do for you. They have only set you free to slaughter and kill you. Don't you wish you were back with your old masters again, for them to take care of you?" He said, "I am a friend of the colored people."

3866. Was he a white man? Yes, sir. He said, "I am the head of this town." But we all knew he was not a commissioned officer. He then went away; nobody would talk with him.

3867. Do you know who he was? I don't know, sir.

3868. Did you see him again? Yes, sir; when the firing commenced he was with the mob. He was in the same lot that burned down the school-house.

3869. What else did you see? After they went away we thought it was all over; but they came back again and set the colored saloon on fire. It was kept by a man by the name of Robinson. When they set the saloon on fire I ran out I was very much alarmed, as it was so near. My husband was just dead and buried, and I had a sick child in my arms, and they had begun shooting at the colored people.

3870. Did you see any one shot? I saw one shot, but I don't know his name.

3871. Did they set fire to your house? After that I went back to my house. I was so afraid, expecting every minute I would be shot down or my house set on fire and burned. Then they set fire to it, when we were all there.

3872. How many of you were there in the house? There was my little babe, seven months old, my little girl, eight years old, and my eldest daughter, about sixteen. We were all in there when it was set on fire.

3873. Was your house fired by the mob? It took fire from the saloon. If they had put out the saloon our house would not have caught fire.

3874. Did you go out when your house caught on fire? They would not let us out.

3875. How long did you remain in there? They would not let us out till the house was all in flames.

3876. What did you save? I saved my children. I took up my shoes, but I was so scared I could not put them on.

3877. Do you say they shot at you when you first went out of your house? Yes, sir. When they set fire to the saloon I ran out and they shot at me when I had my little babe in my arms. The bullets came all around me, and I would have been shot if I had not ran round the corner.

3878. What else do you know of this rioting? When I was running away with my babe a man put a pistol to my breast, and said he, "What are you doing?" "I am trying to save my babe." "Sit down," said he, and I sat down, and they did not trouble me any more.

3879. Was your child injured? It rained, and my babe got wet and it afterwards died.

3880. Did you know any of these men? No, sir; I did not. Some of them had stars.

3881. What did you lose by the fire? I lost everything I had. I lost my clothes and my children's clothes, my bedstead and furniture.

3882. How much was it all worth? I had been working for three years, and trying to save, and my losses, I guess, would be $200.

3883. Had you any money? No, sir; I had no money.

3884. What else do you know about these troubles? When the flames were all around our house I told my children to follow me. My daughter said, "Mother, you will be shot." I said, "Better be shot than burned." It was raining, and I could get no shelter. We stayed out till they were all gone, and they did not disturb us any more. After a while I asked another colored woman to let me into her house, and she let me. Next day I had nothing to eat. After that I asked a white lady to give me some medicine for my babe; it was low and I could get nothing for it. The lady was kind; she gave me medicine for my babe, but it died and the lady buried it; I was not able to bury it. My babe lived nearly two weeks after that night, and then it died.

GUY THOMAS, (colored,) having been examined as to his understanding of the nature of an oath, was duly sworn and examined.

By the CHAIRMAN:

3885. What is your name? Guy Thomas.

3886. How old are you? Going on fifteen.

3887. Have you been a slave? Yes, sir.

3888. How long have you lived here? Five years.

3889. Were you here when the riots took place? Yes, sir.

3890. State what you saw, and what you know about them. Tuesday evening was the first I saw of it. I saw the police and some white men running down towards South street and shooting. I tried to get home, but I could not till dark; I had to wait till they quit firing.

3891. Did you see any one shot? When I got to the corner of Shelby and South streets I heard a shot around the corner. They had shot a woman named Adeline Miller. I saw her lying on the pavement. Some colored people took her into the grocery, but she was dead.

3892. Did you know her? Yes, sir; I had seen her a great deal, and knew her well.

3893. Do you know who shot her? There was a whole gang of them, about a hundred, I suppose. Before she was shot the last time she ran into the grocery, but they kicked her out, when she was shot down. The lady who was with her when she was shot told me this.

3894. Do you know any who were in the crowd? I saw Mr. Boyd. He seemed to be in command of the mob. He is an Irishman.

3895. Did you see any other shooting? I saw them shoot at one colored man as he was crossing at Mulberry street. They shot him three or four times and then robbed him. I do not know his name. He belonged to the United States service.

3896. Did you see any other shooting? I saw another soldier belonging to the 3d regiment United States heavy artillery who was killed.

3897. Do you know his name? I do not, sir. It was William Withers who killed him. He was shot in the breast and did not live more than fifteen minutes. I saw him after he was dead. I knew him by sight. He lay there all day till Thursday evening.

3898. Did you see any one robbed? I saw them rob a man on Friday. They took nine dollars. He was a colored man, and there were three white men who robbed him. They were Irishmen, and all of them had pistols. The colored man had just come off a boat. They halted him and said if he did not give up his money they would take his life. He said he had none, and would not give it up. They then put their hands in his pocket and took what he had.

3899. Did any one see this robbery? There were plenty of white people about, but they said nothing; they just stood and looked at it.

3900. Were these men who did this policemen? No, sir.

3901. What else did you see? I saw Mr. Rankin's school-house on fire. When we went to school on Wednesday he dismissed school that day till Thursday. He said if he kept school that day he was afraid they would kill him.

3902. Did you see any other acts of violence? There was a white woman; her house is by the railroad. She has a colored man for her husband; he is a sergeant. Her house was set on fire and her husband was killed. I heard them say "Let us set this God damned nigger house on fire." I was there when they set fire to it. They went from this house to Mr. Rankin's school-house. Boyd was the first man at that fire. I heard them break open Mr. Rankin's desk.

3903.. Where is Mr. Rankin now? He went off after the riots to lecture, and to try to get money to build another school-house.

3904. Where does Mr. Rankin come from? From Oberlin, Ohio.

3905. How long had you been at school when it was burned down? I had been going about six months.

3906. Have you learned to read and write? Yes, sir.

3907. Did any of your scholars get hurt? Yes, sir; Rachel Hatcher was shot.

3908. Was she a good scholar? She was about the best scholar they had in the school; she sometimes heard the classes.

3909. When do you expect Mr. Rankin back? We look for him this month.

BARBOUR LEWIS sworn and examined.

By the CHAIRMAN:

3910. State your name, occupation, and residence. Barbour Lewis. I have lived in Memphis since January, 1863. My profession is that of the law.

3911. Were you in Memphis at the time of the riots? Yes, sir.

3912. Did you see anything of them? Yes, sir. I did not see much of the firing and shooting.

3913. What did you see? On the evening of Tuesday, 1st of May, about four or five o'clock, I noticed a great excitement; a crowd of citizens were rushing down towards South street.

3914. Of what class was this crowd composed? Of all classes, except our old citizens and thoughtful men. There seemed to be nearly two thousand people, but I suppose there could not have been so many. I observed that almost everybody had arms of some kind or other. It was warm that day, and many in the crowd, who did not carry weapons in their hands, by wearing their coats plainly showed the weapons they carried on their persons. There were some in the crowd who carried shot-guns.

3915. Did you hear any expressions from the crowd? There was no outcry, and nothing was said that I heard; but knowing the feeling that had existed in the community for a long time, I thought I knew what was the matter. There were a good many people in my office at the time, and I was not to leave for an hour or two. About half-past six or seven I sent a boy for my horse and rode down to the market on Beal street, and then south towards South street. My home is in that direction, and I had to pass that way to get home.

3916. Please to state anything you saw or heard. I noticed some squads of from twenty to thirty each with a negro prisoner. The prisoner in each case was without his hat or cap, and some had their shirt-sleeves torn off. I am sorry to say that they pounded their prisoners. The policemen with their clubs would strike them, and every moment or two the colored prisoner would get a bang, which would run him on. I did not myself see any colored men knocked down, though I heard of many such cases.

3917. Did you, at this time, hear any expressions from the crowd? I heard cries from the mob, such as "Kill the damned nigger," &c. A friend that I had met told me that I had better not go any further. He said that a good many persons had been wounded, and that there was great danger. I, however, went on. I saw a great many Irishmen and citizens. There were exaggerated stories among the mob, as that three or four citizens had been killed, and that the negroes had risen upon the whites. When I got within two hundred or three hundred yards of South street there were some bodies of negroes pointed out to me. My impression is that I saw five dead bodies in different places. A couple, I think, were on Elliot street. On one of the bridges I saw a man dead, and a crowd of women around him. I asked a citizen there, who happened to be an Irishman, if the man was killed. "Yes," said he, "he is dead enough, damn him; he has twenty bullets in him." He was shot, he said, as he was runnin to get out of the way, and was unarmed. Besides these five, other bodies were pointed out to me, and if the statements of the crowd were correct, I might have seen half a dozen more; but, of course, the statements of the mob were more or less exaggerated. On my way home, whenever I saw negroes, I counselled them to keep within their own houses, and not to go on the streets. On Tuesday night I heard a great deal of firing, though I was a mile away, and which I have since understood was done by the mob shooting the negroes.

3918. State what you saw on Wednesday. On Wednesday I had duty inside the fort in a case before a military commission. It was nine o'clock when I came down South street, and I saw crowds of people, and I saw that some houses had been burned. I went to the fort, and there I saw three negroes, whom the officer pointed out to me as having been turned out of their houses and shot during the night. The officer vouched for them as peaceable, quiet men. Our court had to break up in consequence of the excitement. The negroes were crying and begging for God's sake to be allowed to have their arms. They assured Colonel Kappner that their wives and children were being murdered by the mob. The officers told them that they could not have their arms; that the government would give them protection, and that if they had their arms it would only make things a thousand times worse. I addressed them, at request of the officers, in order to pacify them. I told them that the government would protect them and see those things righted, and that it would be a hundredfold worse for them and their families if they did not depend on General Stoneman and the authorities here. At about 11 or 12 o'clock, at the request of Colonel Kappner, I came down to see General Stoneman, to get him, if possible, to interfere more actively. General Stoneman said he had not a force sufficient to do much, and entered into a statement of the force he had at his disposal at length, but assured me he would do everything he could.

3919. While you were in the fort were you in a position to see what took place outside the fort? Not fully or thoroughly.

3920. Did you see a considerable number of colored people, armed and unarmed, outside the parapet that morning between ten and twelve o'clock? No, sir; I did not. Sometimes I saw a group of three or four, possibly half a dozen, of men, women, and children, but principally women and children. Men were very scarce that morning. Usually they were scattered, running in every direction they could.

3921. What appeared to be the sentiment of the colored people in the fort after your talk to them? We calmed them down, and they seemed to be waiting for the government to protect them. Sometimes a woman would break out in consequence of the loss of her husband, and the sergeants of their companies and the more thoughtful of them told them they could do nothing.

3922. Did you see any other instances of persons killed or wounded? I rode a little round the city in the afternoon and saw a few dead bodies, but my impression was that they had been killed on Tuesday evening or night. Besides those I saw on Tuesday there were four or six more I saw on Wednesday.

3923. How many did you see in all on Tuesday and Wednesday? I think not more than ten or eleven.

3924. Did you see any more dead bodies? If so, how many do you think you saw in all? My judgment is that I saw more than fifteen. I am confident I saw fourteen or fifteen.

3925. What had been the state of feeling here previous to the breaking out of the riot? The old and more thoughtful of the citizens, the worthy and good men of the city, so far as I knew, have no bitterness of feeling towards the negro—scarcely any unkindness; they would have no wrong done to anybody. But the majority of the population does not consist of the thoughtful and intelligent class, and those were very bitter against the negroes. I think almost all southern people felt rather hard against those negroes who had served in the United States army and fought against the south.

3926. Was that feeling prevalent here in the south? Yes, sir: occasionally there would be exceptions. There were southern gentlemen who were just and kind and considerate towards the negro, felt bitterly towards the colored soldiers, for they regarded the enlistment of the colored troops as the last stroke towards their being conquered.

3927. What was the general conduct of the colored soldiers here? So far as I know, their general conduct was good. I have no doubt they sometimes behaved badly, but I know of no instances myself.

3928. Were you here during the war? I have been here since January of 1863, except a month or two when I was sick.

3929. How would the deportment of the colored regiment compare with the ordinary run of white regiments? Our officers used to say that the discipline of the negro regiments was a good deal better than that of white regiments, not from any superiority in the negroes themselves, but in consequence of the fact that the officers of the negro regiments were selected with more care, and usually for meritorious conduct and efficiency. There were some foolish officers in the colored regiment here, but, as a rule, they were better than those of white regiments. My impression is that the 3d United States colored heavy artillery, the regiment in the fort here, was not disciplined very efficiently, and I have no doubt that the colored soldiers of that regiment used sometimes to commit outrages.

3930. Do you know of any? None came within my personal observation.

3931. Has there been any protection here, through the law, to colored people who received injuries from white men—that is, independently of the Freedmen's Bureau? No, sir.

3932. Have you known of outrages committed upon the colored people where the civil authorities interfered? I think I have heard of policemen interfering, but, as a general rule, the negroes were not protected by the police in any way whatever.

3933. Do you know of negroes being shot by policemen or others? Yes, sir; though I never saw an instance.

3934. Do you know of a negro being shot in front of the Commercial Hotel? Yes, sir; by Maloney, a policeman here; and there was a trial before a military court here.

3935. What were the circumstances? The negro was unarmed, according to my recollection; he certainly did not use any arms. He was shot down by Maloney, one or two other policemen being near. He was shot three or four times, at a distance not further than across this room, and the negro died immediately.

3936. Was this act witnessed by any number of people? Yes, sir; the occurrence was seen by a good many people.

3937. What was done by those people who saw it? A good many expressed their approval of the act; it was a time of very bitter feeling here.

3938. How long ago was this? Four or five months before General Stoneman came here. It was when General John E. Smith was in command here; one or two months after he came here. General Smith came up shortly after the murder, and expressed himself strongly, but declared that the policeman should have a fair trial before the law.

3939. By whom was the approbation of the murder expressed? I would rather not go into that matter, gentlemen.

3940. What was done with Maloney? He was tried before a military commission here in the fort, by order of General Smith, and was convicted and sentenced to the penitentiary. He was detained here some three months, and was finally sent to the penitentiary at Nashville to serve out the term of his imprisonment.

3941. What became of him? Something less than a month ago he was brought before Judge Trigg by a writ of habeas corpus, and released, on the ground that the military commission had no right to try a citizen for offences against the civil law.

3942. Is Maloney in the city? I do not know; I think it is likely. I only learned of his release ten or twelve days ago. General Thomas, I understand, had not been informed of the nature of the case. There was a good deal of feeling about it there when the facts of the case were known.

3943. Do you know what is the feeling of the people of Memphis, generally, respecting northern people? There is a great deal of bitterness against northern people, except those who side with the confederate cause and sympathize with the returned confederates and their friends.

3944. What is the cause of this bitterness of feeling? I attribute a great deal of it to the press of the city which has constantly maligned and abused all northern men whose sympathies were with what is called the radical party of the city.

3945. Does this feeling extend to all these men? Yes, sir; to all radicals and all friends of radicals; to all who do not sympathize with returned rebels and the rebel cause.

3946. Do you know of any threats being made against this class of persons to whom you have referred? Yes, sir; but they have been by irresponsible parties, and were generally to the effect what they would do when their party came into power in Congress.

3947. What was that? It was simply the declaration of individauls that when the South got her rights, the men who sympathize with radicals, like Sumner and Stevens, and all that gang, would have to leave the city.

3948. Was that the spirit of the press of the city? Yes, sir; though the press has not, that I am aware of, uttered precisely that sentiment. Some of our papers here lose no opportunity to indulge in language most inflamatory, the effect of which must be to excite intense hatred and bitterness.

3949. What, in your judgment, would be the effect of the withdrawal of all the military force from the city? Unless the State legislature shall establish a metropolitan police force, so as to give us protection, I should say that in the event of withdrawing the United States forces, no northern man who sympathized with Congress could remain here in comfort.

3950. Would his life and property be in danger? Yes, sir; I should consider it would be hazardous for such a person to remain here, especially any prominent man. Men known and marked as sympathizing with the republicans of the north, their lives here would be almost intolerable.

3951. Are you one of the Union men known as radical? Yes, sir; as one sympathizing with the Union majority in Congress, and I am chairman of the republican committee here.

3952. What do you think would be your condition if all the Union forces were withdrawn? I should leave the place. I and a great many of my friends have talked over this matter, and it has been generally agreed that northern men with national ideas could not remain here without the protection of the military. It has been said a thousand times that all earnest, loyal men, and men who have fought in the late war, would not and could not remain here if the military were withdrawn. Many of us were threatened during the late riots; I was afraid that my office and library would be burned.

3953. From what did that fear arise? Republicans are supposed to be the friends of the negroes, and to disapprove of the prevailing sentiment here. The newspapers here speak of us as "enemies, tyrants, and oppressors of the South," but I know it to be a fact that the very men who use this language do not themselves feel so bitterly, towards us. The editors of the papers are. for the most part, men of education and good sense, but do not sufficiently reflect that the effect of such language upon the crowd is to intensify the bitterness they already feel towards their political opponents. Some men who write very bitter things have kindly feelings toward me personally.

3954. Do you think, then, that the withdrawal of the troops from Tennessee would result in the exodus of any considerable portion of the northern people from Memphis? We have sometimes said amongst ourselves that a thousand men, not including women and children, would have to leave, and of course they would have to take their families. There may be more than that, but many say nothing for fear of injuring their business, and others, if they speak at all, talk on the other side.

3955. Did this condition of things involve a suppression of opinion on the part of men who entertained republican sentiments? Men whose business relations are in a delicate situation, or who are not in independent circumstances, and all men who are timid and sensitive, and anxious for peace and quiet, are kept from speaking out.

3956. What is the prospect of punishing the perpetrators of these recent riots? My opinion is that the civil authorities will never punish any of them.

3957. Have any steps been taken, thus far, towards punishing the offenders? Not to my knowledge.

3958. Do you know what means, if any, there are of redress against the city for property destroyed by the mob? I think that through the civil courts there is none. I have looked over the statutes carefully, and have examined the charters of the city as far back as 1823, and have found nothing. I have also inquired of old lawyers with special reference to the recent riots and the loss occasioned thereby, but cannot find that they know of any law which would compel the city to pay. If the city ever should pay for these things, I suppose it would have to be by military pressure.

3959. Is there, to your knowledge, any other way by which these criminals can be punished, and the parties remunerated to the extent to which they have been robbed? None whatever. I have been consulted by parties, and have given them that opinion, and I know other lawyers who have done the same. I wish to add in regard to the safety and protection of Union citizens here in Memphis, that the State government may possibly protect by its franchise law, and by the metropolitan police bill, which go into effect in a month, the citizens even in the event of the withdrawal of the Union troops.

By Mr. Broomall:

3960. State if the southern men who have sympathized with the government, and are with you in sentiment, are in any better position, with respect to the masses of the people here, than northern men? It is hard to say whether they are or not. They are regarded with special bitterness, as being traitors to their section, and deserters from the cause where their duties lay by birth and residence. There is, on the other hand, a special prejudice against men of northern birth, as being Yankees; a prejudice which has existed in the South for many years.

3961. Are you able to say which of these two classes would fare worse in case of the withdrawal of the military? I am not. I think the men who rendered service to the United States in the late war would be in most danger.

3962. You have said there is little, if any, chance of redress through the civil courts for the injuries done during the recent riots. What is the chance of redress for the wrong done by the white man to the negro, as your courts and juries are now constituted? From my own personal knowledge they do not stand a good chance here, at present, though I think public sentiment will improve; and I know that good southern men very much desire an improvement in this respect.

3963. As a general rule, are your juries taken exclusively from the best class of people? No, sir; the higher class of citizens in the United States usually shirk those kind of duties, and, excepting the juries on criminal cases, juries have not been from the more respectable class of society.

3964. In your opinion would it be possible, in a case between a negro and a white man, to get, under your present system, an unbiased jury? I do not wish to say it would be impossible; I think it would be possible, but the probabilities would be entirely against the negro.

By the CHAIRMAN:

3965. Have you been in the army? Yes, sir; over three years.

3966. Have you occupied any official position in the city at any time? I was captain of company G, Illinois cavalry. I served on some military commissions, and then without my knowledge I was appointed judge of the civil commission, which position I held for about twenty months.

By Mr. SHANKLIN:

3967. Where did you come from to Memphis? Jacksonville, Illinois. I was there from 1856, or 1857, till 1861.

3968. What was your pursuit or business there? Lawyer.

3969. When did you connect yourself with the army? In 1861, shortly after the battle of Bull Run.

3970. Where did you first connect yourself with the military, and in what capacity? At Jacksonville, Morgan county, Illinois. I raised a body of men, and was elected captain of one of the companies I raised. We tendered our services immediately to the governor of Illinois, but the cavalry regiments of Illinois being nearly all made up, he secured admission for us in a regiment formed in St. Louis, the 1st Missouri cavalry, at Jefferson barracks.

3971. Where were you born? In Vermont.

3972. At what age did you leave that State? I left it very early; when I was six weeks old.

3973. Where did you next settle? My father went from there to Canada with all his children. I lived there only a few years. We lived in Canada, about thirty miles south of Montreal, till I was about nine years old. We then lived in Clinton county, New York, till I was about seventeen years old; then moved to Illinois; lived in the State of Illinois till the year 1846; lived part of a year in New Orleans; then in Mobile till 1855; then in the State of Mississippi one year; then I spent most of a year in New York and Massachusetts, and at Washington city; and after that resided at Jacksonville, Illinois, till the war broke out.

3974. How long were you connected with the military after you reached Memphis? Till November, 1864.

3975. Were you in charge of a military commission? It was called a civil commission; our city was without any civil courts. The general could not, in a city of 60,000 inhabitants, have suppressed the courts that existed here without establishing a substitute; without creating a court, though without a jury.

3976. Then you were sole judge of the law and the facts? Yes, sir.

3977. Did you consider it a military or civil court? I considered it a civil court appointed by military authority.

3978. Did you administer justice according to what you consider civil or military law; or did you allow the military to override the civil law when they came into conflict? We had certain orders that would override the law of the State; for instance, we were not to recognize property in slaves. We were not to interfere with the titles of land here, because the records of the city showing title were all down south, and it would not have been safe; and, like all other citizens here, we were bound to obey any military orders that happened to be issued; but orders were to administer justice and law according to the statutes of Tennessee as they existed previous to the rebellion.

3979. Since you were disconnected with the military, have you been practicing law here? Yes, sir.

3980. Have you had any other pursuits? No, sir.

3981. Have you been connected with the press? No, sir.

3982. You have said that you thought the tone and teachings of the majority of the newspapers here were calculated to arouse and excite the multitude, and to have a bad effect upon public sentiment? Yes, sir.

3983. I will ask you if there are not papers published here of a different complexion from those you have spoken of, that are regarded as radical papers? There is one paper published that claims to be a radical or Union paper, the Memphis Post, which may, I suppose, be regarded as a moderate radical paper.

3984. Is there not another paper published here? Yes, sir; the Weekly Republican. I do not see it once in two months; and whether it is published now or not, I do not know; my impression is that it is still published, though I rarely see it.

3985. I will ask you whether the tone and articles of these papers, the Republican and the Post, are not calculated to arouse and excite those persons who entertain feelings which the majority of the people of Memphis entertain? I think not, generally. I do not remember to have seen in the Post anything offensive, or insulting, or violent. There may have been sometimes communications in which there may have been sentiments of which I disapproved. I remember, for instance, a writer in the Post compared the course of the editor of the Avalanche to that of a skunk; but a large portion of the people like these personalities.

3986. I will ask you whether the Post and the Republican newspapers have not advocated a policy on the part of the government of punishing certain members of the community, imprisoning for life certain others, and banishing and exiling a still greater number, and disfranchising all who participated in the rebellion ? Has not that been the general tone and sentiment of those papers, and the policy advocated by them? I do not know much about what the Republican teaches. I do not know that there are a dozen people who read it in the whole town; its influence is so trifling that it has little effect. The Post I read, more or less, every day. I have never seen, in either of these papers, anything calling for the punishment of southern people who participated in the rebellion. On the contrary, I understand the Post to have advocated general kindness, and a merciful treatment towards all classes who have been engaged in the rebellion, excepting those who should henceforth make trouble.

3987. Has he advocated the banishment of men who were actively engaged in the rebellion, or who held offices in the civil and military departments of the confederacy ? I do not know whether he has or not. If he has, it has not been prominent in his paper. My impression is, that he has held that some of the leaders in the rebellion should be exiled: but I do not remember to have read any very strong expressions of opinion in that paper.

3988. Has he advocated that these persons should be disfranchised, federal or State ? The Post never advocated the franchise law of Tennessee till lately; till the last three or four weeks. Perhaps for a month it has occasionally spoken in favor of the franchise law of Tennessee. Colonel Chandler, the acting editor of the paper, has often expressed to me a wish that no such law should be passed, though I think the paper has occasionally spoken in its favor.

3989. Does not that law disfranchise all persons who have been engaged in the rebellion at any period ? My impression is that it does not disfranchise those who voted for the President in 1864, or for the amendment that amended the Constitution. I think it does disfranchise those who actively aided the rebellion, or who held civil offices under it, and who voted against the government.

3990. You think a paper advocating doctrines of that sort in a community such as this would not be obnoxious to the feelings of the people, and calculated to create and excite unkind feelings ? I think it might, in bad men; but reasonable men who served in the rebel armies, many of whom I know, say it is right and just: that it is what they, under similar circumstances, should have done ; and further, they say that the party who conquered in the rebellion should not be expected to give them power immediately.

3991. Do you not think that the advocacy of such sentiments would be calculated to irritate reasonable men ? Possibly not.

3992. I will ask you if these papers in Memphis, which you think inflammatory, have not been zealously advocating the doctrines of the President of the United States upon the subject of the reconstruction of the government ? They would, in a general way, applaud the President of the United States, and say that he was for them; but, on the other hand, they could not be induced to distinctly indorse the doctrines which he announced when governor of Tennessee or while Vice-President.

3993. That is not answering my question. I want to know whether those papers, for the last two or three months, have not been distinctly advocating and approving of the policy of the President of the United States for the reconstruction of the Union ? Only partially ; they have not said a word in favor of his doctrine, in reconstructing the government, that the rebel debt should never be paid; on the contrary, they have more or less explicitly advocated that proposition. They have stated openly and clearly that the southern States are in honor bound to pay the war debt, and that it was despotism to compel the people of the South, in their conventions, to pass laws to prevent the paying of that debt.

3994. How about other points—the emancipation of slaves ? They have generally accepted that as a fixed fact which could not be resisted.

3995. How about the right of secession, as a constitutional right ? They constantly speak of the rights of States, and include in that the right of States to secede. Sometimes they say it has been decided by the sword that they cannot secede, but they maintain that it is one of the inherent rights of States.

3996. Do they not mean that it was the right of a State previous to the rebellion, but that it has been decided by the sword, and that they acquiesce on it ? They often express themselves so, and often speak differently.

3997. You speak of the majority of the people of Memphis being in sentiment hostile to the negroes and hostile to northern men who claim to be loyal in their feelings. That was not the language I used.

3998. I wish to know, not so much what is the present sentiment and feeling of the people of Memphis toward the negroes, so much as what has been their feelings and sentiments ? I think that since the riots the reflecting portion of the people of Memphis have been brought to think upon the subject, and the best citizens we have among us, of southern birth, never wish any injustice done to anybody, white or black, certainly not to the negroes.

3999. What proportion of the people entertain that feeling ? A very insignificant proportion, as to numbers; perhaps five-sixths to nine-tenths are what we call southern in sentiment, in other words, sympathize with the rebellion, and pray for Jeff. Davis ; but a very small portion of that number entertain any unkind feelings towards the negro or hostility to the northern people.

16

4000. You state, do you not, that, in your judgment, it would not be safe for Union men to remain in Memphis if the federal troops were withdrawn? Emphatically that is my conviction; some of them could not remain twenty-four hours with safety.

4001. Is there not a large portion of Tennessee without any federal troops in it? I presume that is so; but there are troops within easy reach, where they could be called upon, and it is felt that there is a military power in the State.

4002. I will ask you if there is not more quiet and order in those sections of the State where there are no troops and no Freedmen's Bureau than in other portions where there are troops and where Freedmen's Bureaus exist? No, sir. In the agricultural portions, where the population is sparse, and where there is a small excitable population, murders do occur.

4003. Do they occur oftener than in the immediate neighborhood where the military are stationed? Yes, sir.

4004. Have you any positive knowledge of that fact? Yes, sir.

4005. Then your impression is, that in the rural districts, where there is no bureau or military, outrages upon the negroes are more frequent than in neighborhoods where the military are stationed and the Freedmen's Bureaus found? My statement is, that in those towns and districts where the bureau cannot operate and the military cannot reach, in those regions the negroes are without redress, and are subject to more violence than where the Freedmen's Bureau does exist.

4006. I will ask you whether or not a large proportion of the people of Memphis who have participated in the rebellion were not disfranchised at the last election by the laws of Tennessee? A large majority of those who participated in the rebellion, according to laws existing till within nearly a year, are disfranchised; but a great number of rebel sympathizers, who should not have voted, have contrived to do so.

4007. To what class do they belong? Those who belong to the civil and those who belong to the military service; they contrived to get certificates of registration which were fraudulent. On the other hand a great many respectable men who have been in the confederate army, according to what I deem correct information, have been offered such certificates by some bad and designing men, but they have refused to accept them, feeling themselves bound in honor to obey the law.

4008. Are not all honorable men who have been engaged in this rebellion, in the city of Memphis, disfranchised by the laws of Tennessee and denied the right to vote? No, sir, not all; those who came in before 1864 and were enabled to take the amnesty oath, all those who have held any office or commission under the present State government, or held office under Governor Johnson, and there are some other exceptions which allowed of their voting by law.

4009. Taking it with all these exceptions, what proportion of all the citizens of Memphis are disfranchised by the laws of the State? Perhaps a half, two-thirds, or possibly three-fourths.

4010. Is there not comprised in that a large proportion of the orderly, quiet, property-holding citizens of Memphis? A respectable proportion of the owners of property and men engaged in business, and a large majority of the rich property-holders, did not enlist in the rebellion.

4011. I will ask you whether, under the disfranchising law of the State of Tennessee, the control and election of city officers in Memphis was not thrown very much into the hands of the foreign population and into the hands of such as had no scruples in taking the oath that was required? I think it was in a very considerable degree thrown into the hands of the Irish who did not participate in the rebellion, and who will always vote, and into the hands of a class of rebels in heart and feeling, who had done no overt act, and of others who will recklessly take any oath to serve their purpose.

4012. Are there not a great many of the population here, as there are in other river towns and large cities, who are regarded as a very bad and low population, and known as wharf rats—a fluctuating population going from city to city, pilfering and committing outrages of every sort? We have our share, perhaps a little more than our share of desperadoes of that class, being, as it were, midway between New Orleans, Cincinnati, St. Louis, and Chicago. I suppose there are two hundred or three hundred thieves here all the time.

4013. What was the character and class of the population you saw congregated together and which constituted the mob here? First, nearly all the police; in the second place, Irish citizens, such as draymen and hackmen; and in the third place there were a great many clerks in stores, American citizens and employés of all kinds.

4014. Were there many of the rebel population mixed up in the rioting? No, sir, not greatly, to my knowledge. I saw many young men who had served in the rebel army and who are now in the stores and houses of business.

4015. Did you see young men who had been in the rebel army, and who are now clerks, participating in any acts of violence? I did not state that I saw any acts of violence committed by this class; they seemed in the mob like all the rest.

4016. Did you see any persons in that mob who were lookers on, brought there from curiosity? Yes, sir; I saw there Germans, northern men and southern men, who were not participators, and who regretted their inability to stop such things very much.

By Mr. BROOMALL:

4017. At the election of the last mayor, what proportion of the white males then here, over twenty-one years of age, were, in your opinion, disfranchised by the laws of Tennessee as they then existed? It is my belief that about one-half of the population was at that time disfranchised.

By the CHAIRMAN:

4018. Have you any knowledge of the robberies which took place on Wednesday night? But little personal knowledge; I know that on Tuesday and Wednesday nights a great number of houses of the colored people were entered and robbed. They were entered on the pretence of searching for arms.

4019. Do you know of any specific instances of robbery? I did; but I do not know that I could give details now. I know there were a great many houses entered, and I saw the occupants with wounds, but I did not see the robberies or violence committed.

4020. What was the proportion of the returned rebel soldiers in the mob of which you have spoken? As most of the rebel soldiers who have returned have adopted the dress of civilians, I cannot speak with certainty. While I think that element was largely represented, I could not state the exact proportion; there were a good many men wearing grey clothes who were engaged in it.

(A pamphlet entitled "Franchise Law," passed at the second session of the 34th general assembly of Tennessee, on the 3d of May, 1866, amendatory of an act passed at its first session on the 5th June, 1865, was produced by witness and ordered to be appended to the record.)

IRA STANBROUGH sworn and examined.

By the CHAIRMAN:

4021. State your name, residence, and occupation. Ira Stanbrough; I live in Chelsea, Memphis; I have a cotton mill.

4022. Were you in Memphis at the time of the riots? Yes, sir.

4023. State what you know about them. While at my place of business I heard that there was a terrible riot in Memphis, and that the Irish and negroes were fighting, and messages came that many had been killed. I remained at home. At the close of that day a messenger came and told me that I had better look out for myself, that my life was threatened. Pretty soon two more came and said that my name had been mentioned, and that I was spotted, and would be killed before morning. They advised me to leave. I told them I should not do it, and I did not.

4024. Did they state any reason why you were spotted? In 1861 I was asked to vote for the ordinance of secession. I was called "one of the six;" but I do not think I was. There were six votes cast against the ordinance of secession. They came for me three times. At last they brought a carriage for me to go with them. I told them I was a peaceable man, but if they forced me to go with them, so help me God, I would vote for the Union. In consequence of this they informed against me, and in a few days I was arrested and shut up.

4025. Was this the reason of your being threatened at the recent riots here? Yes, sir; the hatred still existed, and they threatened to kill me because I was a radical.

4026. Did they threaten you any further? On the second day a white man came to my house and said there were some men inquiring for me and they were armed. He said there were some thirteen or fourteen of them, and that Recorder Creighton was among them. They, however, did not find me. On the Thursday I was told that there was a man on the railroad waiting for me to go along, intending to shoot me, and he said, "For God's sake don't go down." Pretty soon two more white men and two negroes came and told me that the man was lurking about there to shoot me. That night a man who had been in prison with me came and told me that he had come from a secret association. He is a strong secessionist. He said, "I come, as a friend, to give you a last warning." My wife was then much alarmed, and pretty soon the guns began to fire. I finally concluded to leave, and I started through the cotton field. I saw them firing into the nigger shanties, but they did not kill any one. This field, through which I passed, was full of negroes, most of them with little bundles tied up in handkerchiefs. They were trying to fix up to lodge for the time in this field. There were fifty to one hundred of them, mostly women and children, and some men. That night I spent in a counting house; they had a pair of dogs there, and we were pretty well armed.

4027. Do you know who the man was that you say was seeking your life? His name is Clemens; he lives on Third street by the Memphis and Ohio railroad. The night I went away they came to my house and inquired for me; they also called at some other houses.

4028. Who were they you are now speaking of? They were Irishmen.

4029. Had this man Clemens any cause to feel hostile to you? During the war I had some twenty-two bales of cotton, and after the federals came here I sold them. This man Clemens had a great deal to do with burning cotton, and when he found I had some that he had not discovered, when he saw the drays there to fetch it away, he wanted to know whose cotton it was. I told him it was mine, and his reply was, "It is a God damned shame," and he added, "you are a God damned disloyal man." Disloyal to the South he meant. He said, "All your neighbors' cotton has been burned," and he seemed to be outraged that he had not been able to destroy all mine. His grudge has remained, especially as he thought I liked the negroes as well as the Irish.

4030. Do you know of any concerted efforts among these men to do you harm? I know well of the ill feeling of many against Union men. I felt, indeed, that my life was not safe. But I had no desire to retaliate. I have been advised to appear before the Stoneman commission and inform against these men, but I have always said I would not appear before any committee or commission where I myself was personally concerned. I have therefore never retaliated against those who burned my mill and destroyed my property.

4031. Do you think your safety has in any way been secured by the presence of United States troops? If the troops were withdrawn I know I could not speak the sentiments of my heart. If the federal troops were withdrawn, I and twenty more of my friends would have to go away. I have heard these men say that they could push General Stoneman and his handful of troops into the Mississippi river before he knows it.

4032. Do you mean to say that you, and men holding your opinions, would not be safe but for the presence of the federal troops? I know they would not. Not longer than four or five days ago my partner, Col. W. R. Hunt, with whom I am on the best terms, coming into my office, saw the Memphis Post on the table. He made some objectionable remark concerning it. I said, "You take the Avalanche, and that is more radical than the Post." He objected to its been seen in our office, and begged me to desist taking it. I said, "As you so seriously object, I will not have it brought to the office any more, but will direct it to be left at my house." One day I was reading the Post in my office, and a gentleman coming in tried to see what paper it was. The title of the paper was inside, and, while I was reading, he just caught hold of the corner to see what it was. I remarked, "Perhaps you would like to see what paper I am reading;" with that I showed him what paper it was, when he remarked, "It is a damned dirty sheet."

4033. Then am I to understand that you would leave Memphis if the United States troops were withdrawn, because you would not consider your life safe if you were to remain? If General Stoneman were to remove his force from Memphis I will not stay here, because I will not stay where the people are so unfriendly to the flag of their country.

4034. Do you consider, from what you have known and seen here, that the majority of the people here entertain feelings of hostility to the Union and the government as it now is? I just know, for I am associated with them in business, that there is not a bit more love for the laws and the constitution of the United States and the Union than there was in the hottest days of the rebellion. The fires of hatred burn as hot and as deep down as they ever did. A man told me that this morning, and he said it would be so all the time.

4035. Do you see any American flags flying here? I see one on the post office, but I don't see one anywhere else, and I would no more think of raising a United States flag on my mill than I would of putting a match to my property to burn it all up. If I were to do so I know it would be destroyed.

4036. How do you think it would be received if you were to take the American flag and march down Main street with it? I would not do it for my life.

4037. How would a band be received passing through the streets and playing the national airs? All those who have lived here for the last two or three years have lived here long enough to know it would be received with a hiss and a groan. Everybody residing in Memphis knows that the flag of our country is not respected here, and the national airs would be hissed in a minute, if it were not for the force which protects it; but strike up "Dixie" and there is a shout, always a shout; and play it for the twentieth time and every time there is a shout. There is no "Yankee Doodle" or "Hail, Columbia" in Memphis.

By Mr. SHANKLIN:

4038. How long have you lived in Memphis? Ten years.

4039. Where did you come from? From Virginia. I used to live at Harper's Ferry.

4040. Where were you born? In Connecticut; but I left it when I was three or four months old, and have never been back but once since.

4041. Where did you live then? The early part of my education I received in New York; but have been in the south from twenty-five to twenty-eight years.

4042. Have you generally received kind treatment from the southern people? I have been treated with civility and respect by the better class of people. Finding that I hailed from the North the question would come up, "Where do you stand upon the nigger question?"

Being a pro-slavery man, I told them I was with the South on the negro question, but in the spirit of hatred and animosity they manifested against the North, I was against them. I have said the North was not so bad as they thought, but as a general rule, to avoid controversy and unpleasantness, I have waived the question.

4043. Were you at Harper's Ferry when the John Brown raid was made? I came away six months before. I knew three or four of the men who were killed there. I have always been with the South. I am with the South to-day in everything but this unchristian hatred which they bear towards their brethren of the North; and it grieves me to see this disposition to destroy the country that my father fought three years to sustain in the revolutionary war. All that I have said to the South has been to try to get them to desist. I told them if they did not it would become a ruined country. But all my advice was taken the other way, and they thought I advised them thus because I hated them. And now that the war is over, I do not want to ask for admission back into the Union. I have said, "Let us wait." I do not wish to go back unbidden, uncalled for. I want to go back as men, not as beggars.

4044. Your sympathies and affections are still with the South? Yes, sir; but I will not live in it unless I am protected by the government of my country. We have gone from secession to a lower position—to be governed by an Irish mob.

4045. State whether, in your opinion, if all the male citizens of Memphis over twenty-one years of age, who had a residence here, were permitted to vote, it would improve your city government? I think it would. I think it could not be worse than the present state of things. I think it is as bad as it can be, and any change I think would be for the better.

4046. The city government is under the control of the Irish population, is it not? Almost entirely.

4047. Do the Irish control the election of city officers? Yes, sir.

4048. Are you a voter? I do not think I am.

4049. How is that? I did nothing more than this: when they levied a contribution upon me of $20 or $25 to equip a company, I paid my tax. They came and told me how much I had to pay and I paid it.

By the CHAIRMAN:

4050. Are you in business here? Yes, sir.

4051. What does it amount to? I have lately spent $17,000 in adding to my business. When I have got it in full operation my business will amount to nearly $100,000 per year.

CAPTAIN A. W. ALLYN sworn and examined.

By the CHAIRMAN:

4052. State your name and position in the United States service? A. W. Allyn, captain sixteenth United States infantry, commanding the post at Memphis.

4053. Were you present at the recent riots in this city? I was here all the time.

4054. Did you participate in their suppression? Yes, sir; very actively.

4055. Please to state, narratively, what to your knowledge took place? I will submit a copy of my report made on the subject, dated May 21, 1866.

(See Appendix.)

4056. At what time of the day did you first hear the disturbance? It was on Monday that I had heard some disturbance in the neighborhood of my camp, in the northern end of Fort Pickering. Disturbances had been going on perhaps for a week, more or less; pistol firing and carousing.

4057. By whom was this disturbance made? I discovered it was a disturbance made by the negroes at a dance-house where they were in the habit of going to dance. I heard several shots, but I thought the negroes were, as usual, discharging their pistols in the air.

4058. What was done? I did nothing at all that evening. I gave instructions then to the officer of the day, in case of a recurrence of the firing—for some of the shots came very near my men—to move out instantly and disarm and arrest the persons engaged in it.

4059. What knowledge have you of the next disturbance? It was when Major Smyth moved his troops on Tuesday night, about 6 o'clock in the evening.

4060. For what purpose were these troops moved out? For stopping the firing and disarming the persons who were creating the disturbance.

4061. What was this firing on Tuesday evening? It was principally by the police and citizens.

4062. Did he stop it? He reported to me several instances of negroes being arrested and beaten by the police, and of the crowd trying to kill them. He reported that he had taken away one negro from the police. He had also disarmed some of the policemen; but whenever he found that the police were in the discharge of their duty he returned them their pistols.

4063. Have you any knowledge of anything that took place Tuesday evening? No, sir; not till the matter was entirely over.

4064. State what took place on Wednesday. On Wednesday morning, about twenty minutes past nine, being officer of the day and in charge of the guard, I determined to march to the place where the disturbance had been, and I moved directly east, to South street, and down South street as far as Causey street. Everything there was quiet. At the corner of Causey and Beal streets I turned west. I had got but a short distance when a gentleman on horseback told me there was a riot in progress in South Memphis, and that the mayor would probably like to see me.

4065. How many men had you with you? Perhaps about forty. I directed the sergeant to take the men to the navy yard, and I hunted up the mayor. I finally found him. I then saw Sheriff Winters, who ordered me to turn out all the troops necessary to suppress the riot.

On Tuesday evening I received an order from General Stoneman, and on Wednesday morning I received Sheriff Winters's order. Sheriff Winters asked me how long it would take me to turn out my troops. I said in twenty minutes. He requested me to meet him at the Beal Street market in an hour. When I got to Beal Street market I saw no particular disturbance. There was a large crowd of citizens and a large number of policemen who were very much excited. I saw one shot fired by somebody, and I afterwards understood it was fired by a negro. I waited at the Beal Street market three-quarters of an hour before the sheriff came. That must have been about half past ten. I then, under his directions, moved my command back to South street, and held it just east of the Mississippi and Tennessee railroad depot.

4066. How large a command had you then? I had about forty-five men and one officer. Just at that time I received an order to send a guard to General Runkle's office. I sent him a sergeant and ten men. At this time the whole property guard was out, and there were very few men left in the camp.

4067. What was there at the time to guard? There was property to guard worth $25,000, consisting mostly of arms.

4068. Were you near enough to the crowd to hear what was said? I was so busy that I did not pay attention.

4069. Proceed with your narrative. I requested to know where the riot was, and where our services were needed; and, after some time, Sheriff Winters pointed out where the disturbances were going on. I ordered Lieutenant Clifford to take part of the command, and I deployed the rest on South street. I requested that the citizens should be kept away from my troops. I then moved forward; the men loaded their pieces and fixed their bayonets. I instructed them not to fire upon anybody whatever, unless they were fired upon; but if they were, they were to return the fire, and to arrest everybody found with arms creating a disturbance, and to turn the men and arms over to the police.

4070. Was there any mob at this time that you saw except the mob of police, and citizens with the police? No, sir; I saw none.

4071. If arms had been taken from any one, and turned over to the police, would that not in reality have been turning them over to the mob? I thought it would not be so; because, I thought the police were acting under the control of the authorities, and I was acting under the orders of Sheriff Winters.

4072. Did you take any arms from any in the mob? I found no one in advance of my line with arms.

4073. How long did you remain there? I skirmished that locality very thoroughly; then I wheeled the line till I came on a line with the Mississippi and Tennessee railroad. There I halted, and the line of Lieutenant Clifford and my line came together.

4073½. Were not these localities inhabited by colored people? Yes, sir.

4074. Did you find any hostile demonstrations? No, sir.

4075. Did you find any arms? No, sir.

4076. Were any arms taken away? No, sir.

4077. State what further you did. I then went back. I just then received a communication from General Stoneman that he wished to see me in person. I then collected my line, and proceeded towards General Stoneman's headquarters. I noticed that there were several questionable companies coming up Main street, and I concluded it would be best to disperse that crowd of citizens and send them home. This was between 11½ and 12 o'clock. There was a person by the name of Wallace, attorney general here, standing on the Morris cemetery making a speech to the crowd, advising them to organize and arm themselves. As soon as he noticed me on horseback he asked me if everything was quit in the portion of the town I had left. I requested him to disperse the people and tell them to go home; and immediately after this I saw two of these companies of armed men go off. I understood they went off under the immediate control of the sheriff. In twenty minutes—while I remained—the greater portion of the crowd had gone, and the rest were going; and concluding that everything was quiet, I ordered my force to report to Lieutenant Clifford, and I ordered him to remain on the ground to keep the troops together while I went to see General Stoneman. I returned probably at one o'clock, and noticed immediately after dinner that there were two or three fires, which broke out apparently simultaneously. I started off on horseback and despatched a body of troops under Lieutenant Clifford, ordering him to report to me on the ground. I understood that Major Smith had been there endeavoring to save things at the fire, and that there was only one white person assisting Major Smith in putting out the fire. It was impossible to save the school-house which was on fire, but we saved all the adjoining buildings that it was possible to save. There were three or four little shanties on fire, but they burned so rapidly that it was impossible to get into them to put them out.

4078. Did the firemen assist in putting out these fires? I saw none. One of the houses next to the school-house I noticed had been pretty well battered to pieces. Major Smith said when he arrived there he found a lot of people tearing it down. He stopped them and kept them back, but it was too late to save it. I kept the line open as far as South street, and gave instructions to keep the citizens from coming over in that portion of the town, and to keep any negroes from going north of South street. I then returned to camp about three o'clock, and from that time till evening there was no disturbance. In the mean time the troops had driven in and kept all the negroes inside the fort. They were standing on the parapets, and I sent them all back into the fort below. There were no disturbances during the afternoon after that. At night, a little after dark, I ordered those men in who were on South street to get a little rest, as the same men would have to be on guard next day; and at the same time I sent out a skirmish line, running diagonally across from Fort Pickering to the railroad, to keep the negroes in the fort. I knew a large number had wives and families living in South Memphis, in the disturbed districts, and that there would be inducements for the men to leave the fort. I rather expected that in the evening there would be some burning, but it ran along till pretty late, till ten o'clock, before any fire was noticed. As soon as a fire was noticed troops were sent out again, under command of Major Smith, and considerable property was saved that night by tearing down fences and confining the fires to the buildings in which they commenced. They were occupied with that till a little before daylight. That night, in order to protect myself in camp, I retained a small number of men, and sent over to the wagon-yard and got a couple of Parrott guns. I had them loaded. I ordered them there because I saw some fires which I thought were very near General Stoneman's headquarters, so that I might be ready to move in any direction in which I might be ordered with this reserved force; but it was not called for. On Thursday there was no disturbance whatever that occasioned the calling out of the force to South Memphis. Not a shot was fired, nor a building fired, that I saw.

4079. Did you, at any time, see any mob? I saw nothing in Memphis that I should call a mob. I saw that which I was afraid would become an irresistible mob.

4080. Was it a mob of negroes? No, sir; only of white men. I went around among the negroes on Wednesday considerably, knowing that they were mustered out and waiting for their pay. I wanted to know what their feelings were, and whether there was any disposition to be revenged, but I found no disposition to do anything of the kind. Many of them asked me if we were going to allow the mob to burn their houses at night, and I assured them that it would not be allowed, and that I should do everything in my power to prevent it.

4081. Do you know what number of colored people were killed? I saw myself only one negro body; but Lieutenant Clifford reported that he had found eight dead bodies.

4082. If these men had been murdered, and these acts of violence committed, what body of men did it? It was a party of organized citizens who came upon that ground during the time I was away.

4083. By what class of people were these acts committed? It was by a mixture of all classes.

4084. Had you an opportunity to judge of the character of the crowd? My impression of the crowd I saw in South street was that there were a great many people there that did not belong to Memphis. I judge so from various circumstances.

4085. State the reasons for your belief. Men came up on the trains on the Mississippi and Tennessee railroad, and immediately after they came to the depot they jumped off the trains and commenced killing negroes. I do not know who they were; and whether they were employés at the depot I could not say. But taking that fact with a large number of people on the street I did not at all know, I concluded there were many persons there from the country.

4086. Did it seem to you a concerted movement for the disturbance of colored people and the destruction of their property? I am inclined to think it was.

4087. What was your judgment as to the character of the class of people driven back by your skirmish line; were they in sympathy with the negroes or not? My impression was that a large portion of the people who were there were those who had been committing outrages before.

4088. Was that portion you refer to the controlling element? Yes, sir. There were a great many people there looking on. I did not like the appearance of these armed bodies that came up with guns in companies. Judging from the men as I glanced at them, they were not such as I would place much reliance on. I was afraid that with the small force I had there I should have to kill a great many of them before I could drive them away.

4089. When you heard Attorney General Wallace haranguing this crowd, what was there for them to arm against? Nothing whatever.

4090. Did the crowd he was haranguing appear to be excited? Yes, sir, considerably excited.

4091. What was the conduct of the colored people during this whole affair, so far as you could see and judge of it? As far as I could see, I am of opinion that if my regiment had all been here and exposed I do not think it would have been possible to have kept them from interfering in favor of the negroes with their arms; and I think if the negroes had been a regiment of regulars they would have rushed out, unless we could have known it beforehand and placed a heavy guard to prevent it. And, speaking from my own feelings, if they had done so I should not have blamed them for doing it.

4092. You think the provocation had been such that, the wives and children of these soldiers being exposed, their houses burned and robbed, and the women ravished, it was an evidence of good discipline and good behavior on the part of the colored soldiers to abstain from taking revenge in their own hands? It was an evidence of good behavior. Discipline, as I understand, includes something more than mere obedience.

4093. How long had you been in the fort with this discharged regiment? Seventeen days.

4094. What was the conduct of these troops during that time? As far as I could see, their general conduct was very good excepting the disturbance at the dance-house to which I have referred.

4095. Is that sort of amusement unusual with soldiers? It is unusual for men to go armed and to be firing off pistols. One or two men in a company may get pistols without their officers being able to discover them, but for so many to have them surprised me very much.

4096. Did you see at any time on Wednesday, between ten and twelve o'clock, a large crowd of colored people, from three to five hundred outside of the fort, and some twenty to twenty-five of them with arms and shooting? No, sir; I did not see a large number, or amounting to anything like that number of colored people. The only crowd I saw was on the parapet inside the fort, lookers on.

4097. In your judgment, was everything done which could have been done with the forces which were under your command in Memphis? Yes, sir. The officers and men during the first, second, and third of May, did not have a full night's rest; they were kept under arms all the time, arms stacked, and of course in such a position men could not sleep.

4098. What would have been the condition of things if there had been no troops here all during these disturbances? My impression from all I know is, that if there had been no troops here, ten thousand troops would have been needed here a few days afterwards.

4099. Why? Because I think there would have been no fear of any organized force here for the preservation of order, and they would soon have had things their own way.

4100. What would have followed? A universal massacre here, a universal burning; and the Union people of the city would have been compelled to leave; and had they not left they would have been killed, their houses burned, and I am inclined to think that there would have been an organized attempt to get possession of the State government; this is my impression from all I saw and heard, and from the many circumstances which came to my knowledge. As soon as it was known abroad that these men had got the mastery, people would have flocked in from the country and it might have spread through other sections.

4101. When did you get this re-enforcement from Nashville? Saturday evening; but everything was quiet when they got here.

THOMAS O. SMITH sworn and examined.

By the CHAIRMAN :

4102. State your name, residence, and occupation. Thomas O. Smith ; 62 Monroe street, Memphis. I am a funeral undertaker.

4103. How long have you lived in the city ? I have been here twenty-nine years.

4104. Were you born here ? I was born in Tennessee.

4105. Were you here during the riots ? Yes, sir.

4106. Did you see anything of them ? Nothing the first evening ; there was considerable excitement ; I saw the people gathered round the corners, but there seemed to be no general excitement in that portion of the city ; it was all south.

4107. Did you see anything next day ? I went down next day and saw what the excitement was. I saw a great many people on South street and some on the other side, and I saw the federal troops drawn up in line of battle.

4108. Did you bury any of these negroes ? No, sir, I did not ; but we furnished them with plain coffins to the county coroner.

4109. Did you see nothing more of the rioting ? On Wednesday evening a fire broke out ; it was one of the first places set on fire.

4110. Who did you see about the fire ? Fifteen or twenty persons.

4111. What were they doing ? Just standing round.

4112. Were they making any attempt to put out the fire ? No, sir.

4113. Did you see the city clerk there ? No, sir.

4114. Did you see him anywhere during the night ? I saw him on the corner of Linn and Causey streets ; he was going down the street.

4115. Was he with the crowd ? There were some about him ; there was no fire in the immediate neighborhood where I saw him.

4116. Had you any conversation with him ? I believe I did just speak to him. I was trying to avoid this thing, but my brother-in-law, who was with me, remarked, " Let us go along." One of my neighbors also was there, but I told them we had better dodge this thing. About this time there was a pistol shot, and I said we had better dodge this ; the pistol shot I believe was from the Yankee soldiers. The word " Yankee" is a common term in the south.

4117. Is it not a term of reproach ? No, sir ; I think not.

4118. Did you make any effort to put out the fires ? I did not.

4119. Are you in the habit of seeing fires without making an effort to put them out ? No, sir ; but this fire of the government barracks was in an open lot, and there was no water.

4120. What was the building occupied by when it was burned down ? I believe it was occupied as a school.

4121. Was that the reason why it was set on fire ? I do not know.

4122. Have you any idea why it was burned ? No, sir ; I have no idea.

4123. Did you see any other fires ? Yes, sir ; I probably saw four or five or six.

4124. Were any of them colored school-houses ? I do not know.

4125. Did you have any conversation with Mr. Logue, city clerk, that night ? Yes, sir ; I saw him and I remarked to him that some one had fired off a pistol and shot a man down there, and I said that there was a probability that the city would be set on fire. He asked me whether it was a white or black man that had been shot ; I said I presumed it was a white man.

By Mr. SHANKLIN :

4126. When was it you went down to South street ? Wednesday morning.

4127. Did you say there were two lines of soldiers ? No, sir. There seemed to be a line of colored soldiers, and the federal soldiers seemed to be ranged right on South street.

4128. How many were there ? I could hardly tell ; probably seventy-five or one hundred.

4129. Did you see any arms among them ? I could not tell ; they came down on a run, as if they were making a charge.

4130. Where did they come from ? From South street.

4131. Did they come from the direction of the fort ? Yes, sir, from that direction ; the people seemed to be standing on the street.

4132. What were they doing ? They seemed to be doing nothing.

4133. Were they armed ? Some were armed and some not.

4134. What time was that ? It was between ten and twelve o'clock.

4135. Were those negroes you saw in that group soldiers or citizens ? Some were in uniform, and I took it to be the federal uniform.

4135½. Were any of them armed ? I think some were.

4136. Was there any shooting? Yes, sir; there were six or eight shots that I heard.

4137. Did they make any charge in a body at all? Some of them I thought seemed excited.

4138. Did they fire with guns, or pistols? Guns, I believe.

4139. How long did you remain there? I suppose one or two minutes. I had nothing to do with the riot, and I went back to my business.

4140. Did you bury any of these dead? No, sir; I sent some of my hands down to inter some of them.

4141. Have you told all you saw on that occasion? Well, yes; I think I have. There was a man fired on three or four times. I remarked that they were shooting at some persons over there and I was attempting to get away. As I ran around the corner of the house I saw the man shot; they fired at him three or four times. The man who fired was some eight or ten feet from him. The people seemed to be gathering all the time.

4142. Is that all the firing you saw? Yes, sir.

WALTER CLIFFORD sworn and examined.

By the CHAIRMAN:

4143. State your name, position, and where you are stationed? Walter Clifford; I am first lieutenant of the 16th United States infantry, stationed at Memphis.

4144. How long have you been in the service? Since 19th of May, 1860.

4145. Have you been promoted from the ranks? Yes, sir.

4146. Were you in Memphis at the time of the riots? Yes, sir.

4147. What did you see? Between six and seven o'clock on May 1st I heard firing outside the barracks. I took a squad of five men and a non-commissioned officer and went out. We ran across the bodies of two dead negroes, and one severely wounded. I disarmed several negroes and several white men. I took a double-barrel gun from some white man and told him to come to me the next day, but he has never appeared; one barrel was loaded and one was not; it seemed, however, as if it had been recently discharged.

4148. What time did you return? We got back into the fort between ten and eleven o'clock.

4149. How long did the firing continue? It ceased about that time?

4150. What took place on Wednesday morning? 1 went out with Captain Allyn with about fifty men; about ten men were deployed as skirmishers towards the fort, and swept the balance from South street, making a wheel towards the fort. Our orders were to disarm everybody we met, but we met no one at all that was armed.

4151. Did you sweep through the negro portion? Yes, sir.

415 Had they arms? No, sir.

4153. What appeared to be their state and condition? They seemed to be armless, and consequently very much terror-stricken, and the children were crying. There had been pretty sharp firing from whites and blacks.

4154. Where were the blacks firing from? They were firing from South street. There were one hundred and fifty to two hundred citizens who were firing into the cabins of the colored people, and in the direction of the cabins.

4155. Did any of their shot reach the cabins? Yes, sir; I saw probably half a dozen bullet-holes.

1456. Who occupied those cabins? They were occupied by women and children, and a couple of decrepit old men.

1457. What was the character of the white crowd? It was a drunken disorderly rabble.

1458. Of whom was it composed? Policemen, levee men, and railroad men.

1459. Did you hear any expressions from the crowd? They threatened to kill "every God damned nigger they met."

4160. Did you arrest any person? Our orders were to turn over all who were found with arms. We turned over two to the recorder; he said he would be responsible for them. He got up to make a speech. He was very much excited. He said something about killing every "God damned nigger he saw;" and he said something to the effect that from that time he would never fine a white man for carrying arms. There were several city officials there. He was on a horse, and he spoke so loud I distinctly heard him.

4161. What was the effect of the speech on the crowd? I took it that the whole object of the speech was to incite the mob: it was received with cheers and shouts.

4162. Did you see any acts of violence that followed this speech of Creighton? This was the time they commenced burning the shanties. I deployed the men I had in command as patrols. During that time I saw very few black men armed, but I saw a great many white men armed; they said they were policemen, or acting with the police.

4163. Were there many police in the crowd to whom Creighton made his speech? I saw from fifteen to twenty; this was ten or eleven o'clock.

4164. Did you see any mob other than that addressed by Creighton? Yes, sir; this mob Creighton was addressing was out at the end of Second street; he stood in the middle of the road on a slight rising, so that he stood above the rest.

4165. Did you see any firing upon black people? I saw a black man fire twice, but I did not see that he fired at any one.

4166. Did you see any black man fired at by white men? No, sir. The first night I saw a man just attempting to fire; I ordered him to give up his pistol. Just as he was raising the pistol he said, "There goes one of the God damned niggers." I knocked him down with my gun; after he got up he said he was a policeman; he lifted up his coat and showed me his badge.

4167. Were you about the fort on Wednesday from ten till twelve o'clock? No, sir.

4168. State what you saw on Wednesday night? We started out about half-past nine or ten o'clock. After crossing the gully, near the railway, I saw a fire breaking out in one of the negro cabins there. There were three or four men just leaving the cabin, and I captured three of them, and sent three of them, as prisoners, to Captain Allyn, but he let them go. My corporal reported that the bed-tick in the cabin had been ripped open and set on fire, and as the fire had but just started, I knew that these men were the ones who did it. There were fourteen fires I counted that night.

4169. What did Captain Allyn discharge these men for? I do not know.

4170. Did you see any colored men engaged in riotous proceedings that night? During the whole time I was out that night, I did not see a solitary black man. I disarmed several white men who could not account for their presence in that part of the town. We assisted in extinguishing several fires that night.

4171. Did you see any effort on the part of the citizens to put out these fires? No, sir; not in a solitary instance. They set fire to one building which communicated with four others; one of these buildings was occupied by a white man, and this fire they made an effort to put out, but so long as they burned colored people's houses, schools and churches, they made no effort to put out the fires. The only ones I saw who put out fires were the men of our regiment.

4172. Did you see any other acts of violence? I counted the bodies of eight men shot by the mob that day; all of them had bullet holes in them.

4173. What was the language of the crowds of white men you were in? They were cursing the blacks all the while; they were blaming them for the whole of it, and saying that they ought to be driven out of the city.

4174. Did they say anything about white people being the friends of the blacks? No, sir.

4175. What do you think would have been the result if you had not been out with a regular force to stop their riotous proceedings? I do not think there would have been a house left standing in South Memphis.

4176. Why do you think so? Because they were setting fire to the houses as fast as they could; and when I found this to be the case, I gave positive orders to my men to shoot any one they saw setting fire to a house. Not to challenge, but to shoot them. I gave these orders on my own responsibility.

4177. Do you think the rioting would have stopped at setting fire to these buildings in that part of the city? I think they would have gone out to the Asylum, and that they would have burned every negro dwelling in the city.

4178. Did that seem to be the intention of the mob? Yes, sir.

4179. Did you see the crowd of people headed by Attorney General Wallace? No, sir.

By Mr. SHANKLIN :

4180. Did you see any negroes engaged in shooting on Tuesday evening or Tuesday night? No, sir.

4181. Did you see any of them with guns or pistols? I saw one negro; he was very much excited; the tears were running down his cheek; I took the musket away from him; it seemed to have been recently discharged.

4182. Did you see any negroes engaged in shooting on Wednesday, except what you have referred to? No, sir.

4183. Did you see any negroes going toward the fort on Wednesday morning? Yes, sir. There were four or five I saw, and one of them had a double-barrel shot gun which, judging from its appearance, had not been discharged for six months. They were going from South street towards the fort.

4184. Were those all the colored people you saw? Those were all I saw with arms.

4185. Did you see any groups of colored people outside the fort, or between the fort and the depot on Wednesday morning? I saw women and children, but no men. At about fifty yards from the breastworks there is a vacant space all round, between the breastworks and the houses, but I did not see any men there. There were groups of negroes standing on the parapet.

4186. How many might there have been? I saw perhaps one hundred and fifty.

4187. What time did you see them? They were standing there pretty much all day.

4188. Did you see any collection of colored men, consisting as it were of a skirmish line, about three hundred yards from the breastworks? No, sir. My men swept every foot of that ground twice, from South street to the second gate and down by the depot; that was about twelve o'clock. There might have been negroes out in front of the fort before that, but if so, they must have been among the houses.

4189. How far is it from the fortification to the railroad depot? About four hundred yards I think.

4190. Is there not a bluff between the fort and the depot? No, sir; there is a little rise of ground between the depot and sally-port No. 2.

4191. Could there have been any negroes out there that you might not have seen? No, sir.

4192. What time did you leave the fort on Wednesday morning? Between half-past nine and ten o'clock.

4193. Were you at any time, after you left, in sight of this ground? No, sir.

MARTIN T. RYDER (United States marshal) sworn and examined.

By the CHAIRMAN:

4194. State your name and residence? Martin T. Ryder: I reside in Memphis.

4195. Were you here at the time of the recent rioting? Yes, sir.

4196. Did you see any portion of it? Yes, sir.

4197. State what you saw? It was in the evening of the 1st of May, about 6½ o'clock, on my way home I saw a considerable crowd. I inquired what the disturbance was, and was told that there was rioting going on in the south part of the city, and the policemen were getting arms to go down to quell it. I went to my stable to get a horse to go down to see if I could be of any use in quelling it. I rode down Main as far as Beal before I saw anything. The first thing I saw was a negro man running along the street and fifty or sixty men after him with pistols, some firing at him. The negro was not armed, but scared to death. I noticed that there were two or three policemen in the crowd, and I ordered them not to fire, but to take him. Going further, I found a policeman going toward the city, and I asked him if the difficulty was all over. He said it was not; that the negroes were all armed with guns, and that they could not fight them with pistols, but were going back to get guns. I continued my ride to where they said the disturbance had been, but found everything quiet, there was no disturbance whatever. I found one or two negroes lying dead on the street, and the negro people were afraid to go out to take them away. I stopped and spoke to some of them, and told them to take the men in.

4198. How long was this after you met the policemen going back to get guns? It was not five minutes after I met him. He said "they had been repulsed and were going back to get guns."

4199. Was not that a mere pretext on the part of this policeman? I believe there was a good deal of bad feeling, and I think the intention was to kill every negro man they found.

4200. Did you see any violence or mob of rioters except the crowd you have spoken of? No, sir, not at that time.

4201. What else did you see? I rode round and went into some of the negro huts and found some discharged negro soldiers who had been wounded. I found, in an alley, a negro man lying on the ground and a doctor attending him. The negro had a bullet through the shoulder, and one or two through the body. The surgeon told me he saw him shot. He said the negro was going down Vance street and a crowd came upon him, and, without his doing anything whatever, struck him with their pistols, and shot him after he was down. I then rode completely round where the rioting had been, and everything was as quiet as it is in this room. When I saw a colored man at his door I cautioned him to keep within doors, but it required no caution, they were so badly scared. When I got up to the corner of Beal and Causey streets I saw a crowd of men outside a bar-room; some of them were policemen; some of them were armed with guns and others with pistols; they were talking somewhat excitedly. Immediately after this I met some regulars of the 16th infantry, who had been patrolling, but found that there was no disturbance. I then rode to the office of the Post newspaper and gave them a report of what I had seen. From there I went to the Commercial office and reported the occurrence. While in that office I heard a racket in the street as if horses were running away with a carriage. When we got to the foot of the stairs we noticed at the corner of Adams and

Second streets, that there was a hack upset and a crowd round it. How the hack got upset I do not know, but there was a colored man between the horses. He was singly being set upon, and was trying to save himself from the crowd. After this he started to run and the crowd got after him. While they were looking after the negro a man came up to me and asked what I was doing there. I said I was an officer trying to keep the peace. He said, "I know who you are" He had a pistol in his hand. He called me an abolitionist, and said it was men like me that had commenced the disturbance, and he would sooner take my life than that of the negroes, for we were the cause of all the trouble.

4202. Do you know this man? His name is Porter; he is a butcher. He is now under bond of $1,000 to appear at the next term of the United States court. After speaking to me, he turned to the mob and told them I was an abolitionist. He called me a "damned Yankee abolitionist." Said I was "worse than a nigger." He struck me on the head and tried to knock me down, and I expected every moment to lose my life. I had a pistol on, but had not an opportunity to use it. The editor of the Commercial was with me. Soon after I met the editor of the Argus, and I stated the facts to him. He told me the city was in a very dangerous condition; that, as a United States officer, I should see General Stoneman and tell him that the city was in danger of being destroyed; that the mob had full sway, and that innocent lives were being taken. I said, "Where is the Mayor?" He said, "The Mayor is intoxicated." He said, "You had better go up and see General Stoneman."

4203. Did you do so? I went up and told the general the facts. He asked me if the city officers were not able to put the riot down. I told him I thought not; that it had passed that stage; that the officers had no control.

4204. Did you tell him that the city officers were part of the mob? I told him that the police were part of the mob. He said he was sorry for it, for the force he had on hand was not more than sufficient to guard the public property. He said the city government of Memphis did not desire any military interference, and had been writing to the President to have the military removed, and that he would not do anything till he was desired by the civil authorities.

4205. Was anything further said at that interview? He asked me what I thought he should do. I told him the city was really in danger; that the mob was very much excited, and that the men who composed the mob were of the lowest class of the community found in all large cities, and precisely the class of men that composed the rioters in the New York disturbances of 1863.

4206. Who was this crowd composed of in Memphis, as far as you were able to observe? They were butchers and hack drivers and draymen, and that class of men that will gamble for a living; also policemen.

4207. Why should you have been called an abolitionist? I suppose it was because I was an officer of the government.

4208. Why should you have been called a "damned Yankee?" It is a name for every supporter of the government.

4209. By whom were you appointed to your office? By President Johnson.

4210. Has there been any complaint of you for not supporting his administration? There has been complaint here that I did not belong to the Johnson club, and they petitioned for my removal, to give the office to a strong supporter of the President.

4211. Who was he? John C. Creighton.

4212. Who got up that petition? Mr. S. P. Walker, and Mr. Poston petitioned that Creighton should be appointed marshal in my place, on account of his political influence in the city.

4213. Would not the same epithets which were applied to you be applied with equal propriety to all friends of the government who have been friends of Mr. Johnson? I think they would, sir. I know they would be by that class of men.

4214. Where did you come from here? From New York city.

4215. How long have you resided here? Nine years.

4216. Were you here during the rebellion? Yes, sir, and am pretty well known here. I was in the State legislature, and was considered a radical member of that body, and it has always stuck to me since.

4217. Do you know anything of the performances of John C. Creighton during the riot? I saw him once during the riot, near the station-house. He and the sheriff were in a buggy together. That was on Tuesday evening. He was quite excited. There was a great crowd round them, and they were handing round pistols to every one who desired them. He had two or three in his hand, and I saw him hand two of them out.

4218. What else do you know of the rioting? After Tuesday I did not intend to take any part in it unless I was requested to do so. On Wednesday morning it was all quiet, and I did not think there was any reason to believe there would be any more rioting; but there came a report that morning that the police had instructions to go down to South

Memphis and "clean out things." When they commenced gathering round, the county judge came to me and asked me if I would take charge of one of the companies to assist in quelling this disturbance. I told him I would, but not unless he allowed me to pick my men, for I had reason to suppose they might shoot me.

4219. Did you see any prominent men in the crowd on Tuesday? No, sir, I did not see a single person that I knew, except a policeman.

4220. What would have been the result had there been any interference on the part of the military? I think it would have been very bad. On Tuesday night whenever a negro was seen in the street the crowd fired on him for amusement, but if the military had interfered, I think that many more poor unfortunate men would have lost their lives, and much property would have been destroyed.

4221. What, from your knowledge of the state of feeling towards the colored people, and towards those like yourself, who are called "damned Yankees," would be the effect of the withdrawal of the troops from Tennessee? I do not think it would be safe. I think I cou'd live here as well as any, but I do not think it would be safe. There are many men in this town now who could not live here. Personal violence might not be used towards them, but the people would act in such a way as to keep patrons from their business, and in this and other ways compel them to leave. They would perhaps, as they have done in the Avalanche, mark the names of persons attending Union meetings. They have advised to have "small-pox" marked over the door of some because they have attended "unconditional Union meetings." This unconditional Union meeting was denounced by the Avalanche as a radical meeting in order to bring reproach upon it.

4222. Has not the Avalanche publicly assailed men on account of their political views? They have gone so far as to publish a "black list" of all who advertised in the Memphis Post.

4223. What is the Memphis Post? It is a Union paper, supporting the United States government.

4224. Do you know of the Post being threatened with violence? Yes, sir; I so understood; I was there one evening when the mob had been round there threatening it.

4225. What has been the status of John C. Creighton during the rebellion? Politically, he had none.

4226. Was he ever known to be a Union man? I do not think he cared anything about the government. He was a man of no moral character, and but few respectable people would have anything to do with him.

4227. How many times has he been elected? Three times; annually.

4228. Was he elected when the people generally could vote? Not till after the occupation of the city by the federal troops.

By Mr. SHANKLIN:

4229. Who is the president of the Johnson club? Judge Perkins.

4230. Is he regarded as a good Union man? Yes, sir.

4231. Is Mr. Perkins a lawyer of this city? Yes, sir.

4232. Did he run for the legislature? No, sir; it was Poston who was elected to the legislature.

4233. Is Mr. Poston considered a Union man? No, sir; not among Union men.

4234. Does he claim to be a Union man? No, sir; he would not take the oath. I think he did not claim to be a Union man until the close of the war.

4235. Did he remain here all the time? Yes, sir.

4236. Was he recognized as a man of character? Yes, sir; he occupied a high position, and was a man of good, religious, and moral character. He had a son in the rebel army, and he would not act as a lawyer, because he did not think he could take the oath.

4237. But he has been regarded as an honorable man and a man of high character? Yes, sir.

4238. Is he entitled to credit under oath? I would not doubt it.

4239. Did he claim to be a loyal man? Not till the close of the war. He was a law-abiding man.

4240. This sentiment of hostility of which you speak towards northern men, and calling them Yankees, is that sentiment entertained by the respectable portion of this community? There is a good deal of that feeling throughout the country, though, it is frequently suppressed.

4241. Is not that feeling entertained mainly towards those who are extreme in their views? No, sir; I think it is entertained for all Union men, though they may qualify it.

4242. You say, do you not, that you were once elected from this place to the legislature? Yes, sir.

4243. Were you elected by that sort of people? No, sir.

4244. By whom were you elected? I was elected by a general ticket in the State of Tennessee.

4245. What number of votes did you receive in this city? About four hundred and fifty or four hundred and sixty; my oponent beat me one hundred and fifty or one hundred and sixty votes in the city.

4246. How many members did the city of Memphis have? Two, and a part of another for the lower house, and, in connexion with other counties, elects a senator.

4247. You spoke of recorder Creighton having no particular position here. Do you know if he voted at the presidential election for the Lincoln and Johnson ticket? If he voted at all he voted that ticket; all the votes that were cast in the city were all that way; the other ticket had been withdrawn a few days before.

4248. What was the cause? The electors claimed that it was on account of Andrew Johnson; that the oath he required was too strong, and to take that oath, would compel them to vote for Lincoln and Johnson, so the electoral ticket for McClellan was withdrawn.

4249. You think if Creighton voted it must have been the Lincoln and Johnson ticket? Yes, sir.

4250. What is your impression about his vote? I am rather under the impression that he voted; I know he did at the election following. I believe he voted for the restoration of this State.

4251. Is that the same ticket you voted for yourself? Yes, sir.

4252. Then you and Creighton have been voting together? So far as that we have. I do not wish it understood that I have known John Creighton as a republican. In the Union organization of '62 he was a member.

4253. And, as far as you know, has continued to be a Union man up to the present time? I do not know anything to the contrary.

4254. Is he a dissipated man? It is said he is.

4255. Do you know whether he was under the influence of liquor on Tuesday evening? He was not at the time I saw him.

4256. I understood you to state that, in your opinion, if the military were withdrawn from Memphis, this would be an unfavorable location for the northern or Union men to live in? Yes, sir.

4257. But you did not apprehend any personal danger, but that they would not patronize a man in business, and thus break him down. Is that the way you think northern men would be affected by it? Yes, sir; but if such a thing as that riot of the 1st of May occurred, I think that white Union men would be attacked as well as negroes.

4258. Has not this city for the last two years been very much under the control of the Irish population? Politically, it has.

4259. Is there not a hostile feeling between a particular class of the Irish population and the negroes, at least those who come in competition in labor with them, such as draymen, hackmen, and laborers on the wharf? Yes, sir.

4260. Is it from that class that the police force has been taken? Yes, sir.

4261. And with that class there has been a feeling of hostility? Yes, sir.

4262. In the class above that is there the feeling of hostility that exists in the lower classes? Towards the negro, there is no social ill feeling, but politically there is.

4263. So far as you know, do the former slave owners of Memphis, as a class, entertain hostility toward the negro, and do they treat him unkindly and unjustly? I think, as a general rule, they treat him justly.

4264. Are they not now as a general thing employing negroes? Yes, sir.

4265. Are they giving preference to negroes as work hands and hands about the house? I think they are treating them now very much as they did before the war; there is a good feeling towards them.

4266. Have you seen any hostility towards the negroes on the part of former slave owners? I have scarcely seen any instance of that kind amongst them; there was a hostile feeling towards the men who had been inciting the negro to do wrong, but not towards the negro himself; they wished it to be thought that the riot was caused by that class of men called radicals, and that they were the ones to be injured rather than the negro.

4267. Have you, as a northern man, been treated kindly and justly by the mass of people who constitute the better order of society? Yes, sir; but I feel there is a feeling of coldness towards me; that were it not for the position I am in, I would not be treated with respect.

By the CHAIRMAN:

4268. You spoke of the vote of 1864, and of the McClellan ticket being withdrawn. Was that so? Yes, sir.

4269. And that it was withdrawn on account of an oath that was required to be taken?

That was a newspaper report, and I think the McClellan committee went to Washington to see President Lincoln about it.

4270. By whom was it gotten up? By the provisional governor of the State.

4271. You have also spoken of John C. Creighton's participation in that election. Do you know to what party he belongs; does he belong to the radical party, so called? No, sir; he belongs to the conservative party.

4272. You spoke also in that connexion of the talk you heard upon the street, to the effect that white men were more to blame than the negroes, and that in justice the violence should be visited on the white man? Yes, sir.

4273. Was not that the tenor of the conversation that took place when you were assailed? Yes, sir, that was the excuse for assailing me, that I was one of the men who were to blame; it was as I was going down Main street, that I stepped into a store to get a pistol, and the remark was made, "Yes, damn him, he is as black as a nigger."

4274. Did you not understand that it was the class of men like yourself that was more to blame than the negroes? They said the radicals were doing this, and friends of the present reconstruction policy in Congress, and that they were to be held responsible, and that the radicals were no better than niggers.

4275. Did you hear that said? On Wednesday, I heard half a dozen men say it.

4276. Did you see any of the old and respectable citizens of Memphis making any efforts to suppress the mob? No, sir.

4277. Do you know of any public expression of disapproval on the part of the citizens? No, sir; none but what I saw in the newspapers.

4278. Do you know if any meetings were held? I do not.

GEORGE TODD sworn and examined.

By the CHAIRMAN:

4279. State your name, residence, and occupation. George Todd: I live at No. 18 Union street, Memphis, and my business is a plasterer.

4280. How long have you lived in Memphis? For the last nine years.

4281. Were you here at the time of the riots? Yes, sir.

4282. State what you saw, if anything. On the 1st of May, between six and seven o'clock in the evening—it was on the Tuesday I was working on Adams street, and some gentlemen came in hacks and carriages and buggies, and there was a great running of people—it was reported that the negroes on South street had killed four policemen. There was a gentleman, J. C. Creighton, who said, "Stop a minute; I want to make a few remarks." He then put his hand in his pocket and took out his revolver. "By God," he said, "I am a brave man; we are not prepared now, but let us prepare to clean out every God damned son-of-a-bitch out of town," and the crowd then gave him three cheers and said they would vote for John C. Creighton.

4283. Of whom was this crowd composed? It was made up of the lowest class of men; highway robbers, and such like.

4284. What did this crowd do that Recorder Creighton had been haranguing? There was a negro, I noticed, and some one hallooed, "Kill him; kill the damned son-of-a-bitch;" but he was an active chap, and though some policemen fired some four or five shots at him, I think he got away, but it was not the fault of the policemen, for I think it was their intention to kill him.

4285. Did Creighton say he was in favor of killing every negro? His expression was, "Clean them all out, every damned son-of-a-bitch."

4286. Did you see any other acts of violence? On the 2d of May I was in Beal street, and there was a man there had a sort of cowhide, and he cowhided every one he met, male and female; I saw him cowhide five females, and I saw him strike children; he was under the influence of liquor, and was with a crowd like himself; one colored man dressed in federal uniform stood six licks, and the crowd hallooed, "Kill the damned son-of-a-bitch," when he drew his revolver and this man followed him up and fired in the house, but he escaped by the bayou.

4287. Who was the man who followed him up? I believe his name is Parker; I believe he keeps a kind of "shebang," a whiskey shop; I saw all was a humbug and I went home; there was no negro riot.

4288. Did you see anything more? The next day when I was on Main street, between Union and Causey, a fellow put a double-barrel shot-gun in my hand and told me to fall in. We had orders to march for South Memphis; we got orders not to yell or say anything. I think I was nearest the sheriff, who was in command, but we did nothing when we got there, for there was nothing to be done; they said the niggers were kicking up, and we were to shoot them of course.

4289. What did you do then, when you got down? We went there by the orders of the sheriff. We rallied on the corner of Main and South streets, and there we found more citizens, and they said, "Let us go further—follow us." We marched up South street and halted, and then had orders to march. Further on we were stopped a few minutes—perhaps half an hour—but there was nobody there ; then we marched back, and there was an order from General Stoneman to deliver up the arms.

4290. Did you see any mob down there ? No, sir.

4291. Were there any negroes down there ? No, sir ; nothing but white men.

4292. When you were pressed into the service, what orders were given ? To keep in the ranks, and not to yell.

4293. Did you hear such talk as this: "We will kill the damned niggers?" Yes, sir ; but we did not pay any attention to it.

4294. Did you see any negroes killed that day ? I saw one on Beal street.

4295. Was he dead ? I don't know.

4296. Did you see any negroes shot by the crowd ? Negroes were shot at from this crowd.

By Mr. SHANKLIN:

4297. Of what country are you a native ? I am a native of Prussia.

4298. How many were in that crowd that fired at the negroes ? I think there were from sixty to seventy-five.

4299. How many in your crowd fired at the negroes ? There was one man who had a star who fired.

4300. Who was commanding you at the time this policeman fired ? There was no one in command.

By Mr. BROOMALL:

4301. What was the negro doing when the policeman shot him ? He was passing by quietly, and interfering with nobody.

4302. Was he a soldier ? He seemed to be a working man ; I think he was a porter in some store.

TUESDAY, *June* 5, 1866.

PAUL A. CICALLA sworn and examined.

By the CHAIRMAN:

4303. Where do you live ? On the corner of Front and South streets, Memphis. I keep a family grocery there. I have been in business two years, and have lived here about twelve years.

4304. Were you there at the time of the riot ? Yes, sir ; but the disturbance was away east of us. There was a woman killed right there before my door. She was standing looking southeast. She was a colored woman by the name of Adeline ; I do not know her other name. She was between twenty and twenty-five years old, and was a servant, living in the neighborhood.

4305. Who killed her ? I cannot tell. The ball must have come from the east. It struck her in the shoulder, and she must have died immediately. She was just outside of my store door, standing by the wall.

4306. Was there a crowd round there ? I was inside of my store. Somebody called at the store, and I went to attend to him. I saw her fall, but I do not know who shot her. There was a good deal of shooting. This was a little after 6 o'clock Tuesday evening. About three squares below there was a large crowd. They were all mixed together, and, I think, were mostly Irish. When I saw this girl fall I took her in and closed my door immediately. In about half an hour her father and mother sent for her and took her down home. There was a large crowd down there next morning looking round, but they were doing nothing at all.

4307. What were they talking about ? Everybody was saying what a bad thing it was, and they were looking at the crowd in the distance.

4308. Did you see the commencement of the difficulty ? I saw a large crowd, but all I know personally is the killing of this girl.

4309. Was she a respectable negro woman ? I always heard that she behaved very well.

GINNIE MENARD (colored) sworn and examined.

By the CHAIRMAN:

4310. Where do you live ? In South Memphis.

4311. Have you been a slave ? I have been, but guess I am not now.

17

4312. Were you here at the time of the riot? Yes, sir.

4313. What did you see? I did not see but one woman who was shot; that was Adeline Miller.

4314. Who shot her? I am not able to tell you. I was standing right by the side of her—within a foot of her—when she was shot. We were standing together at the door of the grocery talking. I saw the flash of the fire, turned my head around, and she was lying there.

4315. Where did the shot come from? It came from right across the hill.

4316. Who were over there? I do not know. I saw some colored people there.

4317. Did you see any white people there? No, sir; I did not. There were a great many people up above, but so far off I could not tell whether they were white or colored people.

4318. What was done with the body of this girl? Her mother had it taken away and buried.

4319. Did you see anybody else shot? No, sir.

ANN GEORGE (colored) sworn and examined.

By the CHAIRMAN:

4320. Where do you live? I live with Mr. Marsh in Memphis. I have been in Memphis since about two weeks before Christmas.

4321. How old are you? I don't know. I have been a slave all my days until about six months ago.

4322. Were you in Memphis when the riot took place? Yes, sir. I was living to myself, but I cooked and washed for Mr. Wilson.

4323. Who is Mr. Wilson? I cannot tell you. He was a stranger who had just come here. I forget where he came from. He was in a cigar shop somewhere. I cooked two meals a day for himself and wife, and did their washing.

4324. Did they have any children? Yes, sir; one little girl and two boys.

4325. Was Mr. Wilson an Irishman? I reckon he was. He was a very spare gentleman. His hair was black and curly.

4326. Were you at his house when the riot was going on? I was there every day. He was at the cigar shop. He just came every evening.

4327. Did you hear him tell anything about the riots? I got very much excited about the fires that came very close about us. I told him I was going to move away; that it was getting too dangerous to stay there. He said I need not go; that there was no more danger. He said, "We could have burned your house down last night if we had wanted to. I knew you were working for my wife, and I would not let you get into trouble. We had an order to burn down these houses."

4328. Do you know whether he was out burning? He was out at night. I was close from where they were burning as across the street, and heard some one call out "Captain Wilson." I did not know it was him until the next day, when he told me he was the man. He had three men boarding with him. Who he was I do not know. One could not talk plain. He talked in German. These men were all out with him.

4329. Are you married? Yes, sir. My husband has been running the river. He was not with me at the time of the riot.

4330. What was this crowd with Captain Wilson doing at the time you heard him call out Captain? There were six men that I saw. There was a little shebang not far away that some colored people kept. I saw them go there, pull off a plank and set it on fire.

4331. Was Captain Wilson among them? Yes, sir. I heard them call him, and he told me himself he was there. He said he was the head of all burning that was done, and that he had orders to do it. I did not ask him who he had orders from. I was scared any how.

4332. How many houses do you know of their burning down? I could not tell you. They were burning two or three nights.

4333. Where is Captain Wilson now? He went off, and after that I went up to Captain Marsh's to live. He said he was going to Louisiana, I believe. They said that if they ever came back they would want me to live with them, but I said to myself that if I ever got away I would never come back any more, because any person who would burn down houses at all, might burn down mine some time.

4334. Were any of the houses of the colored neighbors burned down? Yes. I could not begin to tell you how many were burned down. They shot at a colored man who was keeping a shebang there as he was getting out of the window. I saw the man shoot at another man because he threw a bucket of water on the fire. The man who shot said, "Never mind, God damn you, we will clean you out to-morrow night."

4335. Did they finish him? They did not come back that night, and did not come again.

4336. Do you know the names of any persons who were burned out? I know the names of a heap of them.

4337. Were there any persons who saw this Captain Wilson when he was engaged in burning down these buildings? Yes. There was Newton, a colored man, and his wife, who lived right there, and a man by the name of Connor. Mr. Wilson rented from him.

4338. When they returned did you see any things they brought with them? The next morning when I went in to set the table for breakfast, there were a couple of pocket-books lying on the table, and a man who was there told me I might have them. I thought they had been taken away from somebody in the riot, and that if I kept them somebody might charge it on me. I carried them down to the kitchen, and as I threw them down two pieces of gold rolled out of one of them. One was a two-dollar-and-a-half piece, and the other a three-dollar piece. Mr. Wilson's son was there and saw it, and they would not let me have the money, though they had given it to me once. They said it was Mr. Wilson's. They did not say where they got the pocket-books.

GEORGE WILLIAMS (colored) sworn and examined.

By the CHAIRMAN:

4339. State your residence and occupation? I live in Memphis. I am a hack driver.

4340. State what, if anything, you saw during the recent riots? I had a load engaged to take to the depot from this hotel, and was standing in front of the hotel, when a policeman came up and said, "There is one of these God damned niggers now, shoot him." One of them fired at me but did not hit me. I started to run away. One of them knocked me down with a pistol, fired at me, and then beat me again.

4341. Were they all policemen? Yes, sir; I took them to be all policemen. I do not know the number of the one that shot me.

4342. Would you know him if you was to see him? Yes, sir. I saw his partner on the same beat right out here. Mr. Cockrell says I lay there senseless about six minutes, and he never expected I would rise. After a while some policemen came along, and one fired at me but missed me. Then another came along and snapped his pistol at me, but it did not go off. Then there was a gentleman who told me he had me put in a carriage and taken away. I was senseless. The first I knew I was down on Main street with my family. Dr. White came to see me about 10 o'clock the next day, and told me he had been there before, btut hat I was unconscious. The ball struck me on the head and glanced off. They beat me on my head and on my arm, so that I have not been able to do anything since.

4343. Do you own the carriage? No, sir; I was driving one of the carriages of the hotel.

4344. Did anybody in the house take any interest in you while they were shooting at you? The clerk had told one of the porters to go out and bring me in. The porter started to go, but the clerk told him he had better not go; they would shoot him. The porter tried to get some white porters to bring me in, but they would not. As soon as Robinson, the colored man who has charge of the carriages, saw me, he had me taken away. It was only six days after that the gentleman I rented from came there, and told me I had better go to the hospital and get out of there. I said I was sick and could not go; that I was paying my rent. He then went and got a policeman, and had me taken away.

4345. Who was he? I know his name well, but I cannot think of it at this moment. The policeman came and kicked me, knocked me with a pistol and abused me. I was very sick, and could hardly get along. A white gentleman, named Jim McCoy, came along, and said he was doing very wrong; that I was a boy who got shot at the Gayoso House. Then he turned me loose and let me go.

4346. Do you know of any other colored man who was hurt? Yes; Sam Brooks, a colored hack driver, got shot down on South street.

4347. Do you know that he was shot? The same doctor who attends him attended me. He has almost got well.

4348. Do you know the name of the colored man who got killed down on the corner? I do not know his name. He was waiting on Dr. Sanders. I did not see it. I was sick and could not get about.

4349. What family have you? A wife and child thirteen years old.

ORRIN E. WATERS sworn and examined.

By the CHAIRMAN:

4350. What is your residence and occupation? I have resided in Memphis three years, and during the last four months have been superintendent of public colored schools.

4351. State the number of colored schools there were in Memphis at the time of the riot, the number of children attending these schools, and the number of teachers. Twelve schools, twenty-two teachers, and, during the last quarter, about one thousand two hundred children.

4352. What were the ages of the children? They varied from five years to forty-five and fifty years of age. We had but two or three adults, however. I think the average age probably would be twelve or fifteen years.

4353. Were the teachers white or colored? Three were colored and the balance white.

4354. What number of teachers were male and what number female? Three were male, the rest female.

4355. Where were these teachers mostly from? They were all from northern States.

4356. Do you know them personally? Yes, sir.

4357. What was their character? Their characters were all excellent. The white teachers were from first-class schools in the North. The colored teachers were educated at Oberlin, Ohio.

4358. Were the colored teachers male or female? Two were male and one female. One white male teacher and the others white lady teachers. They were from Maine, Massachusetts, Ohio, Illinois, and Iowa; generally from New England and the West.

4359. By whom were these teachers employed? They were employed by different associations. The American Baptist Missionary Association, the Western Freedmen's Aid Association, the American Missionary Association, and, I believe, two or three were independent. The teachers were all employed and paid by benevolent associations.

4360. Were you agent for these associations? I was agent for the Western Freedmen's Aid Commission.

4361. How many teachers did you employ and pay? Eight, I believe.

4362. What has become of the school-houses, scholars, and teachers? The school-houses were burnt up during the riot; the teachers have gone home, the most of them; three or four remain here; the scholars, of course, have been scattered to their homes. A few of them have been gathered up for the schools that have commenced.

4363. How many school-houses were burned up? Five government barracks used as school-houses, and three churches used as school-houses. There was also a private school-house, I believe, owned by Rev. Mr. Rankin, a colored teacher, which was burned. One was owned by the Southern Methodist Association, and the other by the Colored Baptist Association.

4364. What was the value of the property destroyed by the burning of these school-houses? The value of the school-houses was estimated at about $2,500 apiece. The property destroyed, such as school furniture, apparatus, &c., was valued at about $1,000 in the aggregate, for the school-houses belonged to the Government. I know nothing about the others.

4365. What did these teachers leave for? Their lives were threatened. I knew very little about the mob myself, for I was sick in bed, and had very little opportunity to judge why they left. They were ordered to leave. I received the order myself for them to go away. The threats from the mob were such that it was deemed prudent by the military authorities for them to leave.

4366. What were the threats of the mob? That they would burn them out and kill them.

4367. What were they going to burn them out for? Because they were teaching colored children, I suppose.

4368. Were they well-behaved persons, and blameless in their lives and conversation? They were in every respect.

4369. They have not interfered in any matters outside of their regular vocation as teachers here? No, sir. I have not heard of an instance. I have been here over three years in connexion with colored schools, and I have never heard of a single instance where they had any difficulty with any person in the city, white or black.

4370. What has been the conduct of this large number of scholars of which you speak, as a general thing, and what progress have they made in the acquisition of knowledge? Their conduct has been uniformly good. They have never, that I know of, given any cause of complaint. In two or three instances, where their schools are in immediate proximity with white schools, difficulties have occurred, such as white children pelting their school-houses with stones. That is the only difficulty I have known. Their progress in their studies has been remarkable, probably excelling that of the white schools. It has been remarked by those who have visited both schools, that the colored children have advanced more rapidly than white schools. I have not visited white schools myself. I know, from my own knowledge, that the colored children have evinced very great interest and eagerness in their studies. The average attendance in the schools has been very good. The deportment has been very good in some schools and not so good in others, owing to the discipline of the teachers.

4371. What proportion of the people of Memphis does the prejudice against the colored schools you have spoken of extend to—I mean the prejudice which induced these teachers to leave? I had not any opportunity of knowing at the time of this mob who they were;

I only know from reports. I only know of threats being made against teachers by reports. I did not know myself what was going on at the time.

4372. Are there any teachers in the city now who were threatened, to your knowledge? The Rev. Mr. Bailey and the Rev. John Cheatham were threatened. They left the city in consequence of the threats.

4373. How many teachers have returned? Two; Miss Mary E. Tyler and Miss Henry.

4374. Did they leave on account of threats? No, sir, they left on account of an order for them to leave, which I received from Gen. Runkle.

4375. What was the nature of that order? I have not it with me. It was an order respectfully asking that the teachers might be sent immediately to Cairo for protection; that he had not protection for them.

4376. Do you know whether these teachers felt any alarm for themselves? I do not think they did. They did not seem to be alarmed. They were out in town visiting among the colored children, some of them. Gen. Kiddoo was here at the time. I advised with him, and he thought it was best to go.

4377. Do you know how many churches were burned? There were two buildings used exclusively as churches.

4378. Were they large churches? One was a brick church, and the other was a large frame church with a brick basement. There were several other buildings burned which were used as churches and schools together.

4379. How many schools have you in operation now? There are two schools now in operation. I do not know the number of scholars. Probably about three hundred. There are also some independent schools which have sprung up in the city, started by private parties. I suppose there are probably three or four hundred scholars in addition.

4380. Were your schools all free? Not altogether; probably one half of the scholars paid. Those who could pay were expected to do so; those who could not were admitted free.

4381. What, from your knowledge, is the general state of feeling on the part of the people of Memphis in regard to these schools? I came to the conclusion some time ago that they were very much opposed to them, and very much opposed to the education of colored people.

4382. Upon what do you found that opinion? Upon their prejudices. There is a large class here who do not wish to see them educated. They fear the negroes; that if they are educated they will become their competitors in business.

4383. Have the schools and school teachers been assailed through the public prints here? Yes, sir.

4384. Do you know of anonymous letters and communications having been sent to parties connected with the schools? No, sir; I do not.

4385. Did you ever hear of an anonymous communication like this having been sent?

"MEMPHIS, TENN., *May* 6, 1866.

"Mr. ——— : You will take notice that we have determined to rid our community of negro-loving fanatics and philanthropic teachers of our former slaves. You are one of the number, and it will be well for you if you are absent from the city by the 1st of June. Consult your safety.   ANONYMOUS."

Yes, sir, I have heard of that, but not until I saw it in print. I do not remember precisely in what paper I saw it. I remember seeing it in some of them. I should have added, in stating the number of buildings burned down, that there was also a storehouse, belonging to the government, which was used by the Western Freedmen's Aid Commission as a storehouse for supplies for freedmen. The total amount of supplies and property belonging to the Western Freedmen's Aid Commission burned was four thousand five hundred and ninety-seven dollars and thirty-five cents. The storehouse belonged to the government.

4386. Please state what this Western Freedmen's Aid Commission is? It is an organization for the support, advancement, and education of the colored people of the South. It originally aided the destitute principally, but subsequently turned its attention more directly to the educational department.

4387. Who are the officers of that commission? Adam Poe, president; Dr. R. A. Rust, secretary. The headquarters of the commission are at Cincinnati.

4388. Where have this commission raised means to carry on this work? By benevolent appropriations all over the country, and also from England and Europe. They have had a large donation from Europe.

4389. What efforts have been made by the citizens of Memphis in the direction of educating colored people here? I know of none.

4390. Have efforts been made by parties here to induce them to take hold of the matter? Yes, sir; General Fisk and others have appealed to them, and done everything they could to interest them in this work.

4391. Did they succeed in exciting any interest? I do not know. There has none come to my knowledge, unless it is the interest taken recently in a colored orphan asylum. I believe the Episcopalians have taken some interest in that during the recent meeting of their convention.

4392. Was that interest general, or merely confined to one class of persons? I think it was confined to one class of persons.

By Mr. SHANKLIN:

4393. Are you here in the capacity of superintendent of colored schools, and also as a teacher, or only in one capacity? I am here in the capacity of agent for the Western Freedmen's Aid Commission, and also as superintendent of the colored schools of Memphis.

4394. You were not then engaged in teaching yourself? No, sir.

4395. Are you also a minister of the gospel? I am not.

4396. Are you connected with any religious denomination? Yes, sir; I am connected with the Union Congregational denomination of the city of Memphis.

4397. Is there not a school taught in the rear of this Gayoso House building? I believe there is.

4398. Who is the teacher of that school? The Rev. Mr. Hubbard. It is a private school.

4399. Do you know the character of the class of persons who were engaged in this recent riot and mob in Memphis? I do not, except what I have learned since the riot. I was sick and knew nothing of what was going on.

4400. From the information you have received, what was the class of persons who composed the mob? The class of persons was rather mixed, and extended from the lowest rebel in the city to some of the leading citizens.

4401. Can you mention some of the leading citizens who were engaged in it? I understand from reports that 'Squire Creighton had something to do with it, and also some persons, whose names I cannot tell, connected with some of the prominent stores on Main street, were engaged in it. I have heard Mayor Park's and other city officials' names mentioned.

4402. Then the principal part of those you consider leading citizens were city officials? They were. I think the policemen had a good deal to do with the riots.

4403. You have spoken of the number of the teachers of colored schools that were here. Do you know whether that class of persons have been engaged to some extent in teaching the negroes their civil and political rights under the laws of the country? I do not know of anything of the kind in any of our schools. I do not know how it is in the private schools. I have had nothing to do with them.

4404. Do you know of any instances of those teachers who have had charge of these colored schools delivering lectures here, in which they have taken occasion to teach the colored people as to their civil and political rights and what they ought to claim? No, sir; I do not know of any such instance.

4405. Will you state whether there were not some of these teachers who were boarding and living in colored families? I never heard of any.

4406. Is there not another class of persons here who are taking some control of colored people, persons who are preaching to colored congregations? Yes, sir.

4407. Do you know what has been the character of their teaching to these colored congregations, whether it has not been of a political character to some extent? I do not know. I have not attended their services, and am not aware what the character of their preaching has been.

4407½. Do you know of any demonstrations of hostility or unkindness to these teachers of colored schools by the old citizens of Memphis, men who formerly owned slaves and who own property here? No, sir; I do not know of any instance.

4408. Have not these manifestations of hostility, as a general thing, been made by the Irish draymen, hackmen, men who work about the wharves, laborers, and men of that sort, who come in competition with the negroes in their labor? I think there have been instances of insult from both classes, but more particularly from Irish policemen and Irish citizens. I have heard of instances where insults have come from a better class of citizens.

4409. Were they demonstrations of hostility? No, sir; merely insults, such as calling out on the street as they passed by and using insulting language. I do not know the nature of the language, but there have been teachers who have experienced it.

4410. Has there been any insult offered to you? No, sir. I have lived here three years and have never had any trouble or difficulty with any one. The transactions I have had with citizens here have been perfectly kind. I have never said or done anything to cause or make any trouble, and I have not had any trouble.

4411. Have you ever apprehended any danger for your safety? No, sir; I never apprehended danger anywhere.

4412. Did you apprehend danger to those persons who acted prudently and discreetly? I could not tell anything about that, for the reason that I was sick and do not know what danger there may have been.

4413. Do you know in what paper the anonymous communication handed you by the chairman was published? I do not remember.

4414. What paper published in Memphis do you generally read? I have read only the Memphis Post.

4415. State whether you did not see that article published in that paper. It may have been. The matter has now escaped my recollection.

4416. The Post is considered the radical paper of the city, is it not? It is so called by citizens here.

4417. Have you heard anything like a general expression of sentiment, on the part of the people of Memphis, in regard to the riots and cruelty practiced towards the colored people? No, sir.

4418. Have you conversed with many of them upon the subject? No. I have been very unwell most of the time since the riot, have conversed very little, and could not undertake to say what were the sentiments and feelings of the people of Memphis upon that subject.

By the CHAIRMAN:

4419. You have been asked in regard to teachings of the civil and political rights of the colored people. Is there anything in the Constitution and laws of the United States that prohibits teaching civil and political rights to colored people or white people? I do not know of anything. I would not hesitate myself to tell them what their civil and political rights were whenever called on.

4420. You have been asked in regard to where some of these teachers boarded. Where have they boarded, as far as you know? The white teachers have principally board provided by the Western Freedmen's Aid Commission, as a Teacher's Home. We had, at one time, eighteen of these teachers boarding at the "Home," but it was removed so far from some of the schools that several of them rented houses to live in. The Baptist Association had a "Home" of their own.

4421. Do you know of any of these teachers who board at the Gayoso House? Mr. Hubbard, the teacher of one of the private schools, told me he boarded at the Gayoso House.

By Mr. SHANKLIN:

4422. Is there a fixed salary for these teachers? Yes, sir. The Freedmen's Aid Commission teachers receive twenty dollars ($20) per month and their expenses paid. The United Presbyterian teachers get forty-five dollars ($45) per month and pay their own expenses. I do not know what the Baptist Association teachers get.

4423. What rate of tuition is paid by the colored scholars in your schools who pay? One dollar a month or less, according to their ability, and one half of them are admitted free. The object of making them pay at all is to encourage them to help themselves as much as possible.

Major General GEORGE STONEMAN recalled and examined.

By the CHAIRMAN:

4424. Since your report made to General Grant on the 12th of May, and since you were before the committee, from further examination into the matter of the riot, have you had any occasion to change or modify that report as to the extent of the riot, the number killed, the amount of property destroyed, and the acts of outrage perpetrated? In my report I was unable to state the number of killed and wounded, or the amount of property destroyed. Since then the testimony collected by the commission that I ordered to investigate the affair has been completed and was handed to me yesterday. I have not yet looked it fully over, nor has a summary of the proceedings been handed in. It will, I understand, be handed in to-morrow, containing a statement of the number killed and wounded and the amount of property destroyed. From what I have seen, the number of killed and wounded exceeds my expectations when I made my report to General Grant, largely.

4425. How in regard to the number of outrages perpetrated, houses burned and amount of property destroyed? The property destroyed has hardly come up to what I expected it would in value. That would not be a modification of my report, but an additional amount of information.

4426. From what has been disclosed since your previous examination, has the proportion of riotous proceedings been enlarged or increased from what you supposed at that time? It has been enlarged.

4427. From your observation and knowledge of the colored troops in Memphis, how did they compare with the ordinary run of white volunteer troops under like circumstances, stationed in the same way? I must say, in justice to the colored troops, that their conduct compared very favorably with that of the same number of white troops under similar circumstances.

4428. State if any steps within your knowledge have been taken by the civil authorities of Memphis to bring the perpetrators of these outrages to justice? None that I have heard of.

4429. Have the massacres been denounced in the newspapers here, or by any public meetings or collections of individuals, to your knowledge? They have not been denounced in the newspapers as I had hoped they would be, and as I thought they would be, nor has any public meeting been assembled to my knowledge, the object of which was to express condemnation of the outrages committed, though I have talked with several leading men here and advised such a course.

4430. Have you at any time, by written or verbal order, forbidden or prohibited the people of Memphis from meeting together for the purpose of denouncing the massacres and taking measures to vindicate the law and character of the city? I have not; further than that, I have encouraged it by my expressions of opinion in regard to it, and by advice to several of the newspaper editors or people connected with the press here, to use their papers for that object.

4431. What response has been made to that? They all acknowledged the propriety of it, but most of them told me they thought it was useless to try to get up any uniformity of expression.

4432. For what reasons did they state that it was useless? For the reason that there is such conflict of ideas and want of harmony among those who control the press here.

4433. Did you state to them what would be the effect of the riot upon the city unless these measures were taken? I did. I have told the people here repeatedly that they had better have taxed the city millions of dollars and thrown it into the Mississippi, than to have had such a thing happen, and that the best thing they could do was to have some expression of opinion such as would fully satisfy the country and world that such outrages were not countenanced by the people of Memphis.

4434. Has that been done? Not to my knowledge.

4435. Have you at any other time given any order or issued any proclamation or paper that could be construed into an order prohibiting persons from meeting or assembling together, other than that of May 3, given in your former testimony, which is as follows:

HEADQUARTERS DEPARTMENT OF TENNESSEE,
Memphis, Tennessee, May 3, 1866.

To the Mayor, City Council, and all civil authorities of the county of Shelby, and city of Memphis:

GENTLEMEN: Circumstances compel the undersigned to interfere with civil affairs in the city of Memphis. It is forbidden for any person, without the authority from these headquarters, to assemble together any posse, armed or unarmed, white or colored. This does not include the police force of the city, and will not so long as they can be relied upon as preservers of the peace.

I am, gentlemen, very respectfully, your obedient servant,

GEO. STONEMAN, *Major General Commanding.*

No, sir; I have not. Subsequent to this I have given no order or direction prohibiting the assembling together of the people of Memphis.

4436. Does this order, either by its language or any interpretation, mean that citizens shall not be permitted to get together for the purpose of denouncing these riotous proceedings or vindicating the character of the city? Certainly not; there was no such intention, and I cannot imagine how such an inference can be drawn from it.

4437. Do you believe, from what you have seen and heard, that the perpetrators of these outrages will be punished by the civil authorities? I can answer by stating I have written to my superior officers that I do not believe the perpetrators of the outrages during the Memphis riots will ever be punished unless the strong arm of the federal government is made use of for that purpose.

4438. Have any steps been taken, as far as you know, by the city authorities, to assess and collect the damages done by the mob? As far as I know there has not, and I have been informed by the mayor that no proceedings will be had for that purpose. In fact, he denies the responsibility of the city for them.

4439. What is your opinion, from your knowledge, of the loyalty and love of a majority of the people of Memphis towards the United States government? If a desire to return to the Union is considered loyalty, I should consider a large majority of the people were loyal that far. If a love for the Union and flag is considered loyalty, I look upon a large majority of the people of Memphis as not being loyal.

4440. How does the state of feeling in Memphis and in the entire State of Tennessee, as far as you know it, compare now with what it was a few months ago? In other words, is there a better or more loyal feeling to the government now than there was six months ago, or is there less loyal feeling and less love for the government and flag? I think at present there is not that disposition upon the part of the people of Tennessee to recognize existing facts that there was six months ago. It may be that the same feeling exists now as then, but they are more outspoken at any rate than they were then.

4441. Then the language they use now is less friendly to the government? As far as you can get it from the press, and from the meeting of the people for various purposes, I do not consider it as loyal, defined in that way—love for the Union—that it was six months ago, and I think it is growing worse and worse every day.

4442. Are there any emblems or signs of nationality displayed in the city, such as flags, &c.? I believe there are three points, and only three; one is over my headquarters, the building in which I reside, another one is over the Freedmen's Bureau, and I have seen another one in front of the building used as a printing office by the Memphis Post.

4443. Have you seen flags displayed over the printing offices of any other newspaper? No, sir; nor any other building.

4444. Have you seen it displayed at public meetings, places of amusement, the theatre, &c.? No, sir; I have seen it sometimes on steamboats that came down the river.

4445. How would a national flag be received if carried through the main streets of the town by the citizens? That would depend a great deal upon the object he had in carrying the flag. If a man started through the streets of Memphis to carry a flag simply as a species of bravado, he probably would be insulted and hooted at. If the flag was carried by an armed body of men, or any procession regularly gotten up, I doubt whether any overt act would be committed.

4446. Suppose a flag was carried unostentatiously by a citizen, without any particular object, how would it be received? It is very possible that by some irresponsible person he would be annoyed; I do not think he would be by the self-respecting class of the community here.

4447. Do you know how loyal sentiments and loyal airs are received at public places, such as theatres, here? I have had but one instance of that kind from which I could judge; that was at the theatre. I was not there myself, but it was reported to me that there was a call for national airs, and that such as Hail Columbia, the Star Spangled Banner, and Yankee Doodle, were hissed by the audience in the theatre. I wrote to the manager of the theatre, Mr. Thompson, informing him that if in the future national airs should be met by expressions of disapprobation by the audience, or if so-called confederate national airs should be received with applause by the audience, it would compel me to interfere, which I should regret very much to do. Since then I believe neither has been played in the theatre.

4448. Did you understand that rebel airs were received with applause? I have known them to be, and it was reported to me that national airs were hissed. I was satisfied of the fact, or I should not have written the letter.

4449. I will ask you your opinion, from your position here, with regard to the necessity of continuing United States troops in the city of Memphis, or in the State of Tennessee? I will answer that question by stating that I was called upon by General Thomas to report to him the number of troops I thought it necessary to be retained in the department of Tennessee, in order that the "public places" might be secured. I interpreted that to mean the public property. I replied, 500 at Chattanooga, 500 at Memphis, and 1,000 at Nashville, and this was supposing that all the rest of the State of Tennessee was turned over to the civil authorities. The amount of public property since then has been reduced very materially, and if I were called upon again I should reduce my estimate in like proportion. The country to be guarded has been reduced in each place. To execute orders which I receive from my superiors I should deem it absolutely necessary to have a force, under my special control, of United States troops. If the State is turned over to the civil authorities entirely, then of course no United States troops would be required. The execution of the laws would be left entirely to the civil authorities; I am called upon every day to use the federal troops for the execution of the laws of the State of Tennessee. Latterly I have pursued the policy of referring these applications to his excellency, Governor Brownlow, and getting his opinion upon the propriety of the application, preferring to not interfere with the the civil authorities of the State of Tennessee without his indorsement. In almost every instance the governor has returned these applications with his indorsement, stating it was absolutely necessary to carry into effect the laws of the State of Tennessee.

4450. By whom are these applications made to you? Sometimes by irresponsible parties, sometimes by self-constituted committees, and sometimes by the executive officers of the State, such as judges, sheriffs, &c.

4451. What do you believe would be the condition of the people here if all military control should be withdrawn? In the present state of affairs, and under the present circumstances, with the laws now in operation in Tennessee, I should consider the state of affairs would not be a good one by any means.

4452. Do you believe all classes of citizens in Memphis would be protected in their lives, liberty, and property, if the military forces were entirely withdrawn? Not with the present officers and executors of the civil law now in power.

4453. What, in your judgment, would have been the result of the recent riots and massacres had there been no United States troops in the city? I reported that I was led to believe that there would have been indiscriminate slaughter of the colored people by the excited mob, and I have no reason to change that report.

4454. Did there appear to be well-grounded apprehensions of violence to a certain class of white people here during the time of these riots and massacres? I am not prepared to say whether the apprehension was well grounded or not. There was an apprehension expressed upon the part of a good many that they would meet with violence at the hands of the mob. I am not prepared to say whether such would have been the fact or not.

4455. On what ground did these persons base that apprehension? They based it upon the ground that they were sympathizers with the negro population.

4456. Did they entertain such apprehensions of violence as induced some of them to leave the city? Many of them did, especially those who had been engaged in Christianizing and educating the colored people here.

4457. Were you of the opinion, from what they told you, and the circumstances you had heard, that they did a prudent act when they left? I told them when they came to me that they must be their own judge of what was best. I did not share myself in the apprehensions they were laboring under; I did not think they would be molested.

4458. What is now your opinion upon the subject, after having learned more fully the facts and extent of the riotous proceedings, as well as the spirit of the mob? I think upon the part of numbers of the mob, how many I am unable to say, there was a disposition to interfere with the class of people I have named, those engaged in the education of and in Christianizing the colored people.

4459. Were there any indications of violence towards the Freedmen's Bureau? Not to my personal knowledge.

4460. Was it deemed necessary to detail a guard to go to the Freedmen's Bureau? Upon the report of General Runkle, I sent him a guard to protect him and his bureau.

4461. Have you had an estimate made of the amount of government property that has been destroyed by this mob? The estimate has not been completed yet.

4462. In your previous examination you furnished the committee a communication you sent to General Thomas, touching an assessment of the damages done in the riot; have you taken any steps in that direction yet? I have not.

4463. For what reason? By direction of General Thomas, who stated that he could not give me instructions; that he had referred the whole thing to Washington for special instructions. I have heard nothing since.

By Mr. BROOMALL:

4464. Recalling your attention to the question about national emblems, what would be the effect upon the business of a merchant here who would put a United States flag over his door without giving any reason for it? I think he would make himself very conspicuous.

4465. What other effect do you think it would have? I do not know whether the papers would notice him or not. It is very likely that some of them would notice him disapprovingly.

4466. What effect would it have on his business? Would it be a profitable mode of advertising? I think it would bring people to him. It would bring him into notoriety, and draw trade to him on the principle that you and I read the Avalanche the first thing in the morning.

4467. Do you think he would be molested in any way? I think not. The Post has a flag out and has not been molested.

4468. Have you ever heard that the order you have given us here has been interpreted by any parties as prohibiting the meeting of any persons to denounce the mob? No, sir.

By Mr. SHANKLIN:

4469. Will you state whether your proclamation or communication dated at Memphis, May 3, 1866, addressed to the mayor, city council and civil authorities of Shelby county and the city of Memphis, was intended by you as a proclamation of martial law in the city of Memphis at that time ? No, sir ; it was not. It was intended to assume no further powers than were already delegated to me by the President of the United States.

4470. Was it intended to suspend any proceedings or prevent any proceedings upon the part of any citizens or civil authorities, except the police force from taking any steps for the purpose of stopping this mob riot which was going on ? In explanation I may say that from what I saw and what I heard, bodies of men were being collected together by various persons in whom I had little or no confidence, and in whom the people of Memphis had little or no confidence, ostensibly for the purpose of quelling what they called a negro riot. The parties assembled together were many of them of bad character and not fit to be trusted with the execution of the duties for which nominally they were collected. I considered that if it was necessary to assemble together any body for that purpose, I could do it through the means at my disposal better than anybody else, and I therefore issued that circular. I issued it, too, after a communication had been handed to me, signed by a number of the people here, which was passed in a body assembled together of respectable and reliable citizens, as follows :

MEMPHIS, *Tennessee, May* 3, 1866.

SIR : I am requested by the citizens composing a meeting held this morning at the court-house to lay before you the following resolutions which passed unanimously, and to request from you your co-operation in any measures that may be taken in pursuance thereof.

Respectfully, yours,

R. C. BRINKLEY.

Major General STONEMAN, *U. S. A.,*
Commanding Department of Tennessee.

RESOLUTIONS.

Resolved, That the mayor of the city and the sheriff of the county, together with the chairman of this meeting, (W. B. Greenlaw,) be authorized to summon a force of citizens of sufficient number, to act in connexion with the military, which shall constitute a patrol for the protection of the city, to serve such time as the mayor, sheriff and chairman of this meeting shall direct.

Resolved, That the chairman, (W. B. Greenlaw,) J. H. McMahon, S. P. Walker and R. C. Brinkley, be requested to wait upon General Stoneman and inform him of the proceedings of this meeting.

W. B. GREENLAW, *Chairman.*

R. C. BRINKLEY, *Secretary.*

Another meeting was had, and I was urged to take the whole control in my hands and set aside the civil authority here. I told them I did not choose to set aside the civil authority further than to issue such a notification to prevent the assembling of possees, armed or unarmed. I did not take the responsibility upon myself, as I informed them, and they knew, to set aside the authority of the mayor or any other civil functionary, further than to prevent them from assembling possees.

4471. Did not you afterwards issue an order to some of your subordinates to disperse any citizens, white or black, that might assemble except the police force of the city ? The night subsequent to the issuing of that circular—the night of the 3d—I directed the officers and soldiers stationed in different portions of the city, if they saw any collections of people that night, to disperse them.

4472. After the order was issued there was no such collection of people so far as you know ? There was not, and I had no occasion to reiterate the order.

4473. The mob was then dispersed and put down ? Yes. The people got together afterwards and had German fairs and Irish fairs, and they were not molested or interfered with in any way by myself or the military authorities.

4474. You stated in your testimony that in your report to General Thomas you had given it as your opinion that the perpetrators of these outrages during this riot, in the present condition of affairs, were not likely to be punished by the civil authorities. I would ask you whether that opinion was not based upon the inefficiency and want of qualification of the city authorities of Memphis ? It was based both upon the inefficiency of the civil authorities here and their indisposition to bring these men to punishment.

4475. And that opinion of yours was based alone upon these two grounds ? Yes, sir.

4476. I ask you whether, in your opinion, from your knowledge of the people of Memphis, if there were efficient, active, and properly qualified city officers here, with a disposition to maintain peace and quiet, it would be possible for them to do so without any military aid ? Certainly ; I think if there were proper officers and agents the civil laws might be maintained and enforced.

4477. You also stated in your report to General Thomas what number of troops you deemed necessary to protect United States property in Tennessee. With the laws now in operation in Tennessee, with the officers charged with the execution of these laws, do you think it safe to withdraw the military force of the general government? I must judge of the facts as they occur from day to day, and taking these facts into consideration, that I am called upon by the civil officers of the State of Tennessee to use military force for the execution of these laws, I may say I should not consider it safe to withdraw them.

4478. From what you know of the public sentiment in the State of Tennessee, if the laws of the State were just and the officers of the State were competent and prudent men, do you think then a military force would be necessary in order to preserve peace and quiet in the State of Tennessee? That is hardly a question proper for me, as a soldier, to investigate or answer. If the laws are just and proper and the executors are honest, it is fair to presume that there ought to be no trouble in Tennessee.

4479. My object is to ascertain whether, in your opinion, the state of feeling and the sentiments of the people of the State of Tennessee are such as that they would submit to the administration of laws of that general character and aid in enforcing them? Whatever the laws may be, experience goes to prove, in my humble estimation, that no community would be satisfied with laws enacted by a small minority, whether the character of these laws may be just or unjust. Such is human nature.

4480. From your knowledge and information in relation to the sentiments of the people of Tennessee, do you think there will be peace, security, and harmony among the people of the State so long as a very large portion of the people are denied political rights? There certainly will never be harmony.

4481. Do you think there will be peace without the aid of military force? Taking human nature as it is, my opinion is that there would not be peace. There is not now, as is shown by the fact that troops have to be used for the execution of the laws.

4482. You stated that public opinion, judging from the expressions you have heard, was not so much in favor of the execution of the laws of the United States as it was some months ago. I asked you whether there has not been some feeling excited and interest manifested in what the people consider a harsh policy exercised towards those people who had participated in the rebellion, both by the State government and general government? Those who had participated in the rebellion no doubt would have been a great deal better satisfied had no steps or measures been taken to make treason odious, and had they been permitted to come back on terms of equality with everybody else, and by everybody else I mean those who differed with them in sentiment.

4483. So far as you have been able to learn the sentiments and feelings of those people in the State of Tennessee who have been engaged in the rebellion, was it a submission to the issues of the war and a determination to acquiesce in that decision, or has it been of a rebellious disposition—a disposition to not submit to the results of the war? I was in East Tennessee at the time of the surrender of Lee's and Johnston's armies, and a large proportion of the people of Tennessee who had been engaged in the rebellion passed through East Tennessee on their way home. At that time they appeared to be satisfied with the results of all their efforts, and were willing to go home and keep out of sight if they were let alone. Subsequently elections have been held, and these people have been instructed by office-seekers to believe that they had rights in addition to privileges. At first they were satisfied with privileges. Now they are not satisfied unless they have rights.

4484. What rights are they seeking? The right to vote.

4485. Has there been any manifestation upon their part, so far as you have been able to learn, to restore the institution of slavery? No, sir. I have never been so unfortunate, or fortunate, as to be thrown into company with any individual in Tennessee who was crazy enough to advance the idea that slavery could under any circumstances be restored in this State.

4486. So far as you have observed the sentiments of this people, have they surrendered the doctrine they once claimed of the right of secession as one of the issues settled by the war? They are willing, apparently, to accept the result after having appealed to the last high court of nations.

4487. That is, arms? Yes, sir. The principle of secession, as I learn through the newspapers of Tennessee, is still advocated by newspaper editors here. They say that to admit they were wrong would be to stultify themselves. They are willing to admit they were mistaken, but not that they were wrong. This I get from newspapers I receive from different parts of Tennessee.

4488. Did they surrender that as a right in consequence of the result of the war? They surrendered it upon the principle that "might makes right." I do not believe, myself, that the feeling of the people of Tennessee in regard to the principle of secession has changed any more than mine would have done had I been the conquered party. They are willing, a large majority of them, to accept the issue, to recognize the facts as they exist; but they are not willing to say they were wrong, or that they have committed treason and should be punished.

4489. In your opinion, from your knowledge of the people of Tennessee, will the feeling of dissatisfaction, which you say has been increasing for the last two or three months, in consequence of being denied the right of suffrage and other political rights, continue to increase so long as that right is denied to them, or will it be given up and acquiesced in ? Before answering that question I will say that probably the committee are well aware of a peculiar state of affairs existing in Tennessee, particularly in regard to the strong sectional feeling that exists between the different divisions of the State. The people of East Tennessee were strongly Union, whereas the people of western and Middle Tennessee were as strongly rebels. When the war closed there was a feeling of proscription raised in both sections. In East Tennessee the rebels that returned were proscribed and warned to leave the country. Many of them were driven out and came to Middle and West Tennessee, particularly the latter. In turn the Union people of this section were persecuted, and many of them left West and Middle Tennessee. This feeling I, as the commanding officer of the department, tried to curb and check, but the animosity which originally existed between the Union people and rebels was heightened and intensified by these irritants and counter-irritants, and I am under the impression that the feeling between the Union people and the rebellious portion of the people of East Tennessee is now more bitter than between the same classes in any State of the Union. This feeling has been intensified by the elections that have taken place. The contests between the advocates of men in different sections of Tennessee have been more bitter than they have been in any of the other southern States. And I am under the impression that this bitterness of feeling will continue to increase from day to day, judging of the future by the past.

By the CHAIRMAN :

4490. In the order which you gave—I think you said to your command, on the third day of the riots, or Thursday—you directed them to prevent the gathering together of crowds or knots of people on the corners of the streets. Did that order have any reference to meetings for the purpose I have stated ? Not in the least ; nor was it so construed by the people of Memphis.

4491. It was simply to prevent further outrages by the mob ? It was, as I have already stated in my testimony.

4492. In answer to questions put by Mr. Shanklin in regard to what the state of things might be in Tennessee in a certain emergency, did you have any reference to the present state of things ? No, sir. I declined to say anything in regard to the civil authorities of the State of Tennessee.

4493. And your answer to that question has no reference to the state of things now existing in the State of Tennessee, which renders it necessary for a military force to be kept here ? No, sir. As I said in my answer to that, the necessity which compels the retention of a military force here does not depend upon the laws or the executors of the laws, but upon the conduct of the people, except in one or two individual instances : as, for instance, in the city of Memphis, where I replied I considered the disorders as much as anything incident to the executors of the city laws here.

4494. Mr. Shanklin has asked you about the feeling on account of the disfranchisement of rebels in this State, and you have spoken of the probability of that feeling being increased instead of being diminished. What would tend to an increase of that feeling ? Keeping the outs out. It will increase as long as the outs are kept out and the ins in.

4495. Will it not increase until the rebels of Tennessee, being vastly in the majority in the State, have the entire control of the State ? In my opinion it will increase until the rebels, as you term them, or the outs, have a voice in the election of officers. Whether they will ever be able to get control or not I am unable to say.

4496. Do you, or do you not, believe, from your knowledge of the State of Tennessee, that a large majority of the voting population were in sympathy with the rebellion ? I believe that a majority of the people of Tennessee now have been in sympathy with the rebellion ; but originally, before the rebellion broke out, I do not think a majority of the people of Tennessee were in sympathy with the rebellion. I judge of that by the vote given in the State.

4497. Do you believe this agitation on the part of the people of the State will go on and increase until they can get control, if possible, of the State government and the offices ? I think it would be diminished very much by removing the restrictions so as to allow the voting population to be in the majority.

4498. You mean that if those men who have been disfranchised as having been in the rebellion could get to vote, they being in the majority in the State, the bad feeling, so far as they are concerned, would diminish ? Certainly.

4499. What then do you believe would be the condition, if that class of men should get control of the State by being enfranchised, of the Union men who now hold control of the State? They would be in the same condition as all minorities are.

4500. Would they not, in your judgment, from your knowledge of the state of feeling in Tennessee, be in a much worse condition than minorities are generally in? I do not think they would be. Although I know there is fear by some persons, I do not and cannot believe there would be any oppression of Union people.

4501. Do you gather that from the tone of the public press? From a portion of the public press, and from conversation with people of the State.

4502. Is not the tone of the great majority of the public press intensely hostile and bitter towards the present governor and legislature of Tennessee? Yes, sir; I think so.

4503. Do not you think the people of the State partake to a greater or less degree of this feeling? Yes, sir; but I do not think the press in Tennessee are any more bitter than a portion of the press in the North is against the administration of affairs in their States. I may say, in justice to the press of Tennessee, that the most bitter articles I have read have been extracts from northern papers they have copied.

4504. Have you not read articles of extreme denunciation and bitterness against the present legislature of this State from the press of the State? Yes, sir; I read them every day.

By Mr. BROOMALL:

4505. You have said that upon the surrender of the rebel armies the returned rebels were satisfied to go home and, being let alone, take no part in the government of affairs. You have also said that state of feeling among them has gone out, and that they are now demanding the right to vote. To what do you attribute that change of feeling? To the teachings of demagogues, office-seekers, and a portion of the press.

4506. Has it not been, to some extent, owing to the idea that they would be countenanced in their demand and aided in it by the administration?

WITNESS. Do you mean by the administration of the President of the United States?

Mr. BROOMALL. Yes.

WITNESS. I believe they looked upon him as their friend.

4507. Has not that been one of the causes that produced this change of demand and feeling on the part of the rebels? I do not know as I could answer that question satisfactorily to myself or anybody else.

4508. Then all you can say is, you look upon the administration as being on their side? Yes; as being friendly disposed to them.

4509. You have said, in answer to a question, that if the laws of Tennessee were just, and the executors of the laws prompt in executing them, the troops might be removed? I think I said if the laws were just, and the administrators competent and honest, the troops might be removed, so far as Memphis was concerned.

4510. The question of enforcing civil laws depends, does it not, upon the punishment of the guilty, and the punishment of crime on the character of jurors? From what you know of the population of Memphis, would an unbiased jury be likely to be obtained in any case arising out of the recent riots, the jurors to be drawn from that class of persons which usually furnish the material for jurors, it being understood, of course, that one juror may stand out against eleven? I think the chances are that the man would escape punishment.

4511. It would require, then, a change of public sentiment here to furnish proper jurors, would it not? I think so.

4512. If you were to throw open the ballot-box and jury-box to returned rebels, would it improve either list in respect to their disposition to do justice in a case where the rights of negroes were concerned? If I wanted justice meted out to the incendiaries and murderers in the recent riots, I should prefer to go to the returned rebels here than to the class of people from whom juries are now drawn. I have heard but one expression on the part of paroled rebels, and that has been condemnation of the recent riots. I have talked with this people as I have met them about town here, and I get it also from the Union people that the returned rebels here have not, to any extent, favored the disturbances that have taken place.

By the CHAIRMAN:

4513. You have spoken of the opinions of the returned rebels, and also of the character of the newspapers of this city, and you have said that none of the papers have published articles in condemnation of these riotous proceedings. Can you tell by whom these papers are edited—whether by paroled rebel officers, or whether by Union men? Are there not two or three paroled rebel officers who are editors of the Avalanche, and one or two paroled rebel officers connected with the Argus and Appeal? I believe there are paroled rebel officers in connexion with the papers you mention; but in conversation with these men they have expressly condemned these outrages committed.

4514. But they have not condemned them in their newspapers? They have not been consistent in their newspapers.

4515. Then, while their conversation privately has been in condemnation of the riots, they have not given any public condemnation through their newspapers? They have not given that condemnation they gave in private, which I urged them to give in public, and which they should have given.

4516. How do you explain that? In one or two instances they told me they were afraid to publish in their papers what they had written to northern newspapers. Two of the editors told me that.

4517. Did you understand that the public sentiment here was so overwhelmingly in favor of the rioters that they dared not confront it by coming out boldly in their papers? I was led to believe that they thought it would make their papers unpopular and unsalable.

By Mr. SHANKLIN:

4518. In response to a question asked by the chairman of the committee you speak of manifestations of hostility on the part of the people of Tennessee. I ask you whether that hostility, so manifested, has not been against the measures which were advocated by a particular party, rather than against individuals? I do not recollect any expressions of opinion personally hostile to the civil officers of Tennessee. I take it for granted that it is against their measures.

4519. Have you seen any indications on the part of those who have been heretofore in sympathy with the rebellion of an intention, if they got into power, to disfranchise or oppress those who differed with them in sentiment? I have seen, through the press, an intention upon the part of some newspapers to proscribe Union men.

4520. In what particular? Socially and in a business point of view.

4521. In a political point of view? In a political point of view, I take it for granted that they would proscribe them; that is, that they would not nominate or elect them to office.

4522. Have you understood they would disfranchise them or deny them any political rights? No, sir. I have never heard the subject mooted of disfranchising the Union people.

4523. If the elective franchise was extended to all male white citizens of the State o Tennessee of the proper age, and with the proper residence, and it should turn out that these men of southern sympathies should not be in a majority in the State, and could not control the elections, do you think they would still acquiesce in the result, although the other party remained in the majority? I think so. I do not know of anything more they could ask.

4524. Do you know how the sheriff, under the laws of Tennessee, selects a jury? Whether he has the discretion to summon such men as he thinks will make competent jurymen, or whether they are selected in a different manner? I cannot inform you of the manner in which they are selected.

4525. If the sheriff of Shelby county and Memphis, under the laws of Tennessee, had the power to select such men as, in his judgment, would make impartial and suitable jurymen, do you think the materials in Memphis are such that a prudent, discreet sheriff could find a jury who would mete out justice to parties engaged in these riots? I think so.

By the CHAIRMAN:

4526. I understand your answer to the question just asked to mean that there are twelve men in Memphis who, if appointed upon a jury, would agree to punish these rioters? I most certainly think they could be found. It would be a terrible state of affairs if they could not get that many.

By Mr. SHANKLIN:

4427. By the exercise of ordinary discretion and prudence on the part of the sheriff, if he had the power, do you think there would be any difficulty in getting proper jurors to try any cases growing out of this riot? I think he would find some difficulty in getting an unprejudiced jury who would do equal justice to white and black in these particular cases of the recent riots.

By the CHAIRMAN:

4528. What is the social status of Union men here in the city of Memphis? I do not know anything about the social status here. I have not had an opportunity of judging personally.

4529. What is the social status of the regular officers of the United States army in the city of Memphis? I do not know of any regular officer of the United States army, within my acquaintance, who occupies any social position here. I mean, who goes into society.

4530. Do you know of an officer of the United States army who has, at any time, been received into society here ? I do not.

4531. And this applies to yourself as well as others ? Yes, sir.

By Mr. BROOMALL :

4532. Would the officers of the army be disposed to be social with the citizens here, if they were invited or encouraged ? Judging from my own feelings, I should think there would be a diffidence upon the part of officers in mixing with society here. I do not think it would be very agreeable.

4533. On what ground ? I do not think they would be as welcome as they would wish to be, or as they have been accustomed to be.

By the CHAIRMAN:

4534. Were any of the soldiers under your command connected with the riot ; and if so, how, and at what time, and what has been done with the parties concerned ? And, if tried and convicted, please furnish a copy of the record of conviction and sentence. On the 4th day of May, 1866, charges and specifications were presented to me by Captain A. W. Allyn, sixteenth infantry, commanding the post of Memphis, Tennessee, against a corporal and two more of his command. The order convening the court was issued on the 5th, and the men were tried the same day. The offences for which they were tried were robbery, and were committed on the morning of the 4th, about 11 a. m. The findings and sentences will be seen by reference to General Orders No. 31, from my headquarters, which I now hand you. The men are now undergoing sentence in Nashville. Two other men of the same command were tried by the same court mentioned for robbery committed on the evening of the 6th. The findings and sentences are set forth in the order before referred to, and they are now undergoing sentences in Nashville. It will be seen that all these men were tried for offences committed subsequent to the riot. Captain Allyn informs me that he knows of no man of his command having been connected with the riots, and none were reported absent from the command during the riots.

The order referred to by witness is as follows :

[General Orders No. 31.]

HEADQUARTERS DEPARTMENT OF TENNESSEE,
Memphis, Tennessee, May 15, 1866.

I. Before a general court-martial which convened at Fort Pickering, Memphis, Tennessee, in pursuance of Special Orders No. 89, from headquarters department of Tennessee, dated Memphis, Tennessee, May 5, 1866, and of which Captain A. W. Allyn, sixteenth United States infantry, was president, were arraigned and tried :

1st. Corporal James Gore, company G, second battalion, sixteenth United States infantry.

CHARGE I.—Conduct prejudicial to good order and military discipline.

Specification 1.—In this: that he, Corporal James Gore, company G, second battalion, sixteenth United States infantry, being in charge of the guard stationed at the commissary warehouse at Memphis, Tennessee, and while returning to the camp of his regiment, at Fort Pickering, Tennessee, did fail to keep his guard together, and did permit the members thereof to straggle without order or discipline.

All this at Memphis, Tennessee, on or about the 4th day of May, 1866.

Specification 2.—In this: that he, Corporal James Gore, company G, second battalion, sixteenth United States infantry, being in charge of the guard at the commissary warehouse at Memphis, Tennessee, and while returning to the camp of his regiment, at Fort Pickering, Tennessee, did, without authority, halt a hack, and under the pretence of searching for arms, did countenance and assist certain members of his guard in robbing David Kane and William Davis, discharged soldiers of the third United States colored artillery, (heavy,) who were riding in said hack, of money to the amount of fifty-five dollars and seventy-five cents, ($55 75,) the property of the said David Kane and William Davis.

All this at Memphis, Tennessee, on or about the 4th day of May, 1866.

CHARGE II.—Robbery.

Specification.—In this: that he, Corporal James Gore, company G, second battalion, sixteenth United States infantry, did, with Private James Farrett, company A, and Private Thomas Gibbons, company H, second battalion, sixteenth United States infantry, feloniously, forcibly, and violently take from David Kane, a discharged soldier of the third United States colored artillery, (heavy,) money to the amount of forty-five dollars, ($45,) the property of the said David Kane, and from William Davis, a discharged soldier of the third United States colored artillery, (heavy,) money to the amount of ten dollars and seventy-five cents, ($10 75,) the property of the said William Davis, and with the intent to appropriate the said sums of money to their own use.

All this at Memphis, Tennessee, on or about the 4th day of May, 1866.

To all of which charges and specifications the accused pleaded, Not guilty.

Findings, Guilty.

Sentence.—And the court do therefore sentence him, the said Corporal James Gore, company G, second battalion, sixteenth United States infantry, to be reduced to the ranks, to be dishonorably discharged the service of the United States, with loss of all pay and allowances now due, or to become due, and to be confined at hard labor in such penitentiary as the commanding general may direct, for the period of ten (10) years.

2d. Private John Farrett, company A, second battalion, and Private Thomas Gibbons, company H, second battalion, sixteenth United States infantry.

CHARGE.—Robbery.

To which the accused each and severally pleaded, Not guilty.

Findings, Guilty.

Sentence.—And the court do therefore sentence them, the said Privates John Farrett, company A, second battalion, sixteenth United States infantry, and Thomas Gibbons, company H, second battalion, sixteenth United States infantry, each and severally to be dishonorably discharged the service of the United States, with loss of all pay and allowances now due or to become due, except the just dues of the laundress and sutler, and to be confined in such penitentiary as the commanding general may direct, for the period of ten (10) years.

3d. Privates Frank Averill, company C, second battalion, sixteenth United States infantry, and John Smith, company G, second battalion, sixteenth United States infantry.

CHARGE.—Robbery.

Specification.—In this: that they, Privates Frank Averill, company C, and John Smith, company G, second battalion, sixteenth United States infantry, did feloniously, forcibly, and violently take from A. J. Lewis, a citizen of Memphis, Tennessee, one pocket-book containing twenty-one dollars ($21) in currency of the United States, and various other articles, the property of the said A. J. Lewis, and with the intent to appropriate the same to their own use.

All this at Memphis, Tennessee, on or about the 6th day of May, 1866.

To which charges and specifications the accused each and severally pleaded, Not guilty.

Findings, Guilty.

Sentence.—And the court do therefore sentence them, the said Privates Frank Averill, company C, second battalion, sixteenth United States infantry, and John Smith, company G, second battalion, sixteenth United States infantry, each and severally to be dishonorably discharged the service of the United States, with loss of all pay and allowances now due or to become due, excepting four dollars and fifty cents, ($4 50,) and the just dues of the laundress and sutler, and to be confined at hard labor in such penitentiary as the commanding general may direct, for the period of ten (10) years.

Before a general court-martial, which convened at Fort Pickering, Tennessee, in pursuance of Special Orders No. 89, current series, from headquarters department of Tennessee, dated Memphis, Tennessee, May 5, 1866, and of which Captain Thomas J. Durnin, sixteenth United States infantry, was president, was arraigned and tried:

Private Philip Duly, company H, second battalion, sixteenth United States infantry.

CHARGE.—Robbery.

Specification.—In this: that he, Private Philip Duly, company H, second battalion, sixteenth United States infantry, did feloniously steal, take, and carry away from the knapsack of Corporal Andrew Ness, company D, second battalion, sixteenth United States infantry, the following articles of clothing: Three (3) government shirts, one (1) pair of drawers, and one (1) pair of stockings, of the total value of nine dollars and four cents, ($9 04,) the property of the said Corporal Ness.

All this at Nashville, Tennessee, on or about the 27th day of April, 1866.

To which charges and specifications the accused pleaded, Not guilty.

Findings, Guilty.

Sentence.—And the court do therefore sentence him, the said Private Philip Duly, company H, second battalion, sixteenth United States infantry, to be dishonorably discharged the service of the United States, with the loss of all pay and allowances now due or to become due, excepting the just dues of the laundress and sutler, and to be confined in such penitentiary as the commanding general may direct, for the period of three (3) years.

III. The proceedings and findings in the foregoing cases are approved, and the sentences in the cases of Corporal James Gore, company G, and Privates Thomas Gibbons and Philip Duly, company H, Frank Averill, company C, and John Smith, company G, second battalion, sixteenth United States infantry, are confirmed, and will be carried into execution by the proper officers.

So much of the pay and allowances due Privates Averill and Smith by the government as is not stopped by the sentence of the court, amounting to four dollars and fifty cents,

18

($4 50,) to each and severally will be stopped against the pay of the said Privates Averill and Smith, and this amount, nine dollars, ($9,) will be delivered to A. J. Lewis, citizen of Memphis, Tennessee, to make good to the said A. J. Lewis the balance of the money taken from him by the said Privates Averill and Smith.

In the case of Private John Farrett, company A, second battalion, sixteenth United States infantry, the sentence of confinement, upon the recommendation of the court that tried the prisoner, to mercy, and its statement that he "is apparently an inoffensive person, and was led into this difficulty by old and designing villains," is commuted from ten (10) to three (3) years' imprisonment. The remainder of the sentence is confirmed, and will be carried into effect by the proper officers.

The penitentiary at Nashville, Tennessee, is designated as the place of confinement, whither the prisoners will be sent under guard by the commanding officer of the post of Memphis, Tennessee.

IV. The general court-martial convened by Special Orders No. 89, current series, from these headquarters, is hereby dissolved.

By command of Major General Stoneman:

WM. L. PORTER,
Assistant Adjutant General.

Brevet Brigadier General BENJAMIN P. RUNKLE sworn and examined.

By the CHAIRMAN :

4535. Please state your position. I am lieutenant-colonel of the twenty-first regiment Veteran Reserve Corps, brevet brigadier general of volunteers, and superintendent of the Bureau of Refugees, Freedmen, and Abandoned Lands for the district of Memphis, embracing western Tennessee.

4536. Under whose command are you? Under the command of Brevet Major General Fisk.

4537. What are the duties devolved upon you? To look after the interests of freedmen in West Tennessee ; to see that the orders of my superior officers are carried out in good faith ; that the freedmen are protected in their rights, and are made to fulfil the obligations devolving upon them under the orders and laws relating to them.

4538. Is the following paragraph a part of the instructions of General Fisk to you ? "The duties devolving upon you as the agent of this bureau are delicate, difficult and important. Upon their proper discharge materially depends the tranquillity and consequent prosperity of your community. See that simple justice is done, and follow after the things that make for peace." Yes, sir ; that is always what I have understood to be my duty, and having seen the importance of it, I have learned to appreciate it.

4539. Were you in Memphis during the recent riots ? I was in the city of Memphis ; sometimes in my office ; sometimes on the streets ; sometimes in the riotous districts, and a part of the time at my home, a mile and a quarter in the country.

4540. Were there any premonitions of this riot, so far as you know ? Not of this riot exactly at that time. I had seen indications of bad feeling, but did not expect they would culminate in any such riot and butchery as occurred. I always thought there was an antagonism on the part of a class of people here, both against the negroes and those they term their friends.

4541. After being ordered here, how did you get that idea ? I was coming with my wife on the cars from Nashville here. I was in company with a number of gentlemen, who had as I supposed from their talk, been members of a mass convention that had just been held in Nashville. There were one or two from Arkansas, one from Panola, Mississippi, and others from Memphis. I was in citizen's clothes, and unknown to them. From their talk I was led to believe there was a very bad feeling in Memphis, both towards the freedmen and persons they termed "Yankees."

4542. What was the tenor of their conversation ? They talked about making some arrangements for cleaning out a certain class of people in Memphis. They were all "judges," "colonels," or "generals," from the titles they gave to each other. One of them remarked, "We will never stop until the last one of them goes out or goes under." Of course I understood that to mean "leave town or be killed." They mentioned some names, and talked about having a meeting. I heard one say to another, "Do not forget to come up to-night." They were on their way to Memphis. I could not tell where the meeting was going to be. One of them said, "I have got no country ; I have nothing to live for ; I don't care a damn ; patriotism is played out." Another said he "thought that was going a little too far." One said, "We have got it all fixed right over at Nashville." Another said, "It may be they will not stick up to the work when they get sober ; we had to get them pretty drunk before they would agree to secede and break up the quorum.'' When I came to the river I had to pick up my sword, and they seemed astonished to find I was an officer. I heard them wondering among themselves which army I belonged to, and remarked that I was wounded and must be a soldier. I heard them say they could buy the bureau for a bottle of whiskey, which was a remark of interest to me, as I was coming here in connexion with the bureau. They seemed to disappear from the hotel about 8 o'clock. I was led to suppose from this conversation that there might be some general understanding, not peaceable in its character.

4542½. State what was the first knowledge you had of the riot, and when you received it. I was coming out of my office on the evening the riot began, talking with one of my officers about the success we had had in carrying out General Fisk's order relative to vagrants, &c., when I saw a large number of people coming up the street. Some were on horseback, some were policemen, having their batons in their hands, and some had their hands on their pistols. They were followed by so large a crowd of people, that I concluded there was something serious. I went back on Main street, walked on through the city and went home. The next morning I came in. During the day it was ominously still. There did not seem to be as much business going on as usual. This was on Wednesday. I began to think there was something the matter. In the afternoon there was firing. In the forenoon, however, some Union man asked me to go with him to see General Stoneman. He said that General Stoneman must turn out the military, and that I must get a guard over the bureau headquarters or they would be burned down. I remarked that they would not burn anything that the United States flag floated over. He said the United States flag had very little consideration with these people, and that I should have a guard. Then the freedmen began to come by dozens and by hundreds to my headquarters for protection. I could do nothing for them, for I had not a soldier at my command. I went down and asked General Stoneman if he would not give me troops under my own personal command, to go down there and protect those people. I had been waited on by a committee composed of certain prominent and respectable colored men, who told me their people were being murdered in South Memphis, and wanted me to protect them. When I arrived at General Stoneman's, as he came down stairs, I heard him tell his adjutant general, Major Porter, to send a detachment of men to South Memphis, and patrol between Beal and South streets, and to direct Colonel Kappner to keep all the negro troops in the fort. I saw then that he had made a disposition of the troops he had. The general told me he had not many troops, and that he had a large amount of public property to guard ; that a considerable part of the troops he had were not reliable ; that they hated the negroes too. I asked him if I should make a fight at my headquarters, or allow the mob to burn it down. He said, '' The United States flag floats over your headquarters, and I will protect them,'' and he sent ten men down there. When I went back to my office, these freedmen still continued to come. I told them I had no troops, and could not protect them ; to go back to their houses, have nothing to do with the riot, and if the government was not able to protect them, it would at least redress their wrongs after the riot was over. While I was on the street that day, I saw men with muskets, pistols, and shot guns, on foot and on horseback, driving around like mad. I began to think it was a very serious business. That night they commenced burning buildings. I had no idea they would do that. I had under my charge some dozen young ladies out at what we call the '' Teachers' Home.'' There were three or four gentlemen there, and among them Major General Kiddoo, whose sister was there. My wife was also there. The next morning after I had seen all those buildings burning, and found out what had been done ; after I had seen men riding up and down calling upon men to turn out to the assistance of the mob, and had seen them turn out ; after I had been down to South Memphis, and had pistols drawn on me, seeing that my own life was in danger, and that I could do no good, I concluded the next thing they would do would be to attack the negro teachers. Doctor Bailey came to me and told me he had heard a reliable statement that such was the intention, and I said to the ladies who were there that I thought they had better leave the city. General Kiddoo said his sister should not stay there for fifty thousand dollars, and that I had better send my wife away, which I did. I then took the ten men I had in my office. Persons would go by my office, make a reconnoissance of it and go away. The soldiers I had were all concealed. I made no display. That night a good many citizens of the place, and some negroes who were afraid to be at large, came to my office, were furnished with arms, and if the mob made us a visit, we intended they should go away with more than they came for.

4543. Did you hear any threats made against the building ? I heard them on Thursday night say, '' Now we'll clean out that damned Freedmen's Bureau.'' That was when they burned the house below, by Caldwell's Hall.

4544. Do you know of their making any threats to burn the Memphis Post ? I had heard of such an intention, and my information was confirmed by sworn testimony before the commission with which I have been connected. While I was on the street, I heard them say '' There go the God damned nigger teachers and God damned Yankees.''

4545. Was any violence offered to you? Nothing but drawing revolvers upon me to my back ; I turned twice and said, " Do you want to shoot me ?" I went with my wife down where they were burning Rankin's schoolhouse ; a big fellow who looked like a countryman, pulled out a revolver to my back ; I turned round and said, " Do you want to shoot me ?" I have had revolvers pulled to my back in this house, and I have had persons put their hands to their revolvers a dozen times in the street here ; they were afraid to shoot me ; that is the reason they have not done it.

4546. Have you heard of any admissions made by men who were in the crowds of an intention on the part of the crowd to burn the Memphis Post? I heard of that in testimony given upon oath.

4547. Who made that admission? M. C. Galloway.

4548. What did he admit? That he was walking down street ; that he saw a large number of people at some engine-house on Jefferson street ; that the crowd cheered for Galloway, Cluskey, and the Avalanche ; that they took him on their shoulders and said, "Let's burn the Post ;" that he advised them not to do it, as it would injure him and injure them ; that about that time a negro came along ; they began shooting at the negro, and he and Captain Cluskey walked off.

4549. Did you see any other or further acts of violence during these days of the mob than you have stated? I saw no man killed ; I saw the people on the street.

4550. Since you have been here in charge of the bureau, what has been the general conduct of the freedmen? The conduct of the freedmen in West Tennessee is all that could be expected under the circumstances ; there have been exceptions, but as a general rule, their conduct, including those in Memphis, has been good.

4551. What kind of counsel have you given the freedmen, in your capacity as superintendent of the bureau? I have always counselled them that liberty meant the right to work for themselves, to get their own living, and live honestly as white people do ; I have always counselled them that they had no right to put themselves on an equality with white people, nor to presume to do anything of the kind ; whenever they have made contracts, I have told them, and instructed my officers to tell them, that they must fulfil their contracts ; that they must always at least work ten hours a day, and, under certain circumstances, more than that ; that they must be obedient to their employers, and peaceable ; that on the other hand their employers were bound to treat them well ; to furnish them with healthy rations and good quarters, and I would see that their employers paid them ; but that it was also my business to see that they performed their contracts.

4552. How were they getting along under the system you adopted? In the city of Memphis there was a manifest improvement from the time I came here until the riot broke out ; Circular No. 9, issued by General Fisk, had been carried out except the clause relating to vagrants ; I had been trying to carry that out, and had succeeded in a very good degree, though, having no men at my command, it was a very difficult thing to do ; the cabins of these people had been pretty generally cleaned and whitewashed inside and out ; a good many had gone into the country, and those remaining here were doing very well ; they had organized a sanitary commission of their own people ; I had collected from them as much as $2,000, which was to be expended by them in caring for their own poor, burying their own dead, &c.; and I had begun to congratulate myself that I could see daylight in the city of Memphis.

4553. What has been the effect of the riot upon them? It has put them back further than they were when I began ; they have lost all confidence, I may say, in everything ; they will not heed my counsel ; when they come to me they say, " You are the man we expected to protect us ;" I had no troops and could not do anything, and they have had very little confidence in me or in the government since that ; I have been doing what little I could to restore it, but I have not succeeded as well as I hoped to have done.

4554. What have been the causes of the riot in your opinion? There have been a good many influences at work which have tended in that direction, and one of the most important has been the course of the press here ; certain papers have published articles which have tended to excite the passions of the lower class of whites against the negroes and their supposed friends, although I do not know that they are really any better friends than a great many others; they have made a crusade against what they term radical Yankees, singling out many of them by name ; they have taught the people to believe that the negroes had no rights ; then there was a standing feud between the negroes and the Memphis police, which is the worst police I ever saw in any city ; their hatred was particularly against the soldiers connected with the 3d heavy artillery ; I do not think the feeling extended to the entire police force, nor to all the negro soldiers, but the feeling that existed had a good deal to do in starting and carrying on the riot ; there was also a conflict of labor between the Irish hack-drivers, dray-drivers, porters, laborers, &c., and the negroes employed in the same occupations ; there was a good deal of bitterness felt upon the part of the Irish, from the fact that these southern gentlemen preferred to hire negro servants ; my wife has been insulted on the streets by them with such expressions as "Damn you, if you prefer a nigger, take him."

4555. Was this feeling you mention of hatred on the part of the Irish, inflamed by the newspapers? It undoubtedly was; they were taught more or less to believe that the negroes had no rights; a policeman could not arrest a negro without knocking him in the head before he carried him to the station-house, while if he arrested a white man he would carry him there in a decent way; many negroes were arrested and taken up when they had done nothing; they were abused a great deal; the natural tendency of that was to make the low class of the population believe they could abuse a negro with impunity; I have known negroes to be shot here, and it seemed impossible for me to get justice done; there was an instance just before I came here of a man who, seemingly for mere amusement, killed three; he was let out on $2,000 bail, and nothing has been done with him since.

4556. What other cases do you know of like violence? Their name is legion; such affairs as knocking down and beating were facts of every-day occurrence almost.

4557. What is the general state of feeling on the part of the people of Memphis towards the negroes and towards the Yankees? There are a class of people in Memphis I call politicians, who, as far as I can judge, have no principle whatever; they go for what is popular; they like the negro as far as the negro can be made to answer their purposes; they have before them the constant bugbear of negro equality, and that sort of thing; the lower class of people hate the negroes most bitterly; taking the community together, the feeling is decidedly antagonistic to the negro, though I should except a large class of people who had nothing to do with this riot, and who served in the rebel army.

4558. What, in your judgment, would have been the final result of this riot and massacre, had there been no troops or United States military authorities here? I cannot say I think the military authorities stopped the riot.

4559. What did stop it? I think they were rather tired out; it has been aptly expressed by a gentleman who said, "They had filled their graveyards."

4560. What would be the result of taking away all the troops here, upon all classes of men? Would the majority of the people be protected in their lives and property? My answer to that question would need this explanation: I mean to say that it was not the physical force of the troops that stopped the riot; it was the fact that it was the authority of the United States, and that if these troops were not sufficient there were more behind them; it was not the strong hand of the federal troops, by firing or charging upon them, that put down the riot, but the feeling that they would put it down if resistance was made.

4561. I ask you again what would be the result, in your judgment, if the troops and military authorities were withdrawn altogether? They would make such men as myself, such people as teachers of colored schools, and such business men as have been talked of in the papers, leave the city. They could not live here. I could not live in this town now without troops here. There would be just the difference there was before and after the colored troops were mustered out. The difference there was between January and February and May and June. After the troops were mustered out they could raise riots, shoot down negroes, and murder men, women, and children. When sixteen hundred colored troops were here they dared not do it. The same result would follow the removal of all troops from the city. We would have to leave, and the teachers would have to leave with us. Those people, also, who compete here with the merchants, and are obnoxious in principle, would have to leave; and, finally, all northern people would have to go, because I do not think the civil law is strong enough here to protect them. I have no doubt there would be a disposition upon the part of some here to protect them, but the other party would be the strongest and drive them away.

4562. Are you acquainted with the teachers of colored schools here? I know them all.

4563. What is their character? They are generally estimable young ladies and gentlemen. They have always been quiet and unobtrusive. They have their principles, politically and otherwise, and just live up to them.

4564. Are the ladies who have been here as teachers of blameless life and conversation? They are as far as I know.

4565. Have they ever made themselves obnoxious to the southern families here? If they have I have never seen it. The most you can say of them is, they have taught the children to sing the "Red, White, and Blue," "Rally round the Flag," and songs of that description, for which they have been abused in the public press of the city.

4566. Is it considered obnoxious to the people here to have national airs sung? I have seen them sneered at, hissed in the theatres, &c. These children have sometimes sung "John Brown," but nobody has been insulted by them, and they have always been discouraged in everything tending to excite these people or hurt their sensibilities. I am free to say that with a confederate soldier, who fought me on the field with his gun in his hand to my face, I have no quarrel whatever.

4567. How is the American flag, the "Star Spangled Banner," regarded in Memphis generally? I do not think they love it. I have never seen it here except at United States headquarters I have seen pictures of rebel generals in all shop windows and stores wherever I have been, but I have never seen those of such men as Lincoln, Grant, Sherman, Farragut, and such as them, displayed.

4568. Did you ever see the picture of our President, Andrew Johnson, in the same crowd? I do not remember. I never should have noticed the thing if I had not seen the pictures of Jeff. Davis, Lee, Beauregard, &c., displayed in such profusion. There is a Lee Academy here.

4569. Who is that academy named after? After Gen. Lee. I have seen the name "Lee Academy" in gilt letters on the sign-board. My attention has been called to matters of this kind so often, that of course it has led me to believe that these people love the southern confederacy now defunct, and of course that is obnoxious to me as a soldier. I have walked the streets here with my wife, and had them insult me, when nothing but her presence prevented me from resenting the insult.

4570. Has the uniform or insignia of the government worn by military men been the subject of insult and reproach here? That is my belief. They hate the sight of it. An officer has been asked here if he was not afraid to wear the uniform of the United States on the streets. I would not consider myself safe in walking the streets at night alone in the uniform of a United States officer, and particularly the uniform of an officer of the obnoxious Freedmen's Bureau.

4571. Why do you say "obnoxious Freedmen's Bureau?" Because they hate it in every shape and form. They call me a pimp. I have served the United States government in the army five years, and I am called a pimp in the public press.

4572. Is it the office of the Freedmen's Bureau, among other things, to issue rations to people? Yes, sir.

4573. Do they issue rations to other than colored people? I know the fact officially. In the district with which I am connected rations are only issued to orphan children under twelve or fourteen years, and people so sick as not to be able to get out of the hospital.

By Mr. BROOMALL:

4574. You speak of newspapers here. Will you name one of the worst in your estimation? The Avalanche.

4575. Who is the editor of the Avalanche? Colonel Galloway.

4576. Will you state whether that was the man who was raised up on the shoulders of the mob? He is the same man.

By Mr. SHANKLIN:

4577. In the commencement of your testimony you spoke of being in citizen's dress on the railroad cars coming from Nashville to this place. Will you give the names of the gentlemen you heard talking in the manner you have stated? I cannot give you the name of one of them. I did the best I could to find them out. I tried very hard to get the name of the gentleman who said he could buy the bureau for a bottle of whiskey, but I could not. I have seen them at the hotels, but have not been able to find out their names. I would be very glad if I could.

4578. How many were engaged in this conversation? About six or eight.

4579. How many of them did you understand resided in Memphis? From their conversation there was one man from Arkansas, one from Mississippi, one, and perhaps two, from out here in West Tennessee. The rest lived in Memphis. That was my judgment from observation.

4580. Were these men under the influence of liquor? One was, but he did not do any talking. The others may have drank somewhat. They talked about drinking—talked about getting members of the legislature drunk, &c.

4581. Were they members of the legislature themselves? No, sir. My judgment was that they were politicians, men who had been to attend what was called the "great Johnson ratification convention," or some convention, I do not remember precisely what it was.

4582. So far as the better class of the people of Memphis are concerned, have you ever heard any similar expressions by them? They would not express anything of that kind before me if they knew it. I know a great many of them, and when they come to my office they are very polite indeed, but outside I have nothing to do with them. They have never extended to me any courtesy I should extend to any gentleman in the United States service who should come where I lived. Consequently, I have had nothing to do with them.

4583. What class of people have offered you these insults on the streets? As far as dress went they were gentlemen, but, to be candid in this matter, I cannot tell by the dress who a gentleman is. Some of the roughest-looking men by their dress, who have come in from the country, I have found to be perfect gentlemen.

4584. Have you ever been openly insulted by these men? No, sir. They have never done that. They have never made remarks except such as I could not take; such as, "Get out of the way; here comes ———." There they would stop, and I could not hear the rest.

4585. These demonstrations of drawing arms on you, you say have never taken place except behind you? No, sir. I have said that a pistol was drawn on me in the hotel here, but I was not aware of it then. Colonel Johnson was behind me and faced the man, but I did not know it until I was out of the hotel.

4586. Did you ever make any remarks to these people? I asked a man if he wanted to shoot me. He said no.

4587. Did you see his pistol? I did. It was a navy revolver. He had it in his hand. My back was turned, but as I turned round I saw him, and I did not shoot him for the simple reason that I had a lady with me and there were too many round there.

4588. Will you state what are your own private feelings towards the citizens of Memphis, whether they have not been irritated and excited? No, sir. I have always been a democrat; I was bred, born, and have lived in the democratic party. I came here ready to take these people by the hand, but they have met me with insults, because I wear the uniform of the government. I have, however, no unfriendly feelings towards them.

4589. What are your feelings towards the masses of the people here? I pity them.

4590. What sort of people have made these hostile demonstrations towards those they term "Yankees" and the colored population? Has it been by those considered the better classes, or the lower classes? They are called respectable men. They stand on the code of honor as it is recognized by gentlemen of the south. I have said I know nothing about their society, for I have never been in it. I assure you I have no bitter spirit against these people.

4591. My question was whether these hostile demonstrations towards the colored people and those they term Yankees were confined to a particular class? I think the weapons are a low class of people, but the instigation, I think, comes from a class called respectable people, and I think they are respectable.

4592. Are they the only men who have instigated these hostilities against the colored people and those they call Yankees? My opinion is made up from a thousand little things. For instance, a respectable planter comes into Memphis to get a girl put into the stockade because she said "what" to his daughter. There are, I say, a thousand things that assist in making up my opinion, and I would not feel like exempting any entire class, unless it would be those who had served in the confederate army. So far as I know they all feel alike in regard to the negroes and Yankees. These highly respectable people would not murder a man because he is a negro or Yankee, but still I believe they have no affection for him. I do not think they feel as much antagonism for the negro as for the people who have placed him where he is and made him free.

4593. Is the conduct and treatment of the colored people by what is considered the better class of southern people, men of property and men of business, as kind and liberal as that of the class of people they call Yankees who live in western Tennessee? If you confine that to the city of Memphis, I answer no, sir.

4594. Then you think the northern people in the city of Memphis, as a class, are more kind and considerate to the negro than southern people here who have been slave-owners? If there is any difference at all, such is my opinion. Outside of this city, the best friends to the negro are soldiers who have served in the two armies. I have met, of course, more who have served in the federal army than have served in the confederate army.

4595. How is it with soldiers in this city? I cannot tell you, because I cannot distinguish between them.

4596. You think the Freedmen's Bureau is odious in the estimation of the whole people of Memphis except the northern portion of the citizens? Not altogether. That part of the Freedmen's Bureau which protects the negro in his rights is obnoxious to them. That part which makes the negro do his duty and work their plantations they would regret very much to lose. I am informed by an agent of mine, that in the country very few would be willing to have the Freedmen's Bureau removed. They say, if the bureau is removed what are we going to do with the negroes? I have written letters by the hundred to thousands, advising them to work faithfully for their masters, and live happily and contentedly, and they have nearly all followed my advice. They do not object to that, but that part of the bureau which takes a man who has knocked down one of his negroes, and fines him $25—that part which makes a man pay what is due the negroes, is obnoxious to the people.

4597. Universally obnoxious? Yes, sir. Obnoxious to this whole country.

4598. Will you state to what extent the bureau requires a negro to comply with his contract? When I have made a contract with a man for the employ of one, two, or five hundred negroes, I have generally gone in person and explained to the negroes the terms of their contract; that they were to get so much money, so many rations, to have such houses and such privileges. That for this they were to work a certain number of hours each day under certain regulations. Then I have told them that I should expect them every one to comply with the contract in every minute particular; that they must not neglect it in anything whatever. They have generally complied with the contract. When they have refused, the planters have come to me and made complaint. When they have seemed to be well grounded on such testimony as I had, I have written letters telling the men they must comply with their contracts. If they still refused, I would send agents there to instruct them as to their duties. If they then remained obstinate, I would have the ringleaders brought to my office, and when they have still absolutely refused, (I do not know whether I have done right or wrong,) I have had them put in the stockade.

4599. In making these contracts do you leave it to the option of the negro to enter into these contracts, or do you require them to do it whether they consent or not? The negro is generally brought to my office by the man who makes the bargain with him, and my duty is simply to see that the contract is equitable and just. I do not require them to do anything.

4600. Do you under no circumstances require these negroes, against their consent, to enter into contracts? I have always been instructed to treat colored people just the same as I would white people under similar circumstances, and if the man is a vagrant, to treat him the same as I would a white vagrant. Whenever I have found a black vagrant, and the civil authorities have taken no notice of him, if he proves on examination to be a vagrant, I have put him in prison as such until he would agree to work, and then have permitted some gentleman to take him away. Many who have been so taken up as vagrants have gone off and made good hands. I have not in any other case required a negro to contract against his consent, unless he is a criminal who is released on condition of his going to work.

4601. As a general thing in contracts made under your supervision, has the contract been more frequently violated by the whites or by the negroes? They have been more frequently violated by the white men than by the negroes, in the proportion, I should think, of about four to one.

4602. So far as the matter has come under your observation, do these white men hiring negroes, as a general thing, treat them justly? In West Tennessee they generally treat the negroes pretty well, and the negroes are doing pretty well, but when you get down into Mississippi, in most of the cases that have come to my knowledge, they have not. My impression is that they amuse themselves down there by abusing the negroes in every shape and form.

4603. Do you make contracts for planters living in Mississippi? Yes; we make contracts for negroes to go anywhere in the country, and it is the duty of the agents where they go to see that they are carried out in good faith.

By the CHAIRMAN:

4604. Have you been in the Union army? I have, for the last five years.

4605. Have you been in any battles? Yes, sir.

4606. Have you been wounded? I have been hit seven times, and have three bullet-marks about me.

EVENING SESSION, *June* 5, 1866.

PITSER MILLER sworn and examined.

By Mr. SHANKLIN:

4607. State your name, residence, and occupation. Pitser Miller. I reside in Memphis, and have been here for the last three years. I am a merchant.

4608. Have you mingled with the people of Memphis pretty freely since your residence here? Yes, sir; very freely.

4609. Are you familiar with the public sentiment of the people of Memphis? Yes, sir.

4610. Will you state, from your knowledge of the sentiments and opinions of the people of Memphis, what is the feeling towards the colored people; is it kind and just, or unkind and unjust? I have heard a great many express themselves, and they sympathize with the negroes; they say that whatever fault there was in regard to the riots, they behaved themselves a great deal better than was expected.

4611. Has this been the expression of the people of Memphis so far as you have heard any expression? I scarcely know an excepting voice, except from the lower orders of the people, that is, the laboring people; and I understood (though I do not know that I so heard myself) that they were opposed to them, on account of the competition of labor.

But from the citizens of Memphis I have never scarcely heard a word against the negro, and I do not know that there is a particle of animosity either in town or country, and I know the opinions of the people of the country as well as of the towns, having talked a great deal with the former owners of negroes, and they do not blame the negroes, but say that they behaved better than they expected, and they felt a disposition to assist them in any way they could.

4612. When you speak of this hostility of the working classes, to what class do you particularly allude? I mean stevedores, boat-loaders, mason tenders, draymen, and the common laborers about the place, such as porters. I should state that this is all hearsay with me, for I have had very little conversation with this kind of people, but I have had a great deal of talk with the former owners of negroes and with the good citizens down here.

4613. Will you state, so far as you are acquainted with the people of Memphis, if there is a hostile and unkind feeling on the part of the people of Memphis towards the people of northern States who come here and locate among the people? I think there is some little jealousy in that respect, particularly where a northern man is a little fussy about politics; it is especially obnoxious to a good many people; but so far as trade is concerned, if he sells a thing one per cent. lower than a native does, they go there to deal; I see no difference made in that respect. In politics, however, they are a little fussy; indeed there is considerable feeling against the northern men; but when they come here and attend to their business, I do not think there is a particle of hostility.

4614. Do you think that among the people of Memphis with whom you are acquainted there is such a state of hostility towards these northern men as to induce them to resort to any violence towards them? No, sir; I have seen men who were the most violent southern men I know of take them into partnership. I saw a man two days before the battle of Shiloh, and he said that if the war did not succeed, the banks of the Amazon would be his resort; four of them made that resolve in my presence. I saw that man two weeks ago, and had a long conversation about his business and his prospects, and he had taken in some man from Ohio as his partner, and he spoke in the most favorable terms of him.

4615. State if there is not a very large portion of the citizens of Memphis, belonging to the better class, who are disfranchised by the laws of the State of Tennessee? Yes, sir; I know a great many people who are disfranchised by the franchise law that was passed a year ago by the legislature; a great many were disfranchised by it; this law is considered more strenuous than the other.

4616. State whether the election of city officers has been under the control of the better classes of society in the city of Memphis in consequence of this franchise law? The present authorities would not get one-tenth—I think not one-twentieth of the votes of the good citizens of Memphis.

4617. Do you mean of those who are disfranchised? The present incumbents would not get the votes of one-twentieth of the citizens of Memphis.

4618. Then it is not with the consent of those men who have been disfranchised that the present officers of the city are in office? Oh, no, sir; I stood by and saw those men who voted in these men getting their authority to vote; they just swore every man a loyal citizen right through; all who voted were draymen, laboring men—Irish almost entirely, who swore to anything that was asked.

4619. I will ask you what has been the general expression of those with whom you are associated in Memphis, with regard to the recent riots and the outrages committed upon colored people? I never heard it approved of by an associate of mine yet, but it was condemned in the most unmeasured terms; I never heard what I call a respectable man but has so condemned it ever since it happened.

4620. So far as you know the sentiment here, is it excused or justified, except by that class who were engaged in it? I have never heard it excused by any man; and it is like knownothingism; I do not know whether you will find anybody that was engaged in it.

By the CHAIRMAN:

4621. You are a native of Tennessee, are you not? Yes, sir; I have been in the State during all the recent troubles.

4622. You are a qualified voter, are you? Yes, sir.

4623. You have spoken of the general expression of the people of Memphis with whom you are acquainted in regard to these riots; do you know whether those people with whom you have associated have taken any measures to bring to justice the perpetrators of these unheard of outrages? No, sir; I have had a conversation with several with respect to getting up a meeting for the purpose of disapprobating the thing; and, in the second place, to appoint a committee to hunt out the rioters and punish them; and thirdly, to pay for the burnings; but they said we can do nothing with the powers that be, and nothing was done; there never was any meeting; I talked to probably thirty or forty, and they all said that would be exactly right, but they did not know whether they could do anything with the existing authorities in regard to it. Indeed, I was not so well satisfied as I would like to have been; I thought some of my friends were a little colder than I liked; shuffling the responsibility, as I thought.

4624. Then these people did not sympathize with your sentiments? They did not to the same extent; they did not go so far as I wanted them to go. I wanted a meeting to disavow the thing.

4625. Did these sentiments of which you have spoken—I mean the expression of condemnation of the better class of citizens in regard to the riots—find a response in the press of this city? They spoke of it. The Commercial disapproved of it; I do not read the Avalanche.

4626. Why do you not read the Avalanche? It is not of my way of thinking.

4627. Wherein does it differ? It is a little more ultra than I am.

4628. You have spoken of northern people coming down here, and you say they would hardly be disturbed unless they became fussy about politics? I mean when they come in as strangers, and take hold of things as though they wanted to rule, which does not meet the approval of people generally.

4629. Do people generally believe that a man coming here from the north should take no part in the discussions of the day? They think they should not take more part than others; and they think that they should, as it were, take the back seat.

4630. If they did not take the back seat, but exercised the privilege of an American citizen in forming an opinion, have not such men been assailed here? I cannot call a case to mind. I know some have been condemned on account of being pretty forward—that is, for being pretty ultra and radical; and I hear about editors quarrelling with and condemning men for their opinion of things.

4631. Is it not a man's business to have an opinion on politics, and to express that opinion? Of course a man is bound to have an opinion.

4632. Do you not know of threats of violence against a newspaper here called the Post? I have never in my life heard any violence threatened to it. I have heard some people speak about its being very radical, and thinking that it was a little like the Avalanche, a little too far to one side.

4633. What do I understand you to mean by being radical? The general understanding of the term radical is, opposed to everything southern.

4634. Mention some particular thing southern? Opposed to the representation of the South. Of course the slavery question is settled; everybody has given that up, and a good many are saying that it is a very good thing, but I suppose it is because they cannnot help themselves; there is no complaint of it at all; but they complain about the people wanting equality of the negro; that they call radical.

4635. Do you mean equal rights before the law? Equal rights before the law, socially, and so on.

4636. Is there any one here in favor of social rights wiping out distinctions? I suppose they think if the negroes were admitted to one thing, they would require another till they were even.

By Mr. BROOMALL:

4637. You have spoken about the good citizens of Memphis. Will you tell me what portion of the citizens you design to embrace in that term? Would it include one-fifth of the entire population? No, sir; not unless you included ladies; I think one-fifth would be a large proportion.

4638. The remaining four-fifths, then, I understand embrace those who have not this good feeling towards the negroes? Well, there are a good many of them that have good morals but are not educated; I could not say that they have not good feelings towards the negroes; many of the common people seem friendly to them.

4639. What proportion of the citizens of Memphis would be impartial in a case between a negro and a white man? I think that the people would be fair towards them, with the exception of a few ignorant people.

4640. Do you say that one-half of the people of Memphis would be impartial in a case of a negro towards a white man? I should say one-half would be.

4641. Has there been any demonstration of any kind, either in the press or in the churches, or in any public meetings, of disapprobation of the late riots on the part of these good citizens? No, sir; I do not think there has been any whatever.

4642. According to your knowledge of the people of Memphis what are the chances of punishing these outrages by the civil law, through the courts? I have not heard of a particle of a movement towards it.

4643. Do you think there ever will be a movement through the civil law ? It don't look as though there would be ; I have my doubts.

4644. These good citizens of Memphis embrace the wealthy, and some quite wealthy ; have you heard of or seen any movement to rebuild the colored schools or churches by private contributions ? No, sir ; none whatever.

4645. Do you think it is likely they will do anything towards rebuilding those schools and churches ? It does not look much like it ; I do not think there will be.

4646. Has there been any movement on the part of these good people, or anybody else, towards educating the negroes except that which came from the north ? My church has undertaken to take care of the orphans ; but that is very recently.

4647. What church is that ? Episcopal.

4648. Has any church or any other body of men here undertaken to educate the negroes ? I have not heard of any ; but there is some excuse for that, for they have enjoyed schools almost equal to the whites.

4649. By movements from the north ? By the military, I believe ; the Freedmen's Bureau.

4650. What is the feeling towards the teachers in those colored schools ? The feeling is not as good as it should be ; they have the epithet of " school marms." I have not heard anything against the character of the teachers in this town ; I have never heard them slandered. I have heard them slandered in Vicksburg.

4651. Do you think there is a good feeling towards these " school marms ?" Are they received in society ? I have never met one.

4652. Are they encouraged ? I do not think they are.

4653. Are they looked down upon ? I do not think any one has ever sought them out to pay particular attention to them ; nor have I ever heard them spoken of with scorn or contempt.

4654. Is the teaching of colored schools a popular business here, or otherwise ? I have heard nothing against it ; I don't reckon it would be called popular. There are a good many people who think the colored people would be better for being educated, but they do not feel like going into it. Our church is teaching them at Bolivar ; they commenced before the rebellion, and a good many people disapprobated it, but they have all given in now.

4655. Outside of your church what has been the feeling about educating them ? Well, it was very unpopular ; it was against the law.

4656. Is it more popular now ? I do not think it is disapprobated ; if it goes on without their help they don't care to pull against it.

4657. If the North were to suspend teaching the negroes would the matter be taken up and carried on by your own population ? I think it would gradually get into that train ; but it would be a slow process.

4658. What proportion of the citizens of Memphis really love the old flag ? I could not say as to the love of it, but there are 19 out of 20 who are determined to support it the balance of their days ; I do not know what proportion really love it.

4659. Does it appear anywhere except upon the buildings of the government ? I do not think it is displayed in any other place.

By Mr. SHANKLIN :

4660. I would ask you, from your knowledge of the destruction of property and the change in the pecuniary condition of the people of this country, whether they are at present able to make suitable provision for the education of *white children*, as a general thing ? They have good arrangements for teaching the white children. There are a great many pay schools and a great may free schools.

4661. Have all the white children of your city the facility of attending schools ? They have a chance to attend school, every one of them, though they do not avail themselves of it.

CHARLES S. CAMERON sworn and examined.

By Mr. SHANKLIN :

4662. State your name, residence, and occupation. Charles S. Cameron ; I have resided in Memphis since the summer of 1862 ; I am by occupation a lawyer.

4663. What place did you come from, and in what capacity did you come ? I came from Chicago, and was a soldier in the Union army.

4664. Did you hold an office in the army ? I was captain in the ninth Illinois cavalry. I continued in the army till December 31, 1863.

4665. How long have you been in Memphis in the practice of your profession ? Ever since then.

4666. Have you mixed with the people of Memphis pretty freely since you have been here? Thoroughly.

4667. You think you are pretty well posted as to the public sentiments of the people of Memphis? Yes, sir; I was elected to the legislature by the people of Memphis in August last.

4668. Will you state what is the feeling existing between the white population of Memphis and the colored population—I mean of permanent residents here? With the classes with whom I am in the habit of associating the feeling is kind; I mean lawyers, and merchants, and property-holding citizens generally; those are the people of my acquaintance.

4669. What is the feeling and sentiment, so far as you have learned it, of the negro towards that population—is it hostile? No, sir.

4670. Is there a class c people in the city of Memphis who are hostile to the negro? If so, state what class that is. I do not know that you could call it a class, but there are people who are hostile; they are generally the ignorant people.

4671. Are they engaged in any particular pursuits by which you could classify them? No, sir; I have heard but few expressions of hostility against the negro except during the riots.

4672. Was it not the foreign population, such as the Irish and those who are employed in the business of draying, driving hacks, &c.? Yes, sir; there is a feeling among the Irish and the policemen against the negro; but that is not confined to Memphis; that class is not friendly to the negro.

4673. What proportion of the whole male population of the city of Memphis is of that class which you consider entertain kind sentiments towards the negro? A large majority, constituting the better portion of the people.

4674. Would it amount to two-thirds of the whole male population of the city? I think it would, sir.

4675. As a lawyer your attention as a matter of course has been directed to the franchise law of the State of Tennessee? Yes, sir.

4676. State what proportion of the population of Memphis you think would be disqualified from voting under the franchise law of the State of Tennessee of June 5, 1865? Very nearly all were disfranchised; a very large proportion. It disfranchised all who participated or aided in the rebellion; all except those who could prove that they were loyal all through the war.

4677. What would be the effect of that law upon the people of Memphis? It would be to disfranchise almost all the people of Memphis, for it would be next to impossible to prove a man's loyalty under such circumstances.

4678. State whether under the influence of that franchise law the election of city officers for the city of Memphis was not thrown into the hands of what you regard here as the lower class of the community? Most undoubtedly so. The voters are principally Irish, Germans, and Jews; they constitute the great majority of the voters here.

4679. Having come here as a federal officer and a northern man, can you state what the feeling of the people of Memphis has been towards that description of people to whom you belong? It has been open, generous, and hospitable.

4680. Has that been the general treatment you have experienced? Yes, sir; it has been of the very kindest character.

4681. Has that treatment, so far as you know, extended to northern men who occupy the position you do? Yes, sir.

4682. Have you seen any feeling of hostility manifested towards northern men who have located here? As northern men, no, sir. There is a class of men who come here to settle and who advocate these disfranchising laws, and it is because they seek to aid in disfranchising people with whom they settle that there has been any feeling against them.

4683. Have you in the practice of law found any discrimination made against you because you were a northern man? No, sir; I at once entered into a very fine practice.

By the CHAIRMAN:

4684. When did you go out of service? On the 31st of December, 1863.

4685. What did you go out for? I received my discharge from the Secretary of War.

4686. By resignation? No, sir; there was a commission ordered to examine officers, before which commission I did not appear.

4687. For what reason? I wanted to go out of the service.

4688. Why did you wish to go out of the service? Because I was running in debt all the time; I was not getting pay enough to support my family.

4689. Were there no other reason? No, sir.

4690. Were there no charges filed against you? No, sir.

4691. You say you were elected to the Tennessee legislature; did you serve? For six weeks.

4692. Did they adjourn then? They voted me out.

4693. On what ground? The ostensible ground was that I had not been, as the law required that I should be, a resident of the State of Tennessee for three years. I claimed that I was such a resident.

4694. There was a difference of opinion then as to your right to sit; and as the legislature had the power they exercised it and excluded you? The difference was that I was a Union man, but all these men were radicals, and all of them had been connected with the rebel service.

4695. Have you recently run for office? Yes, sir; I was defeated by 58 votes; it was for attorney general. I was run for the purpose of testing the constitutionality of the recent disfranchising act. In the American portion of the city, I think I received nearly two-thirds of the votes; but in the Irish ward I was defeated.

4696. You speak of the treatment which northern men have received here; do you mean men participating in feelings like your own? No, sir; not particularly. There is Colonel Hepburn, who has been in the northern army, and is here considered the leader of the radical party; he is a young lawyer like myself, without any means but his profession; he occupies a respectable position, and makes money. His partner is of the same stripe, though I do not know what his politics are. Hepburn is a prominent gentleman here. And there is Mr. Pearce, who was a major in the army; he is well liked here and makes a living from the law. Mr. Channing Richards also makes his living by the law.

4697. Do you know whether or not there is a strong prejudice against people known as republicans or radicals? There is a strong feeling against men who favor this proscriptive policy of disfranchising people; and it does not make any difference whether they are northern men or born here. The feeling is as strong perhaps against the county clerk, Mr. Ware, as against any man; and there are other gentlemen who have been born and bred here against whom exists the same feeling.

4698. Have you not heard threats made, both by people and by newspapers, against the Yankees here; threats of driving them out? No, sir, not by people; but I have seen articles in the newspapers, and particularly in the Avalanche, in which it was said that no exception was taken to northern men as northern men, but that when northern men came down here and assumed rights which they were not willing should be enjoyed by the people among whom they had cast their destiny, that men should not patronize their stores; there was considerable feeling against them, but it was distinctly claimed that the objection was not to the section from which they came, but to their sentiments.

4699. And, in consequence of their sentiments, "small-pox," as was recommended by the Avalanche, should be written over their doors; was not that applauded in the city? It was deprecated by many, and it was agreed to by many, but not applauded I think. It was not because they were northern men, but because they wanted to disfranchise and make aliens of the people among whom they were settled.

4700. What were the grounds for which they would disfranchise? For sympathizing with the rebels, and giving them aid and comfort; and these disfranchising laws were passed by men who got up this rebellion.

4701. Then they could not have voted under them? They could not if they had not voted in the presidential election of '64 and '65.

By Mr. BROOMALL:

4702. Are you a native of Illinois? No, sir; I was born in Canada, of Scotch parents.

TREADWELL S. AYERS sworn and examined

By Mr. SHANKLIN:

4703. State your name, residence, and occupation. Treadwell S. Ayers; I am a lawyer by profession; have resided in Memphis for twenty-two years.

4704. Have you had much intercourse with the people of Memphis; and are you posted as to the general sentiments of the people of Memphis in regard to the colored population here? I have continued here during the war, and have had perhaps equal opportunity with any one else to learn the general sentiment of the people here.

4705. What is the sentiment of the people here towards the colored people? What is the treatment of the people of Memphis towards the negroes; and what is the feeling of the colored people towards the citizens? I was a slaveholder myself; I owned seventeen slaves, and have been brought in contact with the colored people who were associated with me, and with their acquaintances and friends, and I think I know generally how they feel. I know there is no feeling on the part of our people of enmity or dislike to the colored population; but, on the contrary, so far as the older citizens are concerned, I may say that their feelings towards the colored population are almost universally kind. The colored people that belonged to me I believe regarded me as their best friend, and used to come to me for advice, and this I believe was generally the case with those who owned slaves in town. So far as I know the colored population are kindly disposed, and receive kindness from the citizens generally; I have known of no instance to the contrary, except the interruptions which have occurred between certain officials and the colored people who do not belong to the town, and did not heretofore.

4706. What classes of persons are there that do entertain hostile feelings towards the negro, and the negro towards them? The negroes, so far as I know, have been brought occasionally into contact with our municipal authorities and policemen, and there has been some little ill feeling engendered on both sides. The negroes have learned to think that they are not so kind in their treatment, as, for instance, in making arrests, more particularly about the 1st of May; that was a serious affair. There were outbreaks on the part of the colored population before, but they were generally by those who had straggled into the city and thought they were entitled to do pretty much as they pleased.

4707. Was there not a bad state of feeling existing here between those white persons who are engaged as wharf hands, draymen, hackmen, and porters, and the colored population engaged in the same business? I think it is very probable that with that class of people that have come into conflict with each other's interests, there may have been some ill nature exhibited on both sides; but it has never, so far as I know, broken out into anything serious. There is one class of the population that has had some ill feeling towards the negroes, and the negroes have towards them; I mean the Irish. The ill feeling towards the negro has generally been on the part of the foreign population, but it has never assumed a violent character except on the 1st of May. Any one who visits the wharf can see the contests for business between Irish and negro, and words may pass between them; but this has not been characteristic of the last year or two; it has been more or less so at all times.

4708. What has been the sentiment of the people of Memphis, so far as you have heard an expression of it, in relation to the outrages and cruelties that were perpetrated upon the negro population? So far as I know there was but one sentiment among the citizens of Memphis, and that was an expression of regret that any collision should have occurred. and that the negro should have been abused. Many negroes took refuge in the houses of some of the older citizens who had owned them; mine came to my house.

4709. Did you see enough of this mob to form an opinion of the character of the persons who constituted it? No, sir.

4710. Did you see the crowds passing through the streets? Occasionally, as they would move up town, I saw the character of the men that seemed to be the most violent and excited; I did not know them personally; I do not think I saw a single man I knew; they were mostly Irishmen.

4711. Of what nationality are the policemen? Unfortunately for us, gentlemen, we are under a sort of Irish rule; I believe they are Irishmen, and not very reputable at that.

4712. I will ask you whether, under the operations of the franchise law of the State of Tennessee, the election, and the control of the election, of city officers, has not been taken almost entirely out of the hands of the better class of society and placed in the hands of the lower orders? That is true; there is no doubt about that. Of those who have been willing to take the required oath, and conform to the law in that respect, nine out of ten are of that low class, mostly German and Irish; there are but very few of the old citizens of Memphis who are qualified voters under the franchise law.

4713. What proportion of the citizens of Memphis over twenty-one years of age do you think had the right under that law to vote in your last election of city officers? I do not remember distinctly the number of votes polled, but I think I would not be mistaken in saying that not more than one out of three or four had the right to vote under that law. The registry shows, I believe, some 2,500 to 3,000 voters altogether, but, according to our present population, we would be entitled to some 7,000 or 8,000 voters, perhaps more; it is said we have a population of 60,000.

4714. Are you a qualified voter under the franchise law? I got a certificate, but did not vote.

4715. That class which is excluded from the right of suffrage under the franchise law embraces within it a large portion of the more peaceable and orderly portion of the citizens of Memphis? I am satisfied it embraces much the larger portion of the persons who represent the property, and who feel an interest in the welfare of the city—the prominent business men of the town.

JOHN C. PARKER sworn and examined.

By Mr. SHANKLIN:

4716. State your name, residence, and occupation. John C. Parker; I am a resident of Memphis; by profession a banker.

4717. How long have you been in Memphis? Two years.

4718. What was your employment before you located here? I was an officer in the United States navy. I was in the navy four years; on duty in Memphis, before resigning, one year.

4719. Did you hold an office in the navy? I was a lieutenant.

4720. Where was your residence before you went into the navy? Cincinnati.

4721. Are you a native of Cincinnati? Yes, sir.

4722. Since your residence in Memphis have you had an opportunity of ascertaining the public sentiment of the people of Memphis; if so, to what extent in relation to the colored population? Yes, sir; I think I have, both as an officer and as a citizen.

4723. Will you state what the general sentiments and feelings of the people of Memphis are, so far as you have had an opportunity of ascertaining them; whether they are kind and just, or unkind and unjust? So far as I know, the feeling has been kind; more especially between the former masters and those who have been held in slavery.

4724. What has been the feeling of those colored persons towards their former masters and the white persons of Memphis? So far as I know, the feeling of those who were slaves has been uniformly kind; as regards that of the negroes that come here, that we call contrabands, I do not know. I speak with reference to family servants and negroes about town that I know.

4725. Is there a class of persons in the city of Memphis who seem to come into competition with negro laborers; such as draymen, hackmen, wharf hands, porters, &c.? Yes, sir.

4726. What has been the state of feeling between that class of persons and the negroes? It has not been a good one at all; there has always been more or less trouble between the Irish and the negro.

4727. Has that hostility, or hatred, of the Irish population towards the negro been participated in to any extent by the former owners of slaves and the old citizens of Memphis? In reference to that I do not know, sir, except upon the occasion of the late disturbance. I recollect, upon one occasion, seeing a negro killed by an Irish policeman. He was shot by him, and then the policeman emptied the contents of his revolver into the body of the negro. He was arrested, and was convicted by court-martial.

4728. Are not the policemen taken from that population? I believe exclusively. I have never met a policeman in this town who was not an Irishman.

4729. What was the general sentiment of the people of Memphis, so far as you have ascertained, in regard to the destruction of property and the outrages and cruelties perpetrated upon the negro population by this mob? So far as I know, it was universally deplored, condemned, and denounced; more especially by the old citizens. I believe the old citizens were more severe in their denunciations than those who have lived here but a short time.

4730. Have you discovered, on the part of the citizens of Memphis, any feeling of hostility towards that portion of the population living here who have recently come from the northern States? If you have, please state what are the foundations or causes of that hostility. I can speak for myself, that I have never been more kindly received, or treated with more kindness, than by the people of Memphis.

4731. Do you know of any hostile feeling against any portion of the population here on account of their having come to this place from the north? No, sir; I know of nothing except our little newspaper skirmishes.

4732. Is not that hostility you have spoken of, either on the part of newspapers or citizens, more on account of political sentiments than on account of birth? Most decidedly, sir.

4733. Have you, as a northern man, been able to discover any want of kindness or courtesy on account of your northern birth or your former connexion with the navy of the United States? I have yet to receive the least slight from the hands of any one in Memphis, man, woman, or child.

4734. Do you think, if the military force of the United States was withdrawn, that northern people would be in danger of violence from the citizens of Memphis? Not at all, sir. I should consider myself as safe here, if there was not a federal soldier in the department, as I should in Cincinnati or New York.

4735. Is the feeling of hostility between the Irish and negro more intense here than it is in Cincinnati and New York? Yes, sir; I think it is.

4736. Is that hostility between the Irish and the negro laborers common whenever they come into competition? Yes, sir. I have always found that the two races had more or less difficulty as laborers.

4737. Did you notice, before this riot took place, any indications of rudeness on the street, towards white persons, by negro soldiers when off duty and passing through the streets? No, sir. I have heard of such cases, but have never seen anything of the sort.

I have always been treated by the negroes, both soldiers and citizen negroes, with courtesy.

4738. Did you ever see any collision between the police and negro soldiers? No, sir.

MARLAND H. PERKINS sworn and examined.

By Mr. SHANKLIN :

4739. Will you state your name, residence, and profession? Marland H. Perkins ; I reside in Memphis, and my occupation is that of an attorney at law.

4740. How long have you been a resident of Memphis? A little over a year.

4741. Have you been engaged in the practice of the law all that time? No, sir.

4742. State when you first came to Memphis, and in what capacity. I am a native of the State of Illinois ; was raised principally in Chicago.

4743. Have you been in the United States service? At the breaking out of the war I enlisted in the 9th Illinois cavalry, and went into the field with it. In the spring of 1864 I was detached from my regiment and placed on duty as judge advocate in the district of West Tennessee, on the staff of General Washburn. I remained there until I was mustered out, by reason of the expiration of the term of service, in the month of October of that year. I was then appointed by General Washburn as a judge of the civil commission at Memphis, in place of the State courts, which had been suspended by reason of the war, and I remained on that bench until the civil courts were reorganized by the State authorities, some six months afterwards. Since then I have been practicing law at this bar.

4744. State whether, since you have been in Memphis, your intercourse with the citizens has been free, and whether or not you have had an opportunity of ascertaining and learning the general public sentiment of the people of Memphis in relation to the negro population here. I think that I can safely say that I am well acquainted with the people of this city generally. I have been thrown in contact with them officially, and since then I have met them in business and socially, and I feel, perhaps, better acquainted with these people than with any other people anywhere, though I have been here but a short time ; and I have no hesitation in saying that, so far as I have observed, the feeling on the part of the people of this city—of the southern people, the confederates, the old citizens and former masters—is five times more friendly and kind towards the negro than that which exists on my part, or that of any northern man who was not raised among them. And I think that a negro of this city would go for a favor to one of these old citizens sooner than he would to one of my class ; though I feel as kindly towards them as I can feel, but I have not the sympathy that I see my neighbors and friends around me have towards the negroes. It is not a feeling I have in my heart.

4745. What is the feeling of the colored people towards those old citizens? I think it is reciprocated, fully. That is my experience here, and I have observed it with some surprise, but I believe it to be true. I speak positively as to the feelings of the old citizens towards the negro ; and, so far as I have been brought into contact with the negroes, it is reciprocal.

4746. So far as you have had intercourse with families, have they generally had black or white labor to assist about their houses? They have manifested the greatest disposition to retain their old servants ; and wherever the old servants did their duty, they were very grateful for their services and very glad to have them, and pay them well and treat them well. I think they preferred black labor.

4747. So far as you have observed the conduct of the colored people in Memphis, has it been quiet and orderly? So far as my own personal knowledge goes, it has been orderly.

4748. State whether you have been able to discover any sentiment of hostility or unkindness, on the part of the masses of the people of Memphis, towards men who come from the northern States and locate among them, from the fact that they did come from northern States. No, sir. I think that the best and greater portion of this community are anxious for northern men and northern capital to come here and make it what nature evidently intended it should be. They want that element ; they invite and welcome it. That is the feeling, so far as I have been able to discover.

4749. So far as there has been a manifestation of hostility to northern people, if there has been any, has it been on account of their political utterances which they were promulgating and advocating? The only manifestation of that kind I have seen is when reading the newspapers. I never heard any such ideas expressed, and never saw any evidence of it in any way ; and the only reason I have for supposing there is any person in this community that entertains such sentiments is from what I read in the newspapers of the city.

4750. So far as there has been an expression of feeling in the newspapers, has it been hostility to the political utterances they were advocating, or was it to them as northern people? It was not at all on account of their being from the north ; but the publication was made in times of high political excitement, and from the feeling that they were injured by the fact of these men coming here asking for trade, and at the same time attempting to proscribe them. There was nothing personal, but purely political.

4751. What were those utterances to which objection was made and hostility manifested? There has been a great deal of hostility on account of the franchise law in this State, and the effect it has upon our government, both State and municipal. Men who advocate those proscriptive measures, the disfranchisement of the best people of the city and the State, of course must expect to bring down upon their heads the bitter expressions of the press.

4752. Will you state what the sentiment of the people of Memphis was in regard to the outrages and cruelties perpetrated by this recent mob upon the colored people? I never heard a respectable man in the city of Memphis express anything but the most profound regret at the occurrence.

4753. Were the acts of the mob universally condemned? Universally. I never heard a man of intelligence express a contrary opinion.

4754. State whether, under the operation and effect of the franchise law of the State of Tennessee, the control of the offices of your State is not taken out of the hands of the better class of the population, and placed in the hands of the lower and worse population? I believe that to be the effect of the franchise law of this State, and I believe that a large proportion, two-thirds or perhaps three-fourths, of the best people in Memphis are disfranchised by it. I do not know that this city is alone. It used to be so in Chicago, and I have heard of other cities equally unfortunate in having the city affairs ruled by the foreign element. Two-thirds of the voters of this town—those who do vote, are foreigners, but the propertyholders, the good citizens, the old citizens, and a great many new, cannot vote under this law, and especially under the last law. It has placed the city in the hands of the present men, who will rule it for all time to come until that law is changed.

4755. From your knowledge of the people here, and of their sentiments, do you think the present officers of the city, including the police force, hold their offices with the consent and approbation of the masses of the people of Memphis, or against their wish? I think not, sir. There is a very general desire and a very determined effort is being now made to change this administration, and if we can succeed in dividing this vote, which heretofore has been a solid column, we may succeed in electing a better mayor, and our city government will be materially changed.

4756. Is there not a population here, from which the mayor was elected, who entertain hostile feelings towards the colored people, and against whom the colored people entertain hostile feelings? I suppose everywhere there is that feeling between the Irish and the negroes, the Irish feeling that the negroes are trespassing upon their rights, thinking that they have the privilege to do this labor. I have seen this antagonism between these races manifested in many other places besides Memphis, but nowhere more bitterly.

4757. Do you think that the recent riot and these outrages can be traced to that as one of the principal causes? It is my opinion, sir, that that is the principal cause and foundation of the recent riot.

By the CHAIRMAN:

4758. I understood you to state that you belonged to the ninth Illinois cavalry? Yes, sir.

4759. Was Charles S. Cameron a captain in your regiment? Yes, sir.

4760. For what reason did he leave the regiment? I have no personal knowledge on that subject. I am informed he was discharged by order of the Secretary of War.

4761. On what ground? I do not know, but I think it was on the record of our regiment that he was honorably discharged by order of the Secretary of War.

4762. Do you know of any reasons which led to his going out of the service? I do not. I know that he was ordered before a commission for an examination as to his conduct here in Memphis; pending that examination he received his order.

4763. What were the charges against him? Drunkenness, but I am under the impression that I saw the order of the Secretary of War honorably discharging him from service. There were a great many officers of the ninth regiment ordered before that commission, and he was one of them.

4764. Was any officer sent before that commission without some such charge? No, sir.

4765. You spoke of confederates; whom do you mean by that term—the men who have involved this country in this terrible war, costing three hundred thousand lives, and three billions of dollars, and that has clothed the whole country in mourning? I mean men who have been in the confederate army, who have returned and taken the oath of allegiance, and have resumed their occupation in life.

4766. Are they the same men we call rebels? Yes, sir.

4767. You call them confederates. Is that the term generally used? They are called returned confederates.

4768. They are not called rebels? I would not call them that myself.

4769. Do you mean that the man who has attempted to break down this government, and involved us in this terrible war, is a rebel or not? That is a very abstruse question, and would require considerable time to answer. I do not know whether legally he would be called so or not.

4770. Do you consider him a rebel? I consider that notwithstanding all that bloodshed and trouble, he has in good faith come back and taken the oath of allegiance and loyalty to the government. Having fought that man three years in the field, and knowing his bravery as I know it, and knowing his integrity as I have since learned, I believe that man is not a rebel.

4771. Do you consider such a man a rebel to his government? Yes, sir. In the incipiency of the war he was a rebel to the government; whether it did not after that assume proportions that should give it another name I am not sure.

4772. What other name? Belligerents. I do not think that those men should now be punished according to the law for the crime of treason.

4773. Then you do not think Jeff. Davis is a rebel, and deserving of punishment for the crime of treason? I do not think Jeff. Davis should be punished for the crime of treason ; that is, I do not think he should be hung.

4774. That is the punishment for treason—death—is it not? Yes, sir, I believe it is.

4775. You have spoken of the people of Memphis and of their good treatment of the colored people ; and kindness to them; who was it that burned the colored school-houses and churches of Memphis, on the 1st and 2d of May? Who was it that set fire to the houses, and attempted to burn up the inmates? Who was it that robbed the colored people? Who was it that ravished the women? Who was it that shot down women and children in cold blood? You have asked me a good many questions, not one of which have I any personal knowledge of.

4776. Have you any personal knowledge of the recent riot in Memphis? I have no personal knowledge of there having been a riot in Memphis. People told me a riot was going on, and I now believe it, but I was very particular not to go and investigate the matter I was satisfied with their report.

4777. If such a riot took place, and such things happened, who were the participators in it? So far as my knowledge goes—and I have no personal knowledge—the participators in that riot were Irish and negroes. It was nothing more nor less than an Irish and negro fight.

4778. You have spoken of what has been done by the better class of citizens for the negro ; who built the school-houses here in Memphis which were burned, and who furnished the means for carrying them on, and taught the colored children in these schools? That is a subject upon which I have no information.

4779. Have the old citizens of whom you speak given any expression of their regret and detestation of the murders and outrages committed in these riots? At the time when such an expression would have been made, they could not make it ; that is, the people could not assemble in any considerable numbers, by order of General Stoneman.

4780. How long did that order continue in force? I saw the order referred to in the papers, that a public meeting could not be held, and I have never seen the statement refuted.

4781. Is that the reason that nothing of that kind has been done? I suppose that is the reason.

4782. Do you mean to say that no meeting has been held, and no means whatever have been taken by the citizens of Memphis to give any expression of condemnation to these outrages? None that I know of.

4783. If it should turn out to be the fact that General Stoneman never made such an order or anything like that order, neither verbally nor in writing, what excuse is there for the people not publicly making known those sentiments, which you say they have expressed to you privately? They have expressed these sentiments privately, but I do not know that it is necessary for them to express their sentiments in any way. For myself, I would not desire to take any part in it whatever.

4784. You, as a citizen of Memphis, would not then feel yourself called upon to take any means to give any public expression of condemnation of these outrages? I cannot say that I see a necessity for calling any public meeting

4785. It is not a question of necessity, but a question of propriety. I think it is a question to be decided by the people themselves.

4786. I understand you to say then that these people have never given any public expression to that sentiment? No, sir.

4787. Have the newspapers given utterance to any such expression? I read very little of the newspapers here, but I think some of them have ; I think the Bulletin has condemned it. I have not read an editorial for a long time ; I read the local news and the telegrams, but not their editorials. I am under the impression that it was condemned.

4788. But you do not know of its being condemned publicly in any way? I think it was.

4789. Have these old citizens done anything to remunerate those colored people whose property was destroyed? Have they taken them into their churches to worship, or have the pulpits condemned the riots in any way? You are getting me into a field with which I have very little familiarity—the pulpits or churches of Memphis.

4790. I understood you to say that you were well acquainted with everything going on in Memphis; would not that acquaintance lead you to know these things? As to negroes being invited into the churches, I do not think such a thing would ever be done; for myself, I should never do it, at least not at the same time.

4791. Have these old citizens taken any measures to build school-houses? General Fisk has been so energetic in this matter that they have had no chance. I do not think the citizens would rush ahead in spending money to build school-houses and churches in these hard times; I know I would not, and I do not think any gentleman in this room would.

4792. You spoke of northern men here; do you not know of the prejudice existing against northern men who entertain sentiments which are obnoxious to the majority of the citizens? I do not think that sentiment towards northern men holding those political opinions is more deeply felt by others than by myself.

4793. What is your prejudice against them? I think their policy is ruinous to the country.

4794. What is the policy which you believe to be ruinous to the country? The proscribing of and the refusal to admit these States to their original position; the course that Congress has taken through the winter.

4795. Do you think that the men holding that opinion should be proscribed and driven out of Memphis? No, sir; and they never will be.

4796. Has there not been a constant attempt on the part of the newspapers to drive such men out of the city? There may possibly have been an attempt on the part of the Avalanche to bring about such a state of feeling, but I do not think they attempted to drive them out of the city.

4797. Is not the Avalanche the representative paper of the city? I do not believe it is.

4798. Has it not the largest circulation? I believe not.

4799. What paper has a larger circulation? I believe the Bulletin has.

4800. What political organization do you belong to? I belong to an organization here styling itself the Johnson Club.

4801. Who are the officers of that club? I have the honor to be the president of it; and there are some fifteen or sixteen vice-presidents, from various parts of the country. The secretary is Mr. Keating, of the Commercial. I have here a slip which I clipped from a morning paper, containing the proceedings of the meeting which organized this club.

4802. Is John Park one of your vice-presidents? Yes, sir.

4803. Is John C. Creighton, the present recorder of the city, one of your vice-presidents? Yes, sir.

4804. Do I understand you to say that you entertain a very strong prejudice against men denominated radicals? Yes, sir; I do entertain a strong feeling, politically, towards my opponents; very strong, very decided.

4805. Do you or do you not know of threats having been made against this class of men, that they should not be permitted to carry on business? I never heard of such a thing in the world, and do not think that such a threat was made by any sensible or responsible man.

4806. Do you not know that respectable men have been held up as radicals, and people advised not to go near them to trade, and that "small-pox" should be put upon their doors? I have heard of such things, and I have no doubt it was the best advertisement they could get. I believe that the Avalanche published an article of that kind, but that is a very eccentric and unreliable sort of a sheet, and I should not be surprised to see almost anything in it; but it did very little damage.

4807. Have you a partner in your profession? Yes, sir; Duncan K. McRae, of North Carolina.

4808. I see on your card that against your name your former residence, Illinois, is not put down; why did you not give your State? The reason was that Mr. McRae had a good reputation; I was a boy, having no reputation in any part of the world. I had no reputation to bring with me from that State; but in order that people might know who my partner was, I thought it was a good thing to put that down on my card.

4809. Did you think that the fact of your being from the radical State of Illinois would have helped you any? It would have been no injury to me in any way, but perhaps quite an advantage; the idea that anybody is to be injured in his business because he is a northern man is ridiculous.

4810. You have spoken of the hostility to this franchise law, and said that the men who uphold this law are the subjects of bitter hatred; it is a law of the State, is it not? Yes, sir; but I should most emphatically denounce any man who upheld that law.

4811. You would denounce the man who does not permit men to vote who have been traitors to their country? The misfortune is that only the men who voted in the presidential election can vote now; it disfranchises every man who has had any relation or connexions in the confederate army, or who has any sympathy whatever with them.

4812. Do you find that in the oath which is taken? I think it is in the oath; [the franchise law, shown to witness;] I take it for granted this is the law. There are a good many citizens who are loyal to the United States, but who have given comfort to the rebel army; having had acquaintances or relatives in the confederate army, not only have they felt sympathy for them, but they have given them comfort.

4813. For the purpose of aiding the rebellion? No, sir.

4814. Then it would not come within that law, would it? That is the letter of the oath.

4815. Because a man believes that parties connected with this rebellion, this attempt to tear down the government, should not have all the rights which, for instance, you, who were endeavoring to sustain the government, would have, that man you think should be denounced? I do not think it is necessary to denounce him; I think he is mistaken; I differ with him in opinion.

4816. I understood you to say that you would denounce a man holding these opinions? You certainly, sir, had no right to suppose so; I say that a man who does uphold those opinions must expect to be denounced.

4817. Do you think that a man who for three years has been fighting you, and endeavoring to tear down the government, should have the same rights that you should? I am satisfied that that man has been brave and sincere, he believed he was right, and he fought like a man; I have reason to know that, and from his conduct during that time I am satisfied that when he takes the oath of allegiance he will be loyal to the government of the United States, and that he will never take up arms against it; it would be better to take that man back and restore him to his old place, than to pursue the opposite policy and keep him in a state of bondage.

4818. I do not mean any man in particular, but do you think that men who have been in arms against the government, and attempting to destroy it, should be permitted to have the same rights in controlling the government they sought to destroy, as the men who sought to uphold that government? I think if any discrimination is to be made, it should be in favor of the loyal citizen.

4819. That does not meet my question. Do you think that, without any probation, that man should come and have the same rights that you have, after having four years of fighting to maintain that government? I am absolutely willing to place them on an equality with myself in all political rights.

4820. Then you are willing to place the rebels, who have tried to break down this government, in position to attempt to break it down again? That is a matter of argument.

4821. But that would be the result of it? I should be a very simple man to concede anything of the kind.

4822. You say that no southern man can have a greater prejudice against, or would denounce more strongly than you would, the northern man who would be in favor of that franchise law; and yet that franchise law is simply to prohibit a man who has given aid and comfort to the rebellion from now exercising the right of suffrage? I say, most emphatically, that if I should meet such a man publicly, in politics, I should denounce him, the same as you have been in the habit of denouncing your political opponents.

4823. You would do that because the man is opposed to giving to rebels the same rights which you have and which the man himself has? I am opposed to the law on principle, because I think it is bad policy; I think it is ungenerous and unjust; I think it is an infamous law.

4824. It is an infamous law, you think, because it prohibits a man from voting who has been a rebel and has given aid and comfort to the rebellion? But the man has been invited to come back, and I am not in favor of his being held as a serf, but of his being received and entitled to the privileges of an American citizen, whose highest privilege is to be entitled to vote.

4825. What has been the character of the public expression of sentiment in this city? Has it been loyal since the rebellion was suppressed? I never heard a disloyal sentiment uttered in public.

4826. Did you hear the address which was made by Landon C. Haynes at the tournament here? I heard a part of it.

4827. Is that a fair specimen of the speeches which are made here, as far as you have heard them? I refer to the whole address. Did you hear this portion of the address?

[From the Daily Avalanche, May 23, 1866.]

Extract from the address of Landon C. Haynes, at the Memphis tournament.

" The magnanimity and grace with which the people have acquiesced in the issues decided against them by the verdict of the sword, are only equalled by that superhuman high-
mindedness and knightly chivalry which, in the hour of battle, not only extorted admiration
from their stern foes, but made them seem to forget that they had ever heard the name of
death. [Applause] And it can scarcely now be expected by enlightened men that the
people of the South should suddenly transfer their affections personally to those whining,
canting, graceless, godless, christless vipers in the human form, who, cruel in the name of
humanity, nefarious in the name of piety, cowardly in the name of courage, warlike in the
name of peace, and disunionist in the name of union, seek to prevent fraternity and con-
cord, and to reduce a vanquished people to servitude, and to hasten them down into an
abyss of ruin unequalled in this or any other age or country. [Applause.] While we give
our allegiance and fidelity to the government of the United States, we reserve our scorn
for those buzzing insects of the hour, who, with the venomous stings of malignant asps,
would goad us to degradation and to death. [Applause.]'' Did you hear that? I believe
I heard that portion. Well, sir, that is pretty near my idea of it, with the exception of the
exaggeration of expression.

4828. Who are those "godless, christless vipers'' to whom he refers? What class of
people are they? Well, sir, I understand them to be that class of radicals in Congress who
have never smelt gunpowder, and who, now that the war is over, and the enemy has laid
down his arms and the government is restored, are especially warlike and vindictive in
their expressions and feelings. I have just that opinion of these men.

4829. Then your sentiments concur with his? I would not express myself in that way.

4830. But your sentiment is the same, though your expression would be different? I
say that, without the exaggeration of expression, to a great extent that would explain my
political feelings towards that party to whom I am politically opposed ; I am conservative.

4831. That is conservative doctrine then? As I understand it, a part of it, at least.

4832. I understand you to approve of the sentiment, but not of the exact language?
So far as my knowledge of the men he is speaking of goes, they are a godless, christless
set of men.

4833. Does that tend to lead to harmonious and fraternal feelings between the two sections? I do not think the radicals have given any opportunity for such feelings to be exercised.

4834. Do you approve of that sort of expression? I think it would have been well for
them to have set an example of an opposite nature ; but I am sure worse expressions than
those have been uttered on the part of the radicals.

4835. Were these radicals you speak of rebels in arms, or members of the confederate
Congress? No, sir ; they were very careful never to be in arms, so far as my knowledge
goes.

4836. How far does your knowledge go? Do you know that there are fifteen or twenty
men on the radical side of Congress who have been in the service? I should be very much
surprised to learn that fact ; and if it is true, I am very much surprised.

MEMPHIS, TENN., *June 6, 1866.*

HENRY G. SMITH sworn and examined.

By Mr. SHANKLIN :

4837. State your name, residence, and occupation? Henry G. Smith ; I have resided in
Memphis between twenty-three and twenty-four years, and am a lawyer.

4838. Have you been engaged in the practice of the law all that time ? I have.

4839. State if you have had free intercourse with the citizens of Memphis, so as to understand the public sentiment of the people towards the colored population? Yes, sir.

4840. Will you state what is the sentiment and feeling of the people of Memphis towards
the colored population of Memphis? I do not, in that, include the colored soldiers, or the
refugees who stay here temporarily. The relations between the negroes and what are
called the better class of white people are kindly, and always have been so ; the laboring
Irishmen and the negro are and always have been hostile to each other ; the relations of the
German people to the negro are more kind than are those of the Irish ; we have a great
many Irish laborers and German people in Memphis, and have had for many years ; I do not
think the relations between the negroes and the German and Irish people are at all so kindly
as they are between the negroes and the American people ; a good deal of animosity exists
between the negroes engaged as hackmen and draymen, and the white persons who follow
the same occupation ; most of these white persons are not natives here, they come from

abroad ; perhaps the majority of them are foreigners ; I think the great bulk of the population of Memphis are kindly to the negro ; that is to say, I do not think that they are disposed to practice any unkindness, or harshness, or cruelty upon the negro ; the native people here generally, almost universally, prefer to employ a negro to a white laborer, or a negro to a white drayman, and that begets a good deal of competition and animosity between the negro and the white draymen and hackmen ; I am not aware of any general feeling of unkindness existing in the great bulk of this community towards the negro ; but there was for a time, soon after the negroes began to come in here free, a good deal of irritation on the part of nearly everybody with the negro ; although nearly all, if not all, with whom I have had conversation on the subject, think that under the circumstances the negro has behaved remarkably well, probably better than white men under the same circumstances would have behaved ; I mean by this that there has been less outrage and audacity and insolence on the part of the negro than might reasonably have been expected under the circumstances ; almost everybody is aware that the negro does not work as faithfully or as much as he did formerly while a slave, and persons who employ them are irritated a good deal by their shirking ; but, upon the whole, my opinion is that the great bulk of the population live in about as much kindness with the negro people as the population of any country I know of live with the lower laboring class.

4841. Will you state what, in your judgment, is the proportion of the people of Memphis who entertain these sentiments, and practice justice towards the negro ? My answer to that must be greatly conjectural ; but nearly all the people with whom I have had intercourse, or have had conversation, feel that way ; there is a growing good feeling on the part of the white people towards the negro, as the irritation wears off, and partly because the negro has behaved remarkably well under the circumstances through which he has gone, and partly, also, because the negro is a kindly, obliging creature naturally ; but as to the proportion I am unable to answer with any approximation to accuracy, though I should think it is much more than one-half.

4842. Do you think it would amount to two-thirds ? I think it would, but it is guessing rather than knowing.

4843. I ask you, from your acquaintance with the sentiments of the people of Memphis, whether, so far as you know, there is any feeling of hostility towards northern men, or men from northern States who have settled among you, on account of their being northern men ? Yes, sir ; there is something of that ; a good deal.

4844. To what extent is that feeling entertained, so far as you can judge ? Probably the general feeling of the native people is dislike of northern people, but I do not know that it runs out into any personal or practical animosity, not to much extent ; but I have yet to discover that business men from the north are less patronized, that is to say do less business with the people, than the native-born people ; on the whole, the business men of this city of northern birth have been quite as prosperous as the business men of native birth, perhaps more so ; the newspapers contain a great deal of animosity, but I do not think it enters into the practical relations and business of life in any great measure ; merchants of southern birth, struggling to get into business, may be disposed to work through the newspapers somewhat upon what is supposed to be the southern animosity, in order to operate upon merchants of southern birth ; but I doubt whether it accomplishes anything material ; I do not think it does.

4845. State whether it is not a feeling of hostility to the political sentiments entertained by a great many of these northern people, rather than to the fact that they are northern people ? Of course, this dislike of northern people with northern sentiments is strong ; and the dislike is more or less general.

4846. Do you think that feeling towards northern people, whether on account of their place of nativity, or on account of the sentiments they entertain, is of such a character as to lead the masses and class of which you have spoken to acts of violence towards them ? Not here in Memphis, nor anywhere in the region about, as far as I know ; I have witnessed here at Memphis much more cruelty and more intense animosity between the people in political elections towards each other, and leading to a great deal more personal violence between them, than between them and persons of northern birth ; therefore I cannot say that there is, here in Memphis, any disposition to practice or to favor violence of any kind towards people of northern birth, even of that kind whose sentiments and occupations are particularly disagreeable to the native people ; I did not suppose that there was any occasion for any of the persons of northern birth who were here to go off immediately after the mob ; I did not think they were in any danger of personal violence ; those who thought so I think gave way to their fears more than to any real danger ; and yet anybody, I suppose, at that time, who threw himself in the way of the mob would have been run over and destroyed probably ; that is the history of mobs everywhere.

4847. Have you any knowledge or information upon which you can rely as to the character of the people constituting this mob, and the class to which they belong ? Not from any personal knowledge or observation, for I was absent at the time, and I am only able to answer from what I have been told ; I have not heard the name of any person mentioned who was engaged in the mob, or in any acts of violence ; but on the information I had, my opinion is that the chief actors in the mob were of that lower class of people with whom the animosity towards the negro chiefly exists, particularly the policemen of the city, the draymen, hackmen, and others following like occupations, who have become aggravated with the negro by reason of the competition of which I have spoken ; I have no idea that any of what we call the better class of persons, people of respectability, or that pass as such, desired to stir up, or foster, or encourage the mob ; I have no idea that the persons engaged in the newspaper business, and who write much of the inflammatory matter of the papers, desired or encouraged any such mob, or any such acts of violence, and I think I would be likely to know if they did.

4848. Will you state what has been the general sentiment of the masses or of a large majority of the people of Memphis in relation to this mob? State as far as you have been able to learn their sentiments, has it been approved of or disapproved of and condemned? Nearly everybody I have heard speak of it disapproved of it ; I do not know that I would be likely to hear what were the feelings of the classes of people who were more or less actively engaged in it ; but my own opinion has been that, as compared with the whole population, it was but a mere tithe, indeed greatly less than that ; the people who were engaged in the mob were very few compared with the whole mass of the population ; and while there was a strong feeling against the negro on account of his supposed intention to engage in violence against the white people—for at that time that feeling was pretty general—I know, as far as I have been informed, that nearly everybody regrets the mob and the violence, and disapproves of the outrages that were practiced upon the negroes after the actual fighting was over.

4849. Will you state, whether from your knowledge of the feelings and sentiments of the people, either the negro or the northern people here would be in danger if the federal troops, which are now in Memphis, were withdrawn from among them ? I think that the feelings of the negroes and of the people of northern birth who have recently come here are such that there is more safety to them against violence by the presence of the federal troops ; as to any general mob or violence, I do not think there is more danger of that here than almost anywhere ; individual cases of collision would occur if the violent southern and northern people were to come in contact, but I do not think there would be any general or formidable violence of any kind ; I think, sir, the great mass of the people of all sorts, who want order and quiet, prefer the white federal troops to remain ; but I do not think that any of the white people want the black troops here.

4850. Will you state whether, in your opinion, the election of city officers and the appointment of the police of Memphis, under your franchise law of Tennessee, has not been thrown under the control and management of this lower class of people, while a great many or a sufficient number of the better orders have been disfranchised ? I think the government of the city would have been in much better hands for the order and safety of the people if all the white people had been permitted to vote ; upon the whole, the operation of the franchise law has been to deprive of the right of voting a very large class of those who constitute our best people, and who most desire order and security to everybody.

4851. Has that been the effect, to place the control of the elections in the hands of this disorderly class of people ? It has heretofore.

W. F. TAYLOR sworn and examined.

By Mr. SHANKLIN :

4852. State your name, residence, and occupation ? W. F. Taylor ; I reside in Memphis ; I am now clerk and salesman in the house of Pitsor Miller.

4853. How long have you resided in Memphis ? About fifteen years.

4854. Are you a native of Tennessee ? I am a native of Alabama.

4855. Will you state whether you saw any part of the difficulty and contest between those who engaged in it, on the first evening of the riot ? If you did, state what time you first saw it, and what you did see. I was going out home about half-past six o'clock, on the first evening, and discovered a very large crowd of negroes, men, women, and children ; I remarked to my uncle who was with me, "There is a difficulty of some kind," and probably it was not more than a minute after this that I heard negroes hallooing ; this was on South street, at the crossing of the Mississippi and Tennessee railroad, that connects the Mississippi and Tennessee railroad with the Charleston railroad, southeast corner of Morris Cemetery ; after I heard the negroes shouting, they commenced running in every direction, and probably in a few minutes I saw ten or twelve negro soldiers ; then in a few minutes the firing commenced.

4856. What were they firing at ? I did not see any white men, the crowd was so large of negro men, women, and children ; I did not discover who they were firing at, but they were firing north, towards the city.

4857. How many shots do you think they fired while you remained there? Probably fifty, sir, in very rapid succession.

4858. Were they firing with guns or pistols? Pistols were all I saw.

4859. How long did you remain there after the firing commenced? Only a minute or two ; I was uneasy for fear I should receive some of the missiles myself, and I returned.

4860. Did you see anything more of the fight that evening, or the next day? No, sir.

4861. Did you see the character of the white crowd? No, sir ; I did not.

4862. Do you live in the country? I was going to my country home when I saw what I have referred to.

4863. When did you return? At eight o'clock next morning, when everything was uiet.

4864. Did you pass that street again that evening, Wednesday? No, sir, not that place ; I went to Hernando street, and flanked the battle-ground.

4865. Were there any crowds there the next day? None that I saw.

4866. Have you told all you saw? Yes, sir.

4867. Who was with you? My uncle, Mr. Ford.

NEWTON FORD sworn and examined.

By Mr. SHANKLIN :

4868. State your name, residence, and occupation. Newton Ford ; I live about two miles from the court-house, on the Hernando road ; I am a commission merchant.

4869. Have you heard the statements of Mr. Taylor which have been read to you, in relation to what he saw when in your company on the first evening of the riot ; if so, state whether you agree with him in all the facts, or if in anything you differ from him? I do not differ from him. There was a contending party, I presume, on the north side of the street.

4870. Do you concur with him in the statements he has made? Yes, sir ; there was a party on the banks of the railroad, and I presumed there was some party they had shot, but it seemed that they were examining a horse that had been hit, and I observed to Mr. Taylor that we would go through some other street home.

4871. Did you hear any firing in that neighborhood previous to the time you saw those negroes engaged in it? No, sir.

MARCUS J. WRIGHT sworn and examined.

By Mr. SHANKLIN :

4872. State your name, residence, and occupation. Marcus J. Wright ; I reside at No. 110 Madison street, in this city, and am a lawyer.

4873. How long have you resided in the city of Memphis? Since 1850.

4874. Where did you reside previous to coming to Memphis? Where is your place of nativity? McNair county, Tennessee, where I lived till I came here.

4875. Were you in the city during the recent riot? Yes, sir.

4876. Will you state whether you saw any part of that riot, and what you did? I saw no part of it ; I was at my office daily, which was then on Second street above Jefferson ; there was no riotous proceeding in that vicinity, or in the vicinity of my residence.

4877. Did you see passing through the streets any of those mobs, so as to form an opinion as to the character of the people who constituted them? I did not.

4878. Will you state, from your knowledge, or any information on which you can rely, what was the character and class of the mob who perpetrated the atrocities upon the colored people during the riots, and state, also, your sources of information? The ablest source of information I have is the testimony of others who were present, and who stated to me that they saw different riotous proceedings, such as shooting citizens ; that there were no citizens engaged in them, except such as the policemen, and the rabble who were with them were low people whom they did not recognize as citizens.

4879. From your intercou.se, and from the opinions you have heard expressed by the masses of the citizens of Memphis, what is the state of feeling existing between those masses and the colored population in the city of Memphis since and previous to this riot? I do not think there is any unkind feeling among the mass of citizens towards the negro— certainly not among those who were the former owners of negroes. I think their disposition is to be kind to them, and that they prefer them to new servants. I know of instances during these riots—at least I know from information—where the negroes sought protection from their former owners ; but I think there is a hostile feeling towards the negroes entertained by some men of a low class who are engaged in business, and who regard the negroes in the same business as their rivals. As a general rule, these men are foreigners, and are engaged in driving hacks and drays, and a very large majority of the draymen of the city are negroes, and many of them have been doing business for particular houses for years—for many large houses will have so many draymen all the time—and these men will sometimes underbid them in draying, and not being able to get their business, would entertain bad feelings towards the negroes I think the bad feeling towards them is confined to this class, though there may be exceptions. I have heard no expression of unkind feeling towards the negro uttered by respectable people.

4880. What are the feelings and sentiments of the resident colored people towards that better class of white people ? Very kind—exceedingly kind. They feel that they are their friends, and rely upon them in matters requiring advice or assistance, when they generally seek them out.

4881. State, so far as you have been able to learn it, from your intercourse with the business men of Memphis, property holders, and the fixed residents of the city, what is their sentiment in regard to this riot, and the outrages perpetrated upon the negroes. I have heard but one expression from that class, and that is condemnation of it. During the time the riot was going on, a good many persons who had been in the army with me (I had been in the confederate army) came to me and said that outrages were being committed by a low class of people—that they were getting up a riot, and they wanted to put it down. They asked me what they should do ; I said, nothing, unless General Stoneman called upon them. Their object was to suppress it, and they were willing to put it down ; but I told them they were under parole, and they must take no step unless they were called upon by General Stoneman.

4882. Was that the common feeling among the paroled soldiers, as far as you know ? It was the entire feeling, as far as I know.

4883. Did they act upon your advice ? Yes, sir. Some of them were afterwards summoned by the sheriff, and they told him they must do nothing except upon the call of General Stoneman. This was to excuse themselves for not serving under the sheriff.

4884. I will ask if the effect and operation of the franchise law which has been in force for a year or two in Tennessee has been to throw the control of the city elections into the hands of what is considered here an inferior class of people ? That is my opinion, sir. The proof that was required to be made under the law at the last municipal and county elections (I am not familiar with the present law) was a certificate from two witnesses that he had always been an unconditional loyal man to the United States ; and there was a large number of men that went to the polls with certificates and proofs from two men that had not been here for the required length of time—six months—and probably the party whom they proved had not been here six days.

4885. Was the effect of that law to disfranchise a large portion of the citizens of Memphis ? Yes, sir ; it disfranchised perhaps four-fifths of the property holders here. The business men here, with few exceptions, were almost entirely disfranchised.

4886. Is the effect of that law to place the control of the election in the hands of such men as constitute the police force, the hackmen, draymen, and men who work on the wharf ? I think so, sir. It put the power of election in the hands of those who have very little or no material interest in the city, and who had not been resident here for any long time, and were not known to the older business men of the city.

4887. Is it a fact that the police force was taken from that class—draymen, day laborers, hackmen, &c. ? I do not know ; but I know from seeing the police mustered daily at the station-house, and from seeing them frequently, that a large majority of them are Irish. One or two have been here for some time ; Garrett, chief of police, has been here a long time, but the larger portion are strangers to me. At one time I knew nearly everybody here.

4888. Is Garrett an Irishman ? No, sir ; he is not.

4889. Will you state whether you were not selected by General Stoneman as one of the military commission to investigate this riot, and whether you acted on that commission ? Yes, sir ; General Stoneman requested me in person to come. He said he intended to appoint a commission of officers of the army, and he would like to select one citizen of Memphis to act with them ; as I had resided here a considerable length of time, and as he happened to know me personally, he said he would be glad if I would serve, and I did serve on the commission with General Runkle, Captain Allyn, and Captain Colburn, of the quartermaster's department.

By the CHAIRMAN :

4890. What position did you occupy in the army ? I was brigadier general towards the close of the war.

4891. You stated that you were on this commission to examine into this riot ? Yes, sir.

4892. Did your commission make any report as to its judgment and conclusion ? No, sir ; we only reported the facts. General Stoneman told me in the first place that he did not desire an opinion ; he merely desired the facts. Afterwards General Stoneman requested the recorder of the court to inform us that he would like us to make up a report ; but, as the proceedings will show, we asked to be relieved, as there would probably be two or three reports. General Runkle was anxious that it should be so, for, as chief of the bureau, he had a report to make to his superior officer, and he did not want to make two reports.

4893. To what conclusion did you come as to the nature, extent and character of the riots? I became satisfied, from the investigation, that the beginning of it was the arrest of some negroes, who had been soldiers, by the police. They arrested some men, and had them under charge, when other negro soldiers following after them, and probably under the influence of liquor, commenced firing on them. The fighting commenced between the police and discharged negro soldiers, and there had evidently been strong feelings between the police and the colored soldiers. It was at first a sort of skirmish ; then the police called for assistance, and gave notice to their different friends and the rabble, who have no particular property to be preserved, and who are always ready for a row, and it then assumed the proportions of a very considerable riot. I do not think that one-half or one-quarter of the people who went there went from anything but curiosity, but I have no doubt that many shot down negroes without any cause in the world, and that they burnt school-houses, churches and dwellings on Wednesday night, and robbed, and committed very many outrages of that sort.

4894. Was it deemed necessary to call in United States troops to suppress this riot? Yes, sir.

4895. What do you think would have been the consequence if there had been no regular troops to rely upon in the emergency? I think fifty good men could have checked it at any time.

4896. If there had been no troops here? I think the sheriff could have selected a number of men who would have checked it. Such crowds are always cowardly ; and I think they could have been checked. There were many men here ready to go.

4897. Do you think the mob would have been checked had it not been for the regular troops? I think it would, sir, by the old citizens ; I judge so from the expression of feeling on the part of the citizens.

4898. Did they make any attempt? No, sir ; I think they depended upon the troops.

4899. What do you think of the troops being here for the preservation of the peace? I do not think that they are necessary. I think the negro troops here have not tended to the peace of the place ; the city has been more quiet since they left.

MARTIN GRIDLEY sworn and examined.

By Mr. SHANKLIN :

490J. State your name, residence and occupation. Martin Gridley ; I am a cotton factor ; sixty-six years of age ; was born in New York, but have been here twenty-six years.

4901. State whether you have mixed freely with the citizens of Memphis, and interchanged opinions and thoughts upon the subject of the sentiments and feelings of the mass of the people of Memphis towards the colored people ; and if so, state what is that state of feeling on the part of the business men, property-holders, and men of fixed location? So far as my knowledge extends, I think the old citizens, property-holders, and the former slave owners are kindly disposed towards the colored people. I never heard one of them but was anxious for their good treatment and disposed to give them employment. The bad blood seemed to be among the irresponsible people, mostly Irish, who seem to be hostile to the negro ; but the old citizens are not ; they are kindly disposed towards their servants.

4902. Were you here during the recent riot? Yes, sir.

4903. Did you see anything of it? I only saw people going that way, but did not mix with them.

4904. Of what class of people was the crowd composed? Mostly of the lower class, the rabble, rowdies ; I saw but few respectable persons going with it, and those, they said, were subpœnaed by the sheriff.

4905. So far as you know, were the respectable people of the city, the men who make any pretensions to character here, engaged in that difficulty, except the sheriff and some of his officers? No, sir ; I do not think they were. Good citizens kept at home and attended to their business, and did not care to mix up in it.

4906. State what has been the sentiment of the people of Memphis in regard to the outrages and cruelties perpetrated by this mob. So far as I heard anything from conversation with respectable citizens, on street corners, they universally condemned it as an outrage and misfortune on the city ; they said it would give us a bad name abroad.

4907. Was sympathy expressed towards the colored people who suffered? There did not seem to be much sympathy for the discharged soldiers who commenced the riots, but for colored people who were shot down very much sympathy was expressed. I heard some say that some discharged soldiers commenced the riot, and they did not seem to pity them much if they got killed.

4908. Were there not colored people of Memphis who went to their former masters for protection, and was that protection given them? I know that about a dozen of them knocked at my door and begged of me to let them in, for they were afraid of being shot. I told them "Certainly, come in and sit down; keep quiet and out of sight." I let some twelve or fifteen into my house; they were quiet, peaceable negroes, who had nothing to do with the riot.

4909. Do you know if others acted in the same way? No, sir. I stayed at home expecting to be burnt out ourselves, for within forty feet of our house there was burning. I saw a great deal of smoke in our house, and as the wind was setting thàt way I feared we should be burnt out. There were some ladies opposite us who begged them so piteously to put it out, that after putting chairs and tables on it they did put it out. The men were on horseback, but who they were I could not tell. I have been told it was a parcel of Irish police, but I do not know. There seems to be a bad feeling on the part of the Irish towards the negroes; they think they are interfering with their profits.

4910. I will ask you if the majority of the police had not been selected from that population who entertain hostile feeling towards the negro? Almost all the police are Irish; all our public men, from the mayor downward, are for the most part Irish, and they are all inimical to the negro.

4911. I will ask you if the effect of the last franchise law of Tennessee was not to throw the election and the selection of city officers into the hands of that description of people? I think it would have that tendency.

4912. Did the mass of the people approve of the selection of these officers? No, sir; the better portion of the people are hostile to them, but under the franchise law they had no power to prevent it.

4913. Have you discovered any hostile feeling of the masses of the people here towards northern men who have settled among you, on account of their nativity? Not unless it was on account of their politics; but this has been the case with all who attempt to interfere. Men who come from the North, as I did, and leave politics alone, are not interfered with.

4914. What particular doctrine was it these northern men advocated that rendered them obnoxious? The abolition doctrine that negroes should be allowed to vote; southerners here do not believe that.

4915. Were they also advocating the disfranchisement of the southern people who participated in the rebellion? Yes, sir.

4916. And were these the doctrines which created hostility to them? Yes, sir; and nothing else.

4917. Do you think the hostility of the people of Memphis towards these northern men is based upon their advocacy of these doctrines, or upon their nativity in northern States? Yes, sir; there are northern men here who are respected as much as southern men, but they, for the most part, leave politics alone.

By the CHAIRMAN:

4918. Were you here during the rebellion? Yes, sir. I was in Mississippi from January, 1861, to the following fall.

919. Are you a qualified voter? Yes, sir.

4920. Are you a voter under the recent franchise law? I do not know, sir; I have not tried it. I was, under the old law.

4921. What was the state of feeling towards Union men at the time the war broke out, here? It was, I thought, foolishly hostile.

4922. Were Union men called abolitionists and politicians? Yes, sir; I talked as long as it was safe to talk.

4923. Were you called an abolitionist? Yes, sir.

4924. Are not the Union men now called abolitionists, as you were called then? Yes, sir; but they are considerably quieted down.

4925. Were you not considered to be mixed up with politics? Yes, sir.

4926. Were you not obnoxious to a great portion of the southerners? Yes, sir,

4927. The same as a particular class of politicians of the North are obnoxious now? Yes, sir.

J. H. McMAHON sworn and examined.

By Mr. SHANKLIN:

4928. State your name, residence, and occupation. J. H. McMahon; I live in Memphis; I am the editor of the Appeal newspaper.

4929. How long have you been a resident of Memphis? Since 1838, with intervals of absence; once of two years, in 1848-'49, and then within the last four years I have been absent.

4930. What is the place of your nativity? Williamson county, Tennessee.

4931. State if you are familiar with the public sentiment entertained by the people of Memphis towards the resident colored population of the city, not including soldiers, or the freedmen who are temporarily coming in and leaving. I think I am.

4932. What are the sentiments, conduct, and treatment of these people towards the colored population? I think they are entirely kind. I think there is a feeling of entire recognition of its being to the interest of both races to live together in harmony, and in good friendly relations; and those relations do exist between the negro population and the great mass of the people of Memphis.

4933. State whether there is a class of people in Memphis between whom and the negroes there has been a jealousy, hatred, and rivalry. I think there probably is, though if you want me to indicate what that class is, I do not know that I could very distinctly define who compose that class. I judge more from the occurrences during the troubles here than from any previous knowledge.

4934. Do you think there is hostility between that class of foreigners located here and engaged as porters, hackmen, draymen, and wharf hands, and the negro? I think there is, sir. I have not much personal acquaintance with that portion of the population, but from occurrences that have taken place I judge that feeling exists. The killing of a boy at the Gayoso House was, I believe, from that class of people. The boy was here in attendance upon a party that was gotten up for the benefit of the confederate maimed and crippled; he was very well known to the respectable citizens, and was very much esteemed; he was killed just outside here. Some gentlemen had just gone into the hat room, and had given him their arms or pistols. The boy was probably sent down to call a hack; he had been gone but a few minutes when he was killed, and from all the information I could get, it seems he was killed by that class of people, the hackmen. He had indiscreetly buckled these pistols round him, and had them on his person when he went down.

4935. From your knowledge and information, of what class of persons was this mob composed who perpetrated these great outrages upon the colored people? I was not down at the scene of the disturbances, and cannot speak from personal observation of the class of people who composed it; but I know there is an element of disorder in the town, made up of people that I have no knowledge of—that I never saw before. When I see them in the street I cannot imagine who they are, and I know of no one who does know, either. I take it that for the most part they are thieves, pickpockets, burglars, and people of that sort. There is another element of disorder, the magnitude of which I think is not appreciated by the citizens here, and that I think was mainly instrumental in conducting these riots and the burnings; and that is an element we call the "mackerel brigade." It is made up of boys; they are ostensibly newsboys, but mixing with them is a number of boys that are known at the police office as thieves, burglars, and pickpockets. They are precociously shrewd and sharp; and I am quite certain that the excitement that was kept up in town after the first day's occurrences, and the exciting rumors that prevailed and filled the streets with people, originated with these little villains. For instance, on the last day there was an exciting rumor that there were a thousand negroes coming in from the country on the Pigeon Roost road, armed, to assist the negroes here. At the same time there was another rumor that the negro troops in the fort had seized their arms, run out of the fort, and were intrenching themselves. I believe these rumors were started and spread through the town by these little villains, probably under the direction of other and larger villains, burglars, and thieves, who in all times of disorder find their best opportunity to carry on their avocation. I think that element was a more potential one than was generally supposed. From all the information that I was able to obtain, and from the best judgment I can form, I think that after the first day's riot the disturbances and the outrages were continued by that class of people that the citizens of Memphis generally have no personal knowledge of.

4936. Where does that population come from? God only knows. They seem to come from all parts of the world. Among this mackerel brigade you will hear one called London; another Chicago or New Orleans, or St. Louis, or Dublin, &c., and they are blasphemous, obscene, and shrewd beyond conception. The burglars, thieves, pickpockets, and hack-drivers I believe come in the same way, from all parts of the world.

4937. Then that description of population is rather temporary than fixed? I imagine so; I suppose every large city in the Union exhibits something of the kind.

4938. From your central position between St. Louis and New Orleans, do you think you get an undue proportion of that rabble? Yes, sir; it is likely that we get more than our proportion.

4939. Have you heard any expression or sentiment on the part of the people or the newspapers, which, in your opinion, was intended and had the effect to encourage and excite the acts of violence and outrage perpetrated by the mob? No, sir, I do not think I have; I certainly have not from any one with whom I associate, and I do not remember to have read anything in any newspaper the purpose of which seemed to be this. I am quite sure these occurrences were very much deprecated by every good citizen, from the fact that it was calculated to make us very much misunderstood abroad. There is no general feeling among the citizens that is in accordance with these acts of violence; consequently I think I may say positively that I have neither heard nor known of any sentiment of that kind.

4940. You are, I presume, conversant with the newspapers of Memphis. Do you think the articles and teachings in these papers were intended or had the effect to incite or encourage acts of violence towards the colored population or anybody else? I do not know that I am willing to set myself up as a censor of the newspapers; perhaps I have read articles in the different papers that I should not myself have written, and the fact that I have not in my own paper written such articles as appeared in some of the other papers is evidence that I have taken a different view of treating these subjects; but if you ask me if I think these articles were written with that purpose, I unhesitatingly acquit every newspaper here of any such intention. I cannot recall any article in any newspaper that I think would have the effect of producing those acts.

4941. If there is any feeling of hostility existing on the part of the masses of the people of Memphis against persons of northern birth who have settled in the city of Memphis, is that prejudice or hostility of feeling on account of the place of their nativity and former residence, or is it on account of peculiar sentiments which they entertain and which they express? I do not think there is any feeling or sentiment of hostility simply from the fact of northern birth, or emigration from the north. Wherever there may be any feeling of hostility towards such a person, I think it is invariably from the expression of some special sentiments peculiar to that person. The proof that no such general sentiment exists is to be found in the fact that between native southern men here—men who belonged to the confederate army, returned paroled soldiers—and northern men and northern soldiers, in vast number of instances, there exist the most kindly and friendly relations; there exist the most intimate business relations, and every day there is exhibited the most friendly personal intercourse and association mutually sought by both parties. I am not aware of the existence of any special hostility to any northern men, or class of northern men; perhaps if there is, it is to the teachers of negro schools; northern men coming down here to teach the negro schools. I think the sentiment of this community is such that they would not seek personal acquaintance with such. I do not think this feeling would lead to personal violence towards them, but I think the community generally would be very apt just to let them seek their own associates, and that they would be averse to associating with them.

4942. State whether, in your opinion, there would be an equal amount of hostility felt and exhibited towards men of southern birth as towards men of northern birth, if they were contending for and promulgating the political˙sentiments that negroes should be invested with all the political rights—the right of suffrage and the right to hold office—that white men have heretofore enjoyed, and at the same time advocating the doctrine that all men who were engaged in the rebellion should be disfranchised; would there be any discrimination in the feeling towards the persons teaching such doctrines on account of their nativity? There probably would; the feeling would be more intense towards the southern than the northern men.

4943. Would there be a feeling of unkindness manifested or entertained towards people who advocated doctrines of that sort? If you mean personal violence and hostility, I do not think there would be, because the thing is done without being attended with personal violence. One of my most intimate friends is an ultra advocate for universal suffrage, and I differ very widely with him on that subject, but it certainly has not interrupted our personal relations, nor has it interrupted his personal relations with this community. This gentleman, however, I should say, disapproves of the sweeping disfranchisement.

4944. Would not persons teaching those doctrines excite some hostility in the minds of the masses of the people? Undoubtedly; even the worm would turn at such degradation.

4945. Then you think that whatever hostility exists in the public mind of the people of Memphis towards northern people is on account of their own personal deportment and the doctrines they teach, and not on account of their place of nativity? Unquestionably I do.

By the CHAIRMAN:

4946. I understand you are the editor of the Memphis Appeal? Yes, sir.
4947. For how long a period? Since the 5th of November last.
4948. Were you editor of it previous to that time? No, sir; I was not connected with it.
4949. Where were you during the recent troubles? I was confederate quartermaster in that service.

4950. You have spoken of the disapprobation of sentiment at these recent riots ; has that disapprobation found expression through the public press ? I think so, sir, to some extent.

4951. To what extent ? To the extent of expressing disapprobation.

4952. Were they severely denounced ? I do not know that I could say they were severely denounced, but I think they were condemned generally by the press.

4953. Do you, or not, think that the tendency of some articles of the press of this city has tended to excite a turbulent and hostile feeling here in this city previous to the riot? As I said before, I cannot undertake to be a censor of the press.

4954. I understood you to say that you had seen articles on this subject which you would not have written yourself ? Yes, sir.

4954½. In what did you differ from those articles ? I do not know that I could answer.

4955. Were they more violent and inflammatory than you would have written yourself ? I can illustrate : some newspapers gave publication to the rumors that existed at the time, and which no doubt were believed to be true, but in the Appeal I did not.

4956. Was not the tendency of giving publicity to those rumors to inflame the public feeling ? Well, sir, that is a matter that each one must judge for himself ; it would be impossible for me to undertake to determine.

By Mr. BROOMALL :

4957. You have spoken of the sentiments of the people of Memphis towards men of northern brith ; I find in one of the Memphis papers of this morning an article, which appears to be editorial, in which the writer, after giving an account of a white man running away from his wife and taking up with a negro woman, says, "This is the kind of morality which these northern radicals wish to force upon us." State if that is a common sentiment of the newspapers here. I do not think I can answer that question direct ; I have never read the newspapers with reference to the common sentiment here.

4958 I said a common sentiment inculcated here. I think a very common sentiment here would be condemnation of a man guilty of that.

4959. That is not my question ; I want to know if that is the kind of morality the northern radicals want to force upon the South ? I have heard that it is.

4960. State whether or not there is a public sentiment in Memphis more or less extensive, that would respond to a charge of that sort against the northern men ? It is very probable sir, as you will find extreme men in every community, in all phases of politics, who will respond to any doctrine, however outrageous.

4961. State whether in your opinion that kind of assertion is not calculated to keep up a spirit of hostility between the people of the south and the northern men who come here. I do not know that I clearly perceive the scope of your question.

4962. I want to know if the reiteration of that sentiment, that the northern people wish to enforce that kind of morality upon the people of the south, is not calculated to keep up a hostility between the people of the south and people of northern birth who entertain northern sentiments ? If you mean by northern sentiments absolute equality and amalgamation, then I say that a feeling of hostility certainly exists.

4963. I believe you know that I do not mean that. Northern sentiments, as expressed in the North and here, are hostility to the late rebels. Now does not the charge that northern sentiment embraces a disposition to force this species of morality that I have alluded to, but excite and increase animosity between people of the south and men who are hostile to the late rebels ? It is but the expression of opinion, and I think of that just as I think of many things I see in both northern and southern newspapers, that are calculated to keep the breach open between the two sections.

4964. Does not the press of Memphis—I do not speak of your paper—throwing aside the radical papers here, persistently charge that the northern men who are here desire to bring about amalgamation between the races ? Gentlemen, the files of these papers exist, and I am unwilling to make myself a censor.

4965. Then you are unwilling to answer the question ? I am unwilling to be censor as to the manner in which they conduct their papers.

4966. I am not asking you to praise or condemn ; I am asking for the fact ? I do not wish to give an immature opinion, and I should prefer, therefore, not to be called upon to pronounce a judgment and criticism upon the press of Memphis.

4967. I am asking you to give the fact, not to give an opinion upon it ; simply to state whether it is not an idea commonly inculcated by the press of Memphis, that the northern radicals try to force the species of morality mentioned in the article I have alluded to upon the South ? I expect it is a fact that the press of Memphis do attribute to certain classes of northern writers that sort of thing ; I do not know, though, that it is a common habit for them to do so, for I am not prepared, not having perused the press of Memphis with a view to answering any such question.

CHARITY WORMLEY (colored) sworn and examined.

By Mr. SHANKLIN :

4968. What is your name, and where do you live? Charity Wormley; I always belonged to Mr. Wormley, all my life ; I live with Dr. Smith now, in Memphis.

4969. How long have you been free? I have always been free as I can be, because I have always lived well and done well.

4970. What is your age? Seventy-one.

4971. How have the white people, those who owned slaves and property and live here, treated you and other colored people since the war commenced? My family of people, the Wormleys and Walkers, I know all about them, and they have treated them very well ; the others I know nothing about.

4972. Then, as far as you know, the treatment has been good? Yes, sir ; though I see many who appear to be suffering going about here, but they are strangers to me.

4973. You know a good many_colored people in Memphis ; how do those who formerly owned them appear to treat them as far as you know? They appear to treat them very well.

4974. Do the colored people seem to be satisfied with the treatment they get? Yes, sir; but I do not know very much about the people of Memphis ; I go to the north every year.

4975 Where do you go to? To Pekin, Illinois.

4976. Do you go with white people? Yes, sir; with my mistress ; and I shall stay with my master and mistress as long as I live. I am doing better now than if I was free.

4977. If you wanted aid and assistance, to whom would you go? I would go right to them.

4978. As far as you know, how have the colored people been treated by their former owners? They have been kind, so far as I know.

4979. And the colored people are contented and satisfied with the treatment they get? Yes, sir.

By the CHAIRMAN :

4980. Were you in Memphis at the time of the disturbances? Yes, sir.

4981. What do you know of the colored people that were killed? I heard there were four or five or six who were killed.

4982. Who killed them? I cannot say.

4983. What were they killed for? I cannot say anything about that. I saw the light of the fire, but I never came out to see

4984. Why? I was afraid ; I was afraid they would shoot me on the street, for they were shooting there.

4985. Why were they shooting? I do not know.

4986. Had you ever done any harm? No, sir ; and what they were shooting for I never could see, never could tell.

4987. Who did they shoot? I do not know anything about that ; I saw a great many who did see them.

4988. How long have you been a slave? All my life.

4989. Are you a slave now? Yes, sir ; I am a slave to them now, and I shall be still, for they treat me right ; I have worked for them all my life.

4990. Is that the reason why you go to them for assistance? Yes, sir.

4991. You think that in consideration for all the work you have done for them, they can aid you when you need it? Yes, sir

4992. You have worked for them faithfully and industriously, and without compensation? Yes, sir.

4993. And have worked for them all your life? Yes, sir.

By Mr. SHANKLIN :

4994. You have a comfortable home, have you not? Yes, sir, always ; a comfortable room, a comfortable fireplace, and plenty to eat.

By the CHAIRMAN :

4995. And plenty to do? Yes, sir ; plenty to eat, and plenty to do.

L. J. DU PRE sworn and examined.

By Mr. SHANKLIN :

4996. State your name, residence, and occupation. L. J. Du Pre ; I live in Memphis, and am editor of the Memphis Bulletin newspaper.

4997. Please to state the place of your nativity. I was born in Athens, Georgia, and resided before I came here, in 1850, in Noxubee county, Mississippi.

4998. State if your intercourse with the people of Memphis has been such as to enable you to form an opinion as to the general sentiment of the masses of the people here towards the colored population? I have been absent from this city nearly five years, leaving in June, 1861, and my associations here have been for the most part with men I knew before the war. Many new people have settled here.

4999. What service were you engaged in? I never enlisted in the confederate army, but was frequently with it, and acted at times as staff officer.

5000. From your intercourse with the people since your return, what have been the sentiments of the people here towards the colored population? I judge of other men by myself. I was a slave owner; I inherited them; and I may say the relations between ex-masters and ex-slaves are kind. The negroes we owned are sometimes great annoyances, but we take care of them as well as we possibly can.

5001. So far as you know the sentiments of their former masters, you think they are kind? Yes, sir; entirely so. Many that I know have just the same kindly feelings towards them that they had before the war.

5002. Please to state what are the feelings and sentiment of the masses of the people here towards people of northern birth; whether or not it is hostile, and, if so, whether that hostility is based upon the peculiar opinions those people entertain, or whether it is on account of the place of their nativity? We have been discussing that question in the papers, and the controversy between the Avalanche and the Bulletin became a very bitter one. I have thought they have endeavored to excite a prejudice against northern men; but while the quarrel has been going on the circulation of the Bulletin has steadily increased, and I know my course has been approved of by such men as D. R. Cook, Wiley B. Miller, Brinkley, Greenlaw, and others, ex-rebels and large property holders. But I do not think that such a feeling is entertained; it may be by a few young men, but it is not generally entertained by intelligent citizens.

5003. If any hostility is entertained by the people of Memphis towards the class of people I have referred to, is it on account of their being northern people, or on account of their peculiar opinions? It is to a great extent because of the legislation of this State, I mean the franchise law, and their advocacy of it, that any such feeling is entertained.

5004. That law is generally disapproved of by the public sentiment here, is it not? Yes, sir, it is, almost universally.

5005. The doctrine that has been promulgated by some, of conferring upon the negro equal political rights with white men, has that doctrine been advocated here to any extent? There are persons who advocate it. There was a newspaper which did so for a time; but the doctrine is offensive here, and has a bad effect upon the two races. I am told by gentlemen who have been accustomed to get shaved by colored barbers, that since that question has been agitated they have ceased to be shaved by any other than white men.

5006. Do you think that the discussion of the civil rights bill has done harm, so far as the relations between the white and black people are concerned? Yes, sir.

5007. Will you please to state the character and class of persons of which this mob was composed? I can only tell by the general condemnation of the whole thing while it was in progress. For the last eight months I pass the recorder's room daily and I frequently stop and look in. The city government, as you perhaps know, is in the hands of the Irish, and there has always been, both before the war and since, hostility between Irishmen and negroes. Since the war they have fought differently: before, they used their fists and clubs; but since, they have used deadly weapons.

5008. So far as you have been able to acertain, was that mob composed of that class of people and the rabble population? Yes, sir; I have so understood. The whole city government and policemen are all Irishmen. It was as far as I understand an Irish riot, and was mainly between the Irish and the negroes.

5009. I will ask you whether or not the franchise law of the State of Tennessee, which was in operation at the last city election, did not place the control of that election in the hands of the Irish population, such as draymen, wharf-hands, &c.? Yes, sir; the whole city government is in the hands of the Irish, and there is no means of ridding ourselves of it under the existing order of things.

5010. Did not that franchise law of the State of Tennessee take the control of the election out of the hands of the more orderly, quiet, and property-holding citizens? Yes, sir. Some of the leading radicals of the city, good citizens, such as W. R. Moore, Mr. Fitch, and Walcott, and others, at my instigation, signed a petition to Governor Brownlow to the effect that all who owned real estate or paid a rental of $500 per year should be permitted to vote in city elections.

5011. Was that petition acted upon? I know not. I mailed it to Governor Brownlow, but he made no reply.

5012. Then is it not the sentiment of both parties that the legislative law which controls the city elections should be changed so as to permit the citizens to vote without regard to their antecedents? Yes, sir; all with whom I have intercourse believe that. Under the old city charter none could vote unless they held property; and under the old city government everything went on well. All our railways were then built; now there is no money in the treasury, and city scrip is at a discount of twenty-five cents on the dollar, and city revenues are quadrupled.

5013. What was the sentiment of the people of Memphis in regard to this outrage? All the people I associate with condemned it as bitterly as you do, gentlemen; and one reason why there was not a stronger expression of that feeling was that they even feared the Irish. An honest expression of feeling might have resulted in the burning of a newspaper office.

5014. I understand you to mean that the legal authority and power were in the hands of the mob? Yes, sir. At the last election anybody could vote. The Irish, I am told, voted about two thousand one hundred at the last election. I was offered a certificate of citizenship, but not deeming it right to vote, of course I declined. The law deserved obedience because it was the law.

5015. Is it your opinion that if the election was placed in the hands of the whole people of Memphis, you would get competent and good civil officers that would secure the peace and order of the city without the aid of the federal troops? There are too many Irish here, I fear. The city government would be greatly better, because several of the wards would be represented by Americans; but there would be many wards represented and would be governed by the Irish; but we would have an infinitely better government than we have now, and a government that I believe would maintain order and quiet without the presence of the troops. Now a white garrison is deemed essential to the maintenance of good order and personal security.

JACK HARRIS WALKER (colored) sworn and examined.

By Mr. SHANKLIN:

5016. What is your name, and where do you live? Jack Harris Walker. I live in Memphis.

5017. Have you been a slave all your life? Yes, sir.

5018. Who was your former master? My first master was A. O. Harris, near Nashville. He married James K. Polk's sister. After that I lived with Samuel P. Walker, here in Memphis.

5019. Were you staying with Mr. Walker at the time of the riots? Yes, sir.

5020. How long have you been free? Since the rebellion; but I always hired my own time since I have been in Memphis, some fifteen years.

5021. Tell us what the treatment of the white people you have been mixing with has been towards you and other colored persons for the last year or two. As far as I know, I can state that the man I have been with—and I have known him since I was a boy—has always treated me well, and treated all his colored servants well, and allowed us as much privilege as if we were free. He always told us, twenty years ago, that if ever we were to be free, he would rather have us to work for him, and he would pay us good wages. I thought I would see if he was a man of truth or not, and I found that he was, and have remained with him.

5022. What has been the treatment of white citizens towards you? I have been here for fifteen years, and there never was a white man in this town that could say anything against me. I do not think there is a white or black man or anybody in this city that can say a word against me.

5023. What has been the treatment of the citizens here, the property-holders and men of business, towards the colored people, as far as you know? As far as I know, some treat the colored people with a good deal of respect, and others have not treated them well, and that is the reason why they left them; but I have been treated mighty well.

5024. What is the feeling the colored people entertain towards their former masters and white people they have associated with? So far as I know, some of them have very good feeling for some, and for others they have not, because they find them different in language and conduct.

5025. So far as you know the treatment and sentiment of the white and colored population of Memphis, then, it is friendly and kind? Yes, sir. The old citizens here have always been friendly and kind with those they knew, before the war and since, and that has been the case between the white and colored people, as far as I know.

By the CHAIRMAN:

5026. How long have you been free? I have been considered about free ever since Memphis was captured.

5027. Were you living here when Memphis was captured? Yes, sir.

20

5028. Were you Mr. Walker's slave? Yes, sir.

5029. How long have you been his slave? About fifteen or sixteen years.

5030. What did you do? I always waited about his house. I was raised up to that and going on errands through the city and waiting on his office. And then I worked out for wages, and paid him twenty-five dollars a month for my time, and' he always gave me ten dollars out of it every month.

5031. What did he give you for that fifteen dollars? Why, he did not'give me anything.

5032. What did you give him that for? Because I was a slave.

5033. How do you like being free? Of course anybody with any knowledge would rather be free, because we have not to pay anything to anybody now.

5034. Which did you like best, the Union men or the rebels? I like the Union men a great deal the best. I suppose they have done a great deal, a tremendous deal for our race, and we should glorify those who have taken the burden off from us; but still we have feelings of respect and regard for those among whom we were raised as boys.

5035. How were the colored people treated during the recent riots? They were treated tremendous bad; but it was not by all the white men, only the low class.

PRINCE MOULTRIE (colored) sworn and examined.

By Mr. SHANKLIN :

5036. What is your name? Prince Moultrie.

5037. Where do you live? I live in Memphis.

5038. How long have you lived here? For the last ten years.

5039. Have you ever been a slave? Yes, sir; Fraser Titus was my master.

5040. How long have you been free? About a year.

5041. Were you living in Memphis when you obtained your freedom? Yes, sir.

5042. State how the white people have treated you, before and since you were free. My four owners, that I belonged to, treated me very well indeed, but a great many outsiders would seem to despise you as you walked upon the street.

5043. What sort of people are those who despise the colored men? They are the low down class among the Irish; I think they are about as mean a people as we have got here; you are not safe at night.

5044. Outside of them, do the white people treat the colored people well? As far as I know, sir; I have kept myself pretty close at work, and do not run about much.

5045. Were you here at the time of the riot? Yes, sir.

5046. Was it that low down sort of people that committed all these outrages upon the colored people? I think it was altogether among the low down people. There were a good many colored people trying to get to their homes who were very much abused before they got there, and the next day they could not go to work at all.

5047. How have the old citizens of Memphis generally treated the colored people since they have been free, kindly or unkindly, leaving out the low classes? As far as I know the high classes have treated free servants very well indeed, because they prefer their old servants rather than have strangers. I live with the gentleman who owned me.

5048. Is there a good or bad state of feeling existing between the colored people here and this better sort of white people? I think they are inclined to treat them well—better, I think, than they would strangers.

By the CHAIRMAN :

5049. How do you consider an Irishmen in comparison with yourself? I think he is very much below me.

THOMAS BRADSHAW (colored) sworn and examined.

By Mr. SHANKLIN :

5050. What is your name, age, and where do you live? Thomas Bradshaw; I live in Memphis; I guess I am about forty-eight.

5051. Have you been a slave? Yes, sir; I was Mr. Bradshaw's slave.

5052. How long have you lived in Memphis? I have been here about twenty years.

5053. How long have you lived with Mr. Bradshaw? Ten or twelve years.

5054. What has been the treatment of the white people of Memphis towards you and other colored men in the city for the last three or four years? I am an old citizen here, and those who knew me treated me very well in the position I held. I was barber and musician; and as my conduct was straight and quiet they treated me nicely. For myself I was well treated as a general thing.

5055. Since you have been free what has been their course of treatment towards you?

They have treated me pretty well ; during the war I suppose I was flustrated like other people, but I cannot say that they treated me very rough. During war I suppose everybody has to suffer.

5056. What is now and what has been the state of feeling in Memphis, so far as you know, between the white people and the black—I mean the residents ? As far as I recollect, among certain classes, it has been very kind ; with some it is different. Those who knew me treated me very kindly, and seemed willing, if I needed assistance, to assist me.

5057. So far as you know, what has been the general treatment of old residents towards colored people ? I could not say much as to that, for I was not about much ; for myself, I got along very pretty.

5058. Can you say what was the feeling of the colored people towards the white people of the city of Memphis generally ? There was a kind of hostile feeling between some portion of the colored and some portion of the white people.

5059. Has there not been for the last ten or fifteen years a feeling of hostility existing between the Irish draymen, hack-drivers, &c., and the colored people ? There were Irish draymen and colored draymen before the war, and the owners of most of the colored draymen were here in the city, and the Irish did not take the same privileges with the colored men at that time that they do now, because they were afraid of their owners, who would take a stick and come out and maul them. The prejudice was pretty much kept down on that account ; but it has seemed to grow up from what I have heard ; and there seemed to be a prejudice between the soldiers and the policemen.

J. L. CHANDLER sworn and examined.

By the CHAIRMAN :

5060. State your name, residence, and business. J. L. Chandler ; I live in Memphis, and am in business in the firm of Beaumont & Hamilton ; I am also acting as editor of the Memphis Post.

5061. What is your business? Wholesale grocer and commission.

5062. Have you been in the United States army ? Yes, sir.

5063. In what capacity? Private first; then lieutenant colonel and colonel.

5064. Were you in Memphis at the time of the riots? Yes, sir.

5065. What did you see of them ? I saw little of the proceedings of the rioters ; I live outside of the scene of the riots, and I kept away from it. I saw the burning of the two buildings on Wednesday night.

5066. State whether or not the Post building was threatened by the mob. As I was going home on the Wednesday evening about eight o'clock, on the corner of Hernando and Vance streets, I passed through a crowd of strangers to me, and I heard them say, " We're going to clean out that God damn Post to-night ;" and another said, " That must be done, sure."

5067. Had you any well-grounded apprehension that the Post would be attacked ? The lady with whom I board got information of it during the day. She lives on the outer circle of the scene of the rioting, and one or more of the men told her that they were going to kill all the negroes and blow up the Post. She got scared and started down to tell me, but she did not know where the Post was.

5068. Were there any expectations on the part of the employés that it would be attacked ? We had scarcely any doubt about it. On the information I received in town, before I heard what I have referred to, I went down with General Morgan and Doctor Shaw to see General Stoneman, and obtain a guard ; but we were told in the office that the General had gone up stairs with a very severe headache, and unless it was something very important he must not be disturbed. We left our message, but heard nothing from him afterwards.

5069. Did you know any person in the mob ? No, sir.

5070. Do you know of any propositions of the mob other than what you have stated, that they would attack the Post? None that came to my direct knowledge. The lady with whom I board gave her evidence before the commission.

5071. Are you pretty well acquainted with the newspaper press of this city ? Yes, sir.

5072. Do you know who are the editors and proprietors? Yes, sir.

5073. Do you know if any, and if any, what number have been in the rebel service ? I do not think I can say definitely, but I have understood that Colonel DuPre has, and Colonel Galloway, Captain Ray, Captain Cluskey, and Major Hampton, of the Avalanche, have been in the rebel service ; of the editors of the Appeal, I do not know that any have.

5074. Have any of the editors of the Ledger ? I do not know certainly, but I have understood that one of the Whitmore brothers was in the service ; of the Argus I think none have been in the service ; of the Commercial, I think, Colonel Truesdale ; Mr. Keating and the other members, I think not.

5075. How many daily papers are published in Memphis? The Appeal, Bulletin, Argus, Commercial, Ledger, Post, and Avalanche.

5076. Who is connected with the Ledger? It is published by the two Whitmores; one was away during the rebellion and one remained here; he was not in the rebellion.

5077. Do you know that five out of the seven papers published here are controlled, in a greater or less degree, by men who have been in the rebel army? Yes, sir.

5078. Are there any persons on the Post that were connected with the Union army? Almost all were; Colonel Eaton was, and so were all the compositors but one; Mr. Dumars has not been in the service, I believe, but the others were in the service, I believe, during the entire war.

By Mr. SHANKLIN:

5079. You spoke of having passed a crowd on Wednesday evening, and you said, did you not, that you heard some men in the crowd threatening that the Post should be destroyed? Yes, sir; they spoke of it as "the damned nigger concern, the Post," and said they would clean it out.

5080. Will you state what class of persons composed that crowd; were there any respectable citizens among them? I should say there were none among them that could be classed among our quiet, respectable citizens.

5081. Was it not composed of the low rabble of the city? It was about eight o'clock in the evening and I could not see their faces, but the general impression left on my mind was that they were of a rather low class of people.

5082. Was not that mob, so far as you know, composed of that low rabble class and the police of the city? There were some men connected with it who claim a pretty good standing here, men who are mechanics, and merchants' clerks, who, I have heard, were armed during that day and who have been heard talking of what was going on, and were supposed to be connected with the affair; but, as a general thing, the class of men there was of a low description.

5083. Were not those men generally summoned by the sheriff? I do not know, sir. I saw a crowd being armed by the sheriff at Folsome's gun store on Wednesday morning; it had some few respectable men in it, but more than half were a very low class, such as barroom loafers.

JAMES CARROLL MITCHELL (colored) sworn and examined.

By the CHAIRMAN:

5084. What is you name, and where do you live? James Carroll Mitchell; I live in South Memphis.

5085. Were you a soldier? Yes, sir; I belonged to the sixty-first United States colored infantry.

5086. Were you in Memphis at the time of the riots? Yes, sir; I was here when they broke out.

5087. Did you see the shooting that was going on? Part of it I saw.

5088. What did you see? I saw some men shot that I knew.

5089. Did you see any white people shot? Yes, sir.

5090. Did you see any colored people shot? No, sir; I heard the shooting on South street as I stood at my house.

5091. But did you see any men shot, white or black? Yes, sir; I saw John Pendergrast shoot a man.

5092. Who did he shoot? The first man he shot was a white man; he walked up within five paces of him and shot him in the back of the head. He said at the time that he thought it was another man; he said, "I thought he was a damned yellow nigger."

5093. Who was it that was shot? He was a fireman. I was not fifty steps from there, and saw it.

5094. Did he shoot him from behind? Yes, sir. The man was advancing close after the colored soldiers; they were close by and were running up the bayou; the man that was shot was going towards the soldiers. Pendergrast had two pistols in his hand, and the fireman, they said, had no pistols in his. Mr. Pendergrast ran out of his grocery and his mother told him to come back, but he went with his pistols, and as the man's back was turned he shot him in the head.

5095. Did you see him after he was shot? Yes, sir.

5096. Did he say anything? Just as he was turned over he was dead.

5097. Did Pendergrast come up? Yes, sir; he came up and said, "We have killed one of our own men; I thought it was a damned yellow nigger." Then they got a hack and took him away.

5098. Were there any other people about there at that time? Yes, sir; lots of people were there at the same time.

5099. Were there any others who saw Pendergrast shoot him? Yes, sir; a woman was standing at the same place; and my wife saw it.

5100. Are you certain in regard to the shooting of this fireman; and are you certain as to the person who shot him? Yes, sir; I am quite certain.

5101. Were you robbed, or burned out? No, sir; I was renting a house from a white man, giving him $200 a year for it.

5102. Did you see any other persons killed by the mob? The policemen surrounded where the colored people were, and as a young man, a colored soldier, was about to make his escape, Captain Cash was on the bridge, and he shot him right there. The soldier belonged to the heavy artillery in the fort.

5103. Did you see anybody else shot? Yes, sir; I saw Pendergrast—he was so mad that he had shot a white man—go right up to the bayou and told a man, a colored soldier, to come up, he wasn't going to shoot him; so the soldier came up, and he shot him right through the mouth.

5104. Was this the old man Pendergrast? No, sir; it was his son; it was John Pendergrast.

5105. Where is he? •He went away after this.

5106. Have you seen the old man? Yes, sir.

5107. Was the old man engaged in the mob? Not that I know.

5108. When was the fireman killed? It was on Tuesday.

5109. Did you see any one else killed? I came out the next night, when they were burning down the school-house, and I saw a man shoot a woman.

5110. Do you know the man's name? His name is Galloway.

5111. What was the name of the woman he shot? That was Rachel Hatcher. I know Galloway shot her.

5112. How do you know it? I did not see him shoot her; but there were men that did that told me.

By Mr. BROOMALL:

5113. Have you heard the name of this fireman that was shot? No, sir; but I knew it was a fireman that was shot.

ERASTUS CORNELIUS sworn and examined.

By the CHAIRMAN:

5114. State your name, residence, and occupation. Erastus Cornelius; I live in this city; am clerking for Mr. Jones, coal merchant.

5115. Were you in Memphis at the time of the riot? Yes, sir; I was in the employ of Mr. Jones at the time.

5116. Did you see anything of the riotous proceedings? I saw something burning at about twelve o'clock on the second night, Wednesday; I got up and found the freedmen's church was on fire. I went down and found a great crowd round it, but I could not learn who set it on fire.

5117. Did you hear any conversation? I heard a great many saying "Keno's correct."

5118. What did you understand by this? I understood it to mean that it was all right.

5119. Did you hear any orders given to burn the building? No, sir.

5120. Did you see any city officials that you knew about there? I saw John C. Creighton.

5121. What was he doing? He was standing around looking on

5122. Did he make any observation? Nothing more than I have said. Nearly every one made use of that expression.

5123. Did you understand that it was an approval of the proceedings? I took it as such. It seemed to be a watchword of the mob.

5124. Did you hear him give any orders in regard to the fire? No, sir.

5125. Did you see any effort to put the fire out? No, sir.

5126. Did you see any other official there that you know? No, sir. I heard Creighton's name, and I heard him. The evening before, a little before dark, I heard a gentleman remark, "I am going down to South Memphis; I think there will be a fire; that church will go up to-night."

5127. Do you know who he was? He is a German who keeps a grocery right opposite where I board.

5128. What did he mean? I have thought since that he knew it would be burnt, and that if he was not a party to it he knew who the parties were.

5129. What was the name of the church? It is an old established colored Baptist church. I know it very well.

5130. Was there any property burned about it? No, sir; but there was hard work to save the property around it.

5131. All the efforts, then, were to save the property round? They did not throw a drop of water, except on the little house near.

5132. What were the firemen doing? They came up and seemed to be fixing their hose; but they did nothing, except upon the house near.

Dr. JAMES E. LYNCH recalled.

By the CHAIRMAN:

5133. Were you called at any time during the riots to see a man who had been shot? Yes, sir.

5134. What was his name? Dunn. He was a fireman.

5135. Was he dead when you were called to him? He was living, but on the point of death. He lived twenty or twenty-five minutes.

5136. Where did you see him? In the drug store at the bottom of Jackson street.

5137. Where was he shot? In the back of his head. I made no examination whatever. I was requested to call in by some friends.

5138. Describe the nature of his wound. I saw the man lying on the floor, and a couple of the 16th regulars with him. I supposed they had brought him. I looked at him and saw he was about to die. He had quite a prominence on his forehead and found his skull fractured, as if he, perhaps, had fallen forward. I said, "There is no use in doing anything with him; if you can give him brandy, all well." The druggist then remarked, "He is wounded behind;" and putting my hand behind, I found that this prominence on his forehead was the bullet that had passed through his head. At least that was my impression.

5139. Was the ball from a pistol? I should judge that it was a musket ball from the size of the wound.

5140. Was the shot from behind? I should judge so; but I made but a momentary examination, as I saw the man could not survive more than ten or fifteen minutes. The druggist said he had been shot from behind, and that the ball had entered the skull from behind; and I saw that there was a considerable wound behind.

CHANNING RICHARDS sworn and examined.

By the CHAIRMAN:

5141. State your name, residence, and occupation. Channing Richards; I reside in Memphis; I am one of the Metropolitan Police commissioners under the late law.

5142. How long have you resided in Memphis? I came to Memphis in 1863, and have been here ever since, in service and out.

5143. Have you been connected with city affairs here? Yes, sir; I was provisional mayor last year.

5144. Who was the mayor in law? Mr. John Park; he had been elected at the previous election.

5145. When was he elected? At the general election in 1864, and was immediately deposed by General Washburne.

5146. Do you know the probable number of votes he received? I could not state the number; but it was a close competition. His principal competitor was Mr. John Bullock; and some two or three hundred votes were cast for Dr. Johnsn.

5147. Was it a pretty free vote? Almost everybody voted that wanted to. There was no franchise law to prevent them.

5148. Had all the citizens a right to vote at that time? Yes, sir. It had been publicly announced by General Washburn that Park would not be allowed to continue in office another year.

5149. And yet he ran and was elected? Yes, sir.

5150. By what class of citizens was he elected? I only know by common rumor.

5151. He had been elected, then, before that? Yes, sir. I think he was first elected in 1861, and has been annually elected ever since.

5152. And he was elected in the face of an announcement that he would not be permitted to exercise the duties of his office? Yes, sir.

5153. On what ground was that announcement made? On the ground of incompetency and disloyalty.

5154. And yet he was elected? He was elected again in 1865 by a pretty large majority.

5155. Was there a free election then? No, sir; it was the first election under the franchise law. The registration under the new law began about a week before that election.

5156. Do you know the number of votes cast? My impression is that the votes amounted to about 2,000. I took a good deal of interest in that election. It was a straight contest between Mr. Park and Mr. W. O. Lofland, who has been city comptroller for several years.

5157. Is Mr. Park a less competent and more drunken man than when he was first elected? I understand such to be the fact. I think he is more so than when I first knew him, three years ago.

5158. Is he worse than he was in 1864? Yes, sir; he is worse now. He then had some lucid intervals. I see him more frequently drunk now than I did then.

5159. Who is the present city recorder? John C. Creighton.

5160. What kind of a court does he hold? Offenders against the city ordinances are tried by him. He is also magistrate of the county.

5161. Does he still hold that office? Yes, sir.

5162. Is it an important position? Yes, sir; on it depends the order of the city.

5163. Has he been elected by the people? Yes, sir.

5164. How many times? He was defeated in 1864, when the military board was established, but he was elected again last year. When he came here in 1863 he was elected recorder.

5165. Was there any elective franchise in operation when he was elected? No, sir; anybody voted that pleased, but in 1863 my impression is that the vote for mayor was only two or three hundred.

DUDLEY D. SAUNDERS sworn and examined.

By the CHAIRMAN:

5166. What is your name, and where do you reside? Dudley D. Saunders; I reside in Memphis.

5167. Were you here at the time of the riots? I was, sir.

5168. Do you know of any acts of violence committed upon any person or persons during those riots? I know of a boy who was killed on the Thursday night at the hotel here; he was a colored man; we commonly called him William Henry.

5169. State the circumstances under which he was killed. A large ball was given here that night, and as he was a very trusty fellow, he, with another of the boys I have raised, that waits in my office, had to take care of the coats and hats. Many of the young men wore their pistols, and knowing these boys, they would take off their pistols and would say, "Take these and take care of them;" and would add, "Put them in your pocket, or buckle them round you; and don't mix them up with the others." The boy had some buckled on him, and some stuck in his bosom, and of course there was no one in the room to disturb them. But about supper time, at twelve o'clock at night, the other boy missed him from the room; he said he waited some little time and then went to look for him. He heard some one say, "There's a boy shot down on the pavement." He went down, and discovered that it was Will who was shot. I did not know of it for half an hour; some friends then came to me and said, "Is not that your boy?" I was perfectly surprised, and replied, "I reckon not;" but I immediately went out and found the boy lying on the pavement dead. He was shot in the left eye, the shot ranging through his head. A gentleman told me that he told Will about that time to go down and order his carriage, giving him the number, and the boy, thoughtlessly, went down with the pistols buckled on him and some sticking in his bosom; when he got to the door, not finding the carriage immediately at the door, (for the street was full of hacks,) he walked down the pavement to find the hack, and on the corner, some person whom I have never been able to find out, shot him down, I suppose because he had those weapons buckled on him. I inquired of the hackmen if they could tell me anything about how he was killed, or who shot him, but no one knew anything about it; or if they did, would not tell.

5170. Were they colored hackmen? Most of them were white; some were Irish and others not. One hackman said, "All I know of it is, I drove up here just now, and my horses started at the shot, and when I looked I saw the man lying there in that pool of blood." I attribute his being shot to the pistols he wore.

5171. What was the object of the ball? It was for a benevolent purpose; it was for the purpose of furnishing limbs to men who had been in the confederate service.

5172. Was he a good, harmless boy? He was a most worthy, honest fellow, and well known to many gentlemen here. It was undoubtedly some irresponsible fellow among the hackmen who shot him, and the others would not tell of him.

5173. Would a white man have been shot had he those arms about him? I do not know. At that time there was a good deal of feeling and excitement; the rioting was going on, and while it was confined pretty much to the police, the firemen, and the colored soldiery, there were a good many irresponsible characters about town who would shoot a negro if they got a chance. It was a cold-blooded assassination.

General RUNKLE recalled.

By the CHAIRMAN :

5174. You produced a book before the committee purporting to be composed of extracts from certain papers published in the city of Memphis ; I desire you to state whether those extracts are what they purport to be, and if they were cut from the papers as marked, from papers published in the city of Memphis? They are.

5175. Did you select the extracts which appear in manuscript, and marked as editorials? I did.

By Mr. SHANKLIN :

5176. Do I understand that this scrap-book has been made by yourself? Yes, sir ; and I know that each one of those articles comes from the paper it purports to come from.

5177. How did you happen to get up this book? I began to get up these articles for the purpose of substantiating my own opinion, and the markings in the articles are my own.

5178. At whose instance has the book been completed and got up by you? At the instance of Mr. Washburne, and at the suggestion of General Fisk.

5179. How long is it since these requests were made to you, to get up this book? On Monday of this week.

5180. And all the extracts which you have made from the different papers were selected under the request of General Fisk and Mr. Washburne? Yes, sir. You will remember that I gave an opinion that these papers assisted in creating the riot, and that was what induced me to commence making the extracts.

MARCUS EDWARDS sworn and examined.

By the CHAIRMAN :

5181. Did you copy the editorials in this scrap-book? Part of them ; the rest were copied by Mr. Boudinot.

5182. From what papers did you copy them? I made extracts from the Avalanche and the Argus.

5183. Are the extracts copied correctly? They are.

By Mr. SHANKLIN :

5184. Did you do the whole of it? We did.

5185. Were you acting under the instructions of General Runkle? Yes, sir.

H. B. BOUDINOT sworn and examined.

By the CHAIRMAN :

5186. You have heard the questions I have asked Mr. Edwards in regard to the copying of those Avalanche and Argus editorials ; are the copies you made true and correct? They are.

5187. Did you do the whole of it? We did

By Mr. SHANKLIN :

5188. Did you engage in this under the order of General Runkle? Yes, sir.

SILAS A. ANDREWS sworn and examined.

By the CHAIRMAN :

5189. Did you make copies of certain original affidavits taken at the Freedmen's Bureau, in relation to the recent riots in Memphis, for the congressional committees of investigation? I did, sir.

5190. Are such copies made by you and now in the possession of the committee, to the best of your knowledge and belief, true and correct copies? They are.

Captain MICHAEL WALSH sworn and examined.

By the CHAIRMAN :

5191. Please state your official position. Captain, and assistant adjutant general in the Freedmen's Bureau.

5192. Where are you stationed? In Memphis.

5193. Did you, in your official position, take certain affidavits in regard to the recent riots in Memphis? Yes, sir.

5194. Can you state whether copies of such affidavits have been placed in the hands of the congressional committee of investigation? They were.

5195. Are the copies of such affidavits, as far as you know, true and correct copies? They are, sir.

TESTIMONY TAKEN BEFORE MILITARY COMMISSION ORGANIZED BY ORDER OF MAJOR GENERAL GEORGE STONEMAN.

H. N. RANKIN (colored) was duly sworn, and testified as follows:

Question. Do you know anything in regard to the recent riots? If so, state what you know.

Answer. On Tuesday evening, May 1, 1866, between five and six o'clock, I was on South street near Causey, and saw about fifteen policemen come out of Causey street with revolvers in their hands. The policemen commenced shooting at the negroes on South street, but seemed to fire principally at those dressed in uniform. The colored people were very quiet before the shooting commenced. There were not more than five soldiers in one party, though they were passing back and forth all the time. There were also about twelve men, women and children in the street. The squad of five soldiers were going east. When the policemen commenced firing the colored women looked on, but took no part in the riot. I did not see any colored man with a revolver or other weapon that evening. I saw two men shot on the South street bridge. One of the men fell on the bridge, and the other fell off the bridge. There were about thirty citizens, including the policemen, who were shooting at the negroes. There was also one white soldier in the crowd shooting at the negroes. A small boy was shot in the thigh. Do not know who shot the boy. I saw the dead body of Freeman Jones, who was shot in the mouth, about 200 yards from my school-house. Saw the dead body of a small negro man dressed in uniform in the same vicinity; he had three wounds in his head and breast. Saw the dead body of a colored soldier at the corner of Linden and St. Martin streets, who had the appearance of having been stabbed three times in the stomach. Saw a woman who was wounded in the side with a knife, in same neighborhood. Saw the dead body of a colored man between Causey and Shelby streets, south of South street. The two soldiers who fell on the South street bridge were the only bodies I saw on Tuesday night. The other bodies I saw between eight and nine o'clock, Wednesday morning. Saw the dead body of a colored soldier on Reyburn avenue. Saw the dead body of a negro woman on the corner of Shelby and South streets. The shot passed through the stomach. The man killed between Causey and Shelby streets, south of South street, was killed on Wednesday morning. On Wednesday morning about eight o'clock I closed my school-house. About two o'clock I saw my school-house on fire. The house belonged to the colored Methodist society. The furniture belonged to me. The house was frame, double-floored and ceiled overhead, 18x36 feet, not lathed or plastered; it was furnished with two stoves. Witness considers the furniture worth $190, and the building worth $1,000. There were ladders and gas-lighters, worth $15.50, in the building when it was burned. There were fifty dollars' worth of school-books in the house at the time it was burned. When I arrived at the school-house it was burned to the ground. There were a great many white people in that vicinity, and unknown white persons asked me why I did not have school, and what I would do for a school-house. The language used was taunting. There were two white men at the fire, armed with shot-guns, but they did not make any disturbance. On Wednesday afternoon there was a guard of soldiers on South street, who would not permit colored persons to cross South street into the city. When witness tried to cross the street it was about five o'clock p. m. On Thursday morning I saw the dead body of a young woman, formerly one of my scholars, who had been burned. This was on South street, near Causey street. Two buildings were burned on Thursday evening at the corner of Gayoso and Hernando streets. These buildings were the property of the Methodist church, of which witness is trustee. One thousand dollars had been paid on this property.

Question by MR. WRIGHT. Did you recognize any of the people whom you saw coming down Causey street with the police on Tuesday evening, as citizens of this city?

Answer. I did not know any of their names, but their dress indicated they were rowdies. Also saw a party of men commanded by a gentleman on horseback.

Hon. TFJMAS LEONARD, judge of Shelby county, residing on Hernando road, south of city limits, after being duly sworn, testified as follows:

Question. Please state what you know regarding the recent riots.

Answer. I was in my office on Tuesday, May 1, 1866, at five p. m. Saw a large crowd passing on Second street. Was informed that there was a disturbance on South street, between colored discharged soldiers and police. Proceeded to Elliott street, where I saw some policemen pursuing a colored soldier. There were fifteen or twenty policemen and citizens. Saw several men in the crowd level their pistols and fire at the negro. I was informed by the citizens in that vicinity that the negro whom they were pursuing had shot a policeman. I was ordered by the policeman to go with the crowd. I went north on Echols street about fifty yards, when I turned back and went to my house on Hernando road. The policeman who ordered me to join the party threatened to shoot me. The shooting was promiscuous in the vicinity. Do not know whether any of the shots took effect on the negro soldiers.

Question by the RECORDER. Did you see any other negroes in the vicinity of the disturbance?

Answer. I saw five or six colored men, women, and children. None of them had arms. The crowd were not firing at these colored people, but seemed to be looking after and pursuing the colored soldiers. On Wednesday morning I ordered the sheriff of the county to assemble a possee to keep the peace.

Question. Did you see a large crowd of citizens assembled on Wednesday in the south part of the city?

Answer. I did, but did not go near them. I remained with General Stoneman nearly all the forenoon on Wednesday, consulting with him regarding the safety and good order of the city.

Question by RECORDER. Did you hear any expressions by citizens regarding the cause of the riots?

Answer. I heard many prominent citizens who were known to me, and who belonged to different political parties, deprecate the acts of violence. I saw many buildings on fire in different parts of the city on Wednesday night. Every colored church and school-house that I know of in the city was burned.

Question. Do you know the name of, or could you recognize the policeman who levelled his pistol at you?

Answer. I do not know his name, but could recognize him. He was a short, heavy-set man.

WILLIAM WALLACE, attorney general criminal court of Memphis, Tennessee, residing in East Memphis, after being duly sworn, testified as follows:

Question. Please state what you know regarding the recent riots.

Answer. On Wednesday morning about half past nine o'clock I was in the criminal court room, the court being in session, when several persons entered the room and announced that the riots had commenced again. The court was adjourned in consequence of the rumor. I left the room and met Sheriff Winters, who requested me to take charge of a possee and proceed to Beal street. Went to Fulsom & Co.'s gun store, on Main street, and procured thirty or forty double-barrelled shot-guns and rifles, also ammunition, with which the guns were loaded. The guns were distributed to the possee. I proceeded to the intersection of Main and South streets, where I turned the possee over to the command of Sheriff Winters. Sheriff Winters told Captain Gallagher to take command of the possee. There were thirty or forty gentlemen standing in this vicinity. At the request of Sheriff Winters, I requested all the men who had pistols to assemble in a squad by themselves. I started towards Beal street with the men under my orders, but there were not more than six who remained with me, and went to Beal street. Upon arriving at Beal street market-house my party separated, and I went to my house.

Question by RECORDER. Did you see any negroes in South street when you arrived there Wednesday morning?

Answer. I did not see any negroes on the street.

Question by RECORDER. Did you see any disturbances in other parts of the city?

Answer. I did not see any during Wednesday or Wednesday night.

Question. Did you hear any firing in South Memphis while you were there?

Answer. I did not. I did not remain on South street more than half an hour.

Question by Captain ALLYN. How many people were on South street while you were there?

Answer. About one thousand or more. The arms for the possee were procured at my suggestion, and my object in proceeding to the scene of disturbance (thus armed) was to suppress all acts of violence by whomsoever committed.

ORVILLE YERGER, residing on Alabama street, Memphis, Tennessee, after being duly sworn, testified as follows :

Question. State what you know regarding the recent riot.

Answer. On Wednesday morning about 10½ a. m. I went to South street, near Causey ; I saw a large crowd of men pursuing a negro dressed in uniform. The negro suddenly stopped and turned toward the crowd, throwing up his hands and walking toward them in a supplicating manner. A white man stepped out of the crowd with a gun, which he clubbed and struck the negro over the head, breaking the gun at the stock. Three or four men then stepped forward and fired at the prostrate body. Another man, who I do not know, stepped forward, and pointing his pistol at the head of the negro, discharged the contents into the head of the negro. The man who struck the negro with the gun was a policeman. I have seen the man since with a star on his breast. Heard him use the words, after striking the negro, " Yes, damn him, I did it."

JAMES M. LITTLEFIELD, residing at 151 Causey street, Memphis, Tennessee, after being duly sworn, testified as follows :

Question. Please state what you know regarding the recent riots in Memphis, Tennessee, on Tuesday, May 1, 1866.

Answer. On Tuesday, May 1, I saw a white man who had been wounded in the back carried into a blacksmith shop, corner of Causey and Vance streets. This was about 6 p m., Tuesday. I have twenty-six colored men employed at my brick-yard near the Memphis and Tennessee railroad depot. On Wednesday, about 10 a. m., these men were frightened from their work by firing from five or six persons east of my brick-yard, who were firing towards my men. The party firing appeared to be white men. I do not know that any of my men were armed. Did not see any of my men firing in return. My hands left, and did not return until Thursday morning. Some of them have left the city.

M. R. COOK, residing at No. 139 Madison street, Memphis, Tennessee, after being duly sworn, testified as follows :

Question. Please state what you know regarding the recent riot in Memphis, Tennessee.

Answer. On Wednesday I went to South street, near the Memphis and Tennessee railroad depot. Saw a crowd of about fifty persons following a negro. I saw a citizen step up to the negro and strike him on the head with the but of a pistol. A policeman then stepped up and struck the negro over the head with a carbine. The force of the blow broke the gun at the stock. The policeman was dressed in light pants, black frock-coat; was without a vest ; had on a light hat. He was about five feet ten inches high, hair light brown ; had a dark moustache. Did not know the man was a policeman till afterwards. Have seen him on duty as a policeman since that time, wearing a star. The negro struck was killed. He was shot several times after he was down. The negro was dressed in soldier's uniform.

Question. Did you see any further disturbance or riotous parties on Wednesday ?

Answer. I did not.

By Mr. WRIGHT :

Question. Where did you go from the Memphis and Tennessee railroad depot, and what did you see ?

Answer. I visited Fort Pickering, and found the colored regiment at the fort much excited, but there was no disturbance. A man was introduced to me by Captain Mooney, 3d United States colored heavy artillery, as a captain in his regiment. This man told me he had no control over his men, and they knew it. Mr. Cameron was in company with me.

By Captain ALLYN :

Question. Did you see any colored soldiers outside of the fort ?

Answer. I did not see any colored soldiers outside of the fort.

J. H. JOHNSON, who lives on South street, between Main and Bayou bridge, Memphis, Tennessee, and keeps a drinking saloon, after being duly sworn, testified as follows :

Question. State what you know regarding the recent riot in Memphis, Tennessee.

Answer. Between six and seven o'clock p. m. on Tuesday, May 1, 1866, I saw a party of four policemen on South street, near the Bayou bridge, with a negro in their possession, coming from the direction of Main street. They were followed by a party of about seventy-five negroes. The policemen let the negro loose on the bridge. There was a cart loaded with firewood standing near, to and west of the bridge, and some negroes took wood from the cart and commenced throwing at the policemen. Both parties commenced shooting at that time. Some of the negroes were soldiers, and appeared to be intoxicated. The first firing I heard was at that time. I do not remember having seen the policemen in this part of the city before that day. I saw a policeman carried from the bridge, apparently in a wounded condition. The four policemen left the bridge with the wounded man. I did not see any further disturbance in this immediate vicinity, but heard firing and saw a large crowd further east on the street. I saw the dead body of a negro soldier who had been chot on the South street bridge, near Reyburn avenue, between seven and eight o'clock Tuesday evening. On Wednesday morning, about ten o'clock, I saw a colored man shot and killed near the Memphis and Tennessee railroad depot. Saw the dead body afterwards. The negro had on blue pants. About four o'clock p. m., Wednesday, I visited the negro quatrers east of the Memphis and Tennessee railroad depot, and saw the dead bodies of three negro soldiers and two colored citizens. All of them had the appearance of having met their death by shooting. On Thursday morning, about ten o'clock, I saw the dead body of a negro woman near Causey street church on South street, partly burned. Her clothing was burned off. I also saw the dead body of a colored soldier outside the city limits, in the negro quarters.

Question by General RUNKLE. How far distant from you was the crowd of seventy-five colored men who were following the policemen on Tuesday evening?

Answer. They were in front of my saloon. There were colored women and children among the crowd. There was only one negro who threw wood at the police. Do not know who commenced firing; saw one negro fire his pistol in the air. Most of the crowd ran away when the firing commenced. About ten or fifteen negroes, scattered through the street, remained; they were talking among themselves. Before the firing commenced on Tuesday evening, I heard an intoxicated negro who had a stick in his hand say that he would "kill the damned police." This negro was held back by his comrades.

Question by General RUNKLE. How many negroes did you see together on Wednesday?

Answer. Saw three negro women looking over a fence near Main street. This was the largest number of negroes I saw together during the day.

Mrs. P. V. McPHERSON, residing at No. 214 Vance street, Memphis, Tennessee, was duly sworn, and testified as follows:

Question. Please state what you know regarding the riots which commenced on May 1, 1866.

Answer. On the second day of the riot I heard two men who were passing my house, and appeared to be intoxicated, say that they would "kill off the negroes in town, and then kill the Yankees." One of them said they would blow up the Memphis Post printing office. This conversation was about 3 o'clock p. m. One of the men looked like a rowdy; the other looked more genteel. One was a tall man, and the other medium height. The short, heavy-set man was the one talking. They looked like country men.

W. B. GREENLAW, jr., residing on Vance street, corner of Ruth, Memphis, Tennessee, after being duly sworn, testified as follows:

Question. Please state what you know regarding the recent riots.

Answer. On Wednesday afternoon I saw the dead bodies of two negroes, dressed in uniform, lying in the creek south of South street; also saw the dead body of another negro soldier in a shanty east of the Mississippi and Tennessee railroad depot, near extension of De Soto street. One body had a wound in the breast; the other two appeared to have been shot. On Wednesday night I saw the barracks at the corner of Vance and Lauderdale streets burning. There was a large crowd in the vicinity of the fire. I also saw men with muskets at the fire on Echols street about the same time; I took them to be soldiers. I saw three or four men coming from the fire on Vance street, carrying blankets; they were proceeding down Vance street. While looking at the fire two negroes passed by me towards the fire on Echols street; they stopped near me. At this time two white men spoke to the negroes and ordered them to get down on their knees, threatening to kill them. One of the men pointed a pistol at the negroes while speaking. The party of gentlemen with me and myself interceded for the negroes. The two men then ordered the negroes to go to their homes. These men appeared to be Irish.

Question by Captain ALLYN. Do you think the men who ordered the negroes to kneel down intended to kill them?

Answer. I do not think they did. At the time I thought there was danger enough to interfere.

ALEX. McQUARTERS, residing on the corner of Clay street and Reyburn avenue, Memphis, Tennessee, after being duly sworn, testified as follows :

Question. Did you see any of the recent riots in Memphis, Tennessee ?

Answer. About 6½ o'clock p. m. on the first day I was on the corner of Clay street and Reyburn avenue, when I saw a large crowd of police and citizens coming from South street. When I first saw the crowd they were pursuing negroes and firing in every direction. A white man who was twenty feet in front of, and appeared to be leading, the crowd of white men, fell in front of my house. I did not see any negro firing at that time ; and there were no shots coming from the direction in which the negroes were. I heard about fifty pistol shots at the time the man fell. I saw the police firing in the direction the crowd was running when the man fell. About ten or fifteen minutes after the man fell in front of my house I saw the body placed in a hack and taken away. The man was said to have been named Dunn. There were no more colored people in the street before or during the disturbance than usual. There were more women than men.

AMOS BOWLES, (colored—occupation, a hack-driver,) residing on Madison street, near Memphis and Charleston railroad depot, Memphis, Tennessee, after being duly sworn, testified as follows :

Question. Were you wounded during the recent riots ?

Answer. Between 10 and 11 o'clock p. m. on Tuesday I was driving my hack on Main street, near Exchange, when I saw five men walking on the street. Just as I passed them I heard a pistol shot, and felt a sharp pain in the fleshy part of my arm. I turned my hack into Exchange street, going towards Second, and heard four shots as I was turning the corner. The bullet is still in my arm. I was making eight dollars a day, clear of expenses, at the time I was wounded.

ELI ANDERSON, (colored—occupation, deck-hand,) residing on Alabama street, Memphis, Tennessee, after being duly sworn, testified as follows :

Question. When and where were you wounded?

Answer. On Wednesday, about 11 o'clock a. m., I went down on South street to get some tools ; about three hundred yards from South street, near Causey, I saw a large crowd of firemen and citizens. There were two colored men with me. I did not hear any firing until I felt a sharp pain in the fleshy part of my left arm. Just before I was shot six men on horseback rode up to me and ordered me to deliver my money. Two men dismounted and searched my pockets ; they took thirty-five dollars in money. Three of the men belonged to fire company No. 7 ; they had on belts with the number of their company. I did not know the men. Six shots were fired after I was wounded. I was making forty-five dollars per month.

MEMPHIS, TENNESSEE, *May* 12, 1866.

SIR : I would respectfully request that you would correct the statement I made yesterday in reference to Private George Anderson, late company "H," 3d United States colored heavy artillery. I should have said " George Cobb."

Please substitute the name of Cobb for Anderson, and then it will be correct.

Very respectfully,

W. H. PIERCE,
Late Captain 3d United States Colored Heavy Artillery.

Captain COLBURN.

Official copy:

W. J. COLEURN,
Captain and Assistant Quartermaster.

GEORGE ROBINSON, (colored,) residing on Main street, between Beal and Gayoso streets, Memphis, Tennessee, after being duly sworn, testified as follows :

Question. State whether you were injured during the recent riot ; if so, when and where ?

Answer. On Tuesday evening, about sunset, I was returning from work on Main street, south of Beal, when I was set upon by a crowd of white men and beat over the head with pistols. Do not know who the white men were. Before they struck me they asked if I was a soldier. I have not been able to work since that time. I had been working for two dollars per day previous to this occurrence.

E. O. FULLER, residing at the corner of Vance and Main streets, Memphis, Tennessee, (occupation, quartermaster's agent,) after being duly sworn, testified as follows :

Question. State what you saw at the riot in Memphis, Tennessee, about May 1, 1866.

Answer. On Wednesday morning, about ten o'clock, I went to South street, near Main. I saw a white man leading a negro by the collar. The man struck the negro on the head with his fist and let him go. About five minutes later I saw two men on horseback bringing the same negro from the direction of the Mississippi and Tennessee railroad depot, towards South street. When they arrived in the vicinity of the crowd on South street, I heard a pistol shot from the crowd, and immediately afterwards I saw a policeman step out of the crowd with a gun and strike the negro on the head, breaking his gun at the stock. The policeman had on light-colored clothing and a light felt hat; was about five feet ten inches high; had light hair cut short, and a light moustache. The force of the blow felled the negro to the ground. A large man, with a red goatee, stepped up to the negro, aimed a pistol at him, and fired. I do not remember whether there was more than one shot fired. I think there was more than one. I have seen the policeman who struck the negro with the gun since that day. His star was numbered "9." When the negro was first released, about twenty men started after him. They were rough-looking men. There were between one hundred and two hundred men in this immediate vicinity at that time.

JOHN BROWN, (colored,) barber in the Gayoso House, Memphis, Tennessee, being duly sworn, testified as follows:

Question. State the probable or actual value of the church and property of the Colored Baptist Society, on the corner of Overton and Main streets, burned Wednesday night, May 3, 1866.

Answer. In my opinion the church could not be replaced for less than eight thousand dollars ($8,000.) The building was 25x58 feet, two stories high, and was built of brick. There were in the church at the time it was burned, one bible, one testament, one hymn-book, seventy-five benches or pews, two stoves, one table, three chairs, and two book-cases.

SAMUEL PUGH, (colored,) pastor of the colored Baptist church corner of Overton and Main streets, Memphis, Tennessee, being duly sworn, testified the same as John Brown.

BENJAMIN MONROE, (colored,) living corner of Second and Jackson streets, Memphis, Tennessee, being duly sworn, testified the same as John Brown.

Mrs. KATE CURLEY, residing corner of Main and Elliot streets, Memphis, Tennessee, after being duly sworn, testified as follows:

Question. Did you see the beginning of the disturbance in Memphis, Tennessee, on Tuesday, May 1, 1866?

Answer. Between four and five o'clock p. m., Tuesday, May 1, 1866, I saw a crowd of about one hundred colored men, women, and children pass by my house towards South street. There were several colored soldiers in the crowd, who appeared to be drunk. Many of the men had revolvers in their hands. Shortly after they passed I saw firing from a crowd on South street. About two hours after this, I saw ten or twelve negroes pass my house with pistols in their hands. They were going north on Main street, and appeared to be pursuing a crowd of about fifty white men. I also saw a white officer with a colored man in a buggy going towards South street at the same time. I saw smoke around the buggy, and saw the officer put his pistol away. Do not know whether he fired his pistol. I saw a colored man lying on the pavement in front of my house apparently in a wounded condition.

B. F. BAKER, late first lieutenant 3d regiment United States heavy artillery, residing in Fort Pickering, Memphis, Tennessee, after being duly sworn, testified as follows:

Question. Did you know men from your regiment being killed during the riots which commenced May 1, 1866, in Memphis, Tennessee? State their names, and the company to which they belonged.

Answer. Private Joseph Lunde, company E, was killed Tuesday evening; was shot through the breast; saw him die. Private Isaac Richardson, company H, was killed by a gunshot wound on Tuesday night, May 1, 1866 Private William Withers, company H. was killed by gunshot wound on Tuesday night, May 1, 1866; saw his body Wednesday morning. Private George Cobb, company H, was killed on Tuesday evening by a gunshot wound; saw his body that night. Private George Black was killed Wednesday morning; the body was found on South street bridge, at second bayou. I also saw the dead body of a colored man named Levi Baker, at the corner of Main street and Butler's avenue, who was killed Tuesday evening. Baker appears to have met his death from a gunshot wound through the stomach. On Tuesday afternoon, about five o'clock, I was in the southern part of the city and heard firing in the direction of South street, and went to that vicinity. I ordered all the colored soldiers whom I met to go with me to Fort Pickering. Twenty-five or thirty went with me. There was only one colored soldier who refused to go with me. Not more than twelve other soldiers remained in that part of the town. After going to the fort with the colored soldiers, I again returned to the scene of disturbance. This was after dark. The soldier who refused to go to the fort with me was Sergeant Lewis Hurst, of company H ; I saw him on Wednesday morning ; but he was not engaged in any of the riots. My regiment, including the officers and men, was discharged from the service on the 30th of April, 1866.

Corporal Lewis Robinson, company K, was killed on Wednesday morning : did not see his dead body, but know he was reported on the pay rolls of his company as having been killed on that day. Private Allen Summers, company L, was reported on the pay-rolls of his company as having been killed on Tuesday or Wednesday. Private Alfred Turner, company H, was wounded in the fleshy part of the left arm on Tuesday evening ; the wound was from a pistol shot.

Mrs. ANN TIPPING, residing opposite small-pox hospital, Memphis, Tennessee, after being duly sworn, testified as follows:

Question. Did you see any shooting during the recent riots in Memphis, Tennessee ?

Answer. On Wednesday, May 2, 1866, about sundown, I saw a large crowd on Main near Exchange street, and saw seven or eight firemen in the street. I saw one of the firemen fire his pistol twice, and heard expressions in the crowd of "A nigger is shot !" I did not hear any other shots at this time. Do not know the fireman who discharged his pistol.

ALEX. ROBINSON, (colored,) residing at the Gayoso House, Memphis, Tennessee, after being duly sworn, testified as follows:

Question. Did you see any one injured during the recent riots?

Answer. On Tuesday, about sundown, May 1, 1866, I saw several white men beating a colored hack-driver named George Williams with pistols, in front of the Gayoso House, and saw the negro man knocked down, and I saw a white man draw his pistol and fire at him. There were ten or twelve white men in the crowd which was beating the negro. I understood a man named Billy Cook to say that he had three shots at the negro.

ANDREW MEADOWS, (colored,) at No. 9 Linden street, Memphis, Tennessee, after being duly sworn. testified as follows :

Question. State when, where, and by whom you were wounded.

Answer. I formerly resided in a frame house at the corner of Causey and South streets. On Thursday morning, May 3, 1866, about two o'clock, I heard a rapping at my door, and shortly after two men came to the window at the head of my bed ; they broke the window, when a white man stuck a pistol in at the window and fired at me ; the ball taking effect in my left hand. This man and another man then came into my house, and the same man who shot at me struck me on the left side with a sharp instrument. Some one then took my pocket-book, containing twenty-five dollars, ($25.) The two men then broke open my trunk and took four suits of clothing, worth seventy-five dollars, ($75,) and took some clothing belonging to my wife. About one-half hour later, the same white men returned and set fire to my house. There were a large number of white men here at this time, and they burned several other houses besides my own. The man who shot me and struck me is named John Callahan ; he kept a drinking saloon at the corner of South and Causey streets, opposite my house ; I did not know the other man. I heard Callahan say, just before the house was burned, "God damn him ! I know he has got more money than this, and if we can't find it, we will burn up the house!" At the time of this occurrence I was employed as a fireman on the steamer R. M. Bishop, at forty-five dollars ($45) per month and board.

MAGGIE MEADOWS, (colored,) residing corner of South and Causey streets, Memphis, Tennessee, wife of Andrew Meadows, after being duly sworn, testifies the same as Andrew Meadows, and that the clothing which was lost by the burning of the house in which she lived was worth three hundred and five dollars. I also lost two diamond rings, which I valued at one hundred dollars ($100) each. Also one carpet worth twenty-five dollars, ($25 ;) one stove worth fifteen dollars. ($15 ;) six chairs, one dollar and fifty cents ($1 50) each, and other articles worth eighty-four dollars, ($84.)

A. M. GLASGOW, residing on Gayoso, east of De Soto street, Memphis, Tennessee, after being duly sworn, testified as follows :

Question. Did you lose any property during the recent riots in Memphis, Tennessee ? State time of loss, and value.

Answer. On Tuesday night, May 1, 1866, I lost fifty dollars ($50) by fire, which was set in a building belonging to me on Gayoso street, east of second bayou. The building cost twelve hundred dollars, ($1,200,) and was used as a colored school-house, and to rent ; also had rooms to rent. I saw two men set fire to the building ; I do not know who they were. I succeeded in extinguishing the fire. There were about twelve men in the crowd with the two men who fired the building. About twenty shots were fired at me while I was putting out the fire. One of the men who set fire to my building was a tall, red-whiskered man. I fired three shots at the party, and they left. About half an hour later about twelve men made their appearance and threatened to burn my building. Several of them cocked their revolvers and said "They would as soon shoot me as a damned nigger." My building was renting for about one hundred and fifty dollars per month at that time. The tenants—colored people—were frightened away and have not returned, and the school is suspended on account of the riots.

JAMES E. MECHAN, residing on Jones avenue, and tends bar at No. 14 Jefferson street, Memphis, Tennessee, after being duly sworn, testified as follows:

Question. Do you know any of the parties who were concerned in the burning of buildings in the city of Memphis on the 2d of May, 1866 ? If so, state their names.

Answer. I do not.

Question. Did you hear any expressions regarding the burning of school-houses and barracks that evening ; and were the expressions deprecating the fires or encouraging ?

Answer. I heard expressions to the effect that barracks and school-houses were burning. Parties making the expressions did not seem to care whether the buildings were burned or not.

WILLIAM W. WHEEDEN, residing on South street, east of Main street, Memphis, Tennessee, after being duly sworn, testified as follows :

Question. Did you see the origin of the riot on Tuesday, May 1, 1866 ?

Answer. On Tuesday, May 1, 1866, about 4 o'clock p. m., I was standing in the door of my store, on South street near the Bayou bridge, when I saw four policemen coming from the direction of Main street, followed by about fifteen negro soldiers, and the same number of negro citizens. When opposite my door I saw one of the negroes push a policeman. The crowd proceeded as far as the bridge, about twenty rods from my store, when the police stopped on the bridge and faced the crowd. I saw two or three negroes seize wood from a wagon in the street and throw at the police ; they also commenced firing their revolvers in the air, and some of them fired at the police, and the others continued to throw wood. The police then drew their revolvers and fired at the negroes. About thirty shots were fired by both parties, and one of the policemen was wounded and fell on the bridge. A few shots were fired after the policeman was wounded. The parties then separated, the negroes going toward Main street, and the policemen took up their wounded comrade and went toward Causey street. During the firing large numbers of negro women and children had come into the street. Some of the negro soldiers were drunk when they passed my store.

KELSIE BOND, residing on Walker street near Hernando road, Memphis, Tennessee, after being duly sworn, testified as follows:

Question. State whether you lost any property during the recent riots, and its value.

Answer. I had an interest in three buildings on Echols street, between Vance and Elliott. Two of the buildings were two-story, part brick and part frame, and one frame building one-story. These buildings were burned on the same night the colored school-houses and churches were burned. It would cost five thousand dollars ($5,000) to replace the three buildings.

WILLIAM B. HOOD, residing at No. 109 Main street, Memphis, Tennessee, after being duly sworn, testified as follows:

Question. Did you see any persons wounded during the recent riots? If so, state their names, and when and where wounded.

Answer. On the second day of the riots, about 7 o'clock p. m., I was going south on Main street with three colored men in my employ, when I met a party of firemen near the corner of Main and Exchange streets. One of the firemen struck one of my men named George Clapp with a horn, when another firemen said, "Shoot the son of a bitch." I saw a man aim his revolver at Clapp and fire three shots, two of them taking effect in the thigh. One other colored man named Franklin Gross was shot in the small of the back by the same party who shot Clapp. Gross is severely wounded ; Clapp will recover. At the time of this occurrence these colored men were walking quietly along the street, and did not say anything. I tried to protect the negroes, when three of the firemen struck at me with revolvers, and others said: "Shoot him for taking their part." Neither myself nor the negroes had any weapons. These firemen stopped at the engine-house of company No. 6. The man who had the horn was an Irishman, and the whole party looked like rowdies.

A. BOSTWICK, (colored,) residing on Washington near New Orleans street, Memphis, Tennessee, after being duly sworn, testified as follows:

Question. State what you know regarding the burning of the church of the Colored Methodist Society, on the corner of Washington and New Orleans streets, on Wednesday night, May 2, 1866.

Answer. I saw the church burning on Wednesday night, May 2, 1866. The basement was occupied as a school-room.

BENJAMIN SLATER, (colored,) residing on Third between Adams and Washington streets, Memphis, Tennessee, after being duly sworn, testified as follows:

Question. State the value of the Colored Methodist church, on the corner of Washington and New Orleans streets, which was burned on Wednesday night, May 2, 1866.

Answer. The building was built partly of brick and partly of wood. It was fifty by seventy feet, and thirty feet high. It would cost about twenty-five thousand dollars ($25,000) to replace the property as it was at the time it was burned. It was fully furnished with seats, pulpit, lamps, and everything complete.

JULIA YATES, (colored,) resides on South street, east of Main, (a washerwoman by occupation,) after being duly sworn, testified as follows:

Saw the beginning of the riot at 4 p. m., Tuesday, May 1, 1866. Saw a large number of colored soldiers drinking on Main street, at Mr. Wadloe's grocery store. Three policemen stepped up to the crowd and told the soldiers they were not allowed to drink and get drunk. One of the soldiers walked up to the police with a stick and tried to strike him, the rest of the crowd pulled the soldier· back; the crowd then went down Main towards South street, the police in advance, the same soldier still trying to strike the police, but held back by the crowd. As soon as the policemen reached the bridge, they stopped and turned towards the crowd, and one of the police fired at the crowd, and two shots were then fired in return, one of which hit a policeman. Two shots were fired by the police, one of which hit a soldier in the neck. The police then went down South street, leaving the wounded man in a grocery. Soon after a crowd of white men came from Causey street, and killed a colored soldier near a large brick house on South street, near Second bridge. Three men knocked the first negro down, and then shot him four times, and robbed him of his pocket-book and watch. The second negro ran towards Grady's hill, and several shots were fired at him, one of which hit and killed him. The crowd then came up South street, one having a colored soldier in charge. The man having the negro struck him with a pistol three times. The crowd then moved up South street, and killed a negro woman named Emeline. I saw her dead body the next day in Mr. Kelley's store. The crowd went up town and returned almost immediately with shot guns, and remained in the road near Smith's grocery. My husband, Allen Summers, was also wounded. On Wednesday, about 3 o'clock, I saw several houses on Grady's hill, near the school-house, on fire. I saw some citizens going towards these houses, and soon after the houses were on fire.

Dr. E. S. BOWEN, residing at 109 Main street, Memphis, Tennessee, after being duly sworn, testified as follows:

Question. Did you see any one killed or wounded, or that you know to have been injured during the recent riots?

Answer. On the day of the night on which the colored school-houses and churches were burned, a colored man in my employ, by the name of George Clapp, was shot in the hip; another colored man in my employ, by the name of Frank McGue, was also wounded, and has not been able to work since that day. I was paying these men forty ($40) dollars per month at that time. I also saw a colored man shot at in the vicinity of Market square, on Second street, the second day of the riots. Do not know whether the negro was wounded.

GEORGE SHAIF, resides on Popular street, opposite market-house, Memphis, Tennessee, after being duly sworn, testified as follows:

Question. Did you see any buildings burning during the riots?

Answer. About 12½ o'clock a. m., Thursday morning, I saw many fires in different parts of the city. About 1½ a. m., I saw a crowd of about forty persons who had come from the east part of the city. They went toward the south part of the city.

21

S. H. CHAMBERLAIN, residing at No. 6 Court street, Memphis, Tennessee, after being duly sworn, testified as follows :

Question. Did you see the commencement of the riot on May 2d, 1866, in Memphis, Tennessee ?

Answer. About nine o'clock Wednesday morning, I was on South street, and walked from Main to De Soto street, on South street ; everything was quiet at that time. About one hour later, I met Captain McMahon on Vance street, with about one hundred policemen and citizens going toward South street ; I followed the party to South street, when they dispersed in small squads and went among the negro cabins in that vicinity ; ten minutes after this I saw several white men firing ; I saw a few negroes, but did not see any of them have weapons ; I saw a negro who was shot near the Mississippi and Tennessee depot. Mr. Worsett, who was with me, pointed to a policeman who was in the crowd and asked me who it was ; I told him McCormick ; I knew the man from the fact I had served on the police with him. McCormick is about six feet high, and wore light clothes ; he had a light moustache. Worsett said McCormick was the man who shot the negro.

THOMAS FOX, residing on Poplar street, between Main and Second streets, Memphis, Tennessee, after being duly sworn, testified as follows :

Question. State what you heard during the recent riots regarding the burning of buildings in this city.

Answer. I was in front of the Worsham House on Tuesday evening, about half past eight o'clock, on the first day of the riot, and heard a butcher, whom I have frequently seen in the city, but whose name I do not know, trying to organize a party to go to the southern part of the city to take part in the fight ; I saw John C. Creighton there ; he appeared to be greatly excited, and said he would not fine any one for carrying fire-arms. Mr. Creighton said the harness had been shot off his horse, and negro soldiers had fired four times at him ; Mr. Creighton is recorder of the court of Memphis, Tennessee. Alderman Kelly was there and spoke to me regarding the proposed assembly in the southern part of the city in a disapproving manner ; did not hear him address the crowd to that effect. I saw the newsboys running after negroes in that vicinity with sticks and stones ; the chief of police tried to stop them ; other police were present, but showed no disposition to stop the boys ; soon after this I went home. On Wednesday night, I heard parties on the street intimate that buildings were to be burned that night, and, from what I heard, was confident that buildings would be burned ; the part of the city indicated to be burned was the portion occupied by negroes in South Memphis ; I do not remember the names of the persons whom I heard express themselves to that effect.

JAMES MEEHAN recalled.

On Wednesday night, about twelve o'clock, I saw two men ride up to the saloon of John Schools, on Jefferson street ; one of them dismounted and went into the saloon ; as the man came out of the saloon, I heard the man on horseback ask if he had brought some matches ; the party who was questioned said he had not, and went into the saloon again. The two men who rode up to the saloon and called for matches were James Schools and Jacob Herd. At the time these men rode up to the saloon I was conversing with two or three men near there, but do not remember their names. There were a large number of men on the street in that vicinity. I went home after this, and went to bed about half past one o'clock a. m.

WILLIAM CRAIG, residing next door to Tennessee National Bank, Memphis, Tennessee, after being duly sworn, testified as follows :

Question. Did you see any one killed or wounded during the recent riots in this city ?

Answer. On the first evening of the riot, I went down on Beal street and saw about six policemen leading a negro near the bayou ; I saw the negro run behind some buildings, the police following, and shortly afterwards saw policemen return hauling him toward the street and beating him with their clubs ; they beat him till he fell, and afterwards when he was on the ground ; I then heard some one in the crowd say, " Shoot him ;" one of the police then drew his pistol and shot the negro ; I heard the negro groan after the shot ; the police then left the body and started toward Main street, when I saw one of the policemen return, and when about two steps distant, I saw him level his pistol and fire the pistol at the negro ; the negro groaned again as if hit by the ball from the pistol ; there were about twenty men and boys besides the police present when the negro was shot, but none of them looked like the better class of citizens. I did not recognize any one in the crowd. To the best of my recollection, the second policeman who shot the negro was of medium height, had on a linen duster and dark-colored cap, and had brown hair.

JOHN M. C. SMITH, residing at 188 Hernando street, Memphis, Tennessee, after being duly sworn, testified as follows :

Question. State what you know regarding the burning of houses during the recent riots.

Answer. About ten o'clock, on the night the buildings were burned during the riots, I heard a pounding on the negro school-house on Hernando street, near Brown's avenue, and shortly afterwards saw two men dressed in federal uniform come out of the building and run south ; as the men were running away, I saw fire in the building ; as soon as I saw the fire I went to my room and commenced dressing, and when I returned to the door I heard a cry of "fire," and saw a soldier with a musket ; the soldier said to the person who gave the alarm, "Hush, I don't want any such language as that ;" a detachment of soldiers came up at this time. I did not see any effort made to extinguish the fire. There was about one company of soldiers there. I saw a party of citizens there with guns. There were one hundred and fifty or two hundred people present before the building burned down.

THOMAS M. HAYNES, resides at 281 Main street, Memphis, Tennessee, after being duly sworn, testified as follows :

Question. State names of any one whom you saw robbed or otherwise injured during the recent riots in Memphis, Tennessee.

Answer. On Tuesday, May 1st, 1866, about nine o'clock p. m., I saw a crowd of white boys stop a negro man on Main street, between Court and Madison, and demand and take from him his money ; they then told him to run for his life. There were about twelve boys and they had clubs ; did not know the names of any of the parties.

A. J. SHICK, residing at 281 Main street, Memphis, Tennessee, after being duly sworn, testified as follows, viz :

The same as Thomas M. Haynes.

JESSIE WILLIAMS, (colored,) residing No. 13 Jefferson street, Memphis, Tennessee, after being duly sworn, testified as follows :

Question. Did you see a policeman beat Henry Jackson about the 1st of May, 1866, in this city ?

Answer. I saw a policeman seize Henry Jackson, a colored man, by the beard and strike him in the face, and then kick him and tell him to go. There were a large number of policemen present. This occurred on Jefferson street, near Main, about four o'clock p. m., on Wednesday. The name of the policeman who struck Jackson is Curley McEven ; I see him every day.

EDWARD FITZGIBBONS, residing in Chelsea, Memphis, Tennessee, after being duly sworn, testified as follows :

I saw a negro man pass my house about half-past six p. m., on the third day of May, 1866, and shortly after saw a pistol fired at him. Three men came past my house about the same time, and I saw them throw bricks at some of the negroes who live near my house. They appeared to be intoxicated. The negro fired at had no weapons that I saw. I do not know whether he was wounded or not. On Thursday, May 3, 1866, I heard four or five men say that buildings occupied by colored men in Chelsea were to be burned, and I set up to watch houses that night which I had rented to colored people. I did not believe any such attempt would be made.

Dr. D. D. SAUNDERS, residing 37 South Court street, Memphis, Tennessee, after being duly sworn, testified as follows :

A colored servant in employ of Samuel Mansfield, by the name of William Henry, was killed by a gun-shot wound in the head on Thursday night, May 3, 1866. I found the dead body on the side-walk about half-past twelve a m., near the corner of Shelby and McCall streets.

Rev. J. T. C. COLLINS, residing corner of Hernando and Elliot streets, Memphis, Tennessee, after being duly sworn, testified as follows :

Collins Chapel, belonging to the Methodist Church, (colored,) was erected on Washington, near New Orleans street. The church was built during the years of 1860 and 1861. I had charge of the building of the church, and all money expended passed through my hands. I collected and paid out for the house six thousand dollars. There was a debt against the house at the time it was burned of about twelve hundred dollars.

Exclusive of this cost, the church was furnished with two stoves, eighty yards of carpeting, at least twelve lamps, pews for eight hundred people, book-case, and books worth about one hundred dollars, bible and hymn book worth about fifteen dollars, and pulpit cushion. The value of all furniture and books in the Chapel was about seven hundred and seventy-four dollars.

C. H. BOWMAN, residing on South street. opposite Causey street, Memphis, Tennessee, after being duly sworn, testified as follows:

Between five and six o'clock p. m. on the first of May, 1866, I was going east on South street, and met four policemen going towards Main street. Twenty minutes later I saw about one hundred and fifty colored men and women congregated near the Mississippi and Tennessee railroad depot. I went down on South street and saw four policemen coming east on the street with two negroes in custody. I met them on the Bayou bridge, between Main and Causey streets. There were fifteen or twenty negroes who were hallooing and making a great deal of noise. I saw many of the negroes draw their pistols and aim towards the policemen, and heard two shots fired. I was crossing the bridge with a wagon at that time, and my back was turned towards the policemen. Do not know whether they fired at the negroes. Many shots were fired by the negroes while I was crossing the bridge.

WILLIAM H. SMITH, brevet major sixteenth United States infantry, Memphis, Tennessee, after being duly sworn, testified as follows:

On the first of May, 1866, about seven o'clock p. m., I went with a detachment of about twenty-five men through South street. I went to Beal street. I saw several policemen beating a negro, and ordered them to desist, which they did. I returned to Fort Pickering with my detachment about eleven o'clock. About half-past twelve o'clock I went out with another detachment and went to South street. Everything was quiet when we arrived there. On Wednesday, the second, about eleven o'clock a. m. I received an order from General Stoneman to keep all colored soldiers in their quarters at Fort Pickering. At this time the colored soldiers were standing on the parapet of the fort looking towards South street. I walked along the parapet, ordering the soldiers to go to their quarters, which they did without the use of force. About ten o'clock p. m. I went to South street with a squad of twelve men, and stationed them along the street, with orders not to permit white men to come south of the street or negroes to go north of it. About two p. m. I saw a colored school-house on South street, east of Morris cemetery, on fire. There were forty or fifty white men near the fire. They were tearing down negro houses adjacent to prevent the spread of the flames. I directed them to stop tearing down the houses, as there was no danger. I organized a small party of colored men to extinguish the flames. the white men refusing to assist in putting out the fire, when white men commenced stoning the negroes. I then called my guard and drove the crowd to the north side of the street. I then set my men to work and prevented further destruction of property. There were policemen among the crowd, who did not attempt to restrain them, but seemed to countenance the proceedings. I returned to the fort between five and six p. m., with my detachment. About eight o'clock p. m. I went out with twenty men and patroled the southern part of the city. I did not see any negroes. Very few buildings were burned after my patrol arrived in that vicinity. I remained out with my detachment till two o'clock, when I returned to the fort. My detachment was kept well together during the night, and there were no stragglers. On Thursday night I went out with a detachment of forty-six men, whom I stationed at Court square, and sent patrols in every direction through the city. There were some shots fired during the night, and I saw one negro cabin burned on Beal street. There was no further disturbance.

C. E. BUSHNELL, residing corner of Linden and St. Martin streets, Memphis, Tennessee, after being duly sworn, testified as follows:

On Tuesday, May 1, 1866, about six o'clock p. m., on the corner of Linden and Main streets, I saw a party of six men, two or three of them policemen, beating a negro with pistols. They were still beating him when I left. Shortly after I passed down Linden street I heard three pistol shots in that direction.

J. S. CARUTHERS, residing corner of Main and Vance streets, Memphis, Tennessee, after being duly sworn, testified as follows:

On Wednesday night, May 2, 1866, I was sitting up with my brother, who was sick. About eleven p. m. I saw a party of men around the building next to my house, which had been used as a colored school-house and church. I saw the school-house on fire, and walked to the fence between my house and the building and requested the crowd to put out the fire, as it would' endanger my property. No answer was made to my request. I then got over the fence, telling the party of men I would put the fire out myself. The party numbered about fifteen men. One of the men told me not to be alarmed, as they would not let my house be burned. I then told them I would put the fire out, and advanced to the building for that purpose, saying such proceedings were disgraceful to the city. The same man who first spoke to me then said, "Captain, we know you and don't want to hurt you ; but, by God, you can't do that ! " After further altercation with them, becoming fearful that my house would be burned, I asked them to save it, when one of the men said, "Turn in, boys, and save Captain Caruther's house ; by God we will die by it." Some of the men then assisted me in preserving my house and others went to the house west of the building, which was also in danger. The man who talked with me had a pistol in his hand. I did not know any of the party.

Question. Why were you called captain, and what regiment were you with ?

Answer. I was in Richardson's West Tennessee brigade under General Forrest. While the barracks were burning I saw a detachment of soldiers halt near the burning and remain there till the crowd dispersed. The building could not have been saved when the soldiers came up.

Mrs. J. A. GRAY, residing at the corner of Main and Trezevant streets, Memphis, Tennessee, after being duly sworn, testified as follows :

On Tuesday, May 1, 1866, between five and six o'clock p. m., I heard firing in the vicinity of my house, and saw a colored man on the opposite side of the street who appeared to be dead. Saw him taken into the grocery of a colored man named Wadlow, on Main street.

W. J. McKEON, residing on Poplar street, between Second and Third streets, Memphis, Tennessee, after being duly sworn, testified as follows :

On Thursday, May 3, 1866, I was in an omnibus returning to Memphis about sundown from a pic-nic in Chelsea. A party of men who were intoxicated rode on top of the bus. When near the brick church in Chelsea, four of the men on top of the bus got off and two men inside the bus got out. Two of the men, Tom Connell and John Sullivan, had pistols. I saw Sullivan fire one shot at a negro man, but do not know whether the negro was wounded. The man fired at was sitting on a wagon with another negro by the side of the road, and was not doing or saying anything. The name of one of the other men who got off the bus was Dennis Braman. Shortly after the bus left I heard shots in that direction. When Sullivan fired both negroes jumped from the wagon, and I saw one of them run and the other was getting up as the bus drove away.

Thirteenth (13th) day, May 21, 1866, a. m. Present : Brevet Brigadier General B. P. Runkle, Captain W. J. Colburn, A. Q. M., and M. J. Wright, esq., of Memphis, Tennessee.

M. J. GIBBONS, residing on Madison street bridge, Memphis, Tennessee, after being duly sworn testified as follows :

I owned a house on Echols street, between Vance and Elliot, which was burned the 2d of May, 1866. The house was worth one thousand dollars. My house was occupied by a negro family at the time, and was rented for thirty dollars per month.

M. C. GALLOWAY, residing at corner of Court and Third streets, Memphis, Tennessee, after being duly sworn, testified as follows :·

I am chief editor of the Memphis Avalanche. On Wednesday night, May 2, 1866, a proposition was made to me by a party of one hundred or one hundred and fifty men, to mob the Post printing office in this city. This crowd was near the engine house, on corner of Jefferson and Main streets. I was passing by at the time, and the crowd came to where I was, shouting for the *Avalanche*. Some parties in the crowd seized hold of me to raise me on their shoulders, and I heard cries from unknown men in the crowd to mob the Post. I then appealed to them to desist, as I was opposed to anything of that kind, and the pro ceeding would be an injury to them and to me. While this discussion was going on, a ne- gro was passing, and I saw three shots fired at him from the crowd ; I do not know that the negro was wounded. I did not know a single man in the crowd, except Captain Clus- key, who was with me and is an attaché of my office. The crowd appeared to be a low class of community. When I left the crowd, I saw three shots fired at a passing hack driven by a negro, and heard the balls strike the windows ; do not know whether there was any one in the carriage. On Wednesday morning, between nine and ten o'clock, I was in South Memphis with the crowd, and saw the dead bodies of two negroes. I also saw a negro dressed in federal uniform in possession of four men, and heard shouts of "shoot him," "shoot him," from the crowd. I saw Sheriff Winters take the negro and rescue him from the four men.

I saw a negro on one of the huts in that vicinity, waving a black flag. The crowd went toward the flag and it was taken down; I saw the negro when he got off the house. There were several shots passed near us, fired from the direction of the fort, I did not see who fired them. I could not see any negroes in the vicinity of the one waving the flag, and could not distinguished whether he was in uniform or citizens' clothes. I saw men in line of battle near fort Pickering, and saw some standing on the parapet of the fort.

OFFICE COMMISSARY OF SUBSISTENCE,
Memphis, Tennessee, May 21, 1866.

SIR : In reply to your letter of the 19th, requiring a "detailed statement of all expenses incurred by the subsistence department on account of the recent riots in this city," I have the honor to report two items : First, expenses to the subsistence department absolutely ; and second, expenses to the department at this post.

1. Hire of five (5) citizens, whose duties but for the riots could and would have been performed by enlisted men, amounting to one hundred and forty-five dollars.

2. Rations issued to troops brought here only on account of the riots, viz : Five thousand and sixty-four (5,064) rations, at twenty-one cents each, (5,064 rations at twenty-one cents,) amounting to one thousand and sixty-three dollars and forty cents. Total estimate $1,208 40.

I am, sir, very respectfully, your obedient servant,

J. I. LANGDON,
Brevet Major and Commissary Subsistence, Volunteers.

Captain W. J. COLBURN, *A. Q. M.*,
    Recorder, Military Commission, Memphis, Tennessee.

Sworn to before me this 21st day of May, 1866, at Memphis, Tennessee.

W. J. COLBURN,
Captain and Assistant Quartermaster, Recorder.

JAMES HAGGERTY, residing 145 Poplar street, Memphis, Tennessee, after being duly sworn, testified as follows :

On Wednesday night, May 2, 1866, I was at my store on Poplar street. During the day I had information that shanties had been burned during Wednesday in South Memphis. Wednesday night I played cards at a saloon near my house with Peter Boyle, James Brown and Frank Myres.

J. W. WRIGHT, residing 128 Vance street, Memphis, Tennessee, late lieutenant and acting assistant quartermaster, second Iowa cavalry, post quartermaster at Memphis, Tennessee, after being duly sworn, testified as follows :

The buildings at the corner of Lauderdale and Vance streets, burned during the recent riots in Memphis, were built under my direction, and cost about thirty-five hundred (3,500) dollars.

The building at the corner of Echols street and Hernando road, burned during the riots, cost about one thousand eight hundred (1,800) dollars.

The building corner of Hernando and Pontotoc streets, burned during the riots, cost about two thousand two hundred (2,200) dollars.

The building corner of Beal and Wellington streets, burned during the riots, cost about one thousand (1,000) dollars.

The building corner of Main and Vance streets, burned during the riots, cost about one thousand eight hundred (1,800) dollars.

B. G. GARRETT, chief of police, city of Memphis, Tennessee, residing at corner of Pontotoc and St. Martin's streets, after being duly sworn, testified as follows :

The police force of the city of Memphis numbers about one hundred and forty men, with a captain and lieutenant of night police, and a captain and lieutenant of day police. The night force is larger than the day. When the police force are off duty, they are usually about town ; there are no published rules for the regulation of the police force. I have not had entire control of the police force, but the mayor and police committee have hired and discharged men from the force without my knowledge and do not notify me of the fact. On Tuesday evening, May 1, 1866, I learned that there was a riot in the south part of the city, and collected a force of twenty-five or thirty policemen at the station-house on Adams street, and went to the scene of disturbance on South street. As I went down Causey to South, and when near South, I heard firing, and saw an excited crowd of twenty-five or thirty men, and two or three men were firing at a negro lying near a fence. I saw one man, a stranger, walk up to the negro and shoot him. I stepped up to the man and told him "it was a cowardly act." I did not arrest the man. The firing ceased in this vicinity, but the crowd of people continued to increase ; some of the policemen with me went with the crowd, do not know how many. I then went to the bayou on South street, and when I arrived there the negroes commenced firing from the hill opposite, on the crowd. The crowd then became excited, and the police force were also excited. This skirmishing continued about three quarters of an hour, and extended up to the corner of Main and South streets, when I ordered the police to go home. I went to my house on Pontotoc and St. Martin's streets, and the policemen went towards the station-house. About ten o'clock p. m. I collected a force of about forty policemen and citizens, and went to the south part of the city. Everything was quiet, and I left sixteen or eighteen policemen in the south part of the city to preserve order, and ordered the other policemen to their several wards. I returned to the city, and about twelve o'clock went again to see that all was quiet in the south part of the city ; I remained up nearly all night. On Wednesday morning, about seven o'clock, I heard that two white men had been killed, and I collected a force of twenty-five or thirty policemen at the criminal court-room on Second street, and went to South street. I saw Sheriff Winters, who was assembling a posse of men to preserve order.

By Captain ALLYN :

Question. Did you think there was any disturbance ?

Answer. I did not. When I arrived on South street there was no disturbance, but a large crowd of citizens were assembled there. There were a large number of rowdies in the crowd, who became excited and commenced running after and firing at negroes in that vicinity. I saw a colored soldier run under a house, and a policeman by the name of McCormick was about to fire under the house, when I stopped him. He then got down to go under the house, and I pulled him out and took his pistol from him. Did not arrest McCormick. I then told the crowd to disperse, and started with my force of policemen towards Main street. Some shots were fired from near the fort, and the crowd fired in return. I remained there about an hour with my force, when Captain Allyn arrived with some soldiers. When I returned to the city with the police, every policeman I know of who went with me returned with me. I did not go out on Wednesday evening, being very much fatigued and exhausted.

Question. Who appoints the police ?

Answer. The mayor and the police committee.

Question. Who were the police committee that appointed the policemen on duty during the riot ?

Answer. Hitsfield, Green, Grace, Leonard and Kelley.

Question. What are the qualifications required to fit a man for a policeman ?

Answer. He must have been a resident of the city twelve (12) months preceding his appointment ; he must be steady, sober, discreet, and an energetic man ; he should always know how to read and write.

Question. Did a majority of the police of Memphis appointed previous to these riots come up to the requirements which you have mentioned ?

Answer. In every respect they have not.

Question. Were a majority of the police sober men ?

Answer. They were sober sometimes.

Question. How many were discreet ?

Answer. More than half of them.

Question. How many could read and write ?

Answer. Mr. O'Donald reported that they could all read and write.

Question. Has the mayor, to your knowledge, ever appointed police without authority from the police committee ?

Answer. I am not able to say.

Question. Have you not relieved policemen for bad conduct and have not the same policemen been re-appointed by the police committee?

Answer. Yes, sir.

Question. What was the nature of the offence committed ?

Answer. For theft.

Question. Is there not a policeman on duty against whom there are charges of theft, who in fact is held under bonds for theft, yet placed on duty against your remonstrance to the committee, and did not the said committee know that he was under bonds at the time?

Answer. There is such a man ; his name is F. B. Sullivan. The committee knew it when he was appointed the second time.

Question. Did you see the mayor of the city during the riots, and how often ?
Answer. I saw him only once.
Question ? Was he drunk or sober?
Answer. He was tolerable drunk.
Question. Did you see the recorder of the police court during the riots ?
Answer. I did not see him in the vicinity of the riots.

D. A. BROWER, residing in Ayres Block, Memphis, Tennessee, after being duly sworn, testified as follows :

I am the managing editor of the Memphis Daily Argus ; I supervise the editorial and original reading matter of the Argus. Sometimes comments appear in the editorial columns of the paper which are published before I see them. I do not as a general rule examine the editorial items which appear in the local columns. The circulation of the Argus in the city of Memphis is about eighteen hundred (1,800) copies daily.
Question. Please state who wrote the paragraph published in the local columns of the Argus, on the 29th of April, 1866, in words as follows, to wit : "Would to God, they (meaning the negroes) were back in Africa, hell, or some other sea-port town, *anywhere* but here. Not that we have no regard for them, but the idleness and profligacy of the race is such that they are a perfect nuisance, and forfeit all the regard that humanity can offer them in their present condition?"
Answer. Captain Isaac A. Hood, acting as local editor of the Argus, told me he wrote the article.
Question. Did the paragraph appear with your knowledge and consent ?
Answer. No, sir ; I did not see the paragraph until my attention was called to it after publication. I would not have permitted any language embodying such sentiments to be published in the paper.

M. W. CLUSKY, residing at No. 19 Jefferson street, Memphis, Tennessee, after being duly sworn, testified as follows :

I am one of the editors of the Memphis Avalanche. On Tuesday night, May 1, 1866, about nine o'clock, I was walking from the Commercial hotel in company with Mr. Galloway, of the Avalanche, and stopped near the corner of Main and Jefferson streets. There was a large crowd on the opposite corner ; I saw a negro man run by the crowd, and several men fired at him ; the negro escaped. The crowd then commenced gathering about the corner where Mr. Galloway and myself were standing, and rapidly increased in size. It was then I heard the cry of "Let's go for the Post." Colonel Galloway and myself expostulated with the crowd, remarking "that won't do," or words to that effect. There were about one hundred in the crowd, but it was continually increasing. I suggested to Colonel Galloway that we had better get away from there, and acting on my suggestion the colonel walked with me to my room. The crowd did not appear to have a bad spirit, and were not animated with that fury which generally characterizes mobs. They were not the better class of citizens ; I did not know a single person in the crowd ; I heard two or three shots fired at a passing carriage and heard the shots strike the glass. I saw several men take hold of Mr. Galloway, evidently with a desire to receive his encouragement.

GEORGE ARMON, (colored,) residing at No. 108 Fourth street, Memphis, Tennessee, after being duly sworn, testified as follows :

On Wednesday, May 2, 1866, between three and four o'clock in the morning, six (6) or eight (8) men came to my house. The names of one of the men was Boyle, who has a grocery store on Poplar, near Fourth street. Another man was called Haggarty, who has a grocery on Poplar street, near Fourth, told me the next day that he was with the party. The party knocked at the door and ordered me to come out   Some one in the party remarked that they "could not burn the damned niggers out without burning two white families on each side." They remained there five or ten minutes and then went away. About the same number of men came to my house the next night about twelve o'clock ; two policemen were in my grocery at the same time. The party demanded entrance, and the door was opened ; shortly afterwards the policemen and crowd went away together.

SARAH ARMON, (colored,) residing at 108 Fourth street, Memphis, Tennessee, after being duly sworn, testified as follows :

Between one and two o'clock a. m., Wednesday, May 2, 1866, a party of men came to my house and knocked three times at the door ; I knew two of the men ; one of the men was named Boyle, and one was named Haggarty ; I heard some one in the party say, "We can't burn these damned niggers out without burning the two white families each side of them." They remained a short time and then went away. The next night Mr. Kline and

Mr. Moore, policemen, were in my grocery about 12 o'clock, when a party of men came to the door and knocked ; the door was opened, and one man started to come in, when Mr. Moore stopped him ; the man said " We want that nigger." Mr. Moore spoke to some one in the crowd and said " Go home, Joe," there is no negro man here ; I did not know the man spoken to ; the policemen went away with the crowd.

THEODORE PETERSON, residing corner of Seventh and Jackson streets, Fort Pickering, Tennessee, after being duly sworn, testified as follows:

I keep the Cosmopoliton saloon, corner of Jefferson and Second streets. On Tuesday evening about nine o'clock, May 2, 1866, I saw a crowd of forty or fifty white men on Adams street. Some of them were beating a negro ; did not know the negro, or any one in the crowd ; heard expressions that " all negroes ought to be killed or run out of town," or words to that effect.

Mrs. MARY FOX, residing on De Soto, between Beal and Linden streets, Memphis, Tennessee, after being duly sworn, testified as follows :

On the afternoon of the day after the buildings were burned during the riots in Memphis, a drunken man in front of my house said my husband " had command of a negro regiment, and had no business to free them." He also said " the Yankees had no business here."

Question. Did this occur in the month of April or May ?

Answer. I cannot tell.

Question. What day of the week was this conversation held ?

Answer. On Thursday, the day after the burning.

HENRY J. KRYLE, residing on Howard row, Memphis, Tennessee, after being duly sworn, testified as follows :

I have a meat market on Howard row. During the recent riots in the city of Memphis I saw a man named Richard Marsh shoot a negro man near my shop on Howard row. The ball took effect in the negro man's leg near the knee. The negro man was quiet and peaceable, and was not doing anything at the time ?

J. O. PIERCE, residing at 343 Main street, Memphis, Tennessee, after being duly sworn, testified as follows :

I was living temporarily for two months previous to the riot on De Soto street, south of South street, in this city. In that immediate vicinity there were a large number of negro cabins, and a large negro population. During the day time that part of the city was generally very quiet, but at night there was a great deal of disturbance occasioned by the firing of guns and pistols. There was so much firing that it was unsafe to go out of doors in a dark night. I have frequently heard what appeared to be regular skirmishes with pistols in the immediate vicinity of South street.

On Tuesday, May 1, 1866, in the evening, I saw a portion of the riotous proceedings in the south part of the city ; I did not see any of the disturbances on Wednesday.

On Wednesday evening, May 2, 1866, I was at my room, 343 Main street, and saw the lights of burning buildings in the south part of the city, and started for that vicinity. Very soon after I saw the fire I heard an alarm, and when near the corner of Beal and Main streets I saw a steam fire-engine going towards the fires. It passed me at the corner of Beal and Main. Mr. C. A. Stevens, my room-mate, was with me. As we walked down Beal street we saw very few persons. When near the Beal street market another steam fire-engine came from the direction of Union street, proceeding towards the fire. At the Beal street market, and near the corner of Hernando street, I heard some person unknown to me, speaking in a tone of authority, order the engine to halt. The engine stopped near the corner of Hernando street, apparently in obedience to that order. At the same time I noticed that the first engine had stopped at a point midway between Hernando and De Soto streets. It was still two or three blocks from the fire. We then started to return, and proceeded as far as the bayou bridge on Beal street, and then stopped. As the hook and ladder truck was coming from Main street, I heard a voice from behind calling the truck to halt. As it passed us the man still continued calling it to stop, and when about thirty yards east of the bridge the truck halted. After some conversation, which I could not distinguish, between the driver of the truck and the man who I thought from the tone of voice had been hallowing, it again moved on towards the fire. As we reached the corner of Hernando and Beal streets, the second steam fire-engine turned around and went towards Main street, going away from the vicinity of the fire. As we proceeded towards the fire, I observed that the firemen with the first engine we had seen were raking out their fire, and turned the engine around and went toward Main street. The fire was raked out midway between Hernando and De Soto streets, and apparently where the engine first stopped. We went as far as the corner of De Soto street, and the ladder truck which we had passed again came up, turned the corner where we stood, and proceeded slowly northward on De Soto street. There was no fire in that direction. Mr. Stevens and myself then returned to our room. The fire on Hernando road at this time appeared to burn brighter than ever. After reaching my room I heard the bell of the ladder truck proceeding northward on Second or Third street. As we were returning up Beal street towards Main, I saw a patrol of armed men, which I afterward learned was Sheriff Winters going towards the fire. While at my room, about two o'clock Thursday morning, May 3, 1866, I saw a fire in the north part of the city, on Main street, and saw a hose cart turn from Union into Main street, and drove rapidly in the direction of the fire, when some person ordered it to halt. A conversation of which I could not hear the tenor then passed between the driver and the person who had ordered it to halt, when the hose cart again started, going slowly towards the fire.

Question. Did you not say that negro boys in the south part of the city carried pistols?
Answer. I heard the negro servants say that the little boys carried pistols.

JAMES HAGGARTY recalled.

On Wednesday night, May 2, 1866, about two o'clock in the morning, I went to the fire on Main street, near Jackson. The building burned was a church. I remained there a few minutes, and then returned to my house. When on Poplar street, near Fourth, I saw several persons on Fourth street, in front of a house and grocery occupied by a colored man named Armon. I walked toward the crowd, and told them that "it would be wrong to burn the colored man's house, as there were white people in the houses on each side of him." I did not go into the crowd, and did not know any person there. No one in the crowd spoke to me. I left and went to the corner of Fourth and Poplar streets, and shortly afterward saw the party go toward Washington street.

JAMES DUNLAP, (colored,) nurse at Freedmen's Hospital, Memphis, Tennessee, after being duly sworn, testified as follows:

On Tuesday, May 1, 1866, about dark, I saw a squad of twenty or thirty men come down Main street, and as they passed the Freedmen's Hospital they fired at the hospital. Two of the patients in the hospital were wounded by shots from the crowd; one of them in the leg and one in the shoulder. Some of the men in the crowd that fired had stars on their breasts, and were policemen. I saw an Irishman with black whiskers shoot a colored man near the hospital. The man is called Pat, and visits at a grocery near the hospital. The colored man was looking at the crowd at the time, and was not doing anything.

LOUIS BENNETT, (colored,) patient in Freedmen's Hospital, Memphis, Tennessee, after being duly sworn, testified as follows:

On Wednesday, May 2, 1866, about sunset, six white men stopped me in front of the Gayoso house, and one of them asked me if I had been a soldier. I told him I had been on a gunboat. He then called me "a damned smoked Yankee," and struck me on the left arm with a club, and broke my arm between the wrist and elbow. One of the other men struck me on the head with a club, and knocked me down. The men then took my watch and pocket-book containing fifty dollars. I laid where I was knocked down till the next morning.

J. S. WHITE, residing at No. 224 Vance street, Memphis, Tennessee, after being duly sworn, testified as follows:

On Wednesday night, May 2, 1866, about 11 o'clock, I saw some buildings burn on Echols street. I saw a party of five or six men coming from the direction of buildings which had just been fired. The party seemed to be intoxicated, and were firing pistols. A crowd then commenced assembling from every direction. I did not see any of the fire-engines in the vicinity of the fire, but saw five or six men on horseback who gave directions to prevent the spread of the flames. I afterwards learned they were firemen. On Tuesday evening I was called to see a policeman at the corner of Causey and Vance streets, who had a slight wound in the back, which appeared to have been made by a spent gun or pistol shot. The shot did not penetrate through his clothes.

ROBERT PEPLOW, residing corner of Hernando and South streets, Memphis, Tennessee, after being duly sworn, testified as follows:

On Wednesday, May 2, 1866, about 6 o'clock p. m., I saw a policeman come from a house between Clay and South streets on Hernando with a gun. I saw him aim his gun at a negro man standing at the crossing of Clay and Hernando streets. I turned my head, heard the report of a gun, immediately looked in the direction of the negro and saw him lying on the ground. I did not hear any other shots in the vicinity of the negro.

E. C. HASTINGS, residing at No. 12 Overton street, Memphis, Tennessee, after being duly sworn, testified as follows :

On Tuesday, May 1, 1866, about 6 o'clock p. m., I was on South street, and saw a crowd of men running after a negro. I saw the negro fall down near the corner of Avery and South streets. One of the white men ran up to him, jumped on him and kicked him in the face. I then saw a policeman step up to him and shoot him.

Question. What class of community did the parties running after the negro appear to belong to ?

Answer. The most of them were policemen, and the rest appeared to be roughs.

GEORGE HAGAN, first sergeant company G, second battalion, sixteenth United States infantry, stationed at Memphis, Tennessee, after being duly sworn, testified as follows :

Shortly after the riots in the city of Memphis, Tennessee, which commenced May 1, 1866, I heard Mr. Morning Star, proprietor of the National Theatre in this city, say that the "riots were a good thing," and he " wished every damn nigger was massacred, as they had no business to live among white men," and other words to the same effect. I have heard conversations of the same kind at his entertainments among the audience.

JOSEPH TEUFEL, residing on South street, west of Hernando, Memphis, Tennessee, after being duly sworn, testified as follows :

On Tuesday, May 1, 1866, about 3 o'clock p. m., I saw Lieutenant Jericho lead a party of about one hundred and fifty negroes from Morris Cemetery toward South street, and shortly after heard firing in that direction. On Tuesday night, May 1, 1866, about 12 o'clock, several citizens came to my house and searched for Lieutenant Jericho, and said they would hang him to a tree behind the house if they caught him. Lieutenant Jericho was not in the house. I knew several of the party ; one was named Hagan and another Harrigan, Harrigan's stepson, and a man to me unknown was in the party.

J. WANDS, residing on Vance street, between Hernando and Causey streets, Memphis, Tennessee, after being duly sworn, testified as follows :

On the night of the 2d of May, 1866, about 2 o'clock, a shanty on corner of Webster and De Soto streets, which was occupied as negro quarters, was burned, with everything in it. I had ten prints used for stamping oil cloths in the building at the time, and they were destroyed. They were worth two hundred (200) dollars.

Rev. WILLIAM C. HUBBARD, residing under Gayoso house, corner of McCall and Front streets, Memphis, Tennessee,. after being duly sworn, testified as follows :

Question. Did you not tell a gentleman of this city that you knew, from the colored soldiers themselves, that they intended getting up a row here after they were mustered out, and that you had used your efforts to persuade them not to do so ?

Answer. No, sir; I never made use of any such expressions. I often heard expressions previous to the riots, from hackmen and firemen, that "the damned niggers would be cleaned out as soon as they were mustered out of service."

SAMUEL VAN PELT, (colored,) residing on South street, near Hernando, Memphis, Tennessee, after being duly sworn, testified as follows :

On Tuesday, May 5, 1866, about 5 o'clock p. m., I was standing on the South street bridge, and saw a white man dressed in uniform coming down Elliott street. Some policemen were going up that street at the same time, and a large crowd of negroes were following them. I heard some of the negroes halloa "stop that son-of-a-bitch," and saw the man on horseback turn around and fire at a policeman. The policeman fell down. I was about fifty yards distant when the policeman was shot.

LUCINDA LEE, (colored,) residing on South street, near St. Martin street, Memphis, Tennessee, after being duly sworn, testified as follows :

On Thursday morning, May 3, 1866, about two or three hours before day, I saw some policemen set fire to four houses on South street, near the bayou bridge. There were twelve men in the party. In the ruins of one of the houses, on Thursday, I saw the remains of a woman and child who had been burned to death.   I also saw one of the men in the party shoot and kill a woman who was going towards one of the houses to get some clothes she had piled outside of the houses.   The man who shot the woman was a heavy-set man, full face, with light hair and beard.   He had on gray clothes, which I saw him pull off, when I saw that he had on a suit of black.   I saw the son of the lady who lives next door to Ryan's house in the party.   The man is a Dutchman, about five feet nine inches high, light hair.

WILLIS JONES, residing corner of Linden and Mulberry streets, Memphis, Tennessee, after being duly sworn, testified as follows :

I am a blacksmith, and have a shop on Main street.   On Tuesday evening, May 1, 1866, shortly after six o'clock, I was about starting home to supper, when I saw a large crowd of policemen coming up Main street, from the direction of South street.   The policemen passed me, but a thick-set man, about five feet ten inches high, in rear of the crowd, aimed his pistol and fired at me, the ball taking effect in my right eye.   I walked away from him and he fired at me again.

DAVID SMITH, (colored,) residing near Mississippi and Tennessee railroad depot, Memphis, Tennessee, after being duly sworn, testified as follows :

On Tuesday night, May 1, 1866, about 9 o'clock, I was at Mrs. Grady's, in South Memphis, and a party of seven men, with pistols, came to the house.   One of them was named Pat Pendergrass, and another man was named Burns.   Burns jabbed his pistol against my neck and said, "God damn you, I ought to shoot you."   Pendergrass and Mrs. Grady interfered and saved me.

JAMES FINN, residing on Winchester street, Memphis, Tennessee, after being duly sworn, testified as follows :

I am a policeman of the day force, city of Memphis, Tennessee.   On Tuesday, May 1, 1866, about 5½ o'clock p. m., John O'Neil, David Carroll, John Stevens, and myself were on Causey street.   We heard a great noise in the direction of St. Martin's street, and we went in that direction   Near Morris cemetery I saw a crowd of about fifty or sixty negroes, which increased to a crowd of one hundred or one hundred and fifty, among whom were several negro soldiers.   I asked one of them what the trouble was, and he said, "Its none of your God damned business, you damned white-livered son of a bitch; you got no business over here."   This negro was dressed in citizen's clothes.   This man said, "Go for Carroll, that white-livered son of a bitch."   The negroes then formed a half circle around us, and two negro soldiers took hold of Carroll, who finally got away from them.   Stevens and myself then commenced going east on South street, and had reached the Bayou bridge, and were about twenty-five yards from the crowd, when I heard pistol shots from the negroes and saw policeman Stevens fall, wounded through the thigh.   O'Neil and myself then turned toward the crowd and commenced shooting at them.   I fired four shots, and the whole crowd dispersed.   I then started up Avry street, and met a white man dressed in citizen's clothes on horseback, who told me to stop and go with him, saying, "You are my prisoner."

D. McMAHON, residing on Robinson street, Memphis, Tennessee, after being duly sworn, testified as follows :

I am captain of the day police of Memphis, Tennessee.   James Finn and John Stevens, of the day police, were wounded during the riots which commenced in Memphis, Tennessee, May 1, 1866.   John Stevens died soon after he was wounded.   There were no others of the day police who were reported to me as wounded during the riots.   I had twelve men on duty in the seventh ward of this city on the day of the riot.   Four men were on duty in the vicinity of the southern part of the city, where the riot originated.   There is no reserve force kept at the station-house, nor any prescribed rules for assembling the police in case of a riot.   The four men who were on duty on South street the day of the riot were John Stevens, James Finn, David Carroll, and John O'Neil.

MARIA SCOTT, (colored,) residing on Grady's Hill, South Memphis, Tennessee, after being duly sworn, testified as follows :

On Wednesday night, May 2, 1866, about ten o'clock, Chris. Pidgeon and four (4) men came to the house of Mary Black and set fire to the house and burned it up.   I had ninety dollars ($90) burned in the house.

D. A. BROWER recalled :

Question by Captain Allyn. Who was the author of the article published in the Memphis Daily Argus on the 2d day of May, 1866, entitled "The Reign of Bloodshed."

Answer. I am not positive who wrote the article, but, as one of the editors of the paper, I am responsible for it. The words of the article are as follows: "THE REIGN OF BLOODSHED.—Again the irrepressible conflict of races has broken out in our midst, and again our streets are stained with blood. And this time there can be no mistake about it. The whole blame of this most tragical and bloody riot lies, as usual, with the poor ignorant deluded blacks. A full report of the affair will be found in our local columns, to which the reader is referred. But we cannot suffer the occasion to pass without again calling the attention of the authorities to the indispensable necessity of disarming these poor creatures, who have so often shown themselves utterly unfit to be trusted with fire-arms. On this occasion the facts all go to show that but for this much abused privilege accorded to them by misguiding and misjudging friends, there would have been no riot, no deadly attack, in the first place, on sworn officers of the law going forward to make an arrest in the regular discharge of their duty. The universal question asked on all corners of the street is, why are not the negroes disarmed ?"

Question. Who was the author of the article published in the Memphis Daily Argus on the 4th day of May, 1866, entitled "The Memphis Riots—Facts to be Remembered—Radical Organs—Misrepresentations Exposed ;" and an article published the same day, entitled "Churches, school-houses, and shanties burned by the mob, responsibility of the same ?"

I object to the introduction of newspaper articles published after the 3d day of May, and any on the 2d and 3d of May, unless the articles in words encourage riotous proceedings. I object to editors of newspapers being interrogated as to their opinions as to the cause of the riotous proceedings, as their opinions are not evidence any more than the opinions of other men.

MARCUS J. WRIGHT.

Captain A. W. ALLYN says : I believe any article published by any newspaper in the city of Memphis, either before the riot or during it, extending even to the day of the arrival of editorial troops, on Saturday, May 5, 1866, of an inflammatory character, intending to excite the public mind against any class of persons engaged in the riot, to be competent evidence bearing on the remote and immediate cause of the riot.

Answer. Colonel J. P. Pryor wrote the first mentioned article, and I wrote the concluding paragraph of the second. I read the article before it was published, and, as one of the editors, am responsible for it.

Question by Captain ALLYN. What was the object in printing in italics a portion of the second paragraph of the second named article, in words as follows, to wit, "In the late riots the negroes wantonly began the riots," &c.

Answer. We wished to make the fact prominent, as it was our opinion, from what we heard, that the negroes commenced the riots.

J. P. PRYOR, residing at Metropolitan Hotel, Memphis, Tennessee, after being duly sworn, testified as follows :

I am the political editor of the Memphis Daily Argus.

Question. Do you know the names of any of the persons referred to, in connexion with the riots, in the leading editorial article of the Memphis Argus published May 4, 1866, as "certain low bad white men ?"

Answer. I do not.

Question. Did you write the article ?

Answer. I did.

Question. Did you ever hear the names of any of the parties referred to as " low bad white men "

Answer. I do not remember to have heard any names mentioned.

M. C. GALLOWAY recalled.

Question. Who wrote the closing sentence of the second paragraph of the leading editorial article published in the Memphis Avalanche of May 2, 1866, in the following words, viz : " Life has been taken, the result of the incendiary impressions of the radicals upon the public and too willing intellect of the negroes ?"

Answer. I did not write the article ; but saw it before it was published, and am responsible for the assertion.

Question. State the names of any persons referred to as radicals, or any white persons who instigated or encouraged the recent riots in this city.

Answer. I do not know the name of any person who instigated or encouraged the riots.

Question by Captain ALLYN. Who is responsible for the publication of the last clause of the leading editorial article on the second page of the Avalanche on the 5th day of May, 1866, to wit : "The late riots in our city have satisfied all of one thing : that the southern men will not be ruled by the negro. For months past acts of violence, bloodshed and murder have been too common ; but they have almost always had some direct connexion with the negro troops stationed here. Time and again stores have been broken open and plundered, and white men shot down in our city by drunken, brutal negro soldiers ; and we have yet to hear of the first instance where punishment followed the crime. We readily grant that it was often, in fact almost always, impossible to identify the offenders, as the crimes were generally committed after dark. We only speak of the facts, however ; and, believing that negro troops were the prime cause, our citizens again and again petitioned that they should be removed. In all these cases of violence the officers of the law had been left to vindicate the law and protect the rights of the people, whose peace and quiet they are sworn to protect. The citizens themselves took no part in all these altercations, and hence the negro soldiers began to believe that they could manage things their own way. This idea of insolence culminated on Tuesday evening, and they became engaged in a fatal altercation with the police. Then, for the first time, our citizens took part in the fight ; and the negroes now know, to their sorrow, that it is best not to arouse the fury of the white man. Such a thing as a riot never occurred in Memphis till these negro troops came among us to teach us manners ; and, from the lessons these brutes have lately received, we think it will be many a day before a riot will occur here again. The negro population of Memphis—the draymen, hackmen, porters, servants of all kinds—are as respectful and kindly in their deportment as they ever were. With these, save in rare instances, our people would never have trouble. It is only with the negro soldiers that trouble has ever existed. They, as we learn, will soon be gone ; and with their departure will come order, confidence, and the good will of old days. We shall soon have now among us but white troops, and with them we can have no difficulty. They are of our race, and can and do appreciate our position and our wishes. Had we had them all the time, instead of negro troops, neither this riot, nor the many lawless acts preceding it during the past six months, would have occurred. The chief source of all our trouble being removed, we may confidently expect a restoration of the old order of things. The negro population will now do their duty. Already we hear of many in South Memphis seeking houses in the country. A perfect hegira exists in that part of our city. It is a good sign. Negro men and negro women are suddenly looking for work on country farms. This is right, for two reasons : the country farmers need their labor, and can pay for it better than the town can. They must become producers instead of being consumers. In the second place, by going to the country they place themselves beyond the ready reach and contamination of the low pimps of that 'ebony line' whose position and pay depend upon fomenting trouble between whites and blacks. We congratulate the country ; we congratulate our readers. Soon we shall have no more black troops among us ; and we shall thus have peace with it, genuine, real blessings, confidence and hope. Thank Heaven, the white race are once more rulers in Memphis. In this connexion let our people pay a just and merited respect to Major General Stoneman, commanding here. He has had unusual trials to contend with. He has really had to fear that just here, under his immediate eye, would be commenced a war of races. Gradually he has been reducing the negro force here, until it is now a mere squad ; and he has called in white troops to take their place so far as it should be necessary. He has not made himself a fanatic ; he has respected our prejudices, and conciliated our kindness. He has acted upon the idea that, if troops are necessary here to protect the rights of the blacks even, white troops can do this with less offence to our people than black ones. He knows the wants of the country, and sees that the negro can do the country more good in the cotton field than in the camp. In short, he has seen the emergency, and has known how to meet it. Under his military rule our people are about to obtain what they have so often petitioned for—the rule of the white man. Let us all aid him in his wish and effort to procure order and quiet. In doing this we can soon convince him and his superiors at Nashville and Washington that, the negro troops having been removed, the people of Memphis require no others to teach them their duty as good citizens ?"

Answer. I am.

B. G. GARRETT recalled.

Question. Did you state to the local editor of the Memphis Avalanche that you had the affidavit of a negro woman to the effect that the negroes contemplated rising, sacking the city, and robbing the banks four days, or any time, previous to the recent riots ?

Answer. I never had any such affidavit, and never heard a negro woman make such a statement. I never made any such statement to the local editor of the Avalanche, or any other man.

JOHN PARK, mayor of the city of Memphis, Tennessee, residing at No. 304 Second street, after being dulys worn, testified as follows:

The fire department of Memphis, Tennessee, is under my immediate control. James Madden is captain of steamer No. 1, engine house on Jefferson street; John J. Reede is captain of steamer No. 2, engine house on Shelby street; J. B. Sainagel is captain of steamer No. 3, engine house on Poplar street; Michael McFadden is captain of steamer No. 4, engine house on Adams street; Philip Taffe is captain of hook and ladder company No. 1, house on Adams street. These constitute the organized and paid fire department of Memphis, Tennessee. The general orders for the action of the fire department is to proceed to all fires immediately upon the alarm being given. Nos 6 and 7 hand engines and companies are also subject to my orders. They have about forty men each.

Question. Did you or do you know of any orders being given to all or any of the fire engines in the city during the riots, which commenced May 1, 1866, not to proceed to certain burning buildings in this city?

Answer. I know that no such orders were given. I was present at the fire on Gayoso street on Wednesday night, May 2, 1866, and all the engines of the city were present, and did their duty. If the police force of this city had done their duty, there would not have been any buildings burned during the riots, with the exception of the negro church on Washington street.

Question. Did you see all the fire engines of the city present at the fire on Gayoso street?

Answer. I did not see any of them, but saw the pipes. They saved all the property adjoining the burning building.

Question. Why do you except the church on Washington street?

Answer. For the reason that there were very few police stationed in that vicinity.

ASSISTANT QUARTERMASTER'S OFFICE,
Memphis, Tennessee, May 31, 1866.

SIR: In accordance with your request of May 19, 1866, I have the honor to submit the following "statement of expenses" incurred by the branch of the quartermaster's department under my control, on account of the riots which took place recently in this city. These expenses were incurred solely in transporting the negroes to such point, or points, as they desired to go; and the aggregate is computed according to the "mileage rates" expressed in General Orders No. 50, Quartermaster General's Office, dated August 24, 1865:

The total number of miles traveled was 54,181; at the rate of said order, two cents per mile, makes.. $1,083 62

All of which I respectfully submit.

Very respectfully, your obedient servant,

J H. TIGHE,
Captain and Assistant Quartermaster.

Captain W. J. COLBURN,
Recorder Military Commission, Memphis, Tennessee.

Subscribed and sworn to before me this 1st day of June, 1866, at Memphis, Tennessee.

W. J. COLBURN,
Captain and Assistant Quartermaster, Recorder

J. A. HOOD, residing on Second street, between Jefferson and Adams streets, Memphis, Tennessee, after being duly sworn, testified as follows:

I am local editor of the Memphis Argus. On Wednesday morning, about 9 oclock a. m., May 2, 1866, I was in rear of Rankin's school-house, on South street, and saw a boy about fourteen years old waving a piece of black cloth suspended from a pole which he held in his hand. I saw the boy remove the flag. I was about three hundred yards distant from the flag, which was west of the depot. There were only three or four persons in the immediate vicinity of the boy, and I could not tell whether they were white or black. I saw on the hill beyond the boy a party of colored soldiers. Those on the hill were between me and the sky-light; the flag and those around it were under the hill. I do not remember whether the sun was shining at the time The party of colored soldiers on the hill were firing about the same time, and were armed with rifles or muskets.

EDWARD O'NEIL, residing in North Memphis, Tennessee, after being duly sworn, testified as follows:

The fire engines of this city are ordered to proceed to all fires immediately on the alarm being given. During the riots the engines were all out on Wednesday night, May 2, 1866. Every engine was out except steamer No. 2, which was at the machine-shop opposite the

Gayoso House undergoing repairs. The first fire we visited on Wednesday night, May 2, 1866, was on Beal street, east of the bayou. The engines did not play on the fire, for there is no water east of the bayou. Two engines went to the church on Washington street about ten o'clock, and threw water on the fire. When the engines were returning from Washington street I saw a fire in the northern part of the city, and three engines went to the fire and worked till nearly daylight. We saved a portion of the church on the corner of Main and Overton streets. The church on Washington street was so near destroyed when we arrived there that we could not save it. These were the only fires we visited that night. The other fires occurred while the engines were engaged as stated.

Question. There was a fire recently extinguished on the opposite corner from the buildings burned on Beal street; why could not the fire during the riots have been extinguished?

Answer. Because the building was consumed by the time we got there. At the Washington street church we played on the fire till the only cistern in the vicinity was exhausted.

Question. Did the engines go to the fires in South Memphis on Wednesday afternoon, May 2, 1866?

Answer. They went as far as South street, but did not play on the fires. There is no water on South street which we could reach. There is not a public cistern south of Vance street.

AFFIDAVITS TAKEN BEFORE COMMISSION ORGANIZED BY FREEDMEN'S BUREAU.

ROBERT BOYLE, after being duly sworn by Captain M. Walsh, A. A. A. G., of the Freedmen's Bureau, testified as follows:

On the night of the 1st of May, 1866, a party of men came to the house occupied by himself and son, Louis Boyle, and robbed him of carpenter tools and other articles in the house, amounting to the sum of one hundred (100) dollars; one of them told him if he spoke he would put a ball in him.

FRED. TOLES, Memphis, Tennessee, after being duly sworn, testified as follows:

On the evening of the 1st of May, 1866, as I was going home from my work, I met a number of policemen who were after some colored men, firing at them with revolvers. They all passed me but one; he stopped when he came up to me, and shot me through the arm and then passed on. I hid under a pile of lumber near by, and remained until night before I went home.

OBADIAH STOCKLY, Memphis, Tennessee, after being duly sworn, testified as follows:

On the 3d of May, 1866, three white men, names unknown to me, came to my house and inquired if I had any arms; I said there was a gun in the house; they ordered me to bring it out; asked me if I had been a soldier; said I had better not own it if I had; they took my pocket-book, containing seventy-one dollars in greenbacks, and a gold watch. They also took my gun and left it with a man by the name of Johny, who lives near Mrs. Jacobie's, and who knows the names of the parties that robbed me. The men were armed with revolvers, and presented them as they approached the house.

KIT TEMPLE, Memphis, Tennessee, after being duly sworn, testified as follows:

On the night of the 2d of May, 1866, a mob came to my grocery store and fired through the door, and then broke down the door and came in and went to work carrying out all my goods. They started to set my house on fire, but Mr. Casper (stops at the Delmonico House) got them to stop it. He begged of them not to rob my store, but they would not listen to him. I heard some of the party call three of the men by the names of Mike Colton, Johney Reed, captain fire engine No. 2, and Allen Young. I think Mr. Casper would know some of them. Full amount of loss $1,404.

R. H. SIMMONS, Memphis, Tennessee, after being duly sworn, testified as follows:

On the night of the 2d of May, 1866, several men came to my house and broke in and took from me one gold watch and chain, worth three hundred (300) dollars. They took from a man in the house with me seventy-five (75) dollars worth of clothes. I would know the men if I was to see them. One man has a wooden leg, and was a policeman; I would know him, and can get his name and number. They also took from me $5 in silver. They threatened to kill me, and said they were going to burn up the Freedmen's Bureau and run the General out of the city.

COLEMAN DEFAULT, Memphis, Tennessee, after being duly sworn, testified as follows :

On the evening of the first day of May, 1866, David Roach, policeman, and several other policemen, came to where I was, on South street, and fired the house, shot me twice, beat me on the head with pistols, and robbed me of what money I had and my discharge from the army. David Roach shot me the first time, in the thigh, but could not tell who shot me the second time. After Roach shot me, I begged of him not to kill me ; he said, " Yes, God damn you, I will! You, and all the balance of you." I think they left me for dead. That night I rented another house from Captain Barns, and a party of men burned it that night. They shot and wounded a man who was trying to stop the fire. Loss will amount to thirty ($30) dollars.

JANE GOODLOW, Memphis, Tennessee, after being duly sworn, testified as follows :

I live in the city of Memphis, Tennessee. On the evening of the 1st of May, 1866, a party of men, shooting at a colored soldier, shot into my house and wounded me in the breast.

FRANCIS JONES, Memphis, Tennessee, after being duly sworn, testified as follows :

On the night of the 2d of May, 1866, a party of men came to the house of Fanny, a colored woman, where I was living ; they were shooting promiscuously at every person they saw. One shot took effect in my jaw. They also shot and wounded a man in the shoulder named Tom. They shot him because he would not tell where another man went to whom they were after.

NATHAN FENSTER, corner of Causey street and Brown's avenue, Memphis, Tennessee, after being duly sworn, testified as follows :

On the night of the 2d of May, 1866, two houses, situated on South street, and owned by Mr. F. Feldman, were entirely destroyed by fire at the hands of some person or persons connected with the riot then going on in the city. They were occupied by colored people at the time they were burned. I have known the above described property, as belonging to Mr. Feldman, for the past four or five years. The houses were worth seven hundred and fifty dollars ($750) each.

NELSON ROBINSON, Memphis, Tennessee, after being duly sworn, testified as follows :

On the night of the 3d of May, 1866, a party of men came to my house or grocery store, on corner of Maine and Overton streets, tore it down and took away a lot of the articles Loss would amount to two hundred and fifty ($250) dollars.

ELLEN LEE, Memphis, Tennessee, after being duly sworn, testified as follows :

On the night of the 3d of May, 1866, three men came to my house and asked for my husband, Lewis Lee. I told them he was a soldier and was at Fort Pickering. They robbed my house of articles to the amount of one hundred and fifty ($150) dollars. Said if my husband wanted any more clothes he could go to headquarters after them.

FRANK D. BERRY, Memphis, Tennessee, after being duly sworn, testified as follows :

On the night of May 1, 1866, a party of men came to the house of my sister-in-law, Sarah Long, where I boarded, broke open my trunk and took from it, belonging to me, some three hundred dollars in greenbacks, fifteen dollars in silver, a watch, and a lot of clothes worth seventy dollars.

JOHN LEWIS, Memphis, Tennessee, after being duly sworn, testified as follows :

On the night of the 3d of May, 1866, four men came to my house and took from me sixty dollars in money and a gun worth twenty-five dollars ; said they would kill me if I did not leave.

KELLUM MOON, Memphis, Tennessee, after being duly sworn, testified as follows :

On the evening of May 1, 1866, as I was coming down Main street, a party of men coming, (one policeman,) meeting me, commenced shooting at me and killed my horse. I ran away and made my escape. They came into my house, broke open my trunk, and took out of it thirty-seven dollars in greenbacks and $1 75 in silver, a coat and pair of shoes, worth nineteen dollars ; my horse was worth one hundred and thirty-five dollars.

22

HARRIET MOTON, South street, near De Soto, Memphis, Tennessee, after being duly sworn, testified as follows :

On the night of the 4th of May, 1866, four white men came to my house o. a plea of hunting arms ; I told them I had none. They asked me if there were any men there. I told them no. They asked me what I did have there. I told them nothing. They said, "God damn it, we will burn the house up," and did so, with most of the articles it contained. My loss would amount to one hundred and twenty-five dollars.

JOSEPH SIMPSON, Memphis, Tennessee, after deing duly sworn, testified as follows :

On the night of the 2d of May, 1866, some person or persons burned my house and all the articles it contained. My loss will amount to three hundred dollars.

JORDAN BUFFORD, residing on De Soto street, near No. 7 engine house, Memphis, Tennessee, after being duly sworn, testified as follows :

On the night of the 1st day of May, 1866, I was returning from my work—I had been employed by Mr. Botland at the Elmwood cemetery—I had finished work and had been paid off. When near my home I was stopped by the police, who demanded my carpet sack, containing my clothes and fifty dollars in money. One of them struck me over the head with his club. They asked me if I had ever been a soldier. I got away as soon as I could.

Before me personally appeared the undersigned, PHILLIS PREMIER, and, being duly sworn, deposes as follows ·

My name is Phillis Premier ; I am the wife of Samuel Premier ; we live on Gayoso street, in the city of Memphis. On the night of the 2d of May, 1866, policeman David Roach and Smith, with Joe Chambers and Charley Lynn and other citizens, came to my house and demanded our arms. We said we had none. Charley Lynn knocked my husband down with his pistol and robbed him of fifty dollars in money. While I was standing over my husband, Charley said to me, "Get away, you damn bitch," drawing his pistol at the same time as though he was going to strike me. They broke open three trunks and scattered their contents over the floor. They got twenty dollars out of one of the trunks belonging to my brother ; said they wanted to kill him because he was a soldier.   My sister was sick in bed at the time ; they broke the bed down on which she was lying, and frightened her so much that she died in a few days thereafter.

her
PHILLIS + PREMIER
mark.

Subscribed and sworn to before me this 17th day of May, 1866.

MICH. WALSH,
Capt. and A. A. Genl. and P. M. Freedmen.

Before me personally appeared the undersigned, JOHN MUNSON, and, being duly sworn, deposes as follows :

My name is John Munson ; I live in the city of Memphis, Tennessee. On the night of the 2d of May, 1866, a party of white men came to my house and asked me if I had any fire-arms. I told them no. They then demanded that I should give them my money, and I would not do it, whereupon they shot me through the head and took from me fifty dollars in money.

his
JOHN + MUNSON.
mark.

Subscribed and sworn to before me this 12th day of May, 1866.

MICHL. WALSH,
Capt. and A. A. Genl. and P. M. Freedmen.

LEMUEL PREMIER, living on Gayoso street, in the city of Memphis, being duly sworn, testified as follows :

On the night of the 2d of May, 1866, policeman Dav. Roach, Suett, and ten or fifteen other white men, came to my house and demanded my arms. Said I had none. One of the men, called Charley Lynn, knocked me down with his pistol and robbed me of fifty dollars in money.

CHESTERFIELD SANDERS, Memphis, Tennessee, being duly sworn, testified as follows :

On the night of the 2d of May, 1866, some twenty-five men came to my house and robbed me of two hundred and twenty-five dollars in money, a watch worth forty dollars, and other articles to the amount of seventy five dollars, and two guns worth forty dollars.

ASBURY GIBBONS, Memphis, Tennesse, being duly sworn, testified as follows :

On the 2d day of May, 1866, a party of nine or ten policemen took me prisoner, and were going to kill me if it had not been for Sheriff Winters ; he prevailed upon them not to do so. They robbed me of three hundred dollars in money, and broke my trunk open and took out of it and took away fifty dollars' worth of clothing. This was at the house where I was boarding on South street.

SALLIE HAWKINS, Memphis, Tennessee, being duly sworn, deposes as follows :

On the 3d day of May, 1866, a party of men came to the house occupied by myself and husband, Daniel Hawkins, killed him and took from his trunk fifty dollars in money and some clothing to the amount of ten dollars. One of the men is named Mr. Dunn ; he keeps a grocery store on South street, near the bridge, across the bayou.

ISAAC PERKINS, Memphis, Tennessee, being duly sworn, deposes as follows :

On the night of the 2d of May, 1866, a party of men came to my house and robbed and destroyed property from me to the amount of fifty dollars. They threatened to kill me, but I finally begged off from them.

MARIA TROTTER, Memphis, Tennessee, being duly sworn, testifies as follows :

On the night of the 2d of May, 1866, four men came to the house occupied by myself and husband, Ned Trotter, knocked at the door, but I did not answer. They then set fire to the house, and before I could get out the house was all in a blaze. The house and all we had was lost. There was sixty dollars in money in the house which was lost. Our loss without the money would amount to three hundred dollars. My husband was absent at Little Rock at the time. About half an hour before, I saw them shoot a woman, Rachel, and set fire to her after they had killed her.

BARTLEY TAM, Memphis, Tennessee, being duly sworn, testifies as follows :

On the 1st of May, 1866, a party of men came to my house and accused me of firing out of my house at them. They cursed and abused me, and took from me articles to the amount of twenty dollars.

EDWARD JACKSON, Memphis, Tennessee, being duly sworn, testifies as follows :

On the 2d of May, 1866, while I was at my work in the city, the house I occupied was burned down. I had in my trunk one hundred and ninety-five dollars. The woman who occupied part of the house stated that she saw the man who set fire to the house take the money and some other articles out of my trunk. I was afraid to go home until next day, when I learned the disturbance was there. When I did get there I found all I had gone. I also had two diamond rings taken which had been presented to my dead sister by her mistress. I have often been offered one hundred dollars apiece for the rings. Lost carpenter tools and other articles, besides the money and rings, amounting to eighty dollars. The woman who occupied part of the house has since gone to St. Louis.

MATHILDA HAWLEY, Memphis, Tennessee, after being duly sworn, testifies as follows:

On the 1st of May I saw a colored soldier, named Charlie, walking quietly along, when a policeman walked up and hit him on the head with his revolver, breaking the weapon. Then a white man shot the soldier. This occurred in front of my house. After that I saw a colored man, named George Howard, with four white men ; another colored man, named Uncle Dick, who has a house near where I live, was next molested. The white men broke in the door of the house and fired into it twice. The next morning I went into the house and saw the dead body of Uncle Dick with a bullet hole through his breast. After they fired into Uncle Dick's house they passed around the corner and I heard one of them say, " Let us go and burn up these damned nigger shanties ;" another said, " No, we promised the widow (a white woman) that we would not disturb her, and the houses might burn." Then George Howard said, " Let's go and kill them while they are asleep. " One of the white men said, " No, let's wait until they come back." Then Howard said, " It's a good time now while they are asleep." I was close to them, hiding. The next day I met George in the street, and as he met a white man he said, " So you are thinning them out, are you, God damn them."

REUBEN BENNETT, Memphis, Tennessee, after being duly sworn, testified as follows :

On the night of the 2d of May, 1866, some person or persons came to my house and while I was asleep set it on fire. I had to work to save myself ; my house and all its contents was burned. My whole loss would amount to two hundred dollars.

CARY CAMPBELL, discharged soldier, Memphis, Tennessee, after being duly sworn, testifies as follows :

On the night of the 2d of May, 1866, during the riot in the city of Memphis, a mob came to my house and robbed it of most of the articles it contained—the whole amounting to one hundred and twenty-two dollars and forty cents.

HARRY TOWNED, living in portion of the city of Memphis called Chelsea, being duly sworn, testifies as follows :

On the 3d day of May, 1866, four white men came to my house ; two of them passed through after another man. I was in the stable and heard them beating him in the yard ; after they quit beating him he ran into the stable where I was. One of the men followed him to the stable ; looked through a crack and saw me ; put his pistol through and shot me through the shoulder. He was on horseback when he came up, and they called him " Jerry."

ANDREW MINTER, living on South street, Memphis, Tennessee, being duly sworn, testifies as follows :

On the night of the 2d of May, 1866, three or four men came to my house and knocked at the door ; I did not open it ; they then went around to the window and broke it open. There were some buildings burning near by, and by the light of which they saw me lying on the bed. They fired a pistol ; the ball went through my left hand. Two of the men then came into the house. I recognized the voice of one of them as Mr. Clanahan, who lives at the corner of Causey and South streets. This man then stabbed me in the side with a small knife. I feigned death so as to be able to make my escape. They broke open my trunk, took my own and wife's clothing ; finally took my pocket-book containing twenty-five dollars, after which they set the house on fire, and swore they would shoot any one that attempted to carry me out. I waited till the fire was well under way, and pulling a quilt over my head, escaped by a back door.

JOSEPH PATTERSON, of Memphis, Tennessee, after being duly sworn, testified as follows :

On the 1st of May, 1866, a party came to my house, and robbed me of a watch worth seventy-five dollars, and one hundred and forty dollars in money.

EDMOND BRISTOL, of Memphis, Tennessee, after being duly sworn, testified as follows :

On the 1st of May, 1866, after night, a party of men came to my house and demanded of me to deliver to them any fire-arms that I might have. I did so. They made me open a chest, and took from it three hundred dollars, a watch, fifteen dollars, and a revolver worth eighteen dollars. They threatened to kill me, and abused me very badly, striking me with a revolver on the face and head.

MARY A. MERRIWEATHER, Memphis, Tennessee, after being duly sworn, testified as follows :

On the night of the 1st day of May, 1866, a number of white persons came to the house occupied by myself and husband and set it on fire. I ran out and they fired several shots at me. The house and all the contents were burned. My loss would amount to one hundred dollars. My husband's name is Henry Peipers. He was absent at the time in the country.

GEORGE CRUSE, Memphis, Tennessee, after being duly sworn, testifies as follows :

On the night of the 2d of May, 1866, a party of white men set my house on fire and burned it down. My loss would amount to one hundred dollars.

HOUSTON SAVAGE, living near corner of Gayoso and De Soto streets, Memphis, Tennessee, being duly sworn, testifies as follows :

On the night of the 3d of May, 1866, while a fire was burning in my vicinity, I was trying to get my household goods out of danger, and had got my bureau into the street, when a fireman, name unknown, came up and demanded the keys ; not having them with me at the time I was unable to comply with his request, and he broke open the drawers and took therefrom clothing belonging to myself and wife amounting to over one hundred dollars, and one hundred and twenty dollars in greenbacks When I remonstrated with him, he drew his revolver and threatened to shoot me if I did not go in the house.

ANN PATRICK, living on Gayoso street, Memphis, Tennessee, being duly sworn, testifies as follows :

On the night of the 3d of May, 1866, a number of persons came to my house armed, and commenced shooting into it, and ran me and all my family away. They then ransacked my house, and took from it articles to the amount of two-hundred dollars.

MACK PARKER, Memphis, Tennessee, being duly sworn, testifies as follows :

On the 1st of May, 1866, a party of men came to my house, destroyed and took away property to the amount of sixty dollars. I left with my family.

AARON JONES, Memphis, Tennessee, being duly sworn, testifies as follows :

On the 3d of May, 1866, as I was going home from my work, I met three white men ; two of them held revolvers at me, while the third robbed me of twenty-six dollars.

ALBERT WATSON, Memphis, Tennessee, after being duly sworn, testifies as follows :

On the night of the 2d of May, 1866, a party of men came to my house and robbed me of one hundred and twenty dollars in money, watch fifteen dollars, and clothes to the amount of seventy-five dollars. I jumped out of the window when I heard them trying to break open the door, and made my escape.

SHEPPARD ARTIST, Memphis, Tennessee, after being duly sworn, testified as follows :

On the night of the 1st of May, 1866, a party of men came to my house and broke in. I got out of their way with my wife and child. They robbed my house of articles to the value of sixty dollars.

JOHN MALONE, Memphis, Tennessee, being duly sworn, testifies as follows :

On the 5th day of May, 1866, while I was at work in the city, two white men came to my house and wounded Edmund Lacy, and robbed me of three hundred dollars in money. They robbed Edmund Lacy of two hundred and fifty dollars. This I was told when I came home. I did not see the men ; my money was gone when I came back.

S. BRANDONED, Memphis, Tennessee, being duly sworn, testifies as follows :

On the morning of the 2d of May, 1866, four men got off the cars at the depot, (Mississippi,) and came to my house and asked me if I had any money. I told them not here, that it was up stairs in my trunk ; they went up stairs and took from my trunk one hundred dollars belonging to me ; they came down stairs and took from me a silver watch worth twenty-five dollars ; told me not to say a word or they would blow my brains out.

GEORGE WILLIS, Memphis, Tennessee, being duly sworn, testifies as follows :

On the night of the 1st of May, 1866, I was going to the fort to keep out of the way of the rioters. On my way I met four white men. They halted me and asked me if I had ever been a soldier. I told them I had. They then asked me if I had any money. I told them I had my pocket-book. They commenced searching me then, and took from me seventy dollars, and a watch for which I gave fifty dollars.

MONROE JONES, Memphis, Tennessee, after being duly sworn, testifies as follows :

On the evening of the 1st day of May, 1866, as my father was locking his shop, (blacksmith shop,) on the corner of Main and Talbott streets, some police came up and one shot him in the eye. He is not dead yet, but in a very critical condition. Policeman Roach was one of them. My father's name is Willis Jones. The next night they set the shop on fire, but did not burn it up, as we stopped the fire.

BURTON DAVIS, Memphis, Tennessee, after being duly sworn, testifies as follows :

On the night of the 2d of May, 1866, some three or four policemen came to my house and broke open my trunk, taking therefrom my discharge and fifty dollars in silver, and fifteen dollars in greenbacks ; after which they set fire to my house and burned it up, not allowing us to take anything out. The policeman that broke open my trunk was No. 43. When my mother attempted to take anything from the burning buildings she was shot at by the policeman.

ADAM JONES, late private company K, 3d United States colored heavy artillery, being duly sworn, testified as follows :

To-day, May 4, 1866, I started over in Arkansas to work for a man named Stillman ; there were several other colored men along, going for the same purpose. While waiting for a ferry-boat to take us across the river, two policemen came up and searched us all for arms. They then went away, but returned in a short time ; one of them said to me, haven't you got some weapons ? and commenced searching me the second time. Finally, they saw my pocket-book in my waist, took me by the arm and said, come along with us. They cursed me and said I had been giving the police a great deal of trouble lately. They took me into a saloon near the levee, and took from me $160. They then took me to another saloon on Front row, into the back room. I thought they were going to kill me. They asked me where I belonged. I told them I had belonged to Fort Pickering. They then told me to get back to the fort. The money belonged to myself and two other boys, friends of mine, and were going with me to work for Mr. Stillman.

BEN TUCKER, of Memphis, Tennessee, being duly sworn, testified as follows :

On the night of the 1st of May, 1866, while I was absent in the country, a number of persons came to the house occupied by myself and mother, and burned the house and all its contents. Myself and brother lost $100 in money, which was in the house.

LANZIE GILLIMAN, residing six miles from Memphis, Tennessee, after being duly sworn, deposed as follows:

On the night of May 2, 1866, I was on Beal street, and a party of policemen and white men came up to me and knocked me down with a gun and robbed me of $246 and a gold ring worth $10 50. I had just come from the country that evening after a wagon and some forage, &c.

WILLIAM REED, of Memphis, Tennessee, after being duly sworn, testified as follows :

On the evening of the 2d of May, 1866, a party of men came to my house and set fire to it and burned it up, with a great number of the things it contained. My loss would amount to $150.

MAJOR JONES, of Memphis, Tennessee, being duly sworn, testified as follows :

On the night of the 2d of May, 1866, a party of men came to my house and set fire to it. I came out and tried to put it out, when they commenced shooting at me. I retreated into the house ; they kept up the firing. and one ball came through the house and wounded me in the shoulder. I do not know who the men were, but think they were firemen and policemen.

ROBERT BRUSTER, of Memphis, Tennessee, being duly sworn, testified as follows :

On the night of the 3d of May, 1866, a mob came to my house, or grocery, and broke in the door and destroyed and carried away almost everything I had. They got $40 in money. The articles I lost would amount to $250.

THOMAS MOSEBY, of Memphis, Tennessee, being duly sworn, testified as follows :

On the 2d of May, 1866, Pat Pendergraft, John Pendergraft, and Bill Callahan, and two policemen, one called Mike, and a number of other men, came to my house and broke into my trunk and took from it $60 in greenbacks, and a watch worth $35. I jumped out of the window and ran under the house. They then left my house and got after another man and came back ; said that man ran into my house, and to me said I was the man they were after. Several of them drew their revolvers and guns on me. Callahan wanted to kill me anyhow. The two Pendergrafts stopped him and said, don't kill him, he is a good boy, and one of the best neighbors we have.

CLAYBORNE MOSS, of Memphis, Tennessee, being duly sworn, testified as follows :

On the 2d day of May, 1866, some of the mob that composed the riot broke into my house, and into a chest and trunk, took $56 in money, and accounts to the amount of $44, and a number of other articles, clothes, &c., to the amount of $200.

MARSHALL ESCUE, of Memphis, Tennessee, being duly sworn, testified as follows :

On the night of the 2d of May, 1866, a number of persons came to my house and set it on fire, which almost destroyed it. All the contents in it mostly were burned. Loss will amount to $150.

ELIZA GROVES, living on Union street, Memphis, Tennessee, being duly sworn, testified as follows :

On the night of the 3d of May, 1866, policeman Roach and a man named Tracy, and other men, came to my house and asked me who lived there, white men or black men ? I made no reply. They set my house on fire ; also a colored church near by, which burned down. Loss, $75.

CLARY JOHNSON, of Memphis, Tennessee, being duly sworn, testified as follows :

On the night of the 1st of May, 1866, I was stopping at the house of my nephew, Cary Campbell, who was living a few yards from me. One policeman and four men came to his house that night on a plea of searching for fire-arms, and while there robbed the house of some of the articles in it. The policeman stood at the foot of the bed with his club in his hand, while the men searched the house and stole the articles. The next day, May 2d, 1866, a party of men came back and had with them three white women. The men told these women to help themselves to whatever they wanted, and the men and women took away with them most of the valuable articles in the house. On the night of the 2d of May, 1866, they burned my husband's house and all its contents. My loss would amount to $250.

PENNY LE MUIR, residing on Rayborn avenue, south of South street, Memphis, Tennessee, after being duly sworn, testified as follows :

On the 1st of May, 1866, I was standing at my door and saw John Pendergrass pass with a pistol in his hand ; I followed him, and saw him go up to a colored soldier and shoot him, killing him. Do not know his name. The colored soldier was walking along quietly. I then saw Corporal John Robinson (colored) running, with two white men after him. Some one said, there comes another one of the damned rascals. When Pendergrass turned around and met Robinson, and shot him, Robinson fell, and Pendergrass beat him over the head with his pistol. Pendergrass then left, and I went up to Robinson and found him dead.

SAMUEL BROOKS, of Memphis, Tennessee, after being duly sworn, deposed as follows :

On the night of the 1st of May, 1866, I was waiting at the Commercial hotel with my hack for a load. A man came from the engine-house near there, where a crowd of men were congregated. He threw a rock at me, but I took no notice of it. He then came up and asked me what the hack was doing there. I told him that I was standing there at the hotel where it generally stood, as it ran for the hotel. He told me to take my hack and drive it away, or I would get my damned head shot off. I got on my hack and started up Shelby street to get away from him. I saw him following me, and I turned back and drove down Jefferson street, by the engine-house. As I came by the engine-house, there were a number of shots fired at me from the crowd, and one shot took effect in my back. They all stoned me as I went by. If I was to see that man I could recognize him.

HANDY CHRISTOPHER, of Memphis, Tennessee, after being duly sworn, testified as follows :

On the night of the 3d of May, 1866, two policemen and six citizens came to my house and robbed it, and destroyed a great many of the articles they did not take away. They robbed me of $275 in money, a gold watch worth $50, a pair of gold bracelets worth $35, and a suit of clothes that cost me $75 and never was worn, and destroyed articles to the amount of $40.

WILLIAM GREEN, of Memphis, Tennessee, being duly sworn, testified as follows :

On the night of May 1, 1866, a party of white men came to my house and robbed me of a watch, clothing, &c., amounting to the sum of $175. I do not know who the parties were, but think they were firemen.

NORRIS DAVIS, living near the corner of Causey and South streets, Memphis, Tennessee, being duly sworn, testified as follows :

On the night of the 2d of May, 1866, the house in which I live was set on fire and destroyed by policemen and others. My clothing, discharge papers from the army, and one hundred dollars in money, were burned up or taken. I have no means of knowing the names of the policemen, but they wore their uniform. Have had to lie out doors since.

JASPER McCULLAM, of Memphis, Tennessee, being duly sworn, testified as follows :

On the night of the 2d of May, 1866, a number of white men came to my house, and robbed me of and destroyed articles, my own personal property, to the amount of $125.

WESLEY WARE, Memphis, Tennessee, being duly sworn, testifies as follows :

On the night of the 2d of May, 1866, while I was on my house trying to keep it from getting on fire from another house near mine, some persons entered my house and said to my wife, Martha Ware, that they had orders to search my house for fire-arms. My wife opened all the trunks and drawers for them to search, and they robbed me of money, jewelry, &c., to the amount of one hundred and fifty dollars. Think the men were policemen ; could not see any stars.

ALEX. McQUARTERS, residing on the corner of Rayburne avenue and Clay street, being duly sworn, testified as follows :

On the 1st of May, 1866, on my return from work, I stopped at a public house at the corner of South street and Rayburne avenue, and while reading a paper, a large crowd of policemen came down Rayburne avenue. Everything was quiet; there were no negroes armed, nor any indications of a riot—no disturbance of any kind when the policemen arrived. They came down firing at the negroes. The negroes ran away without offering any resistance, the police following and shooting. Dunn, engineer or fireman, was about twenty feet ahead of the police when he fell. No negro fired a shot; the firing all came from the police in the rear of Dunn. When Dunn fell the police passed down Rayburne avenue and South street, and I saw no more of the affair.

JOSEPH CARLTON, Vance street, Memphis, Tennessee, after being duly sworn, testified as follows:

On the 2d of May, 1866, during the riot in the city of Memphis, Tennessee, my brother (a discharged soldier) was shot and killed by some unknown person or persons, and robbed of the sum of $60. I know he had the money, for I gave it to him the day before myself to go to Mississippi to see his family. His name was Robert Carlton. A young man who was clerk in the sutler's store of my regiment told me he saw him a short time after he was killed.

LUCY BEMAN, Memphis, Tennessee, after being duly sworn, testified as follows:

On the night of the 3d of May, 1866, three men came to my house on a plea of searching for fire-arms. They took a stick of wood and broke open my trunk, and took from it a watch worth $45, and a knife worth one hundred cents. They then blew out the candle, and left before I could get it lit. I missed a good many things after they were gone. My loss would amount to sixty dollars, ($60.)

LUMNON DAVIS, Memphis, Tennessee, after being duly sworn, testified as follows:

On the evening of the 3d of May, 1866, a man called Jerry, (I think his name is Jerry Erwright,) and three more men, came to my house and broke in the doors. I ran out when they broke in the doors and went to Second street at a store near there, and in the same square. The man Jerry came there and shot at me three times. He was riding a sorrel horse. The man in the store saw him shoot at me. I can get the name of the man that keeps the store.

PERRY LANE, Union street, Memphis, Tennessee, after being duly sworn, testified as follows:

On the night of the 3d of May, 1866, during the riots in the city of Memphis, six men came to my house and three came inside. I had gone to bed. They made me get up and open the door and make a light for them. They set my house on fire, and each of them held a gun pointed at me, and told me if I moved they would shoot me down. They kept me there until the fire had spread so I could not put it out. They said then, "We will go." My house and all I had was burned up. Loss, $150.

CHARLES HARRIS, corner of Main and Talbert streets, Memphis, Tennessee, after being duly sworn, testified as follows:

On the 1st of May, 1866, I saw a white man, who lives with Policeman Shelby, shoot and kill Eli Cherry (colored) on Main street, near Trezevant. Cherry was passing along quietly. There was a number of police there. Bill O'Hern, a constable, was on horseback urging the crowd to go on. I saw the policemen have a colored soldier in charge, one of them having him by the arm. The next morning I saw the soldier dead near the same place. He had a hole in his breast and a hole in his head as if made by a bullet.

JOHN ROBINSON, residing on South street, Memphis, Tennessee, after being duly sworn, testified as follows:

On the 2d of May, 1866, I saw Thomas Galloway driving a dray on South street. He got off and shot a colored soldier, killing him. The colored man was walking quietly along when it occurred. He (Galloway) went back to his dray, and "old man Pendergrass," to take his mule out of the dray, and took them to the stable.

MARTHA WARE, Memphis, Tennessee, being duly sworn, testified as follows:

On the night of the 3d of May, 1866, two men came into the house occupied by myself and husband (Wesley Ware) on a plea of hunting fire-arms. They said they were policemen. One of them was dressed like a policeman. I opened the drawers of the bureau for them to search for arms, and they robbed us of jewelry, money, &c., to the amount of about $150.

RACHEL HARRIS, living on Beal street, Memphis, Tennessee, being duly sworn, testified as follows :

On the night of the 2d of May, 1866, a number of men came to the house of Mary Ella Brown, where I was living, and robbed her of $180 in money and a gun. I saw my husband count the money the day before for her, and know they took that much.

MASON WALKER, living on Jackson street, near South street, being duly sworn, testified as follows :

On the night of the 2d of May, 1866, a number of men came to the house of my sister, Mary Duncan, where I was staying, and took from me clothing, &c., to the amount of $50.

ELIZA INGRAM, living on St. Martin's street, Memphis, Tennessee, being duly sworn, testified as follows :

On the night of the 3d of May, 1866, three persons came to my house and robbed it of $75 or $80. My husband had the money when they came in ; he gave it to me. They drew a pistol on me, and said they would kill me if I did not give it up.

F. K. STILLMAN, living in the county of Crittenden, State of Arkansas, being duly sworn, testified as follows :

I was in the city of Memphis, Tennessee, during the riot. On the 4th day of May, 1866, I hired a colored man named Adam Jones to work for me. At about 2 o'clock p. m., while waiting for a boat to cross the river, a policeman came up and arrested the said Jones and took him with him. I saw him searching him, and I supposed he had arrested him on the supposition of his carrying concealed weapons. I started up into the city a short time afterwards and saw the man Adams coming back. I asked him what was the matter, and he told me that the police had robbed him of $160. I made complaint to a detective, and he arrested a man whom Adams identified as one of the men who robbed him. This was at the station-house. While there the policeman drew a revolver on Adams and said he had a good mind to blow his head off.

MARY ELLEN BROWN, living on Shelby street, near South street, Memphis, Tennessee, being duly sworn, testified as follows :

On the night of the 2d of May, 1866, a party of men came to my house and asked for arms. I told them there was a gun there which belonged to my husband, who was dead. They said never mind, they would search the house. They found my husband's discharge and $180 I had put away with it. I told them I would give them half of it if they would go away. They told me to hush or they would kill me, and took all and the gun away with them. The gun was worth $6.

DANIEL AUSTIN, Shelby county, Tennessee, after being duly sworn, testified as follows :

On the 2d of May, 1866, I brought a boat-load of wood down the Hatchie river to Memphis. While I was at the landing a number of men—five or six white—came down to the river where I was, and said, "Boys, here is a damned nigger," and commenced shooting at me. I pushed my boat into the river as soon as I could to get out of their way. They fired some twenty shots at me, and one took effect in my shoulder. I jumped into the river and held to the boat with one hand, while the balance of me was in the water ; by that means I kept them from killing me. While I was in the water I lost my pocket-book which contained $35 in money, and my discharge from the army.

BECKY PLEASANT, living on Shelby street, between Union and Gayoso streets, Memphis, Tennessee, being duly sworn, testifies as follows :

On the 3d of May, 1866, about four o'clock in the day, three policemen came to my house on a plea of hunting arms and ammunition. One stood at the door and said, let no person go in or out. The other two took some keys belonging to me, and opened a trunk belonging to one John Cole, left in my care. Out of that trunk they took a little bag, which the said Cole says contained three watches, twenty-five dollars in greenbacks, and three dollars in silver. I saw them take a pocket-book out of the bag, and saw money in it. I told them to leave these things be. They said they knew their business ; that that was what they were looking for. I followed them to the door, and wanted to send to the steamboat for the said Cole, (where he was working.) They told me to go back and keep still ; that the whole house would be arrested for the stolen watches.

JIM WHITECOTTON, Memphis, Tennessee, being duly sworn, testifies as follows:

On the 2d day of May, 1866, I saw a white man, named Dick Marsh, shoot a colored man, by the name of Ben Cotton, on the bank of the river. Dick Marsh lives in the city, but I do not know where at. A white man named A. J. Kriel, who keeps a meat shop near the river, saw Marsh shoot him. I do not know where Cotton is. He was not killed.

JULIUS WOOD, Shelby county, Tennessee, after being duly sworn, deposes as follows:

Had all my clothing burned during the riots. Loss, twenty-five dollars.

GEORGEAN KELLEY, Union street, Memphis, Tennessee, after being duly sworn, deposes as follows:

On the night of the 2d of May, 1866, a man came to the house of Easter Cooper, and burned the house and all its contents. I lost by the fire articles to the amount of forty dollars.

JANE FLETCHER, Memphis, Tennessee, after being duly sworn, deposes as follows:

On the 2d day of May, 1866, as I was going down Main street, I met several men; just as I passed them, one turned around and shot me in the back. There was another colored girl with me, named Lizzie.

JOSEPH COLWELL, Memphis, Tennessee, being duly sworn, testifies as follows:

On the night of the 2d of May, 1866, a party of men during the riot set fire to the "Colwell Hall," which belongs to me, and burned and destroyed furniture and other articles, together with the damage done to the hall, to the amount of two thousand ($2,000) dollars. David Roach, policeman, Charley Galena, and Mr. Johnson, were the parties who set fire to the hall.

CALDONIA McKETCHUM, Memphis, Tennessee, being duly sworn, testifies as follows:

On the night of the 3d of May, 1866, Charley Smith came to my house and asked me if I would wash some clothes for him next day. I told him I would. Charley Toler was with him. I asked him (Smith) what all the fuss was about. He said, the damned nigger, and that the same fight that brought them into freedom would take them back into slavery. The next morning he brought me his clothes to wash. When I unfolded them, I found they, the pants and shirt, were all bloody.

ADALINE CURTMAN, Memphis, Tennessee, being duly sworn, testifies as follows:

On the night of the 1st of May, 1866, a number of persons came to the house occupied by myself and husband, Shedrick Curtman, and robbed the house of twenty dollars in money, and other articles to the amount of thirty dollars, belonging to my husband and self. They took, belonging to brother William Whitley, fifty dollars in money, a watch worth twenty dollars, and a gun worth six dollars. My husband and brother were absent at the time.

ALBERT BUTCHER, Memphis, Tennessee, being duly sworn, deposes as follows:

On the 1st of May, 1866, I was standing near the corner of Causey and South streets, and my attention was called to some colored soldiers (about thirty or forty) who were laughing and shouting, and making considerable noise. About this time two buggies came up, in one of which was a gentleman whom I was told was Recorder Creighton. This man ordered some three or four policemen to arrest the soldiers. The soldiers refused to be arrested, but used no violence toward the policemen. They, the policemen, came by where I stood, accompanied by three or four stout men (colored) who appeared to be aiding the police. After the police had gone some distance they fired back into the crowd of soldiers, and they returned the fire. I am not positive who fired first. There was a great deal of firing going on. I came up into the city, and seeing a crowd going in the direction of South street, I again went down near Morris cemetery; but the crowd was too far away to see who were engaged in the firing which was going on sharply. As I was leisurely returning up Main street, I was overtaken by the crowd returning. They were running as fast as they could, and seeing me cried out "there is a nigger, shoot him!"

PETER JOHNSON, Memphis, Tennessee, being duly sworn, testifies as follows:

On the night of the 1st of May, 1866, a mob came to my house; broke in and robbed it of most of the articles it contained. The next night, May 2d, 1866, it was burned, with all the balance of the articles. Loss, one hundred and eighty-two dollars.

DICK JOHNSON, 145 St. Martin's street, Memphis, Tennessee, after being duly sworn, testifies as follows :

On the 3d day of May, 1866, as I was going to my work, I met a white man on St. Martin's street, who presented a pistol at me, and demanded my money. Said if I did not give it to him he would shoot me down. He took from me twenty-five dollars in greenbacks.

JACOB UNDERWOOD, Memphis, Tennessee, after being duly sworn, testifies as follows :

On the night of the 1st of May, 1866, a party of men came to my house, broke in the door, and robbed me of twenty-five dollars in money, and other articles to the amount of forty dollars. I went to the fort to keep them from killing me.

BOSTON SHERFIELD, Memphis, Tennessee, being duly sworn, testifies as follows:

On the evening of the 2d of May, 1866, as I was going home, I met three men on South street. One of them collared me, while one held a pistol to my breast, and the third robbed me of thirty-six dollars. Said they would kill me if I was not a cripple.

ELIZA GREEN, living on South street, Memphis, Tennessee, being duly sworn, testifies as follows :

On the night of the 2d of May, 1866, a number of men came to my house, and robbed me of twenty-five dollars in money, and other articles to the amount of thirty dollars.

HENRIETTA COLE, living on South street, Memphis, Tennessee, being duly sworn, testifies as follows :

On the night of the 2d of May, 1866, old man Mike Pendergrass, and his two sons, John and Pat, and a number of other men came to the house of myself and husband, and stole from me clothing, &c., to the amount of seventy-five dollars. My husband's name is Henry Cole ; he was in the fort at the time.

DAN CARUTHERS, Memphis, Tennessee, being duly sworn, testifies as follows:

On the night of the 3d of May, 1866, some persons burned the fence around my house, and robbed me of some of the articles I had in it. Loss will amount to forty dollars. Would have burned my house, had not a soldier come up and stopped them.

CHARLEY HOWLET, Memphis, Tennessee, being duly sworn, testifies as follows:

On the night of the 2d of May, 1866, some person or persons came to my house and robbed me of one hundred and seventy-five dollars in money, a watch worth twenty-eight dollars, and clothing, &c , to the amount of fifty dollars. I was a soldier in the fort at the time. My wife had to leave the house to save herself.

JOHN ROBINSON, Memphis, Tennessee, being duly sworn, testifies as follows:

On the night of the 2d of May, 1866, a party of men came to my house and ran me off ; robbed me of carpenter tools, clothing, &c., to the amount of two hundred and fifty dollars. There was a party there during the day and threatened to burn my house, but did not do it on account of some white ladies living in the adjoining room. One of the same party was there that night, but I could not tell his name, nor neither could the white ladies. He told the ladies he lived in "Pinch.'

PLEASANT WOODFALL, Memphis, Tennessee, being duly sworn, testifies as follows:

On the 2d day of May, 1866, the house of James Huston, where I was boarding, was burned up, and all things I had which were in the house. My loss would amount to one hundred and seventy-five dollars.

AARON SMITH, Memphis, Tennessee, being duly sworn, testifies as follows:

On the night of the 4th of May, 1866, three white men came to my house on a plea of hunting for fire-arms; when they found I had none, they asked me if I had any money. I told them I had a little. They told me to hand it over, which I had to do   The amount was fifteen dollars. I can identify one of the men. One of them is a policeman.

FELIX WILSON, Memphis, Tennessee, being duly sworn, testifies as follows:

On the night of the 2d of May, 1866, a party of men came to my house and tried to get in. While they were at that I jumped out of the window to make my escape from them ; as I jumped out one of them cut at me with a big knife and cut one of my fingers. I ran around the corner of the house, and they fired several shots at me as I was trying to get away. I got under the floor of another house and they could not find me.

MARY BRYANT, living on South street, Memphis, Tennessee, being duly sworn, testifies as follows:

On the night of the 3d of May, 1866, a party of men came to my house, broke down the door and came in, and ordered me and my daughter to leave, and they would kill us if we did not. We went to the fort. They broke open the trunks, took eighty-seven dollars in money, four watches, ($125,) and a number of other articles of clothing worth fifty dollars.

NANCY WHITLEY, Memphis, Tennessee, being duly sworn, testifies as follows:

On the night of the 2d of May, 1866, a number of men came to my house, broke in the door, pulled me out of bed and shoved me out of doors, and abused me and my children. They robbed and destroyed property for me to the amount of fifty dollars.

C. WRIGHT, living corner of Madison and Third streets, Memphis, Tennessee, being duly sworn, testifies as follows:

On the night of the 2d of May, 1366, I saw a number of men break open the store of Kit Temple and throw a good many of the articles it contained out into the street. I could not identify any of the men.

CATHERINE EVANS, Memphis, Tennessee, being duly sworn, testifies as follows:

On the night of the 2d of May, 1866, a number of men came to the house occupied by myself and husband, Edmond Evans, and asked for arms; my husband told them he had none; they then commenced beating him with clubs, &c., and stabbed him six times with a knife. My husband is not able to get up yet, and the doctor says it is doubtful whether he recovers or not. Two colored girls who live near me know the name of one of the men.

PETER BLOOM, Memphis, Tennessee, being duly sworn, testifies as follows:

On the night of the 2d of May, 1866, a number of white men came to my house on a plea of hunting for arms. They stole from me fifty dollars and fifty cents in money, a gold watch worth seventy dollars, and other articles to the amount of thirty-five dollars. They took me into the other room, and I heard them trying to ravish my wife, she refusing them.

NANCY SANDERS, Memphis, Tennessee, being duly sworn, testifies as follows:

On the night of the 4th of May, 1866, my husband, William H. Sanders, went to wait on Dr. Sanders, at the ball given at the Gayoso House, on that evening, when he was killed by the mob. I never saw him until next morning, when I took my seven children to see him before he was buried.

JAMES HUNT, Memphis, Tennessee, being duly sworn, testifies as follows:

On the night of the 1st of May, 1866, three white men came to my house and robbed me of two hundred and fifty dollars in money. I heard them fire three shots in the adjoining house before they came to mine, and the next day I saw the man dead in his house. I think he was killed when I heard the shots fired.

ANN ODUM, Memphis, Tennessee, being duly sworn, testifies as follows:

On the night of the 2d of May, 1866, a party of men came to the house occupied by myself and husband, Charles Odum, and set fire to it and burned it up, and all its contents. Loss two hundred dollars.

JOHN W. LANE, Memphis, Tennessee, being duly sworn, testifies as follows:

On the 3d of May, 1866, I met a party of white men, on Mulberry street, who robbed me of twenty dollars and twenty-five cents, and tore up my license for a grocery store. Two of the men I think were soldiers, and the others citizens.

FRANCIS HARRIS, Memphis, Tennessee, being duly sworn, testifies as follows:

On the night of the 2d of May, 1866, a party of men came to my house and set it on fire, and burned it up with all the things, which would amount to seventy-five dollars.

TONEY LUMKINS, Memphis, Tennessee, being duly sworn, testifies as follows:

On the night of the 3d of May, 1866, a party of men came to my house and set fire to it and my stable, and burned them down. Most all the things in my house was lost. My loss would amount to $400.

SOLOMON PICKET, Memphis, Tennessee, being duly sworn, testifies as follows :

On the night of the 1st of May, 1866, a party of men came to my house, and one man came in and asked me who was there—called me to the door. I went to the door; he caught hold of me and jerked me out, struck me with his pistol, and before he got me to the gate he shot and wounded me through the arm ; they then beat me unmercifully with revolvers, swords, &c. They took me to the station-house, and kept me until 10 o'clock next day. They took my name at the station-house. The police did this, but I could not recognize any of them.

ROSE MORRIS, Memphis, Tennessee, being duly sworn, testifies as follows :

On the night of the 3d of May, 1866, three men came to my house on a plea of searching for fire-arms ; they demanded from me the key of my trunk, and took from it $10 in greenbacks, $35 in gold and silver, and some clothing. They took a lot of clothing belonging to gentlemen in the city, which I had taken in to wash. They robbed from me, besides the money, jewelry, clothing, &c., to the amount of $75. The clothing I had taken to wash would amount to $100.

ADALADE PICKET, living on Corinth street, Memphis, Tennessee, being duly sworn, testifies as follows :

On the night of the 1st of May, 1866, a number of persons came to the house occupied by myself and husband, Solomon Picket, (colored.) They were after another colored man. They said, "there he goes up the back yard," and kept straight on into the yard ; one man came into the house. My husband told him he had done nothing ; he said, never mind, come out here, and when he got to the door, he pulled him out, and when he got him to the gate, he shot him through the arm, and commenced beating him with his pistol and took him away. My husband had just come from work about half an hour before, and had not left the house. He had done nothing to cause such treatment. They took him to the station-house.

RICHARD LANE, living on De Soto street, Memphis, Tennessee, being duly sworn, testifies as follows :

I keep a saloon back of No. 7 engine-house. On the night of the 2d of May, 1866, Mike Cotton, Elden Found and Billy Barber, with several other men, came to my house and saloon—came into the saloon, ordered me to deliver to them my arms. I told them I had none. The saloon was closed when they came. Six of them shot at me, and one ball took effect in my shoulder. After they went out they shot into the house and wounded my child.

JOHN H. PERRY, Memphis, Tennessee, being duly sworn, testifies as follows :

On the 3d of May, 1866, as I was going to work, I met two men ; they asked me where I was going ; I told them to work ; when one of them shot me, the ball grazing my chin, but not breaking the bone.

HANNAH HERSEY, living on South street, Memphis, Tennessee, being duly sworn, testifies as follows :

On the 3d day of May, 1866, I had to leave and go to the fort ; two white women that lived near me told me I had better go, that all the colored people had gone, and those that did not go would be killed. I left in the care of these two women a chest containing all my things. When I came back the chest was sitting out in the yard and all the articles taken out. I afterwards identified some of the articles in the house of the two women. One of the women is named Rachel Dobbs.

CORNELIA HALL, living on Exchange street, near Poplar street, Memphis, Tennessee, being duly sworn, testifies as follows :

On the night of the 1st of May, 1866, James Wallock and four other men came to the house of Edmund Evans, knocked him down, beat him, and stabbed him several times with a knife.

ROSS SPAIN, living on South street, Memphis, Tennessee, being duly sworn, testifies as follows :

On the night of the 1st of May, 1866, a number of men came to the house of David Doddson, where I was stopping, and robbed me of $40 and clothes to the amount of $30. They destroyed a good many articles for Doddson in his house.

ALBERT HINTON, Memphis, Tennessee, being duly sworn, testifies as follows :

On the night of the 1st of May, 1866, a man named Pigeon, and a number of other armed men came to my house and robbed and destroyed articles in my house to the amount of $150.

ELIZA ROBINSON, living on Echols street, between Vance and Elliott streets, Memphis, Tennessee, being duly sworn, testifies as follows :

On the night of the 2d of May, 1866, a number of men came to my house, set it on fire, burned it up with all its contents.   My loss would amount to $175.

GEORGE McCORD, living corner of South street and Front Row, Memphis, Tennessee, being duly sworn, testifies as follows :

On the evening of the 1st of May, 1866, as I was going home from work, I met several men.   They asked me where I was going ; I told them home ; one of them, a policeman, pulled out his revolver and shot me through the leg.   They took from me $10.

ANDY POLLIN, Memphis, Tennessee, being duly sworn, testifies as follows :

On the 3d of May, 1866, some person or persons came to my house and burned my house and all its contents.   I was a soldier and at the fort at the time.   My loss will amount to $150.

ANTHONY FRENCH, living on South street, Memphis, Tennessee, being duly sworn, testifies as follows :

On the night of the 2d of May, 1866, a number of persons came to my house, struck me on the head with a brick-bat, kicked me, and threatened to shoot me.   They burned my house and all its contents.   My loss will amount to $350.

SOLOMON HALL, living corner of Beal and De Soto streets, Memphis, Tennessee, being duly sworn, testifies as follows :

On the 4th day of May, 1866, about half past eleven o'clock, I was driving down Shelby street with my hack, and six men inside of it.   As I was passing the corner of Union street I saw several persons standing on the corner.   After I got by one beckoned me to stop.   I thought he wanted a hack, and shook my head at him and drove on, for I had a load at the time.   He hallooed, stop that carriage.   I halted the carriage.   Three or four men ran out of a store and drew their revolvers on me, also two policemen.   The men inside the hack jumped out and ran, and the parties there commenced firing at them.   I do not know whether they hit any of the men or not.   They were after them the last I saw of them.   They were discharged soldiers.   They fired one shot at me, and a policeman drew his revolver to fire another.   I told him not to shoot me, that I had done nothing to be shot for.   He then left me, and started after the other men that got out of my hack. I can identify two of the men that fired the two first shots.   The man that fired the shot at me took good aim at my head.

ROSE HART, Memphis, Tennessee, being duly sworn, testifies as follows :

On the night of the 2d of May, 1866, a party of men came to my house and burned it, and most all the contents in it.   My loss would amount to the sum of seventy-five dollars.

HARRIET WILLIAMS, living on Main street, Memphis, Tennessee, testifies as follows :

On the night of the 2d instant, about nine p. m., a number of persons came to the house occupied by myself and husband, and asked for some skiff oars ; they wanted to follow a man (colored) into the bayou and kill him ; that they had already wounded him.   My husband told them he had no oars.   One said, "God damn him, let's shoot him."   My husband ran into the house and shut the door.   The parties broke the door down ; came in and knocked him down with a pistol, and after he was down one man took out his knife and stabbed him (my husband) twice ; once in each side.   He died yesterday, May 3d, about eleven o'clock.   He had done nothing, and had not been from home since he came from his work.   They had no cause whatever to murder him as they did.

JONAS BEARD, Memphis, Tennessee, being duly sworn, testifies as follows :

On the night of the 2d of May, 1866, some persons came to my house and burned it up, and all its contents.   Loss will amount to two hundred and fifty dollars.

PATIENCE NELSON, Memphis, Tennessee, being duly sworn, testifies as follows :

On the night of the 3d of May, 1866, during the riot in the city of Memphis, some of the rioters burned my house to the ground.   It was on the corner of Causey and South streets.   Loss one hundred dollars.

WALTON WRIGHT, living corner of Broadway and Rayburn avenue, Memphis, Tennessee, being duly sworn, testifies as follows :

On the 3d of May, 1866, when the shooting commenced, I, and another boy named Mitchel, were attracted by the firing, and started in that direction. As I reached Causey street bridge, I saw a policeman shoot a negro who was not doing anything. They (the police) then went down South street, and shot another black man who was walking quietly along. They took a horse belonging to a black man, beat him over the head with their pistols and clubs. The black man was perfectly quiet. When I got to Main street I met a black boy fourteen or fifteen years of age shot in the hip. One of the police was a big fat man ; would know him if I saw him.

SIMON TURNER, living on South street, Memphis, Tennessee, being duly sworn, testifies as follows :

On the night of the 2d of May, 1866, my house was set on fire and burned to the ground by some unknown persons, who were committing depredations during the riot. Loss estimated at one hundred dollars.

SHEDRICK SMITH, Memphis, Tennessee, after being duly sworn, testified as follows :

On the night of the 1st of May, 1866, as I was coming from a drug store, where I had been after medicine for a sick child, I met a number of men on Main street. One asked me for a chew of tobacco. I told him I had none, but would like to accommodate him if I had. One said he would take what I did have. One caught me around the waist and arms. One choked me, while the other robbed me of my money, thirty dollars and fifteen cents. They treated me outrageously. My doctor bill has cost me forty dollars. Several of them were policemen. Mr. M. H. Riley, keeper of the station-house, came up at that time and stopped them.

PATZY TOLLIVER, Memphis, Tennessee, after being duly sworn, deposes as follows :

On the evening of the 1st of May, 1866, I saw some twenty-five or thirty soldiers, who were making a loud noise. Some three or four policemen came up to arrest them. I saw recorder Creighton in a buggy near by. The police attempted to arrest the soldiers, and they refused to be arrested. Soon after shooting commenced, but I could not say which party began first.

REBECCA ANN BLOOM, Memphis, Tennessee, being duly sworn, testifies as follows :

On the night of the 2d of May, 1866, I was in bed, when five white men broke open the door and came into my room, and ordered a light. We had no candle. They took my husband out to get a light. One man remained in the room. He demanded my money. I had none. He wanted to know if I had anything to do with white men. I said no. He held a knife in his hand, and said that he would kill me if I did not let him do as he wanted to do. I refused. He said, " By God, you must," and then he got into bed with me, and violated my person, by having connexion with me, he still holding the knife.

FRANCIS PERKINS, Memphis, Tennessee, being duly sworn, testifies as follows :

On the night of the 1st of May, 1866, a party of men came to my house, set it on fire, and burned it down with all the contents. They shot at me five times while trying to stop the fire. My loss would amount to two hundred and fifty dollars.

RICHARD NEVILLE, living in Chelsea, Memphis, Tennessee, being duly sworn, testifies as follows :

On the night of the 3d of May, 1866, a number of persons came to my house and robbed me of forty-five dollars in greenbacks, and a shot-gun worth fifteen dollars. The men said they were ordered by the Bureau to take all the arms they could find.

THOMAS ROBINSON, Memphis, Tennessee, being duly sworn, testifies as follows :

On the night of the 1st of May, 1866, a party of men came to the house of Humphrey Morris, where I was boarding, and burned it with all the things inside of it. All my things were in it and burned up. My loss would amount to one hundred dollars.

HUMPHREY MORRIS, Memphis, Tennessee, being duly sworn, testified as follows :

On the night of the 1st of May, 1866, a party of men came to my house, set fire to it, and burned it down, and all its contents. Thomas Robinson was boarding with me, and his things were burned also. My whole loss would amount to $350.

HENRY HUNT, Memphis, Tennessee, being duly sworn, testified as follows :

On the night of the 4th of May, 1866, six men came to my house and asked if there were any nigger soldiers there ; my wife (Lucy Hunt) told them "no," that there "was no person there but my husband." They said I had better leave there, and they then went to another house. I took the things out of my house to leave, when they returned and burned them up. They also took from me $325 in money. The loss of my property would amount to $250. My wife knows one of the party.

NED YOUNG, Memphis, Tennessee, being duly sworn, testified as follows :

On the night of May 2, 1866, a party of men came to my house, two were policemen, and demanded entrance ; said they would kill me if I did not let them in. When they got in they put their pistols to my head and demanded my money. I tried to beg off, but they would not let me talk. They broke open my trunk, took out of it $275 in money, $100 worth of clothes, a lot of bed-clothes, barrel of flour, and some meat, worth $50 in all, and a pair of boots worth $11. The policemen appeared to be the leading men. I can identify one of the policemen, if I see him. The policeman that broke open my trunk they called "Pat."

JOHN DEADWILEY, Memphis, Tennessee, being duly sworn, testified as follows :

On the night of the 1st of May, 1866, a party of men came to my house and burned it and most of the articles it contained. My loss would amount to the sum of $50.

HENRY BANKETT, Memphis, Tennessee, being duly sworn, testified as follows :

On the 2d of May, 1866, my house was burned up with all the things it contained. My loss would amount to $500. I was a soldier at the time and was in the fort. My wife said she wanted to go in and save some of the things while the house was on fire, and they told her, "God damn her, if she went in there, they would burn her upon it."

WILLIAM PLEASANT, Memphis, Tennessee, being duly sworn, testified as follows :

On the 3d day of May, 1866, as I was driving through the city of Memphis with a horse and wagon, a party of men came up and arrested me and took me to the edge of town, and kept me there until after night ; they took there with me another man ; after night they brought there two more men and three more women. The women were accompanied by three boys and two girls. One of the men was wounded through the shoulder, and one of the boys through the leg. About two hours after dark they started with us to Mississippi ; from what I could learn I think they intended to go to Panola. One of the men said if they (the men who brought the women and children) had brought five more hands, they (the white men) would have made $300. They made us all take off our shoes, and they tied them on their saddles ; there were four men ; they took us about forty miles, and another man and I made our escape. My companion was a discharged soldier, but do not know what his name was. Previous to our escaping, we were instructed to say that we had hired to them. At night they had us all tied together, the others they kept on with to Mississippi I think there were none brought after us. The next day, on our return, we saw two men and a boy dead along the road They took from me $15 in money and the "bill of sale" of my horse. I have not heard of my horse and wagon since then. My loss amounts to $300.

GEORGE CHAMBERS, Memphis, Tennessee, being duly sworn, testified as follows :

On the night of the 3d of May, 1866, a party of white men came to my house and burned it down, with all its contents. The whole loss would amount to $400.

WILLIAM SMITH, Memphis, Tennessee, being duly sworn, testified as follows :

On the 30th of April, 1866, I went about twelve miles up the river to work for a man, John Harris. I returned on the 6th of May, 1866. Mr. Harris paid me $35 for work I had done for him. On Poplar street I met two policemen the same night about eight o'clock, and they took from me the $35. On my return I found that my house and all its contents had been burned during the riot here. The loss would amount to $200.

JULIA MARSHALL, living in the city of Memphis, Tennessee, being duly sworn, testified as follows :

On the night of the 2d of May, 1866, during the riot in the city of Memphis, some person or persons burned up my house and a great many articles in it. Loss $300.

ALFRED BOYD, Memphis, Tennessee, being duly sworn, testified as follows :

On the night of the 2d of May, 1866, a party of men came to my house and burned it, with all its contents. My loss would amount to $125. Two of the men in the party were named McCormick and Simon Easley. Easley lives on Vance street. The white men were armed, and made the colored people protect the property of the whites while their own was burning.

MOSE PORTER, Memphis, Tennessee, being duly sworn, testified as follows :

On the 1st of May, 1866, after night, Mr. Cash and seven or eight policemen, and a number of other persons, came to my house, broke the door down, came in and robbed me of $160 in money and a watch which cost me $80, and other articles to the amount of $75. They were armed with hatchets and revolvers. They put a pistol to my head and threatened to kill me. There were several policemen with them.

MARGARETTE KENNEY, Memphis, Tenneseee, being duly sworn, testified as follows :

On the night of the 3d May, 1866, some persons came and set fire to my house while I was asleep ; a colored man came to wake me up, and they shot and wounded him twice. They burned the house and all its contents. Loss would amount to $300.

THE MEMBERS OF COLLINS CHAPEL, Memphis, Tennessee, being duly sworn, testified as follows :

That the aforesaid chapel was set on fire and burned down on the night of the 2d of May, 1866, by a mob which helped to compose the riot in the city of Memphis at that time. The said chapel was valued at the sum of $25,000 by the colored citizens who belonged to or were members of the said church.

SAMUEL GREEN, living on South street, Memphis, Tennessee, being duly sworn; testified as follows :

On the night of the 3d of May, 1866, my brother had a mule belonging to me, for which I paid $150, and a horse belonging to himself, for which he paid $135. The dead mule I saw myself, it having been shot. The horse I did not see, but Emeline Wilson and others state that it was stolen. His house was burned up, and I know that it and the horse and mule were valued at $785. He had besides in his trunk $400 in money. He is the man who is missing, and whose wife and child were burned up.

EMELINE WILSON, living on Jackson Bluff, Memphis, Tennessee, being duly sworn, testified as follows :

On the night of the 3d of May, 1866, I was a short distance from the house occupied by John Green, and his wife, Ida Green, and family. I saw their house set on fire by a crowd of policemen and citizens. I saw Ida Green attempting to leave the house, but they drove her back into it ; she begged and prayed them to let her out of the burning house, but they would not let her. She then attempted to come out anyhow, and they shot her. She fell partly in the house ; they then kicked her and rolled her over like a log into the fire, where she was burned up. Her baby was in bed, and was burned up at the same time. Her husband, John Green, has never been seen since that evening, and I heard Mary Black and others say he was killed.

JOHN COLE, employed on steamer Mollie Hambleton, after being duly sworn, deposed as follows :

On or about the 1st day of April, 1866, I left with Becky Pleasant a trunk belonging to myself, for her to take care of for me. In that trunk I had three watches and a pocketbook containing twenty-five dollars in greenbacks, and three dollars in silver. These articles were in a little blue cotton bag, together with some notes and accounts and a receipt for my discharge, which I had left with a claim agent to draw my bounty. About four o'clock to-day she sent her husband for me, stating that the police had been into my trunk and taken away some of the articles it contained. I immediately went to her house, but the police had gone. I examined my trunk and found missing the watches and articles before mentioned.

WILLIAM VAUGHN, Memphis, Tennessee, after being duly sworn, testified as follows :

On the night of the 1st of May, 1866, as I was coming from the Memphis and Ohio depot, I met a party of men ; they asked me if I was a soldier and had any arms. I told them no. Said if I had any they would kill me. They then commenced searching me, and robbed me of $260 in money, a watch worth $80, my discharge, and two notes which called for $560, and belonged to my uncle, George Price. After they had turned me loose, and found out from my discharge that I had been a soldier, they fired six shots at me. One man had a police club in his hand.

23

SHACK ROBINSON, Memphis, Tennessee, being duly sworn, testified as follows :

On or about the 2d of May, 1866, about twelve o'clock at night, a number of persons came to the house occupied by myself and Horace Whitley as a saloon, and set fire to the building. Myself and two other men tried to put out the fire, but they commenced shooting at us, and said, "God damn you, go away and let the fire alone," and did wound one man, Jim Gillam. The house and everything in it was burned up with $52 75 in money. Loss was about five hundred dollars. They also burned the house of Henry Perkins, joining mine.

HENRY PERKINS, Memphis, Tennessee, being duly sworn, testified as follows :

On or about the 2d of May, 1866, about twelve o'clock at night, a number of persons came to the house of Shack Robinson and Horace Whitley and set fire to it, and from his house mine caught fire and burned up with all my household furniture. The fire could have been stopped, but they shot at every person that undertook to put the fire out, and did wound one man. I lost everything I had. The house I had just paid $300 for a few weeks before. Loss, $600.

ALFRICA BAILEY, lives on South street, Memphis, Tennessee, being duly sworn, testified as follows :

On the night of the 2d of May, 1866, a party of men who were around committing depredations and burning houses, burned a house belonging to myself and Cyrus Hardway. I could not tell who the men were. Loss, $400.

MOSE HARRISON, lives on Vance street, Memphis, Tennessee, being duly sworn, deposes as follows :

In the latter part of April, 1866, I went down the Mississippi river to chop wood. When I left here I left my trunk containing a lot of clothes in the care of Shack Robinson, who keeps a saloon on Echols street. He tells me that his saloon and everything he had in it was burned up and that my trunk and clothes were burned also. This was done by the rioters during the riot in the city. My loss would amount to $150.

JOHN WESLEY, Memphis, Tennessee, being duly sworn, testified as follows :

On the night of the 1st of May, 1866, a party of men came to my house and robbed it of $140 in money, two watches worth $55, and a lot of clothing and other articles that would amount to $100.

LEWIS BOYLE, Memphis, Tennessee, after being duly sworn, testified as follows :

On the night of the 1st of May, 1866, my house was robbed of articles to the amount of two hundred dollars. I was a soldier in the fort at the time. My father and mother, Robert and Eliza Boyle, were living in the same house with me and were there at the time.

MARY AUSTIN, Memphis, Tennessee, after being duly sworn, testified as follows :

On the night of the 2d of May, 1866, a party of men came to my house, broke open the door and robbed me of ten dollars in greenbacks, five dollars in silver, and a watch worth ten dollars. Said they had money enough to pay for the damned shanty without burning it up.

THOMAS BOON, Memphis, Tennessee, after being duly sworn, testified as follows :

On the night of the 1st of May, 1866, as I was going peaceably to my home, some persons shot me through the shoulder. I saw them, but could not recognize them. I had to go to the fort after I was wounded, and some person stole from my house articles amounting to the sum of twenty dollars.

JAMES HUSTIN, Memphis, Tennessee, after being duly sworn, testified as follows :

My name is James Hustin. I live in the city of Memphis, Tennessee. On the second day of May, 1866, some person or persons set fire to my house and burned it down with all the contents it contained. I was at my work and started home to save my things, when some white persons near there stopped and kicked me, and one man drew a revolver on me and threatened to kill me if I went any further. Loss, three hundred and fifty dollars.

ANNIE BOYD, Memphis, Tennessee, after being duly sworn, testified as follows :

On the night of May 2, 1866, a number of persons came to my house and run me and my two sick children away. Said they were agoing to burn up every damned nigger shanty there was around there. They burned up mine and everything that was in it. I left my pocket-book there which contained twenty dollars in greenbacks, which was burned or taken away. The loss I sustained would amount to four hundred and fifty dollars.

FANNIE LONG, Memphis, Tennessee, after being duly sworn, testified as follows :

On the 2d of May, 1866, my house was burned by the mob who were committing the depredations at that time. It was worth one hundred dollars.

ALEXANDER MITCHELER, Memphis, Tennessee, being duly sworn, testified as follows

On the evening of the 1st of May, 1866, I saw John Creighton, recorder, mounted on horseback and a crowd of men around him. He was making a speech to them. He said, "Boys, I want you to go ahead and kill the last damned one of the nigger race, and burn up the cradle." The crowd applauded. Creighton continued: "God damn them, they are free, free indeed, but God damn them, we will kill and drive the last one of them out of the city." The men were all unanimous in hallowing " hurrah for John Creighton " They drove me away with pistols, and I did not hear him finish his speech. That night some men set fire to my house, but I succeeded in putting it out by the help of some other colored people. We were fired on all the time we were trying to stop the fire. One man, Major Jones, was wounded in my house.

ISAAC GIBSON, lives on South street, Memphis, Tennessee, being duly sworn, testified as follows :

On the 2d of May, 1866, during the riots in the city of Memphis, Tennessee, four men came to my house and robbed me of $180 in greenbacks, and two silver watches; also broke a violin and case to pieces worth $100 ; have been offered that for it several times. Would know two of the men. They drew a revolver on me and threatened to kill me.

LOUISA GILLIAN, Memphis, Tennessee, being duly sworn, testified as follows :

On the night of the 1st of May, 1866, a party of men came to my house, made me open my trunk and took from it ten dollars belonging to me.

JOHN YOUNG, Memphis, Tennessee, being duly sworn, testified as follows :

On the night of the 2d of May, 1866, a party of men came to the house where I was boarding, and broke open my trunk and took from it all the articles it contained and threatened to kill me. The articles I lost would amount to $150.

COLUMBUS RILEY, Memphis, Tennessee, being duly sworn, testified as follows :

On the night of the 2d of May, 1866, a party of men set my house on fire and burned it down with all its contents. I heard the men say, " Come on Roach," before they got to the house, but could not tell who any of them were. After they set the house on fire they fired five or six shots in the house to keep me from coming out ; but I made my escape with my wife, who was in the family way. It caused miscarriage. Mr. Glassby and Cooper, white men, owned the house and occupied part of it. Mrs. Cooper begged of them not to burn the house ; they told her to go in the house, they would not hurt her, but would kill Cooper and Glassby if they found them. They (Cooper and Glassby) were teachers of colored schools. The portion of the house I lived in was all that was burned of it. My loss would amount to $75. I also lost my discharge from the army.

HENRY RAMBERT, Memphis, Tennessee, being duly sworn, testified as follows :

On the night of the 2d of May, 1866, a lot of men came to my house on a plea of searching for fire-arms, and robbed me of fifteen dollars in money. Two of the men were Dave Roach, policeman, and a McGuire.

LILLY HENDERSON of Memphis, Tennessee, after being duly sworn, testified as follows :

On the 1st of May, 1866, a number of persons came to my house and took from me eighteen dollars in greenbacks and two dollars in silver, also about thirty dollars worth of clothes from Ann Carr, who was living with me. The night of the 2d of May a party came to my house and burned it up and all its contents. Loss would amount to $400.

HARRIET MOTON being duly sworn, deposed as follows :

My name is Harriet Moton ; I live in the city of Memphis, Tennessee, on South street, near De Soto street. On the night of the 4th of May, 1866, four white men came to my house on a plea of hunting arms. I told them I had none ; they asked me if there were any men there, I told them no ; they asked me what I did have there, I told them nothing ; they said, " God damn it, we will burn the house up," and did so, with most of the articles it contained. My loss would amount to $125.

ANNIE BOYD, being duly sworn, deposed as follows :

My name is Annie Boyd ; I live in the city of Memphis, Tennessee. On the night of the 2d of May, 1866, a number of persons came to my house and run me and my two sick children away ; said they were going to burn up every " damned nigger shanty" there was around there. They burned up mine and everything that was in it. I left my pocket-book there, which contained $20 in greenbacks, which was burned or taken away. The loss I sustained would amount to $450.

MARGARET McGHEE, being duly sworn, testified as follows :

I live in the same house that Soloman Picket, colored, lives in. On the night of the 1st of May, 1866, during the riot in the city of Memphis, I heard a number of persons coming to the house in a very disorderly and boisterous manner. I closed my doors to keep them from coming into my room. I heard them go into the room of Soloman Picket and said to him, "Get, you son of a bitch," and could hear them beating him. They fired three shots in the yard after I heard them taking him out, but do not know whether they shot him or not. He had just come from his work about half an hour before, and had not left the house since he came home. I do not know who the parties were, but know they had no cause or provocation to disturb or molest him.

Mrs. BRIDGET LOWDER, being duly sworn, testified as follows :

On or about the 1st day of May, 1866, during the riot in the city of Memphis, about eight o'clock at night, there were a number of persons came into the house of Solomon Picket, colored, and shot at him three times, but could not say whether the shots took effect or not. I think they abused him very badly ; I could hear the knocks of their guns and pistols, and think they were beating him; it was dark and I could not see. He had just come from his work some half an hour before, and had not been out of the house until they took him away. I think the parties were soldiers, policemen, and citizens. I know they had no cause or provocation to molest him.

MARY DUPEE, being duly sworn, testified as follows :

My name is Mary Dupee ; I live in the city of Memphis, Tennessee On the night of the 3d of May, 1866, one Pugg Cartright (colored) came to my house and brought a white man with him to search my house for arms. The white man went away and would not search it. Cartright then went away and came back the second time with three more white men ; these men ransacked the house and destroyed most everything in it. Some steamboatmen, colored men, whom I wash for, had left their valises and satchels containing their clothes with me; these were cut to pieces and destroyed, and Cartright carried off a great many things with him. They also beat and abused me very badly. Cartright has since threatened me.

FRED. A. MYERS, being duly sworn, testified as follows :

My name is Fred. A. Myers; I reside at the French restaurant on Second street, between Court and Jefferson streets. On the 1st day of May, 1866, I left my residence to see what was the matter ; when I arrived at the corner of Monroe and Second streets I saw the sheriff, Patrick Winters, who was enrolling men to go for guns to suppress the riot. I was enrolled and advised to run and get a gun; I did not get any, but went to South Memphis. saw two men beat a negro, heard quite a number of shots fired. On Vance and Causey streets the sheriff made a speech, did not hear it; then Recorder Creighton made a speech to this effect, that every one of the citizens should get arms, organize and go through the negro districts, and that he was in favor of killing every " God damned nigger." At that time a number of regular troops made their appearance and passed along Causey street, when I saw a citizen take a negro out of a yard and shoot him in the head, and one of the United States soldiers (I think a non-commissioned officer) cut the negro several times with his sword ; an officer ordered him to stop, and the negro was then turned over to the police, who beat him until the officer stopped them with his men. I was ordered to leave there by a policeman who held a pistol at my head, because I objected to this wholesale killing of negroes. I left, and on my way down Causey street I met a crowd, who proclaimed themselves (by three loud cheers) in favor of burning every negro shanty in Memphis. I saw a number of negroes pursued by whites, and a number of shots fired at them. I did not see a negro resist, but all appeared to be getting out of the way.

PUGG CARTRIGHT, being duly sworn, deposed as follows :

My name is Pugg Cartright ; I live in the city of Memphis, Tennessee. On the corner of Gayoso street and "Rotten Row," on the night of the 3d of May, Jack Reed, captain of fire-engine number five, and two men who had police stars on, came to my house and demanded entrance. I let them in and they took from me a pistol. They then demanded that I should take them to every negro house around there; I refused, and they told me I had better go or they would kill me, and drew a revolver on me. We went to the house of Jane Dupee; there I saw a hundred porter checks, thought they looked like mine and took them away, have them yet. Reed said he was going to take all the weapons the negroes had.

WILEY MASON, being duly sworn, deposed as follows :

My name is Wiley Mason; I live in the city of Memphis, Tennessee. I am porter at the Tennessee National Bank. On the 2d of May, 1866, Dr. Keller, at the Commercial hotel, came to the bank and asked one of the clerks what my name was. Told the clerk I had better keep close, that he knew of a dozen persons that would kill me on sight. James Quinlin, fireman, at corner of Main and Jefferson streets, said he came there and tried to bribe some of them to kill me. He also asked David Lawrence, barber, what my name was, and said to him he had me spotted.

PETER JONES and GABRIEL CUMMINS, being duly sworn, deposed as follows :

We the undersigned, Peter Jones and Gabriel Cummins, live in the city of Memphis, Tennessee. We keep a shoe shop at number eight Beal street. On the night of the 4th of May, 1866, a party of white men, police and soldiers, came to our shop and stole boots, money and other articles to the amount of $100 ; said if we spoke a word they would kill us. They held pistols to our breasts while they robbed us.

ROSE MORRIS, being duly sworn, deposed as follows :

My name is Rose Morris ; I live in the city of Memphis. On the night of the 3d of May, 1866, three men came to my house on a plea of searching for fire-arms; they demanded from me the key of my trunk and took from it $10 in greenbacks, $35 in gold and silver, and some clothing. They took a lot of clothing belonging to gentlemen in the city which I had taken in to wash. They robbed from me besides the money, jewelry, clothing, &c., to the amount of $75. The clothing I had taken to wash would amount to $100.

MAY BRYANT, being duly sworn, deposed as follows :

My name is May Bryant ; I live in South street, in the city of Memphis, Tennessee. On the night of the 3d of May, a party came to my house, broke down the door, came in and ordered me and my daughter to leave, said they would kill us if we did not. We went to the fort. They broke open the trunks, took $87 in money, four watches, $125, and a number of other articles of clothing worth $50.

RACHEL HARRIS, being duly sworn, deposed as follows :

My name is Rachel Harris ; I live in the city of Memphis, Tennessee, on Beal street, at junction of Union, near Mr. Topp's. On the night of the 2d of May, 1866, a number of men came to the house of Mary Ella Brown, where I was living, and robbed her of $180 in money, and a gun. I saw my husband count the money the day before for her and know they took that much.

NANCY WHITLEY, being duly sworn, deposed as follows :

My name is Nancy Whitley ; I live in the city of Memphis, Tennessee. On the night of the 2d day of May, 1866, a number of men came to my house, broke in the door, pulled me out of bed and shoved me out of doors, and abused me and my children; they robbed and destroyed property for me to the amount of $50.

WILLIAM WHITLEY, being duly sworn, deposed as follows :

My name is William Whitley ; I live in the county of Shelby, and State of Tennessee. Some time in January, 1866, when I was discharged from the army, I went to the country to work. Before going I left with my sister, Adaline Curtman, fifty dollars to take care of for me ; also, a watch worth twenty dollars, and a gun worth six dollars.

JOHN WILLIAMS, being duly sworn, deposed as follows :

My name is John Williams ; I live on Madison street and Third. On the night of the 3d of May, 1866, a crowd broke open my house and took from it one trunk, containing all my things, clothes, watch, &c , valued at three hundred and fifty dollars, and about twenty dollars in cash that was in it. The man who carried off my trunk was Charles Ruffins; he appeared to be leader of the gang.

PETER MITCHEL, being duly sworn, deposed as follows :

My name is Peter Mitchel ; I live in the city of Memphis, Tennessee, on Beal street. On the night of the 1st of May, 1866, a party of men broke into my house ; one of the party was a white soldier. They threatened to kill me. I leaped out of the window, when they fired at me two shots, but missed me. I then ran into the woods, where I laid all night. When I came back next morning I saw all Mrs. Yocktaw's dishes and furniture broken and scattered about the house. I had my money in my trunk, and the trunk and money were taken away by the crowd. I had in it fifteen hundred dollars in money, and my clothes, valued at one hundred dollars. I earned this money (sixteen hundred dollars) freighting on the plains. I was teamster for Mr. W. T. Rose, of Leavenworth City, Kansas, who paid me the money a few days before I came down here. I came down here four days before the riots.

PARTHENIA DICKERSON, being duly sworn, deposed as follows :

My name is Parthenia Dickerson ; I live on Ravine street, in Memphis, Tennessee. On the 3d of May, 1866, a party of men came to the house occupied by myself and husband, Lafayette Dickerson ; they shot and killed him, and robbed him of twenty-five dollars. They put one shot through his head, another through his bowels. The parties that shot him were named Salt Berry and Hoodley, both of them clerks on the levee.

[Exhibit No. 2.]

HEADQUARTERS POST OF MEMPHIS,
Memphis, Tennessee, May 21, 1866.

MAJOR : I have the honor to report the operations of my command during the riots which occurred in this city on the 1st, 2d and 3d days of May, 1866. The muster out of service of the 3d regiment United States colored heavy artillery having been completed on the last day of April, I assumed entire command of this post on the 1st of May. Having noticed considerable pistol firing near Fort Pickering, in the northern extremity of which I was, camped in the barracks formerly occupied by the 11th United States colored troops. On the evening of the 30th of April I went about through that locality, and discovered the cause to be drunken negro soldiers who attended a dance-house kept by one Mrs. Grady, on Grady's hill, South Memphis. These soldiers, inflamed with liquor, coming and going from this house, were in the habit of firing their pistols promiscuously, in all directions, endangering the safety of my command. Having observed the recurrence of this firing for several nights, from six to eleven o'clock, previous to the night I discovered the cause, I determined to abate the nuisance, and instructed my officer of the day on the 1st day of May, in case of its recurrence, to move out a portion of the command and stop it by disarming the parties engaged.

My command, on the 1st of May, consisted of one hundred and eighty men and four commissioned officers. My guard details were sixty-three men daily. I had sick, in confinement, and on extra and daily duty, forty men. The largeness of the extra and daily duty column was occasioned by a detail of carpenters, working to put quarters in order at the navy-yard, and a detail as nurses and cooks at post hospital, not then closed. It will be seen from this that my command was on guard duty every other day, and that for some time after guard mount I had but fourteen men for duty in camp ; and they were principally non-commissioned officers. Soon after parade, at six p. m., on the 1st day of May, firing was heard from the direction of South street, and much more frequent than it had been on any evening previous. The troops in camp were put under arms immediately, and in a few minutes Captain William H. Smyth, 16th United States infantry, and brevet major United States army, was started for the scene of the disturbance with a small detachment, ordered to patrol the streets in the neighborhood of the firing, and disarm all parties engaged in it, and disperse all large bodies of men on the streets. Another detachment, under First Lieutenant Walter Clifford, 16th United States infantry, was also sent in another direction, with the same instructions. These parties patroled South street, Shelby street, and Main street, as far north as Beal street, dispersing the people, moving in the direction of any shots that were heard, disarming all persons, even some of the police, whose arms were, however, returned to them as soon as they were known to be policemen. The shooting this night seemed to be an onslaught on every negro met by the police. Such negroes as the police found they arrested, almost always beating the negroes severely, and in one instance I am confident that they shot one in cold blood. In several instances negroes who had been arrested were turned loose to the excited crowd which followed the police, and killed by the crowd. The presence of the troops on the scene, and the disarming of a few persons, soon dispersed the crowd, and order reigned in that part of the city ; and at 11 o'clock p. m. the troops were withdrawn to allow them time to rest before going on guard the next day. The command, however, was all night held in readiness to move, but the night passed quietly. During the evening I received definite instructions from the major general commanding as to the course I should pursue, if the disturbances broke forth afresh in the morning, viz: owing to the smallness of my command to guard the public property securely, and keep the negroes, as far as possible, inside of Fort Pickering, and the citizens away from them—he deeming this the best way to protect the negroes, as in fact, it was. I was directed to reply to any call for assistance received from the mayor of Memphis, or the sheriff of Shelby county, with such troops as I could readily spare. On Wednesday morning, while I was marching with the new guard to the United States navy-yard, about 10 o'clock a. m., after having passed through the scenes of the disturbance of the previous evening, when near the Beal street market, I was notified that the sheriff desired to see me, as also his honor the mayor, as a riot was in progress in the very part of the city I had passed. I inferred from this, viz., the quickness of the riot after my leaving the ground, that there was an organized attempt on the part of the police and citizens to renew the riot ; and, therefore, rode quite rapidly to see the mayor, and, after much difficulty, found him, only to know that he was powerless to act, when the riot was in progress. I hastened to the sheriff, who ordered out my available forces, and requested me to meet him at the Beal street market. In an hour I rode to camp, moved all my men but the guard—having a force of about forty-five men, as both old and new guard were out at the time—at a double-quick to the appointed place, where I waited three-fourths of an hour for the sheriff. Upon his arrival I moved with him to the scene of the riots, and the localities which were pointed out to me as the spots where the riot was then progressing were immediately gone through by two skirmish lines, at right angles to each other, which, wheeling, one to the right and the other to the left, covered the whole ground. My instructions were not to fire at any one unless fired on, and then only the man fired at should return the shot ; and to arrest all persons bearing arms and turn them over to the civil authorities. I also requested the police to keep all citizens north of South street, which was partially done. I arrested several persons, among whom were several policemen, breaking open negro cabins and robbing them, searching their clothes for money, and turned them over to Recorder Creighton, who vouched for their character and office, and turned the rioters loose. Besides these persons, my command found none engaged in riotous conduct ; therefore, having also been summoned by the commanding general to meet him, I withdrew the skirmish lines, placed them under the command of Lieutenant Walter Clifford, and ordered the men retained under arms near the fort. I then proceeded to direct the crowd of armed and organized citizens on South street to disperse, as their presence conduced to no good result. I did this because I saw many organized, officered, and armed parties, on whom I was unwilling to place any reliance for the preservation of order. The larger part left ; and, having seen order established, I reported to General Stoneman, and received the same instructions in regard to keeping the parties apart as previously stated. About 1 o'clock p. m. fires were seen in the locality occupied by the troops. The command under Brevet Major Smyth, under my superintendence, came to the points where the fires were burning, and did all in their power to save the buildings, many of which were saved. All assemblages of people were dispersed. A skirmish line was kept in the vicinity all day to carry out my instructions. About 11 o'clock p. m. fires were again seen, and again the command, with the exception of twenty-five men retained in camp to man the ten-pounder Parrotts, which I ordered out and loaded with canister, were moved to the fires, and saved much property, although, for want of buckets and water, the buildings already fired could not be saved. By tearing down fences the fires were kept from spreading. After the discovery of the fires, some five or six, which broke out almost simultaneously, no further burning occurred in the vicinity in which I was assigned to preserve order. Although churches and school-houses were burned in the city, no large crowds were noticed in South Memphis ; and I attribute the origin of all the fires to some villians who, residing in the locality, took advantage of the night to fire, almost simultaneously, the buildings burned. No arrests were, however, made, as no one was found in the act of destroying property. Everything remained quiet near the fort, and at 3 o'clock a. m. the troops were withdrawn to rest. The guard details for the morrow coming from the men on duty during the night demanded this. On Thursday all was quiet in South Memphis. In the evening, pursuant to orders from Major General Stoneman, I detailed an officer and fifty men to take post in Court square and patrol the city. Nothing unusual occurred this night, as far as the troops went. The detail returned at 5 o'clock a. m., necessitating the keeping on of the old guard for over thirty-six hours.

I have, also, the honor to state that, on duty each night till daylight, and on guard the next day, even the old guard standing to their arms, day and night, as soon as relieved, during Tuesday, Wednesday, and Thursday, May 1, 2 and 3, I know of no absentees, and heard no grumbling from any of the men under my command. The officers and men of my troops deserve much credit for the willingness and alacrity with which they, one and all, performed the part assigned to them, though none of them had a night's rest for three consecutive days.

I am, major, very respectfully, your obedient servant,

ARTHUR W. ALLYN,
Captain 16th United States Infantry, Commanding

WILLIAM L PORTER,
Captain and Assistant Adjutant General, United States Volunteers,
Brevet Major, United States Volunteers.

Official :

WILLIAM L. PORTER,
Assistant Adjutant General.

HEADQUARTERS DEPARTMENT OF TENNESSEE,
Memphis, Tennessee, May 1, 1866.

SIR : I desire that you should hold your command in readiness to co-operate with the constabulary force of Memphis, in case of any further continued lawlessness on the part of persons, white or black. You will use the greatest discretion, should you be called upon by his honor the mayor of the city, and use your force mainly to assist the civil authorities in quelling disturbances—using fire-arms only in case of extreme necessity, of which you must be the judge.

I am, very respectfully, your obedient servant,

GEORGE STONEMAN,
Major General Commanding.

COMMANDING OFFICER <i>Detachment 16th United States Infantry, Fort Pickering, Tennessee.</i>

A true copy :

ARTHUR W. ALLYN,
Captain 16th United States Infantry.

HEADQUARTERS DEPARTMENT OF TENNESSEE,
Memphis, Tennessee, May 1, 1866.

SIR : I desire that you would see that proper guards be placed over all arms belonging to the United States, and that none of them get into the hands of improper persons.

Please direct Colonel Kappner, 3d United States colored heavy artillery, to have all muskets taken from the hands of the enlisted men of his regiment, and not to permit any to retain theirs after they are discharged.

Very respectfully, &c.,

GEORGE STONEMAN,
Major General Commanding.

COMMANDING OFFICER <i>Detachment 16th United States Infantry, Memphis, Tennessee.</i>

A true copy :

ARTHUR W. ALLYN,
Captain 16th United States Infantry.

SHERIFF'S OFFICE, May 2, 1866.

CAPTAIN : Will you please furnish me with such forces as may be at your command to quell the disturbances now in the city and suburbs.

Respectfully,

P. M. WINTERS,
Sheriff Shelby County.

Captain A. W. ALLYN, <i>16th United States Infantry.</i>

A true copy :

ARTHUR W. ALLYN,
Captain 16th United States Infantry.

HEADQUARTERS DEPARTMENT OF TENNESSEE,
Memphis, Tennessee, May 2, 1866.

CAPTAIN : The major general commanding directs that you patrol, with about fifty men, that portion of the county lying between and in vicinity of Beal and South streets, during the day and night, for the purpose of preserving order and keeping the populace quiet.

To do this, the patrol will be instructed to be very careful as to the use of arms, which will not be used unless absolutely necessary. With the remainder of your command, you will endeavor to keep the men of the 3d United States (colored) heavy artillery within the fort, and prevent them from going into the city.

By command of Major General Stoneman.

WM. L PORTER, *A. A. G*

Captain A. W. ALLYN, *Commanding Detachment*
 16th Infantry, Memphis, Tennessee.

A true copy :   ARTHUR W. ALLYN, *Captain 16th Infantry.*

HEADQUARTERS DEPARTMENT OF TENNESSEE,
Memphis, Tennessee, May 2, 1866.

CAPTAIN : The major general commanding directs that you order a detail of one good sergeant and ten men, to report to Brevet Brigadier General Benjamin P. Runkle, United States volunteers, Superintendent Bureau Refugee Freedmen and Abandoned Lands, Second street, No. 399.

I am, captain, very respectfully, your obedient servant,

WM. L. PORTER, *Brevet Major and A. A G*

Captain A. W. ALLYN, *Commanding Detachment*
 16th United States Infantry, Memphis, Tennessee.

A true copy :

ARTHUR W. ALLYN, *Captain 16th Infantry.*

HEADQUARTERS DEPARTMENT OF TENNESSEE,
Memphis, Tennessee, May 2, 1866.

COLONEL : The major general commanding directs that you allow none of your men to visit the city of Memphis to-day, but keep them within the limits of Fort Pickering.

I am, colonel, very respectfully, your obedient servant,

W. L. PORTER, *Brevet Major and A. A. G.*

A copy furnished me, the original being addressed to Colonel J. G. Kappner, 3d United States colored heavy artillery.

A true copy :

ARTHUR W. ALLYN, *Captain 16th Infantry.*

HEADQUARTERS DEPARTMENT OF TENNESSEE,
Memphis, Tennessee, May 3, 1866.

CAPTAIN : The major general commanding directs that you instruct your officers and men to be specially vigilant to-night. Four additional companies will reach here from Nashville to-morrow.

I am, captain, very respectfully, your obedient servant.

W. L. PORTER, *Brevet Major and A. A. G.*

Captain A. W. ALLYN, *Commanding Detachment*
 16th United States Infantry, Fort Pickering, Tennessee.

A true copy :   ARTHUR W. ALLYN, *Captain 16th Infantry.*

HEADQUARTERS DEPARTMENT OF TENNESSEE,
Memphis, Tennessee, May 3, 1866.

CAPTAIN : Please detail an officer and fifty men (armed) to proceed to this city at once. The command will be halted at the Court square, and the officer in command will report in person to the commanding general at these headquarters for instructions.

By command of Major General Stoneman.

WM. L. PORTER, *A. A G.*

Captain A. W. ALLYN, *Commanding Detachment*
 16th United States Infantry, Fort Pickering, Tennessee.

A true copy :   ARTHUR W. ALLYN, *Captain 16th Infantry.*

AN ACT to alter and amend an act entitled "An act to limit the elective franchise," passed June 5, 1865.

SECTION 1. *Be it enacted by the general assembly of the State of Tennessee,* That every white male inhabitant of this State, of the age of twenty-one years, a citizen of the United States, and a resident of the county wherein he may offer his vote, six months next preceding the day of election, shall be entitled to the privilege of the elective franchise, subject to the following exceptions and disqualifications, to wit :

First. Said voter shall have never borne arms against the government of the United States, for the purpose of aiding the late rebellion, nor have voluntarily given aid, comfort, countenance, counsel, or encouragement to any rebellion against the authority of the United States government, nor aided, countenanced, or encouraged acts of hostility thereto.

Second. That said voter shall never have sought or voluntarily accepted any office, civil or military, or attempted to exercise the functions of any office, civil or military, under the authority or pretended authority of the so-called Confederate States of America, or of any insurrectionary State whatever, hostile or opposed to the authority of the United States government, with the intent or desire to aid said rebellion or insurrectionary authority.

Third. That said voter shall have never voluntarily supported any pretended government, power or authority hostile or inimical to the authority of the United States, by contributions in money or property, by persuasion or influence, or in any other way whatever: *Provided*, That the foregoing restrictions and disqualifications shall not apply to any white citizen who may have served in and been honorably discharged from the army or navy of the United States since the 1st day of January, 1862, nor to those who voted in the Presidential election in November, 1864, or voted in the election for "ratification or rejection" in February, 1865, or voted in the election held on the 4th of March, of the same year, for governor and members of the legislature, nor to those who have been appointed to any civil or military office by Andrew Johnson, military governor, or William G. Brownlow, governor of Tennessee; all of whom are hereby declared to be qualified voters upon their complying with the requirements of this act. *Provided*, That this latter clause shall not apply to any commission issued upon any election which may have been held.

SEC. 2. *Be it further enacted*, That the governor of the State shall, within sixty days after the passage of this act, appoint a commissioner of registration for each and every county in the State, who shall, without delay, enter upon the discharge of his duties, and who shall have full power to administer the necessary oaths provided by this act. The said commissioner, before entering upon the duties of his office, shall take and subscribe an oath to support the Constitution of the United States and the constitution of the State of Tennessee, and to faithfully discharge the duties of his office, and also the oath prescribed in section 3 of this act, which oaths shall be filed in the office of the secretary of state.

The said commissioner shall keep his seat at the county seat of the county, and it shall be his duty to take the proof required by this act, and to register the name of each and every qualified voter, and to issue a certificate that such voter is entitled to the privilege of the elective franchise, and he shall preserve and keep the necessary records of his office, and shall receive from the treasury of the State the sum of one hundred dollars, to be paid upon the warrant of the comptroller of the State; and said commissioner shall make a report to the county court, at each quarterly session thereof, showing the number of voters registered previous to said quarterly session : *Provided*, That all sums of money paid by said commissioner for the United States revenue stamps, in the necessary discharge of his duty, shall be audited and paid out of the county treasury.

SEC. 3. *Be it further enacted*, That said commissioner shall issue certificates of registration to every white soldier who may have served in, and been honorably discharged from, the army or navy of the United States since the said 1st day of January, 1862, upon the production of the proper certificate of such service and discharge, or legal evidence of the loss of such discharge. Said commissioner shall issue certificates of registration to all those who voted in the said November, February, and March elections, upon production of the poll-books of the election at which said voter voted, or a certified copy, under oath, of such poll-book in case the voter may have removed to another county, or upon the affidavit of two enfranchised citizens, known to the commissioner to have been unconditional Union men throughout the rebellion, in case said poll-books may be lost. And he shall issue certificates of registration to those citizens of Tennessee who have been appointed to office by the said military or civil governors, upon the production of the commission showing such issued, in case of loss. But every other person claiming to be entitled to the privilege of appointment, or the proper certificate of the secretary of state, that such commission was the elective franchise, as provided in this act, shall, before he obtains a certificate thereof, prove by the evidence of two competent witnesses, known to the commissioner to have been themselves, at all times, unconditional Union men, that they are personally acquainted with the person so claiming, and that they verily believe that he has not been guilty of any of the disqualifications hereinbefore specially mentioned—which proof shall be taken upon affidavit, subscribed by said witnesses and filed in said office of said commissioner; and said applicant shall also take and subscribe the following oath before the commissioner of registration :

" I do solemnly swear that I have never voluntarily borne arms against the government of the United States for the purpose or with the intention of aiding the late rebellion, nor have I, with any such intention, at any time given aid, comfort, counsel, or encouragement to said rebellion, or to any act of hostility to the government of the United States. I further swear that I have never sought or accepted any office, either civil or military, or attempted to exercise the functions of any office, either civil or military, under the authority or pretended authority of the so-called Confederate States of America, or of any insurrectionary State, hostile or opposed to the authority of the United States government, with the intent and desire to aid said rebellion ; and that I have never given a voluntary support to any such government or authority. So help me God."

Provided, That citizens known to said commisssoner to have always been unconditional Union men, never having sympathized with the late rebellion, or who may be proven to have been such unconditional Union men by the oath of two witnesses who shall be known to said commissioner to have been themselves, at all times, such unconditional Union men, shall not be required to take and subscribe any oath whatever in order to obtain for themselves certificates of their right to the elective franchise.

SEC. 4. *Be it further enacted,* That upon the taking and filing the proof and oath required in section 3 of this act, the said commissioner shall register the name of said voter and issue to him his certificate therefor: *Provided,* That nothing herein contained shall prevent said commissioner from hearing proof from equally competent testimony contrary to and contravening the proof offered and taken in behalf of said applicant ; and said commissioner shall be the judge of the weight of said conflicting testimony, so far as the same may affect the issuance of certificates.

SEC. 5. *Be it further enacted,* That no person shall be entitled to vote at any State, county, district, or municipal election, or any other election held under the laws of this State, unless he shall have been registered and shall have received a certificate thereof as provided in this act ; and any person swearing falsely to any of the facts required to be sworn to by the provisions of this act shall be deemed guilty of perjury, and upon conviction thereof shall suffer all the pains and penalties provided by law for such offence ; and this act, and all the provisions thereof, shall be strictly construed to prevent any evasion thereof, and the judges of all the circuit and criminal courts of this State shall give this act specially in charge to the grand jury at each term of such court.

SEC. 6. *Be it further enacted,* That the secretary of state shall provide, at the expense of the State, the necessary books for the registration of voters, and shall cause to be printed the necessary blanks containing the necessary forms for the oaths, affidavits and certificates, as provided for in this act ; which books and blanks shall be furnished to each commissioner appointed and qualified under this act, and the expense of supplying such books and blanks shall be audited by the comptroller and paid by the treasurer out of any money in the State treasury not otherwise appropriated.

SEC. 7. *Be it further enacted,* That it shall be the duty of the governor, before any State or other general or special election, to issue writs of election to commanding officers of régiments, batteries, or detachments of officers and soldiers, who may be at the time in the service of the State, or of the United States army, wherever located, and it shall be the duty of the officer to whom such writ is directed to open and hold, or cause to be opened and held, the election required by said writ, and make returns thereof to the secretary of state, and the votes of such officers and soldiers shall be counted the same as if such votes had been cast in the counties in which said officers and soldiers may reside, and the returns shall designate the county in which said voters may reside : *Provided,* That the governor shall not be required to issue such writs of election for county, district, or corporation officers.

SEC. 8. *Be it further enacted,* That all certificates heretofore issued under the provisions of the act to which this is amendatory are hereby annulled, and shall not be used at any future election in this State, from and after the passage of this act, except at the election for county officers, to be held on the first Saturday in March, 1866.

SEC 9. *Be it further enacted,* That all candidates for any official position shall, before the day of election, be required to take and subscribe the oath prescribed in the third section of this act, which, in case of a candidate for a county office, shall be filed in the office of the court clerk, and for all other offices in the office of the secretary of state ; and that judges of election or other officers shall reject, and make no return of the votes cast for any person who has not so taken and subscribed said oath ; and the same oath shall be taken and subscribed, as an official oath, by all judges and clerks of all elections, and all deputies in any of the offices of the State or county : *Provided,* That candidates who may have served in, and been honorably discharged from, the army or navy of the United States, since the first day of January, 1862, or who may have been appointed and commissioned to any office by said military or civil governor of Tennessee, shall be eligible to office, except political offices, without taking said oath.

SEC 10. *Be it further enacted,* That in case any county court shall fail or refuse to induct into office any of the officers elected under this act, it shall be lawful for the commissioner of registration, upon orders from the governor, to perform that duty, and to administer all necessary oaths, and to take and approve all necessary official bonds, and the same shall be good and valid in law.

SEC. 11. *Be it further enacted,* That no election shall take place until the registration provided for in this act shall be completed in the county, circuit or district in which said election shall be had, and the report or reports of the commissioner made to the governor, except the said election for county officers in March, 1866.

SEC. 12. *Be it further enacted,* That it shall be the duty of each commissioner of registration to report to the governor when he shall have completed the registration of his county ; and when said reports are all in from any county, district or circuit, or from the entire State, it shall be the duty of the governor to issue his proclamation and writs of election, announcing the completion of such registration, and ordering elections to fill all the vacant offices of the State, counties, circuits or districts.

SEC. 13. *Be it further enacted,* That it shall be the duty of the commissioner, without delay, to proceed with the performance of his duties ; and before completing the same in his county, he shall give at least ten days' public notice, by advertisement in some newspaper, or at least four public places in his county, of his intention to complete and for the time being close his registration. But it shall be his duty, after making his report to the governor, to attend for one day at each quarterly session of the county court, for the purpose of issuing certificates of registration to such persons as may be entitled to them, under the provisions of this act ; and for each day he may so attend he shall receive the sum of three dollars, to be paid out of the county treasury.

SEC. 14 *Be it further enacted,* That every wilful and intentional violation of this act by the commissioner of registration is hereby declared to be a misdemeanor, and upon conviction he shall be removed from office, and shall pay a fine of not less than fifty dollars to the use of the State.

SEC. 15. *Be it further enacted,* That every violation of this act is hereby declared to be a misdemeanor, and punishable upon presentment or indictment, and every person participating in such violation shall, upon conviction, be fined not less than ten nor exceeding one hundred dollars, and may be imprisoned at the discretion of the court.

SEC 16. *Be it further enacted,* That an act entitled " An act to limit the elective franchise," passed June the 5th, 1865, be and the same is hereby altered and amended as provided in the several sections of this act, and the provisions of this act shall be deemed and held in lieu of the said act entitled " An act to limit the elective franchise," passed June the 5th, 1865, with the exception of the preamble thereunto prefixed.

SEC. 17. *Be it further enacted,* That this act shall take effect from and after its pa

> JOHN NORMAN,
> *Speaker, pro tem , of the House of Represen*
> JOSHUA B. FRIERSON,
> *Speaker of the Senate.*

Passed May 3, 1866.

CITY HALL, *Memphis, June 5,* 1866.

The following is a true and perfect statement of the votes cast for the respective candidates for mayor of the city of Memphis at the respective elections held for that officer in June, 1861, in June, 1862, in June, 1863, and in June, 1865. An election was held in June, 1864, for mayor, but no return thereof made. The United States military authorities then in possession of the city appointed a provisional government. &c., say for the 38th corporate year, commencing July 1, 1864, and ending June 30, 1865:

Names of candidates for mayor at the June election.	1st ward.	2d ward.	3d ward.	4th ward.	5th ward.	6th ward.	7th ward.	8th ward.	Total.
35th corporate year.									
John Park	585	143	232	49	127	52	319	124	1,631
Amos Woodruff	80	77	124	86	98	41	105	74	685
Richard D. Baugh	46	69	170	51	80	35	99	30	580
Joseph J. Rawlings	3	4	25	46	50	50	60	9	247
Total 35th corporate year	....	....	....	....	....	....	....	....	3,143
36th corporate year.									
John Park*	293	83	44	17	36	50	100	75	698
37th corporate year.									
C. Kortrecht	113	67	90	70	74	38	116	102	670
John Park	619	123	118	30	153	91	283	136	1,553
G. P. Ware	7	6	11	13	36	7	39	6	125
Total 37th corporate year	....	....	....	....	....	....	....	....	2,348
39th corporate year.									
Joh. .rk									1,356
Wm. . Lofland									835
Total 39th corporate year	....	....	....	....	....	....	....	....	2,191

* No opposition.

This is to certify that the above and foregoing is a true and perfect extract, copied from the duly recorded minutes of the proceedings of the board of mayor and aldermen of the city of Memphis.

In testimony whereof, I, Lewis R. Richards, city register and keeper of the records and corporate seal of the city of Memphis, have hereunto set my hand and affixed the seal of said city this June 5, 1866.

[L. S.]

L. R. RICHARDS, *City Register.*

———

CITY HALL, MEMPHIS, *June 27,* 1866.

The following is a true and perfect list of the duly elected and regularly appointed officials of the city of Memphis that were in the service of the city during the months of April and May, 1866:

Mayor.
Honorable JOHN PARK.

Aldermen.

*E. V. O'Mahoney, first ward.
*John Glancy, first ward.
†G. D. Johnson, second ward.
†Samuel T. Morgan, second ward.
*Thomas Leonard, third ward.
‡Louis Wundermand, third ward.
†Ira M. Hill, fourth ward.
†A. P. Burdett, fourth ward.

*Michael Burke, fifth ward.
*Thomas O'Donnell, fifth ward.
†R. K. Becktell, sixth ward.
*William Harvey, sixth ward.
†John S. Doaf, seventh ward.
*Martin Kelley, seventh ward.
*J. F. Green, eighth ward.
*D. R. Grace, eighth ward.

* Irish.   † American.   ‡ German.

The following is a list of the names of the city officers generally, and in what capacity acting in April and May, 1866:

Names of parties.	In what capacity acting.	No. days in April.	No. days in May.
P .M. Dickinson†	City comptroller	30	31
Lewis R. Richards†	City register	30	31
W. K. Bridges†	City treasurer	30	31
E. De F. Morgan	City attorney	30	31
S. P. Bankhead†	Assistant city attorney	30	31
B. Decker‡	City inspector	30	31
F. L. Warner‡	City property tax collector	30	31
Thomas Fisher*	City privilege tax collector	30	31
John J. Butler*	Wharf master	30	31
Dr. Charles A. Warner‡	Hospital physician	30	31
Charles W. Padgett	Hospital druggist	30	31
Dr. W. C. Cavanaugh*	Health officer	30	31
C. N. Martin†	City scavenger	30	31
J. H. McClure†	City engineer	30	31
James Ford*	Street commissioner	30	31
Thomas Garvey*	Market master, north	30	31
James Ryan*	Market master, south	30	31
Edward Keating*	Superintendent of Court square	30	31
Pat. McCarthy*	Superintendent of Market square	30	31
Edward O'Neill*	Chief of fire department	30	31
W. M. Connelly*	Fire warden	30	31
J. M. Keating	City printer	30	31
Joseph C. Wilson†	Superintendent workhouse force	30	31
D. D. Cook	Assistant sup't of workhouse force	30	31
Dennis Savage*	City stable keeper	30	31
Pat. Hornley*	Dredge boat keeper	30	31

The following is a list of the names of all parties in any manner connected with the police force of the city in April and May, 1866:

Names of parties.	In what capacity acting.	No. days in April.	No. days in May.
John C. Creighton*	City recorder	30	31
W. B. Cotton†	City recorder's clerk	30	31
Benjamin G. Garrett†	Chief of police	30	31
William Jerricho‡	Chief of police's clerk	30	31
Daniel McMahon*	Captain of day police	30	31
Edward Dowling*	Lieutenant of day police	30	31
Bernard Grey*	Captain of night police	30	31
Timothy Hichey*	Lieutenant of night police	30	31
M. H. Rieley*	City prison keeper	30	31
‖W. G. McIlvain†	Assistant city prison keeper, day	30	31
‖James Honan*	Assistant city prison keeper, night	30	31
‖Ed. Rieley*	Prison watchman	30	31
‖Dennis McMahon*	do	30	31
‖John Toomey*	do	30	31
‖Ed. Foley*	do	30	31
¶R. H. Lee*	Detective policeman	30	31
¶Owen Winters*	do	30	31
¶Thomas O'Mahoney*	do	30	31
¶C. L. Morrison	do	30	31
¶C. N. Robinson†	do	30	31
¶P. S. Simons†	do	30	31
M. O'Brien,* No. 1	Day policeman	30	31

*Irish.   †American.   ‡German.
‖ Under charge of city prison keeper.   ¶ Under charge of chief of police.

List of names of parties, &c.—Continued.

Names of parties.	In what capacity acting.	No. days in April.	No. days in May.
M. McKeough*	Day policeman	30	31
P. Baker*	......do......	30	31
Thomas Collins*	......do......	15	31
Angelo Maree§	......do......	30	31
Henry McCormache*	......do......	30	26
John McPartland*	......do......	30	31
P. McMahon*	......do......	30	31
M. O'Brien,* No. 2	......do......	30	26
D. Carrall*	......do......	30	31
D. Roach*	......do......	30	13
F. S. Sullivan*	Detective police	30	30
J. F. Sweatt†	Day policeman	30	31
D. Shevlin*	......do......	30	31
P. Green*	......do......	30	31
J. Joyce*	......do......	30	31
P. Welsh*	......do......	30	31
C. McCarthy*	......do......	30	31
P. Galvan*	......do......	30	31
Walter Joyce*	......do......	22	31
James Connell*	......do......	30	31
Ed. Rowane*	......do......	30	31
John McMahon*	......do......	30	31
J. W. Smith*	......do......	30	31
J. H. Kelly*	......do......	30	31
James McAdams*	......do......	30	31
M. Gallagher*	......do......	30	31
John Canning*	......do......	30	31
J. B. Passell	......do......	30	31
R. Clark*	......do......	30	31
John Winters*	......do......	30	31
P. McMahon*	......do......	30	31
F. McShane*	......do......	25	31
Martin Rogers*	......do......	30	31
Luke Calvay*	......do......	30	31
James Birmingham*	......do......	30	31
William Finnell*	......do......	30	31
P. McDermott*	......do......	30	31
Thomas Shandley *	......do......	30	31
John McMainard*	......do......	30	31
James Finn*	......do......	30	31
P. Burke*	......do......	30	31
T. Marnon*	......do......	30	31
Jeff. Garrett†	......do......	30	31
Thomas Slattery*	......do......	30	31
John O'Neill*	......do......	30	31
John Green*	......do......	30	31
P. Malone*	......do......	30	31
P. Spillman*	......do......	30	31
John Welsh*	......do......	30	31
M. Cane*	......do......	30	31
James Downes*	......do......	30	31
Thomas McNichols*	......do......	30	31
Dennis Gorman*	......do......	30	31
J. W. Lafe*	......do......	30	31
M. Dee*	......do......	3	......
Thaddeus Carmichael*	......do......	30	31
John Helan*	......do......	30	31
Timothy Hope*	......do......	30	31
Roger Sullivan*	......do......	30	31
Michael Brown*	......do......	30	31
John Foy*	......do......	28	31

* Irish. † American. § Italian.

List of names of parties, &c.—Continued.

Names of parties.	In what capacity acting.	No. days in April.	No. days in May.
Daniel McGown*	Day policeman	20	......
John Joyce*	......do	28	......
Dennis Lenehan*	......do	30	31
John Galvan*	......do	27	31
L. Connell*	......do	26	31
B. Cox*	......do	26	31
James Conner*	......do	30	31
John Stephens*	......do	20	
Ed. Powers*	......do	17	......
William Carroll*	......do	16	......
James Dowling*	......do	16	31
J. C. Lee*	......do	30	......
Michael Kelly*	......do	......	31
Pat. Powers*	......do	......	31
Michael Carroll*	......do	......	31
R. H. McIlvain*	......do	......	27
Michael Maloney*	......do	......	15
James Castellos*	Night policeman	30	31
John Calligan*	......do	30	31
Thomas Cayne*	......do	30	5
John Slattery*	......do	30	31
John Kanerge‡	......do	30	31
Dennis Kenole*	......do	30	31
James Cusack*	......do	30	26
Simon Malone*	......do	30	31
John Harvey*	......do	30	31
Pat. Maloney*	......do	30	31
S. Perry*	......do	30	31
Ed. O'Donnell*	......do	30	31
Mike Reagan*	......do	30	31
Thomas Carty*	......do	30	31
John Conry*	......do	30	31
Phil. Moran*	......do	30	31
Franke Faley*	......do	30	31
Pat. Brady*	......do	30	31
D. F. Slattery*	......do	30	31
Pat. Welsh*	......do	30	31
Pat. Cusack*	......do	30	31
Michael Farrell*	......do	30	20
John Glancy*	......do	30	......
W. J. Anderson	......do	30	13
John Eagan*	......do	15	......
Matthew Shelly*	......do	30	29
Louis Barbara§	......do	30	26
James Brown*	......do	30	31
H. Hanson*	......do	30	31
James Murphey*	......do	30	31
Thomas Eagan*	......do	30	31
Thomas Berrigan*	......do	30	31
John Liby*	......do	30	29
Michael Moore*	......do	30	31
Joseph Parker	......do	10	......
Ed. Farrell*	......do	30	29
Condy Burns*	......do	30	28
Frank Murtaugh	......do	30	31
Peter Gillen*	......do	30	31
John Breen*	......do	30	31
Owen Shehan*	......do	30	29
Jas. Lynch*	......do	30	31
John Casgrove*	......do	30	31
Wm. Regan*	......do	25	7

*Irish.   ‡German.   §Italian.

List of names of parties, &c.—Continued.

Names of parties.	In what capacity acting.	No. days in April.	No. days in May.
George Sullivan*	Night policeman	30	29
Frank Brannon*	do	30	31
Frank Grey*	do	30	31
Barney Burns*	do	30	28
Jas. Byron*	do	30	31
Ed. Maroney*	do	30	31
Michael Clarke*	do	30	31
G. W. Rion*	do	30	29
Jas. D. Radigan*	do	30	31
Michael Connell*	do	27	26
Ed. Powers*	do	27	31
John Glancy*	do	27	8
Mike Malone*	do	30	31
Wm. Fox*	do	30	31
Thos. McCormack*	do	11	......
Peter Kelley*	do	30	31
Thomas Cox*	do	11	31
E. H. Wilhelm†	do	30	19
B. Gillooley*	do	30	31
Owen McPartland*	do	30	31
Daniel Slavin*	do	30	31
Wm. Halden*	do	29	29
Thomas McGinty*	do	30	29
John Sherridan*	do	30	7
Nicholas Preweitt*	do	30	31
Michael Anglin*	do	30	31
Michael King*	do	30	31
John Galvane*	do	3	......
Michael Dea*	do	27	31
Pat. Powers*	do	26	......
Jas. Kennedy*	do	22	31
Pat. Drisclol*	do	21	31
Thomas Hichey*	do	20	31
Hugh Degnan*	do	17	31
Bernard Sweeney*	do	13	28
Drury Dee*	do	......	11

* Irish.   † American.

RECAPITULATION.

Nationality of the police force of the city of Memphis.

Irishmen	163
Germans	2
Italians	2
Americans	8
Unknown	5
Total	180

24

POLICE COMMITTEE.

The police committee is composed of five members of the board of aldermen, with his honor the mayor of the city, who is, by virtue of his office, a member of all regular or standing committees. This committee has a general supervisory charge of the police force of the city, in the selection of, as well as trial and dismissal of, all offending policemen.

* JOHN PARK, *Mayor.*
* THOS. O'DONNELL,
* J. F. GREEN,
* THOMAS LEONARD,
* D. R. GRACE,
* MARTIN KADY,
Aldermen.

The following is a true and perfect list of the names of all persons employed in the Memphis fire department during the months of April and May, 1866:

Names of parties.	In what capacity acting.	No. days in April.	No. days in May.
Jas. Madden*	Captain fire steamer No. 1	30	31
Jas. Dolan*	Engineer fire steamers Nos. 1 and 4	30	31
Tim. Ryan*	Laborer fire steamer No. 1	30	31
Dennis Quinlan*	....do............do............	30	31
Michael Waters*	....do............do............	30	10
Barney Brady*	....do............do............	30	31
Dennis Ryan*	....do............do............	30	31
Arthur Dwyer*	....do............do............	30	31
Michael Hart*	....do............do............	30	31
A. J. Matthews†	....do............do............	......	20
J. J. Reed*	Captain fire steamer No. 2	30	31
H. R. Dunn,* (killed in riot)	Engineer fire steamer No. 2	30	......
Andrew Keilly*	....do............do............	......	20
John Hachet*	Laborer fire steamer No. 2	30	31
P. H. Phelon*	....do............do............	30	31
William Carrall*	....do............do............	30	31
J. J. Cavanaugh*	....do............do............	30	31
W. J. Rovoga‡	....do............do............	30	31
Pat. Scott*	....do............do............	24	31
Richard Dougherty*	....do............do............	23	31
Stephen McGinnis*	....do............do............	6	......
John B. Signiago‡	Captain fire steamer No. 3	30	31
A. J. Ward†	Engineer fire steamer No. 3	30	31
Frank Dent†	Laborer fire steamer No. 3	30	31
James Stokes*	....do............do............	30	31
John Waters*	....do............do............	30	31
Thomas Callahan*	....do............do............	30	31
James Canally*	....do............do............	30	31
Pat. Stokes*	....do............do............	30	31
Michael McFadden*	....do............do............	18	......
Nicholas Collins*	....do............do............	10	......
Michael McFadden*	Captain fire steamer No. 4	......	31
Joseph Hiskey*	Engineer fire steamer No. 4	13	31
James Sullivan*	Laborer fire steamer No. 4	......	31
Thomas Prewett*	....do............do............	......	31
Michael Gallagher*	....do............do............	......	5
Thomas O'Brien*	....do............do............	......	3
John McMahon*	....do............do............	......	8
John Cunningham*	....do............do............	......	8
Robert Thompson	....do............do............	......	6
Phil. Daffte*	Captain hook and ladder company No. 1.	30	31
James Harrigan*	Laborer hook and ladder company No. 1.	30	31
Morris Peters*	....do............do............	30	31
Pat. McGown*	....do............do............	30	31
Michael Kenan*	....do............do............	30	......
Tim. Bolan*	....do............do............	......	6

* Irish.   † American.   ‡ Italian.

RECAPITULATION.

Nationality of the employés of the Memphis fire department.

Irishmen	40
Americans	3
Italians	2
Unknown	1
Total	46

FIRE COMMITTEE.

The fire committee is composed of five members of the board of aldermen and the mayor *ex-officio,* making six in number, who have general sapervisory charge or care of the fire department, similar in character to the police committee.

* JOHN PARK, *Mayor.*
* MARTIN KELLY,
† A. P. BURDETT,
* THOMAL O'DONNELL,
* J. F. GREEN,
† R. K. BECTELL,
Aldermen.

CITY HALL, *Memphis, June 2,* 1866.

This is to certify that the within and foregoing contains a true and perfect list of the names of all persons connected officially with the city government, or in the employ of the city of Memphis during the months of April and May, 1866, with the exception of the day laborers on the streets, under charge of the street commissioners, and the laborers employed by and under the general supervisory charge of the health officer of the city, as appears from the records and account books of the city and papers on file in my office.

In testimony whereof, I, Lewis R. Richards, city register and keeper of the records and corporate seal of the city of Memphis, have hereunto affixed my official signature and attached the city seal this 2d day of June, A. D. 1866.

[L. S.]

L. R. RICHARDS,
City Register.

Irish. † American.

INDEX.

NOTE.—Reference to page is indicated in the index by the letter " p ;" all other figures refer to the numbers of questions in the testimony.
ABBREVIATIONS.—" M. C.," Military Commission ; "F. B. C.," Freedmen's Bureau Commission.

A.

Alexander, Henry, testimony of, 1246–'58; blacksmith's shop burned, 1251.
Allyn, Captain A. W., testimony of, 4052–4101 ; commanding post of Memphis, 4052 ; details of suppression of the riot by the United States regular troops, 4059–'78 ; acted under Sheriff Winter's orders, 4071 ; speech of Attorney General Wallace, 4077 ; a great many people in the mob who did not belong to Memphis, 4084–'85 ; good conduct of the negroes, 4091–'96 ; would have resulted in an universal massacre and universal burning but for intervention of troops, 4100 ; official report of the suppression of the riot by troops under his command, pp. 359–361.
Anderson, Charles W., testimony of, 2337–'45 ; attack on negroes at Chelsea the day after the riot, 2338.
Anderson, Eli, witness, M. C., p. 317 ; shot in the arm and robbed.
Andrews, Silas A., testimony of, 5189–'90 ; made copies of affidavits.
Argus, newspaper, quotations from—*Bowers*, pp. 328, 333.
Armon, George, witness, M. C., p. 328 ; house not burned because two white families would have also to be turned out.
Armon, Sarah, witness, M. C., p. 328 ; statement same as George Armon.
Armour, Harriet, testimony of, 2448–'85 ; rape committed on witness by Dunn and another man, 2458–'80.
Artist, Sheppard, witness, F. B. C., p. 341 ; house robbed.
Austin, Daniel, witness, F. B. C., p. 345 ; shot in the shoulder.
Austin, Mary, witness, F. B. C., p. 354 ; robbed.
Avalanche, newspaper, quotation from—*Galloway*, p. 334.
Ayr, Ann Patrick, testimony of, 3781–'97 ; house fired into and robbed.
Ayrs, Treadwell S., testimony of, 4703–'15 ; relations between citizens and colored people : operations of the franchise law, &c.

B.

Bailey, Africa, witness, F. B. C., p. 354 ; house burned.
Baker, Lieut. B. F., witness, M. C., p. 318 ; killing of Lundy, Richardson, Withers, Cobb, Black, Baker, and Robinson ; Turner wounded.
Bankett, Henry, witness, F. B. C., p. 352 ; house and contents burned.
Beard, Jonas, witness, F. B. C., p. 350 ; house burned.
Beatty, John, testimony of, 1260–'71 ; Joe Strickney shot, 1266 ; two soldiers shot, 1267.
Beecher, Dr. D. P., testimony of, 1790–1886 ; in charge of Freedmen's Bureau dispensary, 1799 ; attended six or eight of the wounded—two wounded by a volley fired by the mob into the hospital, 1804 ; colored soldiers not as much addicted to drunkenness as same number of whites under similar circumstances, 1820 ; their great difficulty a want of something to live on, 1822 ; peculiar difficulties and embarrassments of colored soldiers, 1823–'29 ; witness in danger from having purchased property at United States tax sales, 1831 ; threats against radical men, 1838 ; northern men, called radicals, held up by the newspapers as men to be shunned and avoided, 1849 ; many northern men against whom there is no prejudice, 1859 ; no good feeling toward quiet, well-behaved colored people on the part of the citizens of Memphis, 1881 ; list of wounded attended by witness, 1886.
Beeman, Lucy, witness, F. B. C., p. 344 ; house robbed.
Bennett, Louis, witness, M. C., p. 330 ; knocked down and robbed in front of Gayoso House.
Bennett, Reuben, witness, F. B. C., p. 340; house and contents burned.
Berry, Frank D., witness, F. B. C., p. 337 ; trunk broken open and robbed.
Black, Mary, testimony of, 3009–'24 ; house burned by Pigeon and others, 3015 ; colored man shot five or six times and killed, 3023.
Black flag raised—*Cherry*, 2653–'63—*Hood*, p. 335—*Galloway*, p. 326.
Bloom, Peter, witness, F. B. C., p. 348 ; robbery ; abuse of wife.
Bloom, Rebecca Ann, witness, F. B. C., p. 351 ; rape.

Bond, Henry, testimony of, 2970–'89; Willis Jones shot in the eye by policeman, 2975; colored soldier shot by O'Hearn and killed, 2975; Eli shot by policeman, 2979; colored man beaten two hundred or two hundred and fifty licks, 2982.

Bond, Kelsie, witness, M. C., p. 320; three buildings on Echols street burned.

Boon, Thomas, witness, F. B. C., p. 354; wounded and robbed.

Bostwick, A., witness, M. C., p. 321; burning of church corner of New Orleans and Washington streets.

Boudinot, H. B., testimony of, 5186–'88; copied extracts from newspapers.

Bowen, Dr. E. S., witness, M. C., p. 321; wounding of George Clapp and Frank McGee.

Bowles, Amos, witness, M. C., p. 317; shot in the arm.

Bowman, C. H., witness, M. C., p. 324; commencement of riot.

Bower, D. A., witness, M. C., p. 328; editor of Argus; paragraph wishing negroes in "Africa, hell, or some other seaport town," &c., written by Hood, local editor; recalled, p. 333; authorship of other Argus articles.

Boyd, Anne, witness, F. B. C., p. 354; house and contents burned.

Boyd, Alfred, witness, F. B. C., p. 353; house and contents burned.

Boyle, Lewis, witness, F. B. C., p. 354; robbed.

Boyle, Robert, witness, F. B. C., p. 336; robbed.

Bradshaw, Thomas, testimony of, 5050–'59; kind feeling between old residents and colored people.

Brandoned, S., witness F. B. C., p. 341; robbed of money and watch.

Brazier, Wm. H., testimony of, 1271–1319; negro killed on corner of South and Causey streets, 1278; conduct of the mob, 1275–'87; little negro boy brought out and shot, 1288; mayor standing there inactive, 1291; another negro brought out by five or six men, knocked down on his face, and five or six shots fired at him, 1295; a thousand or more persons in the mob Tuesday afternoon, 1311; never have seen any bad behavior on the part of the blacks, 1319.

Brewster, Robert, witness F. B. C., p. 342; store entered and robbed.

Bristol, Edmond, witness F. B. C., p. 340; assaulted and robbed.

Brooks, B. F. C., testimony of, 3301–3374; publisher of the Repbblican, 3301; McElmore boasted of killing five negroes, 3310; burning of tenant houses threatened, 3318; as much prejudice against the radicals as against the negroes, 3327; troops necessary for the protection of Union men, 3336; feeling towards northern men, 3337–'45; policy advocated by the Republican, 3349–'61.

Brooks, Samuel, witness F. B. C., p. 343; shot in the back and stoned.

Brown, Ellen, testimony of, 2998–'9; house burned down, policemen Egan and Clark implicated.

Brown, John, witness M. C, p. 318; $8,000 value of church burned corner Main and Overton streets.

Brown, Mary Ellen, witness F. B. C., p. 345; house robbed.

Bryant, Mary, witness F. B. C., p. 357; house robbed.

Bufford, Jordon, witness F. B. C., p. 338; struck on the head and robbed.

Burning:

Barracks, used as school-houses, Lincoln chapel and other churches—*Tade*, 836–841; house of Primus Lane—*Lane*, 908; houses of Sneed and Adam Lock—*Sneed*, 964, *Lock*, 1227, *Means*, 2371; blacksmith shop of Henry Alexander and George Jones—*Coe*, 1056, *Jones*, 1088, *Alexander*, 1251; three or four shanties—*Tibbs*, 2167–2191; as many as twenty cottages burned on one square—*Townsend*, 2228; Henry Bankins, colored, married white woman, house—*Grady*, 2712; house, clothes, &c., of Mollie Davis, $550—*Davis*, 2995; Ellen Brown's house—*Brown*, 2999; house, clothes, &c., of Lucy Hunt, by Chris. Pigeon and others, $250—*Hunt*, 3003, p. 352: house of Mary Black, with furniture, &c., by Pigeon and his crowd—*Black*, 3015; Mat. Wardlaw's house and contents, $1,600—*Wardlaw*, 3818; Mary Jordan's house and contents, $200 *Jordan*, 3882; counted fourteen fires—*Clifford*, 4168; Rankin's school-house, $1,200 —*Rankin*, p. 313; Andrew Meadows's house—*Meadows*, p. 319; three buildings on Echols street, $5,000—*Bond*, p. 320; school-house on Hernando street, set on fire by a United States soldier—*Smith*, p. 323; house on Echols street, between Vance and Elliot, burned, $1,000—*Gibbons*, 325; building corner of Lauderdale and Vance streets, cost about $3,500—*Wright*, p. 326; building corner of Echols street and Hernando road, cost about $1,800—*Wright*, p. 326; building corner of Hernando and Pontotoc streets, cost about $2,200—*Wright*, p. 326; building corner of Beal and Wellington streets, cost about $1,000—*Wright*, p. 326; building corner of Main and Vance streets, cost about $1,800—*Wright*, p. 326; shanty, oil cloth, prints, &c., corner Webster and DeSoto streets—*Wands*, p. 331; house rented by Colman Default—*Default*, 337; Harriet Moon, house and contents, $125—*Moon*, p. 338; Joseph Simpson, house and contents, $300—*Simpson*, p. 338; Maria Trotter, house and contents, $300—*Trotter*, p. 339; Edward Jackson, house and contents—*Jackson*, p. 339; Reuben Bennett, house and contents, $200—*Bennett*, p. 340; Mary A. Mereweather, house and contents, $100—*Mereweather*, p. 340; George Cruse, house, $100—*Cruse*, p. 340; Burton Davis, house and contents—*Davis*, p. 341; Benj. Tucker, house and contents—*Tucker*, p. 342; Wm.

Reed, house and contents, $150—*Reed*, p. 342; Major Jones, house—*Jones*, p. 342; Marshall, Escue, house and contents, $150—*Escue*, p. 342; Eliza Groves, house, $75—*Groves*, p. 342; Clary Johnson, house and contents, $250—*Johnson*, p. 343; Norris Davis, house and contents, *Davis*, p. 343; Perry Lane, house and contents, $150—*Lane*, p. 344; Julius Wood, clothing burned, $25—*Wood*, p. 346; Easter Cooper, house, $40—*Kelly*, p. 346; Peter Johnson, house, $100—*Johnson*, p. 346; Pleasant Woodfall's property in Jas. Hustin's house, $175—*Woodfall*, p. 347; Ann Odum, house, $200—*Odum*, p. 348; Francis Harris, house, $75—*Harris*, p. 348; Eliza Robinson, house, $175—*Robinson*, p. 350; Andy Pollin, house and contents, $150—*Pollen*, p. 350; Anthony French, house and contents, $350—*French*, p. 350; Rose Hart, house and contents—*Hart*, p. 350; Jonas Beard, house and contents, $250—*Beard*, p. 350; Patience Nelson, house, $100—*Nelson*, p. 350; Simon Turner, house, $100—*Turner*, p. 351; Francis Perkins, house and contents, $250—*Perkins*, p. 351; Thomas Robinson, goods, $100—*Robinson*, p. 350; Humphrey Morris, house, $350—*Morris*, p. 351; John Deadwiley, house and contents, $50—*Deadwiley*, p. 352; Henry Banket, house and contents, $500—*Banket*, p. 352; George Chambers, house and contents—*Chambers*, p. 352; Wm. Smith, house and contents, $200—*Smith*, p. 352; Julia Marshall, house and contents, $300—*Marshall*, p. 352; Alfred Boyd, house and contents, $125—*Boyd*, p. 353; Margaret Kenney, house and contents, $300—*Kenney*, p. 353; Collins Chapel, $25,000—*Members*, p. 353; John Green, house, &c., $785—*Green*, p. 353; Shack Robinson, saloon and contents, $500—*Robinson*, p. 354; Henry Perkins, house and contents, $600—*Perkins*, p. 354; Africa Bailey, house and contents, $400—*Bailey*, p. 354; Mose Harrison, trunk and clothes, $150—*Harrison*, p. 354; James Hustin, house and contents, $350—*Hustin*, p. 354; Annie Boyd, house and contents, $450—*Boyd*, p. 354; Fannie Long, house and contents, $100—*Long*, p. 355; Columbus Riley, house and contents, $75—*Riley*, p. 355; Lily Henderson, house, $400—*Henderson*, p. 355; Harriet Moton, house and contents, $25—*Moton*, p. 355.

Bushnell, C. E., witness M. C., p. 324; beating of negro, corner of Linden and Main streets.

Butcher, Albert, witness F. B. C., p. 346; commencement of the riot.

Bryant, Mary, witness F. B. C., p. 348: driven out and house robbed.

C.

Cameron, Charles S., testimony of, 4662–4702; two-thirds of the people entertain kind sentiments towards the negro, 4676; effect of franchise law, 4676–'78; no hostility manifested towards northern men as such, 4682; strong feeling against those who favor policy of disfranchising people, 4697.

Campbell, Carey, witness, F. B. C., p. 340; house robbed.

Carlton, Joseph, witness, F. B. C., p. 344; killing and robbing of Robert Carlton.

Caruthers, J. S., witness, M. C., p. 324; burning of school-house corner of Main and Vance streets.

Caruthers, Daniel, witness, F. B. C., p. 347; robbed.

Cartright, Bugg, witness, F. B. C., p. 356; went with Jack Reed to Dupee's house.

CAUSES OF THE RIOT:

The newspapers—*report*, p. 30; stimulated by leading disloyal papers; growing prejudice between police and negroes—*Hunter*, 515; intense hatred between the Irish and negroes, fostered by southern citizens to the best of their ability—*Tade*, 828, 829; originated between the lower class of whites and negroes—*Irwin*, 1542; the sons of Erin do not like the sons of Ham particularly when they come in conflict with their wages—*Keller*, 1610; negro soldiers got drunk and raised a fuss, and innocent negroes suffered from the mob—*Edmunds*, 1699; feeling between the colored people and police—*White*, 2240; the negroes against the Irish—*Dent*, 2267; the Irish and thieves had been wanting an excuse to get into a riot with the negroes—*Dent*, 2269; feeling of spite between police and negroes—*Swan*, 2505; feeling between the Irish and negroes—*Perkins*, 4757; was nothing else than a well-appointed thing—*Moller*, 772; often heard hackmen and firemen say the d——d niggers would be cleaned out as soon as they were mustered out of the service—*Hubberd*, 331.

Chamberlain, S. H., witness, M. C., p. 322; negro near railroad depot killed by Policeman McCormick.

Chambers, George, witness, F. B. C., p. 352; house and contents burned.

Chandler, J. L., testimony of, 5060–'83; acting editor of Memphis Post, 5060; threats to burn the Post, 5060; editors of the Post in the Union army, 5078; editors of other papers in the rebel army, 5073; composition of the mob, 5080–'83.

Chapin, J. S., testimony of, 2768–2822; character and conduct of the mob, 2772–'98; colored man shot; lying on the side-walk at Beal street market, 2786; conduct of the colored soldiers, 2802–'07; relations of citizens and negroes, 2808–'22.

Cherry, Tony, testimony of, 2577–2680; colored soldier, 2584; commencement of the riot; arrest of colored soldier by police; resisted by crowd of colored soldiers; resulting in fight between soldiers and police, 2581–'93; Richardson killed, 2593; Withers, Black,

Cobb and another soldier killed, 2595–2608; fight between the police and soldiers on Tuesday, 2612–'30; same on Wednesday; black flag raised by white man, 2631–'68; artillery loaded at the fort, 2670–'75; talk of getting arms from the arsenal, 2676–'78.

Church, Robert, testimony of, 3608–3617; saloon of witness robbed, and fired at, twelve or fifteen shots, by Roach and other policemen; two other colored men wounded, 3611.

Christopher, Handy, witness, F. B. C., p. 343; house robbed.

Cicalla, Paul, testimony of, 4303–'09; killing of Adeline Miller.

Citizens engaged in the riot:

John Callahan, grocer, with party that burned Lock's and Sneed's houses, and killed Rachel Hatcher—*Sneed*, 964; carried away a bed from same house—*Swels*, 1211; *Garey*, 1244; shot, stabbed, and robbed Andrew Minter—*Minter*, 2361; shot and robbed Andrew Meadows—*Meadows*, p. 319

George McGinn, grocer, carried away beds and things from Lock's house, fired at Mrs. Lock, when called on to assist her—*Swels*, 1218; *Garey*, 1244; in the crowd—*Townsend*, 2216.

Wm. O. Hearn, constable, leader of a party of incendiaries—*Oldridge*, 1352–1358; shot a soldier—*Bond*, 2978; *Chapin*, 2978.

—— Porter, a butcher, threatened violence on a negro boy in Doctor McGowan's office; threatened and attempted violence on Doctor McGowan as an abolitionist—*McGowan*, 1402–1404; same on United States Marshal Ryder—*Ryder*, 4201–'02.

—— Palmer and his brother, depot agents, wounded Jos. Walker; killed another negro—*Walker*, 1784–92.

John Pendergrast and three sons, engaged in several cases of shooting and burning—*Tibbs*, 2156–99; *Townsend*—2107–'18; killed Dunn—*Mitchell*; killed Rachel Hatcher—*Porter*, 2280.

—— Gallaway, drayman, killed a negro—*Tibbs*, 2173; *Porter*, 2280; *Robinson*, p. 344; shot Rachel Hatcher—*Mitchell*.

—— Cash, killed and robbed Charley Wallace—*Tibbs*, 2173; *Townsend*, 2211.

Charley Toler, a white boy in the crowd—*Tibbs*, 2200; shoots a negro—*Dawkins*, 2330.

Charley Smith, teacher, arrested for having a dead man's clothes—*McKetchum*, p. 346; *Tibbs*, 2200; *Townsend*, 2225.

—— Dunn, committed rape on Harriet Armour—*Armour*, 2458; robbery—*Hawkins*, p. 339.

—— Wilson, engaged in the robbery of Albert Harris—*Swan*, 2489.

—— Tyler, engaged in the robbery of Albert Harris—*Swan*—2489.

Chris Pigeon, grocer, with others, robbed and burned house of Lucy Hunt—*Hunt*, 3003.

—— Woods, arrested as the man who killed Ben Dennis—*McElvane*, 2938.

—— McElmore, boasted of killing five negroes—*Brooks*, 3310.

Mike Cotton, shooting of Richard Lane and little girl—*Lane*, 3497.

L. D. Young, shooting of Richard Lane and little girl—*Lane*, 3497.

Billy Barber, shooting of Richard Lane and little girl—*Lane*, 3497.

Tom Harris, beat and kicked colored man—*Johnson*, 3530.

—— Boyd, Irishman, in command of the mob that shot Adeline Miller; set on fire Rankin's school-house—*Thomas*, 3894.

—— Clemens, threatened Stanbrough—*Stanbrough*, 4027.

—— Parker, "shebang" keeper, followed a negro up, and shot into his house—*Todd*, 4287.

Captain Wilson, cigar shop, in charge of a crowd of incendiaries—*George*, 4327.

Billy Cook, shot at George Williams—*Robinson*, p. 319.

Richard Marsh, shot negro on Howard row—*Kyle*, p. 329; *White, Cotton*, p. 346.

Pat ——, an Irishman, visits a grocery near F. B. hospital, shot a negro—*Dunlap*, p. 330.

—— Burns, presented his pistol and threatened to shoot a colored man—*Smith*, p. 332.

Charley Lyn, assault on, and robbing of Lemuel Premier—*Premier*, p. 338.

Joe Chambers, assault on, and robbing of Lemuel Premier—*Premier*, p. 338.

Mr. Johnson, set fire to Caldwell Hall—*Caldwell*, p. 346.

Charley Galena, set fire to Caldwell Hall—*Caldwell*, p. 346.

Rachel Dobbs, robbed Hannah Hersey—*Hersey*, p. 349.

James Wallach, stabbing of Edward Evans—*Hall*, p. 349.

Simon Easley, robbed Alfred Boyd—*Boyd*, 353.

Charles Ruffin, robbed John Williams—*Williams*, p. 357.

Citizens of Memphis, conduct and feeling of—*Report*, p. 26; *Minority* do., p. 43; property holders and fixed population discourage riotous proceedings—*Stoneman*, 49–51; a class of agitators who keep up a bad state of feeling—54; desire to return to the Union, but do not love the flag—4439; national airs hissed and rebel airs cheered at the theatre—4447; about one-third loyal, the other two-thirds disloyal—*Davis*, 718; did not see any attempt to suppress the mob—*McGowan*, 1453; no measures taken by the better class of citizens to bring the rioters to justice—1455; two hundred private citizens, patrolling the streets, could have prevented trouble—1466; distinguished men going out and speaking to the crowd could have stopped it—1467; the better class of citizens would have taken any means in their power to have stopped it—*Irwin*, 1542; feeling towards the resident negroes has been perfectly kind—1548; relations with the resident negroes, friendly and agreea-

ble—*Keller*, 1595; nothing but the kindest feelings between the citizens and negroes—
Martin, 1669—*Wormley*, 4978; more kindly feeling between southerners and negroes
than between the negroes and northerners residing in the south—*Edmunds*, 1698; a prejudice since the colored people became free against their being here at all—*Beecher*, 1875; better
class of southern gentlemen have regretted very much what has occurred—*White*, 2241; a
class under the impression the negro was born to steal and lie—*White*, 2249; did not see
one good citizen participate in the riot in any way—*Dent*, 2276; no particular difference
in treatment of colored people between unconditional Union and southern men—*Sterling*—2398; did not care whether the Irish killed off all the negroes, or the negroes killed
off all the Irish—*Chapin*, 2799; saw none of our merchants or business men there; suppose that class of citizens do not usually participate in the doings of mobs—*Chapin*, 2794-
2797; almost all southern people felt rather hard against negroes who had fought against
the south—*Lewis*, 3925; five-sixths or nine-tenths sympathize with the rebellion, and pray
for Jeff. Davis, but very few entertain unkind feelings toward the negroes or northern people—*Lewis*, 3999; the fires of hatred burn as hot and deep down as they ever did—*Stanbrough*, 4034; disloyal conduct of—*Runkle*, 4567–'70; weapons are used by a low class of people, but the instigation comes from a class called respectable—*Runkle*, 4591; riot condemned
in the most unmeasured terms—*Miller*, 4619; no hostility towards northern men, unless
they are fussy in politics—*Miller*, 4613; treatment of northern men, open, generous, hospitable—*Cameron*, 4679; good feeling of better classes towards the colored people and northern people, and condemnation of the riots—*Ayrs*, 4705—*Parker*, 4723–'32—*Perkins*,
4744–'57—*Smith*, 4840–'50—*Wright*, 4879–'83—*Gridley*, 4901–'17—*McMahon*, 4932–'67—
Du Pre, 4998–5003.

Clifford, Lieutenant Walter, testimony of, 4143–'93; lieutenant Sixteenth United States infantry, 4143; in charge of United States soldiers sent out to suppress the riot, 4147; 150
or 200 white citizens firing into the cabins of colored people, 4154; cabins occupied by
women, children, and decrepid old men, 1456; the crowd a drunken, disorderly rabble,
4157; speech of Recorder Creighton, 4160; release by Captain Allyn of men arrested as
incendiaries, 4168; orders to shoot any one setting fire to a house, 4176; but for intervention of troops would not have been a house left in South Memphis, 4175.
Clusky, M. W., witness M. C., p. 328; editor of Memphis Avalanche; dissuaded mob from
"going for the Post;" character and conduct of the crowd.
Coe, William, testimony of, 1049–'84; blacksmith's shop broken open, clothes saturated with
oil and set on fire, shooting of witness threatened, 1056–'73; bad treatment of witness by
white people before and since he has been free, 1074–'83; against every colored person.
1084.
Caldwell, Joseph, witness F. B. C., p. 346; burning of Caldwell Hall.
Cole, Henrietta, witness F. B. C., p. 347; robbed.
Cole, John, witness F. B. C., p. 353; robbed.
Collins, Rev. J. T. C., witness M. C., p. 323; loss by burning Collins Chapel, $6,000.
Collins Chapel, members of, witnesses F. B. C., p. 353; loss by burning of Collins Chapel,
$25,000.
Colored citizens:
   Expression of after the riot was sorrow and depression, not a word or look of envy or hatred—*Tade*, 882–'83; never have seen any bad behaviour on the part of the blacks—*Brazier*, 1319; have acted very well—*McGowan*, 1414; general conduct peaceable—*Keller*,
   1593; indolence the only complaint, 1599; conduct has been first rate—*Martin*, 1670;
   in favor of limited negro suffrage—*Martin*, 1675; have always thought themselves better
   than the Irish—*Dent*, 2267; heard no cause of complaint of them—*Marsh*, 2323; conduct
   as good as that of the lower class of Irish—*Chapin*, 2801; good feeling of towards former
   masters, &c.—*Walker*, 5025; *Moultrie*, 5048; *Bradshaw*, 5058.
Colored soldiers:
   Conduct of—*Report*, p. 31; have not acted very properly several times—*McGowan*, 1414;
   their language sometimes was abominable, 1441; to police and Irishmen they were especially rude, 144; the soldier negroes outdid them all, 1446; have frequently seen them
   drunk and disorderly, using obscene and vulgar language—*Taylor*, 1508–'09; have seen
   white people drunk and using improper language more frequently, 1520; have seen instances of indecorous conduct on the streets, but do not think it has been general—*Irwin*,
   1540; excessively impertinent when drunk; knocked several of them over—*Keller*, 1596–
   '98; more quiet and orderly than other soldiers—*Hewitt*, 1620; have been addicted to
   pilfer and steal; addicted to drunkenness and disorder—*Bercher*, 1817–'21; conduct generally worse than white soldiers, but subject to greater provocation, 1823; conduct of
   very good indeed—*Sharp*, 2084; they have been very orderly and quiet—*White*, 2242;
   conduct as good as the average of white soldiers—*Chapin*, 2802; they have borne it
   (treatment of police) in a manner no other people would—*Garrett*, 3060; with one or
   two exceptions, they behaved very orderly—*Hastings*, 3183; conduct as good as any
   white troops he has ever known—*Helm*, 3390; obedient to orders, well disciplined, and
   respectful—*Pearce*, 3431; no number of white soldiers could be held in such subjection
   when their houses were being burned down as theirs were—*Durnin*, 3574; general

conduct good—*Lewis*, 3937 ; if the negroes had been a regiment of regulars they would have rushed out—*Allyn*, 4091.

Cook, M. R., witness M. C., p. 315 ; colored soldier killed on South street, near railroad depot.

Cooley, C. M., testimony of, 389–467 ; several persons, May 1, commenced beating a negro, who ran into a store on Beale street and escaped ; as they came out they attacked another negro, knocked him down and shot him in the gutter and killed him, 407–'46 ; a negro severely whipped on the street in the same vicinity, May 2, 456–457 ; no steps taken to punish these offences, 467.

Cooper, Mrs. S., testimony of, 3459–'81 ; house burned by police ; men fired on for trying to put out the fire, 3465.

Cornelius, Erastus, testimony of, 5114–'32 ; watchword of the mob at the fires, "Keno's correct," 5117 ; John C. Creighton in the crowd, 2120.

Cotton, Austin, testimony of, 1024–'48 ; was caught by citizen at Hollywood's grocery and held and pounded over the head by policeman, who accosted him, "Halt, you damned nigger," 1028–'33 ; was so much crippled as not to be able to work since, 1037 ; crowd then went after and killed Jackson Godell, 1035 ; has been treated and paid well by citizens, because he was humble like a slave, 1046.

Craig, Wm., Witness M. C , p. 322 ; shooting of negro by police on Beal street.

Cruse, George, witness F. B. C., p. 340 ; house burned.

Cumming, Gabriel, witness F. B. C., p. 357 ; shoe shop robbed.

Curley, Mrs. Kate, witness M. C., p. 318 ; commencement of riot ; colored man wounded.

Curtman, Adeline, witness F. B. C., p. 346 ; robbed.

Creighton, John C., recorder of Memphis, report of committee relative to, p. 23 ; Wednesday night with a crowd of incendiaries, drunk—*Oldridge*, 1352 ; his version of the commencement of the riot—*Sterling*, 2392 ; character of a clever, upright man—*MeElvane*, 2949 ; in the habit of drinking a good deal ; killed a man about six months ago—*McElvane*, 2950, 2951 ; always a very improper man to fill such a position—*Richards*, 3245 ; speeches of to the crowd—*Clifford*, 4160 ; *Todd*, 4284 ; *Myers*, p. 356 ; *Fox*, p. 322 ; *Mitcheler*, p. 355 ; with the sheriff handing round pistols—*Ryder*, 4217 ; recommended as United States marshal—*Ryder*, 4210 ; elections of, character, &c.—*Richards*, 5160–'64 ; Vice President of Johnson Club—*Perkins*, 4802.

Creighton, Dr. R. W., testimony of, 1366–'78 ; dressed the wounds of or attended three policemen, 1370–'73 ; wound of Stevens, which was mortal, probably made by his own pistol, 1373.

D.

Davis, Burton, witness F. B. C., p. 341 : house burned and robbed.

Davis, F. S., testimony of, 695–751 ; president of First National Bank, 695 : negro man killed in front of witness's house, 702 ; witness's coachman, Taylor Hunt, shot and wounded on his way home, 703 ; character of the newspapers, 715, 716 ; have not considered it necessary for citizens to take any action in regard to the matter, 729 ; thinks the negroes were some to blame the first day, after that they were not, 741.

Davis, Lummard, witness F. B. C., p. 344 ; assault by Jerry Erwright.

Davis, Mollie, testimony of, 2990–'97 ; house burned by John Eagan and his crowd ; loss, $550, 2994–'95.

Davis, Norris, witness F. B. C., p. 343 ; house and contents burned.

Dawkins, Daniel, testimony of, 2329–'36 ; negro shot by Charley Toler, 2380 ; witness struck by policeman who was killed five minutes after, 2331 ; black man across the bridge shot and beaten to death by police, 2334.

Deadwiley, John, witness F. B. C., p. 352 ; house and contents burned.

Default, Colman, witness F. B. C., p. 337 ; shot by Roach : robbed and house burned.

Dent, H. G., testimony of, 2260–'76 ; negro badly wounded, 2263 ; character and conduct of the crowd, 2265 ; bad conduct of colored soldiers, 2270–'74 ; mob composed of Irish police and rowdy population of the city, 2275.

Dilts, Mrs. Ellen, testimony of, 167–268 ; collision, April 13, between four police and three or four negroes ; one negro beaten with pistol, another struck with a brick, 172–181 ; May 1, police and negroes had a battle on South street, 190 ; colored man struck and his head knocked against a post by policeman, 190 ; heard policeman say, "Kill every nigger, no matter who," 190 ; one colored man beaten at witness's gate.

Dilts, Mrs. Rachel, testimony of ; same occurrence, April 30, as testified to by Ellen Dilts, 272–292 ; May 1, crowd of colored persons passed down Main street, followed by police, both parties firing, 293–306 ; negro struck with pistol by policeman ; May 1, (See Ellen Diltz,) 307.

Dilts, Samuel, testimony of, 1259–'70 : a large crowd came past house of witness ; shots pretty thick ; kept out of the way, 1264 ; character of the conversation of the crowd was, "Kill every d——d nigger; shoot him."

Donahue, James E., testimony of, 2957–'69 ; three shots fired by policemen at a house in which there were women and children, 2959 ; three colored men badly beaten and used up in charge of police, 2960 ; relations of colored and white people, 2966–'68.

Dunlap, James, witness M. C., p. 330; firing into Freedmen's Bureau hospital; an Irishman shoots a negro.

Dupee, Mary, witness F. B. C., p. 356; beaten and robbed.

Du Pre, L. J., testimony of, 4996–5015; editor Memphis Bulletin, 4996; relations of citizens with colored people, 5000–'01; relations with northern people, 5002–'03; composition of the mob, 5007–'09; franchise law, 5009–'12; riot condemned by people of Memphis, 5013.

Durnin, Captain Thomas J., testimony of, 3533–'92; Captain sixteenth United States infantry, 5534; attempt of colored soldierss to get their arms, 3539; general management and conduct of the colored soldiers, 3547–'74; Mississippi regulators, 3539; testimony of Upman relative to colored soldiers firing from near the fort contradicted, 3562; sorry the men could not get arms; seemed like a brutish slaughter on the part of the mob, 3589.

E.

Edmunds, A. N., testimony of, 1680–1708; cause of difficulty during the riots of the witness Egbert, his living with a colored wife and trading with negroes, 1685; kindly feeling between southerners and negroes, 1697; generality of citizens in favor of stopping the riot, 1702; tried to protect the colored people as much as possible, 1701.

Edwards, Marcus, testimony of, 5181–'85; copied extracts from newspapers under instructions of General Runkle.

Education of colored children, schools for; testimony of *Tade, Waters, Runkle,* and *Miller.*

Egbert, David T., testimony of, 1320–'39; was threatened, as an abolitionist, with violence, 1324.

Erickson, Frank, coroner, testimony of, 1176–1206; held inquest on ten bodies in the neighborhood of South street, and three others, negroes, alleged to have been killed in the riot; also on the body of one white man, (Ben Dennis, 1184; the white man was talking to a negro, when a fireman said, "This is no time to be talking to niggers," and shot him, 1197; inquests held on the bodies of B. Dennis, Henry Williams, William Saunders, Richard ——, J. Hare, Bill ——, Rachel ——, Robert Collins, Jack Robertson, three unknown colored men, William ——, and Daniel Hawkins, 1206.

Escue, Marshall, witness F. B. C., p. 342; house and contents burned.

Evans, Catherine, witness F. B. C., p. 348; husband stabbed six times.

F.

Fenster, Nathan, witness F. B. C., p. 337; burning of two houses.

Finn, James, witness M. C., p. 332; commencement of riot; shooting of Stevens.

Finne, F., testimony of, 344–387; two of the party who robbed Albert Harris, in charge of property taken under execution at witness's store the day of the robbery, 349.

Fire Department, list of persons employed in, p. 370.

Fisk, Major General Clinton B., testimony of, 96–104; organized commission to investigate the riots, 99; instructions of to Freedmen's Bureau superintendents and agents, *Runkle*, 4537–'38.

Fitzgibbons, Edward, witness M. C., p. 323, negro fired at in Chelsea.

Fletcher, Jane, witness F. B. C., p. 346; shot in the back,

Ford, Newton, testimony of, 4868–'71; confirms statement of W. F. Taylor.

Fowned, Harry, witness F. B. C., p. 340; shot through the shoulder by Jerry.

Fox, Mrs. Mary, witness M. C., p. 329; remarks of a drunken man.

Fox, Thomas, witness M. C., p. 322; remarks of J. C. Creighton; conduct of the mob.

Franchise law of Tennessee, p. 361; has operated most injuriously to the preservation of peace and order—*Minority report,* p. 42; no community would be satisfied with laws enacted by a small minority—*Stoneman,* 4479; qualified voters a worse element than those disfranchised—*Hunter,* 514; better class of people disfranchised by present law—*Irwin,* 1560; the law unconstitutional—*Martin,* 1669; *Cameron,* 4695; bad effects of the law, 1673; in favor of limited negro suffrage, 1675; operation of the law—*Lewis,* 4006–'11; *Miller,* 4618; *Cameron,* 4676; *Ayrs,* 4712; *Perkins,* 4754, 4810–'24; *Smith,* 4850; *Wright,* 4884; *Gridley,* 4911–'12; *Du Pre,* 5010.

Freedmen's Bureau, a guard sent to protect—*Stoneman,* 4460; favorable operation of—*Lewis,* 4002–'05; one feature of popular, another odious—*Runkle,* 4596; operations of, in contracts with freedmen—*Runkle,* 4698, 4603.

French, Anthony, witness F. B. C., p. 350; assaulted, and house burned.

Fuller, E. O., witness M. C., p. 317; negro beaten and killed near railroad depot.

G.

Galloway, M. M., witness M. C., p. 325, editor of the Avalanche; shouting for the Avalanche by the crowd; seized hold of witness to raise him on their shoulders; proposals to mob the post; crowd appealed to by witness to desist; violent acts of the crowd; negro waving a black flag. Recalled, p. 333; authorship of articles in Avalanche.

Gardner, Margaret, testimony of, 933, 958; four policemen carried a man to the station-house, May 1st, on a dray; every time he struggled they would strike him with clubs, 937.

Garey, Mrs. Sophia, testimony of, 1234–1259; robbery of Lock's and Sneed's houses by Callahan, McGinn, and others, 1244; Callahan fired at everybody that came along, 1249; shooting of Rhoda Jacobs, 1245; a young man wears off the hoop and balmoral skirt of the girl who had been shot the night before, 1244.

Garrett, B. G., chief of police, report of committee relative to, p. 25; testimony relative to— see *Police*; witness M. C., p. 327; efforts to prevent violence during the riots; Sullivan relieved from police for theft and reappointed by police committee. Recalled, p. 334; did not state the negroes contemplated rising.

Garrett, S. S., testimony of, 3030–3106; was first lieutenant of United States colored artillery, 3031; commencement of riot second day, shooting of negroes by forty or fifty police, no firing by negroes, 3033–'50; conduct of the colored soldiers, their relations with police, &c., 3051–3104.

George, Ann, testimony of, 4320–4338; Captain Wilson in charge of a company of incendiaries.

George, Hannah, testimony of, 3757–3780; acts of the mob.

Gibbons, Asbury, witness F. B. C., p. 339; assaulted and robbed.

Gibbons, M. J., witness M. C., p. 325; house burned on Echols street, between Vance and Elliot streets; loss, $1,000.

Gibson, Isaac, witness F. B. C., p. 355; robbed.

Gillam, Lauzie, witness F. B. C., p. 342; knocked down and robbed.

Gillian, Louisa, witness F. B. C., p. 355; robbed.

Glasgow, A. M., witness M. C., p. 319; house set on fire, and witness fired on while extinguishing it; loss, $50.

Godell, Lavinia, testimony of, 549, 573; husband, Jackson Godell, drayman, killed May 1st; went out to get some meal, and a few moments after found him shot, lying in the gutter; left him and went back to the house, through fear; next morning saw his body at the station-house, but was not permitted to take it away, and does not know where it is buried, 554; while he lay in the gutter a policeman said, "Here's a d—d nigger, if he is not dead we will finish him," 572.

Goodlow, Jane, witness F. B. C., p. 337; wounded in the arm.

Grady, Mrs. Mary, testimony of, 2702–2725; negro man on horseback killed; witness's house broken open and robbed; attempts to violate colored woman and little girl, 2705; witness's store robbed of $200 in money and $90 worth of groceries, 2715; Henry Bankin's house burned, 2712; black man killed by the bayou, 2712.

Gray, Mrs. J. A., witness M. C., p. 325 colored man lying dead on the corner of Main and Trezevant streets.

Green, Eliza, witness F. B. C., p. 347; robbed.

Green, William, witness F. B. C., p. 343; robbed.

Green, Samuel, witness F. B. C., p. 353; house burned, and robbed, &c.

Greenlaw, W. B., jr., witness M. C., p. 316; dead bodies of three negroes; fires; conduct of the crowd.

Gridley, Martin, testimony of, 4900–4927; good feeling of citizens towards the colored people, 4901; not much pity for the discharged soldiers if they got killed, 4907; no hostile feelings towards northerners unless on account of politics, 4913; franchise law, 4911–'12.

Groves, Eliza, witness F. B. C., p. 342; house burned.

H.

Haggerty, James, witness M. C., p. 326; shanties burned in South Memphis. Recalled, p. 329; advised against burning Armon's house, because white people were on each side.

Hall, Cornelia, witness F. B. C., p. 349; stabbing of Edmund Evaus.

Hall, Solomon, witness F. B. C., p. 350; assaulted by police.

Handy, John, testimony of, 3593–3603; Harry Towns, Joe Davis, and witness wounded, 3596–3601.

Hammond, George W., testimony of, 1910–1925; sergeant 16th United States infantry, 1910; conversation with the proprietor of the National theatre, 1914.

Harris, Albert, testimony of, 126–166; house entered by police and others under pretence of searching for arms, 134; robbed by same party of $350, 144.

Harris, Charles, witness F. B. C., p. 344; killing of Eli Cherry.

Harris, Francis, witness F. B. C., p. 348; house burned.

Harris, Rachel, witness F. B. C., p. 345; Mary Ella Brown robbed.

Harrison, Mose, witness F. B. C., p. 354; trunk and clothes burned.

Hastings, E. C., witness M. C., p. 331; negro shot and beaten, corner of Avery and South streets.

Hastings, Lieut. Frederick, testimony of, 3125–3219; first lieutenant 3d United States colored artillery, 3125; commencement of riot, 3131; interview between Mayor Park and officers at the fort, 3134; conduct of posse and crowd, 3138–'40; one shot fired from parapet by colored soldier, 3147; statement of witness Upman, of firing by colored soldiers, incorrect, 3152–'57; good conduct of colored soldiers, 3170; speech to the soldiers by Colonel Kapner, 3166; guarantee of the mayor that there should be no further violence, 3167.

Hawkins, Sallie, witness F. B. C., p. 339; robbed, and husband killed.

Hawley, Matilda, witness F. B. C., p. 339; riotous conduct of colored man, George Howard; acts of the mob.

Hart, Rose, witness F. B. C., p. 350; house burned.

Hayes, Mrs. Molly, testimony of, 2681–2701; house of Harriet Armour broken into, 2689.

Haynes, Landon C., speech of, at Memphis tournament—*Perkins*, 4827.

Haynes, Thomas M., witness M. C., p. 323; negro robbed between Court and Madison streets.

Henderson, Lily, witness F. B. C., p. 355; robbed, and house burned.

Hersey, Hannah, witness F. B. C., p. 349; robbed.

Helm, James E., testimony of, 3375–3411; lieutenant 3d United States colored artillery, 3376; conduct of the colored troops, 3390.

Hewitt, Mrs. Minerva, testimony of, 1610–1620; two negro men abused and shot at, 1615; good character of negro soldiers, 1620.

Hinton, Albert, witness, F. B. C., p. 350; robbed.

Hogan, George, testimony of, 1887–1909; sergeant sixteenth United States infantry, 1887; ordered out to quell the disturbance, 1890; searched colored people for arms—had no orders to search white people, 1891; threats of the mob, 1900–'03; the fires were under full headway Wednesday night before the troops were ordered out, and it was impossible to prevent the buildings from burning down, 1904.

Hollywood, John, testimony of, 990–1000; assault on Austin Cotton, 992; killing of Jackson Godell, 995.

Hood, J. A., witness, M. C., p. 335; saw boy wave a black flag.

Hood, William B., witness, M. C., p. 320; George Clapp and Franklin Gross severely wounded.

Howlet, Charley, witness, F. B. C., p. 347; robbed.

Howley, Matilda, testimony of, 2740–2756; colored soldier named Charley killed, 2743; Uncle Dick killed in bed, 2744; George Howard, a negro engaged in the riots against colored men, 2744–'49.

Hubbard, William C., witness, M. C., p. 331; riot predetermined.

Hunt, James, witness, F. B. C., p. 348; robbed.

Hunt, Henry, witness, F. B. C., p. 351; house burned and robbed.

Hunt, Lucy, testimony of, 3000–'09; house burned—would have been burned in it but for regulars, 3003; robbed of $325, 3004; shooting of Joe Lundy and another colored man, 3007.

Hunt, Taylor, testimony of, 1001–'23; coachman of Mr. Davis, 1002; while going home, night of May 2d, was shot in the head by policeman, who then asked if he was a soldier; wound serious, 1005–'06.

Hunter, William, testimony of, 484–548; judge of criminal court, 484; no steps taken to bring offending parties to justice, 492; no white persons arrested; negroes arrested and taken to station-house for protection, 497; grand jury not called because military were about investigating, 499; chances of white persons being convicted of offences against negroes remote, because of material from which jurors must be selected, 507; qualified voters a worse element than those disfranchised, 514.

Hustin, James, witness, F. B. C., p. 354; assaulted and house burned.

Hutt, Brance, testimony of, 574–602; was living with Albert Harris when his house was robbed, 580; statement of the occurrence, 580–592.

I.

Ingram, Eliza, witness, F. B. C., p. 345; robbed.

Irwin, Dr. William F., testimony of, 1524–'77; attended policeman who had been shot, 1527; suggested that Stevens's own pistol might have caused his wound, 1529; saw Dunn, the fireman, evidently in a dying condition, 1532; dressed wounds of two negroes, 1527; bad conduct of colored soldiers, 1535–'41; the riot a matter of regret with better class of citizens, 1542; originated between lower class of whites and negroes, 1542; sentiments of the people towards resident negroes perfectly kind, 1548; no difference between conduct of negro and white soldiers—equally drunk, 1552; no public demonstration against the riot because of letter of and commission ordered by General Stoneman, 1559; election of and character of Memphis authorities, 1560–'67.

J.

Jackson, Edward, witness, F. B. C., p. 339; robbed and house burned.

Jackson, Henry, testimony of, 468–483; struck under the chin May 2d by policeman until blood ran down all over his clothes, 473–476.

Jackson, Mary A., testimony of, 2130–'49; negro, a stranger from the country, killed in front of witness's house, 2134; white man shot down by negro, 2143.

Jacobs, Rhoda, testimony of, 2031–'40; house broken into at night by white men and witness shot while she was in bed, 2032.

Jean, Lorenzo, testimony of, 2013–'30; ten or twelve shots fired at a negro without hitting him, 2017; negro shot in the arm, 2019; a sick man by the name of Shedd taken out of his house, made to stand against his door-casing, and killed, 2021.

Johnson, Billy, testimony of, 3524–'32; saw Roach shoot two men, 3529; kicked and beaten by Tom Harris, 3530.

Johnson, Colonel Charles F., testimony of, 105–125; president of commission to investigate the riots, 109; order of General Fisk organizing the commission, 111.

Johnson, Clary, witness, F. B. C., p. 342; house burned; robbing of Cary Campbell's house.

Johnson, Dick, witness, F. B. C., p. 347; assaulted and robbed.

Johnson, J. H., witness, M. C., p. 315; commencement of riot; several unknown negroes killed.

Johnson, Peter, witness, F. B. C., p. 346; house burned and robbed.

Jones, Aaron, witness, F. B. C., p. 341; robbed.

Jones, Adam, witness, F. B. C., p. 341; robbed and abused.

Jones. George, testimony of, 1085–'95; Alexander's wagon-shop burned, 1088.

Jones, Major, witness, F. B. C., p. 342; wounded and house burned.

Jones, Monroe, witness, F. B. C., p. 341; shooting of Willis Jones.

Jones, Peter, witness, F. B. C.; shoe-shop robbed.

Jordan, Mary, testimony of, 3860–'84; house set on fire; with her children, was shot at while attempting to escape.

Journal of committee, p. 45–49.

K.

Keller, Dr. J. M., testimony of, 1578–1610; summoned by Sheriff Winters as a part of his *posse*; went in the capacity of surgeon; negro wounded in the hands of the mob, told them stop; they were also ordered to desist by Captain Garrett; called off to attend Policeman Stevens, 1583; shot must have come from a second party, 1589; relations between men of property and business men and the resident negroes kind, 1592; general conduct of resident negroes very peaceable, 1593; bad conduct of negro soldiers, 1596–1603; general conduct of mobs, 1609–'10.

Kelley, Georgean, witness, F. B. C., p. 346; contents of house burned.

Kenney, Margaret, witness, F. B. C., house and contents burned; colored man shot.

Killed during the riot:

Jackson Godell—*Cooley*, 407–422; *Godell*, 557–573; *Moller*, 755; *Hollywood*, 995; negro man, in front of house of F. S. Davis, on Bank street—*Davis*, 702; Rachel Hatcher, shot and burned—*Sneed*, 964; *Tibbs*, 2187; *Townsend*, 2211; *Porter*, 2283; four men, Wednesday morning, killed by posse—*Quimby*, 1099; Henry Williams, *inquest on*, p. 109; B. Dennis, (white,) *inquest on*, p. 109—*Myers*, 3115; *Mitchell*, 5097; Wm. Saunders, *inquest on*, p. 110; Richard ———, *inquest on*, p. 110; James Hare, *inquest on*, p. 110; Bill ———, *inquest on*, p. 110; Robert Collins, *inquest on*, p. 111; Jack Robertson, *inquest on*, p. 111; unknown negro, corner Webster street and Raven avenue, *inquest on*, p. 111; unknown negro, Clay street, near Raven avenue, *inquest on*, p. 112; William ———, corner Avery and South streets, *inquest on*, p. 112; Daniel Hawkins— S. Hawkins, p. 339, *inquest on*, p. 112, Hastings p. 331; unknown negro, 133 Beal street, *inquest on*, p. 112; two colored soldiers shot—*Beatty*, p. 1267; negro knocked on to his face and shot five or six times after he was down—*Brazier*, 1277, 1295; Eli Cherry, corner South and Main streets—*Harris*, p. 344; *Bond*, 2979; *Oldridge*, 1346; two other bodies in the vicinity of the graveyard—*Oldridge*, 1346; negro near the railroad—*Oldridge*, 1350; *Taylor*, 1476; John Stevens, policeman—*Creighton*, 1373; *Keller*, 1583; *Irwin*, 1528; two negroes, one of them on Beal street—*Randolph*, 1381, 1383; negro soldier, lying dead. just killed by a policeman—*McGowan*, 1409; Dunn, fireman, in a dying condition, wound in back of his head—*Irwin*, 1532–'34; *Lynch*, 2254; killed by Pendergrast; *Mitchell*, killing of—*Alex. McQuarters*, 317; negro soldier shot by the Palmers near the railroad depot—*Walker*, 1792; two negroes shot by the mob—*Lloyd*, 1975, 1988; negro man pursued and shot at the bayou—*Turner*, 1996; Shedd, a sick man, taken out of his bed, stood up against the door-casing and shot—*Jean*, 2021; negro from the country chased and shot—*Jackson*, 2124; Bob Taylor killed—*Tibbs*, 2176; Charley Wallace, shot by Cash—*Tibbs*, 2173; *Townsend*, 2210; Fayette Dickerson called out of his house and shot—*Dickerson*, p. 358; *Tibbs*, 2197; *Quimby*, 1154; two colored soldiers killed by Pendergrast and his crowd—*Tibbs*, 2154–'61; colored soldier shot by Roach and Gallaway—*Tibbs*, 2173; *Porter*, 2280; Lewis Robertson's tongue shot out by Pendergrast—*Townsend*, 2217; negro shot from a dray by Roach—*Townsend*, 2210; negro shot on corner of Causey and South streets—*Brasier*, 1277–'95; *Lynch*, 2254; negro beaten and shot on Beal street, near the bridge—*Lynch*, 2254; negro knocked down and stabbed—*Porter*, 2310; negro soldier knocked down, tramped on and stabbed, corner of Vine and St. Martin streets—*Rezzonner*, 2325; negro, near the bridge, shot and beaten to death by police—*Dawkins*, 2334; *Williams*, 2511; Joe Lundy, colored soldier, shot—*Williams*, 2510; *Hunt*, 3007; Shadrack Garret, taken out of bed, made stand up against the door and shot; *M. Marshall*, 2529; *J. Marshall*, 2557; William Withers, George Cobb George Black, Ike Richardson, and another colored soldier shot—*Clurry*, 2608; *Pearce*, 3418; *Baker*, p. 318; black man shot from a horse—*Grady*, 2705; black man by the bayou fired at twenty times—*Grady*, 2712; Charley, a colored soldier, shot by police—*Howley*, 2743; Uncle Dick shot in bed—*Howley*, 2746; negro shot and lying in the gutter—*Pigeon*, 2760; negro lying on sidewalk at the Beal street market—*Chapin*, 2786; colored soldier shot in the neck by O. Hearn, and killed, corner Mulberry street and Brown avenue 2978; colored soldier shot six times by the railroad—*Hunt*, 3007; colored man knocked down and shot by the bayou—*Black*, 3023; Shade Long, sick, taken out of bed, robbed and shot—*Long*, 3519; colored soldier Jim, and another colored man shot by Roach—*Johnson*, 3529; colored man near the railroad, by policeman McCormick—*Worset*, 3708; Robert George, by policemen—*Wardlaw*, 3829; two colored soldiers—*Wardlaw*, 3830; Adeline Miller shot—Boyd in command of the mob—*Thomas*, 3891; *Cicalla*, 4304; *Menard*, 4313; colored soldier shot by Cash—*Mitchell*, 5102; colored soldier at the bayou shot by Pendergrast—*Mitchell*, 5103; Wm. Henry shot at the Gayoso house—*Saunders*, 5169; Freeman Jones, shot in the mouth, near Rankins' schoolhouse; colored soldier, corner Linden and St. Martin streets; two negroes on the bridge; negro woman shot through the stomach, corner Shelby and South streets; colored man, South street, between Causey and Shelby—*Rankin*, 313; negro knocked down with clubbed musket and shot several times while down—*Yerger*, p. 315; *Cook*, p, 315; Levi Baker, corner Main street and Butler avenue—*Williams*, 2511; *Baker*, 318; negro woman, Emeline, shot on South street, near Mr. Kelly's store—*Yates*, p. 321; negro lying dead, corner of Main and Trezevant streets—*Gray*, p. 225; negro, corner Clay and Hernando streets—*Peplow*, p. 330; woman shot on South street, near Bayou bridge—*Lee*, p. 331; Robert Carlton shot—*J. Carlton*, p. 344; George Williams, stabbed—*Williams*, p. 350; John Green, killed; Ida Green and child, killed and burned up—*Green*, p. 353; *Wilson*, p. 353; *Lee*, p. 331.

K.

Kyle, Henry J., witness M. C., p. 329; negro shot on Howard Row, by Richard Marsh.

L.

Lacey, Edmund, testimony of, 1725–1750; was shot through the shoulder and robbed for having been a soldier, 1730–40.
Lane, Emma, testimony of, 3491–3505; husband and little girl shot, by policemen and firemen, 3497.
Lane, John W., witness F. B. C., p. 348; robbed.
Lane, Perry, witness F. B. C., p. 344; house burned.
Lane, Primus, testimony of, 901–932; house entered Wednesday night by six men and set on fire; witness and his wife robbed and kept in the house until house was partially burned up, 908–918; lost all the property he had, 930.
Lane, Richard, witness F. B. C., p. 349; shot at, witness and child wounded.
Lanford, J. T., testimony of, 3618–3698; in charge of posse, statement of what was done.
Lee, Ellen, witness F. B. C., p. 337; robbed of clothes, &c.
Lee, Frank, testimony of, 1709–1724; was turned out of his house while sick with the small pox, 1715–'19; old man Billy saw the crowd coming, ran under his house, but was shot through the bowels, 1722.
Lee, Lucinda, witness M. C., p. 331; woman and child burned and woman shot on South street, near bayou bridge.
Lemuir, Penny, witness F. B. C, p. 343; killing of John Robinson.
Leonard, Hon. Thomas, witness M. C., p. 314; conduct of the mob.
Lewis, Barbour, testimony of, 3910–4020; two negro prisoners beaten and maltreated by the mob, 3916; conduct of the mob and of the negroes, 3917–'18; fourteen or fifteen dead bodies, 3924; feeling of the southern people towards the negroes, 3925; conduct of colored soldiers, 3927–'30; murder of negro by policeman previous to the riot, 3934; murderer released on writ of *habeas corpus*, 3941; condition of Union people in case of withdrawal of troops, 3949–'55; no law for payment of riot damages, 3958; probabilities against the negro in any case in court between him and a white man, 3862–'64; status of military commissions, 3973; effect of newspaper teachings, 3982–'96; good effect of Freedmen's Bureau, 4002–05; franchise law, operation of, 4006–'11; composition of the mob, 4013–'20.
Lewis, John, witness F. B. C., p. 337; robbed of money and gun.
Littlefield, James M., witness M. C., p. 315; white man wounded in the back, carried into blacksmith shop corner of Causey and Vance streets.
Littlefield, Vesta E, testimony of, 1621–'27; negro caught by the mob and shot, 1623–'25; mob composed mostly of policemen and Irishmen, 1626.
Lloyd, Dr. Charles S., testimony of, 1972–'88; they were just hunting up these men, some running one way and some another; negro killed on Main street, 1975; efforts of Captain Garrett to stop the shooting, 1977; violence attempted on the partner of Dr. McGowan, 1983; negro killed right before witness's door, 1987.

Lock, Adam, testimony of, 1212–'45; history of commencement of riot, 1220; house of witness set on fire Wednesday night; shots fired at witness for trying to put out the fire, 1227; robbed by McGinn, Callahan, and others, 1228; Minter shot and robbed by Callahan, 1241; loss to witness by the riots, $1,500.
Long, Fannie, witness F. B. C., p. 255; house burned.
Long, Sarah, testimony of, 3514–'23; robbing and killing of Shade Long, a sick man, 3519.
Lowder, Bridget, witness F. B. C., p. 356; shooting and abuse of Solomon Pickett.
Lumpkins, Tony, witness F. B. C., p. 348.
Lynch, Dr. Joseph E., testimony of, 2252–'59; negro shot corner of Causey and South streets; another beaten and shot to death on Beal street, near the bridge; found Dunn, fireman, in a dying condition, 2254; second examination of, 5133–'40; wound of Dunn, fireman, apparently made with a musket ball from behind

M.

McKeon, W. J., witness M. C., p. 325; riotous conduct of pic-nic party.
McKetchum, Caledonia, witness F. B. C., p. 346; conversation with Charley Smith and Charley Toler.
McMahon, D., witness M. C., p. 332; captain of police; names of men on duty at the commencement of riot.
McMahan, J. H., testimony of, 4928–'67; editor of the Appeal newspaper, 4928; friendly relations between citizens and negroes, 4932; elements of disorder, thieves, pickpockets, and burglars; the "mackerel brigade," 4935; teachings of the newspapers, 4940; relations with northern men, hostility to, only, on account of personal deportment and the doctrines they teach, 4941–'67; the newspapers and the radicals, 4057–'67.
McPherson, Mrs. P. P., witness M. C., p. 316; threats of the crowd.
McQuarters, Alexander, witness M. C., p. 317; killing of fireman Dunn.
Malone, John, witness F. B. C., p. 341; robbed.
McCord, George, witness F. B. C., p. 350; shot and robbed.
McCullom, Jasper, witness F. B. C., p. 343; robbed.
Mackerel brigade, boys, thieves, pickpockets, &c., engaged in the riot—*Winters*, 649; *McMahan*, 4935.
McElvane, W. G., testimony of, 2934–2956; station-house keeper, 2934; arrest and release of the murderer of Dennis, 2938; character of Recorder Creighton, 2949–'53.
McGhee, Margaret, witness F. B. C., p. 356; shooting and abuse of Solomon Pickett.
McGowan, Dr. Robert, testimony of, 1388–1468; attended a policeman shot on Causey street, 1393; police and posse made an indiscriminate charge on all men, women, and children they could see who were colored, 1396; police and mob ran up to one on the bridge, shot him down and beat him to death; another man in the bayou shot down and beat afterwards, 1401; saw three or four more lying dead, 1402; threatened with violence as an abolitionist and for protecting a negro boy in his office, 1402–1406; was brought out and would have been shot but for intervention of captain of police, 1407–1411; negro soldier saw lying dead, just killed by policeman, 1409; attack was made upon citizen and soldier negroes indiscriminately, 1415; fifty or sixty negroes firing towards the police, the police retreating, 1417–1421; crowd composed principally of police, hackmen, draymen, &c., 1439; bad conduct of negro soldiers, 1441–1449; did not see any of the better class of citizens attempt to suppress the mob, 1453; the authorities could have stopped it without difficulty, but a private citizen would have had no chance, 1461; if a force of 200 private citizens had gone out and patrolled the streets it would have prevented trouble, 1466.
Marshall, John, testimony of, 2556–2566; shooting of Shadrach Garrett, 2557; shooting of witness for helping to put out a fire, 2560.
Marshall, Julia, witness F. B. C., p. 352; house and contents burned.
Marshall, Maria, testimony of, 2528–2555; killing and robbing of Shadrach Garrett, a sick man, taken from his bed, 2529–'40; shooting of witness's husband, 2544.
Marsh, P. G., testimony of, 2309–2314; negro knocked down, stabbed, and killed, 2310–'11.
Martin, John, testimony of, 1628–1679; attack of Irish on negroes in Chelsea on Friday succeeding the riot, 1632; co-operated with citizens to investigate the riot, but was ignored entirely by General Stoneman, 1635; did not understand Stoneman's proclamation to prevent the rioters from being brought to justice, 1643; understood it as declaring martial law, 1647; has not seen any respectable gentleman who did not deprecate this thing, 1655; character and antecedents of Mayor Park, 1656; jurors taken from all classes, 1662; satisfied you could get men here who would punish such outrages, 1663; bad effect of the franchise law, 1666; older and better class of citizens acquiesce in the present condition of things, and have the kindest feelings for the negroes, 1669; election held in violation of the franchise law, believing it to be unconstitutional, 1669; conduct of the negroes first rate, 1670; in favor of limited negro suffrage, 1675.
Mason, Wiley, witness F. B. C., p. 357; threatened.
Mayor of Memphis. (See John Park.)
Meadows, Andrew, witness M. C., p. 319; wounded, robbed, and house burned.
Meadows, Maggie, witness M. C., p. 319; robbed and house burned.

Means, Abram, testimony of, 2370–2388; burning of Adam Lock's house, 2371; five colored men shot dead, 2384; commencement of riot, 2387.

Mechan, Jas. E., witness M. C., p. 320; burning encouraged.

Meehan, Jas., witness M. C., p. 322; Jas. Schools and Jacob Herd called for matches.

Menard, Ginnie, testimony of, 4310–4319; shooting of Adeline Miller.

Mereweather, Mary A., witness F. B. C., p. 340; house and contents burned.

Military force, required for guarding public property and executing the laws—*Stoneman*, 4449–4453; no efficient remedy short of—*Hunter*, 516–525; if the troops were away, all northern men of objectionable opinions would have to leave—*Brooks*, 3335; no northern man who sympathized with Congress could remain here in comfort—*Lewis*, 3949; a thousand men, not including women and chidren, would have to leave—*Lewis*, 3954; I and twenty more of my friends would have to go away—*Stansbrough*, 4031; had there been no troops here ten thousand troops would have been needed a few days afterwards—*Allyn*, 4098; they would have burned every negro dwelling in the city—*Clifford*, 4177; if force were withdrawn, there are many men in this town who could not live here—*Ryder*, 4221: more safety in its presence—*Smith*, 4849.

Miller, Pitser, testimony of, 4607–4667; kind feeling towards the negroes, 4610; a little jealousy against a northern man when he is a little fussy about politics—none when they come and attend to their business, 4613; present city officials would not get the votes of one-tenth the citizens of Memphis, 4617; riots condemned in unmeasured terms, 4619; definition of radicalism, 4633–'36; probability of bringing the rioters to punishment, 4642–'43; what Memphis people are doing for the negroes—loyalty, &c., 4644–'46.

Minter, Andrew, testimony of, 2348–2369; saw as many as fifty colored men shot, 2350; eight colored soldiers killed within three hundred yards, 2352; colored soldier killed before Callahan's door by a man on horseback, 2353–'54; over fifty killed, 2356; witness's door broke open, shot and stabbed in bed, robbed, and house set on fire by Callahan, 2361; loss $1,000, 2365.

Mitchell, James Carroll, testimony of, 5084–5113; shooting of white man (Dunn) by Pendergrast, 5097; colored soldier shot by Cash, 5102; colored soldier shot by Pendergrast, 5103; shooting of Rachel Hatcher by Galloway, 5109.

Mitchell, Peter, witness F. B. C., p. 358; robbed and assaulted.

Mitcheler, Alexander, witness F. B. C., speech of J. C. Creighton.

Mob, ultimate purposes of; universal massacre; universal burning; an organized attempt to get possession of the State government—*Allyn*, 4100; would have burned every negro dwelling in the city—*Clifford*, 4177.

Mob, expressions of; "kill every nigger, no matter who, men or women"—*Dilts*, 190; "they were going to shoot every d—d nigger"—*Moller*, 760; "the G—d d—d niggers ought to be killed altogether, no matter, the small and the big ones," 769; character of the conversation of the crowd was, "kill every d—d nigger, shoot him"—*Dilts*, 1269; they were "going to burn every nigger building, every nigger church, and every G—d d—d s—n of a b—h that taught a nigger"—*Oldridge*, 1358; police said there had been a hell of a fight on South street with the niggers; one said, "I am going out to kill a nigger;" he went out and shot the first one he met—*Creighton*, 1370; "you d—d Yankee s—n of a b—h, you can't live here; we'll burn you out"—*McGowan*, 1411; the general talk seemed to be that they were going to shoot down the d—d niggers—*Taylor*, 1475; they wanted every G—d d—d nigger to be cut off from the face of the earth, massacred, burned out, &c.—*Hogan*, 1900; they spoke of the Yankees, abolitionists, and, in fact, the whole northern people as nothing but a pack of fire-eaters and hell-hounds—*Hogan*, 1903; were going round hunting colored men, and were going to kill every d—d nigger they found—*Sharp*, 2066; they allowed they were going to kill the G—d d—d nigger soldiers who were fighting against their rights—the black s—s of b—s—*Summers*, 2346; they would kill every d—d one who had blue clothes on—*Williams*, 2510; it is white man's day now—*Robinson*, 2829; they were going to kill every d—d nigger in Memphis—*Donahue*, 2960; were going to kill every d—d nigger they came across—*Bond*, 2981; threatened to burn out that d—d abolition hell—*Brooks*, 3318; inflamed with hatred against the negroes and their sympathizers, and with a malicious spirit to clean out all the d—d niggers—*Worset*, 3729: they were cursing the blacks all the while—*Clifford*, 4173; would kill off the negroes in town, and then kill the Yankees—*McPherson*, p. 316.

Moller, John E., testimony of, 752–799; a grocer, 752; Jackson Godell was coming into witness's store, when he was attacked, knocked into the gutter and shot, by a policeman and fireman; they went off saying, "they were going to shoot every d—d nigger," 755–760; little negro boy knocked down on the opposite side of the street, 764; lieutenant of police on horseback said, "the G—d d—d niggers ought to be killed altogether," 769; the riot was nothing else than a well appointed thing, 772; attempts to delude the negroes into acts of violence, 773; a class of rebels who will deprecate violence, but use those low-lived Irish rascals as their tools, 774.

Monroe, Benjamin, witness M. C., $8,000, value of church burned corner of Main and Overton streets.

Moon, Harriet, witness F. B. C., p. 338; house burned, loss, $125.

Moon, Kellum, witness F. B. C., p. 337; horse killed, trunk robbed.

Morris, Humphrey, witness F. B. C., p. 351; house burned.

Morris, Rose, witness F. B. C., p. 349; robbed.

Moton, Harriet, witness F. B. C., p. 355; house and contents burned.

Moseby, Thomas, witness F. B. C., p. 342; assaulted and robbed.

Moss, Clayborne, witness F. B. C., p. 342; house entered and robbed.

Moultrie, Prince, testimony of, 5036–5049; outrages committed upon colored people, all by low down white people, 5046; good feeling with better sort of white people, 5048.

Munson, John, witness F. B. C., p. 338; shot and robbed.

Myers, Fred. A., witness F. B. C., p. 356; shooting and outrages of the mob; speech of Recorder Creighton.

Myers, John, testimony of, 3107–3124; killing of Ben Dennis (white man) for speaking to a negro, in witness's saloon, 3115.

Nelson, Patience, witness F. B. C., p. 350; house burned.

Neville, Richard, witness F. B. C., p. 351; robbed.

Newspapers, influence of, two classes of, keep up agitation and bad feeling—*Stoneman*, 65–72; influence of the Post bad, because its doctrines are not palatable, 81; men connected with the Post nearly all in Union army, many of those connected with the other class in the rebel army, 85; disloyal papers have the largest circulation—*Davis*, 715; Avalanche most violent, Argus nearly as much so, 716; press representing both extremes, calculated to arouse the feelings of the people, 733, 734; effect of the press in exciting riotous proceedings, immense, Avalanche the worst, Argus and Evening Ledger echos of it—*Tade*, 832, 833; Memphis Post a little too tender, the purer and more honest any paper would be, the greater disturber it would be regarded by the other city papers, 880, 881; northern men, called radicals, held up as men to be shunned and avoided—*Beecher*, 1849; one sort doing all it can to harmonize, and the other, including the Avalanche and Argus, going just as far in the opposite direction—*White*, 2247–'48; a portion of the press have advised placing the sign of "small-pox" over the doors of people entertaining radical sentiments—*Brooks*, 3338; speak of us as enemies, tyrants, and oppressors of the South—*Lewis*, 3953; political teachings of—*Lewis*, 3982–'96; "black list" of all who advertised in the Post, published the Avalanche—*Ryder*, 4222; Avalanche the worst—*Runkle*, 4574; species of morality ascribed to the radicals—*McMahon*, 4057–'67; editors of, in the rebel army—*Chandler*, 5073; editors of, in the Union army—*Chandler*, 5078; authorship of various articles in the Argus—*Bower*, pp. 328, 333, *Pryor*, p. 333.

O.

Odum, Ann, witness F. B. C., p. 348; house burned.

Officers of the United States army, social status of, in Memphis—*Stoneman*, 4528–'33, *Runkle*. 4582, 4590.

Officials of Memphis city—list of, pp. 365, 366; list of police, pp. 366–369; police committee, p. 370; report of committee relative to, p. 22; would not be safe for any one to be active in bringing police officers to punishment—*Sharp*, 2113; character of, nationality, &c.,—*Richards*, 3233–'45; several city officials with the mob—*Clifford*, 4160; would not be supported by one-tenth the citizens of Memphis—*Miller*, 4617; election returns for mayor, 1866, p. 365.

Oldridge, John, testimony of, 1340–1365. Eli, a yellow man, dead on the sidewalk, May 1, two other bodies in the vicinity of the graveyard, 1346; May 2, great excitement on Main street, most disorderly man in the crowd a policeman, met Mayor Park making an ass of himself and drunk, 1346; negro man lying dead near the railroad, (see Henry W. Taylor,) 1350; burning of churches Wednesday night, Sheriff Winters with a lot of ragamuffins, Creighton and others there, all appeared to be drunk, except Winters, 1352; conversation of O'Hearn and Policeman Mickey relative to the fires, 1354; O'Hearn a leader, the mob threaten to burn Caldwell Hall, "every nigger building, every nigger church, and every G—d d—n s—n of a b—h that taught a nigger," 1358.

O'Neill, Edward, witness M. C., p. 335; efforts of fire department to extinguish the fires during the riot.

Orphans, colored, cared for by the Episcopal church—*Miller*, 4646.

P.

Park, John, mayor, report of committee relative to, p. 23; ditto of minority, p. 40; letter of, asking for troops, 6; reply of General Stoneman, 6; letter to, of General Stoneman, asking action of the city authorities relative to riot, p. 52; answers thereto, p. 53; met John Park, the mayor, making an ass of himself and drunk—*Oldridge*, 1346; was mayor at the breaking out of the war when the better class of people voted; never has been an office a good man could afford to leave—*Irwin*, 1567; when sober probably the best mayor Memphis has had—*Martin*, 1656; interview with officers at the fort—*Hastings*, 3134; an Irishman, &c—*Richards*, 3231; character of, elections to office, &c.—*C. Richards*, 5156–'57.

Witness M. C., p. 335, organization of fire department; police responsible for burning during the riots.

25

Parker, John C., testimony of, 4716, 4738; relations of citizens of Memphis with; northern people and the negroes.

Parker, Mack, witness F. B. C., p. 341; house robbed.

Patrick, Ann, witness F. B. C., p. 341; house assaulted and robbed.

Patterson, Joseph, witness F. B. C., p. 340; robbed of watch and money.

Pearce, William H., testimony of, 3412–3458; captain 3d United States cavalry, 3413; killing of Cobb, Richardson, Withers, and Black, 3418–'20; statement of Upman relative to large number of colored soldiers firing Wednesday morning contradicted, 3426; good conduct of colored soldiers, 3431; difficulties between the police and colored soldiers, 3435–'40; conduct of the mob, 3454–'57.

Peplon, Robert, witness M. C., p. 330; negro shot by policeman corner of Clay and Hernando streets.

Perkins, Francis, witness F. B. C., p. 351; house burned.

Perkins, Henry, witness F. B. C., p. 354; house and contents burned.

Perkins, Isaac, witness F. B. C., p. 339; threatened and robbed.

Perkins, Marland H., testimony of, 4739–4836; position of citizens of Memphis towards northern men, negroes, and the riotous proceedings, 4744–'53; operation of franchise law, 4754; discharge from the army of witness Cameron, 4759–'63; confederates not rebels, 4770; riot nothing else than an Irish and negro fight, 4777; ruinous policy of Congress, 4794; is president of the Johnson club, 4801; Park and Creighton vice-presidents, 4802–'03; ex-rebels entitled to equal political rights, 4819; franchise law an infamous law, 4823; speech of Haynes at Memphis tournament, 4827; radicals in Congress, Godless, Christless vipers, 4828.

Perry, John H., witness F. B. C., p. 349; shot in the chin.

Peterson, Theodore, witness F. B. C., p. 329; crowd on Adams street beating a negro.

Picket, Rose, witness F. B. C., p. 349; shooting and abuse of husband.

Picket, Solomon, witness F. B. C., p. 349; shot and beaten.

Pierce, J. O., witnesss M. C., p. 329; the fire-engines stop short of the fires, and are taken back.

Pigeon, Joseph, testimony of, 2757–2767; one negro killed, one shot in the neck, and another in the arm; 2760; employed six negroes, but shut them up in his cellar for protection, 2764.

Pleasant, Becky, witness F. B. C., p. 345; John Cole's trunk robbed.

Pleasant, William, witness F. B. C., p. 352; kidnapped, robbed, and taken to Mississippi.

Police committee, p. 370.

Police of Memphis; list of pp. 366–369; nationality of, p. 369; conduct of, report, pp. 25 26; minority ditto, p. 40. (See testimony of nearly all the witnesses.)

Police of Memphis, members of, engaged in the riot, p. 40.

Curley McCuen identified as making an assault on Henry Jackson—Williams, 607.

Carroll with three other police, took negro to the station-house on a dray, striking him with clubs every time he struggled; went up to bring crowd down to McGowan's office—McGowan, 1412, Gardner—937.

Slatterly wounded—Creighton, 1372.

John Stevens killed—Creighton, 1372, 1373, Keller, 1383, Jerdin, 1528.

Clark protected Dr. McGowan considerably—McGowan, 1413; implicated in burning house—Brown, 2999.

R. G. Garett, chief of police, rescued Dr. Mcgowan from mob—McGowan, 1404; rescued negro boy from police—Keller, 1583; remarked to some policemen, "My God, men, this man shooting must be stopped"—Lloyd, 1977; with sheriff, rescued a negro from policeman and fireman, and sent him to the fort—Turner, 2001.

David Roach shot colored soldier, Jim; shot another colored man three times and killed him—Johnson, 2529; killed a negro—Tibbs, 2173, Townsend, 2210, Porter, 2280; kept one man from shooting—Marshall, 2564; robbed Hannah Robinson—Robinson, 2824; robbed and shot R. R. Church—Church, 3611; set fire to Caldwell Hall—Caldwell, p. 346.

McCormick rushed at colored man by the railroad, struck him with carbine, breaking it into three pieces—Worset, 3708, Chamberlain, p. 322, Boyd, p. 353.

John Eagan and crowd burned Molly Davis's house—Davis, 2994; threatened to burn Ellen Brown's house—Brown, 2999.

Pollin, Andy, witness F. B. C., p. 350; house burned.

Porter, Ambrose, testimony of, 3266–3300; First Lieutenant U. S. C. A., 3267; contradicts statement of Upman as to large numbers of colored soldiers being collected and firing Wednesday morning, 3281.

Porter, Henry, testimony of, 2277–2308; interview between Pendergrast and colored soldiers; Roach and Galloway shoot a colored soldier, 2280; white soldiers helping the mob; screams of children fastened up in burning houses, 2281; Rachel Hatcher shot by Pendergrast; three or four children fired at, 2283; attempt to burn a boy with clothes, 2290.

Porter, Mose, witness F. B. C., p. 353; robbed.

Premier, Lemuel, witness F. B. C., p. 338; knocked down and robbed.

Premier, Phillis, witness F. B. C., p. 338; house entered by Roach, Smith, and others; husband knocked down and robbed.

Pugh, Samuel, witness M. C., p. 318; $8,000 value of church burned corner Main and Overton streets.

Q.

Quimby, Dr. S. J., testimony of, 1096–1175: commencement of riot on Tuesday; arrest of negro; interference by negro soldiers; policeman shot; police, reinforced, return; fight with colored soldiers; police repulsed; soldiers return to the fort; later in the evening police return with crowd of citizens, and went among houses of colored people; robbed one man of watches and jewelry, and then shot him through the head; shot a woman lying in bed with a child; shot a man in the head and abdomen, and then asked if he had any arms; robbed his house of everything of value, 1099; Wednesday, a. m., not ten colored soldiers to be seen; posse came up and scattered off among the houses; four men killed; one man shot by person on a railroad engine, 1099; saw the body of Rachel Hatcher after it was burned, 1101; all the parties shot on purpose, had on blue clothes, 1166.

R.

Radicals afraid to live in Memphis; not a majority of northerners in the city—*Stoneman,* 39; definitions of the term—*Stoneman,* 71, *Miller,* 4633–'36; in Congress, who have never smelt gunpowder, &c., "Godless, Christless vipers"—*Perkins,* 4828.

Rambert, Henry, witness F. B. C., p. 355; robbed by Roach and McGuire.

Randolph, J. N., testimony of, 1379–1387; one policeman and one colored man shot, the latter shot several times after he was down, 1381; negro beaten and shot down, on Beal street, 1383.

Rankin, H. N., witness M. C., p. 313; two men shot on the bridge; small boy in the thigh; Freeman Jones shot in the mouth; small negro man with three wounds; colored soldier killed corner St. Martin and Linden streets; negro woman killed corner South and Shelby streets; burning of witness's school-house.

Rape committed on—
Lucy Tibbs—*Tibbs,* 2179–'87.
Harriet Armour, by two men—*Townsend,* 2221–'25, *Armour,* 2458–'66.
Francis Thompson, by four men—*Thompson,* 2912.
Lucy Smith—*Smith,* 2930.
Rebecca Ann Bloom—*Bloom,* p. 351.

Reed, William, witness F. B. C., p. 342; house and contents burned.

Report of committee, pp. 1–36.—General Stoneman's testimony, p. 2; riotous proceedings, p. 2; General Stoneman and the city authorities, p. 4; character of the atrocities, p. 5; commencement, p. 6; first outbreak, p. 6; renewal of disturbances, p. 7; shooting negroes, p. 8; murder of Jackson Godell, p. 9; what the riot was, p. 9; robbery of Albert Harris, p. 10; colored hospital fired into, p. 10; the mob and white people, p. 10; the appearance of the mob, p. 10; what Rev. Mr. Tade saw, p. 11; Attorney General Wallace, p. 11; cowardice of the mob, p. 12; burning of Lincoln Chapel, p. 12; rape, p. 13; of Frances Thompson, p. 13; of Lucy Smith, p. 14; of Rebecca Ann Bloom, p. 14; of Lucy Tibbs, p. 14; of Harriet Armour, p. 15; shooting and burning of Rachel Hatcher, p. 15; conduct of Callahan and McGinn, p. 16; other burnings and shootings, p. 16; attempt to burn Lucy Hunt, p. 17; Mary Black and Maria Scott, p. 17; shooting of Joseph Walker p. 17; killing of Ben. Dennis, p. 17; attempt to burn Mary Jordan and her children, p. 18; murder of Long, p. 18; shooting of women and children, p. 18; attempt to burn white children, p. 19; teachers of colored schools, p. 20; the schools, p. 20; churches burned, p. 21; threats against the Memphis Post and Freedmen's Bureau, p. 21; other murders, robberies, &c., p. 22; treatment of United States Marshal Ryder, p. 22; county and city officers, p. 22; John Park, p. 23; John C. Creighton, p. 23; Sheriff T. M. Winters, p. 24; Chief of Police Garrett, p. 25; other officers connected with the mob, p. 25; David Roach, p. 25; John Eagan, p. 25; McCormick, p. 26; citizens of Memphis, p. 26; Swift, witnesses, p. 26; state of affairs at Memphis, p. 27; United States troops, p. 27; the rebels demand rights, p. 28; Colonel Ryder's opinion, p. 29; testimony of Judge Lewis, p. 29; colored witnesses, p. 30; cause of the riot—the newspapers, p. 30; conduct of the colored soldiers, p. 31; feeling towards the government, p. 32; general conclusions, p. 33; results of the riot, p. 34; the killed, pp. 34, 35; wounded, robberies, burnings, property destroyed, &c., p. 36.

Report of the minority, pp. 37–44; committee's investigations aided by reports of military commissions, p. 37; character of the testimony, p. 38; history beginning of riot—colored soldiers the aggressors, pp. 38, 39; progress of riot—evidence conflicting as to part taken by colored soldiers, pp. 39, 40; order of General Stoneman, May 3d, restored peace, p. 40; mayor intoxicated, and made no effort to suppress the riot, p. 40; sheriff's posses added fuel to the flame, p. 41; violence and disorder encouraged by Recorder Creighton, p. 41; mob composed of police, rabble, &c.—most of them voters under franchise law, p. 41;

character and effect of franchise law, pp. 41, 42; good character of the mass of the citizens of Memphis, p. 42; reasons for non-action on the part of the courts and people, pp. 42, 43: the better class of southern people acquiesce in the results of the war, in good faith, p. 43; partisan and prejudiced character of opposing testimony, p. 43; newspaper extracts, pp. 43, 44; proper mode of guarding against a repetition of the Memphis tragedy, p. 44: of Captain Arthur W. Allyn, pp. 358–361.

Rezzonco, Andrew, testimony of, 2324–2328; brutal arrest of negro soldiers by police, 2325; negro soldiers knocked down, stamped upon and stabbed, at the corner of Vine and St. Martin streets, 2325; saw eight dead bodies in all, 2327.

Richards, Channing, testimony of, 5141–5165; elections and character of Mayor Park and Recorder Creighton.

Richards, Lewis H., testimony of, 3220–3265; city registrar, 3220; character, nationality, &c., of mayor, police, and other city officials, 3223–'25; feeling towards the negroes, 3254–'62.

Riley, Columbus, witness F. B. C., p. 355; shot at and house burned.

Robinson, Alexander, witness M. C., p. 319; beating and shooting of George Williams.

Robinson, Eliza, witness F. B. C., p. 350; house burned.

Robinson, George, witness M. C., p. 317; beaten over the head with pistols.

Robinson, Hannah, testimony of, 2823–2830; house broken open by about twenty men: robbed by policeman Roach; other persons in the house assaulted and threatened, 2824.

Robinson, John, witness F. B. C., p. 344; killing of man by Galloway.

Robinson, John, witness F. B. C., p. 347; robbed of tools, &c.

Robinson, Nelson, witness F. B. C., p. 337; house torn down and robbed.

Robinson, Shack, witness F. B. C., 354; shot at and house burned.

Robinson, Thomas, witness F. B. C., p. 351; goods burned.

Robberies: Albert Harris, by police and others, money, $350—Harris, 144; Primus Lane, by six men, money, $13, clothes, hog, chickens, &c.—Lane, 908–930; houses of Snead and Lock, bed clothes, chickens, &c.—Sneed, 964, Lock, 1227; Edmund Lacey, money, $250—Malone, p. 341, Lacey, 1732; Lewis Bennett, watch, and $50 in money—Beecher, 1886, Bennett, p. 330; Henry Baine, $45—Beecher, 1886; James Moore, $20—Beecher, 1886; Bob Taylor, money, $300—Tibbs, 2177; pockets of Charley Wallace searched by Mr. Cash—Tibbs, 2173; $25 taken from the pockets of Fayette Dickerson—Tibbs, 2197, Dickerson, p. 358; Cynthia Townsend, $50 and clothes, quilts, &c.—Townsend, 2219; Allen Summers, $25—Summers, 2346; Andrew Minter, money, clothes, and everything, to value of $1,000—Minter, 2365; Abram Means, bed clothes, &c., value $100—Means, 2375; Shadrach Garritt, clothes and money—Marshall, 2540; store of Mary Grady, $290 in money and groceries—Grady, 2715; Hannah Robinson's house, by David Roach, and damaged to the amount of $100—Robinson, 2824; Elvira Walker, silver watch and chain—Walker, 2839; Frances Thompson, $300 in money, clothes, &c.—Thompson, 2915; Lucy Hunt, $325, by Chris. Pigeon and others—Hunt, 3003, p. 352; Anthony Simmons, $165—Simmons, 3509; discharged soldier, of $25—Simmons, 3512; Shade Long, $68 and clothes—Long, 3521; Robert Church, $290—Church, 3611; Ann Patrick Ayr, clothes, &c., next door neighbor also robbed—Ayr, 3792–'97; Hannah Savage, money, $120, clothes, &c., $200—Savage, 3847; colored man, $9, by three Irishmen—Thomas, 3998; Eli Anderson, $35, by firemen—Anderson, p. 317; Andrew Meadows, $25 and seventy-five dollars worth of clothing—Meadows, p. 319; Maggie Meadows, two diamond rings, worth $100 each, and other articles, worth $150—Meadows, p. 319; negro, of his money, on Main street, between Court and Madison—Haynes, p. 323, Shick, p. 323; Robert Boyle, tools, furniture, &c., $100—Boyle, p. 336; Obadiah Stockly, $71, gun, and gold watch—Stockly, p. 336; Kit Temple, goods in store to amount of $1,404—Temple, p. 336; R. H. Simmons, watch, ($300,) clothes, ($75,) silver, ($5,)—Simmons, p. 336; Colman Default, $30—Default, p. 337; Nathan Fenster, two houses, $750 each—Fenster, p. 337; Nelson Robinson, house torn down, &c., $250; Ellen Lee, clothes, &c., $150—Lee, p. 337: F. D. Berry, money, watch, and clothes, $390,—Berry, p. 337; John Lewis, money and gun, $85—Lewis, p. 337; Kellum Moon, horse, money, and clothes, $190—Moon, p. 337: Jordon Bufford, $50 and clothes—Bufford, p. 338; Lemuel Premier, money, $50—Premier, p. 338; John Munson, robbed of $50—Munson, p. 338; Chesterfield Sanders, money, watch, guns, &c., $365—Sanders, p. 339; Asbury Gibbons, money and clothes, $350—Gibbons, p. 339; Sallie Hawkins, money and clothes, $60—Hawkins, p. 339; Isaac Perkins, money, $50—Perkins, p. 339; Bartley Tam, $20—Tam, p. 339; Edward Jackson, money, rings, tools, &c., $475—Jackson, p. 339; Cary Campbell, contents of house, $122 40—Campbell, p. 340; Joseph Patterson, watch and money, $215—Patterson, p. 340; Edmond Bristol, money, watch, and revolver, $333—Bristol, p. 340; Huston Savage, money and clothes, $270—Savage, p. 340; Ann Patrick, contents of house, $200—Patrick, p. 241; Mack Parker, contents of house, $60—Parker, p. 341; Aaron Jones, money, $26—Jones, p. 341; Albert Watson, money, watch, and clothes, $210—Watson, p. 341; Sheppard Artist, contents of house, $60—Artist, p. 341; John Malone, money, $300—Malone, p. 341; S. Brandoned, money and watch, $130—Brandoned, p. 341; Burton Davis, money, $100—Davis, p. 341; Adam Jones, money, $160—Jones, p. 341; Ben Tucker, money, $100—Tucker, p. 342; Lawzie Gillam, money and ring, $266—Gillam, p. 342; Robert Brewster, money and groceries, $250——*Brewster*, p. 342; Thomas Moseby, money, $60—*Moseby*, p. 342; Clayborne Moss, money, clothes. &c., $300—*Moss*, p. 342; Handy Christopher, money, watch, bracelets, &c., $475—*Christopher*, p. 343: Wm. Green, watch, clothing, &c., $175—*Green*, p. 343; Norris Davis, money ($100) and clothes—*Davis*, p. 343; Jasper McCullom, personal property, $125—*McCullom*, p. 343; Wesley Ware, money, jewelry, &c., $150—*Ware*, p. 343; Robert Carlton. money, $60—*J. Carlton*, p. 344; Lucy Beeman, watch, knife, &c., $60—*Beeman*, p. 344; Mary Ella Brown, money and gun, $186—*Harris*. p. 345, *Brown*, p. 345; Mason Walker, clothing, &c., $50—*Walker*, p. 345; Eliza Ingram, money, $75—*Ingram*, p. 345; John Cole, three watches and $28—*Pleasant*, p. 345, *Cole*. p. 353; Coldwell Hall, $2,000—*Coldwell*, p. 346; Shadrack Curtman, money, &c., $50, Wm. Whitely, money, watch, &c., $76—*Curtman*, pp. 346, 357; Peter Johnson, contents of house, $82—*Johnson*, p. 346; Jacob Underwood, money, &c., $65—*Underwood*, p. 347; Boston Shorfield, money, $36—*Shorfield*, p. 347; Eliza Green, money, &c., $55—*Green*, p. 347; Henry Cole. clothing, &c., $75—*Cole*, p. 347: Dan Carruthers. articles, $40—*Carruthers*, p. 347; Charley Howlet, money, watch, &c., $275—*Howlet*. p. 347; John Robinson, tools, clothing, $250—*Robinson*, p. 347; Aaron Smith, money, $15—*Smith*, p. 347; Mary Bryant, money, watches, &c., $260—*Bryant*, p. 348; Nancy Whitley, property, $50—*Whitley*, p. 348: store of Kit Temple—*Wright*, p. 348; Peter Bloom. money, watch, &c., $157—*Bloom*, p. 348; James Hunt, money, $250—*Hunt*, p. 348; Rose Morris, money, clothing, &c., $225—*Morris*, p. 349; Hannah Hersey, chest full of things—*Hersey*, p. 349; Ross Spain, money, &c., $70—*Spain*, p. 349; Albert Hinton, by Pigeon and others, $150—*Hinton*, p. 350; George McCord, money, $10—*McCord*, p. 350; Shadrach Smith, money, $30 15—*Smith*, p. 315; Richard Neville, money and gun, $60—*Neville*, p. 351; Ned Young, money, clothes, &c., $436—*Young*, p. 352; Wm. Pleasant, money, horse, and wagon, $300—*Pleasant*, p. 352; Wm. Smith, money, $35—*Smith*, p. 352; Mose Porter, money, watch, &c., $315—*Porter*, p. 353; John Green, money, $400—*Green*, p. 353; Wm. Vaughn, money, notes, &c., $900—*Vaughn*, p. 353; John Wesley, money, watches, &c., $295—*Wesley*, p. 354; Lewis Boyle, articles, $200—*Boyle*, p. 354; Mary Austin, money, watch, &c., $25—*Austin*, p. 354; Thomas Boon, articles, $20—*Boon*, p. 354; Isaac Gibson, money, watches, &c., $280—*Gibson*, p. 355; Louisa Gillian, money, $10—*Gillian*, p. 355; John Young, articles in trunk, $150—*Young*, p. 355; Harry Rambert, money, $15—*Rambert*, p. 355; Lily Henderson, money, $20—*Henderson*, p. 355; Ann Carr, clothes, $30—*Henderson*, p. 355; Mary Dupee, articles in house—*Dupee*, p. 356; Peter Jones and Gabriel Cumming, shoe shop robbed, $100—*Jones and Cumming*, p. 357; May Bryant, money, watches, &c., $267—*Bryant*, p. 257; John Williams, watch, clothes, &c., $350—*Williams*, p. 357; Peter Mitchell, money and clothes, $1,500—*Mitchell*, p. 358.

Runkle, Brigadier General Benj. P., testimony of, 4535–4606; Superintendant of Freedmen's Bureau, 4535; premonitions of riot, 4540–'1; guard placed over headquarters of Freedmen's Bureau, 4542½; teachers of colored schools sent away, 4542½; threats against the Freedmen's Bureau building, 4543; good conduct of freedmen of West Tennessee, 4550–'52; riot has put them back further than when witness began, 4553: hatred and violence of police, 4554–'55; riot stopped because they had filled their grave-yards, 4559; without troops, all northern people would have to go, because the civil law is not strong enough to protect them, 4561; disloyalty of Memphis people, 4567–'70; United States officer called a pimp, 4571; feeling towards the freedmen—northern men, 4590–'94; one feature of Freedmen's Bureau odious; another popular, 4596; operation of freedmen's contracts, 4598–4603; second examination of, 5174–'80; extracts from newspapers made at the request of General Fisk and Mr. Washburne.

Ryder, Martin T., testimony of, 4194–4278; United States marshal; character and acts of the mob, 4197–4201; witness assaulted by Porter, a butcher, 4201–'02; interview with General Stoneman, 4203; every supporter of the government called a d——d yankee, 4208; petition for appointment of recorder Creighton as marshal, 4210; Creighton, with sheriff, handing round pistols, 4217; feelings, &c., towards Union men, 4221–'67.

Ryon, Jeremiah, testimony of, 2045–'65; white man shot by three colored men, 2050.

S.

Sanders, Chesterfield, witness F. B. C., p. 339; robbed of money, watch, guns, &c.

Saunders, Dudley D., testimony of, 5166–'73; shooting of colored boy at the Gayoso house.

Saunders, Nancy, witness F. B. C., p. 348; killing of husband.

Savage, Huston, witness F. B. C., p. 340; robbed and threatened.

Savage, Hannah, testimony of, 3837–'57; run out of her house and robbed.

Scott, Maria, witness M. C., p. 332; $90 burned in Mary Black's house.

Shaif, George, witness M. C., p. 321; saw many fires.

Sharp, Dr. J. N., testimony of, 2056–2129; negro in the bayou chased, thirty shots fired at him, several policemen shooting at him and beating him with their pistols; a negro running and the crowd firing at him; negro on Avery street shot through the shoulder, a person afterwards came along, kicked him several times in the face, turned him over and shot him in the breast; his name, Allen Summers; abuse in Dr. McGowan's office by a half drunken Irishman; attacked by the mob, but rescued by Captain Garrett, 2060;

house on South street broken open, and a colored woman stabbed twice while striking a light, 2066; negro shot in the knee by policeman, 2066; little negro boy shot by policeman, 2070: good conduct of colored soldiers, 2080–'85; brutal arrest of a negro by policemen, 2087; other instances of brutality by policemen towards the negroes, 2088–'93; no instance of punishment by city authorities for assaults upon negroes, 2094; threats against the negroes previous to the riot, 2118; no ground for anticipation of outbreak by the negroes at Christmas, 2124–'29.

Sherfield, Boston, witness F. B. C., p. 347; assaulted and robbed.

Shick, A. J., witness M. C., p. 323; negro robbed on Main street between Court and Madison.

Simmons, Anthony, testimony of, 3506–'13; robbed by police and citizens of $165, 3509; discharged soldiers robbed of $25, 3512.

Simmons, Celia, testimony of, 3482–'90; shooting of Rhoda Jacobs, 3490.

Simmons, R. H., witness F. B. C., p. 336; robbed of watch, clothes and money.

Simpson, Joseph, witness F. B. C., p. 338; house burned.

Slater, Benjamin, witness M. C., p. 321; value of church, corner of Washington and New Orleans streets, burned, $25,000.

Smith, David, witness M. C., p. 332; shooting of witness threatened by Burns.

Smith, Aaron, witness F. B. C., p. 347; robbed.

Smith, Henry G., testimony of, 4837–4851; relations of citizens of Memphis towards northern men, negroes, &c.

Smith, John M. C., witness M. C., p. 323; house burned by a United States soldier.

Smith, Lucy, testimony of, 2921–2933; rape committed on, 2930; outrages committed by the mob, 2924–'32.

Smith, Major Wm. H., witness M. C, p. 324; in charge of detachment ordered out to suppress the riot; conduct of the mob.

Smith, Shadrach, witness F. B. C., p. 350; assaulted and robbed.

Smith, Thomas O., testimony of, 4102–4142; undertaker, 4102; conversation with city clerk, 4125.

Smith, Wm., witness F. B. C., p. 352; house burned and robbed.

Sneed, Jane, testimony of, 959–989; commencement of riot; police arrest a negro, knock him down, and carry him off on a dray; firing between police and colored soldiers; policeman killed; police and white citizens shot every body they found; took a man out of witness's house and shot him; Adam Lock's house set on fire; Rachel Hatcher killed; husband of witness told by Callahan to "come over here till I shoot you;" rescued by appearance of regulars; Callahan took bed clothes, chickens, and everything he wanted, and then set the house on fire, 964; Rachel Hatcher's body burned, 965.

Soldiers, paroled rebel, scrupulous in keeping out of the disturbance—Stoneman, 55.

Soldiers, white regular, bad conduct of—Porter, 2321; some of, as bad as the mob—Sterling, 2402; took the work the mob had been doing out of their hands—Dorset, 3724.

Spain, Ross, witness F. B. C., p. 349; robbed.

Stanbrough, Ira, testimony of, 4021–4051; compelled to leave because of threats, 4025–'30; one of the six who voted against secession, 4024; would leave Memphis if troops were withdrawn, 4033; rebel sentiments of Memphis people, 4034–'37; hatred towards the north, 4042–'43.

Sterling, Dr. Allen, testimony of, 2389–2447; relations between the white and colored population, 2397–2407; better class of people thought this indiscriminate slaughter all foolishness, 2408; no steps taken relative to the riot by citizens because of Stoneman's proclamation, 2412–'47.

Stillman, F. K., witness F. B. C., p. 345; robbery of Adam Jones.

Stockly, Obadiah, witness F. B. C., p. 336; robbed of $71, gun, and gold watch.

Stoneman, Major General George, testimony of, 1–95; in command of department of Tennessee, 2; application of Sheriff Winters for troops, May 1, 6; written application of Mayor Park and reply, 6; application of Judge Leonard for arms, 7; troops ordered out and rioting suppressed, May 2, 7; resolutions for patrol of citizens, May 3, 12; city placed under military control, 14; no further riots, 15; teachers of colored schools, &c., leave the city, 15; military commission ordered, 24; letter asking what action the city authorities will take, p. 53; replies of Mayor Park thereto, p. 54; military control of the city withdrawn, 25; confederate soldiers scrupulous in keeping out of the disturbance, 55; a majority of the rioters registered voters, 55; deportment of the resident black population highly creditable, 56, 57; influence and character of newspapers, 65–89.

Second examination of, 4424–4534; no steps taken by civil authorities to bring rioters to justice, 4428; have encouraged citizens and newspapers to publicly disapprove the riots without success, 4429–4436; loyalty of people of Memphis, 4439–4448; national airs hissed—rebel airs applauded, 4437; federal troops required to execute Tennessee laws, 4449; presence of federal troops necessary, 4449–4463; proclamation taking military possession of Memphis was not intended as a proclamation of martial law, 4469; with proper officers the civil law might be enforced, 4476; effect of the franchise laws, &c., 4478–4536; loyalty of the people of Tennessee, 4483–4523; social status of Memphis, 4528–4533; no Union officer received into society, 4530; United States soldiers as rioters, court-martial proceedings, 4534.

Storms, J. S., testimony of, 2726–2739; colored man shot in the leg, 2727; riotous acts of the *posse*, 2737–'39.

Strickney, Joe, testimony of. 1751–1759 ; was playing with some boys when a policeman shot him in the hip, 1754.

Summers, Allen, testimony of, 2346–'47 ; shot, stabbed, tramped, on and robbed by Irishmen and police, 2346.

Swan, James H., testimony of, 2487–2508; deputy sheriff, 2487 ; names of parties placed in charge of Finne's store, identified as engaged in robbing the house of Albert, Harris, Wilson, and Tyler, 2489; relations between Memphis citizens and negroes, 2493–2500; operation of franchise laws, 2501–'05; rabble population, 2507–'08.

Swels, Mrs. Jannette, testimony of, 1207–1233; Callahan came across the street from where Rachel was burned, bringing a bed with him, 1211 ; a man on horseback took things away from the same house, 1217 ; George McGinn carried away beds and things from the same house, 1218; Mrs. Lock called to McGinn three or four times to help her, and every time she called he fired at her, 1218.

T.

Tade, Rev. Ewing O., testimony of, 800–900; May 1, met a crowd on Main street; a po liceman seized a colored man, commenced pounding him over the head, jammed him against the wall, swearing most furiously, 809 ; colored man on the sidewalk chased and struck with a knife, 813; dying colored man in the street being cared for by two colored women, 813; May 2, posse under General Wallace, some on horseback, some drunk, went through drill movements, filed off among negro shanties, immediately afterwards shots heard and shanties seen on fire, shouts of "Kill him," "Shoot him;" when they came back they said, "There are two d—d niggers out of the way," 815; story of flag of truce early Wednesday morning, shots fired by the negroes and the crowd run back into the city, 825; cause of the riot, hatred between the Irish and negroes, 828; fostered by southern men to the best of their ability, 829; would hang, imprison, or banish a portion of the rebels, and disfranchise them all, 829; burning of churches and colored school-houses on Wednesday night, 836; burning and history of Lincoln chapel, 837–841; how to preach to negroes, 843; distribution of books and papers as missionary, 845–855; political teaching of the blacks, 863–866; character and influence of the Memphis Post, 875–881 ; definition of loyalty, 895–893.

Second examination of, 2567–2576; four colored churches burned, 2571; no churches opened after the riot for accommodation of colored worshippers—did not dare open them, 2573.

Tam, Bartley, witness F. B. C., p. 339; abused and robbed.

Taylor, Henry W., testimony of, 1469–1523; the negro gotten up by the sheriff were trying their best to put a stop to it, 1480 ; a negro shot near blacksmith's shop by the depot—the most cool-blooded murder witness ever saw, 1476–1484; bad conduct of negro soldiers, 1505–1517; white people drunk and using improper language more frequently than negroes, 1520.

Taylor, W. F., testimony of, 4862–4867 ; fifty shots fired by a crowd of negroes first evening of the riot, 4855–'57.

Teachers of colored schools, many of the, leave Memphis—*Stoneman*, 15 ; very much frightened, warned to leave, 28–35; negroes not taught by, to assert their political rights—*Tade*, 863–866; number and character of—*Waters*, 4351–'61; left the city because their lives were threatened—*Waters*, 4365; compensation of—*Waters*, 4422; sent away from the city—*Runkle*, 4542½; of blameless life and conversation—*Runkle*—4564; feeling towards, not as good as it should be—*Miller*, 4650.

Temple, Kit, witness F. B. C , p. 336; store robbed to amount of $1,404.

Tenfel, Joseph, witness M. C., p. 331; 150 negroes led by Lieutenant Jericho from cemetery towards South street, May 1.

Testimony taken by committee of House of Representatives, pp. 50–313.

　　　　taken by military commission, pp. 313–336.

　　　　taken by Freedmen's Bureau commission, pp. 336–358.

Thomas, Guy, testimony of, 3885–3909; shooting of Adeline Miller, 3891.; colored man robbed, 3898; colored man near railroad, with white wife, killed, 3902; burning of Mr. Rankin's school-house, 3902.

Thompson, Frances, testimony of, 2906–'20 ; rape committed on by four men, 2912; robbed of $300 in money and clothes, 2915.

Tibbs, Lucy, testimony of, 2150–2206; two negroes killed by Pendergrast and his crowd, 2154–'59; two other bodies lay nearly two days, 2164; houses fired and inmates shot at as they tried to escape, 2167 ; policeman Roach and drayman Galloway kill a colored soldier, 2173; Charley Wallace shot and robbed by Mr. Cash, 2173; witness's brother, Bob Taylor, killed, 2176; witness robbed of $300; rape committed, 2179–'88; killing of Fayette Dickerson, 2197.

Tipping, Mrs. Ann, witness M. C., p. 319; shooting of a negro.

Todd, George, testimony of, 4279-4302 ; speech of Recorder Creighton, 4282; acts of the mob, 4286-'87 ; went with posse, but did nothing, 4288-'89.
Toles, Fred, witness F. B. C., p. 336 ; shot in the arm by policeman.
Tolliver, Patsy, witness F. B. C., p. 351 ; commencement of the riot.
Townsend, Cynthia, testimony of, 2207-'35 ; drayman shot by Roach—Charley Wallace shot by Cash, 2210 ; killing and burning of Rachel Hatcher, 2211 ; men, women, and children shot at while escaping from their burning houses, 2211-'16 ; Lewis Robertson killed, tongue shot out by Pendergrast, 2211 ; rape on Harriet Armour, 2221-'25.
Transportation, cost of, on account of the riots, p. 335.
Trotter, Maria, witness F. B. C., p. 339 ; house and contents burned.
Tucker, Ben, witness F. B. C., p. 342 ; house and contents burned.
Turner, D. W., testimony of, 1989-2012 ; saw several negroes laying in the bayou, who was told had lain there twenty-four hours, 1998 ; saw one negro killed, 1995 ; also one boy shot through the leg, 1999 ; negro shot in the arm, ran into house of Mr. Merriweather, 2002 ; no cause of offence on the part of the negroes, 2003 ; negro pursued by policeman and fireman, and rescued by sheriff and chief of police, 2001.
Turner, Simon, witness F. B. C., p. 357 ; house burned.

U.

Underwood, Jacob, witness F. B. C., p. 347 ; robbed.
Upman, D., testimony of, 2844-'97 ; crowd of from three to five hundred colored soldiers, Wednesday morning outside Fort Pickering, twenty-five or thirty of whom were firing with United States muskets at the crowd of white people for an hour or hour and a half, 2875-'84.

V.

Van Pelt, Samuel, witness M. C., p. 331 ; shooting of policeman on Elliot street.
Vaughn, William, witness F. B. C., p. 353 ; assaulted and robbed.

W.

Walker, Elvira, testimony of, 2831-'43 ; some men came to witness's house at night, abused her, and robbed her of a silver watch and chain, 2838-'39.
Walker, Jack Harris, testimony of, 5016-'35 ; good treatment of by his former master, 5021 ; some entertain good feeling towards their former masters, others not, 5024.
Walker, Joseph, testimony of, 1775-'98 ; shot by Palmer, depot agent, who got down from an engine and fired, 1781 ; Palmer and his brother shot another colored soldier and killed him, 1792.
Walker, Mary, testimony of, 2898-2905 ; Palmer shot and killed a negro by the railroad depot, 2901.
Walker, Mason, witness F. B. C., p. 345 ; robbed of clothing.
Wallace, Wm., attorney general, in command of a posse, committing riotous acts—Tade, 815 ; speech to the crowd, advising them to organize and arm themselves—Allyn, 4077 ; witness M. C., p. 314 ; armed with rifles and shot guns, and commanded a posse.
Walsh, Captain Michael, testimony of, 5191-'95 ; correct copies of affidavits placed in hands of committee.
Wands, J., witness M. C., p. 331 ; shanty, corner of Webster and De Soto streets, burned ; loss, $200.
Wardlaw, Mary, testimony of, 3798-3809 ; house and contents burned.
Wardlaw, Mat., testimony of, 3810-'36 ; house and contents, value, $1,600 or $1,700, burned, 3822 ; Bob George shot by police, 3829 ; two colored soldiers killed, 3830.
Ware, Martha, witness F. B. C., p. 344 : robbed of jewelry, &c.
Ware, Wesley, witness F. B. C., p. 343 ; house robbed.
Watson, Albert, witness F. B. C., p. 341 ; robbed of money, watch, &c.
Waters, Orin E., testimony of, 4350-4423 : superintendent of public colored schools, 4350 ; 12 schools, 22 teachers, 1,200 scholars, 4351 ; character and treatment of the teachers and scholars, 4353-'76 ; prejudice against the colored schools, 4381-'85 ; Freedmen's Aid Commission, 4385-'88 ; Episcopal Colored Orphan Asylum, 4391 ; political teaching, 4403-'7 ; no hostility to these teachers by old citizens of Memphis, 4407½ ; teaching political rights not contrary to constitution and laws, 4419 ; compensation of teachers, 4622.
Wesley, John, witness F. B. C., p. 354 ; robbed.
Wheeden, Wm. W., witness M. C., p. 320 ; commencement of riot.
White, Dr. Robert, testimony of, 2236-'51 ; causes that led to the riot, &c., 2241-'49.
White, J. S., witness M. C., p. 330 ; burning on Echols street.
Whitecotton, Jim, witness F. B. C., p. 346 ; Ben Cotton shot by Marsh.
Whitley, Nancy, witness F. B. C., p. 348 ; assaulted and robbed.
Whitley, Wm., witness F. B. C., p. 357 ; robbed.
Whitlow, Mitchell, testimony of, 1760-'74 ; general description of the fight, one woman shot accidentally in a window, 1773.

Williams, Frank, testimony of, 2509–'22 ; killing of Baker and Joe Lundy, 2510–'12.
Williams, George, testimony of, 4339–'49 ; shot and abused by police.
Williams, Harriet, witness F. B. C., p. 350; husband killed.
Williams, Jerry, testimony of, 603–612 ; was present at the maltreatment of Henry Jackson, 606; knew the policeman who struck him as Curley McCuen, 607.
Williams, Jessie, witness M. C., p. 323; assault on Henry Jackson by police.
Wilson, Emeline, witness F. B. C., p. 353; burning of Ida Green and child.
Wilson, Felix, witness F. B. C., p. 347 ; cut with a knife.
Williams, John, witness F. B. C., p. 357; robbed.
Winters, T. M., sheriff, report of commissioners relative to, p. 24; testimony of, 613–694. made application to General Stoneman for soldiers to quell the riot ; was told to summon a posse ; did so, and proceeded with them to scene of disturbance; met a squad of regulars and asked their captain to assist, which he did, and posse returned; rescued a wounded negro and put him in a hack, 616. Next day summoned another posse and went to scene of disturbance ; met Attorney General Wallace with another posse ; rescued several negroes who were being misused; met a squad of regulars, some of whom behaved very badly ; went to several fires, but too late to save the buildings, 617. Do not know who made the attacks, not reaching there till the fight was over in every instance, 640. Rescued a negro from an organization of boys—little thieves—calling themselves the mackerel brigade ; received no warrants for the arrest of parties engaged in the riot, 669. Do not know what the idea of the people is in relation to the riots, 670 ; heard Recorder Creighton remark that during the riot he would not fine any one for carrying concealed weapons, 679.
Wood, Julius, witness F. B. C., p. 346 ; clothing burned.
Woodfall, Pleasant, witness F. B. C., p. 347 ; James Huston's house burned.
Worset, G. C., testimony of, 3699–3756 ; was proprietor of Southern Loyalist, 3699 ; Charlie Watkins and another colored man wounded, 3705; colored man killed by policeman McCormick, 3708; conduct of the regular soldiers, 3719–'27 ; political status of the Loyalist, 3740–'57.
Wounded during the riot:
Three negroes beaten by the police—E. Dilts, 172–177, 207, R. Dilts, 272, 292; negro beaten about 79 Beal street, May 1—Cooley, 407 ; negro beaten with riding whip, same locality, 457; Henry Jackson struck, May 2, by policeman—Jackson, 473, Williams, 606; six negroes wounded or being maltreated, rescued from the crowd—Winters, 616, 617 ; another taken from the "Mackerel brigade," 649; Taylor Hunt shot in the head by policeman—Davis, 702, Hunt, 1005 ; a little negro boy knocked down on Beale street—Moller, 764, negro pounded and jammed against the wall by policeman ; another chased and struck with a knife—Tade, 809, 813 ; negro beaten with clubs by police while taking him to station house—Gardner, 937, Sneed, 964 ; Austin Cotton, badly beaten in Hollywood's store—Hollywood, 992, Cotton, 1028; Rhoda Jacobs shot in bed—Quimby, 1143, Jacobs, 2032, Simmons, 3490; John Manson, shot through the head—Quimby, 1146; Joseph Walker, shot in the shoulder with buckshot—Quimby, 1146, Walker, 1781; Joe Strickney, shot in the thigh—Beatty, 1266, Strickney, 1754 ; Slatterly, policeman, shot in leg—Creighton, 1372; one negro with arm broken by shot ; another who had been cut—Irwin, 1527; negro wounded, and in the hands of the mob, corner St. Martin and Pontotoc streets—Keller, 1583; two negroes shot at—Hewett, 1615 ; negro shot on the top of his head—Littlefield, 1625; one negro shot through the arm ; another through the leg in Chelsea street—Martin, 1633, Anderson, 2338; old man Billy, shot through the bowels while under his house—Lee, 1720; Edmund Lacey, colored soldier, shot through the shoulder—Lacey, 1731; woman in a window shot through the arm accidentally—Whitlow, 1773, Sharp, 2160, Summers, 2346; Allen Summers, discharged soldier; gunshot wound through right shoulder—Beecher, 1886 ; Robert Davis ; has lost the use of lower limbs; shot through right shoulder while sitting in hospital door—Beecher, 1886 ; Larry Summers; gunshot wound through the calf of the leg; shot while sitting in the door of the hospital—Beecher, 1886 ; Catherine Fletcher, shot in the back while walking along in Main street; ball lies under shoulder blade—Beecher, 1886; Robert Thornton, citizen negro ; gunshot wound in right thigh—Beecher, 1886; Henry Baine, citizen negro, a blacksmith ; shot by some one in a crowd of policemen and citizens, from behind—Beecher, 1886 ; James Jones, citizen negro, was shot through the arm, while standing in the yard of his employer, by a white man—Beecher, 1886 ; Robert Smith, citizen negro ; knocked down with a gun by a citizen, and robbed ; wound over forehead—Beecher, 1886; James Moore, citizen negro; knocked down with a gun in the hands of two citizens, Beecher, 1886; boy 15 or 16 years old, playing, shot in the leg by policeman—Turner, 1999; man shot in the arm while attempting to pass from steamboat to his house—Turner, 2002 ; negro shot in the arm—Jean, 2019; white man shot by three colored men—Ryon, 2050; negro beaten and thirty shots fired at him—Sharp, 2060; colored woman stabbed twice while trying to strike a light—Sharp, 2066; little boy 12 years old shot by policeman—Sharp, white man shot down by negro—Jackson, 2143; woman stabbed—Tibbs, 2186; Daniel Dawkins struck on the head by policeman—Dawkins, 2331; negro shot by Charley Toler—Dawkins, 2330; John Marshall shot in the hip for assisting to put out a fire—Marshall, 2566; colored man shot in the leg—Storms, 2727; negro shot in the neck and

26

another in the arm—*Pigeon*, 2760 ; Willis Jones shot in the eye by policeman—*Bond*, 2975, *Jones*, p. 332 ; colored man beaten 200 or 300 licks by policeman—*Bond*, 2982 ; Tinnon sh t through the arm—*Pearce*, 3420 ; Richard Lane shot through the shoulder— *Lane*, 3498 ; Lane's little girl shot through the arm—*Lane*, 3497 ; Billy Johnson beat and kicked by Tom Harris—*Johnson*, 3530 ; John Handy shot in leg by Jerry, Harry Towers shot in the shoulder, and Joe Davis shot and struck in bed, sick—*Handy*, 3596– 3603 ; Robert R. Church shot in the neck by Roach ; two colored men badly beaten— *Church*, 3611 ; Charlie Watkins knocked down ; another colored man shot—*Worset*. 3705 ; two negroes under arrest, brutally treated by the mob—*Lewis*, 3916 ; George Williams shot and abused by police—*Williams*, 4340, *Robinson*, p. 319 ; woman wounded in the side by a knife—*Rankin*, p. 313 ; white man wounded in the back, carried into black- smith shop corner of Causey and Vance streets—*Littlefield*, 315 ; Amos Bowles shot in the arm—*Bowles*, p. 317 ; Eli Anderson shot in the arm—*Anderson*, p. 317 ; George Robinson beaten over the head with pistols—*Robinson*, p. 317 ; colored man wounded corner Main and Eliot street—*Curley*, p. 318 ; Alfred Turner wounded in the arm— *Baker*, p. 319 ; George Clapp and Franklin Gross shot and severely wounded by fire- men, corner of Main and Exchange streets—*Hood*, p. 320 ; Frank McGee wounded— *Bowen*, p. 321 ; negro beaten with pistols corner Linden and Main streets—*Bushnell*, p. 324 ; negro on Adams street beaten—*Peterson*, p. 329 ; negro shot in the leg on Howard Row by Richard Marsh—*Kyle*, p. 329 ; negro shot near F. B. hospital by Irishman— *Dunlap*, p. 330 ; Lewis Bennett knocked down, beaten, and arm broken, in front of Gayoso House, *Beecher*, 1886—*Bennett*, p. 330 ; Fred Toles shot in the arm by policeman— *Toles*, p 336 ; Colman Default shot by Roach—*Default*, p. 337 ; Jane Goodlow shot in the arm— *Goodlow*, p. 337 ; Jordon Bufford struck on the head with club—*Bufford*, p. 338 ; Lemuel Premier knocked down by Charley Lynn—*Premier*, p. 338 ; John Munson shot through the head—*Munson*, p. 338 ; Harry Fowned shot through the shoulder—*Fowned*, p. 340 ; Edmond Bristol struck on face and head with pistol—*Bristol*, p. 340 ; Lawzie Gillam knocked down—*Gillam*, p. 342 ; Major Jones shot in shoulder—*Jones*, p. 342 ; Samuel Brooks shot in the back and stoned—*Brooks*, p. 343 ; Daniel Austin shot in shoulder— *Austin*, p. 345 ; Ben Cotton shot by Dick Marsh—*White* and *Cotton*, p. 346 ; Jane Fletcher shot in the back—*Fletcher*, p. 346 ; Felix Wilson cut with a knife and shot at— *Wilson*, p. 347 ; Edmund Evans stabbed six times with a knife—*Evans*, p. 348 ; Soloman Picket shot in the arm and beaten—*Picket*, p. 349, *McGhee*, p. 356, *Lowder*, p, 356 ; John H. Perry shot in the chin—*Perry*, p. 349 ; George McCord shot in the leg—*McCord*, p. 350 ; Anthony French struck on the head and kicked—*French*, p. 350 ; Shadrach Smith choked—*Smith*, p. 351 ; colored man shot twice and wounded—*Kenney*, p. 353 ; Thomas Boon shot through the shoulder—*Boon*, p. 354 ; James Hustin kicked, &c.— *Hustin*, p. 354 ; wife of Columbus Riley shot at, causing a miscarriage—*Riley*, p. 355 ; Mary Dupee beaten and abused—*Dupee*, p. 356.

Wormley, Charity, testimony of, 4968–'95 ; kind treatment of the colored people by their former owners.

Wright, C., witness F. B. C., p. 348 ; Kit Temple's store robbed.

Wright, J. W., witness M. C., p. 326 ; cost of government barracks burned.

Wright, Marcus J., testimony of, 4872–'99 ; relations of Memphis citizens with the negroes, 4878–83 ; effect of franchise law, 4884–'86 ; member of military commission to investigate the riots, 4989 ; conclusions of witness from commission investigations, 4893 ; fifty good men could have checked the riot at any time, 4895.

Wright, Walton, witness F. B. C., p. 351 ; shooting of negroes by police.

Y.

Yates, Julia, witness M. C., p. 331 ; commencement of the riot ; negro woman, Emeline, killed.

Yerger, Orville, witness M. C., p. 315 ; negro knocked down and shot several times while down, South street, near Causey.

Young, John, witness F. B. C., p. 355 ; robbed.

Young, Ned, witness F. B. C., p. 352 ; robbed.

O